a passion for identity

4th Edition

Canadian Studies for the 21st Century

Edited by

David Taras

University of Calgary

Beverly Rasporich

University of Calgary

NELSON

TM

THOMSON LEARNING

Australia • Canada • Mexico • Singapore • Spain • United Kingdom • United States

NELSON

™

THOMSON LEARNING

A Passion for Identity:
Canadian Studies for the 21st Century,
Fourth Edition

edited by David Taras and Beverly Rasporich

Editorial Director and Publisher:
Evelyn Veitch

Acquisitions Editor:
Kelly Torrance

Marketing Manager:
Don Thompson

Developmental Editors:
Jenny Anttila and Rebecca Rea

Production Editor:
Natalia Denesiuk

Production Coordinator:
Julie Preston

Copy Editor:
Karen Rolfe

Proofreaders:
Dawn Hunter and Joan Rawlin

Art Director and Cover Design:
Angela Cluer

Cover Art:
Joyce Wieland, *Confedspread,*
1967. Reproduced with permission
from the National Gallery of
Canada, Ottawa.

Compositor:
Alicja Jamorski

Printer:
Webcom

**Canadian Cataloguing in
Publication Data**

Main entry under title:

A Passion for identity: Canadian
studies for the 21st century

4th ed.
Includes bibliographical references
and index.
ISBN 0-17-616828-1

1. National characteristics, Canadian.
2. Regionalism – Canada. 3. Canada
– Civilization. 4. Canada – History.
I. Taras, David, 1950–   .
II. Rasporich, Beverly Jean.

FC97. P38 2001   971   C00-933137-9
F1021.2.P38 2001

the double world

Eli Mandel

it is variously believed that this world is the
double of another, as in Plato, Swedenborg,
    Malebranche,
some of Immanuel Kant, Arthur C. Clarke,
    Isaac Asimov,
Stanley Kubrick
    Two clocks set at the same time in
identical universes should stop at the same time.
This clock is a shadow of that real clock. When I
look at my clock I have no way of knowing
    whether I am in
the first or second universe. It is spring there
    too:
and the other Ann has grown an avocado
    exactly the same
height, greenness, number of leaves as the one
    Ann grew
here or there. My grandfather Berner weighed
    the same
in both universes, sang sweet Jewish psalms, ate
    sour
curds. In the two graveyards Annie Berner is
    dead.
Nothing on either prairie changes though the
    winds blow
across immensities your heart would shrivel to
    imagine
knowing they pass between the worlds and can
    be heard to do
so on the road to Wood Mountain. That is what
    was written
in the rocks.

CONTENTS

SECTION ONE: CANADIAN IDENTITY

Part A: Foundations

Part B: Quebec's Search for National Identity

Part C: Changing Canada

Part D: Canada and Globalization

Part E: The Dynamics of Culture

SECTION TWO: REGIONAL IDENTITIES

Part A: Atlantic Canada

Part B: Ontario

Part C: The New West

Part D: The North

Acknowledgments

We would like to thank all of the contributors for their fine efforts. In each case we turned to people whom we respected as experts in their fields, and we are flattered that so many busy and productive people gave so willingly of themselves. Dean Kathleen Scherf of the Faculty of Communication and Culture provided both enthusiasm and support. Sylvia Mills, the administrative assistant in the faculty's graduate office, went beyond the call of duty in providing help when we most needed it, and Christine Sowiak was very helpful in selecting the cover. We are very grateful to both of them.

David Taras would like to thank Beverly Rasporich for being such a true friend and colleague. Without Beverly's insights and good humour, the book would have lacked the passion that is its guiding spirit. David would also like to thank Debbie Taras and our four boys, Dan, Joel, Matthew, and Michael for their love and support and for giving him faith in a better future. Irwin Taras, his father, continues to be an inspiration and a guide.

Beverly Rasporich is grateful to David Taras for his creative initiatives, his wonderful friendship, and his enthusiasm for this project. She is especially thankful for the constant support and comic vision of her husband, Anthony Rasporich. Beverly would like to dedicate her contribution to this book to her two grandchildren, Kai and Seth Rasporich, and her parents, Irene and George Matson.

And finally, we would like to thank Jenny Anttila for all her hard work and help, and we wish her the best of luck for the future.

Nelson Thomson Learning would like to thank the reviewers for their insightful comments: L. Pauline Rankin, Carleton University; Dr. W.R. McKercher, King's College; Will Shaw, McGill University; Howard Pawley, recently retired from the University of Windsor; and Paul Nesbitt-Larking, Huron University College.

SECTION ONE

Canadian Identity

Introduction: The Dilemmas of Canadian Identity

David Taras

I never imagined while sitting at poet Eli Mandel's kitchen table in
Toronto in 1985 that *A Passion for Identity* would live through four editions. I remember the anxiety and the delight that came from choosing
from a rich tapestry of themes, authors, and possibilities. Attempting to
capture the many dimensions of the Canadian experience has always
proven difficult. Editing the fourth edition has been no less a challenge
than editing the first. Beverly Rasporich and I have debated, commiser-
ated, and struggled over how to present the many realities of Canadian
identity to a new generation of students. The difficulty of our task is perhaps best expressed and symbolized by the cover of the book—a quilt by
Joyce Wieland that weaves together a series of bright and vivid patches,
each representing something different. We have tried to bring to our
readers a sense of the complexity and majesty of the Canadian experience and also leave readers with tough and sometimes uncomfortable
questions about the Canadian identity. The book also expresses gratitude
for all that we as Canadians have achieved together.

When I wrote the introduction to this section in the first edition, I
was confident, almost buoyant, about the country and its future. I argued

1

that the country was held together by a compassionate system of social caring, sweeping economic patterns that flowed along an east–west axis, the prominent role played by the state, and well-understood and agreed-upon habits of compromise. Beneath the surface of regional and linguistic division were tough sinews of unity and loyalty. I was no longer as optimistic, however, when I had to write the introduction to the second edition in 1992. The country had been shaken by a number of convulsions: the failure of the Meech Lake Accord, the Native uprising at Oka, and the struggle over free trade with the United States. Many of the old certainties of Canadian life were under attack, and a deep sense of unease seemed to hang over the country.

By the time the introduction to the third edition was written in 1996, the storm clouds had burst. The fragility of the country was brought home during the 1995 Quebec Referendum. The forces of Quebec sovereignty lost by a hairsbreadth—50.6 percent to 49.4 percent. In a sense, a psychological bridge had been crossed. What was once unthinkable— that the country could split up—had become possible. Quebeckers and Canadians in the rest of the country began, perhaps for the first time, to imagine what it would be like to live without the other partner. One writer argued that the country seemed to be undergoing a nervous breakdown, losing its sense of balance, unable to cope with the stresses that were being placed on it.

The mid-1990s were also a time when governments were making painful cuts to health, education, and social services. Governments found themselves in a financial straitjacket because of mounting debts and deficits, and a new, radical, right wing agenda made inroads in Canadian public life. Reform leader Preston Manning, Ontario Premier Mike Harris, and Alberta Premier Ralph Klein led crusades in favour of smaller government, increased privatization, and wholesale deregulation. Whether government spending needed to be radically curtailed or not, many Canadians saw investments in medicare and public education as ways in which our country distinguished itself from the United States. These programs were the embodiment of the Canadian commitment to be a more compassionate and more caring society, one that had a greater sense of social justice.

Now, in 2001, the panorama has changed yet again. The economic prosperity of the late 1990s, Canada's leadership in the use of new information technologies, and burgeoning government surpluses, have brought a new wave of optimism, even celebration. One might argue that Canada has emerged from its many trials as a stronger and more resilient country.

This new sense of optimism and achievement is reflected in the fourth edition. The moving speech that Adrienne Clarkson gave upon being installed as Governor General, Harold Troper's magnificent description of the immigrant city, and Janice Dickin's superb account of the revolution brought by the Canadian *Charter of Rights and Freedoms,* all chronicle what many believe are stirring examples of social progress. While gains have been difficult to achieve, and far too many Canadians still suffer the knife wounds of poverty and injustice, Canada has become a more prosperous, open, accepting, and "rights-conscious" society.

One can also argue that Canadian culture is flourishing as never before—Canadian writers, artists, musicians, and humorists have attained international status and are reflecting the country in profound and imaginative ways. Articles by Allan Bell, Christine Sowiak, and Charles Acland describe the evolution of this imaginative space and how the country's artists have reflected and reinforced a particular Canadian sensibility. It must be recognized that many of these achievements have been made against tremendous odds—the gravitational pull of American popular and corporate culture have been so strong that maintaining boundaries and identities cannot be taken for granted. Yet those boundaries and identities still remain.

Moreover, it is now quiet on the national unity front. For the time being at least the guns are almost silent. While important articles by Anne Hébert and Réjean Pelletier remind us that the fires of Quebec nationalist sentiment still burn fiercely, the sharpness and immediacy of the Quebec question has receded. Although Quebec Premier Lucien Bouchard promises that his government will hold another referendum, support for outright independence seems to be at low tide. Quebeckers, like other Canadians, have complex identities and mixed loyalties. While many believe that Quebec needs far more power and autonomy in order to preserve the French language and promote the unique ambiance of Quebec culture, strong emotional attachments to Canada remain. Ties based on shared history, economic integration, and daily interactions cannot be easily severed. Yet tension and uncertainty are still in the air. Canadians have to live with the reality that many of our fellow citizens want to see the country broken apart.

One can also argue that progress has been made by Aboriginal Canadians—our country's first peoples. Fine articles by James Miller, Emma LaRocque, and Cora Voyageur describe the arduous struggles for survival and identity that have been endured and fought by Canada's First Nations. Each of the articles contributes something different to the portrait; James Miller provides a broad overview of Aboriginal history, LaRocque focuses on the unique culture of the Otehpayimsuak peoples, and Voyageur takes us on a journey through her family history, explaining how each generation coped with the many changes in Aboriginal life. Although these articles celebrate accomplishment and achievement, they also reveal much about the despair, injustice, and deep wounds that have scarred Native life in Canada. The reality is perhaps best expressed by the title of Voyageur's article, "We Get Knocked down, but We Get up Again."

Karim-Aly Kassam and Graham White describe two other dimensions of the Aboriginal experience, the struggle of Cree and Inuit for control over economic and resource development and political institutions in the Canadian North. Much of the relationship between Natives and other Canadians is being shaped by the creation of new realities in the North, realities that are explained in both of these clear and well-crafted pieces.

Painful questions are also asked in two powerful pieces that appear in the section entitled "Changing Canada." Anne McGrath's description of the barriers that women face at home and in the workplace will leave readers with much to think about. She asks whether Canadian women are indeed the luckiest in the world. The country's high standard of living, the hard-fought battle to have equality rights enshrined in the *Charter,* and the opening of doors that were previously closed in business and the professions might lead many to believe that Canadian women are living the best possible lives. The truth, according to McGrath, is that high walls still exist, and many women live unfulfilled and broken lives. A similar tack is taken in the poignant contribution made by Wisdom Tettey. Tettey gives readers a glimpse into the world of African Canadians. The portrait shows a complex interaction between the old world and the new, between preserving the values of one's culture on one hand and fitting into the broader society on the other. The sting of lingering racism, however, has made integration more difficult for African Canadians than for others.

The injustices of the past, however, are not forgotten. In a fascinating article, Matt James describes the fight by Japanese, Aboriginal, and other Canadians to seek redress from the federal government for the brutal injustices that these groups were forced to endure in the recent past. James asks important questions about the nature of justice and democracy. Do current governments bear responsibility and liability for the actions taken by previous governments during darker and more desperate times? If governments fail to acknowledge past injustices, are they setting a precedent for the future—signalling that those guilty of racism and prejudice will never have to account for their actions?

In a crucial departure from previous editions, the fourth edition features a section on Canada and globalization. Free trade, the advent of new information technologies, and the rise of global conglomerates are creating a global economy and, indeed, a global culture. Many of the decisions that are important in the lives of Canadians are now made by corporations and institutions that are beyond our borders and beyond our control. Finding our place under this new sun—being able to preserve our identity in the face of so many pressures for integration and convergence—is one of the greatest challenges that we now face as a society.

Although Jack Bumsted's masterful piece on "Visions of Canada" appears in the "Foundations" section at the beginning of the book, his article is a good starting point for understanding the vast forces of international change that have continually shaped and reshaped the Canadian identity. The first stirrings of Canadian nationalism occurred in response to British colonial and then Commonwealth policy. But they also emerged as a reaction to threats from the United States. Bumsted describes how Canadian writers and thinkers have imagined their country and its place in the world from the confederation period until roughly the 1980s.

But these thinkers could not have imagined the pace of change and the deep challenges to Canadian identity that are now posed by the new era of digital globalization. Articles by David Taras, Charles Acland, and David Whitson all deal with the impact made on Canadian culture by the forces of economic convergence and continental integration. Some observers would argue that the attempt to create a common cultural experience through distinctive literature, television, film, sport, and music is now under murderous attack. Huge entertainment conglomerates such as AOL-Time Warner, Microsoft, and Viacom are not only at the forefront of new technologies but also have gained a stranglehold over the distribution of cultural products. One result is the growth of a common youth culture based on listening to the same music, wearing the same clothes, playing the same computer games, visiting the same Web sites, and watching the same movies and TV programs. This new globalization threatens to overwhelm the cultural protections, the cultural fortress, which Canada had erected and guarded for so long.

Another aspect of globalization is the threats to international security that still exist even after the end of the Cold War. While Canada does not have to worry about a direct military threat to its territory, strategic studies scholar Rob Huebert asks whether the Canadian Forces can fulfill the many tasks to which they have been assigned. While Canadians are proud of the country's peacekeeping legacy, and indeed see peacekeeping as one of the ways in which Canada distinguishes itself from the United States, the Forces have also had to defend Canadian borders and sea and fishing lanes and fulfill our obligation to the Western Alliance. After years of budget cutbacks, the Forces may literally be "running out of ammo."

Aspects of the new globalization are so threatening because Canada does not have the mechanisms for national integration normally associated with strong nation building. Many of our leading national institutions—the monarchy, the House of Commons, the Senate, and federal–provincial relations—either no longer command the loyalty they once did or seem to be in need of drastic reform. And some of the old stalwarts of national policy and indeed of national identity—medicare, public broadcasting, and peacekeeping—are also in jeopardy.

Yet, despite the many concerns and travails, the country has deep reservoirs of strength. The tolerant spirit of most Canadians, the talent for organization and innovation that has put Canada at the forefront in the new economy, the belief in education, and the sense that Canada remains a country of hope and of the future are deeply engrained. The majestic and intoxicating beauty of the Canadian landscape also continues to weave a special sense of belonging.

The journey through these four editions has been a happy one and indeed something of a celebration. But we have had to confront through our editing the many difficulties and complexities of the Canadian condition and indeed some of the grave disappointments that are part of the Canadian experience. We hope that the fourth edition is a useful guide to the many dimensions of Canadian identity and a reminder to our readers not to forget who they are in this time of change.

PART A

FOUNDATIONS

Cherry Orchards

Leonard Cohen

Canada some wars are waiting for you
some threats
some torn flags
Inheritance is not enough
    Faces must be forged under the hammer
of savage ideas
    Mailboxes will explode
in the cherry orchards
and somebody will wait forever
for his grandfather's fat cheque
    From my deep café I survey the quiet snowfields
like a U.S. promoter
of a new plastic snowshoe
looking for a moving speck
a troika perhaps
an exile
an icy prophet
an Indian insurrection
a burning weather station
    There's a story out there boys
Canada could you bear some folk songs
about freedom and death

Installation Speech

Her Excellency the Right Honourable Adrienne Clarkson,
Governor-General of Canada

Prime Minister, You have expressed to me the affection, loyalty and esteem of the Canadian people, which it will be my honour to convey to our gracious sovereign, Queen Elizabeth II. I am pleased to accept the responsibility of being her Majesty's representative in Canada, with all that entails, through our history and our custom.

Knowing better than anyone my own shortcomings, I undertake this task with humility and ask you all, as Canadians, to help me.

I take on the responsibility of becoming Canada's 26th governor-general since Confederation,[1] fully conscious of the deep roots of this office, stretching back to the governors of New France, and to the first of them, Samuel de Champlain.[2] In our beloved Georgian Bay, which lies on the great water route he took from the French river to Huronia, there is a cairn, placed on a small island, between a tennis court and Champlain's Gas Bar & Marina, which commemorates his passage and quotes from his journal:

> Samuel de Champlain
> by canoe
> 1615
> "As for me, I labour always to prepare a way for those willing to follow."

Those willing to follow have embodied the institution of the governor-general in ways which have demonstrated the evolution and constant reaffirmation of this country. Canada's institutions have never been static. They are organic—evolving and growing in ways that surprise and even startle us. In a mere 30 years, between 1952 and 1982, we repatriated the governor-generalship and our *Constitution*. We adopted our flag, we formalized our understanding of rights and we strengthened and expanded the bilingual nature of our country. The governor-general is one skein in the woven fabric of what Eugene Forsey[3] characterized as our "independent sovereign democracy."

Champlain's successors have had many activists among them. Lord Elgin, who helped Baldwin and LaFontaine to anchor the Canadian model of democracy in 1848, stands out as somebody who appreciated the originality of a country which would promote such a project. He loved to wander about our few small cities, on foot, glorying in snowstorms, eschewing the formality of his office and speaking of his admiration for "this glorious country" and "its perfectly independent inhabitants." He also said, that in order to have insight into the future of all nations, it was necessary to come here.

Vincent Massey, our first Canadian governor-general, laid the groundwork for practically all of our modern cultural institutions—the Canada Council, the National Arts Centre, the Order of Canada, among others. And my predecessor, Roméo LeBlanc, reinforced the central fact of French Canada across this country, culminating in the success of last month's Summit that put New Brunswick and Acadia at the centre of the map of francophone reality. This was only 50 years after the great painter, Paul-Émile Borduas,[4] had exhorted Quebec, and by implication, all of us, to abandon "the smooth and slippery walls of fear" by refusing "to act knowingly (or consciously) ... beneath (our) psychic and physical possibilities."

Allow me a moment of personal reflection. The Poy family, arriving here as refugees in 1942, was made up of my parents, my brother and myself. Three of us are in this Chamber today. We did not arrive as part of a regular immigration procedure. There was no such thing for a Chinese family at that time in Canadian history.

My mother's intense and abiding love is here in spirit today. My brother, Dr. Neville Poy, was seven when we arrived. And my father Bill Poy, is here—extraordinary, in his 92nd year. Lance-Corporal Poy, dispatch rider with the Hong Kong Volunteer Corps, received the Military Medal for his bravery during the battle of Hong Kong. Like many soldiers, he never speaks of those actions, but it is his bravery which is the underpinning of his children's lives. To have been brought up by courageous and loving parents, was a gift that made up for all we had lost.

As I have said before, the city of Ottawa, then, was small and white—like most of Canada. Much of its psyche was characterized by what Mavis Gallant[5] has called "the dark bloom of the Old Country—the mistrust of pity, the contempt for weakness, the fear of the open heart." But it was also the place where our family was befriended by the Molots, who owned the local drugstore, the Marcotes and the Proulx, among whom we lived in Lower town, and our guardian angels, the Potters.

Because my father had a job with the Department of Trade and Commerce and because we lived among French Canadians, I became fixated, from the age of five, with the idea of learning French. I remember the day when I was dressed up in my patent-leather shoes and pink smocked dress, and was taken up the street by my parents to the convent of Ste. Jeanne d'Arc, where I was interviewed by a kindly woman wearing white all around her face, while a dim crucifix glowed in the background. Walking home, I sensed that there was dejection in the air and disappointment. It had been explained to my parents that it was not possible for a Protestant to receive French-language education in Ottawa. In my lifetime, this has changed to such a radical degree that I don't even need to comment on it. But that early sense of something being impossible, which actually was nonsensical, put steel into me.

Farley Mowat[6] has pointed out that a little adversity in childhood is a very good thing for animals—including human ones. Our family, like many others, had lost a great deal but we had also gained an enormous amount: a country with lakes, with small-mouth bass and with free public education. We became addicted to the wilderness because, as Pierre Morency says, "Le nord n'est pas dans la boussole; il est ici." ["The North is not on the compass. It is right here."]

As John Ralston Saul[7] has written, the central quality of the Canadian state is its complexity. It is a strength and not a weakness that we are a "permanently incomplete experiment built on a triangular foundation—aboriginal, francophone and anglophone."

What we continue to create, today, began 450 years ago as a political project, when the French first met with the aboriginal people. It is an old experiment, complex and, in worldly terms, largely successful. Stumbling through darkness and racing through light, we have persisted in the creation of a Canadian civilization.

We are constructing something different here. As Jean-Guy Pilon[8] describes in one of his poems:

> Racines tordues à vaincre le feu
> A cracher au visage des étoiles.
> C'est ici que respirent, grandissent
> les constructeurs.
>
> ["Tormented roots that defy the flames
> Spitting in the face of stars.
> Here the builders breathe, and grow."]

We have the opportunity to leave behind the useless blood calls of generations, now that we are in the new land that stretches to infinity. Wilfrid Laurier[9] understood this clearly. "We have made a conquest greater and more glorious than that of any territory," he said, "we have conquered our liberties."

There seem to be two kinds of societies in the world today. Perhaps there have always been only two kinds—punishing societies and forgiving societies. A society like Canada's, with its four centuries of give-and-take, compromise and acceptance, wrong-doing and redress, is basically a forgiving society. We try—we must try—to forgive what is past. The punishing society never forgets the wrongs of the past. The forgiving society works towards the actions of the future. The forgiving society enables people to behave well toward one another, to begin again, to build a society in hope and with love.

We know, that in joining Canadian society, we will be able to accept the invitation, offered, in 1970, by Grand Chief John Kelly: "As the years go by, the circle of the Ojibway gets bigger and bigger. Canadians of all colours and religions are entering that circle. You might feel that you have roots somewhere else, but in reality, you are right here with us." That the aboriginal circle enlarges to include all of us—native and immigrant—arriving by boat and plane to a vast and beautiful land, has been characterized by Michael Ondaatje,[10] as a "vision of nature beyond the human ego." This is a place, he said, "fixated by the preoccupying image of figures permanently travelling or portaging their past—we are all still arriving. From the *Filles du Roy* to Dionne Brand's new Canadians is a miniscule step."

We must not forget that this complexity is whole. To be complex does not mean to be fragmented. This is the paradox and the genius of our Canadian civilization.

In the contemplation of our wholeness, lies the symbolic importance of the governor-general: the identification of this post with inclusiveness—the inclusiveness that lies at the core of Canadian society, at its best. This is the essence of our notorious decency, our infamous desire to do good. And it is important to recall that with the great waves of immigration, there has been, since the beginning, an underlying motif: the lost, the rejected, and those who dreamed of another life would come here and would make a contribution to the whole.

In a 1913 photograph, a group of Scandinavian immigrants in Larcmont, Ontario is huddled around a blackboard on which is written:

The Duties of the Citizen
1. Understand our government.
2. Take an active part in politics.
3. Assist all good causes.
4. Lessen intemperance.
5. Work for others.

It would be easy to focus obsessively on all the pitfalls and prejudices that undoubtedly landmined this path of good intentions. But in examining the intent, you see the underlying central assumption. It was expected that the immigrant, along with everyone else, would join in the social process, which was democratic, co-operative and other-directed. The fact that it would take another 50 years for this kind of inclusiveness to become colour-blind, means, simply, that it took another 50 years. Too long, of course. Far too long. But in other countries, it would take a hundred. In some, it has never come.

The essence of inclusiveness is that we are part of a society in which language, colour, education, sex and money need not, should not divide us, but can make us more aware and sensitive to difference.

I learned to be a Canadian through a series of eternally virginal public school teachers, who treated me only as bright—and not bright yellow. They were mostly small-town Ontario women who, given some of our history, might have been narrow-minded; but without exception they had the ability to reach out and understood, instinctively, the need for compassion and the stirring of imaginative curiosity.

I believe that my parents, like so many other immigrants, dreamed their children into being as Canadians. And, as the explorers pushed, every day, beyond the limits of their knowledge, what were Cavelier de la Salle, La Verendrye, Hearne and Mackenzie doing, if not imagining themselves spanning this astonishing space. Luckily, all of us came to a land where the aboriginal peoples have always dreamed life into being.

It is customary to talk about how hard immigrants work and how ambitious they are, but those who have lived that process, know that it is mainly the dream that counts.

I'm not talking here of fantasy. I am talking of the true dream that is caught in the web of the past as it meets the wind of the future. All of us have this, even if we do not express it. This is what gives a nation, such as ours, its resonance, its depth and its strength.

The dream pulls us on and transforms us into Canadians. The dream gives us the strength to avoid being stereotyped by the past or limited by the expectations of others. The dream brings openness, adventure and, of course, pain and confusion. But, as Leonard Cohen[11] observes, "There is a crack in everything. That's how the light gets in."

Through the light that is in us, we have created a place of dynamic innovation. Innovation in political structures. New approaches toward social relationships, towards citizenship. Military innovation in peacekeeping. Economic innovation in cutting-edge industries, from the railway of 150 years ago to aeronautics today.

We must not see ourselves as a small country of 30 million people, floundering in a large land mass. We are among the healthiest, best-educated people in the world, with great natural riches. We have two of the world's great languages. We must not see ourselves as people who simply react to trends but as people who can initiate them. We must not see ourselves as people to whom things are done but as people who do things.

Our history demonstrates that we have the self-confidence to act and to act successfully. We can—when we trust ourselves—seize hold of the positive energy flowing out of the choice we have made to be here, and to continue what remains an unprecedented experiment.

The streetcar our family often took on Sunday afternoons to Rockcliffe Park, used to pass the closed gates of Rideau Hall. I'm so glad that has changed. I'm delighted that crowds of people now come through the ground and the Visitor Centre. I look forward to continuing the tradition of welcoming Canadians to what is, in effect, your national house.

But we will not always be in Ottawa. John and I intend to travel and re-travel this whole country by plane, train, car, canoe and kayak. We are initiating the holding of a public levee in each province and territory we visit. You are all invited. In 10 days we will be in Alberta for our first official provincial trip. Our first levee will be held on Saturday, October 16 at 4 p.m. at the Museum of the Regiments in Calgary. In November, we will be in British Columbia and our levee will be on Sunday, November 21 in Vancouver.

We want to meet as many of you as we can, not only on special occasions at Rideau Hall, and at La Citadelle in Quebec City, but where you live and make your lives.

We bring to this new work, a deep commitment to the relationship between francophone and anglophone, which is the essential and central fact of our political history. We have already long-established, personal interests in French immersion schooling, shelter for the fragile in our society and human rights. And I am committed, as I have always been, to affirming and furthering the full expression of that more than half of society to which I belong—a group which modestly calls itself women. We also have a history of deep involvement in and love for the arts. Beauty and excellence are not the property of a select group. They are the means by which we most profoundly express our society and they belong to every one of us.

As I take up this task, I ask you to embark on a journey with me. Together, I hope that we will be able to do it with the Inuit[12] quality of *isuma*, which is defined as an intelligence that includes knowledge of one's responsibility towards society. The Inuit believe that it can only grow in its own time; it grows because it is nurtured. I pray that with God's help, we, as Canadians, will trace with our own lives, what Stan Rogers[13] called "one warm line through this land, so wild and savage."

And in the footsteps of Samuel de Champlain, I am willing to follow.

NOTES

1. Confederation: The union of the British North American colonies of New Brunswick, Nova Scotia, and Canada (Canada being the earlier union, in 1841, of Lower Canada and Upper Canada), took place on July 1, 1867.

2. Samuel de Champlain: Born at Brouage, France, c.1570, cartographer, explorer, and governor of New France. He first voyaged to Canada in 1603 via the St. Lawrence River to chart the coast for possible settlement locations. In 1608 Champlain, who became known as the "father of New France," was sent to establish the settlement of Quebec.

3. Eugene Forsey: Born at Grand Bank, Nfld., 1904, intellectual, Liberal senator, and two-time CCF candidate, known for his socialist politics, and conversely for his close relationship with Conservative Prime Minister Arthur Meighen. He published one influential study, *The Royal Power of Dissolution of Parliament* (1943), but is best known for his numerous acerbic articles, debates, and letters on public affairs.

4. Paul-Émile Borduas: Born at St. Hilaire, Que., 1905, painter, had an enduring influence on art in Canada. During difficult financial times he was forced to take jobs as a church decorator and a drawing teacher in Montreal. His later works showed influences from Renoir and Cézanne. In 1948 he published a manifesto titled *Refus Global* in which he denounced the oppressive power of the establishment in Quebec and proclaimed the right to freedom of expression.

5. Mavis Gallant: Born at Montreal, 1922, began her writing career as a reporter for the *Montreal Standard* in 1944, but relocated in 1950 to Paris—where she still resides—to follow her dream to become a fiction writer. She has since published more than 100 short stories, which are famous for capturing with vivid visual detail a specific time and place. After long being overlooked in Canada she was appointed an Officer of the Order of Canada in 1981 and won the Governor-General's Award for *Home Truths: Selected Canadian Stories* in 1982.

6. Farley Mowat: Born at Belleville, Ont. 1921, author of *Sea of Slaughter.* "All animals require and profit from adversity in order to survive, and that includes the human animal."

7. John Ralston Saul: Born at Ottawa, 1947, an internationally acclaimed novelist and essayist, who is the only Canadian included in the prestigious *Utne Reader's* 1995 list of the 100 leading thinkers and visionaries. He is the partner of the new Governor-General, Adrienne Clarkson, and won the Governor-General's Award in 1996.

8. Jean-Guy Pilon: Born at St. Polycarpe, Que., 1930, writer who co-founded in 1959 the Quebec magazine *Liberté,* known for its biting commentary and role as a forum for French-Canadian culture. His poetry is romantic with a driving sentiment of love and appreciation for nature.

9. Sir Wilfrid Laurier: Born at St. Lin, Canada, 1841, lawyer, journalist, politician, and prime minister of Canada from 1896 to 1911. He is heralded by *The Canadian Encyclopedia* as "the dominant political figure of his era ... a fervent promoter of national unity at a time of radical change and worsening cultural conflict."

10. Michael Ondaatje: Born at Columbo, Sri Lanka, 1943, poet and writer, author of *The English Patient,* who expresses his experience in a diversity of cultures with exotic and sure imagery and wit.

11. Leonard Cohen: Born at Montreal, 1934, poet, novelist, songwriter, and Buddhist. He won a Governor-General's Award in 1968 but declined.

12. Inuit: Meaning "people." The Inuit, who are one of the original groups to inhabit the northern regions of Canada, were previously known by Europeans as Eskimos, a pejorative term roughly translated as "eaters of raw meat."

13. Stan Rogers: Born at Hamilton, Ont., 1949, folksinger and songwriter, *Northwest Passage*. "Ah, for just one time I would take the Northwest Passage. To find the hand of Frank reaching for the Beaufort Sea; Tracing a warm line through a land so wild and savage. And makes a Northwest Passage to the sea."

Visions of Canada: A Brief History of Writing on the Canadian Character and the Canadian Identity

Jack Bumsted

The extent to which the achievement of confederation, a union of some of the provinces of British North America, demonstrated a willingness to see a nation as a new political entity is a subject much debated amongst historians. It is clear, however, that not all the Fathers of confederation, nor their successors, had the same vision of the new Canada. From the beginning there were a number of variant national visions, based upon a series of fundamental philosophical disagreements, perhaps often as much temperamental as intellectual or ideological. Moreover, the questions changed to some extent over time. As a result, there has never been within Canada a single authorized version of Canadian nationalism, no agreed-upon Canadian identity, and certainly no correspondence between political party allegiance and nationalist visions. Instead, there have been a number of basic conflicting points of disagreement for a series of alternate visions of Canada. Nationalism in its more extreme pan-Canadian form—an exceedingly common if not dominant vision—is almost exclusively an English-Canadian notion. French Canadians, especially those resident in Quebec, have increasingly supported a brand of nationalism based exclusively on allegiances within the province. Over the years, the range of possible disagreements over the nature of Canada has increasingly narrowed.

No single term has ever fully captured the search by Canadians for the meaning of Canada. The two most common are "character" and "identity," often with the modifiers "national" or "Canadian" in front of them. Neither term has ever been precisely defined or described, and those who use such concepts fail miserably to define them in completely operational ways. The concept of identity carries more than a suggestion of self-ascription; thus, one simple distinction could be that identity is what people think of themselves, while character is what others think of them. It is also unclear whether the "Canadian" modifier is meant to suggest something overarching and pan-national or merely something that is present somewhere in the country.

In examining the writings about visions of Canada that have often focused on character and identity, we can perhaps identify three periods. The first, lasting from confederation to World War I, saw the nationalists largely in control, at least of the debate over the nature of the nation, and the Tory viewpoint largely in control of nationalism. Much of the Canadian business community, moveover, supported nationalism. The vision-makers were, for the most part, politicians, publicists, and professionals. Virtually without exception, these people believed in progress and in technology. With the aid of improved transportation and communication, Canada would inevitably get bigger and better. World War I permanently estranged French Canada from any view of Canadian pannationalism and helped move many English Canadians away from British imperialist sentiments.

During the period from 1920 to 1960, a transitional period for the meaning of the Canadian identity, Canadian nationalism became more progressive, moving from the Tories to the political left, especially the League for Social Reconstruction and the Cooperative Commonwealth Federation (CCF). The British connection declined and during World War II was replaced by a continentalist cooperation between Canada and the United States in military and economic matters. Both before and after World War II, much of the articulation of nationalist sentiment was left to the academic and cultural communities of Canada, especially the historians. World War I and the Great Depression tempered the pre-war optimism, and major developments of this period included a new concern over the implications of technology and communications for the Canadian nation, particularly for its cultural identity, which became the critical point in the definitions.

In the later 1960s and 1970s, the English-Canadian nationalists—now firmly to the left of the political centre—linked national cultural identity, issues of foreign investment/control, and fears about technology. In some ways, the issues became much more disparate and complex, and the historical dimension was largely lost. Instead of historians, the visionaries became literary critics and philosophers. The international policy of the American government in the later 1960s, especially in Vietnam, helped make many Canadians fearful of the United States. Beginning in the 1960s, Quebec adopted its own nationalism, and after 1968 the Liberal Party under Pierre Elliott Trudeau became the chief exponent of pan-Canadian nationalism. When, in the 1980s, the Canadian business community abandoned protectionism and economic planning, the way was clear for a complete reversal of traditional roles. The Tories became the supporters of free trade and continentalism. Nevertheless, the relationship between nation, culture, and cultural policy continued to be a strong one.

1. 1867–1919

As might have been expected, the period after confederation saw many contending views of what kind of a country Canada should become. The first extended expression of a national vision began just after confederation, in the movement that called itself "Canada First." The original Canada First group was founded in 1868 as a secret society by a small group of intellectuals in Ottawa. Most had been born in Upper Canada and believed themselves above and beyond "party," although they were hardly immune to ideology. Canada First was a pan-nationalist group. It chafed at any colonial status and was certain that Canada's destiny— often confusing Canada West and the new nation—was to control the western part of the continent north of the 49th parallel. Canada First was convinced that Canada needed a distinctive culture, and it developed the concept that the nation's geography made it inevitable that it should be northern. It was not a far jump from northern geography to racialist ideas. One of these young men, Robert Grant Haliburton, insisted in a lecture eventually published as a pamphlet, that Canada "must ever be a Northern country inhabited by the descendants of Northern races." Although Haliburton was prepared to include the French in the "Northern races," the Canada Firsters had little time for French Canada. In one letter to the press, Charles Mair virtually exploded on this subject:

> Ontario and the English-speaking people of Quebec have been milked long enough.... Thank God there is such a thing at last as a purely national feeling in Canada. There is a young and vigorous race coming to the front, entirely in Earnest, and which is no longer English, Scotch or Irish, but thoroughly and distinctly Canadian.... It means strict justice to the French and nothing more—a fair field and no favour. (Quoted in Berger, 1970, pp. 58–59)

The French language, said Mair, stood in the way of Canadians ever becoming a "homogeneous people." For these early nationalists, the United States was less a threat to Canada than was the condescension of the English, but they certainly saw the United States as the home of the "grab," of the worst sort of political corruption that should not be imitated north of the border. The Americans were also seen as weak and "effeminate," because they were not sufficiently northern (Berger, 1966).

Not all Canadians agreed that the United States was unattractive to Canadians. In 1891 historian Goldwin Smith argued in *Canada and the Canadian Question* that Canada's future lay within a continental union with the United States. He insisted that the geography of North America worked against Canadian nationalism and that the continent was Canada's national market, concluding his study by advocating "Commercial Union" with the United States. Smith had long insisted on four factors that would ultimately lead Canada to break with Britain: "distance, divergence of interest, divergence of political character and the attraction of the great mass of English-speaking people which adjoins us on this continent" (Smith, 1878, p. 130). He saw little in common between Canada and most of the rest of the British Empire, which included "an Asiatic dominion extending over two hundred and fifty millions of Hindoos" and "a group of West Indian Islands full of emancipated negro slaves" (Smith, 1891, p. 191). Smith's critics may have exaggerated a bit when they claimed, as did George Parkin, that no political passion in Canada was so strong as "opposition to absorption in the United States" and that "no avowed annexationist could be elected to the Dominion Parliament" (Parkin, 1894, p. 185). However, there was little Canadian support for Smith's views, which were in many ways largely negative pronouncements of what Canada could never become unless annexed to the United States.

Just as incapable of gaining broad-based popular support in the years before 1914 were the views of John S. Ewart (1849–1933), who called for full Canadian sovereignty in a series of books in the early years of the 20th century. Ewart's arguments for independence tended to be legalistic and constitutional. He found colonial status degrading, for "Colony implies inferiority—inferiority in culture, inferiority in wealth, inferiority in government, inferiority in foreign relations, inferiority and subordination" (Ewart, 1908, p. 6). He did not advocate the breaking of the imperial connection with the Crown, but instead envisioned an evolutionary progression by which the government in Ottawa would have the same standing as that of Westminster. Ewart did agree with the anti-imperialists like Smith and some French Canadians that Canada had no responsibility for shouldering any of the burdens of Empire. Canada had ceased to be a subordinate state, and all that remained was "the semblance and appearance of subordination"(Ewart, 1908, p. 364). Insofar as Canadians had an imperial duty, it was to reject the Empire and become truly independent. Like most other nationalists, Ewart was concerned that British sentiment stood in the way of the creation of a genuine indigenous Canadian national consciousness:

> Our unofficial orators have held up to us, not Canadianism, but Imperialism, and their failure to achieve success is similar to that of those who endeavour to love God and yet remain out of sympathy with their fellow-men. How can Canadians love the British Empire which they have not seen when they do not love their own country which they have seen? (Ewart, 1908, p. 80)

Such arguments were as close as Ewart could come to a transcendent vision.

While the federal government of Sir John A. Macdonald strategically associated the Conservative (or Tory) Party with nationalism through the creation of the National Policy—based on a protective tariff, the construction of a national east–west transcontinental railroad, and the settlement of the West through immigration—the ideas of Canada First were gradually transmuted into Canadian Imperialism (Berger, 1970). While at first glance it may seem paradoxical to view imperialists as nationalists, contemporaries saw no inconsistency here between the promotion of a sense of a distinct Canadian identity and membership in a larger British Empire. Linkage to the British Empire provided Canadians with a larger stage. "I am an Imperialist," argued Stephen Leacock in 1907, "because I will not be a Colonial." For some, although not all, Canadian imperialists, the ultimate expression of imperialism became imperial federation, which one of its advocates described "as a union between the Mother Country and Canada that would give Canada not only the present full management of its own affairs, but a fair share of the management and responsibilities of common affairs" (Parkin, 1892). World War I demonstrated just how softheaded this notion had been, as Canada found itself very much a junior partner in the making of wartime policy.

The Empire, of course, also conveniently provided Canada with a bulwark against the United States, economically, culturally, and militarily. Like Canada First, most of the imperialists believed that the distinctive Canadian character was a product of northern geography, severe northern winters, and the nation's inheritance of "northern races" connected to the northern races of Europe who had been the originators of the concept of "liberty." Conversely, of course, southern climates sapped the energy. French Canadians could be included as northern if they liked. According to George Monro Grant, French Canadians were politically "British and their hearts are all for Canada." But others thought the French Canadians lacked energy. According to George Parkin, "One has no hesitation in discussing frankly this question of race inertia in Quebec. The most clear-sighted men of the province admit and deplore it" (quoted in Hodgins and Page, 1976, 322–23). The poet Wilfred Campbell saw French Canada as "useless, despotic, intolerant, and ultra-conservative in her body political and her social ideas" (quoted in Hodgins and Page, 1976, p. 323). Most French Canadians chose to remain apart from sharing northernness.

Newcomers such as Mennonites, Icelanders, and Ukrainians also qualified as northern, provided they were prepared to assimilate to the dominant norm, which was English-speaking Anglo-Canadian. Not surprisingly, most imperialists supported the notion of English-only schools for western Canada and, at least secretly, admired the Americans for their national ceremonies. In his 1917 novel *The Major,* popular writer Ralph Connor allowed one of his Canadian characters to advocate "flag-flapping" American attitudes toward the flag because it provided a common identity for "foreigners, Ruthenians, Russians, Germans, Poles." The narrator described a "flag-saluting" ceremony he had witnessed in Oregon:

A kid with Yiddish written all over his face was chosen to carry in the flag, attended by a bodyguard for the colours, and believe me they appeared as proud as Punch of the honour. They placed the flag in position, sang a hymn, had a prayer, and then every kid, at a signal, shot out his right hand toward the flag held aloft by the Yiddish colour-bearer and pledged himself, heart, and soul, and body, to his flag and his country. The ceremony closed with the singing of the national hymn, mighty poor poetry and mighty hard to sing, but do you know that listening to those kids and watching their foreign faces I found myself with tears in my eyes and swallowing like a darn fool. (Connor, 1917, 130–31)

Sir Wilfrid Laurier gave new life to a Liberal party with an alternative vision to those of the Tories and the imperialists (LaPierre, 1996). "My object is to consolidate Confederation," Laurier wrote in 1904, "and to bring our people long estranged from each other, gradually to become a nation." Unlike the nationalism of the Tories or the imperialists, Laurier's version of nationalism did not involve either racial unity or the creation of an all-powerful central government. His vision instead was of a country in which "all the races, all the creeds and all the religions" could be united by the bonds of "liberty" (Laurier, 1894). Constitutionally, he sought to preserve minority rights by allowing all provincial legislatures to "be absolutely free of each other, and free from supervision." Thus he refused to bring the powers of the federal government to bear upon the province of Manitoba to force it to accept bilingual education (Crunican, 1974). On this as on other issues, Laurier was prepared to compromise to avoid open confrontations between the peoples and the provinces of Canada.

For Laurier, between the Dominion and the provinces "there is no superiority and inferiority; all are equal, with this exception, that the Dominion Parliament is invested with larger powers, that is, powers of a more extended and more important character than the local legislature" (Laurier, 1896, 2740–43) As for the Empire, he argued in 1909, "We are British subjects but we are an autonomous nation" (Laurier, 1909). Laurier was prepared to allow Canada to make token contributions to imperial military activities, but Canadian autonomy rather than imperial cooperation on defence was the more important issue. In principle supporting free trade, Laurier was pleased to be able to negotiate a better trade relationship with the United States in the proposed Reciprocity Treaty of 1911, and he was startled when the electorate rejected his Liberals, at least partly over the treaty, in the election of that year.

A similar if less hazy perception of Canada was that enunciated by the French-Canadian Henri Bourassa (1868–1952), who was a member of a leading Quebec family (his grandfather was Louis-Joseph Papineau). Bourassa first came to prominence in 1899 when he resigned his seat in parliament over the Laurier government's decision to permit Canadian volunteers to assist Britain in South Africa without parliamentary approval. Bourassa was re-elected unopposed and pursued unsuccessfully his insistence on the right of the Canadian Parliament alone to declare war. He helped defeat Laurier in 1911 over the prime minister's willingness to build a Canadian navy that would be turned over to Britain in time of emergency. Virtually alone in his day, Bourassa advocated a fully articulated bicultural Canadian nationalism:

> The only possible basis for the solution of our national problems is one of mutual respect for our racial characters and exclusive devotion to our common land…. We are not asking our neighbours of English extraction to help us develop a political reconciliation with France, and they have no right to use their strength of numbers to break the rules of the alliance, forcing us to shoulder new obligations towards England, even if these were completely voluntary and spontaneous. (Quoted in Monière, 1981, p. 189)

Although he acknowledged that "My *own* people … are the French Canadians," Bourassa maintained that "My native land is all of Canada, a federation of separate races and autonomous provinces. The nation I wish to see grow up is the Canadian nation, made up of French Canadians and English Canadians" (Monière, 1981, p. 190).

Most of the discussion about Canada assumed that culture was important but did not address it directly. Moreover, presentations of the nature of Canada before 1914 were issued with the understanding, usually tacit, that technology was either neutral or, more often, a positive factor in the development of the nation, however defined. The idea of progress was a major assumption of the Victorian era. History recorded steady growth in material and moral conditions. As Carl Berger points out, continual improvement was "confirmed by the technological innovations of the industrial revolution, identified with the ineluctable processes of evolutionary science," and "it was startlingly obvious in the colonial environment" (Berger, 1970, p. 109). Every history of Canada compared "then" and "now," to the obvious advantage of "now." Orators waxed eloquent about "lines of railway connecting us with the whole American continent," about "steam communication with Europe," and about "telegraphic connection with every part of the world" (Hill, 1873, 5–6). Small wonder that Laurier predicted that the 20th century would belong to Canada.

The Great War in 1914 challenged all Canadian efforts at sharing a vision of the nation. Joining the war effort in 1914 marked a triumph of sorts for Canadian imperialism. The war brought extraordinary expressions of patriotic fervour and eventually isolated the French Canadians, whose suspicion of overseas adventurism before and during 1914 turned into absolute hostility to conscription by 1917. The English-Canadian majority succeeded in 1917 in forming a Union Government out of ruling Conservatives and those English-speaking members of the Liberal Party who broke with Sir Wilfrid Laurier and his adamant opposition to conscription. The result was a government that adopted several of the leading reforms of Canadian Anglo-Protestantism, including Prohibition and women's suffrage. Although that government was able to employ Canadian military contributions to the war effort to increase Canadian military autonomy during the fighting and Canadian international autonomy (including separate membership in the League of Nations) after it, in many respects a single Canadian nationalism could not be retrieved—if ever it had been possible.

2. 1919–64

Following the Great War, it was practically impossible to hold seriously a bicultural vision of Canada. Canada achieved full sovereignty with the Westminster Declaration in 1930, but by this time Quebec had retreated into its own "nationalism," which did not extend far beyond its borders. While English Canadians continued to fuss over whether Canada was spiritually a British or an American nation, the inter-war period saw the development of the social sciences in both the United States and Canada, which led to a sort of debate over the meaning of Canada between two groups of North American social scientists. One group, led by Canadian-born academics who had moved on to teaching positions in the United States, worked with the support of the Carnegie Endowment for International Peace to establish Canada—as had Goldwin Smith—as a North American nation with a friendly working relationship with the United States, while the scholarship of a smaller group of Canadian academics still resident in Canada attempted to establish the integrity of Canada's territory as both naturally and historically determined. This group tended to be less sanguine about the future of Canada in an ever-changing world.

The Division of Economics and History of the Carnegie Foundation for International Peace was directed by Canadian-born James T. Shotwell of Columbia University and, in a series of 25 volumes published between 1936 and 1945, concentrated on various aspects of Canadian–American relations in a conscious effort to improve them (Berger, 1972, pp. 32–54). There was no attempt to produce a uniform interpretation, but a focus on the informal as well as formal connections between the two nations inevitably demonstrated that there was more to North American history than antagonism between the United States and Canada. Diplomatic and military relations may often have been tense until the end of the 19th century, but in social and economic terms the processes involved were far more continental and benign. Before the Great War, population crossed the border virtually at will in both directions, and capital continued to do so. In these terms, the boundaries between the nations had historically been artificial. The series describes Canada and the United States as more like each other and utterly different from Europe.

The early findings of the Carnegie people were anticipated and put into a coherent argument by the Winnipeg newspaper editor John W. Dafoe in his 1935 book, *Canada: An American Nation* (Dafoe, 1935; Donnelly, 1968). The book had its genesis in lectures delivered at Columbia University in New York, the academic home of James T. Shotwell, and was dedicated to him. Dafoe began by calling North America "the largest continuous territory in the world given over to a people, the great majority of whom derive from kindred sources—a people moreover who are subject to pressures, environmental, linguistic, social and commercial, which steadily increase their homogeneous elements." As a result of the American Revolution, Dafoe continued, the revolutionaries and the loyalists developed "an indigenous American civilization, now the common inheritance of Canada and the United States." The author traced the development of Canada as a democratic nation, pointing out the continual American influences—many of which had been or were being documented by the Carnegie series—including a substantial immigration north. He pointed out that the United States had been Canada's major trading partner since 1900 and concluded that the Americans must face up to their international responsibilities. Dafoe did not suggest a merger of the two nations of North America, but he did call for greater cooperation between them.

While the continentalists were at work in the academy of the 1920s and 1930s, so too were the nationalists (Berger, 1976, pp. 85–111, 137–59). Two scholars, both at the University of Toronto, were particularly influential. One was the economic historian Harold Innis (1894–1952) (Havelock, 1982; Melody et al., 1981). In the years after the war, Innis sought, through both archival research and extensive travel, to understand the origins of the Canadian economy. What he discovered—and explained in a series of monographs—was that the Canadian early economy was a northern one based on resources traded overseas using the country's natural waterways, which ran in an east–west direction (Innis, 1930). From the beginning, geography had given Canada coherence; by implication, the creation of a political nation did not impose artificial boundaries on the geography but merely continued the traditional ones.

Innis's insights were translated into political terms by Donald Creighton (1902–79). Ironically, Creighton's great study of the economy of early 19th-century Canada, *The Commercial Empire of the St. Lawrence,* was published in 1937 under the auspices of the Carnegie people (Creighton, 1937). Creighton believed that the St. Lawrence river and lake system was the basis not only of Canadian development and expansion before 1850 but also of the creation of a transcontinental nation in the 1860s and afterward. That later theme he began to develop in his very popular textbook, *Dominion of the North* (first published in 1944), and expanded in his magisterial biography of the life of John A. Macdonald after World War II, which viewed the creation of Canada as an inevitable result of character and circumstance. One of the dangers of the "Laurentianism" of Innis and Creighton, of course, was that it turned Western Canada into a colonial appendage of the Central region, and especially of Ontario, and the Atlantic region into a backwater (Morton, 1946, in McKillop, 1980). Such a version of the Canadian "nation" was all too familiar to many Canadians before and after 1945. Nevertheless, Canadian nationalism was given intellectual and academic integrity.

In his later years, Harold Innis became fascinated with the manipulative power of the media. He became globally reflective, producing a series of books, articles, essays, and addresses under the general heading of one of his titles, "The Bias of Communication" (Innis, 1950; Innis, 1951; Innis, 1952). For Innis, command of the media of communication was control of communication, and in turn communication influenced greatly the development of political empires and their societies. In every medium of communication, a monopoly or oligopoly of knowledge was created. Radio and television were ideal media both for demagogues and for the dissemination of American commercial popular culture. The effects on Canadian culture of American wartime propaganda and commercialism in the electronic media, he wrote,

> ... have been disastrous. Indeed they threaten Canadian life. The cultural life of English-speaking Canadians subjected to constant hammering from American commercialism is increasingly separated from the culture life of French-speaking Canadians.... We are indeed fighting for our lives. The pernicious influence of American advertising reflected especially in the Periodical press and the powerful persistent impact of commercialism have been evident in all the ramifications of American life. (Innis, 1952, p. 18–19)

Innis's appreciation of the relationship between technology and culture—and between culture and nation—in capitalistic societies marked an important breakthrough that would become a major Canadian theme in the postwar period (Kroker, 1984; Patterson, 1990).

The period of World War II had seen the total economic and diplomatic realignment of Canada. Before and during the war, Canada found it necessary to prop up Britain rather than be supported by her and had turned naturally to the United States for economic and military assistance. After the war, the economic and international position of Great Britain collapsed utterly, leaving the "North Atlantic Triangle" without one of its legs. In 1944 and 1945, with much of the world in ruin, Canada found itself in an unfamiliar position as a major industrial and diplomatic player, loaning money and grain to the United Kingdom while sitting in on the conference that would produce the United Nations. Much of the discussion of the Canadian identity in this period was carried out by historians in an essentially historical framework.

One of the first Canadians to attempt to place Canada in its new world position was (Charles) Vincent Massey (Bissell, 1986). Having served in turn as Canada's chief diplomatic envoy to both Washington and London, Massey was ideally suited to essay such a task, the results of which were published in 1948 as *On Being Canadian*. Trained as a historian, he saw the background of his subject in historical and chronological terms. Massey began by insisting that while he was in London during the war, it was possible to pick out Canadian soldiers on the streets: "Something in their bearing told the story—a combination of qualities—on the one hand a naturalness and freedom of movement, a touch of breeziness and an alertness which suggested the new world. They also showed self-control, an air of breeziness and good manners, and they had generally taken some trouble about their appearance" (Massey, 1948, p. 3). As this description suggested, Canada was for Massey the meeting ground between Britain and America, both a North American and a British Commonwealth Nation. He insisted that membership in the British Commonwealth was "essential to Canadian independence; we are the more Canadian for being British." Hearkening back to northernness, Massey observed that most of Canada's population came from north-western Europe, where "the elements of human stability" had been "highly developed." Massey described national unity as "the holy grail," and saw acceptance by English- and French-speaking Canadians of each other's culture, which they did not share. He emphasized the diversity of the population, using the metaphor of the mosaic.

Admitting that in everyday life, "our ordinary habits and equipment are little different from the Americans," Massey insisted that it was time that arts and letters should acquire a "reasonable national flavour." Because Canadian unity and the Canadian identity was spiritual and intangible, it required embodiment through the arts, letters, and intellectual life of the community. Massey then proceeded to set forth a shopping list for a national culture, including an enhanced national broadcasting system, film production, a national library, a national gallery, a national portrait gallery, a flag, a national anthem, and a system of non-titular honours. He thus provided the reform agenda for both his own royal commission on the arts, letters, and sciences of 1950 and for the Pearson government in the 1960s. While Massey was pleased that American–Canadian relations were good, he feared the increase of "influences" across the border, particularly cultural and economic ones. "We cannot afford to allow an erosion of our Canadianism," he emphasized. Canada's national characteristics could only be preserved by the strength of national feeling. He concluded by calling for an educational system that taught Canadian citizenship (anchored by Canadian history) and good manners.

The decade of the 1950s saw an increased concern for the protection of Canadian culture, beginning with the royal commission chaired by Vincent Massey in 1950 and extending through other royal commissions and academic writings over the period (Litt, 1992; Bumsted, 1991, pp. 21–28). In the spring of 1960, W. L. Morton served as a visiting professor at the University of Wisconsin, and his lectures there on Canada served as the basis for *The Canadian Identity,* published in 1961 (Morton, 1972). Morton was a "red tory," a species of political animal many Canadians regarded as peculiarly Canadian (Horowitz, 1968). Morton's approach to his subject was quintessentially historical. He began his analysis with a chapter entitled "Canada in America." It emphasized the importance of the Canadian Shield and its penetration by those seeking "the staples by which Canada has lived." Indeed, he saw "the alternate penetration of the wilderness and return to civilization" as "the basic rhythm of Canadian life," forming "the basic elements of Canadian character whether French or English, the violence necessary to contend with the wilderness, the restraint necessary to preserve civilization from the wilderness violence, and the puritanism which is the offspring of the wedding of violence to restraint." In that chapter Morton recognized the United States as the dominant power on the continent, but he stopped short of declaring Canada to be an American nation. In his second chapter, Morton discussed the British connection. With Massey and earlier commentators, Morton thought the British Empire had enabled Canadians to seek liberty through self-government. Building Canada was hardly easy, he wrote. "To build on the basis of the northern economy, within a world empire, under the influence of a dynamic neighbour, at once alien and kin, in such circumstances to build a nation out of two peoples of two cultures without the compulsion of war or revolution, was an undertaking of unique dimensions and unprecedented conditions."

As for relations with the United States, argued Morton, it was part of Canada's destiny to be an independent nation in America. What differentiated the Canadians and Americans were "things far deeper than the mass culture of North America which both countries share and both created." Canadian governments had to deal with issues on Canadian terms, "and when necessary at Canadian cost." In the final chapter to the first edition of *The Canadian Identity,* Morton argued that Canada had but one history and "but one narrative line," which resulted from four permanent factors in that history: "northern character, a historical dependence, a monarchical government, and a committed national destiny."

Massey and Morton were still optimistic about Canada's future. A few years later, George Parkin Grant, another "red tory," and a professor of philosophy, produced *Lament for a Nation* (Grant, 1965). Unlike Morton and Massey, who had written measured—even stately—accounts of the meaning of Canada, Grant's book was partisan and emotional. Because Grant was a philosopher rather than a historian, the book had a distinctly abstract edge to it in which fine historical detail did not matter. *Lament for a Nation* was cast as a threnody for Canadian prime minister John Diefenbaker, whose "confusions and inconsistencies" were "a bewildered attempt to find policies that were adequate" to his noble cause of national survival. Grant saw the 1957 election as the "last gasp of nationalism," and Diefenbaker's fall as the triumph of "the homogenized culture of the American Empire" (Grant, 1965, p. 5). Diefenbaker was not only a populist who antagonized the business classes, argued Grant, but also a nationalist who "appealed to one united Canada, in which individuals would have equal rights irrespective of race and religion; there would be no first- and second-class citizens." Such a vision of Canada failed to recognize the rights of French Canadians and was more American than Canadian, Grant wrote, as was Diefenbaker's concern for individual rather than collective rights. On the other hand, the prime minister's opposition to Canada's disappearance in the American defence umbrella was "noble." Diefenbaker was not anti-American, Grant argued, simply not pro-American, still bound up in British assumptions that no longer mattered.

Grant now turned to discuss "the Canadian establishment and its political instrument, the Liberal party." The Liberals were realists who understood that Canada would be gradually swallowed up in "a richer continentalism." In *Lament for a Nation,* Grant fully acknowledged that Canada's collapse was not simply because of the Americans. Instead it was part of a universal movement in the modern world toward homogeneity and progress anchored by technology. True conservatism was dead. He insisted that the "current of modern history was against us" (Grant, 1965, p. 68). In subsequent writings, Grant elaborated on his opposition to the modern technocratic society, which found its highest embodiment in the United States (Grant, 1969). His anti-American critique of technology — or anti-technological critique of the United States—helps explain why such an admittedly conservative thinker could, in the late 1960s and early 1970s, become the darling of young Canadian radicals (Emberly, 1990).

3. AFTER 1965

After the mid-1960s, attempts to explain Canada splintered in a vast variety of directions, many of them contradictory. Profound ideological shifts combined with new socio-economic complexities to produce a Canadian society that was regarded by many observers as virtually indescribable. Much of the modern Canadian writing on the nature of Canada turned on explaining why Canadians are different from Americans, and the casual reader of this literature and much other might well conclude that the basic feature of the Canadian character/identity—at least in English-speaking Canada—is that it is "un-American." It is clear that the chief Anglo-Canadian "other" is to be found in the United States rather than in Europe. To a considerable extent, this reflects the fact that Canada—apart from New France—developed historically as an offshoot of or alternative to the United States. Canadian commentators have always used Canada's acceptance of its European heritage as part of the Canadian distinction from the United States, which is seen as having a "revolutionary" new beginning cast in terms of Lockean individualism. In all the discussion, Canadian nationalism increasingly focused on the cultural dimensions, and by the 1970s, "cultural nationalism" had come front and centre (Baskevkin, 1991).

While the establishment of the meaning of Canada by reference to the United States was a familiar technique, after the mid-1960s it gained a new vehemence because of the strength of the hostility of Canadian artists and intellectuals to what was happening in the United States. This virulent anti-Americanism was fuelled by the war in Vietnam. Hostility to American policy in southeast Asia was the central feature of a collection of opinions about the United States collected by Al Purdy and published as *The New Romans: Candid Canadian Opinions of the U.S.* (Purdy, 1968). Even when anti-Americanism was not explicit, it was often implicit in the discussion.

In 1972 feminist writer Margaret Atwood completely altered the traditional terms of debate over the Canadian character in her book *Survival: A Thematic Guide to Canadian Literature* (Atwood, 1972; Cooke, 1998). Although others (such as Northrop Frye) had occasionally employed Canadian literature to explain the nation's psyche, Atwood was the first to set such an analysis squarely in the writing. Her basic assumption was that in writing the reader saw "not the writer but himself, and behind his own image in the foreground, a reflection of the world he lives in" (Atwood, 1972, p. 15). Atwood thus made the great leap from literary themes to the collective persona in positing the central patterns of Canada (and Canadian literature) as survival within the context of victimization. One of the exploiters of the Canadian victim was obviously the United States, although Atwood preferred not to be very explicit on this point.

The Americans may have had as their unifying symbol the Frontier, while the British had The Island. But for Canada, wrote Atwood, the central symbol was Survival/Survivance. In a series of witty chapters she described through literary examples what she called the "basic victim positions," ranging from denial through interpreting victimization as fate through refusing to accept the victim's role as inevitable to becoming a creative non-victim. Along the way Atwood offered many seemingly unsystematic insights into the Canadian psyche that added up to a new way of looking at the Canadian experience. Many of these insights involved contrasting Canadian literary perspectives with those in Britain and especially in the United States. In discussing immigrant novels, for example, she insisted that while American immigrants could escape into a new identity, English-speaking Canadians had no alternate identity to assume. Americans wrote about Aboriginals as either noble savages or inferior beings, argued Atwood, but Canadians saw Aboriginals either as instruments of Nature the Monster or as victims. Atwood's accomplishment was impressive. Not only had she successfully linked feminism, Canadian nationalism, and not-Americanism, but also turned Canada's creative writers—rather than its politicians or historians—into both its cultural makers and its cultural arbiters.

Reinforcing the best-selling work of Atwood were the later writings of one of Canada's great academics and thinkers, the critic and teacher (Herman) Northrop Frye (1912–91). The bulk of Frye's scholarly work was devoted to William Blake, mythology, and the Bible, but as a Canadian teacher of literature, he could not entirely avoid Canadian writing, Canadian culture, and the Canadian identity. Frye did not write systematically or at book length about any of these subjects, but his occasional forays—mainly in the 1970s—were collected and published by James Polk in 1982 as *Divisions on a Ground: Essays on Canadian Culture* (Polk, 1986). Frye had once described Canada in its formative years as suffering from a "garrison mentality." As early as 1965, in his well-known "Conclusion" to the first edition of *The Literary History of Canada*, Frye was insisting that Canadian writers "have identified the habits and attitudes of the country, as Fraser and Mackenzie have identified its rivers" (Frye, 1965, p. 849). For Frye, Canada should be distinguished by its culture, a culture made by its writers. Frye was one of a newer breed of thinkers who saw culture in abstract rather than in concrete tangible terms. Central to Frye's vision of Canada was the recognition that cultural movements marched to a different drummer than political and economic movements. While politically and economically, "the current of history is toward greater unity," Frye insisted, "culture has something vegetable about it, something that increasingly needs to grow from roots, something that demands a small region and a restricted locale." For Frye, Canadian culture might well survive the integrating tendencies of the modern world to become our defining characteristic.

Versions of Canada, cast in the mould of comparison with the United States, continued to be popular. Pierre Berton's *Why We Act Like Canadians* (1982), for example, was cast in the form of letters to an American friend named "Sam"(Berton, 1982). Berton's six chapter titles are a series of historical and environmental cliches: "Peace, Order, and Strong Government," "Big Daddy in a Scarlet Coat," "Once a Loyalist…," "Of Kilts and Babushkas," "When Mercury Freezes," and "The Solemn Land" tell the tale. According to Berton, Canadians do not resist authority, putting order first and freedom second. They remain loyal to the Crown. Ethnically, Canada is a mosaic that revels in its bracing northern winter and is defined by the harshness of the Canadian Shield.

Commentators who have wanted to distinguish Canada from the United States in more complex ways than Berton—or to describe the Canadian identity—have often in recent years taken refuge in the notion of paradox or dialectical oppositions. One example of the paradox approach is by journalist Richard Gwyn in *The 49th Paradox: Canada in North America* (Gwyn, 1985). Perhaps the chief paradox described by Gwyn is that the greater the benefits to Canada of closer ties of all kinds with the United States, the greater the risks. A dialectical approach is adopted by Robin Matthews in *The Canadian Identity: Major Forces Shaping the Life of a People.* "Canadian identity," Matthews argues, "lives in a process of tension and argument, a conflict of opposites which often stalemate, often are forced to submit to compromise, but which—so far in our history—have not ended in final resolution" (Matthews, 1988, p. 1). A combination of paradox and dialectic is employed by John Ralston Saul in his *Reflections of a Siamese Twin: Canada at the End of the Twentieth Century* (Saul, 1997).

In his 1995 book *Nationalism without Walls: The Unbearable Lightness of Being Canadian,* Richard Gwyn has argued that Canada was the world's first postmodern state, a state without any defining national identity whatsoever (Gwyn, 1995). This was, of course, yet another variation on George Grant. As we enter the 21st century, it seems safe to predict that the exercise of attempting to pin down and explain Canada and Canadians will continue, with as much conflict and disagreement as before. Perhaps significantly, the statement that has achieved the most popularity in the year 2000 has appeared in a beer commercial.

In some ways, however, the range of interpretive options has narrowed considerably from the time of confederation. Most of the open-ended issues of 1867 have now been closed. The possibilities for Pan-Canadianism appear unlikely at least as long as Quebec remains a part of Canada. Ethnic homogeneity is even more unlikely, since it is a concept that flies in the face of the data of the Canadian census. The British connection and the notion of Canada as British have both been diminished if not eliminated. Canada is now indisputably a North American nation, whatever its history. Even closer integration with the United States appears difficult to avoid.

While it may well be that Canadian culture will be what identifies Canada, the questions remain: what is Canadian culture and who are the Canadians who will make it? Whether associating Canadian culture with its writers will work remains uncertain. Many of the finest writers now resident in Canada are immigrants or exiles who do not really write about the country. Fitting writers like Rohinton Mistry, M.G. Vassanji, and Shyam Selvadurai—and their novels of life in Southeast Asia—into a coherent picture of Canadian culture provides a real challenge (James, 2000). What Canadians can make of the choices still available to them remains to be determined.

REFERENCES

Atwood, Margaret. *Survival: A Thematic Guide to Canadian Literature*. Toronto: Anansi Press, 1972.

Baskevkin, Sylvia. *True Patriot Love: The Politics of Canadian Nationalism*. Toronto: Oxford University Press, 1991.

Berger, Carl. "The True North Strong and Free." In *Nationalism in Canada*, ed. Peter Russell. Toronto: McGraw Hill, 1966.

———. *The Sense of Power: Studies in the Ideas of Canadian Imperialism 1867–1914*. Toronto: University of Toronto Press, 1970.

———. "Internationalism, continentalism, and the writing of history: Comments on the Carnegie series on the relations of Canada and the United States." In *The Influence of the United States on Canadian Development: Eleven Case Studies*, ed. Richard Preston. Durham: Duke University Press, NC, 1972.

———, Carl. *The Writing of Canadian History: Aspects of English-Canadian Historical Writing, 1900–1970*. Toronto: Oxford University Press, 1976.

Berton, Pierre. *Why We Act Like Canadians*. Toronto: McClelland and Stewart, 1982.

Bissell, Claude. *The Imperial Canadian: Vincent Massey in Office*. Toronto: University of Toronto Press, 1986.

Bumsted, J.M. "Canadian Culture in Peril, 1949–1961." *The Beaver* 71:1 (1991): 21–28.

Connor, Ralph. *The Major*. London: McClelland, Goodchild and Stewart, 1917.

Cooke, Nathalie. *Margaret Atwood: A Biography*. Toronto: ECW Press, 1998.

Crunican, Paul. *Priests and Politicians: Manitoba Schools and the Election of 1896*. Toronto: University of Toronto Press, 1974.

Dafoe, John. *Canada: An American Nation*. NY: Columbia University Press, 1935.

Donnelly, Murray. *Dafoe of the Free Press*. Toronto, 1968.

Emberly, Peter C., ed. *By Loving Our Own: Goerge Grant and the Legacy of Lament for a Nation*. Ottawa: Carleton University Press, 1990.

Ewart, John. *The Kingdom of Canada: Imperial Federation, the Colonial Conferences, the Alaska Boundary and Other Essays*. Toronto: Morang, 1908.

Frye, Northrop, "Conclusion." In *Literary History of Canada*, ed. Carl F. Klinck. Toronto: University of Toronto Press, 1965.

Gagan, David. "The Relevance of Canada First." In *Canadian History since Confederation: Essays and Interpretations*, 2nd ed., eds. Bruce Hodgins and Robert Page, 78–90. Georgetown, Ontario: Irwin-Dorsey: 1970.

Grant, George. *Lament for a Nation*. Toronto: McClelland and Stewart, 1965 (reprinted 1971).

———. *Technology and Empire: Perspectives on North America*. Toronto: McClelland and Stewart, 1969.

————. *Technology and Justice*. Toronto: Anansi, 1986.

Gwyn, Richard. *The 49th Paradox: Canada in North America*. Toronto: McClelland and Stewart, 1985.

————. *Nationalism without Walls: The Unbearable Lightness of Being Canadian*. Toronto: McClelland and Stewart, 1995.

Havelock, Eric A. *Harold Innis: A Memoir*. Toronto: Harold Innis Foundation, 1982.

Hill, James H. *The Landing of the Loyalists*. Saint John, 1873.

Horowitz, Gad. *Canadian Labour in Politics*. Toronto: University of Toronto Press, 1968.

Innis, Harold. *The Fur Trade in Canada: An Introduction to Canadian Economic History*. Toronto: University of Toronto Press, 1930.

————. *Empire and Communications*. Toronto: University of Toronto Press, 1950.

————. *The Bias of Communication*. Toronto: University of Toronto Press, 1951.

————. *Changing Concepts of Time*. Toronto: University of Toronto Press, 1952.

James, Jamie. "The Toronto Circle." *The Atlantic Monthly* (April 2000): 126–30.

Kroker, Arthur. *Technology and the Canadian Mind: Innis/McLuhan/Grant*. Montreal: New World Perspectives, 1984.

LaPierre, Laurier, *Sir Wilfrid Laurier and the Romance of Canada*. Toronto: Stoddart, 1996.

Laurier, Wilfrid. "Speech at Quebec City, 4 January 1894."

————. "Speech in the House of Commons, 3 March 1896," in *House of Commons Debates 1896*, 2740–43.

————. "Letter to W.D. Gregory, 19 November 1909," Laurier Papers, National Archives of Canada.

Litt, Paul. *The Muses, the Masses and the Massey Commission*. Toronto: University of Toronto Press, 1992.

Massey, Vincent. *On Being Canadian*. London and Toronto: J.M. Dent, 1948.

Matthews, Robin. *The Canadian Identity: Major Forces Shaping the Life of a People*. Ottawa: Steel Rail, 1988.

Melody, William et al., eds. *Culture, Communication, and Dependency: The Tradition of H.A. Innis*. Norwood, NJ: Ablex Pub. Corp., 1981.

Monière, Denis. *Ideologies in Quebec: The Historical Development*. Toronto: University of Toronto Press, 1968.

Morton, W.L. *The Canadian Identity*. Toronto: University of Toronto Press, 1972.

Murrow, Casey. *Henri Bourassa and French-Canadian Nationalism: Opposition to Empire*. Montreal: Harvest House, 1968.

Parkin, George. *Imperial Federation: The Problem of National Unity*. London: Macmillan, 1892.

————. *The Great Dominion: Studies of Canada*. London: Macmillan, 1894.

Patterson, Graeme. *History and Communications: Harold Innis, Marshall McLuhan, the Interpretation of History.* Toronto: University of Toronto Press, 1990.

Polk, James, ed. *Divisions on a Ground: Essays on Canadian Culture* [by Northrop Frye]. Toronto: Anansi, 1982.

Purdy, Al, ed. *The New Romans: Canadian Canadian Opinions of the U.S.* Edmonton: Hurtig, 1968.

Rumilly, Robert. *Henri Bourassa: la vie publique d'un grand Canadian.* Montreal: Editions Chantecler, 1958.

Saul, John Ralston. *Reflections of a Siamese Twin: Canada at the End of the Twentieth Century.* Toronto: Viking, 1997.

Sheffe, Norman. *Goldwin Smith.* Don Mills, ON: Fitzhenry & Whiteside, 1976.

Smith, Goldwin. *The Political Destiny of Canada.* Toronto: Willing & Williamson, 1981 (London, 1878).

———. *Canada and the Canadian Question.* Toronto: Hunter Rose, 1986 (London, 1891).

FURTHER READING

Bashevkin, Sylvia. (1991). *True patriot love: The politics of Canadian nationalism.* Don Mills, ON: Oxford University Press.

Berger, Carl. (1970). *The sense of power: Studies in the ideas of Canadian imperialism 1867–1914.* Toronto: University of Toronto Press.

Litt, Paul. (1981). *The muses, the masses and the Massey commission.* Toronto: University of Toronto Press.

Monière, Denis. (1981). *Ideologies in Quebec: The historical background.* Toronto: University of Toronto Press.

Russell, Peter, ed. (1966). *Nationalism in Canada.* Toronto: University of Toronto Press.

Smith, Allan. (1994). *Canada: An American nation? Essays on continentalism, identity, and the Canadian frame of mind.* Montreal and Kingston: McGill-Queen's University Press.

First Nations at the Centre of Canadian Memory[1]

J.R. Miller

At the opening of the 21st century, Canadians find that the First Nations are an ever-present reality. Morning or evening, in newspapers or television news programs, stories on myriad topics concerning First Nations peoples occupy a prominent place. At its most dismal, this presence takes the form of reports on social ills that mar the lives of many First Nations families and communities. Stories of violence, family breakdown, political corruption, and heavy involvement with the criminal justice system have become all too familiar to non-Native Canadians. But the news of First Nations people is by no means all bad, and, increasingly, developments that highlight the progress of Aboriginal groups have become familiar. The creation of the new territory of Nunavut out of the former Northwest Territories, and parliamentary approval of the Nisga'a treaty in British Columbia were major news stories in 1999. They joined more numerous items about smaller negotiations and litigation concerning land claims and treaties. Finally, news from the courts provided constant reminders that First Nations and their interests are now at the centre of public debate, both in important individual cases such as the *Marshall* decision concerning Maritime fishing rights and collective issues such as the large and growing array of litigation by former residential school students who suffered physical, sexual, and cultural abuse at the hands of Christian missionaries. Indeed, the prominence of Aboriginal issues in the public forum shows that First Nations are front and centre in public consciousness in Canada.

First Nations' prominence in journalistic, political, and judicial events is less a novel development than a return to a pattern that prevailed during the first period of interaction between indigenous and immigrant peoples in Canada. The place of First Nations in the consciousness and memory of Canadian society has gone through an evolution from prominence to obscurity and back to prominence again that reflects the way in which First Nations interacted with Euro-Canadians. The place of First Nations in the awareness of Canadians has resulted from the reasons that First Nations and Europeans interacted and the nature of the relationship that their interactions created. To sketch this pattern, First Nations have gone from being essential partners to being largely irrelevant to the aims and aspirations of newcomers, and back once again to being critical to the success that Canadians seek in pursuing their economic and political objectives. In order to demonstrate how this undulating pattern in the relations between First Nations peoples and Euro-Canadians developed, it is necessary to review briefly the history of Native–newcomer relations in Canada over the past 500 years.[2]

PROMINENT PARTNER

The Europeans who came to Canada's eastern shores in those early years came for four reasons: fish, furs, exploration, and faith. More important, each and every one of those motives made them dependent on the indigenous peoples whom they encountered in the Atlantic and central Canadian regions, and that dependence compelled the newcomers to develop relations that were relatively harmonious with the Algonquian and Iroquoian societies they met. To explain how First Nations were essential to Europeans in this early period also helps to explain why relations deteriorated later.

The first Europeans to arrive on the eastern shores of North America came from many lands, but they came primarily for one purpose. For Spaniards, Portuguese, Basque, French, and English mariners, the object of their western voyages were the rich fisheries along the Atlantic coast. The fishing grounds of the region held a wealth of fish protein that lured fishers of countries that were constantly in need of inexpensive food. For Roman Catholic countries such as Portugal and France, the church's dietary rules meant that there were many days in the year—adding up to as much as five months of the twelve—in which the faithful were not to consume animal flesh. Even in England, which broke with the papacy in the 1500s, state policy favoured the fishery in order to encourage a healthy marine sector that would serve as a training ground for men to staff the navy of the island country in the event of war. The consequence of these influences was that the countries of Western Europe annually dispatched vast numbers of small fishing boats to the grounds off Newfoundland and Nova Scotia, where their crews sometimes came into contact with indigenous people, particularly when the strangers landed to dry fish or take on fresh water or wood.

From the occasional interactions between European fishers and Mi'kmaq, Maliseet, and other First Nations emerged the second major industry in Canadian history, the fur trade. Jacques Cartier, the French mariner whose voyages in the 1530s and 1540s provide us with much of our knowledge of early interactions, described how in 1534 he encountered a group of Mi'kmaq in the Bay of Chaleur who shouted at the French sailors, gesturing that they should come ashore, and holding up some furs to suggest that they wanted to trade. Cartier and his men landed and quickly traded for all the furs that the group had, including some that they were wearing as garments. The incident suggests dramatically how other ship captains probably encountered indigenous people who wanted to trade when they came to fish. In this way the fur trade evolved from the fishery, first as a sideline, but in the 1600s as a major economic activity in its own right.

Cartier's voyages also lead us to an understanding of the third motive for European contact with First Nations in eastern North America. Cartier was an explorer and map-maker rather than a fishing-boat captain, and his forays represented the third motive for contact: exploration. By the 1500s Western European nations had two recent discoveries that stimulated maritime exploration to the west. From the accounts of Marco Polo and other sources, they knew of the great riches, especially spices, of the Far East. And from early scientific writings, they were now aware that the earth was round. To princes and entrepreneurs in Western Europe who sought a pathway to Asia that was shorter than overland routes, sailing west was the obvious solution. And when navigators, such as John Cabot or Jacques Cartier, sailed west, they encountered North America and its inhabitants. At first, as is well known, these mariners thought they had reached Asia, as the mistaken terminology of adventurers such as Christopher Columbus and Cartier indicates. Columbus called the local people "Indians" because he assumed they were dwellers of the East Indies. Cartier named a spot just west of what is now Montreal Lachine (*la chine* = China) because he thought he was in Asia. Once the explorers realized they had reached not Asia but a landmass between Europe and Asia, they refocused their search. Explorations in the 1600s and first half of the 1700s sought a route through North America to Asia. Naturally, probing for a route through the continent to the riches beyond brought European explorers into contact with more First Nations.

The final motive for early European presence in North America, the desire to convert the indigenous people to Christianity, was also prominent in the contacts that occurred in the 1600s and later. By 1600 Western Europe was experiencing a resurgence of Christian religious zeal that caused kings and princes to sponsor missionary activities in various parts of the world. The French Crown particularly was motivated to support such evangelical efforts, and in the 1600s the king insisted that French fur traders must take missionaries to Canada and support their labours there. In this way the fur-trading colonies that France planted in Nova Scotia and Quebec early in the 1600s also supported an energetic campaign by Roman Catholic missionaries to convert the First Nations to Catholicism. Obviously, missionary activity meant extensive interaction with First Nations communities.

What is critical to understanding the nature of relations between Native and newcomer that resulted—and also, consequently, the place of

First Nations in the consciousness of the Europeans—was that for the successful prosecution of each and every one of the Europeans' four motives for contact, Native peoples were essential. Fishers needed the cooperation of Mi'kmaq and others if they were to be able to catch fish and dry them on shore without danger. Fur traders, especially those in the trade in beaver fur that dominated the 1600s, were even more reliant than captains of the vulnerable fishing boats. Not only did French fur traders depend on the First Nations to locate, capture, skin, and transport the furs to locations where French merchants would buy them, but in addition Algonquin and other traders also processed the beaver pelts prior to trading then. The prime pelt that European fur traders sought in this period was what the French called *castor gras d'hiver*, a term that translates literally as "greasy winter beaver." Native people in effect "processed" a pelt taken from the beaver in winter, when its fur was thickest, by wearing it as a garment for a season with the fur side of the skin on the inside. Wearing the fur in this way wore away coarse guard hairs, leaving the soft downy fur, and made the skin more supple through the absorption of oil from the human body. The entire process nicely symbolized the importance of First Nations people in the fur trade. Without their cooperation, the European would not be able to get any of the desired furs, and especially not the "greasy winter beaver" pelt that was most prized of all.

Native cooperation was as essential to the missionary as it was to the fur trader. Unless good relations existed between Native and newcomer, First Nations would neither visit the missionaries in their towns such as Quebec and Montreal nor permit the evangelists to establish missions among them. In the early decades of missionary activity the priests had to travel with migratory First Nations bands such as Algonquin or Montagnais or try to establish settled missions among bands such as the agricultural Huron (Wendat), who lived in large villages. Either way, if cooperation was not forthcoming, missionaries would not have even an opportunity to carry out the work that had brought them to the New World. This was illustrated in the 1640s in Huronia, where the Jesuit missionaries found themselves a target of Iroquois war parties who attacked Huron villages and by 1649 dispersed the Huron Confederacy, killing a number of Jesuits and eliminating their largest missionary enterprise in the process. Without a healthy relationship between Natives and newcomers, both the missionaries and the French Crown who promoted their efforts would be frustrated in their desire to convert the First Nations to Christianity.

What held true for those who came to the northern half of North America for fish, fur, and souls, held as well for those who sought to explore and map the interior of the continent in hopes of finding a route to Asia. Explorers were dependent on indigenous cooperation, knowledge, technology, and labour. If First Nations opposed exploration in their territories, it would be too dangerous to go there. If they withheld their knowledge of the water routes and portages, the strangers would probably perish in the vast and dangerous woods and waterways. Many of the maps that explorer-cartographers such as Champlain or La Vérendrye later put together were based on First Nations knowledge and expeditions permitted and facilitated by indigenous people. Explorers needed First Nations transportation technology such as birchbark canoes, moccasins, snowshoes, and toboggans to be able to travel into the interior. They needed Native foodstuffs, such as the corn that Iroquoians grew, to support extended travels during which they found it difficult to stop to search for food. Native guides, paddlers, porters, and assistants all were essential to carry out French exploration. And, obviously once again, if the French did not establish good relations with the First Nations communities, none of these vital forms of assistance would have been forthcoming. If French explorers were able to explore to the mouth of the Mississippi by the end of the 1600s and to the Western plains by the 1740s, while the English colonists to the south of them were penned up east of the Appalachian mountains in dread of Native hostility, the fact that New France enjoyed much better relations with First Nations than New England and the other English colonies did is the most important part of the explanation.

Until about 1700, then, the French presence in northeastern North America stemmed from motives that drove the newcomers to establish reasonably good relations with the Native people they encountered. To catch fish, to trade for furs, to campaign for converts to Christianity, and to explore and map the interior of the continent in hopes of finding a route to Asia—every one of these objectives could not be achieved if the First Nations opposed the newcomers. Indigenous people had to tolerate the newcomers' presence and facilitate their activities, or the strangers would not be able to achieve their goals. The reasons that brought the French to eastern Canada led them to attempt to get along with the indigenous people they encountered. This reality did not mean that the European presence did not cause problems for First Nations. The strangers introduced diseases to which the First Nations communities, because of no prior exposure, had little or no resistance. The consequence was that diseases, such as measles, that bothered Europeans very little because of acquired immunity were devastating in First Nations populations, and other diseases, such as smallpox, that Europeans found damaging were enormously destructive to First Nations. Other problems that the Native–newcomer relationship created were the negative impact of alcohol, introduced by the use of brandy or rum in the fur trade, on societies that had previously not had alcoholic beverages. Finally, the long-term impact of missionaries, as will be seen, was destructive for Native communities.

When French motives for interacting with First Nations expanded at the beginning of the 1700s, the underlying importance of having good relations was only strengthened. At the root of the French desire to add diplomacy and military alliance to the four motives that earlier had governed their approaches to Native people was the fact that in the 1700s the Crown was preoccupied with a struggle with England (United Kingdom after 1707) for dominance. In the worldwide struggle for preeminence and wealth, North America, with its English colonies in the south and its smaller French colonies to the north, was one part of the larger confrontation. The rivalry of the European powers led each government to plot the defeat of the other's colonies in the New World. From 1700 onward the French Crown pursued a strategy of trying to encourage and maintain close alliance with First Nations so that they would either assist the French and their colonists in any clash with New Englanders and British, or at least refrain from supporting New France's opponents. To that end, France subsidized a network of fur-trade posts in the interior south of the Great Lakes, attempting thereby to secure close economic relations with First Nations. In the 1700s France emphasized diplomatic relations with First Nations, forcing Britain in turn to pay systematic attention to Native military relations as well. If prior to 1700 Europeans perceived First Nations people as trading partners, exploration facilitators, and targets of Christian preaching, from about 1700 to 1814 they also regarded them as allies and, if necessary, fellow warriors. Particularly for the French in the north, who had relatively small numbers of their own settlers on the continent, reliance on First Nations' alliance was absolutely essential. In the strategy of European powers, a desire for Native friendship and support again compelled the newcomers to seek and maintain good relations.

In the alliance relationship, as in the earlier ties flowing from trade, evangelization, and exploration, a generally positive character did not mean there were not serious negative effects on First Nations peoples from their diplomatic and military ties to Euro-Americans. Involvement in warfare in a succession of clashes that ended only with the War of 1812, obviously, led to loss of life as various First Nations fought with one European partner against the other power. Moreover, the politics of alliance could be divisive, as the Six Nations Iroquois found at the outset of the American Revolution. Competing calls for alliance with Americans or with British, or for neutrality, disrupted the Council of the confederacy, leading to the extinguishing of the Council fire—the symbolic declaration that League unity was at an end. Finally, and most damaging of all, the strategy of alliance did not work as First Nations hoped it would. They had selected their European or colonial partners in the expectation that the result would be a victory by a power who would respect their territorial rights, but, unfortunately, that did not occur. An especially bitter example of this harsh reality was the War of the American Revolution, after which both those First Nations who had opposed the Americans and those who had supported them ended up losing their lands, the latter a little bit later than the former.

To recapitulate, during this era in which First Nations occupied a prominent place at the centre of newcomers' consciousness and memory, their prominence was attributable to the fact that they played roles that Europeans considered vital to their own success. First Nations' tolerance was a prerequisite for a peaceful and successful fishery, while their active cooperation was necessary if the fur trade was to succeed. Similarly, Native tolerance of and cooperation with both explorers and missionaries were needed if these interlopers were to be successful. Newcomers' needs made them seek reasonably good relations with First Nations, and the consequence was a relationship that, though certainly troubled by major drawbacks such as disease, alcohol, and losses in warfare, on the whole was positive and mutually beneficial.

This first era of relative Native–newcomer harmony typified relations in all regions of Canada, although the onset and precise nature of these relations differed somewhat from area to area. The commercial partnership began in eastern Canada in the 1500s and was supplemented by the diplomatic relationship in the 1700s. In the Western interior, commercial relations began after 1670, when the Hudson's Bay Company was created, and intensified after 1770; and in the fur-trade west there was no military era such as occurred between 1700 and 1814 in the east. On the Pacific the pattern resembled somewhat the western interior, with the commercial relationship beginning in the 1770s and never being complicated by a diplomatic-military partnership. In the far north, the fur-trade relationship dated from the middle of the 1800s, supplemented by cooperation in the whaling industry that was often troubled by violence directed against Inuit. In the north, too, there was no phase of military partnership. What is consistent and important, however, is that in this first long era of Native–newcomer cooperation, First Nations played a central role in the lives of Euro-Canadians. First Nations' relevance to newcomers' needs and aspirations made them valued.

FROM PARTNER TO OBSTACLE

In the era that followed, unfortunately, First Nations were neither needed nor valued as partners. The onset of this period in which First Nations were pushed to the edges of Euro-Canadians' consciousness also varied from region to region. In Atlantic Canada it began late in the 1700s, while in central Canada it occurred shortly after the War of 1812. On the Prairies it dated from the decline of the buffalo economy in the 1870s, on the Pacific from the end of the fur trade in the middle of the same century, and in the north early in the 20th century. What initiated the new period was a change, either military or economic, that rendered First Nations much less vital to the newcomers. In Atlantic Canada it was the end of English–French warfare in the 1760s, in central Canada the termination of a need for military allies after 1814, on the Prairies the development of a wheat economy, in British Columbia the arrival of a disruptive mining frontier, and in the north the replacement of fur dominance by mining.

In all of these transitions Euro-Canadians shifted their economic interests from activities that made them dependent on First Nations' cooperation to economic pursuits for which they viewed their former allies and fur-trade partners as either irrelevant or, worse, an obstacle. The clearest example of the shift is found in central Canada, where the end of the War of 1812 rendered First Nations allies unnecessary. Permanent cessation of hostilities in the interior was soon followed by heavy immigration, particularly from Great Britain, of homesteaders whose purpose was to establish an agricultural colony. The transition from alliance to agriculture was fateful for First Nations communities in places such as the future province of Ontario. Once they were no longer needed as allies, and as agricultural immigrants began to come into the colony in large numbers, hunter-gatherer groups such as the Mississauga found that their presence was little appreciated and that their lands were coveted. Simultaneously, their use of the territory for hunting, fishing, gathering, and trading came into conflict with settlers who wanted to cut down the pine forests to make farms, open the lands along the lakes and rivers for towns, and, sometimes, dam the streams and rivers for water power or canals. The combined effect of these changes was to transform First Nations in Ontario from people perceived as essential trading partners and military allies to people whose presence held up the kind of economic development that newcomer Euro-Canadians wanted to carry out. Similar developments took place in other regions of the country, particularly where settled agricultural population growth occurred. In the 1900s the only region that was exempt from the general pattern of pushing First Nations out of a central role in the eyes of newcomers was the north.

The consequence of the shift, both for non-Natives and First Nations, was drastic and destructive. First, the changed role of First Nations led to their dispossession from their lands by means of a series of land treaties by which the newcomers secured peaceful access to Native territories for agriculture, mining, and forestry development. In Ontario and the Prairies treaties were made that consigned First Nations to reserves, relatively small pockets of land on which they would make their living by some hunting-gathering and newly introduced agriculture. Whether there were treaties or not, reserves were usually provided for First Nations during the 1800s in the Maritimes (Quebec already had a number of reserves that had been established mainly as religiously oriented refuges), Ontario, the Prairies, and British Columbia. As agriculture, mining, and forestry developed on lands that had previously been theirs, First Nations found themselves transformed in the eyes of their Euro-Canadian neighbours from useful partners to irrelevant onlookers.

As harmful as this dispossession was for First Nations, the other major consequence of their shifting role was worse. Once First Nations ceased to be seen as useful to Euro-Canadians, and once their lands were peacefully obtained, the non-Native population, by 1900 the majority in every region of the country but the far north, ceased to value their distinct ways and began to desire their transformation into people who behaved and, if possible, thought like the Euro-Canadian majority. In other words, in addition to dispossession from their lands, this new era in which First Nations were no longer considered vitally useful to the dominant newcomers led to systematic attempts to assimilate them. The campaign to remove First Nations as distinctive individuals and communities took many forms, from voluntary efforts by religious organizations to aggressive action by the Canadian state. What united throne and altar in their campaign of attempted assimilation was the desire to eradicate Aboriginal identity and culture, and to replace them with Christian Euro-Canadian beliefs, practices, and identity. In short, the majority population sought to eliminate First Nations culturally by assimilating them through policies carried out by church and state.

While missionaries had been working among First Nations since the early 1600s, after the War of 1812 the nature of their efforts began to emphasize cultural change as well as religious conversion. In part, this effort, which became increasingly aggressive as the century wore on, reflected the increasing racism of British and British-Canadian society. However, after confederation in 1867, the churches' efforts also became allied with a recently developed desire by the Canadian state to impose assimilation on First Nations, too. Perhaps the single clearest example of this church–state cooperation to bring about the assimilation of First Nations was the residential schools, which from the 1880s to the 1970s were run by four of the churches on behalf of the federal government. Although officially the schools had a variety of purposes, in practice they attempted to assimilate First Nations communities through their young. Not content to promote Christianity and Euro-Canadian ways in general, they also denigrated Aboriginal beliefs, languages, and practices. Residential schooling was a stark example of the assimilative campaign directed against First Nations in an era when they were no longer central to the needs and goals of the Euro-Canadian majority.

Through legislation and other measures the Canadian state carried on an assimilation program of its own that was guaranteed to keep First Nations at the margins of non-Natives' consciousness in this period. The *Indian Act*, passed in 1876, treated First Nations legally as minors and attempted to oversee and control both their political and economic behaviour. Indian agents were authorized to supervise band councils, control the sale of produce and other goods in off-reserve markets, and, most notoriously in the case of the Prairie reserves after 1885, control movement off reserves by the infamous pass system. Under the pass system, a reserve member who wished to leave the reserve temporarily, say to visit relatives elsewhere, had to get permission from the agent to leave. These measures of oversight and attempted control were reinforced by policies that tried to curb traditional First Nations spiritual practices, such as the Potlatch on the Northwest coast or Thirst or Sun Dance on the Prairies. The aim of these policies was to eliminate Aboriginal identity and culture, thereby transforming First Nations into imitation Euro-Canadians. The same objective lay behind the residential schools: to Christianize and assimilate First Nations children in order to change the whole First Nations community culturally.

The cumulative effects of these government campaigns to move First Nations to the margins of society through control and assimilation were, first, demoralizing First Nations and, later, provoking militant political action to resist the programs. From the late decades of the 1800s until the 1940s, First Nations found themselves beaten down, marginalized, and ignored on the fringes of Canadian society. That is not to say that they were not still involved as casual labour or producers of handicrafts for sale in non-Native markets during this period, but they were no longer central, as they had been earlier, to economic and other activities that were vital to the newcomer majority. This marginalization, in combination with poverty, and decades of health problems in the west and north in particular, resulted in population decline and political impotence for most First Nations. By the 1920s the total number of First Nations that government recognized as "status" Indians dipped to about 100 000. In spite of the weakness of poverty and declining numbers, some First Nations tried to pursue their rights. However, when they tried to resist government control, as a coalition of British Columbia First Nations did in a decades-long campaign for recognition of their Aboriginal title to their unsurrendered lands that culminated in an appearance before a joint parliamentary committee in 1926, Parliament responded with an amendment to the *Indian Act* in 1927 that made raising or giving money for pursuit of land claims illegal, effectively barring First Nations from making use of lawyers. This legislation was an eloquent statement of how poverty, population decline, assimilative schooling, and legislative oppression had utterly marginalized First Nations by the end of the 1920s.

RE-EMERGENCE

With difficulty First Nations began in the inter-war period to move away from their position on the margins and back toward the centre of non-Native consciousness. The reasons for this re-emergence of First Nations in the eyes of the majority society were numerous and extended over several decades. Slowly, probably because some of the worst health problems had been dealt with, the long population decline of First Nations began to reverse in the 1930s, and by the 1940s their communities were experiencing rapid growth that would accelerate from the 1960s onward, particularly as a result of a high birth rate. During the 1940s First Nations began to play a more significant economic role in the eyes of non-Natives, not so much because of their direct involvement in cooperative economic activities with non-Natives as because they occupied territories that were now needed for military and economic purposes. Such wartime ventures as the Alaska Highway, built from northern British Columbia to Alaska through Yukon by the U.S. Army Corps of Engineers, and the Canol Project, a wartime oil pipeline from Norman Wells in the Northwest Territories to Whitehorse in Yukon, ran through First Nations lands. After 1945 Canada entered on a decades-long natural resources boom that created enormous wealth, especially for non-Native Canadians, from oil, gas, uranium, base minerals, hydro-electric energy, and uranium in lands occupied by First Nations, who in most cases had not signed treaties. This phase of Canada's economic history underlined the importance of First Nations once more, because in many cases their permission for access to their lands was required by non-Native developers. Perhaps the height of this phase was a project in Quebec in the 1970s. Promoted by the Quebec government, the James Bay hydro-electric development was briefly derailed by the James Bay Cree's successful application for a court injunction in 1972. Although the court's ruling was overturned, the event underlined the importance of taking First Nations seriously and negotiating in advance with them in an era in which access to resources of Inuit and First Nations territories was vital to Canadian prosperity.

Also important in changing the place of First Nations in the consciousness of others were mental changes that were occurring in the non-Native majority from the 1940s onward. Briefly, the assumptions of racial superiority and inferiority on which measures such as the *Indian Act* and residential schools had been based came under attack, particularly by the 1940s. Fighting against Nazi Germany, a system of institutionalized racism, in World War II made many Canadians re-examine what their government was doing at home. It was difficult to fight racism abroad and carry on ignoring its poisonous effects in Canada. These mental, or ideological, changes were accelerated by the influence of social science, especially anthropology and sociology, on government policy from the 1940s onward. The social sciences by the middle of the 20th century had abandoned many of the racist ideas they had held in earlier times and now taught moral relativism. All cultures and races, the social scientists argued, were morally on the same level; the differences among them were largely the product of environmental forces, not inherent, or racial, characteristics. Such thinking, bolstered as it was with the authority of scholarship, discredited such racist policies as segregated residential schools for First Nations and Inuit children, forcing the federal government to move away from them and adopt policies of integrated schooling for Native and non-Native children in the 1950s and 1960s. Such new social policies, based directly on a rejection of racism as a foundation of government policy, helped to move First Nations back onto the mental landscape of non-Natives.

Also extremely important in ending the social and political marginalization of First Nations was their increased political organization and assertiveness. First Nations had been trying to organize nationally since the early 1920s, but the hostility of the federal government to their actions, as the 1927 *Indian Act* amendment showed, was a major barrier. Nonetheless, they persisted with great difficulty, and often clandestinely in their political efforts, and in the 1930s and 1940s succeeded in forging provincial First Nations organizations in a number of the Western provinces. The 1951 repeal of the *Indian Act* prohibition on raising or giving money for pursuit of land claims made fundraising and open organization much less difficult. An enduring national political organization for First Nations was forged in 1961 in the National Indian Council. It would experience growth and redefinition, becoming the National Indian Brotherhood in 1968 and the Assembly of First Nations in 1982. Such pan-Canadian organizations, not to mention the effectiveness of many of the First Nations political leaders, helped to raise the profile of First Nations communities in general.

The government of Canada strengthened this political awakening in 1969 when it undertook a spectacularly ill-advised policy proposal known as the "White Paper." A White Paper was a statement of possible government policy that the cabinet issued to get feedback from groups who were interested in the area with which the policy dealt. In June 1969 Indian Affairs minister Jean Chrétien released a White Paper on policy toward First Nations that, in essence, called for the elimination of their special status, the winding up of their treaties, the termination of their distinctive relationship with the federal government, and their absorption into provincial social programs such as education, health, and welfare. The White Paper was, in short, a proposal for legislated abolition of First Nations. The recently formed National Indian Brotherhood (NIB) spearheaded a revolt by First Nations organizations across the country against the policy, arguing that it was a betrayal of First Nations' special relationship with the Crown and an abandonment of them to the provinces, which historically had shown them less sympathy than the federal government. The nation-wide outcry against the White Paper's proposals forced the government to abandon its proposed policy, thereby handing the NIB an enormous political victory that strengthened it in the eyes of First Nations people everywhere. In the early 1970s the government also assisted the NIB by beginning to provide it with annual block funding that supported its day-to-day operations, thereby putting the organization on a stable financial basis and freeing it to concentrate on its political objectives. The NIB had been heard from on the White Paper; it would be heard again before too long.

In the 1970s, 1980s, and early 1990s a new preoccupation of non-Native Canadians also involved First Nations and helped to move them to the centre of Canadians' consciousness in a spectacular fashion. This concern—an obsession, really—was the campaign to modernize the Canadian *Constitution*, which dominated the national political agenda from 1977 to 1992. Briefly put, this campaign by the federal government to modernize the *Constitution* was conceived by Prime Minister Pierre Elliott Trudeau as a response to the threat of Quebec separatism. In Trudeau's vision Canada would counter the lure of independence with a modernized *Constitution* that would end colonial status by bringing the power to amend the *Constitution* from the United Kingdom to Canada and would guarantee French Canadians' place in confederation by inclusion of a new charter of rights that would protect bilingualism. In the face of great provincial opposition to his campaign, Trudeau persisted and by 1982 succeeded in creating a revised *Constitution* with a domestic amending power and a *Charter of Rights and Freedoms*.

As this process began in the late 1970s, First Nations and other Aboriginal political organizations tried unsuccessfully to participate in the talks in an effort to get Aboriginal rights, such as self-government, recognized in the emerging *Constitution*. They were unsuccessful at first, the depths of their frustration being reached in November 1981, when a draft agreement on constitutional change that completely ignored Aboriginal concerns was signed by the federal government and all provinces but Quebec. However, Aboriginal political leaders were able to join a lobbying effort by women's organizations, who also were angry at the omission of gender equality rights in the proposed *Charter*, that succeeded in gaining the inclusion of gender equality rights and Aboriginal rights in the 1982 revised *Constitution*.

The pattern established in the 1977–82 phase of constitutional talks—Aboriginal groups ignored at first, only to triumph in the end—was repeated in the next stage, which involved the Meech Lake Accord. Meech Lake was the brainchild of Conservative Prime Minister Brian Mulroney, who sought to end Quebec's alienation from the 1982 pact by reaching a new agreement that would respond to Quebec's constitutional desires. The first fruit of this effort was the 1987 Meech Lake Accord, signed by all First Ministers, which recognized Quebec's "distinct society" status in confederation. First Nations political leaders looked on helplessly as their request for inclusion of Aboriginal rights was again ignored. However, the political fates handed them an opportunity three years later during the last days of the Meech Lake effort. Mulroney believed it was desirable to have the changes in the Accord ratified by all 11 governments in the three-year period specified for such changes. However, by 1990, as the deadline loomed, some provincial governments had changed, and support for the Accord was not as strong as it had been in 1987. The Prime Minister, in a strategy of political brinksmanship, let the process wind almost to the last day before reaching an agreement that would secure the support of the most reluctant provinces, Newfoundland and Manitoba.

Mulroney's strategy had ignored First Nations. In the Manitoba legislature there was an Oji-Cree Member named Elijah Harper who was prepared to oppose ratification of the Meech Lake Accord, and Mulroney's tactics had left legislative action in Manitoba so late that it was only with the unanimous consent of all Members that the Assembly could deal with the motion to ratify the Accord before time ran out. With the encouragement of the Assembly of Manitoba Chiefs as well as the national First Nations political organization, Harper day after day refused to give unanimous consent. The Meech Lake Accord failed, Mulroney was humiliated, and the forces of separatism in Quebec gained enormously from the collapse. Meech Lake formed the background in Quebec to the Oka crisis that began in July 1990. Efforts to expand a golf course on lands the Mohawk of Kanesatake, the community near the town of Oka, considered sacred provoked Mohawk resistance, resulting in a raid by the provincial police in which a corporal was shot to death and a 78-day standoff of the Natives and police and military forces. For First Nations, Oka was an energizing force, akin to the aftermath of the White Paper in 1969–70, that united them in opposition to what they saw as high-handed and disrespectful behaviour toward them.

The final phase of the constitutional wars, the Charlottetown Accord and Referendum (1992), detracted from First Nations prestige, but once more registered the centrality of their role in issues that were of vital national concern. Aboriginal political organizations—First Nations, Inuit, and Métis—this time were part of negotiations that fashioned an agreement for constitutional change that recognized a form of Aboriginal self-government in the *Constitution*. However, widespread opposition to this and other parts of the Charlottetown agreement led to its defeat in a national vote in the autumn of 1992, a consultation in which First Nations, like most other groups in the country, rejected the deal. The Charlottetown round of constitutional talks effectively ended First Nations involvement in attempted constitutional change. Not even the recommendations of the Royal Commission on Aboriginal Peoples (RCAP) of extensive new constitutional arrangements to implement Aboriginal self-government could resurrect the campaign for constitutional recognition of Aboriginal political rights (RCAP, 1996, vol. 2). Nonetheless, the battles in the long constitutional war that stretched from 1977 to 1992 had helped to convince non-Native Canadians that they could no longer ignore First Nations and other Aboriginal political organizations in national discussions.

The final force that has brought First Nations to the centre of Canadian public life has been the courts of the country. First Nations individuals and political groups over the past quarter-century have made effective use of the judicial system to protect their rights and advance their causes. The James Bay Cree's success in halting Quebec's power project and forcing the government to the negotiating table in 1972 was followed the next year by the important *Calder* or *Nisga'a* ruling concerning the Nisga'a First Nation of northern British Columbia that recognized the legal existence of Aboriginal title to lands that had never been covered by treaties between the Crown and First Nations. This ruling forced the government of Canada and many provincial governments to recognize that they could no longer ignore land claims based on First Nations assertion of unsurrendered Aboriginal title. This recognition led to the federal government's creation in 1973–74 of a system for dealing with land claims that, although much less successful than its creators had hoped, still exists.

The ability of First Nations to use the courts to pursue their causes was strengthened enormously by the constitutional changes that came into effect in 1982. The new *Constitution* declared that the "existing Aboriginal and treaty rights of the Aboriginal peoples of Canada are hereby recognized and affirmed." The significance of this constitutional recognition and protection of Aboriginal and treaty rights has been that First Nations have been able to use the courts to get satisfaction when governments have refused to negotiate settlements First Nations considered acceptable. A couple of examples of this lengthy and complex story must suffice. In 1990 Ronald Sparrow, a member of the Musqueam First Nation in Vancouver succeeded at the Supreme Court in having his Aboriginal right to fish for food recognized, thereby overturning his own conviction for using improper nets and opening a claim to a larger share of the Pacific fishery for First Nations. A variation on this was the *Marshall* decision in 1999, in which the treaty right of Donald Marshall, a Mi'kmaq man in Nova Scotia, to fish for a modest income was upheld by the Supreme Court. As in British Columbia with *Sparrow*, the *Marshall* decision greatly expanded the Mi'kmaq and Maliseet share of the Atlantic fishery. Finally, in December 1997, the Supreme Court handed down the *Delgamuukw* decision, which ended a lengthy battle by the Gitksan First Nation of northern British Columbia with a victory that set aside a lower court ruling on the grounds that the judges there had not taken into account Gitksan oral history. This, too, was an enormous victory for communities whose principal type of history, evidence that is needed in court cases of all kinds, is oral accounts passed down from generation to generation. The *Delgamuukw* decision helped to pave the way for ratification of the Nisga'a treaty, which had been concluded in 1996, putting an end to a 110-year-long struggle by the Nisga'a to have their territorial rights recognized.

Individual court actions have also helped to keep First Nations front and centre in Canadian public life as the 21st century opens. The bitter legacy of the horrific residential school system has, particularly since

1997, taken the form of thousands of lawsuits by former students who allege that they suffered physical or sexual abuse or both and cultural deprivation at the hands of the missionary staff who operated these schools on behalf of the Department of Indian Affairs. By 2000 some 7000 former students were involved in litigation directed against the government of Canada, Roman Catholic agencies, the Anglican Church of Canada, the United Church of Canada, and the Presbyterian Church of Canada. So large is this mountain of litigation that the Anglican Church and the Oblates, a Catholic missionary organization that ran most of the Catholic schools, have announced that they face bankruptcy from legal costs and compensation to victims if the government does not shoulder a larger share of the financial consequences of the residential school lawsuits. Almost daily in 1999 and 2000 Canadians read in their newspapers or heard on radio or television news of the horrors of residential schooling and the bitter harvest of that system.

PARTNER AGAIN?

At the beginning of the 21st century, First Nations are back where they started: at the centre of Canadian consciousness and memory. They have come back to that central role only over the past 60 years, emerging from an era in which non-Natives did not recognize their worth and importance to Canada's strategic and economic well-being. Earlier they had gone from being vital to Euro-Canadians' needs and aspirations to being relegated to the sidelines as a newly majoritarian non-Native community no longer needed them. In the earliest phases of Native–non-Native relations, First Nations had been critical to the success of newcomers who sought fish, fur, souls for Christ, and knowledge of the North American continent. To all these purposes First Nations' knowledge and skills were essential. So, too, it was in the next phase, in which the Europeans sought First Nations allies who would fight alongside them in the struggle between, first, Britain and France, and, later, the United States and Britain for control of the continent. These phases of commercial and military partnership gave way after the War of 1812 to a long era in which First Nations were driven to the margins of a Canadian society that no longer valued them because they did not see First Nations as critical to their success. Instead, they coveted First Nations lands for settler farms and generally obtained them by treaty, force, or fraud. In the aftermath of the dispossession of First Nations, they also suffered the indignity of almost a century of Canadians' efforts through their government and Christian churches to control and transform them politically and culturally. The product of policies of attempted control and assimilation during this long era was the impoverishment and demoralization of Canada's original peoples. They paid the price of Canada's establishment and growth between the 1820s and 1940s.

Finally, First Nations emerged from the margins and moved steadily back to the centre of the Canadian public stage between the 1940s and the present day because of a number of factors. Their own revitalization and political organization were major influences; Canadians' growing awareness of the moral indefensibility of the racist bases of government policy was a more minor one. First Nations occupied territories that the majority population sought for economic growth, and now First Nations' leadership had the skills and confidence to stand up to developers, whether entrepreneurs or the governments that served them. Clear examples of the skill and determination of First Nations leadership to defend their community and re-establish its central place in Canada are found in the constitutional struggles from 1977 to 1992 and in First Nations' effective use of the courts to advance their Aboriginal and treaty rights, as well as to defend the victims of oppressive policies such as residential schooling. It's been a long and harrowing path to travel, but once again First Nations are back at the centre of Canadian consciousness.

NOTES

1. The support of the Social Sciences and Humanities Research Council of Canada, whose Research and Strategic grants funded the research on which this essay is based, is gratefully acknowledged.

2. These patterns are explained in greater detail in J.R. Miller, *Skyscrapers Hide the Heavens: A History of Indian–White Relations in Canada* 3rd ed. (Toronto: University of Toronto Press, 2000); and, with some variations, in the first volume of the Final Report of the Royal Commission on Aboriginal Peoples (RCAP), *Looking Forward, Looking Back* (Ottawa: RCAP, 1996).

REFERENCES

Miller, J.R. *Skyscrapers Hide the Heavens: A History of Indian–White Relations in Canada,* 3rd ed. Toronto: University of Toronto Press, 2000.

Royal Commission on Aboriginal Peoples. Final Report. 5 vols. Ottawa: RCAP 1996. See especially vol. 1, *Looking Forward, Looking Back,* and vol. 2, *Restructuring the Relationship.*

FURTHER READING

Dickason, Olive P. *Canada's First Nations: A History of Founding Peoples Since 1500.* Toronto: McClelland and Stewart, 1992.

Dyck, Noel. *What Is the "Indian Problem"? Tutelage and Resistance in Canadian Indian Administration.* St. John's: Institute of Social and Economic Research, Memorial University, 1991.

Miller, J.R. *Shingwauk's Vision: A History of Native Residential Schools.* Toronto: University of Toronto Press, 1996.

Ray, Arthur J. *I Have Lived Here Since the World Began: An Illustrated History of Canada's Native Peoples.* Toronto: Key Porter, 1996.

Being Stigmatized and Being Sorry: Past Injustices and Contemporary Citizenship[1]

Matt James

Groups seeking redress for past injustices have made history a crucial focal point for contemporary Canadian debates about citizenship.[2] This role is fitting, because understandings about the past affect how we practise citizenship in the present.

Alan Cairns has established the significance of redress campaigns for Canadian citizenship by linking them to Canada's postwar search for a constitutional framework that is capable of attracting support from a multinational and pluralistic society. Cairns suggests that the increased constitutional emphasis on equality, which followed the 1982 entrenchment of the *Charter of Rights,* has encouraged redress movements to seek "compensatory treatment ... for past injustice[s] whose lingering effects are still visited on survivors" (Cairns, 1995, p. 25). As Cairns explains, these movements insist that transforming Canadian understandings of the "constitutionally significant past" is crucial to the larger project of fashioning a more acceptable future (Cairns, 1995, p. 22).

This article explores redress campaigns as bids to confront problems of civic marginalization and unequal political power. It emphasizes the importance of redress for groups whose capacity to participate in citizenship has been hampered by histories of stigmatization. In turn, I link this group interest in redress to the remarkable symbolic power of apologies. Historical episodes that violate contemporary standards of equal citizenship become potent political tools when they are made to symbolize what others must learn about and then repudiate in order to produce a more satisfactory future. For example, Ottawa's 1988 apology for the World War II Japanese-Canadian internment proclaimed that "the shame on [Japanese Canadians'] honour, their dignity, their rights as Canadians is now removed forever" (Weiner, 1998, p. 2). And in January 1998, after being forced to apologize for its past policy of forcing Aboriginal children to attend residential schools, the federal government officially admitted that "the contributions made by all Aboriginal peoples to

Canada's development ... have not been properly acknowledged"
(Stewart, 1998, p. A19).

As the contrast between these statements and the racist policies for
which they are offered in apology may suggest, groups seeking redress
strive to replace the undeserved stigma of the past with a new imagery of
group honour. This imagery is usefully understood as comprising a
"symbolic capital" of honour (Bourdieu, 1977); a resource of political
power that traditionally marginalized groups can employ as they pursue
recognition as fully accepted civic participants.

The article begins by discussing the various redress claims and the
episodes from which the claims derive. It then proceeds to explain redress
campaigns as responses to problems of citizenship experienced by historically stigmatized communities. This point is important to consider in the
case of Aboriginals, to whom the desirability of Canadian citizenship has
often seemed extremely doubtful. But neither can the differences
between the residential-schools campaign and the other redress movements be ignored. Thus, I distinguish between demanding redress as an
unambiguous project of citizenship inclusion and doing so in order to
assess the desirability of achieving such inclusion in the future.

This article also examines the debate between redress supporters and
their critics. The critics condemn what they see as the unduly divisive
emphasis on historical grievances that accompanies redress politics.
Although redress campaigns are often confrontational, I argue that they
are potentially useful vehicles of civic integration. As the example of South
Africa's Truth and Reconciliation Commission suggests, to demand apologies for past wrongdoing is also to seek more harmonious future relations
with former antagonists. Thus, I conclude that the increasingly influential
opposition to treating past wrongs as issues of contemporary citizenship is
extremely dangerous. This opposition encourages Canadians to avoid the
important work of understanding and reconciliation upon which a more
inclusive and durable citizenship must rest.

REDRESS POLITICS IN CANADA

Among non-Aboriginal redress movements, the successful campaign
waged on behalf of the approximately 22 000 Japanese-Canadian
internees of World War II is the most well known. In September 1988, the
National Association of Japanese Canadians elicited a Parliament Hill
ceremony, $450 million in financial compensation, and an official
apology from the federal government. Other movements have also
demanded redress for historical wrongs, such as the World War I internment of roughly 5000 Ukrainian Canadians and the racist policies (of
which the notorious "head tax" is the most widely remembered) that,
until 1947, severely restricted Chinese immigration to Canada.

These movements have not matched Japanese-Canadian success. The National Congress of Italian Canadians was forced in 1990, after failing to win financial redress for the World War II internment of approximately 1000 Italian Canadians, to settle for an informal apology from Prime Minister Brian Mulroney (Mulroney, 1990). The Congress has continued to lobby for an official apology, the establishment of university chairs in Italian-Canadian studies, and the payment of unspecified amounts of compensation to remaining survivors (de Santis, 1997, p. A4). In 1993, the other non-Aboriginal redress movements, most notably Canadians of Chinese and Ukrainian ancestry, ended negotiations with the Mulroney administration when it became clear that financial compensation would not be forthcoming ("Hefty price tag, 1993," p. A12).

These groups were rebuffed entirely in 1994, when Liberal Heritage Minister Sheila Finestone announced her policy of refusing to offer monetary restitution or apologies of any sort (Canada, 1994). In protest, the Chinese Canadian National Council took its claim to the United Nations to publicize the "spectacle of elderly pioneers ... bringing forth their individual cases of human injustice before the world community" (Wong 1995, p. A15). The Ukrainian Canadian Civil Liberties Association, like its Italian-Canadian counterpart, has persevered in pressing its case. The Association seeks the erection of memorial plaques at all 24 former internment sites (it has persuaded Ottawa to establish two such memorials), an official parliamentary acknowledgement, and $563 000 to cover the costs of documenting the internment experience (Ferguson and Cunningham, 1997, p. B7).

In contrast to Italian Canadians, who received an apology but no compensation, the movement seeking redress for the hundreds of Inuit who were relocated under federal government auspices in the 1950s experienced a setback of the opposite sort. In March 1996, the Department of Indian Affairs agreed to offer $10 million in monetary compensation for the coerced relocation, which buttressed Canadian sovereignty in the High Arctic by sending the Pond Inlet and Grise Fiord Inuit thousands of kilometres north as "human flagpoles" (Aubry, 1994b, p. A6). But the Department refused to apologize, and the Inuit accepted what appeared to be Minister Ron Irwin's final offer (Lowi, 1996, p. B5). Ottawa also adopted the compensation-without-apology approach in response to First Nations demands for atonement and restitution for a residential-schools policy that, for many survivors, led to the near-destruction of their families and languages. In December 1997, the Department of Indian Affairs agreed to set up a $200 million fund (raised subsequently to $350 million) to help meet the health care and counselling needs of survivors but refused steadfastly to apologize or to accept responsibility for the residential-schools fiasco (Anderssen, 1997, p. A1). After difficult negotiations with the Assembly of First Nations, the Chrétien government relented: "To those of you who suffered this tragedy at residential schools," said Minister Jane Stewart, "we are deeply sorry" (Stewart, 1998 A19).

Past Wrongs and Contemporary Citizenship

Many of the past policies for which redress has been sought are ones that unfairly excluded particular Canadians from some of the most basic rights of citizenship. In the case of the federal government's World War II internment operations, the denial was almost total. The vast majority of the interned "Japanese" and "Italians" were Canadian citizens who, with absolutely no proof of their disloyalty, were removed from their communities, incarcerated, forced to work without compensation, and, in many cases, stripped of their homes and possessions (Miki and Kobayashi, 1991, pp. 17–49; National Congress of Italian Canadians, 1990, pp. 7–12). Little wonder that Italian Canadians doubted "that they were dealing ... with a democratic state" (Ramirez, 1988, p. 80) or that Japanese Canadians came to see internment as "a betrayal of democracy itself" (National Association of Japanese Canadians, 1986, p. 1).

Like internment, other past policies for which redress has been claimed also shattered communities by separating innocent individuals and their families against their will. For instance, until the early 1970s the federal government's residential-schools policy aimed to eliminate what authorities viewed as "backward" cultures by removing thousands of Aboriginal children from their homes (Assembly of First Nations, 1994, p. 13–19). At the church-run institutions to which these children were sent, Aboriginal cultures were condemned as inferior and barbaric, discipline was often vindictively enforced, and sexual and physical abuse were remarkably common. The 1994 Assembly of First Nations report, *Breaking the Silence*, has spoken powerfully about the damage inflicted by this policy on First Nations communities. Even excepting the horrific experiences of abuse that are now the schools' most well-known legacy, prolonged periods of near-total familial separation under degrading conditions meant that children who attended residential schools "found themselves becoming alone—silent and isolated and without any hope of belonging to a sensible world" (Assembly of First Nations, 1994, p. 34). The ban on Aboriginal languages, which all the residential schools enforced, though with quite varying degrees of brutality, indicates the thoroughness of this assault on First Nations identities (Miller, 1996, p. 200).

The Inuit who were relocated from their northern Quebec homes to the High Arctic also experienced the shock of an unexpected community breakup brought about by state policy. As survivor John Amagoalik has recounted, "We just went into a panic because [the RCMP] had promised that they would not separate us" (in Marcus, 1992, p. 21).

Rather than fracturing an already existent Canadian community, Canada's "Chinese exclusion" policy (1885–1947), which made "married bachelors" (Bolaria and Li, 1988, p. 114) of two generations of Chinese men drawn to Canada by the lure of work and wages, helped to prevent viable Chinese-Canadian communities from forming. The onerous head tax and subsequent ban on Chinese immigration consigned many of these men to permanent separation from their wives and families. With a 1911 ratio of 2790 men for every 100 women, there would be virtually no second Chinese-Canadian generation until after World War II (Bolaria and Li, 1988, p. 114).

Redress movements remember these episodes as unjust assaults launched by a hostile government and society against the very existence of their communities. As former residential-school student Gilbert Oskaboose wrote in 1996: "When we returned to our own communities we had become strangers.... [T]he policies of assimilation ... brought pain, suffering, lost lives, vicious in-fighting, divisions, waste and sorrow"(Oskaboose, 1996). Unsurprisingly, redress-seekers find it difficult to discharge with enthusiasm the major obligation that accompanies citizenship: loyalty to the state within which citizenship has been assumed. In 1984, for example, an angry Roy Miki of the National Association of Japanese Canadians told the federal minister for multiculturalism that "Your government instituted a policy which was meant to destroy the community, and that policy worked" (in Miki and Kobayashi, 1991, p. 132). To seek official atonement for past injustices may thus be one way of endeavouring to reconcile citizenship's demands of loyalty with the awareness of equal citizenship denied. As one Japanese-Canadian internee remarked four years prior to the historic redress settlement of 1988: "A sense of incompleteness gnaws at me. I need to feel right about my country" (in Miki and Kobayashi, 1991, p. 15).

Redress may also be valued for reasons of a more private nature. In particular, individuals who trace severe personal difficulties back to past injustices may seek apologies and restitution in order to help further their often painful recoveries. For example, Inuit leader Martha Flaherty urged the Royal Commission on Aboriginal Peoples to understand that "the High Arctic exiles ... deserve ... recognition so that they can start the healing process and rebuilding their lives" (in Royal Commission on Aboriginal Peoples, 1994, p. 77). Thus, official repudiation of the relevant historical wrong is welcomed as evidence that the victims will find support from the wider society in their rehabilitation. One survivor, for instance, reacted to Ottawa's apology for the residential-schools disaster by saying: "It's a nice feeling ... to think that the government was listening. It's certainly a better day today than it was yesterday" (in Steffenhagen, 1998, p. A3).

Although internment burdened many Japanese Canadians with psychiatric problems (Omatsu, 1992, p. 171), the focus on personal recovery has been most evident in the residential-schools campaign. With many First Nations people suffering problems of low self-esteem and family dysfunction because of the abuse they experienced in residential schools, recognition of their undeserved suffering is valued as the "beginning of respect, of feeling that [they] are capable of making a contribution to the world" (Assembly of First Nations, 1994, p. 125). This focus on the personal needs of survivors has also driven demands on behalf of former residential students for monetary compensation, which, as one advocate has argued, is necessary "to start healing, because we don't have adequate therapy, addiction treatment, child care or education" (in Fournier, 1997, p. A3). Ottawa's major response to these demands has been the $350 million healing fund announced at the January 1998 reconciliation ceremony. However, because the monies will be disbursed only to selected community healing projects, victims of residential-schools abuse continue to bring claims for individual compensation before the courts (Barnsley, 1999, p. 10).

Redress and the Symbolic Capital of Honour

Redress-seekers insist that Canada has a responsibility to help traumatized communities overcome the ongoing manifestations of past suffering. But their critics wonder why claimants do not seek reconciliation through the more customary routes of psychiatry or forgiving by forgetting. Indeed, opponents often leap from asking this question to portraying redress politics as a cynical attempt to raid the public purse. Thus, *Winnipeg Free Press* editor John Dafoe has complained: "The theory used to be that time healed all wounds. Now there is a growing belief that time plus about $30 million might just do the job" (1994, p. A6). Prominent columnist Jeffrey Simpson has depicted the emphasis on financial compensation similarly as a "crass multicultural politics" that aims at forcing "today's generation to pay for policies and attitudes of generations past" (Simpson, 1990, p. 78).

But redress politics is a more complex phenomenon than such comments leave room to admit. More useful is Cairns's point: redress movements employ an "adversarial, accusatory history" as they seek a "more dignified future" (Cairns, 1995, p. 24). The advocacy literature on redress abounds with references to the public humiliation that can attach to a community even after the original episode or policy that gave rise to its initial official stigmatization has passed. According to the Chinese Canadian National Council, "having been singled out by law for unequal treatment," Chinese Canadians have been labelled as "inferior and undesirable" (1988b, p. 11). The anniversary of July 1, 1923, the date the *Chinese Immigration (Exclusion) Act* was passed, is remembered as "Humiliation Day" (McEvoy, 1982, p. 26). For the National Congress of Italian Canadians, "Canadians of Italian origin were denigrated and discriminated against in their own country.... For that stigma there can never be sufficient compensation" (1990, p. 21). And Japanese Canadians, as Maryka Omatsu explains, have been "scarred by our history in this country," by a "debilitating virus that ... filled me with a shame that I could not understand as a child" (1992, p. 39).

Undeserved stigma is an extreme form of disrespect, which can make "outsiders" or "foreigners" of persons whose citizenship histories ought to support a quite different response. For example, Chinese-Canadian redress-seekers blame the exclusion, disfranchisement, and head-tax legislation for preventing other Canadians from relating to them as civic partners. One member of the Chinese-Canadian redress movement has remarked that despite being able to trace his Canadian family history to 1906, his children were still told to "go back to Hong Kong" while attending Simon Fraser University some 80 years later (in Bolan, 1995, p. A3). As the Chinese Canadian National Council put it, "the bitter legacy of the Canadian government's 62 years of legislated racism is a Chinese Canadian community that is still seen as a new immigrant community" (in Bolan, 1995, p. B3). Similarly, the National Association of Japanese Canadians found that the public was unaware that internment "was carried out against Canadians who happened to be of Japanese ancestry, and not against Japanese nationals who happened to find themselves in Canada" (Miki and Kobayashi, 1991, p. 80).

Because they associate these problems with difficulties in becoming truly accepted and equal civic participants, redress campaigns rebel against the hesitancy and withdrawal that may follow from experiences of official stigmatization. For example, as novelist Joy Kogawa has remarked, "internment worked beyond the wildest dreams of politicians. [F]orty years later, most of the people of my generation are still hiding in the woodwork and wanting to speak" (in Miki and Kobayashi, 1988, p. 10). Omatsu, too, has written of a "passivity ... fashioned by our history in this country, that, like some invisible undertow, pulls us down on bended knees" (1992, p. 69). A similar reaction was noticed after the World War I Ukrainian-Canadian internment. One school principal remarked that his Ukrainian-Canadian pupils, who had felt before internment that "they were really becoming Canadians[,] ... are now hurt, bewildered, shy and drawing back into their half-discarded alien shells" (in Thompson, 1983, p. 40). Internment "conditioned the entire community to be very apprehensive about their ... status as Canadians" ("Ukraine," 1988, p. F5). These remembrances indicate how a citizen's formal right to public participation can be compromised significantly by the (historically justified) perception that others do not regard him or her with respect.

Achieving redress is thus prized as highly public proof that the stigmatization of the redress movement's constituency was ill deserved. For example, the federal government's "Statement of Reconciliation," the outcome of extensive negotiations with the Assembly of First Nations, spoke of "the assistance and spiritual values of the Aboriginal peoples who welcomed the newcomers to this continent," of "diverse, vibrant Aboriginal nations," and of "the strength and endurance of Aboriginal people"; contributions that "too often have been forgotten" (Stewart, 1998 A19). For the National Congress of Italian Canadians, redress would "restore the positive image of Italian Canadians as significant contributors to this country of ours in this century" (1990, p. 21).

A key aspect of redress campaigns is their focus on eliciting increased civic respect by demonstrating virtue. To display public-spirited virtue can be crucial in the arena of citizenship, where people are often condemned for pursuing "special" interests. Accordingly, a prominent theme in redress politics is the movement's insistence that its aim is to prevent similar racist acts from being visited on others. The National Association of Japanese Canadians emphasized that "it is as an act of citizenship and because we refuse to see democracy betrayed that we seek an honourable resolution to the injustices of the war years" (1986, p. 1). Similarly, the Chinese Canadian National Council called for "a trust foundation ... to ensure that similar discriminatory government actions do not happen again" (1988a, p. 21). And the Ukrainian-Canadian movement sought to "ensure that no other ... minority in Canada will in the future experience the injustices Ukrainian Canadians did in the past" (Ukrainian Canadian Civil Liberties Association, 1988).

The successful Japanese-Canadian campaign produced lasting symbols of the community's struggle to enhance the future well-being of other Canadians. For example, because the 1988 *Emergencies Act*—which replaced the old *War Measures Act* that had enabled the various internments—was largely a federal government response to Japanese-Canadian protests, the *Nikkei Voice* newspaper could call the new Act the Japanese-Canadian community's "Gift to Canadians" (Miki and Kobayashi, 1991, p. 121). The establishment of the Canadian Human Rights Foundation as part of the terms of the 1988 redress settlement stands similarly as proof of Japanese Canadians' concern to help protect other Canadians from potential future acts of racist oppression. By no means irrelevant to the argument that a "Japanese-Canadian human rights foundation" would "help other groups" in the future was the aim of establishing a visible reminder of Japanese-Canadian virtue (National Association of Japanese Canadians, 1986, p. 10).

However, critics ask, why do redress movements seek "conscience money ... to appease" ("Post no bills," 1988, p. 50); why do they demand "cash to expiate the perceived sins?" (Drache, 1990, p. 84). This question is important. After all, Conservative Multiculturalism Minister Gerry Weiner's 1993 offer of a parliamentary ceremony and formal apologies for the various movements seeking redress was refused on the ground that redress without money was not redress at all ("Hefty price tag," 1993, p. A12). The need for better health and addictions services has given an understandably consistent monetary emphasis to the First Nations and Inuit claims. But money is not just prized by redress-seekers for what it can directly buy; it is integral to the symbolism of redress as well.

With this monetary emphasis, redress movements indicate that they are willing to forgive the wrongs of the past but only if they can elicit a persuasive indicator that those wrongs will not be repeated. One cannot, after all, be brutally robbed, accept a casual "sorry" from the thief and feel that the exchange bodes well for the future. As the National Association of Japanese Canadians insisted, "Significant individual compensation acknowledges the severity of the injustices [and provides] an honourable and meaningful settlement" (in Miki and Kobayashi, 1988, p. 7). Indeed, Ottawa itself emphasized at the Japanese-Canadian redress ceremony that its sincerity was financially guaranteed. The $450 million compensation package, Prime Minister Mulroney declared, "is symbolic of our determination to address this issue, not only in the moral sense but also in a tangible way" (Mulroney, 1990, p. 1).

A cash settlement can also help to make the gravity of the apology more closely approximate the magnitude of the original misdeed. Groups whose past victimization caused them direct and significant financial hardship insist that an honourable apology must contain a significant financial component.[3] Thus, the Chinese Canadian National Council deplored the federal government's failure to offer "a symbolic sum to acknowledge the injustice of the [head] tax" (in "Hefty price tag," 1993, p. A12), while the Ukrainian Canadian Civil Liberties Association protested that a proposed memorial at a former internment site was utterly insufficient: "a small plaque, valued at $15,000, is not enough. The internees suffered substantial economic losses" (Luciuk, 1994, p. A7).

Perhaps most importantly, struggles for financial redress aim to show other Canadians that the redress movement has forced the government to respond to the injustices of the past with more than just vague declarations of good intent. To return to the mugging analogy, accepting apologies from absconding thieves is only likely to boost one's reputation in circles where masochism is a cherished value. Redress movements, then, view the importance of financial compensation from two major perspectives. The first perspective sees the state's willingness to pay restitution as a symbol of the integrity of its apology: it seeks to determine whether the expressed regret is appropriately sincere. The second perspective on financial restitution is concerned with what a settlement is likely to tell other Canadians about the redress movement and its constituency: it judges the settlement as potential symbolic capital.

Financial restitution as a form of symbolic capital became particularly important after the Japanese-Canadian settlement. In the wake of Japanese-Canadian success, winning financial redress has been seen as an indicator of whether the group is regarded as sufficiently worthy to deserve an "honourable and meaningful settlement" (Miki and Kobayashi, 1988, p. 7). Failure to elicit financial compensation, it is feared, will create an unflattering contrast between the apparent disregard with which the unsuccessful movement's constituency has been handled with the concrete demonstration of respect already accorded its victorious counterparts. Indicating the prevalence of this fear are remarks such as: "redress offered to ... Japanese Canadians would be dis-

criminatory if it ignored the experience of the Ukrainians in Canada"
(Civil Liberties Commission of the Ukrainian Canadian Committee,
1987, p. 49); "compensation [was] given to the Japanese[,] the Inuit ...
deserve the same recognition" (Martha Flaherty, in Royal Commission
on Aboriginal Peoples, 1994, p. 77); "how could the federal government
redress ... other past wrongs but not the ... Chinese Head Tax?" (Wong,
1995, p. A15).

Redress and Citizenship Inclusion

Opponents of redress argue that the "search for restitution for past
wrongs ... risks piling up more division in a country already quite
divided" (Simpson, 1990, p. 79), and that the "rush for compensation for
past slights and indignities is likely to open old wounds" (C. Dafoe, 1994,
p. 40). At the extreme, redress-seeking is depicted as a vehicle of
vengeance rather than of reconciliation: "Everybody has a horror story
to tell about what used to go on. The time has now come to get even" (C.
Dafoe, 1994, p. 40).

But strategies that seek to secure apologies reveal with particular
clarity that the aim is reconciliation rather than rupture. An apology
allows the offended party to relate to the offender in a way that would not
be possible if the offender failed to convincingly disavow her actions. For
instance, whereas a victim may signal his desire to sever relations with a
tormentor by demanding punishment, the apology-seeker demands reas-
surance that the attitudes that gave rise to the past offence have been
repudiated. Like the victim whose condition for undertaking future relations with the mugger is receiving persuasive evidence that the former
wrongdoer has renounced thievery, redress movements are motivated by
the desire to engage in future interaction with other Canadians, not to
reject it.

Residential Schools and Citizenship Ambivalence

The residential-schools campaign is a different case: it cannot be portrayed
unequivocally as a push for integration within the larger Canadian society.
On this point, its quite different approach to the question of honour is particularly revealing. When the movement has described itself as a vehicle for
attaching honour to First Nations, the context of interaction most often
cited has been that of particular status Indian communities. This focus contrasts with that of the Inuit, who spoke of their campaign as a struggle for
citizenship inclusion: the relocated Inuit were described as "Canadians who
suffered for Canadian sovereignty and deserve ... recognition" (in Royal
Commission on Aboriginal Peoples, 1994, p. 77).

This theme has not been as conspicuous in the residential-schools
campaign, which has been more overtly concerned with using redress as
a remedy for interaction problems that it sees within First Nations communities. As the Assembly of First Nations summarized the consensus

among residential-schools survivors: "People realized they needed to work on themselves first, help family next, and then their communities" (Assembly of First Nations, 1994, p. i). Recalled with painful regret are the tendencies of many abuse survivors to either shun interaction with their families and former neighbours (Assembly of First Nations, 1994, pp. 93–97), or to return only to inflict their own suffering on others (Lazaruk, 1995, p. 3). Thus, the idea of speaking out about past abuse has been seen as a means of ending a cycle of "dishonourable behaviour" (Assembly of First Nations, 1994, p. 55) in order to create more healthy communities. Encapsulating this project has been the phrase, "the honour of one is the honour of all" (Assembly of First Nations, 1994, p. 159).

This tendency to focus primarily on the movement as a vehicle for producing respect and healing within First Nations communities, and to place less stress on the notion of Canadian citizenship, helps to point out the immense difficulty that Canada's historical legacy poses for Aboriginal peoples. Canadians cannot expect First Nations to view redress in the same way as non-Aboriginal movements, which have emphasized atonement repeatedly as a symbol of meaningful inclusion within the political community. For the First Nations campaign, redress does not necessarily lead straightforwardly to an enthusiastic push for further integration within the Canadian polity. At least equally significant has been the understanding of redress as a precedent for bolstering future court attempts to make the federal government financially accountable to individual abuse survivors (O'Neil, 1998, p. A1).

The historical legacy of Canada's "Indian policy" underscores one of the most important reasons for the distrust with which many First Nations view Canadian citizenship. As Darlene Johnston argues, past federal government policies (like the ban on traditional practices such as the potlatch and the assimilative thrust of the 1969 White Paper proposals) have conveyed the notion that equal Canadian citizenship requires repudiating—or simply becoming dispossessed of—Aboriginal lands, heritages, connections, and identities. It is only against this background, Johnston (1993) writes, that "the ambivalence and resistance that First Nations display toward Canadian citizenship [can] begin to be understood" (p. 349).

But those who worry that the First Nations stress on past wrongs augurs poorly for a common Canadian future should consider the potential implications if First Nations stopped attempting to discuss history with other Canadians. The analogy should not be pushed too far, but the near-total breach in Canada–Quebec relations following the 1990 collapse of the Meech Lake Accord has also been accompanied by a marked shift in the role played by historical grievances in Quebec nationalism. Complaints directed at English Canada about historical attitudes and policies toward Quebec were prominent in the Meech debates (Cairns, 1991, pp. 226–29). But since Meech's failure, angry remarks about Quebec's history in Canada seem much less appeals to English-Canadian consciences than bids to consolidate independence sentiment among Quebeckers. As Charles Taylor (1991) writes: "With the demise of Meech, something snapped.... A certain kind of compromise was for ever over" (pp. 65–66).

Of course, First Nations nationalism lacks the economic and institutional advantages that make independence a far more immediate prospect for Quebec. But there are other alternatives to joint historical discussion that First Nations may come increasingly to find as the only honourable basis from which to create future relationships with Canada. These alternatives could include, and indeed have included, engaging in campaigns of civil disobedience, launching embarrassing international complaints, or even—more subtly but also indicative of an increasing apartness that would bode ill for a common future—adopting the sullen posture of inauthentic acceptance with which inhabitants of the former Soviet empire awaited their captor's demise.

Therefore, it is important to note that the Assembly of First Nations has sought redress as part of an attempt to "forge a more conciliatory relationship with the federal government" (Anderssen and Greenspon, 1998, p. A4). The co-chair of the Nuu-chah-nulth Tribal Council, Nelson Keitlah, told the Royal Commission on Aboriginal Peoples that an apology "would go a long way toward patching up the differences between Canada's Indians and the federal government. When a person hurts another person, the first thing that comes about before a friend-ship can start again is that [they] say, 'I'm sorry'" ("Apologize for residential schools," 1997, p. 1). *Breaking the Silence* has also drawn a connection between redress and seeking greater inclusion within the Canadian polity: "Today, First Nations are reclaiming their history and affirming their place in Canada, a trend which includes speaking out about their residential school experience" (Assembly of First Nations, 1994, p. 2). Individual survivors, too, have recognized that pursuing redress is a move that involves the risk of adopting a certain openness toward non-Aboriginal Canadians. As one woman expressed this feeling: "Sometimes we have to reach out ... I guess that's what we're doing here. Trusting the government that somehow things are going to be ... dealt with" (in Gummerson, 1997, p. 3).

Certainly, the Métis National Council, the Native Women's Association of Canada, and the Native Council of Canada condemned the reconciliation agreement for focusing primarily on the needs of on-reserve status Indians (Anderssen and Greenspon, 1998, p. A4). Comparing Minister Stewart's statement with the stronger apology given to Japanese Canadians has also occasioned bitterness (O'Neil, 1998, p. A1). As one former residential-school student put it: "If any kind of apology is going to have any meaning, it's got to come from the top. It meant nothing because one of Prime Minister Chrétien's flunkies gave it" (in Barnsley, 1998a, p. 4). Others have pointed out that Stewart apologized only to those who actually attended residential schools and thus ignored the related suffering of the former students' friends and families ("Ottawa," 1998, p. 2). The fact that Ottawa failed to admit responsibility and remorse for undertaking policies whose intent was cultural assimilation and simply expressed "regret" for the abuse associated with the schools has also invited the important criticism that the Statement of Reconciliation was intended more to assuage the guilt of non-Aboriginal Canadians rather than to repudiate colonialism (Barnsley, 1998b, p. 3). And, for many, doubtless the enormity of Canadian wrongs and Aboriginal suffering simply militated against receiving the agreement with undue enthusiasm in any case.

But it is also clear that seeking redress has been understood as a means of reaching out, of attempting to gauge the sincerity of a polity that claims to want partnership with First Nations. Many First Nations individuals reacted to the apology and healing package as an appropriate basis from which to begin reconciliation with non-Aboriginal Canadians: "I felt that we didn't have hope, that this was ever going to materialize. And today it did" (in Steffenhagen, 1998, p. A3); "It's a good first step" (in Laghi, 1998, p. A4); "[it's] a historic step to break from the past" (in Steffenhagen, 1998, p. A3). As one Aboriginal editorialist summarized the mixed First Nations reaction to Minister Stewart's Statement of Reconciliation: "The minister went miles ahead of where other colonial governments have gone. That much is true. But ... if the goal was really to put paternalism to bed and call an end to cultural suppression, we've still got miles and miles to go.... But it's a start and it's about time" ("Give us strength," 1998, p. 6).

Ottawa's previous refusal to admit that the residential-schools policy constituted an injustice for which it would accept responsibility meant that survivors seeking healing did so in an unpromising atmosphere of majority-group denial. To many First Nations, therefore, redress symbolizes a welcome shift in non-Aboriginal thinking about the residential-schools issue. In the wake of Minister Stewart's apology, First Nations people reading the newspaper could find that the quotation marks once used to signify doubts about their reports of mistreatment, as in, "'Atrocities' alleged in mission schools" (Aubry, 1994a, p. A1), had now been replaced with a forthright admission: "Residential schools: A sad history of abuse" ("Residential schools," 1998, p. A1). It is unwarranted to expect that such symbolism will in itself alleviate the mistrust with which many First Nations regard non-Aboriginal society and Canadian institutions. But Canada's official acceptance of responsibility and communication of belief has already begun to make a small but not insignificant difference. In British Columbia, for instance, calls to a provincial sexual-abuse helpline from First Nations persons doubled (up from 12 to 25 calls a day) immediately after Minister Stewart's announcement, while the RCMP experienced a dramatic rise in abuse complaints from former residential-school students (Bell, 1998, p. A1). And approximately 2000 lawsuits from former residential-schools students surfaced in the year after the reconciliation ceremony. Ottawa has since paid out over $20 million (a figure that is expected to reach into the hundreds of millions) in out-of-court settlements ("Abuse claims," 1999, p. 5802).

The point is not that redress is a workable substitute for settling land-claims agreements or that it can solve the political impasse between demands for self-government and opposition to "special status." Rather, it is that a willingness to address past wrongs can help First Nations people to connect with Canadian institutions, such as provincial health and counselling services, the RCMP, and the civil and criminal courts, on a footing of respect. By acknowledging its role in facilitating and perpet-uating abuse, the federal government has encouraged former residen-tial-schools students to contact institutions and authorities that history has given them good reason for distrusting. Canada has therefore earned an important opportunity to show Aboriginal peoples that a common cit-izenship can provide a basis from which to address pressing problems in concert with other Canadians.

CONCLUSION

Redress movements have made respect a politicized issue of contempo-rary Canadian citizenship. The movements have reacted against legacies of civic stigmatization by struggling to achieve the elusive status of civic honour. This status is prized for its utility as symbolic capital, which, by helping to elicit the esteem of others, makes the promise of equal par-ticipation in citizenship more attainable. As sociologist William J. Good puts it, without the "respect or esteem of others [we] can not as easily elicit the help of others" (1978, p. vi).

As this essay has shown, redress politics attracts criticism. Critics hold that the project of repairing historical injustices has no natural limits; they contend that redress politics is unduly divisive; and, like former Prime Minister Pierre Trudeau, they argue that the past is the past and that we can only "be just in our own time" (in Weaver, 1981, p. 179). These criticisms warn that attempting to amend historical wrongs will unleash a torrent of aggrieved claimants, with an ensuing politics of vic-timization pitting group against group. Critics insist further that this prospect is particularly real because there is no end to the list of past practices, such as discrimination against people with disabilities, gays and lesbians, communists, and others, that violate contemporary moral stan-dards. In short, the critics say that redress politics is no way to go about building a healthy citizenship.

Only the foolish would dismiss these criticisms outright. However, it is important to warn against the notion that ignoring injustice is the best way to achieve harmony and that once the door is open to historical grievances it cannot ever be closed. These objections can easily become an argument against democracy itself. Indeed, their basic similarity to the 19th-century objections against giving working-class and poor people the vote is striking.[4] Enfranchisement, argued the conservative critics of the workers' movement, would pit class against class and therefore be unduly divisive. Politics, the conservatives insisted, must be conducted in the general interest rather than be held hostage by "special interests." And this general interest, the propertied critics of mass democracy believed, was best determined not by succumbing to the particular demands of the aggrieved but by ensuring that politics was approached from a rational distance capable of ascertaining the best interests of the whole. Thus, the similarity of the criticisms of redress to an older political position, which no serious observer would attempt to maintain today, suggests that both sides of the argument about redress can easily be extended to the point of absurdity. It is far better, then, to at least remain open to the possibility that some historical injustices may be appropriate candidates for reconsideration, and perhaps even restitution.

Contemporary problems of racism and colonialism might seem to suggest the existence of clear-cut criteria according to which the frivolous redress movement may be separated from the worthy. One might, for instance, distinguish claims animated by lingering, and perhaps unwarranted, perceptions of disrespect from those that aim to confront actual contemporary experiences of racism. From this perspective, the Italian- and Ukrainian-Canadian redress claims might be viewed as unjustified to the extent that group members do not face forms of disrespect that include direct instances of public discrimination or racist threats. But it is important to understand that citizens may also find their equality hampered by a comparatively benign form of subordinate status. In the words of Thomas Hobbes (1991), "to neglect is to Dishonour" (p. 64).

Because Canadian citizenship so often revolves around questions of French-English dualism, other ethnic groups may find their collective civic identities collapsed into a near-faceless membership in a larger "English Canada." As former Liberal MP Sergio Marchi has objected, "not all the people of this country have been dealt the same constitutional card, nor have they been equally credited with being a dignified and contributing part of this country" (in Cairns, 1995, p. 124). This problem of civic recognition is key to redress politics. By demonstrating the role of past experiences of racism in producing movements that are dedicated to building a healthier future, these campaigns aim to establish their traditionally overlooked constituencies as the "founding peoples" of a better Canada.

The tendency of historical patterns of inequality to furnish some groups of citizens with more promising bases of civic respect than others poses a problem that the government and citizens of Canada, if they take the notion of equal participation seriously, have a responsibility to consider. However, many Canadians seem increasingly inclined to deny the relevance of historical injustices to the practice of contemporary citizenship. An angry right-wing populism, whose slogan is "equal rights for all, special rights for none," rails against what it sees as a divisive preoccupation with the past. Wondering whether "anyone [has] told France that England is sorry it burned Joan of Arc?" ("Good guys," 1991, p. 100), the neoconservatives mutter darkly about a wrong-headed fixation on "long-forgotten administrations" (Drache, 1990, p. 85) and "claims that go back to the Dark Ages" (Philip, 1990, p. 94). Some opponents of the Nisga'a land-claim deal reveal a similar zeal to forget the history of a country that is barely 130 years old. They pose as defenders of "the integrity of Canadian democracy" (Lautens, 1998, p. A23) by contrasting the "Pandora's box ... of attempting to resolve historical 'wrongs'" with the justice of living "as equals without special status for anyone" (Lipsey, 1998, p. A10).

When offered in relation to First Nations issues, the suggestion that the past has no moral bearing on our present belies a self-serving indifference toward the contemporary outcome of a legacy of conquest. More generally, the insistence that past wrongs are unreasonable items of political discussion involves a refusal to confront historically derived civic problems of undue neglect, misrecognition, and stigmatization. To the degree that it is through participation in democracy that we shape our futures, these problems carry an importance that goes far beyond psychological issues of self-esteem.

Enjoying the benefits of equal citizenship depends, in an important and often unacknowledged sense, on being able to command the positive regard of others. Without this crucial prerequisite of successful interaction, the civic arena is a remarkably intimidating, and in extreme cases even an unthinkable forum to enter. Demands from redress movements that Canada must revisit unflattering episodes and practices from its past thus afford an opportunity. This opportunity is to seek to realize in a more thorough and inclusive manner the potential of citizenship, which is the most basic instrument of solidarity that Canadians have.

NOTES

1. This article is a revised, edited, and updated version of "Redress Politics and Canadian Citizenship," which appeared in *Canada, The State of the Federation 1998/99: How Canadians Connect*, eds. Harvey Lazar and Tom McIntosh (Montreal and Kingston: McGill-Queen's University Press, 1999), pp. 247–82.

2. The following analysis is indebted to Cairns ("Whose Side Is the Past On?" in *Reconfigurations*, 1995) and to Strong-Boag (1994).

3. For example, the Price-Waterhouse accounting firm has estimated that the federal government confiscated $450 million in current dollars from interned Japanese Canadians (Miki and Kobayashi, 1991, p. 93).

4. On these latter objections, see Hobsbawm, 1988, pp. 297–99.

REFERENCES

"Abuse claims swamp Ottawa." (I)1999, January 1. *Canadian News Facts,* p. 5802.

Anderssen, Erin. (1997, December 16). "Natives to get $200-million fund." *The Globe and Mail,* p. A1.

———. and Edward Greenspon. "Federal apology fails to mollify native leaders." (1998, January 8). *The Globe and Mail,* p. A4.

"Apologize for residential schools says Indian leader." (1997, March). *The First Perspective,* p. 1.

Assembly of First Nations. (1994). *Breaking the silence: An interpretive study of residential school impact and healing as illustrated by the stories of First Nations individuals.* Ottawa: First Nations Health Commission.

Aubry, Jack. "'Atrocities' alleged in mission schools." (1994a, August 8). *Vancouver Sun,* p. A1.

———. "Compensation urged for 'coercive' move of Inuit to High Arctic." (1994b, July 14). *Vancouver Sun,* p. A6.

Barnsley, Paul. "Healing foundation making decisions." (1999, June). *Windspeaker,* p. 10.

———. "Apology, a compromise." (1998a, February). *Windspeaker,* p. 4.

———. "Gathering strength not strong enough." (1998b, February). *Windspeaker,* p. 3.

Bell, Stewart. "Abuse claims soar in wake of apology." (1998, January 27). *Vancouver Sun,* p. A1.

Bolan, Kim. "Chinese group asks UN to act on redress." (1995, March 22). *Vancouver Sun,* p. B3.

———. "Liberal's refusal to redress head tax 'betrays' Chinese-Canadians' trust." (1994, December 15). *Vancouver Sun,* p. A3.

Bolaria, B. Singh and Peter S. Li. *Racial oppression in Canada.* 2nd ed. (1988). Toronto: Garamond Press.

Bourdieu, Pierre. *Outline of a theory of practice.* (1977). Trans. Richard Nice. Cambridge: Cambridge University Press.

Cairns, Alan C. *Reconfigurations: Canadian citizenship and constitutional change.* (1995). Ed. Douglas E. Williams. Toronto: McClelland and Stewart.

———. *Disruptions: Constitutional struggles, from the Charter to Meech Lake.* (1991). Ed. Douglas E. Williams. Toronto: McClelland and Stewart.

———. (1989). Political science, ethnicity, and the Canadian Constitution. In David Shugarman and Reg Whitaker (eds.), *Federalism and political community: Essays in honour of Donald Smiley* (pp. 113–40). Peterborough, Ont.: Broadview Press.

Canada. Ministry of Canadian Heritage. Ministry of Canadian Heritage News Release. (1994, December 14). "Sheila Finestone tables and sends letter on redress to ethnocultural organizations."

Chinese Canadian National Council. (1988a). *It is only fair! Redress for the Head Tax and Chinese Exclusion Act.* Toronto: Chinese Canadian National Council.

———. *Then, now and tomorrow.* (1988b). N.p.

Civil Liberties Commission of the Ukrainian Canadian Committee. Presentation to the House of Commons Standing Committee on Multiculturalism. (1987, August 12). *Minutes of proceedings and evidence.* No. 11. Ottawa: Queen's Printer.

Dafoe, Christopher. Lining up for compensation. (1994). In Lubomyr Luciuk (ed.), *Righting an injustice: The debate over redress for Canada's first national internment operations* (pp. 40–41). Toronto: The Justinian Press.

Dafoe, John. "The cash that heals wounds." (1994, 19 August). *Winnipeg Free Press,* p. A6.

de Santis, Agata. "Canada's Unknown PoWs." (1997, 14 April). *Montreal Gazette,* p. A4.

Drache, Arthur. "Little basis for redress of long past injustices." *Financial Post* (Toronto) (1990, 6 September). Rpt. in Luciuk (ed.), *Righting an Injustice* (pp. 84–85).

Ferguson, Eva and Jim Cunningham. "Ukrainians to get federal hearing." (1997, 1 February). *Calgary Herald,* p. B7.

Fournier, Suzanne. "Abused Natives seek $1 billion." (1997, 4 December). *Province* (Vancouver), p. A3.

"Give us strength." (1998, February). *Windspeaker,* p. 6.

"Good guys." (1991, 23 May). *Ottawa Sun.* Rpt. in Luciuk (ed.), *Righting an Injustice* (p. 100).

Goode, William J. *The celebration of heroes: Prestige as a social control system.* Berkeley: University of California Press, 1978.

Gummerson, Penny. "Residential school inquiry releases report." (1997, July). *Raven's Eye,* p. 3.

"Hefty price tag delays settlements." (1993, 1 June). *Calgary Herald,* p. A12.

Hobbes, Thomas. *Leviathan.* (1991). Ed. Richard Tuck. Cambridge: Cambridge University Press.

Hobsbawm, E.J. (1988). *The Age of Revolution: 1789–1848.* London: Cardinal, 1988.

Johnston, Darlene. First Nations and Canadian Citizenship. In William Kaplan (ed.), *Belonging: The meaning and future of Canadian citizenship* (pp. 349–367). Montreal: McGill-Queen's University Press.

Laghi, Brian. "Residential school left lasting scars." (1998, 8 January). *The Globe and Mail* (Toronto), p. A4.

Lautens, Trevor. "Let's preserve the integrity of Canadian democracy." (1998, August 1). *Vancouver Sun*, p. A23.

Lazaruk, Susan. "77-year-old pedophile sentenced to 11 years." (1995, June). *Windspeaker*, p. 3.

Lipsey, Adrian. [Letter]. (1998, July 28). *Vancouver Sun*, p. A10.

Lowi, Emanuel. "A shameful episode." (1996, April 6). *Montreal Gazette*, p. B5.

Luciuk, Lubomyr. "Time to correct injustice." (1994, October 17). *Winnipeg Free Press*, p. A7.

Marcus, Alan R. *Out in the cold: The legacy of Canada's Inuit relocation experiment in the High Arctic.* (1992). Copenhagen: International Work Group for Indigenous Affairs.

McEvoy, F.J. 'A symbol of racial discrimination': The Chinese Immigration Act and Canada's relations with China, 1942–1947." (1982). *Canadian Ethnic Studies* 3:14, pp. 24–42.

Miki, Roy and Cassandra Kobayashi, eds. (1991). *Justice in our time: The Japanese Canadian redress settlement.* Vancouver: Talon Books.

———. *Justice in our time: Redress for Japanese Canadians.* (1988). Vancouver: National Association of Japanese Canadians.

Miller, J.R. (1996). *Shingwauk's vision: A history of Native residential schools.* Toronto: University of Toronto Press.

Mulroney, Brian. (1990). "Notes for an address by Prime Minister Brian Mulroney to the National Congress of Italian Canadians and the Canadian Italian Business Professional Association."

———. (1988). "Notes for an address by the Right Honourable Brian Mulroney, P.C., M.P., Prime Minister of Canada, on Japanese-Canadian Redress."

National Association of Japanese Canadians. Presentation to the House of Commons Standing Committee on Multiculturalism. (1986, May 27). *Minutes of proceedings and evidence.* No. 9. Ottawa: Queen's Printer.

———. (1984). *Democracy betrayed: The case for redress.* Vancouver: National Association of Japanese Canadians.

National Congress of Italian Canadians. (1990). *A national shame: The internment of Italian Canadians.* N.p.

O'Neil, Peter. "Natives say Ottawa's apology may sway judges in civil suits." (1998, January 8). *Vancouver Sun*, p. A1.

Omatsu, Maryka. (1992). *Bittersweet passage: Redress and the Japanese Canadian experience.* Toronto: Between the Lines.

Oskaboose, Gilbert. (1996, December). "To the Government of Canada." *The First Perspective*, p. 4.

"Ottawa acknowledges mistakes." (1998, February). *Windspeaker*, p. 2.

Philip, Tom. "Haunted by history: Ukrainians, Italians and Chinese seek redress for Historical ill-treatment by Ottawa." (1990, December 17). *Alberta Report.* Rpt. in Luciuk (ed.), *Righting an Injustice* (pp. 93–96).

"Post no bills." (1998, November 10). *Ottawa Sun.* Rpt. in Luciuk (ed.), *Righting an Injustice* (p. 50).

Ramirez, Bruno. (1988). Ethnicity on trial: The Italians of Montreal and the Second World War. In *On guard for thee: War, ethnicity, and the Canadian state, 1939–1945.* Eds. Norman Hillmer et al. (pp. 71–84). Ottawa: Minister of Supply and Services.

"Residential schools: A sad history of abuse." (1998, January 8). *The Vancouver Sun,* p. A3.

Royal Commission on Aboriginal Peoples. (1994). *The High Arctic relocation: Summary of supporting information.* Vol. I. Ottawa: Minister of Supply and Services.

Simpson, Jeffrey. "The trouble with trying to compensate groups for historical wrongs." (1990, June 14). *The Globe and Mail* (Toronto). Rpt. in Luciuk (ed.), *Righting an Injustice* (p. 78–79).

Steffenhagen, Janet. "Apology to abused Natives elicits powerful emotions." (1998, January 8). *Vancouver Sun,* p. A3.

Stewart, Jane. (1998, January 8). "Statement of reconciliation: Learning from the past." Rpt. in *The Globe and Mail* (Toronto), p. A19.

Strong-Boag, Veronica. (1994). "Contested space: The politics of Canadian memory." *Journal of the Canadian Historical Association* 5: 3–17.

Taylor, Charles. Shared and Divergent Values. In Ronald L. Watts and Douglas M. Brown (eds.), *Options for a new Canada.* (pp. 53–76). Toronto: University of Toronto Press.

Thompson, John Herd. (1983). "The enemy alien and the Canadian general election of 1917." In Frances Swyripa and John Herd Thompson (eds.), *Loyalties in conflict: Ukrainians in Canada during the Great* War (pp. 25–46). Edmonton: Canadian Institute of Ukrainian Studies.

"Ukraine: In the shadow of Lenin: 'enemy aliens' remember." (1988, October 8). *Edmonton Journal,* p. F5.

Ukrainian Canadian Civil Liberties Association. (1988). *A time for atonement.* N.p.

Weaver, Sally M. (1981). *Making Canadian Indian policy: The hidden agenda, 1968–70.* Toronto: University of Toronto Press.

Weiner, Gerry. (1988). "Speaking notes for the Honourable Gerry Weiner, Minister of State for Multiculturalism and Citizenship, at the Japanese Canadian Redress Agreement press conference."

Wong, Victor Yukmun. "An old wrong stays wrong." (1995, January 13). *The Vancouver Sun,* p. A15.

FURTHER READING

Brooks, Roy, ed. *When Sorry Isn't Enough: The Controversy over Apologies and Reparations for Human Injustice.* New York: New York University Press, 1999.

Cairns, Alan C. Whose Side is the Past On? In his *Reconfigurations: Canadian Citizenship and Constitutional Change.* Ed. Douglas E. Williams. Toronto: McClelland and Stewart, 1995, pp. 15–30.

Goffman, Erving. *Stigma: Notes on the Management of Spoiled Identity.* New York: Touchstone, 1986.

Luciuk, Lubomyr, ed. *Righting an Injustice: The Debate Over Redress for Canada's First National Internment Operations.* Toronto: The Justinian Press, 1994.

Strong-Boag, Veronica. "Contested Space: The Politics of Canadian Memory." *Journal of the Canadian Historical Association* 5 (1994), 3–17.

PART B

QUEBEC'S SEARCH FOR NATIONAL IDENTITY

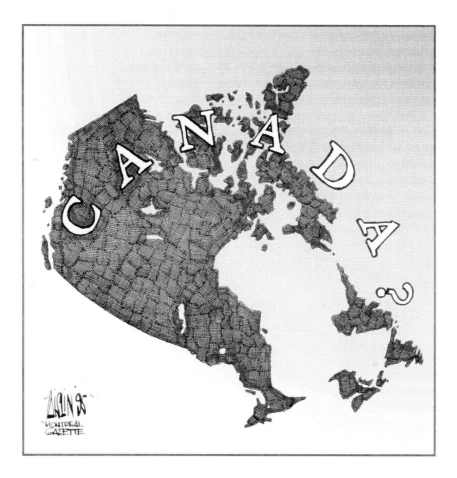

Quebec: The Core of First Time

Anne Hébert

This province is a country within a country. Quebec the Original Heart. The hardest and deepest kernel. The core of first time. All around, nine other provinces form the flesh of this still-bitter fruit called Canada.

The creation of the world took place on the rock of Quebec. Face to the river. Adam and Eve were Louis Hébert and Marie Rollet. The first dwelling. The first land tilled. The first sheaf of grain reaped. The first bit of bread. The first child brought into life. The first body laid in earth.

The first written word. It was in 1534: "In the name of God and of the King of France." A cross planted at Gaspé by Jacques Cartier. The vocation of writing begun in the wilderness wind.

And then we were surrendered to time. Time followed its course. By turns we were shaken or lulled by time. Like logs drifting down rivers, we slipped by. A defeat in the heart. A rosary between the fingers. Like the dead. Musing on the song of Lazarus. But see the thought give way to the word. The word becomes flesh. To possess the world. The Tree of Knowledge. Not in the centre of the garden. Those soft prenatal limbs outside of paradise, in the accursed open land. At the hour of birth, a gate opens upon the round and total world.

"In Quebec nothing changes." Once this was truth. Immobile, peasant-like. Beneath the snow, or the summer sun. Yet no Sleeping Beauty can pass unchanged the test of slumber. Beneath so many dreams and sorrows a duty is discerned. Take up thy bed and walk. The heaped-up treasure-board cracks and splits. Reclaim the heritage from foreign imposts.

The river is salt like the sea. Waves beat upon seaweed-laden shores. Here the wind blows free for ten leagues around. The adventure is boundless. Who can merely tell of it? One must shout it, hands forming a loud-hailer. The two banks narrowing together are thickly black with trees. It is on no human scale. Here we may labour only. Whoever speaks will speak savagely. With a voice of earth and water mixed.

Helter skelter land of wood and sea. North bank South bank. Kamouraska, Saint-Vallier, Cap à l'Aigle, Saint-Jean-Port-Joli, lie aux Lièvrews, Rimouski, Father Point, Sainte-Luce, Anse Pleureuse, Coin du Banc, Pic de l'Aurore, Gros Morne, Cloridorme, lle Bonaventure.

Sea birds by thousands encrust the rock. Lift. Wheel. Raucous cries on the swell of the sea. Gannets, grebes, cormorants, gulls. Beneath the wind the rock seems to shake itself, like a wild beast attacked by superbly fantastic swarms of bees. Above, the sky.

A hundred thousand lakes. Streams with the strength of a river. Forests entangled by deadfalls. An axe in the hand like a cane. The tracks are those of caribou. Mosquitoes smoke upon your body like your own breath.

Burnt-over land as far as the eye can see. New growth of birch on the green moss. Long tendrils of moss, drawn from the soil, like garlands with fine sandy roots. Gathering blueberries. The barrens laden with flue fruit. That silvery mist clouding the fresh berries. That was when I was a child. Now the reign of the birches is threatened. The face of Charlebois is pitted by dead birches. Sad little white bones against the green of the forest.

Calm lakes, like water in the hollow of a hand. Lake Edward. We children were forbidden to go near the water. "Your hair the colour of the fallow deer, your body of peacocks"—hunters might fire in error. The midges, the blackflies ambushed us. Thousands of needles. Was that the sound of a moose? It crosses the lake, swimming. As if it ploughed a mirror. Deer! A deer in the hayfield! A prodigy of a leap! There it is, out of range. Sheltering in the black spruce.

Sainte-Catherine. Each summer's end a brown bear ventured from the forest. Prowled the edges of the fields. While the golden hay assumed the colour of fresh-baked bread. Children saw enormous tracks in the sand of the little strawberry woods. Games were erased. Sand castles crushed. The children gravely enchanted. As if in the night a heraldic beast had come from the high plaints of the Countess de Segur, née Rostopchine, claiming her tribute in Canadian land.

Sainte-Foy. Named for a bitter victory. There where the city, the new university city, now expands. During my childhood it was a little wood. A whole summer of holidays. A brook. Green grass-snakes. Symphonies of tree-frogs. Strawberries bordering the fields. Orchards. Apples succeeding apples—the green, the white, the transparents, the Fameuses. Four houses thick-shelled with white brick. Each with its garden and its orchard. The road was called the Avenue of the Four Bourgeois. It was the country.

Quebec. That city where my parents were born. Where my ancestors prospered and were undone. The city is lived in. Above. Below. The city is ours. We need only plainly speak its name, this city. City on a crag. City of the New World. Upper Town. Lower Town. The secret province. Homogeneous. Certain of its identity. Dreaming behind its jalousies. Taking its time. Sauntering through the narrow streets. Through the summer evenings. Releasing in full bloom the beauty of its daughters.

The long length of Dufferin Terrace. Rue Saint-Louis, rue de la Fabrique, Esplanade, rue des Grissons, rue des Glaçis, ruelle du Trésor, côte à Coton, côte de la Négresse, Latin Quarter, rue Dauphine, Jardin du Fort, Jardin du Gouverneur, rue sous le Cap, Petit Champlain. Little by little the aristocratic quarters move from the old city. A whole floating population camps within the walls. The tall dwellings divide into rented pigeonholes. They sell souvenirs. The port overflows with shipping. Whirlpools of gulls. Vast gates of the water. The sea begins. Clerical bands and coifs. A city of terraces and convents.

Sugar and syrup from the Beauce. Honey from Saint-Pierre-les-Becquets. Mushrooms from Waterloo. Cider from Saint-Hilaire. Brome Lake duck. Valcartier turkey. Real geography is learned at the table, in the breaking of bread.

Boucherville, Varennes, Verchères, Contrecœur, Saint-Antoine-de-Tilly, Sorel, Saint-Jean-sur-Richelieu. Old villages of the French régime. Fine stone houses in the style of manors. Elms, of all trees the most civilized; maples; an amiable river. A domesticated landscape. Ripe and reassuring age.

Rapid, rugged ice hockey. The log drive, perilous leap without a net, on rivers in full flood. Twenty-five thousand white geese alight on Cap Tourmente. Take to the sky. Perfect formations. Passing above Quebec. Their faraway raucous yelping, solid, unhearing, almost unreal, dominating the whole autumnal night sky—if you have never heard it, you have never felt the strange sensation of physical envelopment in a dream, never escaped above the earth.

Once this city was called Hochelaga. François-Xavier Garneau wrote of it, "a half-hundred wooden habitations, fifty paces long and twelve to fifteen wide. In each house, walls hung with skins skilfully sewn together, several rooms opened upon a square room containing the hearth. The settlement was surrounded by a triple palisade." This city was called Ville-Marie. There mass was celebrated by the light of fireflies. "Should every tree on Montreal Island become an Iroquois, it is my duty there to found a colony, and I will go." Thus spoke Maisonneuve. This city is called Montreal. More than two million inhabitants. A vigorous, enterprising life. Creates. Defies. Struggles, gains, loses, rejoices in its destiny. Multiplies. Becomes complex. Accepts or rejects. Melting pot. Cultural broth. Constructs. Demolishes. Reconstructs. A perpetual factory. A city which had no age. Which burns its past. Of which its present pride is its future. At the high heat of its energy. At the peak of its endeavours. Victorian Sherbrooke Street is earth-bound. Vive Dorchester Boulevard and its proud, fine skyscrapers. The calm of Westmount's little streets: Mount Stephen, Oliver, Kensington. Men, ideas, politics, commerce; business, the arts and daily life assert themselves, confront each other. With the rhythm of the neon. Flashing in the immense city. By day as by night.

Country of water. Of the tumultuous strength of water. Untamed water harnessed. Like a hot-blooded team. Proud water tamed and mastered. The powerhouse of La Gabelle. the Beauharnois dam.

Manicouagan. The greatest workshop in the world. Man's all-powerful hand set over the energy of the water.

Asbestos. Noranda. Bourlamaque. Gagnon. Arvida. Matagami. The darkness of the earth opened. The black heart of the earth delivers up its treasures. Asbestos, copper, gold, zinc, aluminum, iron. The shadows are heavy. The miner's lamp scarcely lights the depths of the workings. The patient slow efforts of the young master of the premises. Claiming his entire share.

To seize this land in *flagrante delicto*, in the very act of existence. To understand. To do it justice. To put it into words. The task of a poet. The honour of living.

Lucien Bouchard and the Politics of Quebec Independence

Réjean Pelletier

In recent years, Quebeckers have frequently been asked to express their opinion on the Canadian federation. In October 1992, they expressed their views through a referendum on the Charlottetown Accord, which they rejected with a no vote of 56.7 percent. A year later, they elected 54 Bloc Québécois MPs (giving the party 49.3 percent of the vote), to defend Quebec's interests and promote sovereignty in Ottawa. In September 1994, they chose the Parti Québécois (PQ) to form their provincial government with 77 members of the National Assembly (MNAs) (with 44.8 percent of the vote). In October 1995, Quebeckers opted to remain in Canada by a narrow majority of 50.6 percent and a record voter turnout of 93.5 percent. This result contrasts with the referendum of 1980, when 20 percentage points separated the two sides (with a voter turnout that year of 85.6 percent).

In November 1998, Quebeckers chose the Parti Québécois to form their provincial government for the second time with 76 MNAs, but the party received fewer votes (42.9 percent) than the Quebec Liberal Party (QLP) (43.5 percent). However, with the arrival of Jean Charest, the former leader of the federal Conservatives, at the head of the Quebec Liberal troops, federalist forces had hoped to win a majority of seats and to form the government. Liberal strategists did not take into account the strength of the Action Démocratique led by Mario Dumont, which received 11.8 percent of the vote but only one seat. If this party was able to grab votes from the PQ, it mostly did harm to the QLP in francophone regions, where the Liberals were supposed to make some gains. Lucien Bouchard presented himself as the best defender of Quebec's interest facing up to Ottawa while Jean Charest did not have a coherent vision concerning the place of Quebec in the Canadian federation.

Facing this result, Lucien Bouchard was forced to declare that he could not hold a new referendum on sovereignty until "winning conditions" existed. In other words, he could not hold a referendum until support for sovereignty made substantial gains. A second setback in such a short period would have meant not only the death of the sovereignist option but also the dislocation of the PQ.

On February 4, 1999, two months after the election, an agreement relative to a "social union" was concluded by the federal government and all provincial governments except Quebec. This agreement recognized the federal government's right to spend in areas of provincial jurisdiction, while Quebec demanded that it recognize an unconditional right to opt out with full financial compensation in regards to all new federal initiatives in the social sphere.

Following the failures to renew Canadian federalism in 1990 and 1992, and the unwillingness of the rest of Canada to amend the constitution so Quebec could assent to the *Constitution Act, 1982*, the country faced an impasse once again. These failures led to strong reactions from Quebec, which sent a clear message to Canadian federalists through: the support for the Bloc Québécois in three federal elections, the two provincial victories of the Parti Québécois, and, above all, the near-victory in the referendum. These events suggest that the failure of constitutional reforms could cause the break-up of the country.

In the French edition of his book, *Misconceiving Canada*, Kenneth McRoberts concluded his analysis of the 1995 referendum with these words:

> … three years [now five years] after the referendum which almost led to the dismantling of Canada, francophones from Quebec and Canadians outside Quebec are still unable to agree on the nature of the country to which most of them are still strongly attached. At the roots of the impasse is the conception of Canada which was inscribed in the Canadian institutions during the Trudeau years. Adopted with enthusiasm almost everywhere in the country, it is more than ever rejected in Quebec. (McRoberts, 1999, p. 335)

Before turning to this point, it is important to consider, as background, two important events that have influenced political life in Quebec and Canada in the 1990s and to analyze Bouchard's view of sovereignty. In the third part of the paper, we will ask "why sovereignty?" and in the final part, we will outline some factors that could influence the future of Quebec and thereby affect the future of the Canadian federation.

BACKGROUND: TWO POLITICAL TURNING-POINTS[1]

Considering the recent events of Quebec political life, we can note two major factors which have changed the course of things. First, the defeat of the Meech Lake Accord in June 1990, was strongly resented in Quebec, strengthening the sovereigntist movement and almost giving it a victory in the 1995 referendum. We do not need to look beyond this, and especially the rejection of the Accord's recognition of Quebec as a "distinct society," for reasons for the strength of sovereigntist sentiment at the start of the 1990s. We must also remember that the progression of sovereignty-association since 1989 followed several events which generated strong reactions in Quebec. In December 1988, the Supreme Court declared that the requirement of unilingual French signs violated the Quebec and Canadian *Charters of Rights*. Then after Quebec decided to use the notwithstanding clause[2] to pass a new sign law, various cities—mostly in Ontario—saw demonstrations against the French language and declared themselves English-only in the Fall of 1989. As well, the Premiers of Manitoba, Newfoundland and New Brunswick threatened to not ratify the Meech Lake Accord unless significant amendments were brought forth (Cloutier, Guay and Latouche, 1992, pp.62–66). Analysts of this period submit that the progress of various sovereigntist options was highly sensitive to these events (Cloutier et al, 1992, p.67). We will return to this later in the essay.

We must also consider the arrival of Parizeau as the leader of the PQ in 1988 and his replacement by Bouchard in 1996. Parizeau has always promoted a "*hard-line*" ideal of independence, tirelessly repeating that it is essential to speak of independence "before, during, and after elections"—never hiding this goal for electoral reasons and always making it the ultimate objective of the sovereigntist movement.

After support for sovereignty had peaked at 58 percent in 1990 (support for sovereignty-association had even peaked at 70 percent in November of that year), nationalist fervour declined, with support for sovereignty stalling at around 40 percent in 1994 and early 1995 (Monière and Guay, 1996, pp.181–202). After he had postponed the referendum from Spring until Autumn of 1995, Parizeau agreed in June to a compromise to try to increase support for the sovereignty cause: he signed an agreement with Lucien Bouchard and Action Démocratique leader Mario Dumont, adding the idea of partnership to that of sovereignty. This is reminiscent of René Lévesque's idea of sovereignty-association, which caused tension within the sovereigntist camp years earlier.

Despite the "instantaneous" rise in support for sovereignty in June 1995, the gains soon slipped away, and it seemed that sovereigntists could not hope for the yes vote to exceed 45 percent.[3] An abrupt change occurred during the referendum campaign when, on October 7, Parizeau introduced Bouchard as the leader of Quebec's negotiation team in the event that the sovereigntists won the referendum. Bouchard rapidly gained a high profile in the media, and at the same time he personified the partnership option. This option would mute the most harmful consequences of separation and softened the hard-line position of Parizeau on independence. The more moderate Bouchard became the uncontested leader of the sovereigntist forces, a leader with whom many francophone Quebeckers could identify.

What lessons for the future can we draw from these two turning points? The first of these was an unprecedented rise in support for the sovereignty option in the early 1990s, and its decline in the years that followed. One lesson emerges right away: Quebeckers' sensitivity to the events of the moment causes support for sovereignty to fluctuate[4] in accordance with the importance of these events for Quebec.

The second turning point relates to the role of Lucien Bouchard on the Quebec political scene, first as leader of the Bloc Québécois, then as leader of the PQ, and finally as Premier of Quebec. Unlike Parizeau, who was firmly committed to the idea of independence, Bouchard embodied moderation and the notion of partnership as well as sovereignty, and he even reflected a certain ambivalence felt by a large number of francophone Quebeckers. The cold, rational thinker (Parizeau) was replaced by a more passionate and emotional leader (Bouchard). This shift dramatically changed the political landscape of Quebec and the province's relationship with the federal government.

BOUCHARD'S VIEW ON SOVEREIGNTY

Lucien Bouchard's position on sovereignty contrasts with that of Jacques Parizeau. We may classify Parizeau as a "*hard-line*" sovereigntist, for whom the goal of sovereignty is always paramount, even without association or partnership. Lucien Bouchard is more wavering and doubtful. Parizeau aims at a single objective: sovereignty. While Bouchard shares the same goal, his faith is less steady. Yet he better reflects the ambivalence of the Quebec population.

Although he was once a Liberal, Lucien Bouchard joined the PQ in the early 1970s. A friend of Brian Mulroney, Bouchard wrote speeches for him and helped to prepare the Conservative party platform for the 1984 election (Bouchard, 1992, pp. 137–57). Named Canada's ambassador to France in 1985, he entered electoral politics as a Conservative candidate in a by-election in June 1988. Two years later, he resigned from Mulroney's cabinet and from the Conservative caucus to protest the amendments proposed to the Meech Lake Accord as part of an effort to make provincial legislatures agree to ratify it. He concluded his resignation letter with these words:

> It is definitely better to have honour in disagreement than agreement in dishonour. Anyway, nothing would be worse than dishonour in disagreement, which I believe will be reserved for those who try, in vain I do believe, to convince Quebec to come to a conference to be trapped into final, humiliating concessions. (Bouchard, 1992, pp. 325)

After his resignation, the Bloc Québécois was born in Ottawa and Bouchard became involved in the sovereigntist movement—the same Bouchard who had agreed to support the "*beau risque*" card announced by René Lévesque, a new orientation that led Parizeau at that time to leave the PQ as both minister and MNA.

The routes travelled by the two leaders are very different. Once he became a sovereigntist, Parizeau never wavered in his ideology, always embodying the *"hard-line"* face of sovereignty. On the other hand, Bouchard's nationalist convictions and his will to defend the interests of Quebec led him to found the Bloc Québécois, which obtained unexpected success in the 1993 federal election. Then he entered the 1995 referendum campaign, and would later become leader of the PQ and Premier of Quebec in January 1996. Although sovereignty is important to him, not everything is reduced to this single question. Above all, sovereignty must be achieved on terms which are acceptable for Quebec's entire population.

One of these conditions involves partnership. For Parizeau, the goal is sovereignty, with or without partnership; for Bouchard, partnership is more closely linked to the sovereigntist project. Although he pledged in 1990 to "remain in politics to work for the sovereignty of Quebec" (Bouchard, 1992, pp. 334), clearly he has not travelled in a straight line. If there is one constant in his trajectory, it is his faithfulness to the aspirations and interests of Quebec. At present, this trajectory carries Bouchard towards a sovereigntist position, but this is a sovereignty based on a European model of partnership and the preservation of Canada's economic structure (Bouchard, 1993, pp. 87–95).

With support from Mario Dumont, leader of the Action Démocratique du Québec, Bouchard virtually imposed this policy of partnership on Parizeau prior to the 1995 referendum. This agreement of June 12, it is useful to note, has two important differences from previous PQ projects. First, the idea of a treaty on economic partnership adds a number of provisions to the kinds of agreements the PQ had previously indicated it would pursue, namely shared customs and currency, and free circulation and mobility of labour. The new provisions deal with internal trade, international trade, Canadian representation in international affairs, transportation, defence policy, financial institutions, budgetary and fiscal policies, environmental protection, and postal services. More than a simple treaty of economic partnership, this proposal would reshape relations between Quebec and Canada in a confederal union covering numerous areas of activity.

This agreement also breaks new ground in its proposal for shared *political* institutions. To the three traditional bodies outlined in previous PQ documents—a council, a secretariat and a tribunal—the agreement adds a parliamentary assembly. This would be comprised of Quebec and Canadian representatives nominated by their respective legislatures and would make recommendations to council and approve resolutions. This proposition takes the partnership concept closer to the European model that Bouchard had discussed previously. This is not to say that institutions based on a partnership of two members would necessarily be any more harmonious than one of six, twelve or fifteen.[5]

A further subject remains to be explored: the identity of Quebec. For Parizeau, "anyone who wishes to be a Quebecker can be." Of course, Quebeckers are of diverse backgrounds, but "neither race, nor colour define them, it is language." From this definition, Parizeau therefore recognizes that anglophone rights would be maintained in a sovereign Quebec, although he follows by adding "[p]erhaps it would be preferable, in this case, to add nothing and bring ourselves closer in line with what English Canada wishes to do with regards to francophones outside Quebec ..." (Parizeau, 1997, p. 350). However, he stresses that a people who knows who they are does not abandon the principle of equality of rights of all citizens, and that therefore a sovereign Quebec would respect its minorities.

While Bouchard shares Parizeau's views on the question of defining the identity of Quebeckers primarily in terms of language, he has, however, disassociated himself from the idea of tying the rights of anglophones in Quebec to those of francophones outside the province. These rights are not to be bargained with, says the present leader of the PQ, who follows René Lévesque in opposing a reduction of the rights of anglophones in Quebec. In a speech to anglophone representatives in Montreal's Centaur Theatre on March 11, 1996, Bouchard firmly stated:

> As a sovereigntist and as Premier of Quebec, I believe that it is my duty to solemnly reaffirm our commitment to preserving the rights of the anglophone community at present, and in a sovereign Quebec. They shall continue to administer their schools, their colleges, and their universities; have access to courts and government in English; have access to social services and health care in their language; have radio and television in English. (Bouchard, 1996, p. 6–7)

He added this forceful sentence: "When you go to the hospital and you are suffering, you may need a blood test, but certainly not language control."

In sum, Parizeau's uncompromising position on sovereignty contrasts with the consistent defence of Quebec's interests by Bouchard, who believes that these interests would be best defended, in practice, in a sovereign Quebec which will reach agreement on an economic and political partnership with Canada. Sovereignty is not a panacea to Bouchard; it must be achieved under the best possible conditions for Quebec. To him, it has become a necessity for Quebec in the wake of the failures of the "*beau risque*" idea, Meech Lake, and Charlottetown Accords. Such a position resonates not only with the nucleus of sovereigntists, but also with more moderate, "softer" nationalists, for whom independence is not an absolute necessity, but rather an option which may become necessary if other alternatives fail. Bouchard's record of more varied thinking, doubts, and ambivalence reflects the feelings of Quebeckers, especially francophone Quebeckers, better than the certainty and uncompromising nature of Parizeau.

WHY SOVEREIGNTY?

A number of studies on the determinants of Quebec sovereignty have shown that the expected cost-benefits of sovereignty in terms of economic prospects and the perceived effect of this potential status on the condition of the French language have an impact upon the constitutional choices of Quebeckers (Blais, Martin and Nadeau, 1995; Nadeau and Fleury, 1995). Another study suggests that these two factors may not be genuine causes of sovereignty support but rather rationalization of other, deeply embedded sentiments, such as national identity (Howe, 1998).

According to a recent study (Guérin and Pelletier, 2000), identity was the key determinant of the referendum vote in 1995. Identity affected the referendum vote both directly and indirectly through constitutional preferences. Moreover, identity has been found to be an important determinant of constitutional preferences as well, and language has been found to be the most important determinant of identity.

Why are identity and language so important? Quebeckers mostly define themselves as a nation or a people. More exactly, one can apply to them Kymlicka's definition of "national minorities," that is, "historically settled, territorially concentrated, and previously self-governing cultures whose territory has been incorporated into a larger state" (Kymlicka, 1998, p. 30). A sense of belonging to a community, a common past, the will to preserve the unique character of the community, and a territory are fundamental elements of a nation (Herb and Kaplan, 1999, p.16). A great number of Quebeckers feel they fit the requirements of such a definition.

When they are asked "Do you think of yourself *first* as a Canadian or as a Quebecker?" about half the people of Quebec (49 percent) see themselves first as Quebeckers (Gallup Poll, Dec. 1993 and June 1999). Many Quebeckers may indeed have a real sense of loyalty to both Quebec and Canada. But, if you ask them to chose between the two, they will chose Quebec first.

As Kymlicka would recall (1998, pp. 131–32), the language of nationhood serves a number of valuable functions. Among other things, it serves to differentiate the claims of national minorities from those of other groups. That's why multiculturalism is seen by most Quebeckers as a threat to their national identity. This multiculturalism policy makes them an immigrant group like a Ukrainian, Italian, Greek, or Chinese immigrant group, not a national community. A national community can be defined not only by its own language and culture but also by its own territory and political institutions. No other immigrant group in Canada may have such claims.

Another function of the language of nationhood, evoked Kymlicka, is to equalize the bargaining power between a majority and national minorities, to see them as co-equal partners. That's exactly the case in Quebec. The sovereignty-association projects, and now the idea of sovereignty-partnership, defended by the Parti Québécois assume the logic of co-equal partners. While some Quebeckers wish for a total independence, a complete separation from the rest of Canada, most of them would rather associate with projects that oscillate between sovereignty-partnership, the recognition of an asymmetrical federalism, or changes to the Canadian federalism (Gallup Poll, November 16, 1995). With the sovereignty- partnership, as previously seen, the Parti Québécois not only wants to maintain strong economic ties with Canada but also wishes for the creation of common political institutions that would translate this idea of a co-equal partnership according to the often-cited European Union.

Finally, as Kymlicka underlined (1998, p. 132), "it is worth remembering that the power to name itself is one of the most significant powers sought by any group in society." To define oneself as a Quebecker and to be recognized as a distinct society are part of this logic. Quebeckers have the feeling of constituting a distinct society that is a different national community than the Canadian community by its language, its culture, its civil code, the particular role of its provincial government, and by a certain number of political, social, and even economic (like the Caisse de dépôt et placement du Québec) institutions. This claim for recognition was at the heart of the Meech Lake Accord that English Canada rejected first and foremost because it refused the notion of distinct society in the name of equality for all provinces (Blais and Crête, 1991).

Language, as previously noted, constitutes one of the foundations of this national identity. As Jean-William Lapierre (1988) rightly put it, language is not only the means of communication proper to human beings but also an instrument of power and the symbol of a collective identity; that is why it often becomes the source of passionate and sometimes violent political conflicts, thus prompting the active intervention of the state.

The 1982 *Charter of Rights*, the *Official Languages Act* of 1969 and then 1988 focus on the absolute primacy of individual rights, that is the right of individuals to demand federal government services in the official language of their choice—English or French—by virtue of the 1969 and 1988 Acts and the *Charter*, or the right for their children, under certain conditions, to receive, by virtue of the *Charter*, instruction in the official language of their choice.

Although both the *Charter* and the *Official Languages Act* guarantee individual language rights, they do not give linguistic communities the means to ensure their own survival and development (Burelle, 1995, p. 72), as if individual linguistic rights can be uprooted or separated from the communities from which they arise. Trudeau's legacy, wrote Burelle (1995, pp. 66–67), "does not recognize communities as a necessary instrument for transmitting language and culture, which are, for all human beings, a social legacy much more than an individual right." This same idea is upheld by Lenihan et al. (1994, p. 64): "Language, they suggest, is by its very nature a collective enterprise. Its existence presupposes the existence of a community of users." And they add: "In practical terms, this makes the preservation and vitality of a language community a condition for the exercise of language rights ..."

Because French is a minority language in Canada, it is important that the francophone community be recognized in a special way, especially since, no matter how the situation is analyzed, francophones as a proportion of Canada's population are steadily declining. For example, Canadian census data show how many people with French as their mother tongue can still understand it (without necessarily speaking it). One can see that the number of francophones in Canada has been in decline for 60 years, having plunged from 29.2 percent of the population in 1941 to only 24.5 percent in 1991 and 23.5 percent in 1996 (see Table 1). Moreover, since Quebec's Quiet Revolution 40 years ago, this trend has accelerated. This is simultaneously a reflection of the rate at which francophones outside Quebec are assimilated into the anglophone community, the drop in French Quebec's birth rate and the reluctance of immigrants who speak neither French nor English to blend into the francophone community.

Table 1: Canadians with French as Mother Tongue

(1941–96)

%	Total Population	French as Mother Tongue	
1941	11 506 655	3 354 753	29.2
1951	14 009 429	4 068 850	29.0
1961	18 238 247	5 123 151	28.1
1971	21 568 310	5 792 710	26.9
1976	22 992 605	5 966 707	25.9
1981	24 343 185	6 252 603	25,7
1986	25 309 345	6 359 741	25.1
1991	27 073 450	6 639 821	24.5
1996	28 528 125	6 711 630	23.5

In 1991 and 1996, including non-permanent residents.

Source: Canadian census data (since 1981, data have included an adjustment for multiple responses, which are evenly divided between the reported languages).

Everywhere in Canada, the rate of assimilation of francophone populations has reached a level never before seen: 72 percent in Saskatchewan, 65 percent in the Toronto-Windsor Ontario peninsula, 55 percent in the

Winnipeg-Saint-Boniface region of Manitoba, 55 percent in British Columbia, and even 7 percent in New Brunswick where a strong francophone minority is protected by laws recognizing French language and culture (*Le Devoir*, 1996, p. 1).

Census data also show that French is more often a mother tongue than a language spoken at home. In 1971, 25.7 percent of Canadians said they spoke French at home; in 1996, only 22.6 percent said French was the regular language of the home. In 1991, in all Canadian provinces except Quebec, the number of people whose mother tongue was French was higher than the number of people who use French more often at home. However, the number of people speaking English at home, in all provinces including Quebec, is higher than the number of people with English as their mother tongue, indicating a transfer to English by members of other linguistic groups (Harrison and Marmen, 1994, p. 10). According to the 1996 census, outside Quebec and New Brunswick, between 84 percent (in Ontario) and 99 percent of the population speak English at home. All these results clearly indicate the attraction of English in Canada. That is why Marmen and Corbeil (1999, pp. 81–82) concluded: "It is difficult to imagine a reasonable scenario which would reverse the trend towards a reduction in the proportion of Francophones in the overall population of the country." And they added: "If immigration continues to favour the growth of the Anglophone group and fertility of the two official language groups remains similar to current levels, it is likely that both the number and proportion of Anglophones will increase in the future."

The fact that Quebec—the heartland of francophone Canada—constitutes an ever smaller proportion of the Canadian population makes for a much more sombre picture (see Table 2). The population of Quebec as a percentage of the total Canadian population has not stopped dwindling for the last 60 years, dropping from 29 percent in 1941 to 25.3 percent in 1991 and 24.1 percent in 1999 (estimated figures).

In short, the linguistic rights recognized by the *Charter* and the *Official Languages Act*s of 1969 and 1988 are based on the primacy of individual rights and the notion of equality of citizens. On the one hand, this leads to a refusal to recognize the distinct nature and cultural uniqueness of Quebec, making it a province like any other. Just as all citizens are equal, so are all provinces, but this is not the case for the two "founding peoples."

On the other hand, advocating equality in a situation of inequality can only magnify the inequality. Applying symmetrical rights to asymmetrical situations can only heighten the asymmetry between anglophones and francophones. All data confirm this, especially when we consider the linguistic assimilation of immigrants and francophones outside Quebec, and even immigrants inside Quebec despite Bill 101 (63 percent of Quebec immigrants adopt English as their second language according to the 1991 census; 61 percent according to the 1996 census[6]).

Table 2: Quebec Population in Canada

(1941–99)

	Canada	Quebec	%
1941	11,506,655	3,331,882	29.0
1951	14,009,429	4,005,681	28.9
1961	18,238,247	5,259,211	28.8
1971	21,568,310	6,027,764	27.9
1981	24,343,185	6,438,403	26.4
1986	25,309,345	6,532,461	25.8
1991	27,296,859	6,895,963	25.3
1996	28,846,761	7,138,795	24.7
1999*	30,491,300	7,345,400	24.1

* In 1999, estimated figures.

Source: Canadian census data.

Individual bilingualism of an egalitarian sort, in the context of language inequality, leads directly to domination by the strongest language.

Quebeckers are sensitive to this situation. They consider that French is threatened not only in Canada as a whole but also in Quebec. They believe that Pierre Elliott Trudeau's bilingualism policy was a failure and that, as Kenneth McRoberts expressed it, "… the Trudeau government's language policy impeded national unity rather than strengthened it" (McRoberts, 1997, p. 116).

WHAT TO EXPECT IN THE FUTURE?

Quebeckers, as previously observed, are very sensitive to the way events unfold: their support for sovereignty tends to rise during periods of crisis and fall during periods of calm. But sensitivity to the moment cannot explain everything: it is more useful in explaining short-term mood changes than long-term trends. The latter certainly have more significance for Canadian unity than events of the moment, without denying the importance of these events.

Is the mobilization of Quebeckers around events that might produce anger or indignation still possible? We should note that it is becoming increasingly difficult to mobilize Quebeckers against interventions or attacks by the federal government. According to a poll commissioned by the federal government, a majority of Quebeckers already believe that the federal government should have a say in a referendum question, and that more than 50 percent plus one of the votes are necessary to declare sovereignty. Furthermore, it is becoming more difficult to stir up indignation by simply recalling the 1982 repatriation of the *Constitution* without Quebec's consent, or the defeat of the Meech Lake Accord in 1990. The memory of these events has faded with the passing of time (it has been 20 years since the repatriation) and there is a weariness resulting from the many constitutional debates that resolved nothing.

But we should not assume that this weariness is a permanent and irreversible element of Quebec political life. The sovereigntists can still mobilize the Quebec population following major events that are perceived as unfavourable to Quebec's interests. It is, therefore, less the references to past events than the impact of new ones that might aid the sovereigntist movement. Similarly, reference to past events must be linked to personalities who are still playing a role in politics (for example, connecting Jean Chrétien to the repatriation of 1982 and the defeat of the Meech Lake Accord) if sovereigntists wish to have a real impact. At the present time, references to personalities like Jean Chrétien favour the Bloc Québécois on the federal scene more than the Parti Québécois on the provincial scene.

The second observation is more fundamental and deals with the nature of support for sovereignty. The sovereigntist movement begins with a base of about 35 percent of the electorate. To this, we can add 5 to 10 percent of voters who generally support the sovereigntist option. Added to this fairly stable number is the support of others, which will often vary from poll to poll in response to political events, both at the federal and provincial levels. In this manner, 54.8 percent of Quebeckers were favourable to sovereignty when it was accompanied by an offer of economic and political partnership with the rest of Canada, in the month following the 1995 referendum. Eighteen months later, in May 1997, no more than 42.9 percent expressed the same opinion. However, between November 1995 and August 1996, an average of 52.4 percent of Quebeckers supported sovereignty-partnership; on average, only 46.4 percent took the same position between September 1996 and May 1997. In January 1998, 44.4 percent of decided respondents said they would vote Yes, 43.7 percent in November, but 49.2 percent in March 1999, 44.3 percent in June and only 41.4 percent in September of the same year. According to the president of Léger and Léger, the decline was explained by the dissatisfaction with the Bouchard government at that time.[7]

What conclusions can we draw from these numbers? Support for sovereignty, or more precisely sovereignty-partnership, usually lies between 40 and 50 percent. It is only after important events such as the defeat of the Meech Lake Accord in 1990 or the near-victory in the 1995 referendum that support passes the 50 percent mark. It stays at this level for a short time and then declines. Therefore, it is difficult to consistently mobilize a majority of Quebeckers in support of the sovereignty-partnership option. In these circumstances, Quebec may not find it easy to attain sovereignty and negotiate the kind of economic and political partnership that it might like, even after a majority vote for sovereignty. Such a majority would seem too volatile and unstable to provide a solid basis for sovereignty. Moreover, at this time, a majority of Quebeckers show little enthusiasm for a referendum.

In pursuing the sovereigntist cause, Lucien Bouchard must therefore take into account some factors that point in different directions. These include the sensitivity of Quebeckers to political events although there are great difficulties in mobilizing Quebeckers against past and even present federal actions, such as the so-called clarity bill (Bill C-20); and the support for sovereignty-partnership, which occasionally exceeds the 50 percent mark but is frequently below this level.

The third observation is a crucial one: it relates to the notion of nation or people. The simple act of grouping individuals together does not create a people, just as the simple coexistence of cultural communities or groups does not. What is needed is a desire to live together based on shared values, a common understanding of the political community, and a common understanding and agreement on the principles of government laid down in a constitution.

However, the simple sharing of common values is not a sufficient condition to create a national or political identity. Even if shared values could reinforce identity, it cannot do it alone. It is also necessary to share a sense of solidarity with, and an identification to, the same political community. This solidarity and this identity arise progressively from a common history, common experiences, and, to different degrees, common values. But sharing the same values does not necessarily mean sharing the same experiences, the same memories, the same history. And sharing the same history does not always mean that we interpret the same historic events in the same way.

As was argued by Wayne Norman, shared values "do not necessarily give peoples and polities a reason to share a country." And, he adds, "... shared history is of little value in cementing a shared identity and values if there are radically different interpretations of that history" (Norman, 1995, p. 148). This is precisely the case in Canada where francophones and anglophones (and now Aboriginal people) do not necessarily celebrate the same heroes, and, above all, have often interpreted the same historic events differently .

For example, the *Charter* can certainly impart common values to the citizens of Canada, but the repatriation in 1981–82 that enshrined the *Charter* and the amending formula in the Canadian *Constitution* has been interpreted differently as an historic event. Quebeckers felt "betrayed" at the time of the repatriation, which was completed without the consent of

Quebec. Since then no Quebec government has given consent to the repatriation (even though the *Constitution* is imposed throughout Canada, including Quebec) without insisting on further constitutional modification to satisfy Quebec's aspirations.

For the past 20 or 30 years, although Canadian francophones and anglophones have been said to increasingly share the same political and social values, we have witnessed a re-emergence and not a decline of Quebec's nationalist sentiment. Stéphane Dion (1991) argued this when he referred to the de Tocqueville paradox: the more values of groups converge, as de Tocqueville suggested, the more they put the accent on the differences that exist between them. Contrary to what we may believe, cultures getting closer and nationalism rising are not necessarily a contradictory occurrence.

In this context, what is needed in the Canadian federalism is the recognition of its "national minorities," a term previously defined by Kymlicka. An egalitarian recognition allowing each national minority the same treatment cannot successfully recognize diversity; an asymmetrical federalism referring to particular arrangements to accommodate the needs and demands of national minorities can do it better than an egalitarian federalism. As McRoberts said: "Asymmetry would give the Quebec government the powers that follow from its responsibility for supporting and promoting Quebec's distinctiveness, without undermining the ability of the federal government to assume the responsibilities expected of it in the rest of the country" (McRoberts, 1997, pp. 262–63). But most Canadians refuse asymmetry in the name of equality. Moreover, they do not want to recognize national minorities in Canada and Quebeckers as a nation. This is the heart of the problem.

NOTES

1.   This section and the next are reprinted from Réjean Pelletier, "From Jacques Parizeau to Lucien Bouchard: A New Vision? Yes, But…" in *Canada: The State of the Federation 1997. Non-Constitutional Renewal,* ed. H. Lazar (Kingston: Institute of Intergovernmental Relations, 1997, 295–310). With permission of the publisher.

2.   Section 33(1) of the *Canadian Charter of Rights* reads as follows: "Parliament or the legislature of a province may expressly declare in an Act of Parliament or of the legislature, as the case may be, that the Act or a provision thereof shall operate notwithstanding a provision included in section 2 [fundamental freedoms] or section 7 to 15 [legal rights and equality rights] of this *Charter.*"

3.   Adopting a "realistic" method (rather than a proportional one) to estimate the views of the "discreet" or non-respondents, the average support for the Yes side in fifteen polls published between August 23 and October 12, 1995, was 45 percent. (Support for the Yes side saw a slight increase at the end of

September.) From the moment when the "Bouchard effect" became evident, support for sovereignty-partnership increased to 48.2 percent based on an average of the eight following polls. (The last two polls saw the Yes side at 49.5 percent and 49.8 percent.) This method of estimating the distribution of support of "discreet respondents" (those who refuse to respond) was developed by Pierre Drouilly. It allocates three-quarters of this group to the No side and one-quarter to the Yes side. See Pierre Drouilly, "Le référendum du 30 octobre 1995: une analyse des résultats" in *L'année politique au Québec 1995–1996*, ed. Robert Boily (Montréal: Fides, 1997, 199–43).

4.   It should be noted that the sovereigntist camp (like the federalist camp) is able to count on a base of stable support of about 35 percent, even 40 percent of the electorate.

5.   For a more detailed analysis of these institutions in a new Canadian framework, see Réjean Pelletier, "Institutional Arrangements of a New Canadian Partnership" (especially the section entitled "A Partnership between Equals") in *Beyond the Impasse*, ed. Roger Gibbins and Guy Laforest (Montreal: Institute for Research on Public Policy, 1998, 301–30).

6.   In other words, non-official-language immigrants who learn an official language show a much greater preference for English over French in Quebec.

7.   These results on sovereignty-partnership were published at different times by *Le Journal de Montréal* and *The Globe and Mail*. All these polls were conducted by Groupe Léger & Léger. Satisfaction with the Bouchard government has increased since that time and was over 50 percent in June 2000.

REFERENCES

Blais, A. and J. Crête. (1991). Pourquoi l'opinion publique au Canada anglais a-t-elle rejeté l'Accord du lac Meech? In R. Hudon and R. Pelletier (Eds.), *L'engagement intellectuel: Mélanges en l'honneur de Léon Dion* (pp. 385–400). Sainte-Foy: Les Presses de l'Université Laval.

Blais, A., P. Martin, and R. Nadeau. (1995). Attentes économiques et linguistiques et appui à la souveraineté du Québec: une analyse prospective et comparative. *Canadian Journal of Political Science* 28(4): 637–57.

Bouchard, Lucien. (1992). *À visage découvert*. Montreal: Boréal.

———. (1993). *Un nouveau parti pour l'étape décisive*. Montreal: Fides.

———. (1996, March 11). "Vivre ensemble, avant, pendant et après le référendum." Notes for a speech by Premier Bouchard to the anglophone community of Quebec.

Burelle, A. (1995). *Le mal canadien: Essai de diagnostic et esquisse d'une thérapie*. Montreal: Fides.

Cloutier, E., J. H. Guay, and D. Latouche. (1992). *Le virage: L'évolution de l'opinion publique depuis 1960 ou comment le Québec est devenu souverainiste*. Montreal: Québec/Amérique.

Dion, S. (1991). Le nationalisme dans la convergence culturelle: Le Québec contemporain et le paradoxe de Tocqueville. In R. Hudon and R. Pelletier (Eds.), *L'engagement intellectuel: Mélanges en l'honneur de Léon Dion* (pp. 291–311). Sainte-Foy: Les Presses de l'Université Laval.

Guérin, D. and R. Pelletier. (2000). A path analysis of the determinants of sovereignty support in Quebec. Paper submitted for publication.

Harrison, B. R. and L. Marmen. (1994). *Les langues au Canada.* Scarborough: Prentice Hall Canada. Published jointly with Statistics Canada.

Herb, G. H. and D. H. Kaplan. (1999). *Nested identities: Nationalism, territory and scale.* Lanham: Rowman & Littlefield Publishers.

Howe, P. (1998). Rationality and sovereignty support in Quebec. *Canadian Journal of Political Science* 31(1): 31–59.

Kymlicka, W. (1998). *Finding our way: Rethinking ethnocultural relations in Canada.* Toronto: Oxford University Press.

Lapierre, J. W. (1988). *Le pouvoir politique et les langues.* Paris: Presses Universitaires de France.

Lenihan, D. G., G. Robertson, and R. Tassé. (1994). *Canada: Reclaiming the middle ground.* Montreal: The Institute for Research on Public Policy.

Marmen, L. and J. P. Corbeil. (1999). *New Canadian perspectives: Languages in Canada 1996 Census.* Ottawa: Canadian Heritage and Statistics Canada.

McRoberts, K. (1997). *Misconceiving Canada: The struggle for national unity.* Toronto: Oxford University Press.

———. (1999). *Un pays à refaire: L'échec des politiques constitutionnelles canadiennes.* Montreal: Boréal.

Monière, D. and J. H. Guay. (1996). *La bataille du Québec: Troisième épisode—30 jours qui ébranlèrent le Canada.* Montreal: Fides.

Nadeau, R. and C. Fleury. (1995). Gains linguistiques anticipés et appui à la souveraineté du Québec. *Canadian Journal of Political Science* 28(1): 35–50.

Norman, W. (1995). The ideology of shared values: A myopic vision of unity in the multi-nation state. In J.H. Carens (Ed.), *Is Quebec nationalism just? Perspectives from anglophone Canada* (pp. 137–59). Montreal and Kingston: McGill-Queen's University Press.

Parizeau, J. (1997). *Pour un Québec souverain.* Montreal: VLB éditeur.

Pelletier, R. (1997). From Jacques Parizeau to Lucien Bouchard: A new vision? Yes, but … In H. Lazar (Ed.), *Canada: The state of the federation 1997: Non-Constitutional Renewal* (pp. 295–310). Kingston: Institute of Intergovernmental Relations.

———. (1998). Institutional arrangements of a new Canadian partnership. In R. Gibbins and G. Laforest (Eds.) *Beyond the impasse, toward reconciliation* (pp. 301–30). Montreal: Institute for Research on Public Policy.

FURTHER READING

Burelle, A. (1995). *Le mal canadien: Essai de diagnostic et esquisse d'une thérapie.* Montreal: Fides.

Carens, J.H. (Ed). (1995). *Is Quebec nationalism just? Perspectives from anglophone Canada.* Montreal and Kingston: McGill-Queen's University Press.

Gibbins, R. and G. Laforest, (Eds). (1998). *Beyond the impasse, toward reconciliation.* Montreal: The Institute for Research on Public Policy.

Kymlicka, W. (1998). *Finding our way: Rethinking ethnocultural relations in Canada.* Toronto: Oxford University Press.

McRoberts, K. (1997). *Misconceiving Canada: The struggle for national unity.* Toronto: Oxford University Press.

Webber, J. (1994). *Reimagining Canada: Language, Culture, Community, and the Canadian Constitution.* Montreal and Kingston: McGill-Queen's University Press.

Bill 1: An Act Respecting the Future of Québec

Québec National Assembly

PREAMBLE: DECLARATION OF SOVEREIGNTY

The time has come to reap the fields of history. The time has come at last to harvest what has been sown for us by four hundred years of men and women and courage, rooted in the soil and now returned to it.

The time has come for us, tomorrow's ancestors, to make ready for our descendants harvests that are worthy of the labours of the past.

May our toil be worthy of them, may they gather us together at last.

At the dawn of the 17th century, the pioneers of what would become a nation and then a people rooted themselves in the soil of Québec. Having come from a great civilization, they were enriched by that of the First Nations, they forged new alliances, and maintained the heritage of France.

The conquest of 1760 did not break the determination of their descendants to remain faithful to a destiny unique in North America. Already in 1774, through the *Québec Act,* the conqueror recognized the distinct nature of their institutions. Neither attempts at assimilation nor the *Act of Union* of 1840 could break their endurance.

The English community that grew up at their side, the immigrants who have joined them, all have contributed to forming this people which became in 1867 one of the two founders of the Canadian federation.

We, the men and women of this place,

Because we inhabit the territories delimited by our ancestors, from Abitibi to the Iles-de-la-Madeleine, from Ungava to the American border, because for four hundred years we have cleared, ploughed, paced, surveyed, dug, fished, built, started anew, discussed, protected, and loved this land that is cut across and watered by the St. Lawrence River;

Because the heart of this land beats in French and because that heartbeat is as meaningful as the seasons that hold sway over it, as the winds that bend it, as the men and women who shape it;

Because we have created here a way of being, of believing, of working that is unique;

Because as long ago as 1791 we established here one of the first parliamentary democracies in the world, one we have never ceased to improve;

Because the legacy of the struggles and courage of the past compels us irrevocably to take charge of our own destiny;

Because it is this land alone that represents our pride and the source of our strength, our sole opportunity to express ourselves in the entirety of our individual natures and of our collective heart;

Because this land will be all those men and women who inhabit it, who defend it and define it, and because we are all those people;

We, the people of Québec, declare that we are free to choose our future.

We know the winter in our souls. We know its blustery days, its solitude, its false eternity and its apparent deaths. We know what it is to be bitten by the winter cold.

We entered the federation on the faith of a promise of equality in a shared undertaking and of respect for our authority in certain matters that to us are vital.

But what was to follow did not live up to those early hopes. The Canadian State contravened the federative pact, by invading in a thousand ways areas in which we are autonomous, and by serving notice that our secular belief in the equality of the partners was an illusion.

We were hoodwinked in 1982 when the governments of Canada and the English-speaking provinces made changes to the Constitution, in depth and to our detriment, in defiance of the categorical opposition of our National Assembly.

Twice since then attempts were made to right that wrong. The failure of the Meech Lake Accord in 1990 confirmed a refusal to recognize even our distinct character. And in 1992 the rejection of the Charlottetown Accord by both Canadians and Quebecers confirmed the conclusion that no redress was possible.

Because we have persisted despite the haggling of which we have been the object;

Because Canada, far from taking pride in and proclaiming to the world the alliance between its two founding peoples, has instead consistently trivialized it and decreed the spurious principle of equality between the provinces;

Because starting with the Quiet Revolution we reached a decision never again to restrict ourselves to mere survival but from this time on to build upon our difference;

Because we have the deep-seated conviction that continuing within Canada would be tantamount to condemning ourselves to languish and to debasing our very identity;

Because the respect we owe ourselves must guide our deeds;

We, the people of Québec, declare it is our will to be in full possession of all the powers of a State: to vote all our laws, to levy all our taxes,
to sign all our treaties and to exercise the highest power of all, con-
ceiving, and controlling, by ourselves, our fundamental law.

*For the men and women of this country who are the warp and weft of it
and its erosion, for those of tomorrow whose growth we are now wit-
nessing, to be comes before to have. And this principle lies at the very
heart of our endeavour.*

Our language celebrates our love, our beliefs and our dreams for this
land and for this country. In order that the profound sense of belonging
to a distinct people be now and for all time the very bastion of our identity, we proclaim our will to live in a French-language society.

Our culture relates our identity, it writes of us, it sings us to the
world. And through varied and new contributions, our culture takes on
fresh colour and amplitude. It is essential that we welcome them in such
a way that never will these differences be seen as threats or as reasons for
intolerance.

Together we shall celebrate the joys, together we shall suffer the sorrows that life will set upon our road. Above all we shall assume not only
our successes but our failures too, for in abundance as in adversity the
choices we make will have been our own.

We know what determination has gone into achieving the successes
of this land. Those men and women who have forged the dynamism of
Québec are eager to pass down their efforts to the determined men and
women of tomorrow. Our capacity for mutual support and our appetite
for new undertakings are among our greatest strengths. We commit ourselves to recognize and encourage the urge to put our hearts into our
work that makes us builders.

Along with other countries of like size, we share the virtue of
adapting quickly and well to the shifting challenges of work and trade.
Our capacity for consensus and our spirit of invention will enable us to
take a good and rightful place at the table of nations.

We intend to uphold the imaginative powers and the abilities of local
and regional communities in their activities of economic, social and cultural development.

As guardians of the land, the air, the water, we shall act in such a way
as to be respectful of the world to come.

We, the men and women of this new country, acknowledge our
moral duties of respect, of tolerance, of solidarity towards one another.

Averse to authoritarianism and violence, honouring the will of the
people, we commit ourselves to guarantee democracy and the rule of law.

Respect for the dignity of women, men, and children and the recognition of their rights and freedoms constitute the very foundation of our
society. We commit ourselves to guarantee the civil and political rights of

individuals, notably the right to justice, the right to equality, and the right to freedom.

To battle against misery and poverty; to support the young and the elderly, are essential features of the society we would build. The destitute among us can count upon our compassion and our sense of responsibility. With the equitable sharing of wealth as our objective, we commit ourselves to promote full employment and to guarantee social and economic rights, notably the right to education and the right to health care and other social services.

Our shared future is in the hands of all those for whom Québec is a homeland. Because we take to heart the need to reinforce established alliances and friendships, we shall safeguard the rights of the First Nations and we intend to define with them a new alliance. Likewise, the English-speaking community historically established in Québec enjoys rights that will be maintained.

Independent and hence fully present in the world, we intend to work for cooperation, humanitarian action, tolerance and peace. We shall subscribe to the Universal Declaration of Human Rights and to other international instruments for the protection of rights.

While never repudiating our values, we shall devote ourselves to forging, through treaties and agreements, mutually beneficial links with the peoples of the earth. In particular, we wish to formulate along with the people of Canada, our historic partner, new relations that will allow us to maintain our economic ties and to redefine our political exchanges. And we shall marshal a particular effort to strengthen our ties with the peoples of the United States and France and with those of other countries both in the Americas and in the Francophonie.

To accomplish this design, to maintain the fervour that fills us and impels us, for the time has now come to set in motion this country's vast endeavour;

We, the people of Québec, through our National Assembly, proclaim:

Québec is a sovereign country.

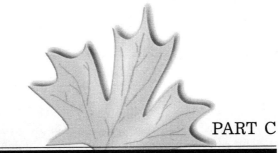

PART C

CHANGING CANADA

Benvenuto

Mary di Michele

The same chickens are scratching in the yard,
the same light is making tracks across the hills,
the same wind is beating its head against the stucco
walls of the houses in the village,
as evening settles into itself,
the light pulling up its seat in the valley
and tucking its legs under it.

Twenty years and my Canadian feet formed of prairie wheat
can still find their own way, can run ahead
while my thoughts seem to resist and find
the pomegranate, the fig and the olive
trees of my grandmother's orchard, in the back of a house
tucked into the pocket of a hill, leaning into it
with the declining light. I stop under a pomegranate tree,
a favourite retreat, under the ripening fruit,
old dreams are pricking at the back of my mind.
I tear one open to eat and it recognizes me
with *benvenuto* in all its myriad, ruby eyes.

The People's Charter?

Janice Dickin

INTRODUCTION

The Canadian *Charter of Rights and Freedoms* was born into dramatic circumstances. Introduced during the 18-month struggle to "patriate" Canada's *Constitution,* the *Charter* has since its passage on April 17, 1982, become an accepted part of our lives. Indeed, most of the people who read this chapter will have lived their entire lives under its umbrella. While, in terms of content, the *Charter* did little more than codify freedoms most Canadians already took for granted, procedurally it gave those freedoms a legal status only partially explored at the time of its passage. The last two decades of the 20th century saw exploration of that status displace almost all other types of legal questions taken under consideration by the Supreme Court of Canada. The Supreme Court has become a *Charter* court, with a crushing workload.

Ironically, as the intellectual challenge of *Charter* interpretation has increased, public sense of ownership of the so-called "People's Charter" has led to expressions of impatience with and even downright contempt for some of the Court's decisions. Indeed, popular outrage over the infamous *Sharpe* child pornography case in 1999–2000 (to which I will return) led Chief Justice Beverly MacLachlin to release an unusual public statement that the Court will not in any way be swayed by public emotion, that it will as always base its deliberations on the law of the land.[1] While Canadians have taken the *Charter* to heart, we have not generally undertaken the taxing job of educating ourselves as to just what the legal system can and cannot do for us. Many are surprised to learn that justice has to do with process, not outcome. In order to understand our *Charter* rights, we must consider the onerous process our courts must undertake of juggling the rights of the individual against the good of the community.

HISTORICAL BACKGROUND

The home page for Constitutional Chat Links and Discussion Groups maintains that "[t]here are those who think that the central unifying trait of all Canadians is our obsession over the *Constitution*. As such, you can always strike up an interesting conversation on the topic."[2]

While this may be going a little too far for most of us in ordinary circumstances, certainly Canadians were plugged into their various media outlets during the patriation process from May 1980 to November 1981.[3] Emotions ran high. When Pierre Trudeau's Liberal government moved to patriate the *Constitution* unilaterally in October 1980, fist-shaking Tories stormed the Speaker's chair, protesting closure of debate. The provincial premiers who formed a united front were called "the Gang of Eight," in imitation of the Gang of Four that headed China's bloody Cultural Revolution of 1968. Women's and Aboriginal groups lobbied vociferously; almost 1000 individuals and nearly 300 groups petitioned to be heard by a special joint parliamentary committee; and Quebec Premier René Lévesque, whose February 1980 referendum on what type of relationship Quebec should have with "Canada" kicked off the process in the first place, claimed that he had been "screwed" by Trudeau.[4]

To give the chat link its due, Canadian constitutional discussion *has* sometimes resembled a national sport. Between 1927 and 1980, ten separate rounds of negotiation made it clear that a consensus among Canadian governments was not going to be easy to get. Canada was in an anomalous position as a constituted state. It did not in fact have control over reform of its own *Constitution*. The *British North America Act* of 1867 was British legislation, not Canadian. This would be rubbed in when the British Parliament delayed patriation by extended debate even after a federal–provincial deal finally was reached. In doing this, the British Parliament made plain a lack of autonomy that had rankled for years. The term "patriation" is a distinctly Canadian one. It was possibly coined by Prime Minister Lester B. Pearson in January 1966 when he vowed to "do everything we can to have the constitution of Canada repatriated, or patriated." Pearson's struggle for the right word had to do with the fact that, while the idea of repatriation (returning something to its native land) is a concept common to all English-speaking peoples, the idea of patriation is not. "Patriation" is defined in the *Oxford English Dictionary* directly in line with the Canadian process, which culminated in the proclamation of the new *Constitution* in April 1982: "to bring (legislation) under the constitutional authority of an autonomous country, used with reference to laws passed on behalf of that country by its former mother-country."[5]

Two things were key to patriation of the *Constitution*. One was an amending formula that could find support from provincial leaders. The other was the *Charter of Rights and Freedoms*, which caught the imagination of the general populace. Popular support, the meat of politicians, kept premiers going when they might have turned back. Trudeau had his own reasons for wanting the *Charter*. One was his long-term interest in civil liberties. Another was his legal training at Harvard where he learned to admire the American *Constitution*. But yet another was his passion for federalism. With a *Charter of Rights* in place, any individual could appeal the laws of any government up to the Supreme Court of Canada. That court has a history of being pro-federal. With the *Charter* in hand, it could "declare and enforce common values and practices in an otherwise diverse federation."[6] Separatist Lévesque had good reason to feel screwed. While the Charter did, in the end, make provisions whereby individual provinces could opt out of certain sections, this power was limited. Section 33 limits provincial rights to legislate out of the *Charter* by insisting on reenactment every five years. In effect, this means that any government striking down a Fundamental Freedom, Legal Right, or Equality Right must meet the electorate at least once between enactment and any proposed reenactment. The *Charter* and the *Constitution* it is part of—both federal legislation, both in the hands of a federalist court—had the ability to tie the country together in ways not possible before.

THE SUPREME LAW OF CANADA

It is the *Charter*'s location within the *Constitution Act* itself—its so-called entrenchment—that makes it so very powerful. Canada had in fact had a similar document since 1960, the Canadian *Bill of Rights*. The Supreme Court, after upholding the *Bill of Rights* in the case of *R v Drybones*,[7] struck it down in *AG (Can) v Lavell*.[8] Both were split decisions, involved Aboriginal people, and considered separate sections of the *Indian Act*. While Joseph Drybones was found to be discriminated against on the basis of race for being charged with being drunk off a reserve, Jeannette Lavell lost her case, charging discrimination on the grounds of gender for having had her Indian status revoked upon marriage to a white man. The point is not, at this long remove, whether the cases were rightly or wrongly decided. The point is that the Supreme Court wavered when it came to upholding the guarantees of the *Bill of Rights*. In order for such an instrument to have supremacy over all other laws, it had to be part of the supreme legal instrument of the land, the constitution. Section 52 of the *Constitution Act, 1982* declares it to be "the supreme law of Canada, and any law that is inconsistent with the provisions of the *Constitution* is, to the extent of the inconsistency, of no force or effect." Section 32 of that same act, located within the *Charter* itself, declares that the Charter applies to the federal and all the provincial governments. The only out is Section 33 mentioned above.

Early commentary on the *Charter* pondered just what its effects would be. Courts had, after all, interpreted statutes for years. In that regard, courts have always had power to limit the effect of legislation. One of my early lessons in this was watching a judge get around a prohibition against fences above a certain height by declaring the structure in question a sound barrier. An early and influential discussion of just how the Supreme Court might interpret the *Charter* was written by Madam Justice Bertha Wilson in 1986.[9] The first woman to be appointed to the Court, in 1982, Wilson grew up with the *Charter*. She made it clear that this was a statute that altered the role of the court system. Under it, judges had been given a new job, that of balancing the fundamental rights of citizens with the right and obligation of governments to govern. Legal scholars had for some time, she pointed out, argued that modern courts needed judges who were more contextually anchored in the society and less reliant on legalistic arguments. She also pointed out that there was no time to wait for such people to be trained. The Court was simply going to have to make things up as it went along. Among other things, it would have to allow an expanded evidentiary role to social science research, much in the manner that the American courts had been doing since black civil rights cases started in the 1950s. We have come to accept this reality to the point where it seems impossible that we could ever straighten out such questions as Aboriginal land claims and women's issues without reliance on the testimony of anthropologists, psychologists, and other social scientists.

Wilson openly admitted the reality of concerns stated by some scholars that, more than ever, the Courts would now be making law, not just interpreting it. While these concerns are still regularly expressed in public forums, they have little place in the courtroom. As one legal scholar has pointed out, "[d]ebates about whether judges interpret law or make law have become irrelevant; the *Charter* requires judges to set aside legislation that contravenes a protected right."[10] The only grounds on which judges can set aside the right rather than the legislation is under Section 1 of the *Charter*, the only section that puts the community before the individual. This is not something the Court undertakes to do lightly. It formulated a complex process for striking down *Charter* rights in 1986 in the case of *R v Oakes*, to which I will return after a discussion of some of the provisions of the *Charter* itself.

INTERPRETATION OF THE CHARTER

One of the most interesting things about a new piece of legislation is waiting to see which sections will have the more active life. Some sections will never get much of a hearing in court, usually because they refer to practice so entrenched that the issue never arises. An example of this for the *Charter* is Section 5 mandating that Parliament and all legislatures must sit at least once every 12 months. Since our law-making bodies, unlike those in some other countries, have never shown any serious inclination to waver from such practice, it does not seem to address a matter of pressing concern. But imagine a war or a revolution or an environmental collapse. What might happen in such a case? Section 5 is there to help us straighten matters out and to hold us to account for any change of our political tradition.

There can even be sections that seem utterly redundant. Section 28 is an example. Why does the *Charter* state there that "Notwithstanding anything in this *Charter*, the rights and freedoms referred to in it are guaranteed equally to male and female persons?" Section 15 includes "sex" under equality rights, and there is nothing else in the *Charter* that would seem to undermine this. The answer lies outside the statute itself, in a long line of cases that defined away women's rights, including the so-called Persons Case itself.[11] Section 28 is in the *Charter* due to direct political agitation by the feminist movement at the time. Even with its inclusion, feminists have voiced concerns about the ability of the *Charter* to protect women's rights.[12]

Other sections paint a picture not clear to the naked eye. Section 27 plays this role in the *Charter*. It mandates that "this Charter shall be interpreted in a manner consistent with the preservation and enhancement of the multicultural heritage of Canadians." This section offers possibility for considerable public outcry. What multicultural heritage? At most, multiculturalism has been part of our public discourse since only the 1960s, significantly before we started to become a visibly multiracial population. For most of its history, Canada has been Anglo-centric and still is to a large extent. Multiculturalism seemed to come out of nowhere in the midst of the deliberations of the Royal Commission on Bilingualism and Biculturalism (1963–71). Interpretation of rights and freedoms in light of "multicultural heritage" need not be limited to whether Sikhs can wear turbans in the Mounted Police but might extend, for example, to questions such as whether a case can be made for female circumcision, for denial of education to girls, or for insistence that boys endure certain rites of passage. I, one lawyer among many, wait patiently for just the right fact situation to arise to really put Section 27 to the test. It may never happen or it might happen next Tuesday.

CHARTER PROVISIONS

The most powerful sections of the *Charter* are Sections 2 (Fundamental Freedoms), 15 (Equality Rights), and 7 (under Legal Rights). Section 2 states:

Everyone has the following fundamental freedoms:
(a) freedom of conscience and religion;
(b) freedom of thought, belief, opinion and expression, including freedom of the press and other media of communication;

(c) freedom of peaceful assembly; and

(d) freedom of association.

These freedoms (now "rights" due to their enshrinement in the *Charter*) are our old civil liberties, built over centuries of legal history extending back to the *Magna Carta* of 1215. The difference between our new "rights" and our old "liberties" is that there is now a strict process in place for anyone wishing to curtail them. They can be legislated away only by use of Section 33 or interpreted away under Section 1. The power of this new regime was made plain by *RJR-MacDonald Inc. v AG (Can)*.[13] In that case, involving tobacco advertising, the Supreme Court decided not to follow American judicial consideration of that country's similar guarantee of "freedom of speech." The Court extended freedom of expression to business organizations, not just individuals, thereby bringing "commercial speech" under our *Charter*. It is important to keep in mind that freedoms and rights belong not only to nice people and good causes. In two notorious cases to do with Holocaust denial, the defendants argued (albeit, unsuccessfully) Section 2 and made some reference to Section 15 as well.[14] It is their right to do so.

Subsection 15(1) reads:

> Every individual is equal before and under the law and has the right to equal protection and equal benefit of the law without discrimination and, in particular, without discrimination based on race, national or ethnic origin, colour, religion, sex, age or mental or physical disability.

This subsection has been heavily litigated, and its cases make some of the most riveting reading of Supreme Court decisions. The fact situations seeking shelter under its umbrella extend from a terminally ill patient seeking assistance in committing suicide[15] to a gay couple seeking to redefine the term "spouse"[16] to a lawyer wanting to deduct child-care expenses as a business expense.[17] We can expect further heavy litigation under this section, since as a society we make discriminatory decisions all the time. Obvious examples of age discrimination are limiting access to certain pensions to those over 60 and denying certain rights to those under 18. Subsection 15(2) in fact makes direct provision for systematic discrimination. It pertains to what we have come to call affirmative action programs aimed at improving the lot of disadvantaged individuals and groups. The term "disadvantaged" is of course open to interpretation— by the Supreme Court of Canada, in the last resort.

Section 7 is one of the Legal Rights protections of the *Charter*. It states:

> Everyone has the right to life, liberty and security of the person and the right not to be deprived thereof except in accordance with the principles of fundamental justice.

Contrast "security of the person" with the American right to the pursuit of happiness, guaranteed in that country's *Constitution*. The American term is not only based on a different philosophy but also would seem open to wider interpretation than ours. Security of the person, however, has been given wider interpretation by our courts than one might be led to expect from what follows it in the rest of the Legal Rights heading. The remaining sections under Legal Rights focus on rights of individuals who come into conflict with the police: rights regarding search or seizure, imprisonment, arrest, proceedings in criminal and penal matters, cruel and unusual punishment, interpreters, etc. However, one of the earliest and most important readings of Section 7 focused not on the security of a person charged but on the balance between the security of the person of a fetus and of the mother seeking to abort it.[18] An immensely important case, *Morgentaler* played out against a backdrop of deeply divided social sensibilities.

Democratic Rights (Sections 3–5) pertain to voting rights and to the duty of legislative assemblies to hold regular sittings. Section 6 pertains to Mobility Rights, guaranteeing to Canadians the right to move to and earn their living in any part of the country. Several sections make guarantees regarding our two official languages, and it is of note that New Brunswick is mentioned in the document by name. Every student of Canada knows the contentious role language plays in this country. This drama is played out in more arenas than our *Charter*, but never since 1982 has the debate been possible without reference to the *Charter*.[19]

All rights, however, are subject to Section 1:

> The *Canadian Charter of Rights and Freedoms* guarantees the rights and freedoms set out in it subject only to such reasonable limits prescribed by law as can be demonstrably justified in a free and democratic society.

This section starts out with a blanket guarantee followed by a three-part limitation. Any limit on the rights and freedoms of Canadians must be reasonable, must be prescribed by law, and that law must not only be justified but demonstrably so. Note also that, rather than simply stating that this must be demonstrated within Canadian society, it stipulates a free and democratic society. This guards against the possibility that the *Charter* might be made a dead letter should Canadian society take a dramatically unfree and undemocratic shift. As phrased, the *Charter* can survive such political accident.

The Supreme Court fleshed out Section 1 in 1986 in *R v Oakes*,[20] a case in which a section of the *Narcotics Act* was found to be in conflict with the *Charter* guarantee of presumption of innocence until proven guilty. Conflict with the *Charter* alone would not strike down the relevant section (clearly prescribed by law, to wit, the *Narcotics Act*) so long as it could be shown to be a reasonable limit, demonstrably justified. In finding that it was not, the Supreme Court established the *Oakes* or proportionality test. This test requires that the objective of the conflicting legislation "must be of sufficient importance to warrant overriding a constitutionally protected right" *and* that "the means chosen are reasonable and demonstrably justified." To establish this, one must demonstrate three components:

> First, the measures adopted must be carefully designed to achieve the objective in question ... Second, the means ... should impair as little as possible the right or freedom in question ... Third, there must be proportionality between the effects of the measures and the objective which has been identified as of sufficient importance.[21]

The *Oakes* test has been used by the courts very successfully ever since, sometimes in upholding the legislation under scrutiny, sometimes in striking it down.

SCOPE OF THE CHARTER

I mentioned at the beginning of this chapter that legislation can take on a life of its own and that the *Charter* is no exception. In 1995, the Supreme Court handed down a decision that extended the effect of the *Charter* beyond its designated target. While Section 32 makes it clear that the *Charter* is to apply to Canada's various legislative assemblies, *Hill v Church of Scientology of Toronto*[22] extended the reach of the *Charter* to the common law. Common law is made up entirely of case law (sometimes called judge-made law because it is based solely on "precedent" as expressed in judges' decisions), not by any statutory instrument of any government whatsoever. In *Hill v Church of Scientology*, the case law under examination pertained to defamation. Clearly, the law of defamation forms a control over freedom of expression as guaranteed by Section 2 of the *Charter*. The Court decided that the underlying values of the *Charter* had to be taken into account in arriving at a balance between "reputation" (protected by the common law of defamation) and freedom of expression (protected by the *Charter*). In effect, this means that the same proportionality test used to balance "public law" against *Charter* values would be used to balance "private law." In this case, the Court found no conflict between the common law of defamation as it stands and the *Charter*. However, it also made it clear that it could do so if it felt justified. This is nothing new. Since judges are clearly in charge of judge-made law, they have always been free to alter it, keeping always of course within the various checks and balances that they are bound to respect. What is extra in this case is the explicit inclusion of the *Charter* and *Charter* "values" in this process. For all intents and purposes, the *Charter* has escaped its bounds and infiltrated every aspect of our legal system with this case. This area awaits further exploration. Will provinces now have to legislate some aspects of common law in order to exempt them from *Charter* scrutiny? Will Section 33 allow them to do so?

In one way, Section 33 can be read as the section of the *Charter* that grudgingly allows regionalism. It is ironic that we have a section that recognizes our "multicultural heritage," a trend of very short standing, and none that recognizes our "regional heritage," a trend of ancient lineage in this country. This difference speaks volumes about the federal thrust of the document. The irony is not lost on the provinces. It was no surprise to anyone when Quebec used Section 33 to "opt out" of Sections 2 and 15 of the *Charter* in its own *Charter of the French Language*.[23] It may seem surprising that the section is not used more often than it is, given the warmth with which the public has taken the "notwithstanding" clause to its bosom. In my own province of Alberta, it has been called for by "family values" groups on a number of occasions. One example was the *Charter* case of *Vriend v Alberta*,[24] which disallowed discrimination on the basis of sexual orientation. The courts accomplished this simply by reading Alberta human rights legislation to include sexual orientation in its definition of sex. In order to change this situation, a bill would have to be voted through the legislature stating directly that certain rights were denied to gays notwithstanding the protections of the *Charter*.

Although any backbencher could initiate such a bill, in practice it would need the support of the party in power in order to pass. Whereas a Quebec government can count on strong support for entrenchment of the French language, an Alberta one could never muster anywhere near the same enthusiasm for anti-gay discrimination. It would take a truly "regional" issue specific to Alberta (perhaps oil) to garner sufficient support. Alarm expressed by some civil liberties lawyers over the power of the notwithstanding clause[25] has so far remained largely unjustified. This is not to say that special interest groups do not sometimes manage to find a niche in the provincial political agenda. An example of this is Alberta's challenge of federal gun-control legislation, recently decided in *Reference re Firearms Act (Can.)*.[26]

TRADITIONAL CONSTITUTIONAL LAW: REFERENCE RE FIREARMS ACT

Federal–provincial legal struggles over power-sharing started long before 1982, and Alberta governments have been anything but backward in testing federal legislative jurisdiction. A notorious example is the *Reference re Alberta Statutes* case,[27] in which the federal government successfully challenged Alberta legislation involving, among other issues, freedom of the press. In *Reference re Firearms Act*, the tables turned, and it was the Attorney General for Alberta challenging the Attorney General for Canada. The issue was whether the federal government has the right to pass legislation that requires gunowners across Canada to register their weapons and to comply with other ancillary requirements, as it did in its *Firearms Act*.[28] What are called "heads of power" were allotted to one or other level of government by Section 97 of the *Constitution Act, 1867* and reaffirmed in 1982. Under the federal list falls criminal law; under the provincial list falls property and civil rights. In an (unusual, these days) unanimous decision, all nine members of the Supreme Court, in a fairly short decision, sided with the argument of the Attorney General of Canada that control of guns had to do with control of crime, not to do with control of property.

The point I want to make here is that this issue, one that has been publicly contested by organizations such as the Law-Abiding Unregistered Firearms Association[29] and citizens such as Retired Major-General Lewis Mackenzie, internationally acclaimed for his peace-keeping role in Sarajevo,[30] has virtually nothing to do with the *Charter*. The courts have had weapons in their arsenal for years with which to settle constitutional issues of this type. Reading the case is like going back to pre-*Charter* days. All the old constitutional phrases are there: "pith and substance," "intra vires," ultra vires," "valid exercise of jurisdiction," and "colorable intrusion." Basically, the Court decided that the "impugned" (questioned) legislation in pith and substance had as its objective public safety through control of access to firearms, that it was intra vires (within the powers of) Parliament, that it constituted a valid exercise of federal legislative power, and was not a colorable intrusion on provincial legislative power. There is one brief mention of the *Charter*, of Section 1. The work of David M. Beatty[31] was cited by Alberta in arguing that considerations of rationality and proportionality should be imported into discussions of legislative competence. Applying this test, Alberta argued, would uphold its view that the gun-control legislation "trenches" on provincial powers. In other words, Alberta sought to extend *Charter* methods of interpretation to non-*Charter* public cases in the same manner that *Hill v. Church of Scientology* extended *Charter* values to private law. The Court in *Reference re Firearms Act* decided that it did not need to consider this matter, since "it is beyond debate that an appropriate balance must be maintained between the federal and provincial heads of power."[32] A statement such as this in a decision is obiter dicta, "other things said." While this does not set precedent, it can be argued in later cases. The Supreme Court has not ruled on whether rules of *Charter* interpretation will be allowed to entrench on traditional areas of constitutional analysis but, with *Reference re Firearms Act*, it has started thinking about it.

With this case, the Court has upheld a piece of federal legislation over provincial objections, but that need not be the end of the matter. The right of individuals to press a case using *Charter* arguments has not been ruled out by this decision. Whether gun-control legislation is federal or provincial makes no difference when it comes to a *Charter* challenge. The problem will be in finding a legal hook on which to hang any challenge. In 1982, there was pressure by special interest groups to enshrine the right to property in the *Charter*. Unlike women's and Aboriginal groups, these groups did not succeed in achieving an amendment. The obvious issue that comes to mind when thinking of a right to property is protection of one's "real" (i.e., to do with land) property from expropriation by the state. Given the nature of statutes to take on lives of their own, however, arguments could be made to extend such rights to "chattels," in this example, guns. Had we such a head of protection under the *Charter*, there would be reason to expect arguments that any control of weaponry is unconstitutional.

Failing this, the most obvious *Charter* possibilities are Section 8, which states that "Everyone has the right to be secure against unreasonable search or seizure" or Section 7's guarantee of "security of the person." While the latter may seem to fly in the face of logic, some gun-lobby groups have argued that we would indeed be more secure if legislation were passed stipulating that all property owners have guns! This is certainly a different perspective on security than most of us hold, but that is what courts are for—to sort out perspectives. While semantically possible, challenge under either section is a long shot. And, sans the *Charter*, there is no opting out. In other words, should a gun lobbyist take such a case forward and lose it, there is no use in pressuring a provincial government to opt out. Section 33 pertains only to the *Charter*. There is no provision for opting out of the *Firearms Act*. Valid federal legislation, as it has just been held to be, the Act can be changed only by pressure on the federal government. Unlike gun lobbyists in the United States, Canadians have no constitutionally protected "right to bear arms."

OPTING OUT: A POSSIBILITY IN THE SHARPE CASE?

Opting out is available not only to the provincial governments but also to the federal government. As mentioned above, the *Sharpe* case[33] was greeted by considerable public outrage when the Supreme Court heard it on January 18, 2000. The earlier British Columbia Court of Appeal decision had sparked such public expressions of emotion as a postcard campaign to MPs organized by the Canada Family Action Coalition.[34] Should the Supreme Court uphold the B.C. court decisions striking down the offence of possession of child pornography, the federal government will be in the same situation it was when the Supreme Court declared the abortion section invalid in *Morgentaler* in 1988. Since the *Criminal Code* is a federal statute, it is Parliament that would have to opt out under Section 33. It may instead have the option of rewriting the section in such a way that it would not conflict with the *Charter*. If the Supreme Court thinks this can be done, it will provide direction on how it might be accomplished. And, indeed, Parliament need do nothing at all if it just wants to let the matter sit there. After *Morgentaler*, no immediate move was made to take the abortion offence off the books. However, although still written into the Code, the law was of no force and effect. No court in the land would convict under it given the knowledge that the Supreme Court would surely grant any appeal and probably chastise the lower court to boot. The political advantage of such a move on the part of the ruling federal party is that to repeal or even tone down the offending section could be portrayed as "softening" on the issue of child pornography. Just letting the possession prohibition lie there makes a moral point, if not a legal one.

POPULAR USE OF THE CHARTER

Inaction also of course makes a political point, and it is clear that the *Charter* has even more popular appeal now than it did when the idea was introduced two decades ago. We are used to it being part of our everyday discourse. Within a four-day period in mid-1999, my local newspaper featured stories in which an oilpatch vandal, a panhandler, and curfew-challengers all called on the *Charter* to strike down the offending laws in question.[35] But just raising the *Charter* like a cross before a vampire does not make your problem vanish. The *Charter* provides a direct conduit to the Supreme Court of Canada, but going to court, any court, is expensive. The oilpatch vandal in question was already on trial, facing prison, and seeking to use Charter freedoms to defend his actions. Curfew-challengers were contemplating whether it was worth it to stay out after midnight, given the possibility of a fine. Only the panhandler directly contemplated a constitutional challenge to the city of Ottawa's anti-begging bylaws. In doing so, he would be joining two similar initiatives from Winnipeg and Vancouver. Which begs the question of how beggars can afford lawyers.

In the beginning, individuals seeking to challenge laws under Canada's new *Charter* could take advantage of a publicly funded Court Challenges Program. This was cancelled in 1991 by the Conservative government of Prime Minister Brian Mulroney.[36] Inability of all but the well-heeled to initiate *Charter* challenges arguably makes ludicrous the guarantee of "a free and democratic society." Nonprofit organizations have stepped into the breach. The best-known is LEAF (Legal Education and Action Fund), which funds challenges pertaining to women's issues.[37] Two other nonprofits are the Court Challenges Program[38] of Canada and the *Charter* Committee on Poverty Issues.[39] All allow issues important to the individual involved—but also to Canada as a society—to feed into the system. All that these organizations need is the right fact situation. Various public interest groups also piggyback as "intervenors" onto cases already in court, taking the opportunity to state their case in regard to their own particular issue. The *Sharpe* decision of the British Columbia Court of Appeal, for instance, lists as intervenors the B.C. Civil Liberties Association, the Canadian Police Association, the Canadian

Resource Centre for Victims of Crime, CAVEAT, Beyond Borders, ECPAT International, the Evangelical Fellowship of Canada, and the Family (Canada) Foundation. *Reference re Firearms Act* had 17 intervenors, representing governments, Aboriginal groups, firearms groups, representatives of women and children, and the Canadian Association of Chiefs of Police. All are granted permission to state their position to the court, and the court is allowed to pay as much attention to their points of view as to those of the original parties involved. LEAF has been particularly successful in gaining the ear of the Supreme Court in recent years.[40]

It is crucial to our legal system that cases continue to be brought before the courts. Trying issues raised by individuals or groups of individuals is how we put our laws to the test, both our case law and our statutory law. Reference cases, in which one government asks the court to consider issues between itself and another government, are a rarity. There is no need to demonstrate that harm has been done, only that the legislation of one government stands to usurp the power of another. In other words, the challenging government need make no case that the impugned legislation interferes with legislation it itself wants to pass. It need never legislate under its heads of power if it doesn't wish to. All that is established in a reference case is that all other legislative bodies must stay out of the field. With individual plaintiffs bringing cases, however, and with intervenors seeking "standing" so that their case might be heard, it is necessary to demonstrate that one's legal right to act in a certain manner has been curtailed. One wants to commit the act in question or, as is the case with criminal cases, one has been charged with committing a prohibited act and, under the *Charter*, the defendant attempts to get the proscription struck down. No legitimacy, no offence. The case is over, and the prisoner goes free.

In addition to a *Charter* challenge, private individuals also have a right to ask for a declaration that legislation is ultra vires (outside the powers of) the legislating body. While not well-situated (as discussed above) for a *Charter* argument, organizations opposed to the legislation could have moved on their own initiative to have the *Firearms Act* declared ultra vires Parliament. They, not just a provincial government, could have sought to have it struck down. The fact that it was the Alberta Attorney General who took the case forward tells us something about that government's relationship with both firearms associations and the federal government. Given such evidence of the political importance of paying attention to provincial interest groups and the propensity of all provinces to resist the centralizing power of federal legislation, opting out under Section 33 is an option any time the payoff seems of sufficient importance.

CONCLUSION

The Supreme Court will, for the foreseeable future, continue to devote itself heavily to creating *Charter* precedent. There remain plenty of social issues still to interpret in the *Charter's* light, and new situations arise all the time. The difficulty of the Court's deliberations is underlined by the fact that *Charter* decisions are, as a rule, very lengthy and are often split. Lower courts, lawyers, and laypeople all need to understand relevant law on the *Charter* in order to guard against offending it. Its principles are so broad and its influence so vast that it affects the lives of every one of us. It is a fact that *Charter* interpretation can never suit all of us equally. The job of the Court is to strike a balance between the interests of the individual and the interests of the community. Arguably, then, both sides could end up dissatisfied with any decision. But remember that justice is a matter of process, not outcome. If our courts employ fair procedures and provide consistent reasons for their decisions, we can be said to be a just society. The Supreme Court, in its extensive *Charter* work, seeks to guarantee that Canada is also a free and democratic society through a People's *Charter*.

NOTES

1. Canadian judges in general have started to fight back at what has been called "judge-bashing." See "Judges Preparing to Answer Critics," *The Globe and Mail*, 7 February 2000, p. A3.

2. Canadian Constitutional Discussions and Chat Links, <www.constitutional-law.net/chatlink.html>.

3. A readable and reliable source on the patriation process is David Milne, *The New Canadian Constitution* (Canadian Issues Series: Toronto: James Lorimer & Co., 1982). My summary of the drama is very abridged.

4. According to Trudeau. Pierre Eliott Trudeau, *Memoirs* (Toronto: McClelland & Stewart, 1993), p. 326.

5. *Oxford English Dictionary*, 2nd edition, 1989, <www.oed.com>.

6. Milne, p. 36.

7. *R v Drybones* (1970) 3 CCC 355. The Supreme Court split 6:3.

8. *AG (Can) v Lavell* (1974) SCR 1439. The Supreme Court split 5:4.

9. Bertha Wilson, "Decision-Making in the Supreme Court," *University of Toronto Law Journal* 36 (1986): 238–48.

10. Neil Boyd, *Canadian Law: An Introduction,* (edition 2nd Toronto: Harcourt Brace Canada, 1998), p. 94.

11. In litigation instigated by five women from Alberta, Britain's Privy Council overruled Canada's Supreme Court in declaring that women were "per-

sons." *Edwards v AG (Can)* (1930) AC 134 (PC). The Privy Council remained Canada's final court of appeal until 1949.

12. See for example Gwen Brodsky and Shelagh Day, *Canadian Charter Equality Rights for Women. One Step Forward or Two Steps Back?* (Ottawa: Canadian Advisory Council on the Status of Women, 1989).

13. *RJR-MacDonald Inc. v AG (Can)* (1995) 3 SCR 199.

14. *R v Keegstra* (1990) 3 SCR 697 and *R v Zundel* (1992) 2 SCR 731.

15. *Rodriguez v AG (BC)* (1993) 3 SCR 519.

16. *Egan v Canada* (1995) 2 SCR 513.

17. *Symes v Canada* (1993) 4 SCR 695.

18. *R v Morgentaler (No. 2)* (1988) 1 SCR 30.

19. See, for example, *AG (Que) v Quebec Protestant School Boards* (1984) 2 SCR 66.

20. *R v Oakes* (1986) 1 SCR 103.

21. Chief Justice Dickson in ibid, p. 138–39.

22. *Hill v Church of Scientology of Toronto* (1995) 2 SCR 1130.

23. See revisions in *An Act to Amend the Charter of the French Language*, SQ 1988, c. 54.

24. *Vriend v Alberta* (1998) 1 SCR 493.

25. For example see *The Charter with Cases and Commentary by Peter Landry, a Barrister of the Supreme Court of Nova Scotia*, <www.blupete.com/Law/ Charter/mainpage.htm>.

26. *Reference re Firearms Act (Can.)* [2000] 1 SCR 783.

27. *Reference re Alberta Statutes* (1938) SCR 100.

28. *Firearms Act*, SC 1995, c. 39.

29. For a list of Web sites against gun control, check out <www.fedupcanada.org/ links.htm>.

30. See Linda Slobodian, "General mired in gun registry backlog," *Calgary Herald*, 16 June 2000, p. A4.

31. David M. Beatty, *Constitutional Law in Theory and Practice* (Toronto: University of Toronto Press, 1995).

32. *Reference re Firearms Act*, p. 35.

33. *R v Sharpe* (1999) BCCA 416, available at <www.courts.gov.bc.ca/jdb-txt/ca>.

34. See "Child Porn Crackdown Urged," *Calgary Herald*, 30 September 1999, p. A1.

35. "Boonstra 'at War to Preserve Freedoms,'" *Calgary Herald*, 22 July 1999, p. A1, A3. "Crusader Calls Panhandling Law Unconstitutional," *Calgary Herald*, 23 July 1999, p. A12; "Legal Experts Dismiss Curfews," *Calgary Herald*, 25 July 1999, p. A1.

36. Boyd, p. 100.

37. See <www.leaf.ca>.

38.   <See www.ccppcj.ca>.

39.   <See www.web.net/ccpi/>.

40.   As an example, see *R v Butler* (1992) 1 SCR 452 in which LEAF won a startling victory involving another *Criminal Code* section to do with pornography.

FURTHER READING

The Canadian Charter of Rights and Freedoms (available on many Web sites).

Gibson, Dale. *The Law of the Charter.* Calgary: Carswell, 1986.

Mandel, Michael. *The Charter of Rights and Freedoms and the Legalization of Politics in Canada.* Toronto: Thomson Educational Publishing, 1994.

Monahan, Patrick. *Politics and the Constitution: The Charter, Federalism and the Supreme Court of Canada.* Toronto: Carswell, 1987.

Weiler, J. and Elliot, R.M. *Litigating the Values of a Nation: The Canadian Charter of Rights and Freedoms.* Calgary: Carswell, 1987.

The Luckiest Women in the World?

Anne McGrath

Canadian women are frequently told that we are the luckiest women in the world. We are told by our politicians, the leaders of our social institutions, our families, and each other that we have the most opportunities, the least discrimination, and the most promising circumstances of any women on the planet. This is both true and untrue.

Canadians are often self-congratulatory about the relative prosperity and freedoms enjoyed by many in this country. In the second-richest country in the world, we are constantly reminded that, according to the United Nations, Canada is the best place in the world to live. Indeed, these reminders are often used as a club to beat back the demands of those who do not share in the wealth, prosperity, and freedom that some Canadians take for granted. These reminders are used as justifications of increasingly regressive and punitive actions of all levels of Canadian government. Women's demands for equality and justice are scrutinized and placed alongside the perception that there is little to complain about in such a prosperous and progressive country. Thus, a common objection to feminism contains the charge of whining and complaining, that nothing could possibly satisfy feminists. You can hear the collective exasperated sigh and see the collective eyes roll when feminists point out yet another example of sexism, racism, heterosexism, or other forms of oppression.

It is true that many of the most overt, open features of discrimination are now prohibited. There are an array of laws, rules, regulations, and procedures in place that forbid discrimination and guarantee equality. Canada has had a woman Prime Minister, women Supreme Court justices, women lawyers, university and college professors, doctors, administrators, and executives. The list of public accomplishments by Canadian women is very impressive. The creation of a context where these could happen is a testament to the work of an active and vibrant women's movement and the actions of individual women with intelligence, humour, and tenacity. Formal equality structures are now in place. In the face of this truth, there is a strong desire, on the part of many women and men, to believe that women's equality has been won. Feminism is

passé. Many people insist, that while feminism might have been necessary in the past, it is outdated and irrelevant. The idea that women have
rights that need protection and promotion is almost old-fashioned. The
media proclaim we have entered a post-feminist age. Women are stopped
only because of their own individual inadequacies. The battle is over. The
evidence, however, is overwhelming that there is a vital need for a strong,
vibrant, and vigilant feminist movement. Feminists, with a renewed commitment to liberation and emancipation for all women, contrast the success of entrenching formal equality structures in Canadian society with
the failure to achieve substantive equality (Day and Brodsky, 1998;
Razack, 1991). Formal equality measures that treat men and women as
equal, and refuse to acknowledge the disadvantages attributed to certain
groups in society, tend to be very individualistic and narrow. In an
analysis of the 1995 federal *Budget Implementation Act,* Shelagh Day and
Gwen Brodsky state:

> ... formal equality can never solve the real problems of
> inequality. To embrace it as a sole model is, in effect, to refuse to
> fulfill social commitments to equality. This highly individualistic
> version of equality, which refuses to deal with the disadvantage of
> groups, which also accepts that the right to equality applies only
> to the form of laws, and not to social and economic inequality,
> and which precludes a role for the state in promoting equality
> among groups, cannot adequately serve the interests of women
> (1998, p. 5).

Day and Brodsky demand that we must do more than "Just Say No"
to inequality. We must struggle for real equality meaningfully reflected in
the day-to-day lives of people and communities. Day and Brodsky
describe the fuller notion of substantive equality with its focus on group
and collective rights and preoccupation with the results or effects of laws,
policies, and practices. Substantive equality refers to the deeper changes
that need to be made to ensure that the structures, policies, and practices
that discriminate against women through "gender blindness" are transformed. Refusing to acknowledge the gender, race, and class inequities
in society does not work in the pursuit of equality. Neutrality and blindness to gender, race, class, and other forms of oppression serve only to
entrench existing inequalities.

The conflict between the perception of women's progress versus the
reality of women's persistent inequality is one of the major challenges
facing Canadian women today. It is hard to maintain a drive for change
when the key social messages promote complacency and inertia and
facades of justice are used to silence critics.

FEMINISM—PLEASE DON'T LET ME BE MISUNDERSTOOD

A key barrier to discussion of the many challenges facing Canadian women is the variety of meanings associated with the term "feminism." Although dictionary definitions generally refer to notions of equality between men and women and an improvement in women's status in society, there are a host of other meanings attributed to feminism. "I myself have never been able to find out precisely what feminism is," declared feminist journalist Rebecca West in 1913, "I only know that people call me a feminist whenever I express sentiments that differentiate me from a doormat ...." (quoted in Elliot and Mandell, 1998, p. 2). Women's opinions in opposition to mainstream thinking, particularly when they are put forcefully, are treated with suspicion, and the women are left open to accusations of being feminist. Many women can attest to the pressure to stay silent on issues that highlight the disparities between men and women. While there are several descriptions and definitions of feminism, most feminists would agree that feminism is about working for an improvement in the social, economic, and political condition of women. This entails working to end sexism and other forms of domination and oppression in our society. In her critique of the relationship between feminism and anti-racism, bell hooks puts forward a definition of feminism: "Feminism is the struggle to end sexist oppression. Its aim is not to benefit solely any specific group of women, any particular race or class of women. It does not privilege women over men. It has the power to transform in a meaningful way all our lives. Most importantly, feminism is not a lifestyle nor a ready-made identity or role one can step into" (1984, p. 26). This description of feminism is both unifying and clarifying. The movement to end sexist oppression is lined up clearly with other movements. Feminism places issues of race and class at its centre. It is common for feminists to note, with some amusement and a great deal of frustration, that many people who agree with the main positions put forward by feminists are quick to distance themselves from any association with the feminist label. The cliched phrase, "I'm not a feminist, but ..." describes the common practice of dissociating from the movement and then going on to agree with many of the central demands for equal pay, an end to violence, equality in relationships, etc. In the film *My Feminism* (Cardona, 1997), Gloria Steinem makes the point that while many people are so resistant to feminism because they don't know what it is, some people are opposed because they do know what it is. "Feminism is a revolution, not a public relations movement," she says. In a desire to be nonthreatening and conciliatory many feminists try to water down feminism to a concept that anyone can accept. However, feminism is and should be a challenge to the status quo. "Feminism is a big, massive world threat to the system that is in place," says Irish feminist Ailbhe Smyth in *My Feminism.*

It is difficult to have a calm, reasoned discussion about feminism. "By its very existence it provokes people," says Maria Mies (1991, p.6). Ranging between hostility and aversion to support and advocacy almost everyone has an opinion about feminism. Many women report that the pressure to resist feminism is intense and have suggested that a name change might make feminism more palatable. Some suggest that the term has become so unpopular that it acts as a barrier to attracting new adherents. Judy Rebick rejects this idea. She recalls the time when the original term "women's liberation" was perverted into an epithet, and feminists were derisively called "women's libbers." She explains that, "it's not the name, it's the struggle for equality that's being vilified" (1996, p. 90).

There is no doubt that resistance to feminism is widespread. Many women who have so much to gain from both the historic and contemporary feminist struggles, even those who believe in feminist goals, feel uncomfortable and defensive. Several reasons have been put forward to explain this resistance and fear of feminism. Media descriptions of feminism are often unflattering and highly distorted. Many women are intimidated by the perception that they need to know everything about every feminist issue. Students in Women's Studies classes often report feeling nervous about the contentiousness of feminist issues and are timid about the level of argument and conflict associated with feminism. The relationship of feminism to sexuality debates and the support of lesbian sexuality is another factor. Many people have been subjected to such intensely homophobic attitudes and practices that they are scared and nervous about the stigma of lesbianism. One very significant factor is reaction from men and fear that feminists are somehow against men. In *My Feminism,* American lawyer Mary Becker says, "One cannot be at all critical of men without being called anti-men" (Cardona, 1997). Canadian feminists Adamson, Briskin and McPhail state that, "... there is no doubt that a large part of women's discomfort with the label 'feminist' is related to what they assume men's response will be" (1988, p. 15).

Opening our eyes to the ugliness of the discrimination and oppression experienced by women and other oppressed groups in our society is not a pleasant experience. It is much more comfortable to refuse to see what is going on. While this is not always a fully conscious choice there is an element of denial in many women's refusal to acknowledge and accept the relevance and importance of feminism. Exposure to feminist insights can make it difficult to enjoy media and popular culture in the same way, family dinners may become less convivial, relationships are sometimes challenged and altered, everything in our environment can be questioned and examined under the light of what it means for gender, race, and class.

SECOND WAVE FEMINISM

Feminist historians have written extensively about the dearth of attention paid to the women who have sustained the homes, toiled in the factories, marched in the streets, and worked in the public realms of business and politics. Much of the scholarly work of feminist historians over the past 30 years has been to uncover and make the individual and collective contributions of women visible. Any account of history, they have pointed out, reveals the biases of the narrator. The stories of women have been ignored and silenced. The stories of people of colour, Aboriginal people, poor people, and other oppressed communities have also been shut out of the official accounts of history. As these inaccuracies are redressed through the development of social and feminist history, there remain biases and distortions related to the social location of the person telling the story. Any account of the past 30 years of feminist activism is subject to a variety of interpretations, and different women will highlight and privilege different factors, different stories. Even the decision about how to bracket the period of time, often referred to as second or second and third wave feminism, is connected to our understanding about what particular events are significant and merit recording. It is common to refer to the Royal Commission on the Status of Women, which reported in 1970, as a critical and important event in Canadian feminist activity. The significance of the panel is a matter of some debate but it is, at least, accurate to state that it drew country-wide attention to the concerns and growing activism of Canadian women. Although Canadians have become somewhat more jaded over the past decade about the relevance, importance, and usefulness of Royal Commissions generally, the Royal Commission on the Status of Women was no doubt a watershed moment. The efforts to convince the government of the need for a Commission came from Canadian women who were waking up to the inequities in society and the completely explicit and obvious unfairness of profound and pervasive sexist practices. Even the call for a Royal Commission was greeted with the ridicule and paternalism that characterized public and private life. Roberta Hamilton (1996) describes some of the media responses and quotes a 1967 *Ottawa Journal* editorial on the subject:

> By all means let the girls gather facts and opinions about women's rights in Canada and see how they can be strengthened where they need it. Bosh! But we suggest to them for their own good, of course, that they do it in the same way that they have advanced their cause in recent years—quietly, sneakily and with such charming effectiveness as to make men wonder why they feel they need a Royal Commission (p. 51).

Despite such dismissive and offensive attitudes, the Royal Commission spent over two and a half years travelling to communities, hearing from women, documenting their stories, gathering facts, and producing a report in 1970 with 167 recommendations for change. Concurrently, many feminists were actively organizing collectives to struggle on the many issues facing women. Women's caucuses were organized in the student movement, trade unions, and service organizations. Women's liberation groups were established in most Canadian cities and many smaller communities. In 1970, the same year that the Royal Commission reported, a group of feminists from Vancouver organized the Abortion Caravan and travelled across the country holding community meetings for women on the issue of abortion. They arrived in Ottawa and visited Parliament with their demands, attended Question Period, and chained themselves to the railings in the Speakers' Gallery. This radical action shook up debate on the issue of abortion rights and the legitimacy of the federal abortion legislation, which required women seeking abortions to submit to the ruling of hospital therapeutic abortion committees.

The years following the Royal Commission and the Abortion Caravan saw the development of feminist services across the country. An array of women's centres, rape crisis centres, battered women's shelters, and status of women action committees were established. In 1973 the National Action Committee on the Status of Women (NAC) was formed to lobby for the implementation of the recommendations of the Royal Commission. As more and more new feminist groups were formed, some postsecondary courses dealing with women's issues began to be offered in universities and colleges.

Constitutional and legal reform struggles dominated much of the activity of the women's movement in the 1980s. The implementation of the *Charter of Rights and Freedoms* early in the decade (1982) focused the attention of many women on the need for equality rights guarantees. The acceptance of Sections 15 and 28 of the *Charter* entrenched these rights in the *Constitution* and provided the basis for many campaigns for legal reform. One particular victory was the 1988 Supreme Court decision striking down the abortion legislation that restricted women's access to abortion. The next year Canadian women mobilized in force to support women's rights to abortion in the case of a Quebec woman whose ex-boyfriend tried to use the courts to prevent her from having an abortion. The Supreme Court again upheld women's rights in this case.

Economic issues also came to the fore in the 1980s as the federal government entered into the first Canada/U.S. Free Trade Agreement. The National Action Committee on the Status of Women (NAC) campaigned vigorously against the free trade deal and entered into coalition with several other Canadian social movement groups opposed to economic integration with the United States. Faced with opposition from the Conservative government, including many women in the government, and allied with those who identified themselves as feminists, NAC adopted the slogan 'the economy is a woman's issue'.

Many women's groups were challenged to address the dominance of white middle-class priorities and values that characterized most feminist organizations. Women of colour, immigrant women, women with disabilities, lesbians, Aboriginal women, and poor women have been critical of the inability and unwillingness of feminist organizations to represent and transform their memberships and leaderships to attempt to meet the needs of all women. Through organized activity and sustained pressure, many organizations and groups went through organizational review processes to change their internal workings and place racism, sexism, heterosexism, and classism at the front of their agenda. Over the past decade the feminist movement has increasingly been challenged by the growth of right wing opposition. The election of radically right wing governments in Alberta and Ontario, sustained by an intensely fiscally conservative federal Liberal government, has intensified cuts to social programs, decreased funding for women's organizations, and empowered socially conservative forces opposed to women's rights. The cuts to social programs initiated by the Ralph Klein government in Alberta left many women's groups reeling. The Calgary Status of Women Action Committee produced a video and a series of papers called "*Bleeding from Alberta's Budget Cuts*" that analyzed the impact of government budgetary actions on women. In one of the papers Alberta NAC Representative Sylvia Hawkins states:

It is glaringly obvious that women are suffering the consequences of government cuts and restructuring. On the one hand, the most marginalized women in our society—those trying to escape poverty and violence—have an almost insurmountable task before them. On the other hand, there are those women who have jobs helping women in need, who are expected to do more and more with less and less. In addition, as services are eliminated or privatized, women have less choices, but are expected to pick up the slack in caring for families and communities" (1996, p. 6).

As governments implement more and more conservative economic agendas, financial support for women's organizations has also declined. Successive changes in the funding apparatus and guidelines have led to sporadic and minimal funding levels for local women's centres, provincial status of women action committees, and national women's organizations. Concurrently, antifeminist women's groups have been more and more favourably received within governments and by the media. Groups such as the Alberta Women United for Families, and its federal counterpart R.E.A.L. Women, strongly antifeminist organizations of men and women, are regularly asked for media commentary on women's issues and have been progressively more successful at securing funding to attack feminism. Buoyed by the success of right wing political parties such as the Klein and Harris governments in Alberta and Ontario, and the rise in federal parties such as the Reform Party and its offspring, the Canadian Alliance, right wing social groupings have been active in their denunciations of feminism and women's rights.

BACKLASH

It is no surprise that feminists and others working for a change in power relations in society would be subject to a backlash. The term "backlash" was popularized by American feminist Susan Faludi in her 1991 book *Backlash: The Undeclared War against American Women.* Faludi's book captured the sense of attack that the women's movement was experiencing. Her description of the assault against women's rights resonated with many feminists. She described the prevailing mythology that feminism had succeeded and that even though women are now equal and have achieved everything they ever wanted, they are now miserable. She contends that the backlash tried to convince women that the very things that would lead to improvements in social conditions would actually lead inevitably to unhappiness:

> The truth is that the last decade has seen a powerful counterassault on women's rights, a backlash, an attempt to retract the handful of small and hard-won victories that the feminist movement did manage to win for women. The counterassault is largely insidious: in a kind of pop-culture version of the Big Lie, it stands the truth boldly on its head and proclaims that the very steps that have elevated women's position have actually led to their downfall (p. xviii).

Another message of the backlash is that feminism has won at the expense of men's equality rights. It is time now, say the backlash advocates, to stop and push back the gains of feminism. Evidence of continuing wage discrimination, violence against women, inadequate child-care, sexual harassment, the glass ceiling and sticky floor of the employment market, sexist and demeaning media images, and deepening women's poverty pose no barrier to the purveyors of the backlash message. The message of "overwhelming feminist success at men's expense" screams out at us from government leaders and media pundits. Feminists and others are described as "special interest" groups with agendas that run counter to democratic society. The notion that the norms of society are threatened by groups opposed to racism, sexism, and other oppressions begs the question about what exactly the interests of that society are. If equality and justice are "special interests," what are the interests of the dominant society?

A particularly effective silencer of social justice individuals and groups has been the charge of "political correctness." Originally coined as a self-critical reflection about particularly zealous approaches to language, and the ways that language can reflect and promote biases and stereotypes, the term has been directed against critics of discrimination and oppression. The view that objections to social prejudice and discrimination are in some way a violation of free speech is a complete distortion. It is ironic that those who fight to protect the rights of free speech for a small, privileged few have so little respect for the rights of people marginalized by hateful speech and practices. There is no evidence to suggest that the proponents of sexist and racist policies and practices are cowering in corners or are reluctant in any way to advance their right wing social and economic agendas. However, they have been very effective at silencing the voices of those most damaged by racism, sexism, classism, and heterosexism.

ONE, TWO, THREE, FOUR—WHAT ARE WE FIGHTING FOR?

Many of the issues that women have coalesced around over the past 30 years remain remarkably and often depressingly current. Employment issues such as pay equity, minimum wage legislation, sexual harassment, date rape, wife abuse, incest, educational equity, part-time workers rights, child-care, domestic responsibilities, sex-role stereotyping, criminal justice, pornography, prostitution, media images, women's health, birth control, abortion, custody and access, new reproductive and genetic technologies, lesbian rights, immigration policies, mental health issues, medical research, popular culture, body image, eating disorders and so on, continue to preoccupy many feminists. Many of these issues can be grouped into two overwhelming and broad categories—the feminization of poverty and violence against women. These are the two key issue areas identified by most contemporary feminist organizations in Canada and other countries.

Increasing numbers of women in poverty has been identified as a major priority in the Canadian women's movement because not all women have gained from feminist organizing. For the most part, women with significant privileges have benefited and accelerated their ability to make money. Other women have experienced substantial declines in their ability to achieve economic security. The feminization of poverty refers to the processes that drive more and more women into poverty and deepen the levels of poverty that women experience. A recent report by the Canadian Centre for Policy Alternatives suggests that, "... it is surely time—thirty years after the Royal Commission on the Status of Women—to end the feminization of poverty in Canada" (Townson, 2000, p. 13). Evidence is mounting that women's economic security is on a downward spiral and that successive government actions, at all levels, are increasing the levels of women's poverty. Monica Townson points directly to government policies and points out that, "... many of the policies they have implemented recently have exacerbated the problem and have undoubtedly contributed to increasing poverty rates for women" (p. 8). Cuts to social assistance, reductions in eligibility and funding for Employment Insurance, reductions in social housing, and federal transfer payment cuts have all contributed to the acceleration in women's and children's poverty. It is often the plight of children in poverty that evinces the most reaction from media and government. The concerns about child poverty are, of course, often expressed as if children live in a vacuum, unrelated to poor mothers. Townson says, "... it is the poverty of women that is behind the poverty of so many of our children" (p. 1).

VIOLENCE AGAINST WOMEN

In 1982 a female federal MP rose in the House of Commons to report startling news about the extent of wife battering in Canada. Quoting from a recently released report compiled for the Canadian Advisory Council on the Status of Women, Margaret Mitchell tried to inform the members of the House that the abuse of women within the family was a critical issue. She was unable to adequately make her point, however, since the laughter and guffaws from the male politicians was so overwhelming. The hilarity that overcame the male MPs was greeted by shock and outrage among women's groups and much of the public. Even though violence against women was not an issue identified by the Royal Commission, the consciousness of its prevalence and effects grew over the 1970s and into the 1980s. Grassroots women's services dealing with violence against women were established throughout this period, and women organized politically to bring the issues to public attention and identify the root causes of the violence.

The public debate around violence against women shifted in December 1989. On December 6, 1989, 14 young women were shot by a gunman in Montreal's Ecole Polytechnique. Francine Pelletier, a Quebec journalist, describes the event:

> A young man enters a classroom armed with a rifle, and evacuates the men from the room. To the women, he says: "you are all feminists. I hate feminists!" He kills some of them. He leaves, and moving from one floor of the building to another, he kills a few more as he goes. He kills himself in turn, leaving a message which says that women are hell, and that he would have liked to slay a few other particular women (in Malette and Chalouh, 1991, p. 34).

The killer's note identified several prominent Quebec women as the target of his rage. Francine Pelletier was, herself, one of the targeted women identified in the note. The collective horror that descended over the country was acutely expressed by women. Several commentators noted that women's everyday experiences of violence began to be expressed openly. The shootings touched off a tidal wave of grief and anger. Ironically, in the days and months following this, the largest single-day massacre in Canadian history, several media and political commentators scurried to separate the massacre from the issue of violence against women. Remarkable contortions were used to frame the massacre in terms other than those elucidated so clearly and articulately by the gunman. The act was "isolated" said the experts. He was a madman said media and government leaders. And then, unbelievably, feminists who pointed out the links to generalized violence against women were accused of manipulating the event for their own ends. Feminists were accused of exaggeration and urged to moderate their tone. The bastions of society were eager to go to any lengths to interpret the act as an isolated act by a desperate, mad individual. Francine Pelletier says:

> If this is madness, never has it been so lucid, so calculated. Never has madness left such a clear message. The message is: there is a price for women's liberation and the price is death. Yes, the killer was mentally ill and yes, this was a desperate act, but killing fourteen women goes beyond "pathological homicide." It was an act of reprisal, well thought out, calculated, and directed against women in general and feminists in particular (p. 35).

Despite the backlash directed against feminists and the attempts to turn the table and blame feminists for the existence of misogyny, there was concerted activity in the women's movement to end violence against women. The poster released by NAC and taken up by many other organizations proclaimed, "First mourn, then work for change." The federal government initiated a series of hearings that resulted in a report called *The War against Women*. Women's groups across the country travelled to Ottawa to appear before the committee and present their views. Ironically, when the committee finally reported to Parliament the focus of attention was on the title of the report. It was denounced as provocative and inaccurate. The accounts and recommendations of the women who worked to bring their stories to the committee were lost in the furor over the title.

In December 1993 NAC released a report detailing some of the steps the federal government could take to deal with the issues of violence against women. The 99 recommendations covered funding for grassroots feminist services, changes to the criminal justice system, racism in the systems that deal with violence, civic safety initiatives, judicial reform, public education, and consultation measures for women's groups in the development of antiviolence policy. Controversy surrounded the decision by several national women's groups to boycott the federally appointed Canadian Panel on Violence against Women. The boycott action initiated by NAC, the Congress of Black Women, the National Organization of Immigrant and Visible Minority Women, and the DisAbled Women's Network followed months of controversy and the inability of the Panel to deal with issues of race equality in the process.

GLOBAL ORGANIZING

Some have predicted that the next wave of feminism will be global in nature (Cardona, 1997; Grown and Sen, 1987). The development of United Nations–sponsored conferences focusing on women's rights, beginning in 1975 in Mexico and held every five years since, has intensified the links between women and women's groups internationally. The impact of globalization through international trading bodies has solidified resistance to corporate domination of economies at the expense of women's human rights. The world conferences of the last decade have been important meeting places for women from around the world to meet together, share experiences and analyses, and strategize for specific measures to pursue equality and identify barriers. The Fourth World Conference on Women, held in Beijing, China brought together over 30 000 women in the Parallel Forum hosted by nongovernmental organizations. Canadian feminists in attendance reported remarkable unanimity in the description of the major barriers facing women. Women from around the world identified the rise in conservatism and the globalization of free market economic policies as major threats to the advancement of gender equality (Day, 1995; Rebick, 1995). The oft-quoted statement from the United Nations Report of 1980 is a rallying point for many:

> Women constitute over half the world's population, perform two-thirds of the world's work, earn less than ten percent of the world's income and own less than one percent of the world's property. For those who like to think that the situation has improved remarkably since 1980, feminists note that the decades since the United Nations made this statement have seen a remarkable deterioration in women's economic security worldwide. A report to the Beijing conference prepared by the United Nations notes that on every continent women work longer hours, earn less money and are even more likely to live in poverty than men (*United Nations Human Development Report*, August 1995).

In *Women and the World Economic Crisis* Jeanne Vickers notes:

> When we speak of the 'poorest of the poor', we are almost always speaking about women. Poor men in the developing world have even poorer wives and children. And there is no doubt that recession, the debt crisis and structural adjustment policies have placed the heaviest burden on poor women, who earn less, own less and control less (1991, p. 15).

The impact of economic and social fundamentalism for women in all parts of the world has been profound. The lessons from Beijing include women's growing knowledge, expertise, and activism. Women are prepared to take action to force governments to listen and be accountable for gender equality. Many women attending the Beijing conference were excited to hear about the successful Quebec and Canadian marches against women's poverty and violence against women. In 1995, a march of 2500 Quebec women succeeded not only in raising awareness and debate about women's poverty and violence against women but also resulted in legislative changes, including a raise in the minimum wage. In 1996, the National Action Committee on the Status of Women (NAC) and the Canadian Labour Congress (CLC) organized a successful march across Canada. Hundreds of women drove, marched, and flew to Ottawa to bring their demands for Bread and Roses, for Jobs and Justice, to the attention of the Canadian government and the country. In Beijing in 1995, the Federation des Femmes du Québec brought the idea of a world march of women. The support was overwhelming. From March 8, 2000 (International Women's Day) to October 17, 2000 (International Day for the Elimination of Poverty), women around the globe were marching, rallying, singing, shouting, writing, publishing, and teaching in support of women's human rights. Over 2700 women's groups from 139 countries participated.

Nevertheless, Canadian women have consistently been told that we have nothing to complain about. The Canadian government crows enthusiastically about its high rating in the United Nations. Human Development reports but never acknowledges that women are slipping further and further behind when it comes to gender equality. The Canadian government was reprimanded in 1998 by the United Nations Committee on Economic, Social and Cultural Rights for its treatment of vulnerable citizens, particularly women, poor people, and Aboriginal people (*NAPO News*, February 1999). Yet the Canadian government has refused to acknowledge the impact of its economic policies on marginalized groups. Report after report boasts of the exaggerated achievements of the Canadian government in promoting and ensuring equality. A recent Canadian government report to the United Nations went so far as to take credit for the work of the social justice groups that are chronically underfunded and fighting government policies that diminish equality rights (Morris, 1999).

The limited reforms supported by different levels of Canadian governments are not enough. They advance the interests of certain groups of women but do not address the underlying flaws in the system. Gender equality cannot be achieved piecemeal, and it most certainly cannot be achieved for only some women. If equality measures are not directed first and foremost at the most vulnerable then justice will not be realized. The Canadian feminist movement has matured and developed into an articulate, conscious, and active force for change in Canadian society. The challenge for the economic and political elites is to acknowledge the legitimate demands of feminism and the value of a society that encourages and supports the organized feminist movement. The challenge for feminists is to move past the formal rhetoric of equality and press for structural changes that will bring about concrete changes in the day-to-day lives of women in Canada.

REFERENCES

Adamson, N., Briskin, L. and McPhail, M. (1988). *Feminist organizing for change: The contemporary women's movement in Canada.* Toronto: Oxford University Press.

Cardona, D. and Colbert, L. (Directors), and Colbert, L (Producer). (1997). *My feminism.* Toronto: Cardona Colbert Films.

Calgary Status of Women Action Committee. (1996). *Bleeding from Alberta budget cuts.*

Day, S. (1995, December). What was left out of the platform? In *Onward from Beijing: The final newsletter of the Canadian Beijing Facilitating Committee.* Ottawa: Canadian Beijing Facilitating Committee.

Crow, Barbara and Gotell, Lise, eds. (2000). *Open boundaries: A Canadian women studies reader.* Toronto: Prentice Hall Allyn and Bacon Canada.

Day, S., and Brodsky, G. (1998). *Women and the equality deficit: The impact of restructuring Canada's social programs.* Ottawa: Status of Women Canada.

Elliot, P. and Mandell, N. (1998). Feminist theories. In *Feminist Issues: Race, class and sexuality* (2nd ed.), edited by N. Mandell. Scarborough, ON: Prentice Hall Allyn and Bacon Canada.

Faludi, S. (1991). *Backlash: The undeclared war against American women.* New York: Crown Publishers.

Grown, C. and Sen, G. (1987). *Development, crisis and alternative visions: Third world women's perspectives.* New York: Monthly Review Press.

Hamilton, R. (1996). *Gendering the vertical mosaic: Feminist perspectives on Canadian society.* Toronto: Copp Clark Ltd.

Hooks, B. (1984). *Feminist theory: From margin to centre.* Boston: South End Press.

Malette, L., and Chalouh, M. (1991). *The Montreal massacre.* Montreal: Gynergy Books.

Mandell, Nancy, ed. (1998). *Race, class and sexuality,* 2nd ed. Scarborough: Prentice Hall Allyn and Bacon Canada.

Mies, M. (1991). *Patriarchy and accumulation on a world scale: Women in the international division of labour.* New Jersey: Zed Books.

Morris, M. (1999). *The other side of the story: A feminist critique of Canada's national response to the UN questionnaire on the implementation of the Beijing platform for action.* Ottawa: Feminist Alliance for International Action.

Razack, S. (1991). *Canadian feminism and the law: The women's Legal Education and Action Fund and the pursuit of equality.* Toronto: Second Story Press.

Rebick, J. (1995, December). Beijing diary: The women's conference the media missed. *Canadian Forum.*

Rebick, J. and K. Roach, (1996). *Politically speaking.* Toronto: Douglas and McIntyre.

Townson, M. (2000). *A report card on women and poverty.* Ottawa: Canadian Centre for Policy Alternatives.

United Nations Report. (1980). Geneva: United Nations.

United Nations Human Development Report. (1995). Geneva: United Nations.

Vickers, J. (1991). *Women and the world economic crisis.* London and New Jersey: Zed Books.

We Get Knocked down, but We Get up Again: Surviving and Adapting as First Nations in Canada

Cora J. Voyageur

Adapt or perish! These words have been the hallmark of Aboriginal[1] life in Canada since time immemorial. Since the first indigenous people set foot on the North American continent,[2] adaptation has been vital. Climatic variation, changes in habitat, and living with the uncertainty— the abundance or scarcity of food—meant change was a way of life.

Aboriginal peoples' resilience and adaptability was put to the test when European explorers came to North America. The original inhabitants of North America were forced to undergo change at a rate never before experienced. There were economic, social, and political changes. With the advent of the fur trade in the mid-1600s, Indians[3] had access to trade goods for the first time. The indigenous people welcomed some of these. For example, women liked the convenience of metal cooking pots while men found the rifle handy for hunting. However, some items, like the gun, required subsequent contact, thus causing change within the indigenous peoples' economic and social realms. Although the rifle revolutionized the hunt by making it easier to kill animals, it also allowed the animals to be harvested at an accelerated rate, resulting in over-hunting. The fur trade's increased demand for pelts meant both hunters and trappers were forced to go farther afield to locate animals (Ray, 1974). Again, this meant changes to social and family life with domestic adjustments needed to accommodate the prolonged absences of the group's able-bodied men—most of whom were husbands, fathers, and grandfathers. Moving farther and farther from their own traditional territory caused encroachment on others' terrain. This resulting conflict with neighbouring tribes altered social and political relations between them.[4]

European contact also meant changes to familial arrangements with Indian women becoming the fur trader's spouses. Women served an important part in the social and economic development of the Canadian frontier through their roles as wives, mothers, interpreters, and guides (VanKirk, 1997).

In Canada's early days, mainstream society thought Indians faced extinction.[5] As a result of this belief, the government regulated us, anthropologists recorded us, and photographers took pictures of us—all for the sake of posterity.

Indians were viewed as a "dying breed" due in part to the drastic decline in indigenous populations through epidemics (Moyles and Owram, 1988). This ideology was further buoyed by mainstream society's view that we would meet our demise through our own wanton behaviour. Green states that we Indians were viewed as lazy, simple, wild, inept, lascivious, and immoral (1995, p. 87). In any event, we were not expected to be around for very long. But until we did eventually die out, we would have to be dealt with. Adaptation has been the key to survival in a country with a shameful record of treating Aboriginal peoples. We say the fact that we are not all dead, given government policies and the regulations that we were subjected to, speaks to our resilience as a people. We have proven that we are here to stay. We have survived, and we are working hard toward elevating our role in Canadian society. We are doing this by continually adapting to our environment, just as we did in the past.

Our society is rapidly changing. Items and events that were the stuff of science fiction in our grandparents', or even our parents' day, are now a reality. In this paper I highlight some changes that occurred in First Nations peoples' lives[6] in Canada during the past century from a personal and family narrative.[7] I explore some societal, economic, and political changes that occurred during the lifetimes of my grandfather, Isadore Voyageur; my mother, Alice Voyageur Adams; and me, Cora Voyageur. [8] I also write from a personal perspective and about my identity as a First Nations person. I provide background information to place my narrative in a historical and societal context. However, before I begin I must clarify whom I am speaking of when I use the term "First Nations."

Speaking about Canada's indigenous people as one homogenous group is a mistake. Canada's indigenous people consist of four separate and distinct groups: First Nations (Indian), non-Status Indians, Métis, and Inuit.

"Indian" is a legal classification defining those individuals governed by the *Indian Act,* 1868 and its subsequent amendments. Shortly after confederation, the Dominion government defined "Indian" as:

All persons of Indian Blood, reputed to belong to the particular tribe and their descendents;

All persons residing among such Indians, whose parents were or are … descended on either side from Indians.

The term "non-Status Indian" was used much more broadly in the past when it was a more encompassing term and included the Métis people and others of mixed Aboriginal and non-Aboriginal descent. The Métis are descendants of mixed marriages between Europeans and Indians. The Métis distinguish between two types of Métis: "the Red

River" Métis, descendants of the Red River district in Manitoba who adapted to the new settlement society; and the "nomadic" Métis, who essentially lived a traditional hunting and trapping lifestyle (Hatt, 1985). The Inuit are the Aboriginal people of Northern Canada, who live above the tree line in the Northwest Territories,[9] Northern Quebec, and Labrador (Dickason, 1997).

OUR LIVES AS FIRST NATIONS CITIZENS

As First Nations members, my family lives under the *Indian Act,* which basically governs every aspect of our lives. As wards of the government, we are among the most regulated people in Canada. In addition to living with more regulation, we have also lived with fewer basic privileges than other Canadians.[10] The government has a fiduciary duty[11] toward us as First Nations people, which means they must look out for our best interests. In spite of this duty to do the best by us, we have still been subjected to some of the most regressive and detrimental policies in Canadian history. One such policy forms the basis of historian Sarah Carter's book *Lost Harvests.* Carter explores how Indian farmers' attempts at farming (at the behest of the Dominion government) were undermined by government policy (1990). These backward policies, such as prohibiting Indian farmers from using mechanized implements and restricting their sale of goods, made it virtually impossible for them to succeed (Carter, 1990). Indian Agents were also to discourage First Nations from dancing or attending country fairs because these activities would distract them from their farm duties (Scott, 1921, p. 1).

We also had little legal or political power. For example, from 1927 to 1951 Indians were not allowed to bring charges against the government. In fact, lawyers could be charged and fined if they represented or raised money for an Indian claim against the government (Ray, 1996). Additionally, Indians could not vote federally until 1960 and were virtually without a political voice (Ray, 1996).

My narrative concentrates on northeastern Alberta, but many of our experiences had similar consequences for First Nations people across Canada since we all live under the paternalistic, patriarchal *Indian Act.* My family, the Voyageurs, are treaty Indians and trace our lineage back to the days before European contact. My family comes from a small, isolated, and primarily Aboriginal community[12] called Fort Chipewyan. Fort Chipewyan was established as a fur trade post in 1788 and is the oldest European community in Alberta. Of course, the indigenous peoples of the region, the Chipewyan, Slavey, Beaver, and Cree, have occupied the area for between 9 000–10 000 years. John Ives, the Director of the Archeological Survey of Alberta, has determined that artifacts from Eaglenest Portage and Clear Lakes in the Birch Mountains (southeast of Fort Chipewyan) represent 10 000 years of prehistory (1990, p. 35).

My family lives in the Treaty 8 region of Alberta. Treaty 8 was signed between the First Nations[13] of the region and the government of Canada in 1899 and 1900. Frank Oberle states that Treaty 8 involved a land surrender of 324 000 square miles of land—an area about 3/4 the size of Ontario (1986, p. 1). Although the Dominion government seemed in no hurry to deal with the Indians (First Nations), and or even to issue scrip to the half-breeds (Métis) within the Treaty 8 area, until that point (Treaty No. 7 was signed in southern Alberta more than 20 years before), there now seemed to be some urgency. The Klondike Gold Rush brought scores of travellers through the region, and the government wanted to ensure their safe passage through Indian territory. Kesterton and Bird estimate that as many as 40 000 individuals passed through the Treaty 8 area on their way to the Yukon Gold Rush (1995, p. 35). In addition, Canadian politicians were becoming increasingly anxious about possible American expansion northward and wanted the Northwest Territories settled as quickly as possible (Owram, 1980, p. 5).

Treaty 8 was signed in my community between the Chipewyan and Cree Indians and the Queens' representative on July 13, 1899. My great grandfather, Alexande Laviolette, signed[14] on our behalf. The Treaty Commissioners wrote that, "The Chipewyan confined themselves to asking questions and making brief arguments. They appeared to be more adept at cross-examination than at speech making" (Mair, 2000, p. 174). The Commissioners further stated:

> ...the Chief at Fort Chipewyan displayed considerable keenness of intellect and much practical sense in pressing the claims of his band. They wanted as liberal, if not more liberal terms, than were granted to the Indian of the plains. (Mair, 2000, p. 174)

First Nations celebrated the Treaty signing at the time. However, the government made many promises to us—some of which have never been delivered. These unfulfilled promises are the basis of specific claims.[15]

The Commissioners were surprised by the "civilized nature"[16] of the Indians of Fort Chipewyan. They commented on our dress and demeanor. *The Alberta Plaindealer* reported:

> The Commissioners found no Indians wearing blankets or any other relic of savagery but men were all dressed in good suits, wore hats and white shirts, collars and frequently boots. The women wore well-made dresses and hats on their heads instead of shawls (September 1, 1899, p. 1).

The fact that we were so "civilized" could be expected since we had been in contact with Europeans for over 100 years when the Treaty was signed. Charles Mair, in his report on the Treaty 8 expedition stated, "There was no paint or 'strouds' to be seen, and the blanket was confined to the bed" (Mair, 2000, p. 117). Although Whites were surprised to see the adaptations of the "Indians," First Nations had in fact made adaptations to European contact over the previous century.

Adaptation and Survival

Our community had undergone many changes to its traditional lifestyle since our first encounter with the fur traders. For example, our town is almost entirely Christian with a long history of European religion. Fort Chipewyan had one of the first Roman Catholic missions established west of St. Boniface (Carney, 1990, p. 291). The Holy Angels residential school, an institution employed to assimilate Indian children into European culture, opened in 1874 and closed exactly 100 years later in 1974 (Brady, 1985, p. 119). By law, First Nations families in the area were obliged to send their children to be educated in these "total" institutions.[17] The results of this separation from family, the lack of parental care and nurturing, and the recently discovered physical, psychological, and sexual abuse perpetrated against the Aboriginal children in these institutions have had devastating effects on our community (Chrisjohn et al., 1997).

One might think that a region so isolated and so far north would remain relatively untouched by southern development and settlement. However, this is not the case. Now, as then, many northern dwellers lament that Southerners develop policies that profoundly modify Northerners' lives. Furthermore, Northerners say that few Southerners ever set foot in the regions that their policies affect.

Aboriginals in northern Canada, particularly in the West, began to see increased settlement. Not only did increased settlement mean more people to contend with, but along with those people came more rules and regulations. Most of these laws were unilaterally imposed, and Indians were not consulted or alerted until after they became law (Calliou, 2000a).

Two examples of such unilateral regulation were the *Migratory Birds Convention Act* of 1917 and the *Natural Resources Transfer Agreement* (NRTA) of 1930. This legislation breeched the terms of Treaty 8. Indians were told that they could live as before and were assured a continuation of their traditional hunting and fishing rights. Treaty 8 Commissioners stated:

> Our chief difficulty was the apprehension that the hunting and fishing privileges were to be curtailed. The provision in the treaty under which ammunition and twine is to be furnished went far in the direction of quieting the fears of other Indians, for they admitted that it would be unreasonable to furnish the means of hunting and fishing if laws were to be enacted which would make hunting and fishing so restricted as to render it impossible to make a livelihood by such pursuits. (1899, p. 6)

The *Migratory Birds Convention Act* prohibited the hunting of ducks, geese, and other migratory birds that formed a large part of the First Nations' diet; while the NRTA allowed for provincial game laws to restrict the trade and barter of products of the hunt (Calliou, 2000b). These regulations severely hampered the Indian's ability to obtain food.

The Fort Chipewyan Indians' freedom to hunt and fish was restricted in 1922 and further restricted when the park was expanded in 1926, with the government's unilateral decision to create Wood Buffalo National Park. The park, along with its restrictions and regulations, was foisted upon the same people who less than 30 years before had been given the promise under Treaty 8 that nothing would interfere with their traditional lifestyle. When interviewed for the Treaty and Aboriginal Rights Research Elders' Program,[18] 100-year-old Isadore Willier remembered what the Indians had been told at the Treaty 8 signing:

> ... The way you have been struggling for a livelihood—no one will ever stop that form of livelihood. If you should take treaty, this is the way you will make your livelihood. Moose, caribou, and any other wild bush animals, no one will ever stop you from obtaining these animals anywhere ... You will always make your livelihood that way. If you make treaty, ... nothing will stop you from fishing and duck hunting....(Daniel, 1999, p. 93)

First Nations' mobility was restricted when they were placed on reserve lands. Reserve lands were surveyed and set aside in the early 1900s for the Chipewyan and Cree Indians of Fort Chipewyan. While some continued to hunt, trap, and fish, others did various work in the broader economy. One such First Nations person who worked in the mixed economy was my grandfather, Isadore Voyageur.

ISADORE VOYAGEUR

My grandfather, Isadore Voyageur, was born in 1910 in Fort Chipewyan, Alberta. He was orphaned at the age of nine when his mother died of the Spanish Flu epidemic that swept the region. The Birds, a local Indian family, raised him through traditional adoption. My grandfather told me about being relocated as a child from the land that was to become Wood Buffalo National Park. He talked about being moved across the lake to one of the Chipewyan Reserves at Richardson Lake (known to the locals as Jackfish Lake).

The park's creation, with the intent to conserve and replenish the depleted buffalo stocks, meant hunting there became prohibited, and hunters were limited in the areas in which they could hunt (McCormack, 1984). It also meant their hunting practices could be criminalized. The people who formerly had only to deal with the scarcity of game now had to deal with licensing, possible fines, or possible prison terms. Thus, my grandfather had to carry out his hunting, trapping, and fishing practices in areas outside the park (once traditional hunting territory) and within the rules set out in both the *Migratory Birds Convention Act* and the *Natural Resources Transfer Agreement.* He was forced to adapt to the imposed regulations.

Treaty promises made to the Indians were to exist for eternity—"for as long as the sun shines and the water runs" (Mair, 2000, p. 62). In the case of Fort Chipewyan, *eternity* lasted about 30 years. First Nations were forced to adapt to the new legal regime or risk criminal sanctions.

One would not think that a small, northern, isolated community like Fort Chipewyan could be so impacted by outside forces. Major resource developments to the south (Great Canadian Oil Sands) and to the east (uranium mining at Uranium City) both had a tremendous impact on the community.

Uranium discoveries in northern Saskatchewan in the late 1940s and early 1950s caused many Fort Chipewyan men to move their families across the lake to Uranium City where they joined the wage labour force. Although these jobs were new to those from Fort Chipewyan, the wage labour market was not. First Nations people had worked at and worked for the fur trade posts in a variety of wage labour jobs. The community's mixed economy consisted of both wage labour and subsistence from hunting, fishing, gathering, and trapping. My grandfather participated in the mixed economy, working for the Hudson's Bay Company as a boatman and tracker[19] in the summer months and as a trapper during the winter. He was also one of the men who left the community to work in the resource exploration sector in Uranium City. He was employed by an Irish mining firm called Northern Explorations where he worked as a guide and staked claims. Anthropologist Patricia McCormack, who has conducted extensive research in the Fort Chipewyan region, has documented these changes to the Indian employment pattern. She points out that postwar inflation and plummeting fur prices produced a need for additional revenue to purchase essentials (2000, p. 280).

The Athabasca Tar Sands, to the south of our community, also caused increased exploration and subsequent environmental pollution in the region. The presence of oil in the sand south of Fort Chipewyan was a well-known fact. In 1793, explorer Alexander Mackenzie stated, "tar and oil could be found oozing from the banks of the Athabasca" (in Daniel, 1999, p. 58). However, it was not until 1912 that serious exploration began (Ferguson, 1985). Many First Nations people left our community to take jobs in the Tar Sands plants.

My grandfather also saw changes to the environment from outside development. For example, the creation of the W. A. C. Bennett Dam in British Columbia significantly lowered Lake Athabasca's water level, having a devastating effect on the trapping and fishing activities in the area. Hunters, trappers, and fishers had to contend with dried-up marshes that were no longer as conducive to wildlife.

My grandfather passed away in 1994 at the age of 83. In his lifetime he adapted in order to survive and seized opportunities as they presented themselves. He was the patriarch of a large family[20] and saw many of his children, grandchildren, and great-grandchildren adapt to changes brought on by mainstream society, obtain employment, and gain educational credentials. One of his children, my mother Alice Voyageur Adams, experienced many changes.

ALICE VOYAGEUR ADAMS

My mother was born in the early 1940s. By the time she was born, the residential school had been operating in our community for more than half a century (Brady, 1985). This meant that she and most of her siblings were forced to attend since my grandparents spent most of the school year on the trapline.

The presence of the residential school in our community is seen as positive by some but devastating by others. My mother attended the Holy Angels Residential School when Indian children were treated very badly. The nuns called them "savages" and made them feel ashamed to be Indian. Children were severely punished for speaking their Native language, talking to the opposite sex, or for a myriad of trivial offences.[21] My mother and aunts would tell stories of physical abuse at the hands of the nuns. They would laugh about it, but they always seemed to stare off into space afterward as they recalled those events.

My mother lived through some of the most oppressive times for Indian people in Canada, and the abuse experienced in residential schools extended into mainstream society. First Nations had essentially been deemed extraneous to Canadian society. This was a dark period in Canada history[22] where Indians were violated by Whites with impunity. For example, a recent court case saw a former policeman and Member of Parliament, Jack Ramsey, convicted of attempting to rape a 14-year-old Indian girl when he was an officer stationed in a small Indian community in Saskatchewan in 1969. When convicted, a Ramsey supporter and a Camrose resident, 78-year-old Robert (no last name given), stated that Ramsey should not be punished, because as Robert put it, "screwing Indians was the thing to do. Squaws were there to be picked up" (Thorne, 2000, p. A17).

Another example of disregard for us as Indian women was shown by the brutal rape and stabbing death of Helen Betty Osborn in the northern Manitoba town of The Pas by four young white males in the early 1970s. The identity of the murderers was well known within the community, but no charges were laid against the killers for many years. As a result of this perceived "availability" of Aboriginal women, we had to adapt to this hostile environment and be very cautious about our safety and on guard at all times.

However, amongst this abuse and pain, my mother's generation experienced many new freedoms. For example, the pass system,[23] introduced following the Riel Rebellion in 1885 (Carter, 1997, p. 147) was repealed in 1941. In addition, changes to the *Indian Act* in 1951 made it possible for Indians to participate in ceremonial activities such as the Sundance and Potlatch that had been previously banned. First Nations could once again observe their traditional and spiritual practices. The prohibition had also been lifted on raising funds to support land claims against the government.[24]

Despite these new freedoms, Indians in Canada were in a relatively desperate state. In the early 1960s University of British Columbia anthropologist Harry Hawthorn headed a research team to investigate the social and economic condition of Native communities. The results were alarming. Research showed Indian people living in dreadful conditions, with First Nations occupying the lowest economic position in Canadian society. My mother, Alice Voyageur Adams, also lived in relative poverty although she adapted and was able to gain employment and survive.

The report also recommended that all forced assimilation programs be abandoned (Hawthorn, 1966 and 1967). It seems the government had not done well by "its Indians." There needed to be a change. This change began with the emergence of the Indian movement.

Although there had been various forms of First Nations political organization over the decades, modern advances began in the late 1960s. In 1969 the Trudeau government's White Paper on Indian Policy sparked the "Indian Movement." This policy sought to radically change the relationship between the government and the Indians by proposing that the *Indian Act* and the Department of Indian Affairs be abolished. The White Paper stated:

> The Government of Canada believes that its policies must lead to the full, free and non-discriminatory participation of the Indian people in Canadian society. Such a goal requires a break with the past. It requires that the Indian people's role of dependence be replaced by a role of equal status, opportunity and responsibility, a role they can share with all other Canadians. (Government of Canada, 1969, p. 6)

The unique relationship between the Indians and the federal government was to be severed. In essence, the treaties under which the Indians had surrendered their land to the Crown in return for certain promises were to be reneged upon. Needless to say, this caused an uproar in the Indian community, and we rallied like never before. Indians' lobbying and vocal opposition forced the government to abandon its plans. The Indians had won a significant victory! Yet despite the moral victory over the White Paper, much more needed to be done. As mentioned in the Hawthorn Report, Indians were living in depressing social and economic conditions (1966 and 1967). This needed to change, and steps had to be taken to improve the length and quality of Indian life. My mother saw the beginning of the "Indian Pride" movement that still continues today.[25] She passed her adaptive skills and her hard work ethic on to her children—one of whom is me, Cora Voyageur.

CORA VOYAGEUR

I was born on the Saskatchewan side of Lake Athabasca in the late 1950s. I, like my grandfather and mother, have seen major changes in the First Nations community during my lifetime. As First Nations people, we have become increasingly politicized, urbanized, educated, and more vocal. Increased calls for self-government by First Nations and a devolution policy[26] implemented by the Department of Indian Affairs has increased First Nations' control over our everyday lives.

I see a changing relationship between First Nations and mainstream society. One factor greatly altering this relationship is land authority. First Nations are currently negotiating outstanding comprehensive and specific land claims with the federal government. If all current land claims succeed, First Nations will control up to 30 percent of the Canadian land mass (Sloan and Hill, 1995, p. xi).

Land authority also changes the power base between us, as First Nations, and the resource companies hoping to extract raw materials from our territory (Calliou and Voyageur, 1998). We are actively involved in negotiations and expect to receive benefits and jobs from resource-extraction projects. We are prepared to be forceful. For example, the Janvier First Nation in northeastern Alberta blocked the road to their reserve in 1996 to protest the fact that resource companies were not hiring the local Aboriginal population. Companies in the Fort Chipewyan/Fort McMurray area now consult First Nations, hire local employees, and contract out to First Nations businesses. Industry Canada states that there are currently more than 20 000 Aboriginal businesses operating in Canada (http://strategis.ic.c.ca/SSG/ab00002e.html). Many First Nations entrepreneurs have set up e-commerce and Internet businesses, while others are involved in other high-tech ventures.

Perhaps one of the most significant policy changes in my adult life has been the implementation of *Bill C31*.[27] The bill, which amended the *Indian Act*, came into effect on April 17, 1985. *Bill C31* became a reality because of the hard work, determination, and tenacity of a dedicated group of women (Voyageur, 1996).

The law had previously discriminated against Indian women by forcing them to lose their Indian status if they married non-Indian men. Significantly, Indian men marrying non-Indian women did not lose their status. In fact, non-Indian women gained Indian status and were able to retain their Indian status even after divorcing their Indian husbands (Jamieson, 1978). Women and children could also be enfranchised if their father or husband chose enfranchisement; the male's choice affected the entire family. Thus, many First Nations women had no voice in choosing their identities and were forced to leave their communities.

When Indians met the minimal requirements for citizenship—education and "acceptable" moral character—they were allowed the rights of full citizenship through voluntary enfranchisement pursuant to sections of the *Indian Act*. They would be allowed to vote, purchase alcohol, and obtain land under the homestead system, and would no longer have to live under the aegis of the repressive *Indian Act* or have to tiptoe around the government's resident reserve babysitter—the Indian Agent. The Indian Agent system was eliminated in 1969 (MacKenzie, 2000, p. 327).

Bill C31 had a significant impact on me since I was able to regain my Indian status after a brief, unsuccessful marriage to a non-Indian. It meant a lot to my family as well. It meant that my aunts, Emma Laviolette and Janet Dashcavich, were also able to regain status as Indians. It seemed ironic that their grandfather had signed the Treaty on behalf of our band, and yet they should lose their status after marrying non-Indians. Regaining status also meant we received the benefits of status such as living and being buried on a reserve, receiving limited medical and educational benefits, and the annual $5 treaty money.[28] The educational benefits were especially relevant to me since I was able to obtain band scholarships, which allowed me to pursue extended postsecondary studies and obtain a Ph.D.[29] Successfully completing one undergraduate and two graduate degrees required discipline and a strong work ethic and adaptation to an alien, sometimes hostile, environment, which at times was not kind to me as an Indian.

Perhaps the most important aspect of regaining my Indian status was that I was able to identify myself as "Indian. " I was accepted as a band member and was given full membership privileges. I no longer had to add the explanation that I had "married out" when I explained my Indian heritage.[30] I could say that I was a First Nations person from Fort Chipewyan and lay claim to its rich and proud heritage without hesitation. Who your family is and where you are from are very important in the First Nations community. These identification markers help set you in context within the community.[31] They also serve as a form of community acceptance, affiliation, and acknowledgment.

Reinstatement means I can vote in band elections and have a say in how our band is operated. We, as band members, also have an interest in our band-owned businesses. One band-owned businesses, Denesuline Environmental Services Limited, contracts with Syncrude Canada Limited in Fort McMurray and provides employment for band members. Members of my extended family have adapted and taken advantage of opportunities in such economic ventures.

My generation has witnessed an explosion of educational attainment. The Indian and Inuit postsecondary student enrollment has increased steadily over the past three decades. However, we are still behind mainstream society. In the 1995/96 academic year, First Nations enrollment in postsecondary institutions stood at 6. 9 percent,[32] while the postsecondary enrollment rate for Canadian society was 11 percent (INAC, 1998, p. 33). In the early 1960s there were about 200 Status Indians enrolled in Canadian colleges and universities. By 1997, the number had increased to about 27 500 (INAC, 1998, p. 32). First Nations people are recognizing society's need for an educated workforce and gaining credentials at a rate never before seen in our community.

For many years, First Nations people faced many barriers and were discouraged from pursuing a higher education. Most communities, like mine, did not have a high school. This meant that students entering Grade 10 had to leave home. Some of my aunts and uncles went to Grouard in central Alberta. These students lived in a residence much like the residential school in Fort Chipewyan. Others lived as boarders with primarily white families in Fort McMurray and Edmonton. My aunt Bernadette lived with us in Edmonton when she went to school, and my Uncle Don lived with another family. They did not particularly like having to move away from their community, but they said it was something they had to do to complete their education.[33] These young students were placed in a foreign environment, and many had trouble adjusting. A high school was finally opened in Fort Chipewyan in the 1980s.

Education is an important issue in our community, and there is concern over the high dropout rate. The Social Services Reform Committee held a career fair in our community in February 2000. Its intent was to show local children the benefits of higher education by inviting professionals from the community. This included many people of my generation: business person and entrepreneur David Tuccaro; education administrator Roy Vermilion; lawyer Ivan Ladouceur; registered nurses Betty McDonald and Claudia Simpson; police officer Eddie Shortman; and me, a university professor. We spoke to the youth about the hurdles that we encountered and how we adapted and overcame obstacles in pursuing our careers.

Aboriginal students are now enrolling and graduating from a variety of disciplines. The diversity of study is beneficial to the Aboriginal community and a departure from earlier enrollment, which showed a heavy concentration in the social work and education fields. The University of Alberta's Aboriginal Admission Policy aspires to make Aboriginal students 5 percent of the University of Alberta student population. The majority of First Nations enrollments are found in undergraduate studies, but there are increasing numbers enrolled in both graduate and professional programs such as law school (http://www.inac.gc.ca/stats/facts/possec.html). The University of Alberta graduated approximately 70 Aboriginal students in the spring 2000 convocation, including five Aboriginal dentists (Angela Wolfe, Personal Interview, June 30, 2000).

First Nations students tend to be older than other postsecondary students. A study conducted at the University of Alberta showed Aboriginal students were on average 10 years older than non-Aboriginal students (Angela Wolfe, Personal Interview, June 30, 2000). However, this is changing with more students coming to university straight from high school (Donna Meckling, Personal Interview, June 30, 2000). As with most older students, life is a juggling act between academics and other domestic responsibilities. Somehow, we adapt and find a way to work things out.

I have seen, and continue to see, many changes in my community. We are adapting and gaining power and demand our voices be heard, even over the voices of those who feel there should not be any "race-based" rights in Canada.[34] We are beginning to use the courts to force the government to fulfill its obligations to us. Recall that approximately 30 years before the *Constitution Act, 1982* we were forbidden to bring land claims against the government. Today we have many legally trained First Nations members arguing our cases at negotiations and litigation.

A number of important Supreme Court decisions have recognized Aboriginal and Treaty rights. An example of the legal recognition of our rights was when Aboriginal and Treaty rights were given constitutional status in the *Constitution Act, 1982*. This means that Aboriginal and Treaty rights are now entrenched in the highest law of the land and now receive constitutional protection.

CONCLUSION

First Nations have adapted, and continue to adapt, to the changing environment and circumstances in order to survive, grow, and evolve. This chapter examined the changes between First Nations society and mainstream society by discussing adaptations by three generations of First Nations people over the last century.

My grandfather lived during a time when Indians had few rights and very few choices. As Indians, we were told how to live (under the *Indian Act*), where to live (on reserves), and where to go (literally, under the pass system). The *Indian Act* was restrictive and repressive, but the only recourse we had was to relinquish our Indian status. Some choice! It is ironic that people from other countries could immigrate to Canada to find new opportunities and obtain religious and political freedoms while we, the first peoples of this country, were given little opportunity for advancement in this land of plenty, no religious freedom, and no political voice. There was little consultation or negotiation with Indians after the Treaty was signed. It seems the government got what it wanted from the Indians—the land. Everything was on mainstream society's side—the law and the legislation. In my grandfather's time, Indians were supposed to go away, be quiet, and not bother mainstream society.

My mother's generation still lived with many of the repressive policies implemented during my grandfather's time. In fact, she inherited
many of the social and economic consequences of earlier oppression.
Her generation suffered tremendously from the residential school
system. However, the healing is now under way. The federal government
has recently apologized to the Aboriginal community for its role in the
residential school system. Some accept the apology, while others say it
does not go far enough.

My mother's generation had more choices than my grandfather's.
One of these choices was to move to urban areas. This trend began in the
1960s and continues today with approximately 50 percent of our First
Nations population living in cities (Statistics Canada, 1998). Although
urbanization was a remedy for the high unemployment rates and lack of
housing experienced on reserves, it was no panacea. Indians were not
always welcome in the city. My mother, and many of her generation,
endured tremendous racism and discrimination at the hands of mainstream society members who deemed them inconsequential. Despite the
chilly welcome, they adapted and remained in the cities where we
obtained jobs and gained educational credentials. My mother's generation witnessed a transformation in the Indian community; a resurgence of
Indian pride and increased personal and political freedoms. My mother's
generation was largely ignored by mainstream society, but this disregard
manifested itself in new political movements. First Nations peoples began
to fight for their rights and reclaim their place in Canadian society.

My generation has seen, and continues to see, remarkable changes
in our community. We can no longer be ignored by mainstream society
because we have learned the rules of the game. We have adapted and are
beginning to prosper in both worlds. We have moved from a community
that had virtually no political rights at the beginning of the century to
one that altered the Canadian political scene as witnessed by Elijah
Harper's refusal to allow passage of a bill in the Manitoba legislature that
would have endorsed the Meech Lake Accord. Harper's refusal essentially halted the Meech Lake Accord. The Oka Crisis[35] of 1990 was a wake-
up call for the government and spawned the Royal Commission on
Aboriginal Peoples (RCAP), which examined virtually all aspects of the
relations between Canada and its Aboriginal peoples.

Today, First Nations people are taking part in mainstream society at
a rate never before witnessed by our society. It is exciting to observe our
First Nations leaders sitting across the table from the prime minister,
provincial premiers, and industry executives. In fact, many members of
Parliament, members of legislative assemblies, ministers of government
departments, and senior civil servants are Aboriginal.

In spite of changes to our environment and the rules under which we
have lived, we have also retained continuity. While adapting, we retained
our identity as Indians. We retained our religious and spiritual practices

although they were forced underground by law. We are maintaining our identity and culture through traditional teachings, ceremony, and language. In fact a resurgence is occurring. We can no longer be viewed as a "dying race. " Our numbers are burgeoning, and our cultures are thriving. This has many implications for society in general since we are increasing our population at twice the rate of mainstream society. This means that we will make up a larger segment of the labour pool in the future and are a larger portion of the consuming public. Indeed, corporate Canada has noticed this trend and now courts the Aboriginal community.

Many things have changed, but many issues remain the same for us as First Nations people. We respect our Treaty and Aboriginal rights and expect that Canada will live up to the promises made to us. First Nations' understanding of the Treaty was to share the land and resources and live together peacefully and prosperously. After all, we gave up our land for those promises. The same land from which much of Canada's wealth is derived.

Although we have gained much over the past century, we have a long way to go. We see ourselves as contributors to our great society and one of the many fibres woven into our multicultural Canadian society. We have proven we are survivors and that we can adapt to our environment and changing circumstances. Adaptation is the Indian way of life. It has been that way since time immemorial. Our history shows that we get knocked down, but we get back up again.

NOTES

1. I will use the terms Aboriginal, indigenous, and Native interchangeably throughout this chapter.

2. Olive P. Dickason in *Canada's First Nations: a History of Founding Peoples from Earliest Times* states that there is general agreement that humans were present in the Americas as late as 15 000 B.C. and as early as 50 000 B.C. (1997:15).

3. The indigenous inhabitants of North America have had many names supplanted upon them by the newcomers. The term "Indian" was given in error and two stories are told about this moniker. The first story says that Columbus was on his was to India when he was "discovered" by the indigenous people of the "new world." He called the inhabitants "Indians" (INAC). The other is that Columbus was on a journey to the West Indies. In any event, Columbus was way off course. Another term, "Red Indian" (used to distinguish First Nations from people from India) was given to the inhabitants of what is now Newfoundland by explorer, John Cabot, when he observed them covering their bodies with red ochre, a plant-based dye (Stefaniuk, 1996). In spite of all names given to us by others, we refer to ourselves as "the People." Indigenous words used to describe us, "Dene"

(Chipewyan), "Neheyaway" (Cree), "Wendat" (Huron), "Inuit" (Inuktitut), translate to "the People."

4. For more information on the trade rivalries and inter-tribal warfare associated with the fur trade see Ray, 1974.

5. In fact, one tribe, the Beothuk of Newfoundland became extinct with the death of Shawnadithit in 1829 (Dickason, 1997).

6. Here I define First Nations (Indian) as those with a legal relation with the federal government through the *Indian Act.*

7. I got the idea to do a family narrative over a century by the recent passing of the 97-year-old Alberta historian Grant McEwen in June 2000. As I thought about all the changes he must have seen throughout his life, having been born in 1902, I was struck by the vast societal changes that can occur within a person's lifetime. I then began to think about the changes experienced by Firtst Nations people in this time period.

8. There are too many changes to mention within the confines of this short paper. I will concentrate on only two events from each generation and draw contrasts and continuities between them. Nevertheless, this examination should provide an illustration of the development of Indian policy in Canada over the past century.

9. This also includes the newly formed territory of Nunavut.

10. This will be explored more fully later in the chapter.

11. The term fiduciary duty was first recognized in the *Guerin* case 1984 where the Supreme Court of Canada declared that the government of Canada must always act in the best interest of the Indians when surrendering land. This fiduciary duty was broadened in the *Sparrow* case 1990 to cover all matters the government conducts on behalf of Indians.

12. The 1996 Census of Canada shows Fort Chipewyan has approximately 1600 residents with 89 percent of whom are Aboriginal (Cree, Chipewyan, or Métis) (Statistics Canada, 1996).

13. Treaty 8 was signed with the First Nations of the region but the Métis also settled their land entitlements with the government through accepting land scrip or cash scrip. Some Métis sold their scrip to land speculators. See Voyageur in *Lobstick: An Interdisciplinary Journal Special Premier Issue.* Volume 1 for a more detailed account on this issue.

14. The Indians did not actually sign the treaty with their signature or with an "X" but touched the pen with their finger to signify their agreement. The "X" and their signatures were written by the commissioner.

15. There are two types of land claims: specific and comprehensive. Specific land claims occur when a First Nation has entered Treaty and has not received certain provisions promised in the Treaty or when reserve lands have been surrendered without the proper legal procedures being followed. Comprehensive land claims occur when no treaty has been entered into by the First Nations, thus Aboriginal rights to the land still exist.

16. It appears that the Commissioners expected to find "savage" Indians rather than "civilized" ones. The term "civilized' has Euro-centric connotations. We have always viewed ourselves as civil.

17. The "total institution" is a term coined by sociologist Erving Goffman to describe a residential environment in which people are isolated from society and hence resocialized. Residents spend most of their time in these institutions such as prisons, mental institutes, residential schools, and boot camps (Spencer, 1992:92).

18. The Treaty and Aboriginal Rights Research (TARR) Elders' Program was carried out by the TARR branch of the Indian Association of Alberta and sought to determine the Elders' understanding of the treaties.

19. Boatmen and trackers moved trade goods and furs up and down the region's rivers and lakes. Trackers pulled boats up the river with long ropes.

20. When he passed away Isadore Voyageur had nine surviving children (three deceased) and eight stepchildren, approximately 100 grandchildren, and numerous great-grandchildren.

21. My mother tells a story of being sent to clean the priest's bedroom and being beaten for opening the door to the priest's bedroom.

22. For more information on the abuse of Indian women and children see among others, Anderson, 2000, and Larocque, 1996.

23. The pass system involved Indians receiving a pass (permission) from the Indian Agent to leave the reserve.

24. For a historical analysis of the restrictions on ceremonies see Pettipas, 1994 for a discussion of the restrictions on bringing claims against the government see Titley.

25. I refer to the Indian Pride movement as a phenomenon in which Indian people began feeling proud about their rich culture and heritage. This was a change from the "shame" that many felt about themselves being Indians as a result of assimilationist socialization measures.

26. The devolution policy was implemented by the Department of Indian Affairs to give administrative powers to the local bands and tribal councils. However, many of the resources were taken out of the programs so the Indians were given control of programs but not the money to run them effectively. Thus, although First Nations have greater control, they do not necessarily have the resources. Essentially, Indian Affairs now gets free administration for many of its programs.

27. Bill C31 states that those eligible to be registered as status Indians include: women who lost status as a result of marriage to non-status men; individuals who lost status or were denied status under other discriminatory provisions of the *Indian Act*; individuals who lost status through enfranchisement, a process under the old act whereby persons could voluntarily give up status; and children of persons in any of the proceeding categories (Paul, 1993:6).

28. As Treaty Indians, we receive $5 treaty money a year. It is now more symbolic than a monetary necessity for the band members. The event is marked by

ceremony with the Chief dressed in his official "chief suit", the Royal Canadian Mounted Police (RCMP) dressed in "Red Serge," a representative from Indian Affairs and Northern Development, and the band's membership clerk. The sum was fixed in 1899 when the treaty was signed in our region. The amount has never been increased.

29. I received my Ph.D. in Sociology at the University of Alberta in 1997. I was the first Ph.D. from my territory and the first First Nations person to receive a Ph.D. from the University of Alberta.

30. "Marrying out" is the term given to people who married someone who was not Indian. It is viewed with varying degrees of acceptance within the community.

31. In the Indian community, one of the first questions you are asked when you are introduced to someone is: Where are you from? After your connection to a specific land mass (reserve) is determined, you are then asked who your parents and grandparents are. This exchange reaffirms your membership and signals your acceptance into the group.

32. This was an increase from 6.0 percent in 1993/94.

33. Neither my aunt nor my uncle completed Grade 12 in Edmonton at that time. However both completed it at a later date.

34. The Reform Party (now the United Alliance) has campaigned vigorously against our "special rights" in Canada by characterizing them as "race-based" rights. They ignore the unique historical and constitutional relationship First Nations have with the Canadian state. They fail to recognize that these rights are legal rights based on our prior occupation of this land.

35. The Oka Crisis occurred in Quebec when the Town of Oka wanted to expand a golf course on land that the Mohawks held as sacred. This led to a 78-day standoff between the Mohawks and the Sureté du Quebec and later the Canadian military. A policeman, Marcel Lemay, was killed.

REFERENCES

Aboriginal Business Canada. (2000). <http://strategis.ic.gc.ca/SSG/ab00002e.html>

Alberta Plaindealer. (1899, September 1). "Treaty commission returns." Strathcona, Alberta, p. 1.

Anderson, Kim. (2000). *A recognition of being: Reconstructing native womanhood.* Toronto: Second Story Press.

Brady, Sister Archange J. (1985). *A history of Fort Chipewyan: Alberta's oldest continuously inhabited settlement,* 2nd Edition. Athabasca: Gregorash Printing.

Calliou, Brian. (2000a). The imposition of state laws and the creation of various hunting rights for Aboriginal peoples of the Treaty 8 territory. *Treaty 8 revisited: Selected papers on the 1999 Centennial conference. Lobstick: An interdisciplinary journal special premier issue* (pp. 151–93). Grande Prairie: Lobstick Editorial Collective.

————. (2000b). *Losing the game: Wildlife conservation and the regulation of First Nations hunting in Alberta, 1880–1930.* Unpublished Master of Laws Thesis. Edmonton: University of Alberta.

Calliou, Brian and Cora J. Voyageur. (1998). Aboriginal economic development. *Power and resistance: Critical thinking about Canadian social issues,* 2nd edition. Wayne Antony and Les Samuelson (eds.). Halifax: Fernwood Publishing, pp. 115–34.

Carney, Robert. (1990). The grey nuns and the children of Holy Angels, Fort Chipewyan, 1974–1923. Patricia A. McCormack and R. Geofrey Ironside, (eds.). *Proceedings of the Fort Chipewyan and Fort Vermilion Bicentennial Conference.* Edmonton: Boreal Institute for Northern Studies, pp. 289–98.

Carter, Sarah. (1990). *Lost harvests: Prairie Indian reserve farmers and government policy.* Montreal: McGill-Queen's University Press.

————. (1997). *Capturing women: The manipulation of cultural imagery in Canada's Prairie West.* Montreal: McGill-Queen's University Press.

Chrisjohn, Roland, Sherri Young, and Michael Maraum. (1997). *The circle game: Shadows and substance in the Indian residential school experience in Canada.* Penticton: Theytus Books.

Daniel, Richard. (1999). The spirit and terms of Treaty 8. *The spirit of the Alberta Indian Treaties* 3rd Edition. Richard T. Price (ed.) Edmonton: University of Alberta Press, pp. 47–100.

Dickason, Olive Patricia. (1997). *Canada's First Nations: A history of founding peoples from earliest time.* Don Mills: Oxford University Press.

Ferguson, Barry Glen. (1985). *Athabasca oil sands: Northern resource exploration, 1875–1951.* Edmonton: Alberta Culture and Canadian Plains Research Centre.

Francis, Daniel. (1993). *The Imaginary Indian.* Vancouver: Arsenal Pulp Press.

Fumoleau, Rene. (1974). *As long as this land shall last: A history of Treaty 8 and Treaty 11, 1870–1939.* Toronto: McClelland & Stewart.

Government of Canada. (1868). The *Indian Act.* Ottawa: Department of the Interior.

————. (1899). Department of Indian and Northern Development. (1966). *Treaty No. 8, Made June 21, 1899 and Adhesions, Reports, Etc.* Ottawa: Queen's Printers.

————. (1969). *Statement of the government on Indian policy.* Ottawa: Department of Indian and Northern Development.

————. (1998). *Basic departmental data, 1997.* Catalogue No. R12-7/1997. Ottawa: Information Management Branch.

Green, Joyce A. (1995). Towards a détente with history. *International Journal of Canadian Studies: Aboriginal Peoples and Canada* 12 (Fall): 85–106.

Hatt, Ken. (1985). Ethnic discourse Alberta: Land and the Métis in the Ewing Commission. *Canadian Ethnic Studies* (17): 65–85.

Hawthorn, H.B. (1966 & 1967). *A survey of the contemporary Indians of Canada: Economic, political, educational needs and policies.* Ottawa: Indian Affairs Branch.

Indian and Northern Affairs Canada (INAC). (1998). *Basic Developmental Data.* Catalogue No. R12-7/1998. Ottawa: Minister of Indian Affairs and Northern Development.

Ives, John W. (1990). The ten thousand years before the fur traders. Patricia A. McCormack and R. Geofrey Ironside, (eds.). *Proceedings of the Fort Chipewyan and Fort Vermilion Bicentennial Conference.* Edmonton: Boreal Institute for Northern Studies, pp. 33–38.

Jamieson, Kathleen. (1978). *Indian women and the law in Canada: Citizens minus.* Ottawa: Advisory Council on the Status of Women and Indian Rights for Indian Women.

Kesterton, Wilfred and Roger Bird. (1995). The press in Canada: A historical overview. *Communications in Canadian society,* 4th Edition. Benjamin Singer (ed.). Toronto: ITP Nelson Canada, pp. 30–50.

Larocque, Emma. (1996). The colonization of a Native woman scholar. Patricia Chuchryk and Christine Miller (eds.). *Women of the First Nations: Power, wisdom, and strength.* Winnipeg: University of Manitoba Press, pp. 11–18.

Mair, Charles. (2000). *Through the Mackenzie Basin: An account of the signing of Treaty No. 8 and the Scrip Commission, 1899.* Edmonton: University of Alberta Press and Edmonton and District Historical Society.

McCormack, Patricia A. (1984). *How the (North) West was won: Development in the Fort Chipewyan region.* Ph.D. Dissertation. Edmonton: University of Alberta.

———. (2000). Overcoming the differences of treaty and scrip: The community development program in Fort Chipewyan. *Treaty 8 revisited: Selected papers on the 1999 Centennial Conference. Lobstick: An interdisciplinary journal special premier issue.* Grande Prairie: Lobstick Editorial Collective, pp. 277–95.

MacGregor, J.G. (1974). *Paddle wheels to bucket-wheels on the Athabasca.* Toronto: MClelland & Stewart Limited.

MacKenzie, Patrick. (2000). The Indian agents of Fort Chipewyan: An example of Treaty 8 administration. *Treaty 8 revisited: Selected papers on the 1999 Centennial Conference. Lobstick: An interdisciplinary journal special premier issue.* Grande Prairie: Lobstick Editorial Collective, pp. 315–27.

Moyles, R.G. and Doug Owram. (1988). Specimens of a dying race: British views of the Canadian Indian. *Imperial dreams and colonial realities: British views of Canada, 1880–1914.* R.G. Moyles and Doug Owram (eds.). Toronto: University of Toronto Press.

Oberle, Frank. (1986). *Treaty 8 renovation: Discussion paper.* Ottawa: Department of Indian and Northern Affairs.

Owram, Doug. (1980). *Promise of Eden: The Canadian expansionist movement and the idea of the West, 1856–1900.* Toronto: University of Toronto Press.

Paul, Pamela Marie. (1993). *The Trojan Horse: An analysis of the social economic and political reaction of First Nations people as a result of Bill C-31.* Master's Thesis. University of New Brunswick.

Pettipas, Katherine. (1994). *Severing the ties that bind: Government repression of indigenous religious ceremonies on the Prairies.* Winnipeg: University of Manitoba Press.

Ray, A.J. (1974). *Indians in the fur trade: Their role as hunters, trappers and middlemen in the land southwest of Hudson Bay, 1660–1870.* Toronto: University of Toronto Press.

———. (1995). Commentary on the economic history of the Treaty 8 Area. *Native Studies Review:* 10(2), pp. 169–95.

———. (1996). *I have lived here since the world began: An illustrated history of Canada's Native people.* Toronto: Lester Publishing Limited and Key Porter Books.

Scott, Duncan Campbell. (1921, December 15). *Department of Indian Affairs Circular,* p. 1.

Sloan, Pamela and Roger Hill. (1995). *Best employment practices in the Aboriginal community.* Toronto: Sloan Hill Publishing.

Spencer, Metta. (1992). *Foundations in modern sociology,* 6th Edition. Scarborough: Prentice Hall Canada Inc.

Statistics Canada. (1996). *Profile of enumeration areas: Fort Chipewyan.* Ottawa: Statistics Canada, Catalogue No. 95F0185XDB-1.

———. (1998, January 17). *The Daily.*

Stefaniuk, Walter. (1996). *You asked us about Canada: The ultimate fact and trivia book.* Toronto: Doubleday Canada Limited.

Thorne, Duncan. (2000, May 4). "Riding split as Ramsay awaits his sentence." *Edmonton Journal,* p. A17.

VanKirk, Sylvia. (1997). Women in between: Women in fur trade society in western Canada. *A passion for identity: An introduction to Canadian studies,* 3rd Edition. David Taras and Beverly Rasporich (eds.). Toronto: ITP Nelson, pp. 41–51.

Voyageur, Cora. (1996). Contemporary Aboriginal women. *Visions of the heart: Canadian Aboriginal issues.* David Long and Olive Patricia Dickason. Toronto: Harcourt Brace Canada, pp. 93–115.

———. (2000). Contemporary Aboriginal women. *Visions of the heart: Canadian Aboriginal issues,* 2nd Edition. David Long and Olive Patricia Dickason (eds.). Toronto: Harcourt Brace Canada, pp. 81–106.

Voyageur, Cora J. and Brian Calliou. (2000). Various shades of red: Diversity within Canada's indigenous community. (Under Review). *London International Journal of Canadian Studies.*

PERSONAL INTERVIEWS

Alice Voyageur Adams. Fort Chipewyan. 28 June 2000.

Bernadette Voyageur. Fort Chipewyan. 2 July 2000.

Donald Voyageur. Edmonton. 3 July 2000.

Angela Wolfe. Edmonton. 30 June 2000.

Donna Meckling. Calgary. 30 June 2000.

FURTHER READING

Anderson, Kim. (2000). *A recognition of being: Reconstructing native womanhood.* Toronto: Second Story Press.

Grande Prairie Regional College. (2000). Treaty 8 revisited: Selected papers on the 1999 Centennial conference. *Lobstick Interdisciplinary Journal.*

McCormack, Patricia and R. Geoffrey Ironside (eds.). (1990). *Proceedings of the Fort Chipewyan and Fort Vermilion bicentennial conference.* Edmonton: Boreal Institute for Northern Studies.

Ray, A.J. (1996). *I have lived here since the world began: An illustrated history of Canada's native people.* Toronto: Lester Publishing Limited and Key Porter Books.

Titley, Brian. (1986). *A narrow vision: Duncan Campbell Scott and the administration of Indian affairs in Canada.* Vancouver: University of British Columbia Press.

What Does It Mean to Be African-Canadian? Conflicts in Representation, Identity, Integration, and Community

Wisdom J. Tettey

INTRODUCTION

Transnational migration has assumed unprecedented global proportions as we begin the twenty-first century. By the mid-1990s, over 100 million people were resident in countries other than those in which they were born *("Workers of the World,"* 1997, p. 81; Weiner, 1996, p. 128). There is no doubt that this trend is continuing unabated, and that current figures are likely to be significantly higher. In Canada, the 1990s saw the largest number of immigrants since the early 1900s—about 200 000 a year (Ley 1999). Africans have not been left out of this global trend and have left their home countries in large numbers for a variety of reasons. These include the search for better economic and educational opportunities, as well as the need to escape political persecution and turmoil. These imperatives have been at the base of the increasing number of Africans entering Canada (see Konadu-Agyemang, 1999).

In the five-year period between 1991 and 1996, 76 260 Africans immigrated to Canada, compared to 64 265 for the whole decade of the 1980s (Statistics Canada, 1996). Canadian census data for 1996 shows that there were about 247 240 African-born immigrants in this country, excluding those who have obtained Canadian citizenship. Of this number, 17 945 were non-permanent residents. The breakdown is as follows: 26 250 West Africans; 107 420 East Africans; 74 890 Northern Africans; 8 940 Central Africans; and 29 735 Southern Africans (Statistics Canada, 1996).

The focus of this chapter will be on first-generation African immigrants, most of whom came to Canada after 1961. 1 have chosen this focus for a variety of reasons. First, in spite of their increasing numbers, there is a dearth of literature about African immigrants in the Canadian context. Secondly, they have generally been subsumed under the category "black." But, as the ensuing discussions will show, this categorization not only shows the importance of race in Canadian constructions of identity but also loses cognizance of the specific circumstances of African immigrants and the multiplicity of experiences that define groups within the black community. This study therefore seeks to highlight specific experiences, perceptions, feelings, values, and conflicts within this group. The analysis will bring out the commonalities between African-Canadians and other minority immigrant communities, while increasing the larger society's understanding of this group. Such an understanding is important in ensuring competent intercultural communication between African-Canadians and other communities.

Whilst African immigrants are clearly a part of the Canadian mosaic today, it is important to recognize that this has not always been the case. In order to appreciate the place of Africans in Canada, it is necessary to take a retrospective look at the characteristics of immigrant populations across time and examine the determinants of qualification for Canadian residency and citizenship from a historical perspective. The chapter will argue that the qualifications have been value-laden with prescriptions that have given white Europeans pride of place as the standard of Canadian identity. In short, residency status and citizenship have been socially constructed in a manner that subordinates certain ethnic groups and races (including the original inhabitants of this country) while elevating one racial group—white Europeans. We need to appreciate these social constructions of the ideal Canadian if we are to understand the largely marginalized location of African immigrants in Canadian society.

In the following discussion, I will explore how antecedent constructions of Africa have shaped the dominant society's ideas about Africans, the historical connections between Africans and Canada, and the circumstances under which people of African descent and African-born immigrants became a legally accepted and recognized community within Canada. I will also critically analyze the complexities surrounding the definition of African-Canadian and what it means for these Africans to be "hyphenated" Canadians. The last section addresses issues of community and intra-African zones of contestation. It engages in a discussion of how African-Canadians have devised mechanisms to provide mutual support for each other, sustain their cultural heritage, and maintain linkages with their societies of origin. It also examines some of the tensions and clashes that characterize what is by no means a homogeneous community.

PEOPLE OF AFRICAN DESCENT IN CANADA: REPRESENTATION, DENIGRATION, AND RESENTMENT

In order to understand who an African-Canadian is, and what that identity signifies, it is important to unpack the various constructions of "Africanness" across history and how the meanings emanating from those constructions have positioned Africans in Canadian society today. This problematization of "Africanness" from a historical perspective is necessary in view of the fact that identity is a relational construct that cannot be understood in isolation. The origins of the African-Canadian identity can, therefore, be understood only vis-à-vis other groups in this society. The focus of this section is on the historical representation of black Africans and people of black African descent. To capture this perception of Africans/Blacks/people of African descent, the section will look at these groups as a single analytical category, and the terms will be used interchangeably. This is because their race and common origins in Africa subject all of them to similar experiences and elicit similar kinds of response from other groups.

Kanneh (1998, p. 2), in a very articulate observation, draws a sharp connection between colonial anthropology, with its construction of a derogatory "other," and racism. She argues that analyses of works of "colonial anthropologists, travel narratives, ethnophilosophies and literary representations ... reveal how the histories of colonial narratives locate and imagine the concept of Africa." In the late 18th century, David Hume, for example, asserted that Blacks were intrinsically inferior to Whites (in Pieterse, 1992, p. 41). These outside textual descriptions of Africa, such as Joseph Conrad's *Heart of Darkness*, have conspired to give Africans a negative image among most Euro-Americans. It is, therefore, not surprising that J.S. Woodsworth, who was superintendent of the People's Mission in Winnipeg and a co-founder of the Cooperative Commonwealth Federation (CCF), uttered the following damning description of Blacks at the beginning of the 20th century: The "very qualities of intelligence and manliness which are the essentials for citizens in a democracy were systematically expunged from the negro race." He argued that the American Black was still "cursed with the burden of his African ancestry.... All travelers speak of their impulsiveness, strong sexual passion and lack of will power ... Hardly a desirable settler" (Troper, cited in Henry et al., 1995, p. 66).

These (mis)representations of Africa cannot be dismissed as uninformed constructions of eras gone by. They continue to shape how most Westerners view Africa. The continent is, for example, still depicted as a jungle, a description whose subtext seeks to portray its inhabitants in animalistic terms such as those uttered above by Woodsworth. The frustrations that these views generate among Africans is captured by Busia (1998, p. 275) who laments thus:

> A jungle is a tropical rain forest, and such forests cover less than 10 per cent of the entire continent. I have yet to find anyone who can tell me the difference between an 'adobe ranch house' and a 'mud hut', except that when a single-storey structure made of building blocks fabricated from sand is found in New Mexico it is called the former, and when found in Mali it is called the latter. It is depressing to begin at ground zero, even in university classrooms, but such is the tenacity of pernicious stereotypes.

The connection between people of African descent and Canada can be traced to the early 17th century when a black man, Matthew da Costa, was said to have worked with Champlain as an interpreter in some Canadian communities (Saney, 1998). In 1629, a native of Madagascar became the first slave to be brought to Canada directly from Africa (Henry et al., 1995, p. 64). Between then and the mid-19th century, various black communities sprang up as slaves accompanying their masters, fleeing slaves, and "free" slaves settled in different parts of Canada. Prejudice and animosity characterized the attitude of the white population toward these early black settlers. Segregation was the best that the former could do to accommodate the latter. In 1784, this resentment toward blacks reached a head when the first race-related riots in Canada took place in Nova Scotia. As a result of the riots, Blacks lost their property and were forced out of the communities of Shelburne and Birchtown.

The vehement opposition to black settlement in Nova Scotia mirrored the national mood and continued into the late 19th and early 20th centuries. In Alberta, for example, various organizations, such as the Edmonton Board of Trade and the Imperial Order of the Daughters of the Empire, registered their opposition to black migration to the province through petitions to the federal government. These organizations also built public support for their cause by fabricating lies about African criminal activity that perpetuated racial stereotypes and were meant to incite public resentment against black migration (Kelly, 1998, pp. 38–39). Blacks were not given any reprieve against these acts of discrimination when they sought recourse through the courts. A Quebec court decided in 1919 that racial discrimination was not inconsistent with public order or morality, while the Supreme Court of Canada ruled in a 1939 case that black customers could be refused services, arguing that the practice was "legally enforceable" (Henry et al., 1995, p. 66).

Unfortunately, these discriminatory acts and attitudes have largely been sanitized from mainstream Canadian history as the experiences and contributions of people of African descent have become part of the absent histories that define minority groups in the country (see Saney, 1998). Consequently, Canada has been erroneously depicted (through such symbols as the Underground Railway, protection of the Lion's paw, and the guiding North Star) as a sanctuary for beleaguered Blacks escaping the inhumanity of American slavery.

WHO IS AN AFRICAN-CANADIAN? EXPLORING CONFLICTING DEFINITIONS OF IDENTITY

As noted earlier, the literature on Africans in Canada, whose voluntary sojourn started in Africa, is very sparse. As a result, certain parts of the following discussion will draw from material based on the situation of

African immigrants in the United States, and the relationship between them and North American-born Blacks. I will then extrapolate from applicable parts of that material to make deductions about African-Canadian identity.

The designation "African-Canadian," on the surface, suggests an unquestionable signifier of a monolithic group of people of African ancestry. The term is, however, more convoluted and complex than it appears, and there is no consensus about who is a part of this group. The lack of concurrence about interpretations of who is covered by the term results from the fact that "Africanness" as an identity is defined by several criteria that are not necessarily congruent. In the ensuing discussion, I provide a framework that isolates four approaches by which the identity of Africanness, and hence African-Canadianess, is defined or rejected. These are the immigration authorities' approach; the "Black equals African/African equals Black" approach; the self-exclusion approach; and the "authentic African" approach.

From the perspective of the immigration authorities' approach (which reflects the Canadian state's view), African-Canadians are immigrants who directly trace their country of origin to the African continent. This approach to classification, however, makes the term a geographical construct. This definition eliminates those for whom the identity of Africanness transcends geographical boundaries to encompass a shared historical, spiritual, ancestral, and cultural ethos.

Critics of this approach argue that "Africanness" is an innate identity that should not be limited by geographical confines. This view emanates especially from people who, while they cannot identify their specific roots in Africa, feel that they have spiritual and ancestral connections to the continent in a manner that gives them a legitimate place in the community of Africans and, by extension, of African-Canadians. African-Canadians therefore include descendants of slaves who have been domiciled in Canada since the 17th century.

This parallels the concept of "African-American" in the United States. This interpretation of the phrase also includes Blacks from the Caribbean, South America, etc. whose geneological links to the continent are difficult to trace.

On the basis of this view, others bring a racial dimension to the definition of African identity, namely the "Black equals African/African equals Black" approach. For this group, the African identity is shared by all black people, both on the continent and in the Diaspora, irrespective of where their sojourn to Canada may have begun. In this view, then, African is equated to Black. For this group, therefore, black people in the Diaspora should be recognized as Africans. In fact, some go as far as to argue that they are more qualified to be called African-Canadians than non-Blacks who may be recent immigrants from Africa but whose ancestral roots do not go as deep as those of Blacks in the Diaspora. This view is rooted in Anderson's (1991) notion of an "imagined community,"

which, in this case, comes from a belief in and expression of a black consciousness and an identification with Africa. These internalized linkages
to the continent define their African-Canadian heritage.

Whilst there are definitely some historical and cultural affinities
between these groups and recent immigrants from Africa, there is no
denying the fact that they are, indeed, different in significant ways
(Lewinberg, 1999, p. 195). Adeleke (1998) argues that the notion of a
Pan-African identity is flawed. He insists that the worlds that continental
Africans and non-African-born Blacks in the Diaspora experience, as well
as the struggles they are engaged in, are fundamentally different. He
argues that "[r]egardless of the degree of African cultural retentions,
regardless of how far Black Americans went in changing their names and
wearing African clothes, they remain in large part, products of the
American historical experience, an experience that has left its mark
indelibly on black American culture and identity" (Adeleke, 1998, p. 187).

Jones (1995) observes that a critical variable that distinguishes North
American Blacks is their inability to identify their ethnic roots in Africa,
which were lost as a result of the horrors of slavery. This situation, he
posits, cut off native African-Americans from their African origins and
immersed them in another reality that redefined them differently from
the recent African immigrants. While these African migrants can clearly
define their ethnic roots, and everything that comes with it (e.g., mother
tongue), their African-American cousins have to limit their signifiers of
identity to a nebulous construct—Africa as a geographical entity, a racial
origin, and a cultural imagination.

The differences in the experiences and, hence, perspectives of
African-born and diasporic Blacks of African descent create conflicts
between the two groups that the notion of a common identity tends to
ignore. One area where these conflicts are evident has to do with the
unpleasant attitude that some North American-born Blacks display
toward recent African immigrants with regard to economic opportunities
and social struggles. In the context of economic opportunities, the
former resent the fact that the latter, who were not participants in civil
rights struggles for socioeconomic and political opportunity, are now
equal beneficiaries of the fruits of those struggles (see Adeleke, 1998).
This tension, based on a nativistic consciousness, is heightened by the
fact that the African immigrants are generally better educated and hence
more employable than their native North American counterparts (see
Djamba, 1999). With respect to social struggles, North American Blacks
are incensed that African immigrants do not usually display an appre-
ciable level of passion for issues that are of concern to the former community. This lack of passion, it is argued, is due to the fact that the
African-born has not experienced, and so does not understand, the historical struggles of their cousins born on this side of the Atlantic.

Based on the preceding observations, Kanneh (1998, p. viii) contends that "modern African-American pan-Africanisms appropriate ideas

of 'Africa' for American agendas," but they tend not to engage with the African reality, and their primary loyalty is not to the continent. Echoes of the difference that recent African immigrants recognize between themselves and their diasporic cousins is illustrated by the main character in Alice Walker's *Possessing the Secrets of Joy* (1992, p. 17): "I felt negated by the realization that even my psychiatrist could not see that I was African. That to him all black people were Negroes." These distinctions, which characterize the relationship between African immigrants and diasporic blacks, threaten the pan-Africanist and cultural nationalist perspective of the Afrocentric paradigm (see Asante, 1990). This paradigm is not only engaged in a political project of unity between diasporic blacks and continental Africans but also argues that they have a shared identity, common traditions, and similar experiences vis-à-vis Euro-American imperalism and domination.

The problem with the "Black equals African/African equals Black" conception is that it is an exclusionary construct. It does not take cognizance of those who may not be black but whose traceable historical, cultural, and cultural origins may be in Africa. Examples of these groups are East Indians and Whites from Eastern and Southern Africa who have known no other place of origin but Africa. Whilst these groups may not have originated in Africa as a racial or ethnic community, they may have no traceable origin to any other place but the continent. This may be where they call home and where they trace their roots. Out of the about 247 240 people who identified themselves as Africans in the 1996 Canadian census, about 30 percent were Blacks, 27 percent Whites, 20 percent South Asian, and the remaining 23 percent comprised other races (Statistics Canada, 1996). The "Black equals African/African equals Black" approach, therefore, effectively dismisses the African origins of 75 percent of African immigrants in Canada.

We now turn to the third approach to identity—the self-exclusion approach. There are two strands in this approach. The first has to do with people who originate geographically from Africa, while the second deals with children of African immigrants. What is at play in the first strand is a reversal of the scenario above where non-black Africans assert their avowed ties to the continent in spite of ascribed designations that seek to deprive them of that identity. It is significant to note that Blacks are not the only critics of the immigration authorities' notion of an African. In fact, there are non-Blacks from Africa who refuse to be identified as African for a variety of reasons. Some non-Blacks seem to contest their portrayal as African because, for them, race is a more important factor in the construction of identity than geographical origin. A number of black Africans have recounted incidents where North African Arabs, East and Southern African Indians, as well as white Southern Africans have refused to describe themselves as Africans and have made the subtle distinction between being African and being from Africa.

The second strand of the self-exclusion approach introduces another dimension to the already complicated definitional issues surrounding the designation of African-Canadian. This dimension is brought to the fore when identity is analyzed with a special focus on children of African immigrants. Such an analysis quickly reveals a tension between ascribed and avowed identities among these individuals and groups. The tension stems from the fact that even though some of these people may have genealogical ties to the continent, they do not necessary feel a part of that group. They do not perceive themselves as sharing a common identity with their progenitors who have their origins in the continent. They see themselves primarily as Canadian, since their sense of self is constructed from the peculiar experiences that they have had in Canada, which may, in fact, be totally different from what characterizes an authentic African experience. Consequently, the definition of these individuals as African, based solely on the origins of their forebears or on the colour of their skin may appear inaccurate to them.

In addition to the above-mentioned approaches is the "authentic African" approach. It is valuable in helping us to understand the perceptions that individuals and groups, who fit into the immigration authorities' definition, have about each other's "Africanness." These perceptions are based on a supposedly measurable standard of "authentic Africanness." In spite of arguments that there is no common African worldview (e.g., Appiah, 1992), there is a general perception that all African cultures share a fundamental ethos that is imbibed by all (i.e., there are certain values that are supposed to be shared by all Africans). This perspective is consonant with Jahn's notion of a spiritual or philosophical "common denominator" of Africanness, which is expressed in a Bantu worldview that is shared by all of sub-Saharan Africa (Jahn, 1961). Abraham (1962, p. 42) also argues that "there is a type of African culture ... this type finds expression in the art, the ethics and morality, the literary and the religious traditions, and also the social traditions of the people." Any African who deviates from this culture is not considered a true embodiment of what it means to be an "authentic African." Such deviation is sometimes construed as a rejection of one's identity or its subordination to the dominant culture. In short, there is a continuum of Africanness in which the most authentic form is manifested in a static preservation of cultural values and norms. Static preservation and adherence to the cultural values and social norms that characterize African societies is, therefore, a key manifestation of what it means to be a true African.

This "authentic African" approach has implications for Canadian-born children of African immigrants. In spite of the fact that some of these children reject an African identity, most of them are more likely to identify in some way with Africa. Based on the "authentic African" approach, however, some first-generation African immigrants do not consider these children to be African enough. This denial of

Africanness is based on the view that the children do not exhibit those cultural characteristics that "truly" define an African, such as knowledge of indigenous African languages, rituals, etc. As Ngugi Wa Thiong'o argues in *Decolonising the Mind* (1987), language and culture are considered to be defining characteristics of a people and a nation. "Language as culture," he contends, "is the collective memory bank of a people's experience in history" (p. 15). Based on this understanding, some Africans have argued that since some of those born in the Diaspora cannot speak indigenous African languages, lack a deep understanding of the African experience, or do not express the ritual forms of the continent, they are more Canadian than African and so cannot legitimately claim an African identity.

Adeleke (1998), for instance, argues that there is a "sovereign power" of African culture that has the force of authority and imposes obligations and responsibilities. Adherence to the dictates of this "sovereign power" is a core element in his definition of African identity. He provides the following illustration to support his argument. According to him, there is general agreement among Africans that children, no matter the legal definition of adulthood, are under the perpetual authority of their parents and so must obey them at all times. Children born to first-generation African immigrants, however, tend to imbibe a different cultural ethos that gives them legal control over their lives when they reach the age of majority. They find the African norms suppressive, refuse to abide by them, and therefore get caught up in intra-personal conflicts and acts of resistance that "emotional transnationalism" brings (Rumbaut, 1997, p. 337). In the view of Africans like Adeleke, this resistance to the "sovereign power" of African culture disqualifies these children from claiming an authentic African identity, even if they profess to be Africans.

Proponents of the "authentic African" approach have, at least, one shortcoming. They suggest that in order to qualify as genuine African-Canadians, all African migrants and their children need to conform to a monolithic worldview, which involves shared values and attitudes. Such a criterion is an attempt to slot all these people into a category that presumes commonalities in backgrounds, historical experiences, worldviews, and so on. Such a presumption overlooks the significant diversity that characterizes Africans, based on race, region, religion, ethnicity, gender, etc. It is important, when we talk about African-Canadians, to recognize these sub-identities and their impact on the definition of how people conceptualize themselves as Africans, the collaborations and contestations between various groups, and their relationship to the meta-identity of "African." These issues will be explored further in the last section of the chapter.

The purpose of the preceding discussion has been to bring out the complexities and subjectivities that surround the designation

"African-Canadian" and to draw attention to the diversity within that group no matter what definition is used. It is quite clear that the debate about the acceptable criteria for "Africanness" will not end any time soon. For the purposes of this essay, however, I have chosen to limit my definition of African-Canadians to first-generation, black, sub-Saharan Africans who have immigrated to Canada in the last three decades and who still have identifiable geneological links to the continent. This is because they constitute the only group in the preceding discussion whose claim to "Africanness" elicits the least, if any, dispute.

AFRICAN-BORN CANADIANS: IMMIGRATION AND THE CHALLENGES OF INTEGRATION

Extensive legal immigration to Canada of those who designate themselves "African," without having had any links to slavery, did not start until the late 1960s at the earliest. This is due to the fact that, until that time, official immigration policy reflected the sentiments of mainstream white society that were discussed earlier. Consequently, immigration laws were deeply steeped in racist, Eurocentric prescriptions for qualification (see Troper and Weinfeld, 1999; Henry et al., 1995, pp. 72–78). While these policies did affect peoples from all areas that were not part of the traditional European sources of immigration, it is clear that that the situation of Africans was even worse. They were, after all, the most likely to "make a fundamental alteration in the character of our population," something that Prime Minister King was not comfortable with (see Troper, 1997). Calliste (1994) provides an illustration of the bogus excuses that were used by immigration officials in the 1950s to justify discrimination against people of African descent and other minorities:

> [C]oloured people ... don't assimilate readily and pretty much vegetate to a low standard of living ... many cannot adapt themselves to our climatic conditions [p. 133].... There are certain countries from which immigration is encouraged and certain races of people as suited [Canada] and its conditions, but Africans no matter where they are from are not among the races sought, and, hence, Africans no matter from what country they come are in common with the uninvited races, not admitted....
> (pp. 35–36)

After 1967, however, a new *Immigration Act* that incorporated a point system (see Henry et al., 1995, p. 75) opened the doors for hitherto undesirable non-European groups to become Canadian residents. These developments in immigration policy were not a voluntary act of magnanimity by Canadian authorities but were necessitated by numerous extraneous factors. These included a decline in the number of skilled European workers, who were no longer attracted to North America because they had bright opportunities on their own continent. This shortage compelled Canada to look elsewhere for substitute labour. There was also pressure from minority and civil liberty groups in Canada who wanted to see a change in immigration policy that was non-discriminatory. Furthermore, state officials were sensitive to the damage that the country's reputation had suffered as a result of its inhumane treatment of Japanese Canadians and Jewish refugees during World War II. Thus, they thought it politically prudent to amend immigration policies in order not to ride against the prevailing tide of international efforts at eradicating racism.

As a result of this new dispensation, the number of African-born immigrants admitted into Canada over the period 1961–96 increased progressively from the 4940 who had entered the country before 1961 (Table 1).

TABLE 1
Migration of Africans into Canada: 1961–96

1961–70	25 680
1971–80	58 150
1981–90	64 265
1991–96	76 260

Source: Statistics Canada, 1996 Census.

This increase does not, however, mean that discriminatory practices were eliminated altogether. What Troper and Weinfeld (1999) call "coded racism" served, and continues, to limit Africans' ability to avail themselves of Canadian residency to an extent far greater than is probably the case with other ethnic minority groups. After all, the motivation behind the revision of the racist immigration policies did not emanate from a sudden epiphany about the equality of all races but was necessitated by political and economic expediency (Troper, 1997, p. 195). In fact, just after the policy changes in the late 1960s, racial discrimination in immigration matters persisted. While not one white immigrant who disembarked at the Toronto International Airport in 1967 was asked to post a bond, every single non-white immigrant was required to do so (Boyko, 1995, p. 168).

Over three decades later, while entry of Africans into Canada has become less premised on overt acts of discrimination, it nonetheless remains a difficult experience. The emphasis, in Canadian policy, on entrepreneurial and family class immigrants, and the de-emphasis on the assisted relatives category means that Africans will be constrained in their ability to avail themselves of immigration opportunities (Konadu-Agyemang, 1999). Most of them do not have the capital to qualify as entrepreneurs, and those who do not have parents, spouses, or children in Canada cannot apply under the family class option. The chances of entering Canada as an independent applicant, when one files an application in Africa, are very slim. Canadian immigration officials there are perceived as prejudiced against African migration to Canada, because they see potential immigrants as "economic refugees" seeking to sponge off Canadian society. The authorities also use their discretionary power to deny applications on the basis that the applicants are not adaptable to life in Canada. This judgment is rendered especially in the case of applicants who have never travelled outside the continent. The experience of similar people who have been able to come to Canada, however, shows that that criterion is not a good measure of adaptability.

In view of the above-mentioned impediments, a large number of Africans, like other minority groups facing similar situations, has been compelled to devise ingenuous ways of entering this country. The most common of these is claiming refugee status, even by those who may not be genuine refugees. That is, they are neither victims of civil strife nor calamities of nature, and they are not being persecuted in any way. As Konadu-Agyemang (1999, p. 404–405) points out, this

> should be seen as a coping mechanism devised by Africans to deal with an international migration system which does not offer them ample opportunities to migrate in the conventional way, a situation which leads to an overrepresentation of Africans in the refugee and undocumented aliens stream and woeful underrepresentation in the landed immigrant (for Canada) and permanent resident category.

Now let us move the discussion to the situation, within Canadian society, of those who are able to enter this country. How Canadian are these African immigrants? Troper and Weinfeld (1999, p. 4) note that, following the coming into force of Canadian citizenship in 1947, "the state [for the first time] addressed the legal equality of all, irrespective of heritage, time of arrival in Canada, religion, languages spoken, and of any proprietary claim that any group might make to being more Canadian than any other." It is worth pointing out, however, that while citizenship in Canada derives from law, nationality appears to be premised on race or ethnicity. Africans are constantly reminded that they are not Canadian enough in their interactions, not only with members of the dominant Euro-Canadian culture but also, ironically, with other ethnic minorities as well.

Notwithstanding the Canadian state's official stance on multiculturalism and the value of different cultures living in unified diversity (Troper and Weinfeld, 1999, p. 9), African immigrants are made aware of their lack of "authentic Canadian" stock by such questions as "where are you originally from?" While this question may be asked without malice, the frequency with which it is directed at Africans, even when they identify themselves as Canadian, creates a feeling among them that no matter how much they identify with this country, they and their children will always be seen as outsiders. Philip (1992, p. 16) captures these feelings when she says:

> Being born elsewhere, having been fashioned in a different culture, some of us may always feel "othered," but then there are those—our children, nephews, nieces, grandchildren—born here, who are as Canadian as snow and ice, and yet, merely because of their darker skins, are made to feel "othered."

Many Africans have recounted experiences where they have been told to "go home" because their expressions of their African identity were not considered acceptable in a society that is ostensibly a mosaic of cultures. It has been documented in Edmonton, for example, that African students' subjection to racist attitudes and behaviours far exceeds that of any other ethnic or racial group (in Kelly, 1998, p. 16). A related report from Ontario confirms that Blacks are the most discriminated against in all facets of social life (Lewis, 1992, p. 2, cited in Kelly, 1998). What we see then is a dialectical contradiction that pits the legalism of citizenship with the reality of racial and ethnic qualifiers of citizenship. Consequently, the idea of a harmonious pluralism of diverse cultures that undergirds the *Canadian Multicultural Act* of 1988, does not seem to have found resonance within the dominant culture. Many African-Canadians, therefore, feel that their identity as Canadians is devalued in their socioeconomic interactions with the rest of society.

They argue that whilst they do not voice any misgivings toward affective and cultural expressions by members of the dominant white majority to their English, Irish, or German heritage, the reaction within the dominant group to similar expressions among African-Canadians is not always pleasant. Some members of mainstream groups perceive the expression of African worldviews and attitudes, which may be different from their own, as tantamount to an adulteration of an ostensibly definable Canadian culture. A 1993 poll validates the Africans' argument and reflects intolerance for "foreign" (i.e., minority) cultures within the dominant population. It shows that 72 percent of Canadians wanted a movement away from multiculturalism toward requiring immigrants to assimilate "Canada's values and ways of life" (cited in Roy, 1995, p. 207). This attitude is based largely on the premise that anything short of cultural suicide by minority groups disqualifies them from becoming full-fledged members of their host societies (see Schutte, 1998, pp. 58–59). It also flows from the spurious view that preservation of minority cultures weakens immigrants' affinity to their new homes. In fact, there is evidence to the contrary that indicates that "non-English- and non-French-speaking immigrants embrace Canadian citizenship in proportionately much higher numbers than do immigrants from the United States or Britain" (Troper and Wienfeld, 1999, p. 16).

One of the areas where the two parts of the hyphenated identity of African immigrants seems to come into constant conflict is with respect to cultural norms, values, and practices, when these do not dovetail neatly into what the dominant culture considers to be acceptable or appropriate. What makes this arena of contestation very tense is the fact that some of these cultural phenomena may be considered illegal, based on an ostensibly universal standard of propriety. It is the zone where there is a clash between respect for diverse cultural expressions and their subordination to a presumably higher standard. Most Africans, for example, do not see anything wrong with meting out corporal punishment to children or scolding them loudly as a form of discipline. In mainstream Canadian society, however, these acts are generally labelled child abuse and African-Canadian parents risk losing custody of their children or facing legal charges if they do not conform. There is, at once, a recognition of the rights of different cultures to celebrate their heritage and retain the practices that sustain it and an abrogation of those rights once they conflict with the values of the dominant culture. The African values are then portrayed, in postimperial Western cultural terms, as primitive and requiring adjustment to the modernity of mainstream society (Bennett, 1998).

When new immigrants come to Canada, they are welcomed to their "new home" through the rituals of landing and citizenship. For most African-Canadians, however, there is always a sense of not really being at home in this country. In the midst of their devaluation and marginalization within mainstream society, the only place where Africans feel at home is back on the continent, where they are not constantly "othered" and denigrated. Most feel that they get their greatest sense of dignity when they are with their own kind. As Busia (1998, p. 273) laments:

> When you are born in a land where everyone seems made in your likeness, you do not, as a group, have to learn strategies of self-affirmation and self-love to counter the opposing, culturally dominant force of mirrors in which you don't figure, have no reflection, or are given to images of yourself which do not in any way reflect the selves you see inside.

This explains why a lot of Africans tend to socialize more with other Africans than with other ethnic groups and feel most comfortable within social spaces that are controlled by themselves (see Fanon, 1967, p. 82; Stodolska, 1998, p. 544). It is also a big part of why they maintain strong ties to their places of origin not only emotionally but also through culturally obligatory acts. The latter include remitting their families back home, attending and/or contributing to funerals at home, replicating traditional rituals here, etc.

The belief that one can find ultimate solace only in the midst of one's own people explains why a number of Africans, albeit a decreasing number, prefer to be buried in their hometowns if financial resources allow. The most vivid representation of this spiritual attachment is symbolized by the phenomenon whereby most first-generation African-Canadians set as one of their primary objectives the construction of a house in their countries of origin. The need to realize this objective remains very important even though they know that they might never live there permanently.

There is overwhelming documentation to support the view that ethnic minorities are subject to workplace discrimination in a variety of ways—being paid less for equal work, being denied promotions, etc. (see Stodolska, 1998, p. 545; Henry et al., 1995, pp. 92–96). While indicating that increased discrimination cannot offer full explanation for the decline in the absorption of recent immigrants into the Canadian labour market, Bloom et al. (1995) do not rule it out as a possible reason. They acknowledge that post-1980 immigration saw a shift in composition toward large numbers of developing-country immigrants, who are likely to be visible minorities and hence more likely to be discriminated against (Bloom et al., 1995, p. 1000).

Evidence has been adduced, in Canada, to support the thesis of employment discrimination in the particular case of African immigrants and other Blacks (see Croucher, 1997, p. 328; Torczyner, 1997). Various studies in the United States show that African immigrants are among the most highly educated immigrant populations there (Djamba, 1999, p. 213). It is estimated that more than 60 percent of people from the largest African immigrant groups in that country (Ghanaians, South Africans, and Egyptians) have a tertiary education (Carrington and Detragiache, 1999, p. 46). The situation is similar in Canada because educational levels are critical determinants in granting permanent resident status in the independent applicant category (see Hou and Balakrishnan, 1996). For a lot of these highly qualified individuals, however, the prospects of securing jobs commensurate with their qualifications remain very bleak. There is widespread perception among African-Canadians that their continent of origin and the racist stereotypes that it engenders in Canada constrain their employment opportunities. It is true that graduates from outside Canada are generally not accorded the same recognition as their Canadian-educated counterparts. But it must be pointed out that African certificates tend to be on the bottom rungs of the accreditation hierarchy.

While there is no evidence that African students who continue their education in Canada are less capable than their Canadian counterparts, there is a tendency among employers not to value certificates awarded in their countries of origin. This attitude can be attributed in large measure to the low intellectual capabilities accorded Africans as a result of some of the stereotypes that were discussed earlier. The logic then is that certificates from there cannot be equivalent to those awarded in Canada. Thus, in spite of the fact that higher institutions on the continent are internationally accredited by organizations such as the Association of

Commonwealth Universities (of which Canada is a member), the view among most employers is that degrees from those institutions are less valuable than those handed out by Canadian universities. Furthermore, any job experience gained in Africa is either ignored or played down. Consequently, most immigrants suffer unfair earning penalties (see Stelcner and Kyriazis, 1995). Africa-educated female graduates, for example, suffer an earning penalty of about 16.4 percent relative to their compatriots educated in Canada. While Canadian-educated, African-born men may have some edge over those educated elsewhere in terms of securing jobs, they are still likely to earn 16.2 per cent less than their Canadian-born white counterparts with the same level of qualification (Pendakur and Pendakur, 1998, p. 531). It is worth noting that African-Canadians' reactions to employment discrimination and the nature of their integration into the Canadian labour market depends very much on their level of education. Their reactions support Stein's hypothesis, according to which immigrants "entering the labour market in occupational categories equivalent or superior ... to those occupied in their country of origin will adapt more easily than [those] ... who do not" (cited in Dorais, 1991, p. 552). Thus, while those Africans with less education may be content with the jobs that they have, highly qualified Africans are invariably very frustrated by the difficulty of securing jobs and the absence of job satisfaction that comes with employment in positions that are not commensurate with their qualifications.

Social and economic opportunities for most first-generation African immigrants are further constrained by the "heavy" accents that characterize their spoken English or French. While acknowledging the difficulty involved in readily understanding what an individual with a heavy accent may be saying, it is still possible to grasp what they are saying if the interactant is willing to listen attentively and to pose follow-up questions. Africans, for example, say that even though they find North American accents to be quite different from what they were used to in their places of origin, they still make a special effort to understand them. In a lot of cases, however, most members of the dominant language groups seem unwilling to make this effort. As a result, "the native speaker will treat the non-native speaker as if she were linguistically or intellectually incompetent. From the perception 'I don't immediately understand what the other is saying,' the dominant speaker will draw the invalid conclusion, 'the other is speaking nonsense,' 'the other is incompetent,' the other does not belong here,' and so on" (Schutte, 1998, p. 63). These conclusions do not only denigrate and silence other voices based on the norms of dominant language groups but also mean that an African immigrant may not get a job that he/she is otherwise qualified for or may not have access to a particular service. I have encountered a number of African-Canadians who have been denied jobs, or specific positions within organizations, because employers want to save clients the trouble of dealing with their accents.

THE AFRICAN-CANADIAN COMMUNITY: ARENAS OF EMPATHY AND CONTESTATION

One of the means by which Africans have tried to provide mutual support for each other and to maintain links to their societies of origin is through the establishment of ethnic and/or country associations. These associations help to preserve indigenous symbols of identity, values, and histories as well as supporting development in their countries of origin.

This collaboration notwithstanding, we must not lose sight of the differences within the African-Canadian community. Similar to what Henry (1994) and Langer (1998) found in relation to other immigrant groups in Canada, these African associations are varied, heterogeneous, and, in some cases, antagonistic to each other. This reality reflects the postmodernist critique of "community as consensus" and shows that "each of us is a member of many shifting communities, each of which establishes, for each of its members, multiple social identities" (Barbara Hermstein Smith, cited in Bennett, 1998, p. 5). Examples of "internal ethnicity" can be found between Hutus and Tutsis in the Rwandese community, Asantes and Ewes in the Ghanaian-Canadian community (see Sorenson, 1991). These differences replicate, in Canada, the animosities, mutual suspicions, and conflicts that characterize these ethnic groups in their countries of origin.

Ethnic differences are not the only areas of contestation among African-Canadians. Others have been shaped by the clash between dominant African worldviews and those of the host society. Of particular significance is the resistance that immigrant African women are exhibiting toward the gendered social constructs that have subordinated them. In Canada, these women are beginning to assert their autonomy. This assertion is influenced by an admittedly still evolving Canadian world view of gender equality, legal protection for women, and supportive public policies. The African women's acts of resistance and the attendant cultural conflicts that they spawn are captured by the following observation, which is by no means limited to Ghanaian- Canadians:

> Among Ghanaian men and women in Toronto there is a deep contestation over gender relations and an evolving consciousness among women. A persistent complaint is that the Canadian state is "spoiling" the women by making them conscious of their rights and that this consciousness is leading to high divorce rates. Men also contend that state benefits available to unmarried women with children ... undermine the authority and power of husbands to maintain particular kinds of relations with their wives. Indeed, some men believe there has been a complete reversal of roles in Canada, claiming that "women have become men, and men have become women." Whereas some men contend that physical spousal abuse is a cultural right in Ghana, in

Canada it can lead to ejection from home, restraining orders, and jail time. (Manuh, 1998, p. 487)

It is important not to conclude that these women, and other Africans who imbibe host culture norms, want to discard all their African traditions. In fact, they do cherish and wish to preserve a significant amount of their original cultures. Consequently, they experience deep intrapersonal conflicts as they try to negotiate their existence around the values of the two cultural worlds—a defining characteristic of situations where "culture's in between" (see Bhabha, 1998).

CONCLUSION

An overwhelming majority of African-Canadians, if not all, believe that the second part of their "hyphenated" identity is a matter of convenience both for themselves and for Canadian political authorities who promote the idea of a multicultural society. The convenience for the Africans stems from their recognition that obtaining legal status in Canada is a *sine qua non* if they are to function within this country with a minimum level of legal protection and sociopolitical entitlement. Most have concluded, based on a variety of experiences in this country, that in spite of their legal equality to other groups, they are seen first and foremost as Africans and hence as outsiders. The African origins of these immigrants also determine the level of legitimacy and authoritative voice that they are accorded in a variety of settings.

In spite of their common experience of marginalization and being "othered," however, it would be erroneous to present African-Canadians as a single, homogenous community. As discussed above, there are differences within the community that derive from a variety of sources. Some are imports into Canada of historical animosities and tensions that have shaped relations among various groups in Africa. Cultural clashes have also arisen as some immigrants imbibe aspects of the host culture that are at variance with their home cultures and contest the positions of others who continue to cling religiously to their indigenous traditions.

As African immigrants become a visible part of the Canadian landscape, it is important that the rest of society understands their history in this country, the social constructions that have shaped that history, and the specific features that characterize the African-Canadian community. Such a movement toward understanding their circumstances and appreciating who they are will then give African-Canadians a sense of belonging, encourage them to seek partnership with other segments of society, and provide them with the environment to develop their potential in ways that will bring benefits to society as a whole.

REFERENCES

Abraham W.E. (1962). *The mind of Africa*. Chicago, IL: University of Chicago Press.

Adeleke Tunde. (1998). Black Americans, Africa and history: A reassessment of the PanAfrican and identity paradigms. *Western Journal of Black Studies* 22(3), 182–94.

Anderson, Benedict. (1991). *Imagined communities: Reflections on the origin and spread of nationalism*. London: Verso.

Appiah, Kwame A. (1992). *In my father's house: Africa in the philosophy of culture*. New York, Oxford: Oxford University Press.

Asante, Molefi K. (1990). *Kemet, afrocentricity and knowledge*. Trenton, N.J.: Africa World Press.

Bennett, David. (1998). Introduction. In David Bennett (ed.), *Multicultural states: Rethinking difference and identity* (pp. 1–25). London and New York: Routledge.

Bhabha, Homi. (1998). Culture's in between. In David Bennett (ed.), *Multicultural states: Rethinking difference and identity* (pp. 29–36). London and New York: Routledge.

Bloom, David E., G. Grenier, and M. Gunderson. (1995). The changing labour market position of Canadian immigrants. *Canadian Journal of Economics*, 28 (4b), 987–1001.

Boyko, John. (1995). *Last step to freedom: The evolution of Canadian racism*. Winnipeg: Watson and Dwyer.

Busia, Abena. (1998). Relocations—Rethinking Britain from Accra, New York, and the Map Room of the British Museum. In David Bennett (ed.), *Multicultural states: Rethinking difference and identity* (pp. 267–81). London and New York: Routledge.

Calliste, Agnes. (1994). Race, gender and Canadian immigration policy: Blacks from the Caribbean, 1900–1932. *Journal of Canadian Studies* 28(4), 131–48.

Carrington, William J. and E. Detragiache. (1999, June). How extensive is the brain drain? *Finance and Development*, pp. 46–49.

Croucher, Shiela L. (1997). Constructing the image of ethnic harmony in Toronto, Canada: The politics of problem definition and nondefinition. *Urban Affairs Review* 32(3), 319–34.

Djamba, Yanyi K. (1999). African immigrants in the United States: A sociodemographic profile in comparison to native Blacks. *Journal of Asian and African Studies*, 34(2), 210–15.

Dorais, Louis-Jacques. (1991). Refugee adaptation and community structure: The Indochinese in Quebec City, Canada. *International Migration Review*, 25(3), 551–573.

Dunn, Robert. (1998). *Identity crisis: A social critique of postmodernity.* Minneapolis and London: University of Minnesota Press.

Fannon, Frantz. (1967). *Black skins white masks.* New York: Grove Cross.

Henry, Francis. (1994). *The Caribbean diaspora in Toronto: Learning to live with racism.* Toronto: University of Toronto Press.

Henry, Frances, C. Tator, W. Mattis, and T. Rees. (1995). *The colour of democracy: Racism in Canadian society.* Toronto: Harcourt Brace and Company Canada.

Hou, Feng and T.R. Balakrishnan. (1996). The integration of visible minorities in contemporary Canadian society. *Canadian Journal of Sociology* 21(3), 307–26.

Jahn, Janheinz. (1961). *Muntu: An outline of neo-African culture.* London: Faber and Faber.

Jones, Rhett. (1995). Why pan-Africanism failed: Blackness and international relations, *The Griot* 14(1), 54–61.

Kanneh, Kadiatu. (1998). *African identities: Race, nation and culture in ethnography, pan-Africanisms and black literatures.* London and New York: Routledge, p. 32.

Karnik, N.S. (1998). Rwanda and the media: imagery, war and refuge. *Review of African Political Economy,* no. 78, pp. 611–23.

Kelly, Jennifer, (1998). *Under the gaze: Learning to be black in white society.* Halifax: Fernwood Publishing.

Konadu-Agyemang, Kwadwo. (1999). Characteristics and migration experience of Africans in Canada with specific reference to Ghananians in Greater Toronto. *Canadian Geographer* 43(4), 400–14.

Langer, Beryl. (1998). Globalisation and the myth of the ethnic community: Salvadoran refugees in multicultural states. In David Bennett (ed.), *Multicultural states: Rethinking difference and identity* (pp. 163–77). London and New York: Routledge.

Lewinberg, Adam. (1999). The black polity and the Ontario NDP Government. In Harold Troper and Morton Weinfeld (eds.), *Ethnicity, Politics, and Public Policy: Case Studies in Canadian Diversity* (pp. 193–223). Toronto, Buffalo, and London: University of Toronto Press.

Ley, David. (1999). Myths and meanings of immigration and the metropolis. *Canadian Geographer* 43(1), 2–19.

Manuh, Takyiwaa. (1998). Ghanaians, Ghanaian Canadians, and Asantes: Citizenship and identity among migrants in Toronto. *Africa Today* 45(3–4), 481–94.

Ngugi Wa Thiong'o. (1987). *Decolonising the mind: The politics of language in African literature.* London: James Curry.

Pendakur, Kristina and R. Pendakur. (1998). The colour of money: Earnings differentials among ethnic groups in Canada. *Canadian Journal of Economics,* 31(3), 518–48.

Philip, Marlene N. (1992). *Frontiers: Essays and writings on racism and culture.* Ontario: Mercury.

Pieterse, Jan N. (1992). *White on black: Images of Africa and blacks in western popular culture.* New Haven: Yale University Press.

Roy, Patricia E. (1995). The fifth force: Multiculturalism and the english Canadian identity. *Annals of the American Academy of Political and Social Science, 199–209.*

Rumbaut, Ruben G. (1997). Introduction: Immigration and incorporation. *Sociological Perspectives,* 40(3), 333–38.

Saney, Isaac. (1998). The black Nova Scotian odyssey: A chronology. *Race and Class,* 40(1), 78–91.

Schutte, Ofelia. (1998). Cultural alterity: Cross-cultural communication and feminist theory in North–South contexts. *Hypatia,* 13(2), 53–71.

Sorenson, John. (1991). Politics of social identity: "Ethiopians" in Canada. *Journal of Ethnic Studies,* 19(1), 67–86.

Statistics Canada. (1996). *1996 Census.* Ottawa: Statistics Canada.

Stelcner, Morton and Nota Kyriazis. (1995). An empirical analysis of earnings among ethnic groups in Canada. *International Journal of Contemporary Sociology,* 32(1), 41–79.

Stodolska, Monika. (1998). Assimilation and leisure constraints: Dynamics of constraints on leisure in immigrant populations. *Journal of Leisure Research,* 30(4), 521–51.

Torczyner, James. (1997). *Diversity, mobility, and change: The dynamics of black communities in Canada.* Montreal: McGill Consortium for Ethnicity and Strategic Social Planning.

Troper, Harold. (1997). Canada's immigration policy since 1945. In David Taras and Beverly Rasporich (eds.), *A passion for identity: An introduction to Canadian Studies* (3rd Edition) (pp. 189–206). Toronto: Nelson.

Troper, Harold and Harold Weinfeld. (1999). Diversity in Canada. In Harold Troper and Moreton Weinfeld (eds.), *Ethnicity, politics, and public policy: Case studies in Canadian diversity* (pp. 3–25). Toronto: University of Toronto Press.

Walker, Alice. (1992). *Possessing the secret of joy.* London: Jonathan Cape.

Weiner, Myron. (1996). Nations without borders: The gifts of folk gone abroad. *Foreign Affairs* 75(2), 128–34.

Workers of the world. (1997, November 1). *The Economist,* 81–82.

FURTHER READING

Henry, Frances, C. Tator, W. Mattis, and T. Rees. (1995). *The Colour of Democracy: Racism in Canadian Society.* Toronto: Harcourt Brace and Company Canada.

Konadu-Agyemang, Kwadwo. (1999). Characteristics and migration experience of Africans in Canada with specific reference to Ghanaians in Greater Toronto, *Canadian Geographer* 43(4), 400–14.

Manuh, Takyiwaa. (1998). Ghanaians, Ghanaian Canadians, and Asantes: Citizenship and identity among migrants in Toronto. *Africa Today* 45(3–4), 481–94.

Sorenson, John. (1991). Politics of social identity: 'Ethiopians' in Canada. *Journal of Ethnic Studies,* 19(1), 67–86.

PART D

CANADA AND GLOBALIZATION

Surviving the Wave: Canadian Identity in the Era of Digital Globalization

David Taras

The much-venerated Canadian scholar Northrop Frye was invited regularly to teach at leading American universities. His American students often asked him whether teaching an American class was different from teaching Canadian students. His answer was that nine out of ten times the experience was the same "... but the tenth time I know that I'm in a foreign country and have no idea what the next move is" (Frye, 1982, p. 58). Frye believed that his American students had a powerful sense of their own identity. They were self-confident in the notion that their country was a superpower with a global mission. Canadians, however, "are conditioned from infancy to think of themselves as citizens of a country of uncertain identity, a confusing past, and a hazardous future" (Frye, 1982, p. 57).

Frye is correct in pointing out that not only are there uncomfortable moments when Canadians realize that they are different but that Canadians have a less certain and less coherent identity than do others. Canadians are still filling in the map of their identity, discovering who they are. Canada has never had the supreme moments of self-definition—bloody revolutions, ringing declarations of independence, or moments of catastrophic defeat—that have characterized the political histories of countries such as the United States, France, Israel, Ireland, or Japan. Lacking a great historical moment or a common language, and having few national institutions, heroes, or symbols that provide unity, Canadians have little of the "hardwiring" that can be found in other countries. Indeed one of the themes of *A Passion for Identity* is that the search for identity has itself become one of the defining characteristics of Canadian life, a passion that has yet to be fulfilled. As Northrop Frye has written:

> Canada never defined itself as a unified society ... there is no Canadian way of life, no hundred per cent Canadian, no ancestral figures corresponding to Washington or Franklin or Jefferson, no eighteenth-century self-evident certainties about human rights, no symmetrically laid out country. (Frye, 1982, p. 48)

Literary scholar Bill New explains that walking the borderlands with the United States means having a different attitude toward nationalism, caring more about health care than guns, and seeing the world in terms of multiple possibilities. Philosopher John Ralston Saul argues that while "We are overcome by a desperate desire to present ourselves as a natural and completed experiment, monolithic, normal, just another one of the standard nation-states," Canada doesn't fit the mould (Saul, 1997, p. 14). Canada, because of its many uncertainties, is complex, amorphous, tolerant, postmodern, and open to the world in ways that many countries are not.

My argument in this essay is that Canada has, to a large degree, been shaped by the forces of globalization. Canada has not only withstood the challenges presented by vast global economic change but also has been at its forefront. The country has had to adapt to waves of postwar immigration, the powerful and relentless pressures imposed by free trade and our proximity to the United States, and vast changes in communication technology that have altered our sense of time and space. Yet even as we have learned to swim in this turbulent and often dangerous sea of globalization, there are fears that the next wave—the changes being brought by a new era of digital globalization—may be the most difficult for a country like Canada to survive.

This essay will describe the ways in which Canada has adapted to the forces of globalization in the past and the degree to which Canadian values have been shaped by these changes. I will then focus on the challenges to Canadian identity that are emerging as a result of the new era of digital globalization and its twin sisters—technological and corporate convergence. It is not so much that the old globalization has been supplanted or erased by the new; it is that the effects of the old globalization have now been deepened and sharpened by unprecedented change. At the heart of these changes is the fact that countries like Canada are caught between two giant pincer movements. To some degree Canada has lost control and authority to a new regime of international investors and corporate actors on one hand and to the fragmentation created by the new information technologies on the other. In a world where many of the old institutions are crumbling or becoming irrelevant, Canada will have to search for new ways to glue itself together.

CANADA AND THE OLD GLOBALIZATION

Canada is the most international of countries. The most obvious form of globalization that would be apparent to any foreign visitor to Canada is immigration and the ethnic and racial diversity of Canadian society. But the imperatives of international trade, the conflict between Canadian and Quebec nationalists that is at the heart of Canadian political life, and the need to contend with the power of the United States, have also been important factors in shaping Canada's global identity.

Walk on the streets of any large Canadian city and you will see a veritable United Nations of peoples and faces. As historian Harold Troper explains in his portrait of multicultural Toronto, new immigrants went from occupying small enclaves on the periphery to taking centre stage in the life of the city. While the push to adapt to the majority culture is undoubtedly a powerful force, people from many different identities and traditions—Asian, Caribbean, Scottish, Italian, Jewish, etc.—find themselves caught in the swirl of the unique social mixing and matching that takes place in Toronto and other large Canadian centres. The number of Canadians who can trace their origins to only one ethnic group is quickly diminishing. By some accounts, Canada is the most multicultural and indeed multiracial society on the planet. There is no greater testimony to Canada's place in the world.

Another important force in globalization has been Canada's resource economy. Canada's very founding, its genetic makeup, is the result of international competition for fish, furs, and religious converts. The original colonists and their Indian allies or adversaries were pawns in a much larger chess game that was being played out in Europe. In the wars and cut-throat diplomacy of the seventeenth and eighteenth centuries, English and French and Aboriginals lived in edgy and often bloody conflict with, and suspicion of, the other. What motivated European monarchs was the drive for economic wealth, what Donald Creighton described as the dream of the Empire of the St. Lawrence. According to Creighton, the St. Lawrence had a magnetic hold on all those who encountered it:

> The river meant movement, transport, a ceaseless passage west and east, the long procession of river-craft—canoes, bateaux, timber rafts and steam-boats—which followed each other into history. It seemed the destined pathway of North American trade: and from the river there rose, like an exhalation, the dream of western commercial empire. The river was to be the basis of a great transportation system by which manufactures of the old world could be exchanged for the staples of the new.... The dream.... runs like an obsession through the whole of Canadian history: and men followed each other through life, planning and toiling to achieve it. (Creighton, 1956, pp. 6–7)

Creighton's majestic prose describes what was in fact the basis of settlement; Canada was part of a metropolis-hinterland economy that stretched from the rivers, forests, and portages of the interior to trading houses in London and Paris. Harold Innis has argued that Canada was shaped by the natural contours of the continent and by trade routes that flowed along an east–west corridor (Innis, 1956). The economy was continually structured and restructured by foreign investments in and the dictates of European and then largely American markets for Canadian staple products.

Indeed, Canada is still to a large degree a resource-based economy subject to fluctuating demands for lumber, oil and gas, hydro power, agriculture, and minerals. Canadian farmers, loggers, oil workers, and miners live and breath the ups and downs of international commodity prices. The recent downturn in the Asian economy, the so-called Asian flu, for example, struck with particular force in British Columbia whose resource-based economy is hinged more and more to developments along the Pacific Rim.

Another determining factor in Canada's global identity is the fact that Canada consists of a fragile political coalition between English Canada and Quebec. The results of the 1995 Quebec Referendum on Quebec sovereignty attest to a national nervous breakdown—the federalist forces defeated the sovereigntist option by a mere whisker—50.56 to 49.4 percent of the vote. The basic geometry of Canadian existence is predicated on the fact that the country consists of more than one nation. There are at least two societies, speaking different languages, having different religious traditions, and maintaining different codes of law that have had to live side by side. Although the two societies remained largely separated from each other, with English- and French-speaking Canadians sharing the same house but sleeping, if you will, in separate bedrooms, dualism has been at the heart of the Canadian political compromise. Some observers believe that there is a third nation—the First Nations— that has legitimate claims to self-government and a form of sovereignty.

Canadian politicians have long realized that the country's survival is based on policies that acknowledge and accept differences, and that there is no single vision, no single identity, no single definition of what it means to be Canadian. A Canadian can have multiple allegiances and identities. While this tolerance, this understanding, has been intrinsic to Canadian survival and is in fact the very backbone of Canada's political existence, it has also placed Canada at the forefront of global developments. After all, the notion that citizens can have multiple loyalties and identities is at the heart of one of the most profound developments of the twentieth century—the formation of the European Union. The EU, which operates under a single currency and is governed by a complex myriad of councils, tribunals, and courts, has taken significant power away from nation-states and attempted to promote a broader European vision and allegiance.

Canada's francophone identity has also helped to shape Canada's global presence. The federal government has had to accommodate Quebec's interests by having strong relationships with francophone countries in Europe and in North and West Africa. Because of the French fact, our global relationships are markedly different from what they might be in a Canada without Quebec. One obvious example is TV5, a television network that links a number of francophone countries.

Because of TV5, Radio-Canada's programs can be seen almost anywhere in Europe. The Quebec government has forged its own broad network of exchanges and relationships, and it can be argued that many in the Quebec elite have spent far more time in France than they have in other parts of Canada.

Perhaps the most difficult problem for Canada is our proximity to the United States. Sharing a border with a global colossus, the most powerful country in the world, has given Canada both unique dilemmas and opportunities. The overriding concern is, as historian Robert Bothwell has written, that the United States is "friendly, familiar, foreign and near" (Bothwell, 2000, p. 165). For many Canadians the gravitational pull of the American economy, culture, and lifestyles is simply overwhelming. For Canadians, globalization has mostly meant Americanization.

Some observers believe that the border that divides the two countries is being gradually eroded. In fact, a TV ad mounted by the Liberal Party during the "free trade" election of 1988 seemed to touch a raw nerve when it suggested that the border might someday be erased. The ad showed Canadian and American officials negotiating the free trade deal. The American official tells the Canadian that only one problem remains. He then leans over a map and erases the border. Twelve years later *Time* would run a cover story entitled "What border?" and *Vanishing Borders* would be the title of a book about Canada–U.S. relations ("What border?" 2000; Molot and Hampson, 2000). In October 2000 various federal government departments sponsored a conference on Canada–U.S. relations that was entitled "Rethinking the Line."

Here the statistics tell much of the story. In 1999, there were close to 90 million visits by Americans travelling to Canada or by Canadians entering the United States. Over 85 percent of Canadian exports are to the United States, while over 75 percent of our imports come from the United States. Much of that trade—close to 45 percent—is between branches of the same company. Almost two-thirds of all foreign investment in Canada comes from south of the border—a massive $115 billion in 1999. Culturally the numbers are equally dramatic. Two-thirds of the TV programs that we watch, and 95 percent of the movies and videos that we go to or rent are American. American magazines account for roughly 80 percent of newsstand sales.

There are two pressure points that are of particular concern to Canadian nationalists. The first is the harmonizing effect of free trade on the Canadian economy. The second is the difficulty that Canadians have had maintaining a vibrant and distinctive Canadian culture in the face of the onslaught of the American entertainment industry.

During the intense debate over what became the Canada–U.S. Free Trade Agreement, some Canadian nationalists argued that the east–west economic axis on which the country had been built would be offset and pulled apart by the more powerful pull of the north–south economy.

Under free trade, Canada could no longer protect its key industries through subsidies or high tariffs. Moreover, Canada would have to "harmonize" its policies with those of the United States. Corporate taxes would be slashed, American business practices adopted, unions discouraged, and Canadian interest rates would have to be line with those south of the border. Critics also predicted that there would be a brain drain as talented Canadians migrated to corporate head offices or to more lucrative jobs in the United States. The lion's share of the better-paying and more creative positions—"front end" jobs in finance and communications, planning, and research—would be housed at corporate head offices in places like New York, Chicago, or in Silicon Valley. The lower-paying "back end" assembly and warehouse jobs would be located in Canadian branch plant operations.

Those advocating free trade saw a different scenario. While Canada would give up some aspects of its sovereignty, Canadian companies and products would have guaranteed access to a much larger market. Canadian corporations would be forced to become more international and more competitive. They would be pushed to rationalize production, invest in research and development, and aggressively expand their overseas markets. It was further argued that greater competition would produce lower prices and a wider range of choice for consumers. While the invasion of big-box stores like Walmart, Costco, and Home Depot might destroy old style main-street shopping, these retail giants would create jobs and spur competition.

Advocates of free trade also argued that the deal would benefit Canadian culture. A higher standard of living would mean that people had more money to buy Canadian books, attend concerts, plays, or sports events, or collect Canadian paintings. They also believed that Canadian culture was strong and vibrant enough to withstand the full force of an American cultural invasion. Pessimists who warned about the loss of Canadian culture didn't have faith in the country, didn't understand its underlying strength and resilience. The country didn't have to hide behind protective barriers—it could take on the world.

But critics argued that these economic changes would eventually have an impact on Canadian cultural values. American corporate values would slowly seep into the Canadian body politic, corroding old traditions and understandings and ultimately undermining the Canadian capacity to forge an independent identity. In the description of Ontario Premier Mike Harris's political agenda that Reg Whitaker has written for this volume, he warns about not only the increased continentalization of Ontario's economy but also of its public life. It can be argued that political leaders such as Mike Harris, Stockwell Day, and Ralph Klein have more in common with American Republicans, from whom they have borrowed many of their ideas, than they do with Canadian Tory traditions.

Although Canadian culture has survived both the FTA and NAFTA, it has done so only with considerable effort. The articles in this volume by

Charles Acland, Allan Bell, and David Whitson describe the difficulty of carving out a distinct cultural niche, of keeping some measure of cultural autonomy, in the face of enormous pressures for continental integration. Nominally excluded from NAFTA, cultural industries in Canada have survived because they are highly subsidized. Music, films, magazines, TV programs, and even the NHL have benefited from a veritable smorgasbord of tax incentives, protective barriers, or government grants. In addition, crown agencies such as the CBC-Radio Canada, the National Film Board, and Telefilm Canada—institutions that are the brick and morter of our cultural ramparts—have benefited from direct public support and involvement. The brutal choice that Canadians have always had to make, according to Graham Spry, one of the early supporters of public broadcasting, is the "state or the United States." Either Canadian governments intervened to tilt the balance in favour of Canadian culture, or Canadian culture would be drowned in a sea of American mass entertainment.

Some observers contend that Canadian television programming, for instance, exists because of a number of life supports. The CRTC limits foreign ownership, mandates Canadian-content regulations, and allows simultaneous substitution—the blocking of signals from the U.S. when Canadian and American stations are airing the same programs in the same time slots. Simultaneous substitution allows Canadian advertisers to have the entire playing field to themselves and brings increased ad dollars to Canadian networks. In addition, government programs offer partnerships, tax relief, and grants to TV and film productions. While support for the CBC-Radio Canada has been cut by as much as 50 percent since the mid-1980s, the annual grant from Parliament maintains a spinal chord of programming that reaches across the country.

The end result is a cultural pattern that is hazy and mixed. On one level, Canadian TV production has thrived. Canada is the second-largest exporter of TV programs in the world, and private networks such as CTV and Global now have the reach and capitalization needed to produce first-rate programming. The CBC, wounded and drained as it has been by seemingly endless rounds of budget cuts, reorganizations, and uncertainty, can still produce a big canvas series such as *Canada: A People's History*. The 30-hour, $25 million series portrays 12 000 years of Canadian life in panoramic majesty.

Despite these developments, "Canadians remain strangers in television's world of the imagination" (Report of the task force on broadcasting policy, 1986). American TV programs such as *Who Wants to Be a Millionaire*, *Survivor, Friends, Ally McBeal, ER,* and *The West Wing* as well as broadcasts of big-league American sports such as the NBA and the NFL dominate viewing time and dinner table and coffee break chit chat. When it comes to drama or sitcoms, Canadian programming has long been relegated to the sidelines, its viewers a distinct minority within the country.

Yet Canadians, one can argue, have a sophisticated understanding of their own interests and their own identity. We have been able to absorb the full blast of continental pressures still knowing who we are and who the Americans are. While economic and cultural borders may be evaporating, there are mental maps and borders and allegiances that have remained intact.

But this multilayered world, this necessary compromising of identity is now being shaken by even deeper changes. Digital globalization threatens to reorder the world and reshape our identities in ways that are only now becoming apparent.

CANADA AND THE TECHNOLOGY REVOLUTION

Thomas Friedman points out in his book *The Lexus and the Olive Tree* that ten years ago, few people had ever heard of the Internet (Friedman, 2000, p. 15). Most people had also never thought about or envisioned digitalization, miniaturization, e-mail, fibre optics, cell phones, DVDs, hard drives, and multiplayer games (MUDs). Yet in the brief space of a decade, the digital revolution has transformed the workplace, entertainment, education, and nature of community. In economic and social terms these new technologies have hit with the devastation of an earthquake. They have created vast movements toward increased centralization and control and new directions for individual and community expression. The new globalization has also challenged the authority of states and governments as never before.

One of the most important developments of the past decade, and indeed its economic engine, has been the convergence of technologies. The computer is being merged with the telephone, television, satellites, cable, and visual libraries. What has made it happen are advances in digital technology that provide a common language (the conversion of signals into codes) that can be translated and used in all mediums. The results are breathtaking. We are entering an age when, in the words of Ray Smith, the President of Bell Atlantic, "Your computer will speak, your TV will listen and your telephone will show you pictures" (in Taras, 1999, p. 63).

An immediate problem for governments is that the Internet and e-mail, the most obvious and powerful examples of this new technology, are difficult and some would say virtually impossible to regulate. The World Wide Web may mean that policies designed to protect national cultures shatter into a thousand pieces. Observers ask how a country like Canada can maintain Canadian-content regulations on TV and radio or adhere to advertising standards with regard to alcohol, tobacco, or even nudity when everyone with a computer has access to the vast ocean of the Internet. And soon every program on radio and TV will be readily available through the Internet. One of the most vivid and agonizing examples of the dilemmas now faced by governments occurred when Adolf Hitler's grotesque manifesto *Mein Kampf* became available through the Internet. Despite the German government's ardent stance against hate propaganda and its deep commitment to fight all forms of racism and extremism, the book soon became a bestseller (Friedman, 2000, p. 37). Parents know that while the Internet may provide their children with access to deep reservoirs of knowledge and to the great libraries, newspapers, and educational institutions of the world, it is also a cornucopia of pornography, violent games, hate-mongering, and shady operators. The reality is that the Web is unregulated territory, a kind of Wild West with no boundaries and few rules.

A second aspect of the convergence revolution has been increased corporate concentration. The shattering of barriers to international trade that has occurred in the past 20 years, the scale of investments needed to achieve economies of scale and develop and adapt to new technologies and the sheer velocity of international competition has led to an unprecedented number of corporate alliances and takeovers. America Online (AOL) is a prime example of the vastness of the corporate empires that are now emerging. While AOL is a towering giant in its own right, with more than 70 million visitors to its online properties per month in 2000, it recently acquired media behemoth Time-Warner for a reported $159 billion (U.S.). Time Warner owns a host of marquee media properties such as *Time, People, Sports Illustrated, Fortune*, CNN, HBO, Warner Brother Studios (*ER, Seinfeld*), Marvel Comics, Warner Books (home of Harry Potter), as well as a forest of popular record labels. Baseball stadiums, theme parks, and sports franchises (baseball's Atlanta Braves and basketball's Atlanta Hawks) are also part of the mix. In addition, AOL has partnerships with companies such as Motorola, Nokia, Research in Motion, BellSouth, and Sprint among others.

Corporate convergence is occurring in every sector of the economy. Vivendi, the huge French utility conglomerate, has taken over Seagram, itself a mammoth media conglomerate, owning Universal Studios and a huge swath, by some estimates as much as 30 percent, of the world music industry. Pharmaceutical giant Pfizer swallowed rival Warner Lambert. One of the mainstays of the German auto industry, Daimler-Benz, has merged with Chrysler. Exxon and Mobil have combined forces, and General Mills has bought Pillsbury. WorldCom and Sprint merged to become a dominant force in telecommunications. And all of these companies have alliances and partnerships that stretch across the globe.

At the hub of the new global system are new information technologies that give these corporate giants the tools that they need to manage far-flung research, buying, inventory, production, and marketing operations. As Dan Schiller, a distinguished Professor of Communication Studies at the University of California at San Diego has observed, "... the Internet comprises nothing less than the central production and control apparatus of an increasingly supranational market system" (Schiller, 1999, p. xiv). Before the Internet, such a tight binding of global corporations and markets was impossible.

Global corporations such as Microsoft, Intel, Oracle, General Electric, and AOL have value far in excess of the gross national products of most of the world's countries. Microsoft alone produces more economic activity than countries such as Denmark, Ireland, Mexico, and Belgium combined or more than all of Africa. In fact, corporate barons such as Microsoft founder Bill Gates, Oracle CEO Larry Ellison, or Intel's Andy Grove have personal fortunes that rival the GNPs of some European countries.

The sheer size of these conglomerates presents difficult problems for cultural industries in a country like Canada. The CBC, with a total budget of roughly $1 billion, and a mandate to provide a wide range of services, has to produce TV programs that compete directly with shows that have big studios and generous budgets behind them. Not only can General Electric, which owns NBC, or Disney, which controls ABC, bring enormous resources to the table—spending millions of dollars on each episode of a major TV series—but they can promote their programs across a wide range of other media outlets. But the CBC is not the only cultural institution that is outgunned by mammoth rivals. A more poignant example for some readers might be the buying of the Toronto Blue Jays' young star Sean Green by the Los Angeles Dodgers for a reported $84 million. Rupert Murdoch's News Corporation, which owns the Dodgers, made an offer that no Canadian sports franchise could possibly resist or match. The key to the kingdom for Murdoch is that the Dodgers are central to a wider media strategy that includes the ownership of numerous TV stations, a cable sports network, and a phalanx of newspapers and magazines. Perhaps the steepest mountain has to be climbed by the Canadian film industry. As Charles Acland has pointed out in his contribution to the book, multinational conglomerates control the distribution pipeline to such a degree that the vast majority of Canadian films are refused admission at the major theatre chains.

The basic chemistry of global power has changed. To some degree, countries have to play by the rules that have been established by these global giants in order to have access to technology and jobs. If companies aren't satisfied with conditions in a certain country, they can move their sizable investments and the jobs that they have created elsewhere. Indeed many corporations have developed strategies that will allow them to be light on their feet. They now work through affiliates and subcontractors rather than build factories of their own. Another control mechanism for the new global economy is the power of large mutual fund and institutional investment managers. At the click of a mouse tens of billions of dollars can be moved almost instantaneously from one part of the world to another. The power of these new "masters of the universe" and the monstrous egos associated with Wall Street have been described with great relish in Tom Wolfe's novel *Bonfire of the Vanities*. Markets or countries that fail to provide a healthy climate for investment can have the oxygen sucked out of their economies almost overnight. This brutal lesson was learned by Indonesian and Thai leaders after the international investment community all but pulled the plug in the late 1990s.

Thomas Friedman, the Pulitzer prize–winning global business correspondent for the *New York Times,* has described the new rules as a "Golden Straitjacket" (Friedman, 2000, p. 105). Countries have to maintain a package of policies that will make them attractive to these highly mobile investors and corporations. They have to remove barriers to trade and foreign investment, trim the size of government, privatize state or crown corporations, maintain low taxes and interest rates, and balance budgets. The formula, according to Friedman, produces two results: your economy mushrooms because it attracts investment while "your politics shrink" (Friedman, 2000, p. 105). Governments lose the power to make decisions about entire areas of public policy that are important to their citizens. To some degree, politics becomes a battle over personalities because the basic rules that will govern economic and social policies have already been decided. Deviate from the rules, Friedman warns, and investors will flee, bond ratings will drop, and the stock prices of the country's major corporations will tumble.

Even if one disputes the validity of the "Golden Straitjacket" argument, it is clear that governments can't control events to nearly the same degree that they once did. Many of the decisions that the Canadian government once had within its grasp are now made by international players who have little interest in or allegiance to countries like Canada.

The second prong of the pincer movement that threatens to undermine the authority of the nation-state is the fragmentation created by new technologies. While new means of communication have helped create global markets and corporations through their centralizing power, they have at the same time fractured and splintered media audiences. In the 1960s and 1970s, for instance, Canada had only a handful of TV networks. This forced millions of Canadians to come together at the same time and place and watch the same TV programs. In a sense, we all shared a "national living room" and with it a set of common experiences and understandings. That world has long since crumbled. The 150-channel universe, the endless horizon of the Internet, and the creation of niche formats on radio have broken national audiences into small micro-communities. In a sense audiences have moved from department store to boutique shopping. Joseph Turow, author of a book entitled *Breaking Up America,* argues that we have undergone a shift from a "society-making media" to a "segment-making media" (Turow, 1997, p. 3). CBC producer Mark Starowicz has gone even further arguing that there has been an "atomization" of the audience (Starowicz, 1996).

The reality is that audiences now enjoy a veritable kaleidoscope of media choices. People can graze the cable universe watching channels devoted exclusively to programming about pets, golf, speed sports, food, news, music, children, the elderly, Aboriginal life, travel, business, and religion among a long list of options. The Internet connects people to every imaginable interest, hobby, institution, organization, or event anywhere on the planet. And, as was the case when photos from the Mars Pathfinder mission were broadcast over the Internet, we can even be linked to other planets. And, more important perhaps, new technologies allow people to in effect become their own broadcasters—anyone who has a Web site can publish and produce his or her own media products.

The possibilities for exchange and learning and indeed for community building are endless. But the relationships that are being built don't necessarily coincide with national communities or national interests. Indeed national boundaries mean very little as people increasingly do business, exchange information, develop relationships, and play games with those living in other countries. And to the extent that people shop online, they not only weaken the local economy by spending money and creating jobs elsewhere but also deprive governments of the revenue that they normally would have generated through taxation.

Some observers believe that what appears to be a tidal wave of choices is in fact the opposite. The same giant corporations that control so much of the global economy also control vast stretches of cable and the Internet. Critics warn that the new media are as top-down as the old media.

There are still others who believe that audience segmentation is destructive to the building of national communities. Elihu Katz, one of the founders of modern Communication Studies, is astonished by the decisions taken by regulators in countries such as Canada to open the floodgates of cable TV so widely. Katz asks:

> Why are governments contributing to the erosion of nation-states and national cultures? Why don't they see that more leads to less to insignificance.... to endless distraction, to the automization and evacuation of public space? Why don't they see that national identity and citizen participation are compromised? Why don't they realize that they are contributing directly to the erosion of the enormous potential which television has to enlighten and unite populations into the fold of national cultures? (in Starowicz, 1996)

Joseph Turow sees similar dangers. He believes that having too many media choices aggravates social divisions because it prevents "people from coming into contact with news and entertainment that other parts of society find important" (Turow, 1997, p. 7).

In summary, the new globalization has shifted the geological plates on which the economy is based. Governments are threatened by a loss of sovereignty on at least two fronts. New and exceedingly powerful global corporations and fund managers dictate the rules of international commerce and have reduced the power that governments have over the lives of their citizens. At the same time, countries such as Canada may find it more difficult to connect meaningfully with their citizens because new technologies have scattered and diffused audiences and connected people to different kinds of communities. These new and powerful waves of change threaten to overwhelm some of our old assumptions about loyalty and belonging.

SURVIVING THE WAVES

To a large degree Canada was built on and is the product of globalization. The Empire of the St. Lawrence was nothing less than an economic dream that linked the Canadian hinterland to world markets. The country also came of age as a result of the honourable and extraordinary sacrifices that Canadians made in two World Wars. Canada was also a fulcrum in the establishment of the postwar international security system, playing leading roles in the founding of the United Nations, the North Atlantic Treaty Organization, and international peacekeeping. And Canadians are now part of a continental relationship in which there is dramatic and increasing economic and cultural integration. Indeed one can say that to Americans, we have become invisible foreigners—we appear to be so similar that it is difficult to tell us apart.

What is most interesting perhaps is the extent to which Canadians have become comfortable with a complex identity and with the powerful forces of continental integration that shape their lives. This reality was recently brought home to me when I was invited to speak to the annual meeting of a group that brings together the graduates of Canadian universities who live in the Chicago area. The group consisted of precisely the kind of people that Canada fears it is losing in a "brain drain" to the United States. They were young, highly educated, and working mostly in the finance or high-tech sectors for large multinational corporations. When I spoke to some of them after the talk was over, I found that they had a mixture of reactions to living in Chicago. Many loved the excitement of being in the thick of the corporate game, some loved what the city had to offer, and a number had already settled down with American partners. Yet I also noticed a strong commitment to remaining Canadian even if their attachments to the country were increasingly intermittent and distant. One person even spoke to me with great emotion about his feeling for the flag and Canadian contributions to peacekeeping.

What is most interesting perhaps is the sheer vibrancy and success of Canadian culture at a time when the forces marshalled against its survival seem to be so overwhelming. Indeed, John Meisel, one of Canada's most celebrated scholars and a former Chair of the Canadian Radio-Television and Telecommunications Commission, argues that Canadian writers, artists, filmmakers, and musicians have reached new levels of brilliance and creativity and that these achievements are being recognized around the world (Meisel, 1996). The survival of Canadian culture, and indeed of Canadian nationalism, is more deeply rooted, more potent and durable, than the pessimists would have us believe.

Northrop Frye reminds us that in comparing Canada to the United States "no difference is unique or exclusive: we can point to nothing in Canada that does not have a counterpart, or many counterparts, south of the border. What is different is a matter of emphasis and of degree" (Frye, 1982, p. 59). One can argue that the Canadian *Charter of Rights and Freedoms,* for instance, is not so very different from the values articulated in the American *Bill of Rights.* The vast multicultural experiment that defines cities like Toronto or Vancouver has its counterparts in the United States. Nonetheless, Canadians by "emphasis and degree" have made different choices about how our country is constructed and about the nature of citizenship and identity.

Yet the new waves of globalization are pounding our country with tremendous force. Maintaining our differences and indeed a strong measure of sovereignty will take a concerted effort in the years ahead. Whether Canadians can meet these new challenges or even fully understand their vast scale, their enormous dimensions, remains to be seen. An observation made by Northrop Frye many years ago still has relevance today:

> Identity in Canada has always had something about it of a centrifugal movement into the far distance, of clothes on a growing giant coming apart at the seams, of an elastic about to snap. Stephan Leacock's famous hero who rode off rapidly in all directions was unmistakably a Canadian. This expanding movement has to be counterbalanced by a sense of having constantly to stay together by making tremendous voluntary efforts at intercommunication.... (Frye, 1982, pp. 77–78)

Finding ways to connect with each other, and to know ourselves, will determine whether we continue to have a passion for identity.

REFERENCES

Bothwell, Robert. (2000). Friendly, familiar, foreign and near. In *Vanishing Borders,* edited by Maureen Molot and Fen Hampson. Toronto: Oxford University Press.

Creighton, Donald. (1956). *The empire of the St. Lawrence.* Toronto: Macmillan.

Friedman, Thomas. (2000). *The lexus and the olive tree.* New York: Anchor Books.

Frye, Northrop. (1982). *Divisions on a ground: Essays on Canadian culture.* Toronto: Anansi.

Innis, Harold. (1956). *The fur trade in Canada.* Toronto: University of Toronto Press.

Meisel, John. (1996). Extinction revisited: culture and class in Canada. In *Seeing ourselves: Media power and policy in Canada*, edited by Helen Holmes and David Taras. Toronto: Harcourt, Brace and Co. Canada.

Report of the task force on broadcasting policy. (1986). Ottawa: Queen's Printer.

Saul, John Ralston. (1997). *Reflections of a Siamese twin: Canada at the end of the twentieth century*. New York: Viking.

Schiller, Dan. (1999). *Digital capitalism: Networking the global market system*. Cambridge, Massachusetts: The MIT Press.

Starowicz, Mark. (1996). The Gutenberg revolution of television: Speculation on the impact of new technologies. In *Seeing ourselves: Media power and policy in Canada*. Toronto: Harcourt, Brace and Co. Canada.

What border? Together, Canadians and Americans are redefining the nature of their common frontier. (2000, 10 July). *Time*.

Taras, David. (1999). *Power and betrayal in the Canadian media*. Peterborough, ON: Broadview Press.

Turow, Joseph. (1997). *Breaking up America*. Chicago: University of Chicago Press.

FURTHER READING

Fraser, Matthew. (1999). *Free for all: The struggle for dominance on the digital frontier.* Toronto: Stoddart.

Friedman, Thomas. (2000). *The lexus and the olive tree*. New York: Anchor.

Schiller, Dan. (1999). *Digital capitalism: Networking the global market system*. Cambridge, Massachusetts: The MIT Press.

Taras, David. (1999). *Power and betrayal in the Canadian media*. Peterborough: Broadview Press.

Thomas, David, ed. (2000). *Canada and the United States: Differences that count*, 2nd edition. Peterborough: Broadview Press.

Running out of Ammo? The Future of Canada's Military

Rob Huebert

INTRODUCTION

During the summer of 2000, the world watched as Canadian land forces equipment was held hostage in a contract dispute involving the Canadian government, a company that had been contracted to ship the equipment from overseas duty in the Balkans, and a third subcontractor. As a result of this dispute, the owner of the GTS *Katie* ordered the ship to remain at sea. After efforts to negotiate with the company failed to produce a satisfactory result, the Canadian government ordered the Canadian navy to board the vessel and to ensure that it reached its designated harbour. This incident clearly illustrates some of the more recent challenges that the Canadian Forces face as they continue to adjust to their new roles and duties in the post–Cold War era.

This incident arose in the context of the Canadian Forces increasingly engaging in overseas operations while facing continued budget cuts. The navy has a limited sea-lift capability and therefore must hire civilian contractors to move its heavy equipment whenever it engages in overseas operations. In the GTS *Katie* situation, when the Canadian government decided to pull most of its troops out of Kosovo, a civilian company was hired to charter a civilian container vessel to carry army equipment from Kosovo to Canada. During the Canadian navy's boarding of the *Katie*, only one Sea King helicopter was used in landing Canadian troops on the vessel despite the fact that two helicopters were onboard the Canadian naval ships shadowing the *Katie*. The Sea Kings are now almost 40 years old, and one of the Sea Kings was inoperable because of mechanical problems. Although the two naval vessels shadowing the GTS *Katie* could have had at least one more helicopter on board, there are not enough in the Canadian inventory to have allowed each ship to carry the maximum number of helicopters. The crew members included in the boarding party were armed. Fortunately, there was no physical resistance to the boarding, short of some irresponsible manoeuvres by the *Katie*'s captain. Although the boarding crew was well trained, its ability to train for weapons use is severely limited as only a small number of bullets for training exercises are allocated each year. Unless the crew members have been specifically assigned to vessels engaged in UN–sponsored blockades, it is unlikely that they have had more than four to six opportunities per year to fire a weapon!

In summary, the Canadian Forces successfully boarded, and the vessel did reach harbour safely, albeit after the *Katie* had run out of fuel. In many respects, the episode proves a metaphor for the state in which the Canadian Forces now finds themselves. A small number of well-trained personnel, using some very old equipment in conjunction with some capable and modern pieces of equipment, is being asked to perform new and dangerous duties. The end of the Cold War had been expected to curtail the demands on the Canadian Forces and to allow for the exploitation of the "peace dividend" that was to occur as a result of these reduced requirements. Instead, the Canadian Forces are now being called on to act in ways that would have seemed inconceivable only 10 years ago. However, this is countered by the Canadian government's continued reduction in the allocation of both funding and personnel to its national defence. Thus the forces are now asked to do much more with much less. Hence the question: are the Canadian Forces running out of ammunition? The objective of this chapter is to assess the challenges that these new realities impose on the Canadian Forces as they enter the 21st century and to determine if indeed the Canadian Forces are running out of ammunition and, if so, why.

THE CANADIAN FORCES IN THE COLD WAR ERA

Throughout the Cold War, the primary purpose of the Canadian Forces was to provide support to their allies (*White Paper on Defence*, 1964; *Defence in the 70s*, 1971; and *Challenges and Commitment*, 1987). They did so through the Canadian commitment to Nato and Norad. In turn, these commitments were designed to deter the Soviet Union from launching aggressive action in Western Europe by demonstrating the resolve and capability of the alliance to defend all of its members if attacked. In doing so, the member states of Nato believed that they could discourage a Soviet attack. However, if deterrence failed and the Soviet Union did launch an attack, all of the members of the alliance were expected to contribute to the common defence of the Western world. The net result of these requirements on Canadian defence policy was that its main mandate was quite simple: to deter and defend against the Soviet Union.

During the Cold War, the greatest challenge for Canadian defence planners was determining how Canada could make a meaningful contribution to such a deterrence and defence. By itself, Canada could not hope to deter or defend against the Soviet Union. Its contribution would be made in showing political solidarity and in providing some military assistance. The question that continually challenged Canadian decision makers was how much was enough (Middlemiss and Sokolsky, 1989)? The United States and, to a lesser degree, the United Kingdom, West Germany, and France, provided the real military power of the alliance. Canada's problem was how it could make a meaningful contribution. For the most part, the Canadian solution was the development of a highly trained, modern armed force that could perform certain tasks very well. For example, the navy developed a proficient antisubmarine warfare capability. The air force maintained a small but relatively modern arm of fighter aircraft throughout the Cold War. Although it was expected that the Canadian contribution would be small in number, the forces would nevertheless match the abilities of their allies.

However, at the same time, there were repeated criticisms that the Canadian Forces faced a capability-commitment gap (Sokolsky, 1987). Some analysts suggested that Canadian decision-makers tended to undertake commitments that the existing forces could not have fulfilled in the event of the outbreak of war (Shadwick, 1985). At one point during the Cold War, Canadian Forces were committed to providing naval units for convoy protection; land and air units for the defence of northern Norway; and fighter aircraft and tanks for use at the Central Front on the West German border. It was doubtful in the event of a Soviet attack that the Canadian Forces committed to Norway would be properly supplied before the area was taken by Soviet forces. Likewise, it also appeared difficult to sustain the commitment to the Central Front in the event of an actual war. This illustrates the current pattern of Canadian decision makers to accept tasks on behalf of the Canadian Forces without providing adequate resources to support these tasks.

Another challenge for the Canadian Forces came in the form of Canada's commitment to UN peacekeeping exercises (Keating, 1993). Since the 1956 Suez Crisis, which was in part resolved by Lester B. Pearson's creation of the modern day peacekeeping force, Canadian policy has been committed to peacekeeping. Both policymakers and Canadians in general have come to believe that such actions provide an important contribution to the maintenance of international peace and security (Byers and Slack, 1984; Morrison, 1993). Consequently, Canadian Forces were posted to almost all of the UN peacekeeping operations throughout the Cold War.

CANADIAN FORCES IN THE POST–COLD WAR ERA

The end of the Cold War was supposed to usher in a new era of international peace and security. As events were soon to demonstrate, this in fact was not the case. The collapse of the Soviet Union unleashed many new conflicts, including the disintegration of Yugoslavia and ethnic conflict in Africa. But the end of the Cold War did reduce the reluctance of Western states to intervene in these conflicts in order to end them. During the Cold War, most conflicts were perceived to be related to the power struggle between the main superpowers. Thus, most states were hesitant to intervene on the grounds that their actions could escalate tensions between the USSR and the United States. However, once the Cold War was over, a greater willingness to use force to resolve conflict developed. Thus, the UN conducted a military action led by the United States to expel Iraq from Kuwait. Nato used military force to end the siege of Sarajevo and more recently to resolve the conflict in Kosovo. Even when force was not used, for example during the ethnic violence in Burundi and Rwanda, some believe that a multilateral military force *should* have been used.

However, unlike the Cold War, none of these conflicts directly threatened Canada's security. Nevertheless, the Canadian public and most policymakers still believed that Canada should have participated in resolving these conflicts. But, at the same time, there was also a belief that Canada should benefit from the peace dividend that was expected with the end of the Cold War. Thus, the Canadian military now finds itself caught in the paradoxical expectation that it must be involved in international operations while at the same time needing to reduce its budget. The net result has been an armed force that is expected to do much more with much less and faces an even more uncertain future.

Status of Canadian Forces

The Canadian Forces were unified in the early 1970s. In theory, this meant that there is no separate Canadian navy, air force, or army, only a Canadian armed force. The idea behind unification was that the duties and requirements of the forces could best be met by a single force, and that the traditional divisions would serve only to duplicate the costs of maintaining and operating the forces (Middlemiss and Sokolsky, 1989). This included having only one type of uniform and rank structure. In practice, unification did not deliver the savings that were anticipated. Furthermore, the forces can still be divided into naval, land, and air requirements. As such, although the forces are still officially unified, there has been a gradual redevelopment of separate identities. In the mid-1980s, the three main services were given their own distinctive uniforms and were allowed to revert to their traditional rank systems. For example, the top leadership in the navy once again became admirals instead of generals. The current Canadian Forces are now divided between naval, land, and air commands.

Government Defence Spending in the Post–Cold War Period

Since the Korean War, Canadian government defence expenditures have steadily declined. At the end of the Korean War, Canadian policymakers agreed with their Western allies that the Soviet Union was preparing for aggressive action in Western Europe. At that time, Canadian defence expenditures reached almost 8 percent of GDP (*Into the New Millennium*, 1999, C1). This figure dropped to 4 percent by the beginning of the 1960s. By the mid-1960s, when Soviet intentions appeared to be less hostile, Canadian defence expenditures were further reduced to approximately 2 percent of GDP, where they remained until the end of the Cold War. In 1999, defence expenditures dropped to approximately 1.2 percent of GDP. In terms of government spending, defence now receives 6.1 percent, which is the lowest level it has been at since World War II (*Into the New Millennium*, 1999, 2-1). Actual government spending on defence declined from $12 billion in 1993–94 to $9.38 billion in 1998–99. This declining trend reversed slightly in fiscal year 1999–2000 when there was an increase in defence spending (*Defence Planning Guidance*, 1999, 1-1, 1-2).

The decline in the defence budget has resulted in the reduction of the number of regular forces personnel. In 1958 there were 120 000 regular forces (*Into the New Millennium*, 1999, 2-1). This was reduced to 98 000 in 1968 and was further reduced to 84 600 in 1988. In 1998 this number was reduced to slightly under 60 000.

In addition to the reduction in the number of forces personnel, the standard of living of the remaining personnel began to decline. Media reports commented that members of the forces were required to take on additional employment in order to make ends meet. In 1997, the House of Common's Committee on National Defence and Veterans Affairs (SCONDVA) undertook an examination of the issues that were affecting Canadian personnel (House of Commons, 1998). It concluded its work and tabled its report in October 1998. Its 89 recommendations made it clear that the cuts to the Canadian Forces had serious negative impacts on the "quality of life" of serving personnel. In response, the government allocated $175 million in new defence spending and reversed an earlier cut of $150 million specifically to improve funding for improved medical services, pay increases, improvements in married quarters, and increased assistance for family support. Given that this is a recent increase in defence spending, it is currently impossible to determine whether these increases will continue or whether this will be the only increase.

Canadian Forces Capability in the Post–Cold War Period

According to the main document of Canadian defence planning, the 1994 White Paper, the Canadian Forces have three main objectives: (1) the protection of Canada, (2) Canadian–American cooperation, and (3) contributing to international security. In order to do this, the White Paper called for "multi-purpose, combat-capable armed forces to meet challenges to Canada's security both at home and abroad" (*1994 Defence White Paper*, 1994, 3).

An examination of the force structure of the Canadian Forces in 2000 shows that the equipment that the forces operate is a mix of old and new. It is beyond the focus of this chapter to provide a detailed examination of the entire Canadian Forces inventory, but it is possible to note the major elements of the three main services.

Navy

Of the three branches of the Canadian Forces, the navy is probably the best equipped. Most Canadians tend to be quite surprised to learn that Canada has a very capable modern navy. It is built around a core of vessels that include four destroyers (Iroquois class) completed between 1971 and 1973 and rebuilt in 1988–95; 12 frigates (Halifax class) completed between 1992 and 1996; 12 coastal defence vessels (Kingston class) completed between 1995 and 1999; two auxiliary oiler and replenishment vessels; and four submarines (Victoria ex-Upholder class) built between 1991 and 1993, which are to be delivered to Canada in 2000–01 (*Into the New Millennium*, 1999, D-1).

As this list makes evident, the Canadian navy has a large number of relatively new ships. What this list does not reflect is the fact that in order for the frigates and destroyers to operate at their maximum capabilities, they must be outfitted with a modern helicopter. The 32 Sea King helicopters that are currently in operation were acquired in 1963 and will soon be 40 years old. As anyone who has owned an old car will know, the older the vehicle, the greater the maintenance requirement. The Canadian government has indicated that acquiring new helicopters has been a defence priority since the end of the 1980s. To this end, the Mulroney government had agreed to purchase the EH-101. However, this decision was overturned when the Chrétien government came to power in the early 1990s on the grounds that the EH-101 helicopter was too expensive for Canadian needs. However, no replacement has since been found, and the navy has had to struggle with using a helicopter that it does not find dependable due to its age.

The navy is also struggling to deal with the recent retirement of one of its replenishment vessels and with the need to soon replace the remaining two vessels, which are now 30 years old. With only two replenishment vessels, the navy faces difficulty in deploying beyond its coastal waters. In order to go beyond the distance allowed by the fuel capacity of the destroyers and frigates, the Canadian navy needs either to depend on the cooperation of its allies, or to have its own capabilities to refuel its ships. This is also true in the deployment of Canadian ground forces. With their own sea-lift capability, Canadian Forces must either be moved by commercial carrier (as was the case with the GTS *Katie*) or be carried by a friendly or allied country. The *Katie* incident demonstrates the difficulty of relying on commercial carriers. The difficulty of relying on allied assistance is that in most instances they are also involved in transporting their troops to the problem area and therefore may have limited room for carrying Canadian equipment. Thus, if Canada is to continue to deploy forces overseas, it will need to have some form of sea-lift capability. To this end, the Canadian Forces have begun to explore an "Afloat Logistic and Sea-lift Capability" project. However, it is not known when such a project would receive funding, let alone have a vessel ready for use.

Air Force

The air force has had a substantial reduction in the number and type of aircraft that it operates. At the end of the Cold War, it had 20 different types of aircraft totalling 700 aircraft in number. It is expected that by 2002 the air force will have been reduced to 11 types of aircraft totalling 336 aircraft in number (Hobson, 2000, 30). The air force is operating with substantially older equipment than the navy. Because technological advances are making any new purchases extremely costly, the air force is currently attempting to maintain its existing forces. However, each of its main elements will need to be replaced toward the end of this decade. It is uncertain how the government will respond. Further complicating the picture is the recent willingness of the Canadian government to deploy air units to combat situations; CF-18s were first used in combat during the war with Iraq and again with Nato forces in Kosovo.

Currently the Canadian Forces have 122 CF-18 fighter/bombers. Of these, 60 are operational, 23 are used for training, and three are test aircraft. These aircraft are now 15–20 years old. In order to maximize their capabilities, the Canadian government decided in 1998 to provide a $1.2 billion upgrade in the avionics for up to 100 of the CF-18s. This will include mission computers, flight software, jamming-resistant radios, an identification friend or foe (IFF) interrogator and a datalink (Hobson, 2000, 32). In addition, the Canadian Forces have also begun purchasing precision-guided munitions (PGM), upgrading aircraft for Maritime and Arctic surveillance flights, and replacing most of their helicopters.

Lastly, the air force is also examining means by which it can improve its air-lift capability. Currently the Canadian Forces rely on their 32 C-130 Hercules aircraft. The bulk of these aircraft were purchased in the mid-1960s, with some additional aircraft being bought as recently as 1997. However, the effort to send two Hercules to East Timor demonstrated that the general state of these aircraft is beginning to deteriorate. Both aircraft were forced to return to base due to mechanical problems. The aircraft arrived safely after several aborted attempts to land. The Canadian government is currently considering the possibility of entering into a cost-sharing arrangement with allies for a strategic air-lift capacity (Hobson, 2000, 32).

Army

Of the three services, the army has been most called upon in the last decade but has received the least amount of funding. Peacekeeper or peacemaker forces comprise primarily members of the land forces. However, the army has the oldest equipment. Canadian Land Forces, comprising 19 000 regular personnel organized into three mechanized brigade groups, are not well equipped to respond to the increased demands that have been placed on them since the end of the Cold War (Hobson, 2000, 29). Until recently, the bulk of the land forces equipment dated to the late 1970s and early 1980s. For example, Canada bought 114 Leopard I tanks from Germany in 1978 (*Into the New Millennium,* 1999, D-2). Although these tanks have received some upgrades with respect to sighting capabilities, it is uncertain as to whether they will be replaced when they reach the end of their serviceable life. Armoured Combat Vehicles, built in the 1970s and 1980s, are, however, being replaced as is the existing tactical communication system.

Despite these new additions, the land forces are considered to be overcommitted. Insufficient funding is available for training exercises involving large deployments of Canadian troops (*Strategic Operations and Resource Plan 2000–2002, n.d.*), and serious shortages in personnel have been reported. The three brigade groups have a shortfall of 300–400 personnel (Hobson, 2000, 29). Thus, given the fact that the land forces contribute the bulk of overseas troops, it is easy to understand how the post–Cold War era has been the most difficult for the army.

THE PARADOX OF CANADIAN SECURITY POLICY IN THE 21ST CENTURY

So far this examination has discussed only a reduced Canadian Forces capability. It is clear that the Canadian Forces' budget has been substantially reduced since the end of the Cold War and that there are important gaps in terms of equipment. However, the Canadian Forces have increasingly been assigned additional roles and tasks, and the Canadian Forces are now in danger of "running out of ammunition."

A close examination of the current state of the Canadian security policy reveals multiple paradoxes and contradictions. Canadian policymakers want to be active in as many international peace-resolution operations as possible. However, they are reluctant to acknowledge that such a proactive policy inherently entails more resources, not fewer. The question arises as to what these security policies are and how they are affecting the Canadian Forces.

International Operations

The most significant challenge facing the Canadian Forces, and most central to an understanding of the future of the Canadian Forces, is the dichotomy that exists between the increased duties of the forces since the end of the Cold War and the expectation of Canadian decision makers and the Canadian public that the end of the Cold War would result in a lesser, not greater, need for military force (Hampson and Maule, 1991, 9–14). Many expected that the end of the Cold War would provide a "peace dividend." For many states, the end of the Cold War was an opportunity to reduce their defence expenditures. However, in Canada, the defence budget had steadily decreased throughout the Cold War. Consequently, by the time the Soviet Union dissolved, the Canadian Forces had already been reduced to a level that did not readily allow for further cuts. Yet as this chapter has already discussed, cuts were still made.

At the same time, the end of the Cold War also allowed for the deployment of military forces in new endeavours and, in particular, in support of the United Nations. During the Cold War, the animosities between the Soviet Union and the United States and its allies meant that the Security Council of the United Nations was effectively frozen. Any action that one side would take would be vetoed by the other side and vice versa. Once the Cold War ended, this deadlock was broken, and the UN could involve itself in a vastly larger number of peacekeeping and peacemaking operations. In the period from 1945 to 1989, Canadian Forces were involved in 25 international operations. Since 1990, Canadian Forces have been deployed on 65 missions, 32 of which have occurred since 1998 (*Building on a Stronger Foundation*, 2000, 5).

The period of 1999–2000 has been one of the most demanding years for the Canadian Forces. More than 4500 troops were deployed overseas on 23 missions. This number represents only the number of troops that are physically on site. It does not consider the number of personnel who remain based in Canada and who dedicate some or all of their actions to supporting these troops. Thus, the actual Canadian commitment is much larger than 4500.

Not only are Canadian Forces being asked to contribute to more operations but the nature of the activity has changed dramatically. Canadian Forces were actively involved in the UN Security Council action against the Iraqi invasion of Kuwait in 1990. In 1999, Canadian CF-18s were used in support of Nato attacks on the former Yugoslavia during the intervention on behalf of the Kosovo Albanians. The net result of this development is that the Canadian Forces are continually being asked to do more with less.

Canadians and their leaders have somewhat contradictory beliefs regarding Canadian security policy and Canada's role in the international system. On the one hand, most Canadians take pride in the Canadian legacy. Since the days of Lester Pearson, most Canadians have come to accept that Canada makes important contributions to world peace and security through the deployment of Canadian Forces (Legault, 1992, 13–17). On the other hand, Canadians tend to view Canadian defence expenditures with suspicion. As a result, Canadians favour Canadian involvement on the international stage but do not like to bear the costs of such action nor do they like to think of these actions as being military.

What further complicates the situation is the misperception that peacekeeping in the 21st century requires little more than a physical presence of lightly armed Canadian personnel wearing blue berets. It is doubtful that this was ever the case, but the reality in the post–Cold War era is that peacekeepers need to be properly equipped and trained and that neither can be done cheaply. Furthermore, the nature of peace-keeping has altered substantially. Current UN operations can be more correctly referred to as peacemaking not peacekeeping (Sens and Stoett, 1998, 249–93). Peacekeeping operations normally involve the placement of troops to maintain an existing cease-fire, such as in Cyprus, while peacemaking or peace enforcement refers to the use of UN troops to create the peace, even using force themselves if necessary. Such actions require any deployed troops to be outfitted for possible conflict and risk being killed themselves. As seen from the brief overview of the status of Canadian Forces equipment, there is a recognition by policy makers that the Canadian Forces' equipment needs to be improved if the current tempo of oversea operations is to be maintained. For the fiscal year of 1999–2000, some resources were allocated to this task. However, it is clear that much more is necessary if the Canadian Forces are to maintain their current level of commitment.

The most immediate problem that the Canadian Forces face con-cerns their ability to transport personnel and equipment overseas. Current Canadian sea-lift and air-lift capability is limited. Canada has two naval replenishment vessels that can be used to transport peacekeepers as in the East Timor operation. However, when these vessels are used in this manner they cannot support any other naval operation. These ships are essential to the ability of all Canadian vessels to operate any distance beyond Canadian waters. Without a resupply capability, the Canadian navy has to either keep its vessels close to Canadian ports or depend on allies for refuelling at sea. The difficulty that the Canadian Forces faced in the GTS *Katie* situation has served to underline the problems in trans-porting equipment from oversea actions. As well, the Hercules aircraft are old and will continue to experience mechanical problems.

One solution that is now being considered is the possibility of entering into a shared program with other allied nations and investing in both heavy-lift aircraft such as the C-17s and new replenishment vessels. While there are economic benefits to sharing the purchase with other states, problems may occur in developing a joint-use program. In most instances, the crises that Canada responds to also involve its allies. So how would the nations decide whose shipment will be moved? Regardless of how this issue is resolved, it is clear that the Canadian government will need to invest substantial resources if it wants the forces to remain as active as they have been in the 1990s.

One issue that Canadian policymakers have not had to confront during overseas commitments is Canadian casualties. The Canadian Forces have been fortunate in that, while they are being asked to participate in increasingly dangerous missions, they have incurred few casualties, and those that have occurred have been in the form of accidents or mine explosions. What would be the reaction of Canadian policymakers if Canadian troops involved in an overseas operation are killed in battle? It is not clear what the reaction of the Canadian public or the government would have been if a Canadian ship deployed to the Persian Gulf during the 1990 war with Iraq had been hit by a missile or had struck a mine. What would have happened if a Canadian CF-18 had been shot down? These are always risks in these types of operations. One of the most difficult questions to answer is how much should be spent on new equipment to protect Canadian personnel as they face these increasingly dangerous missions.

Domestic Operations

Overall, the Canadian Forces tend to operate beyond the notice of most Canadians. However, the forces occasionally are required to respond to domestic crises and challenges. In most instances, these are not problems that the forces are expected to respond to. However, by virtue of their training, they are often the most capable institution that exists within the Canadian society to do so.

Canadian Forces have been asked to provide assistance to local authorities in times of local emergency. The Manitoba flood and the Ontario/Quebec ice storms are the best examples of the willingness of local authorities to perceive the utility of the forces in this light. While requests for Canadian Forces participation in domestic operations occur occasionally, they still place a tremendous strain on the available resources. Equipment must be used, and operational expenses arise. Furthermore, it is possible that these storms are not a rare occurrence (i.e., the storm/flood of the century) but may be the result of global climate change. If this is the case, the Canadian Forces may increasingly be called upon to provide assistance to the civil authorities.

Canadian Forces have also dealt with Chinese illegal immigrants who have attempted to enter Canada. Four vessels were intercepted by Canadian naval vessels and escorted into Canadian waters. While the West Coast fleet was able to handle four vessels, it is unclear how well Canadian Forces would be able to respond to a much larger number of refugee vessels. This may be a new challenge in the near future.

The end of the millennium was also viewed as a possible threat to national security. While most observers are now willing to acknowledge that the threat was exaggerated, prior to the New Year, many Canadians were concerned that computer problems could result in widespread difficulties. As such, the Canadian Forces instituted Operation Abacus, which was to provide assistance in the event that computer systems failed. Over 2500 personnel were deployed with another 14 000 of the regular forces on standby (*Building on a Stronger Foundation*, 2000, A-1).

Canadian Forces have also continued to be called upon to respond to the more traditional threats arising from drug smuggling and search-and-rescue operations. In recent years, the Canadian Forces have responded to 7000 to 9000 incidents per year, and in 1998–99 alone over 1000 lives were saved by the Canadian Forces (*Into the New Millennium*, 1999, 1-5). Once again, such a capability does not come cheaply or easily.

Canada—United States Relations

The Canadian Forces also face the challenge (and benefits) of being the neighbour of the sole remaining superpower. While Canada is fortunate that it has a close relationship with the United States, there are certain demands still placed on the Canadian armed forces that require considerable resources. The American forces are currently committed to developing the technological capabilities of their forces to the farthest extent possible. Often referred to in American strategic planning as the Revolution in Military Affairs (RMA), American policy planners are developing military practices that make the greatest use of their computer, satellite, and communication technology (Cohen, 1999, 122). The planners believe that this will ensure that their forces remain the most advanced in the world (Gray, 1999, 200–5; 243–54).

Consequently, in order for the Canadian Forces to maintain their ability to operate with American forces, they must ensure that their communication systems are compatible (interoperable) with the Americans'. This requirement of interoperability is expensive and will influence the future shape of the Canadian Forces. The more funding that is allocated to this equipment, the less available for other requirements. As such, the Canadian Forces are now debating the degree to which the Canadian Forces are to be shaped in order to operate with the American forces.

The debate is being guided by a National Defence document entitled *Shaping the Future of Canadian Defence: A Strategy for 2020*. It argues that unless the Canadian Forces are fully capable of operating with the American forces, Canadian defence capabilities will deteriorate. Furthermore, since the Americans set the standard of communications for all other allied and friendly states, the issue of interoperability goes beyond the Canadian–American relationship to our relationship with other allies. On the other hand, concerns have been raised that by focusing on maintaining such an advanced capability, the Canadian Forces will run the risk of becoming an appendage to the American forces. More important, the costs involved in maintaining these advanced capabilities could prove to be such a drain on limited resources that the Canadian Forces would not have the resources to perform other less technologically intensive requirements. This debate is far from being resolved. However, the manner in which it is resolved will have important ramifications for the future shape and capability of the Canadian Forces.

Quality of Life

An issue that is currently affecting the Canadian Forces' capability pertains to the ability to meet the needs of its personnel, which is referred to in the Canadian Forces as "quality of life." One of the key costs of the armed forces of any nation is the salaries of its service personnel. As discussed earlier, senior Canadian policy officials became concerned in the mid-1990s that Canadian personnel were suffering economically. Some states require compulsory service and pay their draftees a minimum salary. States, such as Canada, that do not have the draft and that have a professional armed force must attempt to provide a higher remuneration in order to retain their personnel. Nevertheless, in the 1990s, the salary levels fell behind those of the general population. Although the government has recently increased the pay scale for armed forces personnel, the force's ability to retain highly skilled and highly trained personnel will become more acute as time progresses.

In addition, the Canadian Forces will also have to address the issue of burnout. The recent budget increase has not addressed the number of times that personnel are required to serve on overseas operations. While some forces personnel enjoy such a lifestyle, many of those with families find overseas operations to be a strain as they entail significant periods of separation. While the increased defence budget does attempt to provide increased funding for family services, the additional funding does not resolve the core problem that can be summarized as too many commitments for too few personnel. This problem can be resolved only by either increasing the number of personnel or decreasing the commitment. There is currently no indication that the Canadian government intends to do either. Therefore, the problem will continue to exist for the foreseeable future.

CONCLUSION

This chapter has addressed the core issue of the overcommitment of Canadian Forces in the post–Cold War era. With the end of the Cold War came the expectation that the Canadian Forces could be reduced in terms of personnel. At the beginning of the 1990s, Canadian policymakers simply assumed that the Department of National Defence could quickly reduce the number of personnel without impacting overall performance. However, rather than ushering in an era of a more peaceful international system, the end of the Cold War has signalled a period of increased conflict in many regions of the world. In addition, the Western world has also developed a greater willingness to directly involve itself in the resolution of some of these conflicts and has demonstrated a greater willingness to use force if necessary. Canada has been at the forefront of such action. Unfortunately, it is hard to reconcile substantial budget cuts with increased commitments. As a result, the Canadian Forces now face important decisions. If Canadian Forces are to be used as extensively as they have been in the last decade, the Department of National Defence will require an increased defence budget. If this budget increase is not produced, the Canadian commitment will suffer. Either it will become a token effort with few troops, or it will place an increasingly difficult strain on the personnel and the equipment of the Canadian Forces.

There is little question that the Canadian Forces are professional, well-trained forces. It is also difficult to dispute that Canada contributes to its own security by participating in collaborative efforts to preserve and foster international peace and security. The questions that remain are what is a reasonable effort, and what should Canadians pay for this effort? If careful thought is not given to this question, the forces may soon run out of ammunition.

REFERENCES

1994 Defence White Paper. National Defence. Ottawa: Minister of Supply and Services, 1994.

Building on a Stronger Foundation: Annual Report of the Chief of the Defence Staff 1999–2000. National Defence. Ottawa: Minister of Supply and Services, 2000.

Byers, Rod and Michael Slack, eds. *Canada and Peacekeeping: Prospects for the Future.* Toronto: Research Program in Strategic Studies, York University, 1984.

Challenges and Commitment: A Defence Policy for Canada. National Defence. Ottawa: Supply and Services Canada, 1987.

Cohen, William S., Secretary of Defence. *Annual Report to the President and the Congress.* Washington, 1999.

Defence in the 70s: White Paper on Defence. National Defence. Ottawa: Information Canada, 1971.

Defence Performance and Outlook 2000: Making a Difference at Home and Abroad. National Defence, n.d.

Defence Planning Guidance 2000 (DPG 2000). National Defence. 1999.

Dewitt, David and David Leyton-Brown. *Canada's International Security Policy.* Scarborough, ON: Prentice Hall, 1995.

Granatstein, J.L., ed. *Canadian Foreign Policy: Historical Readings.* Revised edition. Toronto: Copp Clark Pitman, 1993.

Gray, Colin. *Canadian Defence Priorities: A Question of Relevance.* Toronto: Clarke Irwin, 1972.

Gray, Colin. *Modern Strategy*. Oxford: Oxford University Press, 1999.

Hampson, Fen and Christopher Maule. "After the Cold War." In Fen Hampson and Christopher Maule (eds.), *Canada among Nations 1990–92: After the Cold War*. Ottawa: Carleton University Press, 1991.

Hobson, Sharon. "Country Briefing—Canada Stretching to the Limit." *Jane's Defence Weekly*, February 2, 2000.

House of Commons, Standing Committee on National Defence and Veterans' Affairs. *Moving Forward: A Strategic Plan for Quality of Life Improvements in the Canadian Forces*. Ottawa: Minister of Supply and Services, 1998.

Into the New Millennium: Annual Report of the Chief of the Defence Staff 1998–1999. National Defence. 1999.

Keating, Tom. *Canada and World Order: The Multilateralist Tradition in Canadian Foreign Policy*. Toronto: McClelland and Stewart, 1993.

Legault, Albert. *The End of a Military Century?* Ottawa: International Development Research Centre, 1992.

Middlemiss, Dan and Joel Sokolsky. *Canadian Defence: Decisions and Determinants*. Toronto: Harcourt Brace Jovanovich, 1989.

Morrison, Alex, ed. *The Changing Face of Peacekeeping*. Toronto: Canadian Institute of Strategic Studies, 1993.

National Defence. Current Operations. *D-Net*. <http://www.dnd.ca/menu/Operations/index_e.htm>. Updated August 3, 2000.

National Defence: Report on Plans and Priorities—2000. National Defence, n.d.

Sens, Allen and Peter Stoett. *Global Politics: Origins, Currents, Directions*. Toronto: Nelson, 1998.

Shadwick, Martin. "Canada's Commitment to NATO: The Need for Rationalization." *Canadian Defence Quarterly* 15:1 (Summer 1985).

Shaping the Future of Canadian Defence: A Strategy for 2020, National Defence. 1999.

Sokolsky, Joel. "Canadian Defence Policy: Coping with the Gap." In Brian Tomlin and Maureen Appeal Molot (Eds.), *Canada Among Nations 1986: Talking Trade*. Toronto: James Lormier, 1987.

Strategic Operations and Resource Plan 2000–2002. National Defence, n.d.

White Paper on Defence. National Defence. Ottawa: Queen's Printer, 1964.

FURTHER READING

Gray, Colin. *Modern Strategy*. Oxford: Oxford University Press, 1999.

Keating, Tom. *Canada and World Order: The Multilateralist Tradition in Canadian Foreign Policy*. Toronto: McClelland and Stewart, 1993.

Legault, Albert. *The End of a Military Century?* Ottawa: International Development Research Centre, 1992.

Middlemiss, Dan and Sokolosky, Joel. *Canadian Defence: Decisions and Determinants.* Toronto: Harcourt, Brace Jovanovich, 1989.

Tom Thomson
Autumn Foliage
n.d.

Lawren S. Harris
Above Lake Superior
c. 1922

By permission of the family of Lawren S. Harris. Art Gallery of Ontario, Toronto.
Gift from the Reuben and Kate Leonard Canadian Fund, 1929.

Paul-Émile Borduas
Expansion rayonnante/Radiating Expansion
1956

Collection of the Montreal Museum of Fine Arts.
Gift of Dr. and Mrs. Max Stern.

Greg Curnoe
Mariposa 10 Speed
25 March 1973–25 April 1973

Reproduced with permission from the National Gallery of Canada, Ottawa.

Joyce Wieland
I Love Canada – J'Aime Canada
1970

MacKenzie Art Gallery, University of Regina Collection.

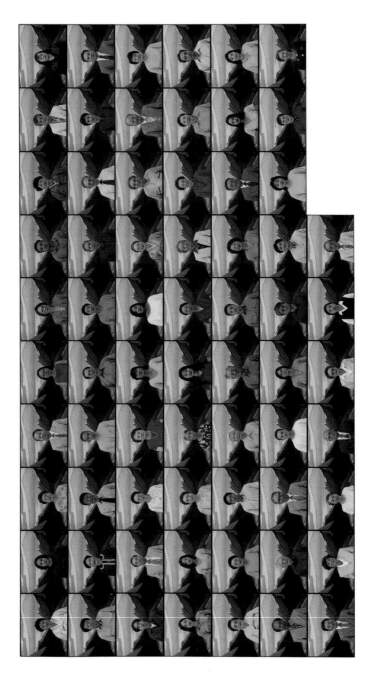

Jin-me Yoon
A Group of Sixty-Seven

Courtesy of Jin-me Yoon and the Vancouver Art Gallery.

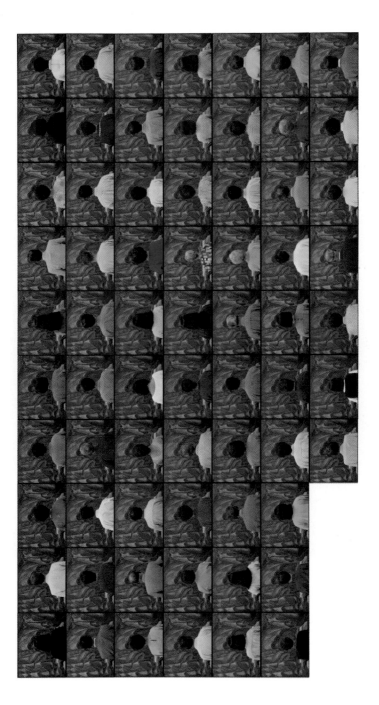

Lawren S. Harris
Maligne Lake, Jasper Park
1924

Reproduced with permission from the National Gallery of Canada, Ottawa.

Hockey and Canadian Identities: From Frozen Rivers to Revenue Streams

David Whitson

In January 2000, Canada's Industry Minister, John Manley, announced an aid package designed to help keep our six remaining National Hockey League teams in Canada. However, after three days of virulent public opposition, the offer of aid was withdrawn. This was an about-face almost unprecedented in Canadian politics.[1] In June 2000, the Montreal Canadiens, Canada's (and hockey's) most-storied franchise, were put up for sale, apparently unable to make money despite a 1996 move from the historic Forum to the new Molson Centre.[2] On the ice, meanwhile, in between these two economic "events," only the Toronto Maple Leafs from among the NHL's Canadian teams managed to make the second round of the playoffs. Clearly, changes in the business of professional sport may threaten the future of most of the Canadian NHL teams. However, the public reaction to the Manley proposals, and later the muted response to season-ticket campaigns in all of the smaller NHL cities, also suggested that hockey no longer means as much as it once did to many Canadians, and that beyond the somewhat self-contained world of the game itself and the sports media, hockey no longer enjoys the place in Canadian life that it maintained throughout much of the 20th century

One could argue, perhaps, that 2000 was a bad year. Yet, the last five years of the 20th century saw a succession of events that chipped away at popular notions that hockey was somehow "our game"—a notion that once mattered to a great many Canadians. In 1995, the Quebec Nordiques were sold to new owners who moved the team to Denver, where, in their first season as the Colorado Avalanche, they promptly won the Stanley Cup. In 1996, it was the Winnipeg Jets who flew off to the greener environment (financially, at least) of Phoenix, after a long campaign by local boosters to raise money for a new arena in Winnipeg ended in failure (Silver, 1996). Indeed, these moves to larger American markets were simply the final acts in stories played out over several years, in which teams that had made money into the late 1980s found themselves facing large and continuing losses as players' salaries escalated beyond what local revenues could support. In 1997, the future of the Calgary Flames and the Edmonton Oilers was secured temporarily through the use of federal infrastructure grants (augmented by civic and provincial funds) to fund renovations to their buildings that provided more luxury seating, as well as enhanced possibilities for advertising and concession revenues. In the larger Canadian NHL cities, meanwhile, team owners pressed ahead with new privately funded arenas, venues that were again designed to maximize the potential of the new "revenue streams" that have become essential to survival in contemporary professional sport. And with the opening of the Molson Centre and the Air Canada Centre, in particular, there was brief optimism that the revenues generated by these new facilities would enable their storied tenants, the Canadiens and the Maple Leafs, to regain something of their former glory.

However, this was not to be—at least not right away. As their individual and collective representations to the Mills Committee and Industry Canada make clear, Canadian teams that were successful only 10 years ago now have trouble competing in a business where their U.S. competitors enjoy higher revenues and lower taxes and often play in venues that have been provided at public expense. Moreover, these financial disparities are now increasingly manifest on the ice. The Oilers and the Canadiens have lost many good players to free agency, including players who have gone on to play leading roles on successful teams. Meanwhile, Canadian teams have rarely, in recent years, made significant free-agent signings of their own, and it was 1994 when a Canadian-based team last contested a Stanley Cup final. This erosion of Canada's historical pre-eminence in hockey also shows on other fronts, as well: in our failure to win a medal in hockey at the Nagano Winter Olympics in 1998 (or in the World Championship in 2000), in our decreasing representation among the elite players in the NHL (and among the high picks in the entry draft), and in increasing agreement that our development system is no longer competitive in a world where many other countries now play hockey at increasingly high levels.

The discussion that follows offers an analysis of contemporary developments in professional sport, developments that challenge some of Canadians' traditional feelings about the game, and threaten the future of most Canadian teams in the NHL. The discussion will begin with some comments on the place of professional sport in the commercial popular culture that developed in North America in the early 1900s, and how the Canadian media of that period constructed the National Hockey League as a Canadian institution, even when it was already by 1930 a league based mostly in American cities. We will then proceed to examine how, since the 1960s, the cultural significance of teams like the Canadiens and the Leafs has been steadily undercut: by expansion, by the draft, by the influx of international players, and by the progressively stronger presence in Canada of other "major league" sports. It will be suggested that in the now-familiar process we call "expansion," sports that were once national or regional in their cultural roots have sought to promote themselves in places where they have no tradition as popular recreations, bringing them into direct competition for audiences with the sports traditional to those places.

This, of course, is consistent with the dynamic now known as "globalization": a set of related commercial developments in which producers of many kinds of goods and services have sought to grow by seeking first national, then continental, and finally global markets for their products. There is, of course, a familiar argument that globalization benefits consumers by bringing them a wider choice of better quality products; certainly in sport there is ample evidence that Canadians have become enthusiastic consumers of a wide range of "world-class" sports entertainment. However, by the late 1990s, it was also clear that some traditional "national" sports are threatened by the spread of global culture, while even those that succeed in globalizing become more like sports *products*, in the ways they are promoted, than the national institutions they once were. Indeed, as sport becomes more fully integrated into a global "promotional culture" (Wernick, 1991), the promotion of "new" sports—whether basketball in Canada or hockey in the American sunbelt—becomes inseparable from the promotion of such other global brand names as Nike, Disney, Coke, etc. The analysis concludes with some thoughts on what globalization may mean for the place of hockey in Canadian culture as well as some questions about the identities that global marketing seeks to construct.

PROFESSIONAL SPORT AND POPULAR IDENTITIES: THE EARLY YEARS

Sociologist David Chaney (1985, 1993) argues that the essence of ritual is that collective identities are postulated and publicly celebrated, identities that might otherwise have only an ambiguous social existence. In this section, we trace the emergence of spectator sport as one of the most powerful civic and national rituals of the 20th century and consider how professional hockey, in particular, developed its now time-honoured place in the rituals of Canadian identity, even though our "National" Hockey League was already substantially American by the late 1920s. Social historians have suggested that one feature of the urban cultures that developed in Europe and North America in the late 19th century was the growth of new forms of crowd experience and spectator entertainment (Butsch, 1990; Riess, 1989).[3] Sport was not alone here; theatres and cinemas, and of course music and dance halls, all became popular venues for going out and for the mixing of the sexes. However, spectator sports quickly attracted large and partisan male crowds, and sports events took on the aura of popular civic rituals. Sports competitions offered occasions for the dramatization of communal rivalries and for public demonstrations of collective allegiances and animosities.

At the turn of the 19th century, most sporting competition in Canada still took place within cities rather than between them, and sports "clubs" served as representatives of the ethnic, class, and sometimes religious rivalries that divided Canadian cities of that period. Historian Alan Metcalfe (1987) has documented how early sports competitions in Montreal were organized and staged by social clubs that gave institutional form to upper- and middle-class social consciousness, as well as to Protestant and Catholic affiliations and, of course, the English and French communities. Accounts of sport in the early 1900s in Edmonton and Winnipeg are likewise filled with team names like Thistles and Shamrocks, or Strathcona and St. Boniface, and this pattern of teams representing ethnic, religious, and neighbourhood communities (often overlapping) was common in most Canadian cities of that era (see Betke, 1975; Mott, 1985). However, as improved communications made intercity competition more feasible, and as professionalism became more normal, the meanings associated with "representative" sport would undergo significant transformations.

Professionalism involved a shift toward the use of paid agents, acting in the name of the community; and once it became common practice to hire outsiders, relationships between communities, the teams that bore their names, and the professional athletes who played for those teams would inevitably change. People were provisionally loyal to the local representatives; however, management was expected to assemble the best team local money could buy, and players were expected to give "value for money," in terms of skill, commitment, and ultimately results. Indeed, as sports promoters learned to sell the promise of winning, it soon didn't matter where players came from so long as they won, and the whole city could be encouraged to identify with their success (Gruneau and Whitson, 1993, pp. 67–72). Now clearly, it is in the interest of sports promoters to seek city-wide support and to promote the idea that professional teams represent the whole community—a challenge that is still germane to sports promotion in Montreal today, for both the Expos and the Alouettes. However, one has to ask whether the "city-as-a-whole" that is celebrated in professional sport is not both ambiguous and problematic. When the legitimate pride that citizens might take in the accomplishments of native sons (and, very exceptionally, daughters) is transformed into pride in the success of their hired agents, the celebration of collective achievement becomes a more vacuous kind of civic boosterism. Moreover, the regular ritualization of "civic" identity papers over important and enduring differences within cities—exactly the function of ritual that Chaney points to—and invites popular identification with the projects and ambitions of civic elites.

In the first two decades of the 20th century, when the structure of professional hockey was less clearly dominated by one league than it is today, teams were established in many small communities across Canada and the northern United States. Without any restrictions on player mobility, barons in remote lumber and mining towns like Renfrew and Cobalt in Ontario and Houghton, Michigan, spent big money importing players who might bring success and fame to their small communities. In 1909–10, for example, M.J. O'Brien of the Renfrew Millionaires paid Cyclone Taylor a salary that briefly made him the highest-paid athlete in North America on a per-game basis. Yet salaries like this could not be recouped from the revenues available in towns like Renfrew, with the result that the heyday of these teams was short, and some lasted only a couple of years. The survivors moved quickly to stabilize professional hockey, and by 1911 the National Hockey Association, the precursor of the NHL, had established itself as the "major" league in Ontario and Quebec, with teams based in the major cities of those two provinces and agreements to limit salaries and honour each other's player contracts. For about 15 years, this league's domination of the hockey business was limited somewhat by the existence of good regional professional leagues in Atlantic Canada and in the West. The Maritime league would soon fold, as a result of World War I and the diminishing health of the Atlantic economy. However, the Pacific Coast Hockey Association (PCHA) grew, as a result of the Patrick family's lumber fortune and business acumen. The PCHA's claims to "major" status were strengthened when first the Vancouver Millionaires (in 1915) and then the Seattle Metropolitans (in 1917) won the Stanley Cup in a challenge series with the NHA champions. Soon after the war's end, moreover, good-calibre professional hockey was again being played on the Prairies, and when the Prairie league merged with the PCHA in 1924, the resulting Western Hockey League (WHL) seriously aspired to compete with the (now re-named) National Hockey League for status as hockey's top league. The Victoria Cougars bolstered their ambitions by winning the 1925 Stanley Cup (Gruneau and Whitson, 1993, pp. 87–92).

At the same time, there was also considerable team movement within the NHL, as well as rapid rises in franchise values. In 1920, the Quebec Bulldogs were sold to Hamilton for $7500; but by 1924 the owners of the Montreal Canadiens could sell half their "rights" to the Montreal market for $15 000 to owners who would operate a rival English team (the Maroons). In that same year, the league granted its first U.S. franchise to Boston, followed by Pittsburgh in 1925, each also for $15 000. In 1925 the Hamilton franchise was purchased by Madison Square Gardens for $75 000 (five times what Boston and Pittsburgh had paid), and that prompted a syndicate in Chicago to pay $150 000 for rights to operate a franchise in that city. In this atmosphere, Conn Smythe had to appeal to patriotism to get the owners of the Toronto St. Patricks to sell him the team that would become the Maple Leafs for $160 000, rather than sell to higher American bidders. Quickly, with hockey moving into 15 000-seat arenas in the large eastern cities, the WHL owners realized that they couldn't compete. They sold their players to the NHL to be distributed around the new U.S. franchises, and by 1927, the National Hockey League had put all serious competition out of business. These developments prompted a writer in *Macleans* to ask questions that sound familiar in the 1990s: "Will U.S. cash cripple hockey? How long will Canada be able to hold its teams?" (Mills, 1995).

My purpose in this brief history is to highlight several features of professional hockey in the 1920s that prefigure present developments. First, the movement of hockey teams (and players) from smaller Canadian centres to larger American ones is not new, nor are Canadian concerns about the loss of our game to the Yankee dollar. Yet despite some expressions of patriotic concern about the Americanization of hockey, it is also noteworthy that popular Canadian interest in the National Hockey League was not at all diminished by these events. The prowess of the Montreal and Toronto teams, the continued location of the league headquarters in Montreal, and the fact that almost all the players were still Canadian, together made for a widespread popular belief that the game remained Canadian. Indeed, interest in NHL hockey continued to expand across the country, and a populist nationalism was given daily voice in the Canadian media's cheerleading for the Leafs and Canadiens. This, in turn, serves to highlight the role of the popular media in magnifying interest in "big league" professional sports. By the early 1920s, newspapers across Canada carried regular coverage of major league baseball, and media historian Paul Rutherford (1993, p. 265) remarks that, especially in the cities, Canadians quickly became enthusiastic and knowledgeable followers of all American professional sports.

However, it was the magic of radio that would take the live drama of sports into homes across North America, making the major league seasons into ubiquitous features of popular life and conversation, and making their annual championships—the World Series, the Stanley Cup playoffs, etc.—into national events. Hockey didn't get national radio coverage in the U.S. in the 1930s, and hence it never achieved the national presence in America that baseball and football did. In Canada, though, hockey broadcasts from Maple Leaf Gardens began in 1931, and by 1934, games from either Toronto or Montreal were reaching more than 1 000 000 listeners in every part of the country. *Hockey Night in Canada* was the first radio program in Canada to reach anything like a national audience, and the broadcasts made hockey stars like Howie Morenz, the Conacher brothers, Max Bentley, and Eddie Shore (the latter two, of course, playing for American teams) into Canadian legends. By the outbreak of war, audiences for hockey broadcasts had grown to over 2 000 0000, and *Hockey Night in Canada* on CBC radio had become one of the most widely shared Canadian experiences (Gruneau and Whitson, 1993, pp. 100–01). The introduction of televised games on CBC in 1952 served only to reinforce hockey's role in bringing Canadians together around a common interest, as across the country the children who made up the baby-boom generations would grow up watching NHL hockey every Saturday night from autumn until spring. By the late 1950s, the NHL season was simply part of the rhythms of Canadian life, the Stanley Cup playoffs a ritual of Canadian spring, at least for most men and boys of that period. What English historian Eric Hobsbawm (1983) has aptly called "the invention of tradition" had been accomplished, in this instance, in less than 25 years.

It is worth noting here that hockey's cultural significance in postwar Canada owed much to the game's popular following in both the English- and French-speaking populations and to the way that the Montreal Canadiens had constructed themselves, since the 1930s, as French Canada's team. Although Canadiens teams have never excluded English players, it was the individual and collective excellence of their francophone players—players like Lafleur, Beliveau, and especially Richard—that regularly gave rise to the collective pride of French-speaking Canadians and gave the team a "representative" significance that has no parallel in North American professional sport.[4] English and French identifications remained an important subtext in how many Canadians watched hockey in the early postwar decades, and there was probably no other common interest that brought the "two solitudes" of these years into the same kind of regular and passionate engagement with one another. Moreover, although migrants from Eastern and Southern Europe had not been prominent in pre-war hockey to any extent, when their children and grandchildren became postwar hockey stars, the folk-hero status of men with names like Sawchuk, Mahovlich and Esposito signalled for many the arrival of "new" Canadians into a different and more inclusive Canadian culture (Gruneau and Whitson, 1993, p. 101). What one can conclude is that popular institutions like sports can be important in the production and reproduction of national identities, precisely because they construct regular rituals of collective identification and pride. They do so, moreover, among many people who take little interest in the "national" agendas of their political and intellectual elites. Yet Canadians' stewardship of what we considered our national game was about to be challenged by foreign influences and by processes beyond our control.

EXPANSION AND TELEVISION: 1960–80

Between 1942 and 1967, the makeup of the NHL had remained stable: the Montreal Canadiens, Toronto Maple Leafs, Detroit Red Wings, Boston Bruins, Chicago Black Hawks, and New York Rangers. This stability now stands revealed as an historical anomaly, contrasting both with the competition and instability that marked professional hockey's formative years and the expansions and team movements that were to come. In the early years of the postwar boom the owners of the "original six" teams (which were not original, as we have seen) saw little reason to alter a successful structure in which their monopoly control of the game kept players' salaries low and profits comfortable. However, the geography and economics of professional sport would soon be altered irrevocably: by television, by commercial air travel, and by a steady shift of population and wealth from the eastern and Great Lakes regions—the old industrial heartlands of North America—to the west and south. Oil and gas booms, the growth of computer and aerospace industries, and climatic and lifestyle attractions all contributed to rapid population growth in California and across the American south, and in British Columbia and Alberta in Canada. As these regions boomed, their affluent populations constituted obvious markets for professional sports, and they wanted to be part of major leagues that television was making even more popular than before.

The first changes came in baseball, in the 1950s, with the dramatic relocation of the New York Giants and Brooklyn Dodgers to San Francisco and Los Angeles, respectively. These moves shocked not only local fans but also many others who believed in the traditions of "representative" ties between teams and their communities and had believed that, in some organic way, teams belonged at least partly to their fans. What would be demonstrated repeatedly, though, was that teams that had been thought of as civic institutions, organic parts of local culture and of the social history of their cities, could be moved to other cities for business advantages. It quickly became clear, as well, that the demand for major league sport could not be satisfied by the transfer of existing teams; thus, all of the major leagues were soon discussing expansions, if only to pre-empt potential competition. In hockey, Canadian fans hoped that expansion would bring teams to Vancouver and Winnipeg, thereby increasing Canadian representation in the NHL. However, from the league's perspective, a primary purpose of expansion was to dislodge the American perception of hockey as a Canadian sport and to establish a more national presence for the game in American popular culture. To this end, the first expansion franchises were granted in 1967 to Los Angeles, Oakland, Minnesota, St. Louis, Pittsburgh, and Philadelphia: choices partly determined by investor interest but also by the NHL's desire to establish itself across America. Canadians were disappointed and angry at the league's disregard of Canadian cities that we believed "deserved" franchises more than places like Oakland and St. Louis; and the issue was briefly taken up in Parliament (Gruneau and Whitson, 1993, pp. 258–59). In this context, the NHL moved belatedly to assuage nationalist sentiments by granting Vancouver a franchise in 1969.

However, interest in professional hockey was such that a rival league was formed in the early 1970s, including teams in several other Canadian cities. The World Hockey Association (WHA) staked its claim to major league status by signing one of the top stars of the day, Bobby Hull, away from Chicago and by competing with the NHL to sign top junior players, including (later) Wayne Gretzky. Competition with the WHA led to big increases in NHL players' salaries, and to the NHL placing new teams in the Colorado and Atlanta markets. Nevertheless, without regular exposure on American television, many of the new teams (in both leagues) lost money, and in 1979–80, the competition ended when the NHL absorbed the strongest franchises from the WHA into a renewed "major league" monopoly. This was how Edmonton, Quebec, and Winnipeg (along with Hartford) gained access to the NHL, and Calgary would join them a year later, with the purchase and transfer of the struggling Atlanta Flames. These Canadian provincial cities were always small markets by American standards, which take into account the size and spending power of the surrounding television audiences, and some U.S. owners saw their admission as a setback to the league's strategic effort to reposition itself in American popular culture. Yet Edmonton, Calgary, Quebec, and Winnipeg were all centres of hockey enthusiasm, and *so long as strong gate receipts were a sufficient condition of success*, they were able to support major league hockey very well. In the 1980s the two Alberta clubs, in particular, played to sellout crowds and were conspicuously successful on the ice too. By the 1990s, however, changes in the economics of professional sports would threaten the viability of all these "small-market" franchises, leading to demands for publicly funded arenas and other forms of subsidy that might help them remain competitive (Gruneau and Whitson, 1993, pp. 228–34).

We shall return to these changes shortly, but first I will make a few observations about the effects that expansion and television would have on professional sports. First, it is clear that there has been a lot of money made in the franchising of professional sport. Even where teams have been poorly supported and have shown operating losses, these have been typically offset by the dramatic rises in franchise values that each major league has been able to sustain by virtue of its monopoly position. In hockey, the $50 million franchise fee paid by Ottawa and Tampa Bay in 1991 represented an exponential increase over the $2 million paid by the initial expansion franchises in the 1960s.

The other important influence, of course, is television. It is now a truism that television has magnified the place of major league professional sports in North American popular culture, and that, in doing so, it has transformed the economics of professional sports. At first, ironically, it was feared that television would undercut live audiences. It soon became obvious, though, both from viewer ratings and attendance figures, that the regular televising of games was actually increasing the number of people who followed professional sports. Television brought faces into living rooms, which would play no small role in turning athletes into celebrities. Commentary, meanwhile, helped to explain play to new fans, made it sound exciting, and included fans in the serial narratives that are the sporting seasons. All of this helped to make sports television appeal to wider audiences than the traditional "hard-core" male blue-collar fans. Indeed, so successful was sports television in attracting large audiences that networks were soon offering unprecedented sums for rights to the most popular sports. When they lost the bidding for traditional favourites, moreover, they wanted sports audiences badly enough to begin offering new alternatives. Indeed, it was the CBC that first brought NFL football to Canada, after CTV had won the rights to the CFL and Grey Cup. The cumulative effect of all of this was to make major league sports more widely watched and talked about than ever before.

Another effect, however, was to dramatically increase the revenues of all major league sports, and it would not be long before players were pressing for a larger share. Athletes' salaries had remained low through the 1950s because of "reserve" clauses, in all sports contracts, which served to prohibit players from seeking higher salaries from other teams. Owners in all the major leagues historically contended that free player movement would destroy "the game," and had invited fan sympathy with this position. But, what owners have called "the good of the game" has equated, always and in every sport, with the profitability of their leagues as businesses, and once the courts ruled that reserve clauses constituted unlawful restraints on labour mobility, all the major leagues moved to make rules governing player mobility (i.e., the conditions for free agency) the subject of collective agreements with players' unions. Free agency initially led to long-overdue increases in players' salaries and to curbs on the arbitrary and paternalistic management practices of earlier years. However, since the early 1990s, exponential rises in salaries have seriously undermined the viability and competitiveness of small city teams, in both Canada and the United States.

Together, it can be suggested that expansion and franchise relocation, television, and free agency have multiplied, and in some ways redistributed, the money that constitutes the economy of professional sport. They have also accelerated the "delocalization" of sports loyalties (Euchner, 1992). At one level, this simply recognizes a gradual but steady decline in the old norm of "cheering for the home team," and an increase in support for famous teams that are followed through the media. This was always present: for example, in national followings for the Canadiens or the New York Yankees. However, free agency and television exposure have made it easier for wealthy teams like the Dallas Cowboys and the Atlanta Braves to buy success and attract national followings. At a more important level, moreover, television enabled all the major league sports to pursue new markets, and those that used television most effectively, notably the NFL and the NBA, vastly increased their followings across North America. From the 1960s onward, indeed, television has brought sports into ever more direct competitions for audiences, competitions in which local and regional traditions would be no guarantee of continued fan loyalty, especially among the young. In this context, sports that did not increase their continental profile have risked losing their traditional fan base to more actively promoted and trendy rivals. This, of course, is one reason why the Canadian Football League has struggled for more than a decade, and it is why the NHL must now compete with the NBA for the interest of young Canadians.

A NEW ERA: CORPORATE SYNERGIES AND CONSUMER IDENTITIES

In the 1990s, pay-television technologies and strategic consolidations in the communications industries, dramatic increases in players' salaries, and further changes in the North American economy all contributed to a new business equation in which some of the same cities that gained major league franchises between 1960 and 1980 began to lose them. The threat was sharpest in those regional cities where traditional manufacturing had been "downsized," or whose "raison d'être" was as a government and commercial centre for a regional hinterland. Such cities have lost some of their importance in an increasingly continental economy; and while this has affected a few U.S. cities like Hartford and Minneapolis, Canadian cities like Edmonton, Quebec, and Winnipeg are smaller and more peripheral and thus more vulnerable. This is the context in which the corporate and civic elites of these cities lobbied to keep their NHL franchises, both for the economic activity it is claimed they generate and for the visibility and status that are widely believed to be attached to being in the same league (literally) with New York, Los Angeles, etc. However, the continuing explosion in players' salaries has made it increasingly difficult for what are now described as "small-market franchises" to survive. Average NHL salaries tripled between 1989 and 1994, from $180 000 to over $500 000, and have more than doubled again since then, to over $1 000 000 (US).[5] Thus, where the Edmonton Oilers could win Stanley Cups in the mid-1980s with total players' salary budgets of less than $5 million, now teams like Edmonton and Calgary spend in excess of $20 million and still find themselves losing their better players as free agents. Owners in small Canadian markets have thus claimed with some justice that they can no longer ice competitive teams unless they gain access to more revenues. Yet salaries are rising precisely because owners in the major metropolitan markets, and owners for whom sports "properties" represent a useful kind of corporate synergy, are making money, and it is useful to explore just how these new "revenue streams" work, as well as why they put "small-market" teams at a significant disadvantage (Rosentraub, 1998; Quirk and Fort, 1992).

The most visible of the new revenue streams that are changing the economics of professional sport comes from premium seating, especially luxury boxes for corporate entertaining. This isn't entirely new, of course; box seats have been a time-honoured form of conspicuous consumption, separating elites from crowds before postwar affluence and democratic attitudes began to erode such distinctions (Chaney, 1993). However, in the 1990s, luxury boxes and "club" seats became a standard feature of North American professional sports venues, because premium seating, with its large charges for exclusive privileges and its upmarket catering, brings in much more revenue than the cheaper seating it typically replaces. This is what produced a 1990s building boom in new stadia and arenas around North America[6] and has made the capacity to sell corporate seating a necessary condition of survival in the National Hockey League. However, the effect of replacing cheaper seats with seating geared to corporate entertaining is to move the game increasingly upmarket, out of reach of even middle-income fans.

Another highly visible source of revenues comes from licensed merchandise. Replica jerseys and caps historically provided a small source of additional revenues for the most famous teams (e.g, the Montreal Canadiens, the New York Yankees). However, since the early 1980s, when the NBA demonstrated that a vigorous approach to trademark protection, together with aggressive promotion of sports insignia clothing as fashion wear, could produce enormous revenues, licensed merchandising has become big business. When combined with the promotion of celebrity stars like Michael Jordan and Wayne Gretzky, the effect has been to make sports brand names—and team logos and colours—into popular texts of identity, especially among the young.

The most important new revenue streams, though, flow from the growth of regional cable and satellite television, offering choices of special-interest channels—including sports channels—on a subscription or pay-per-view basis. Revenues from pay television (as opposed to "free," broadcast TV) have become increasingly important in the economics of professional sports, because they generally belong to the (local) teams whose games are shown, rather than being divided among league members the way that national network revenues are (Quirk and Fort, 1992; Bellamy and Walker, 1995). This accords significant advantages to the large-market franchises, and not just because TSN and the Madison Square Gardens Network can show games with little effect on live gates. What is most important here is that the advertising revenues generated in Toronto or New York reflect the size and affluence of the audiences they reach. In addition, regular exposure in these metropolitan markets adds to the values that teams can realize from rink board advertising, from leasing the name of the arena, and from the marketing of marquee players. This is why Wayne Gretzky was "worth" more in Los Angeles and New York than he was in Edmonton (or St. Louis), and why the large metropolitan clubs can pull away, financially, from their small-market competitors. What subscription television has facilitated, and what sports and media interests have actively pursued, is a new degree of integration between sports and marketing that can be exploited most fully in large markets.

In the new economy of professional sport, the promotion of professional sport, and the use of sports events and sports figures to promote other products have become virtually indistinguishable. This has led to new kinds of corporate ownership in sport and to strategic cross-marketing in which the different products in a corporate empire are used to promote each other. The earliest form of this saw the ownership of teams by brewers, such as Molson and Labatt, whose beer sales and brand visibility were promoted by their associations with the Canadiens and the Blue Jays, respectively. However, it was becoming clear by the end of the 1990s that the ownership of sports teams was no longer seen by major brewers as a profitable enterprise. The Blue Jays have been on the market for several years, ever since Labatt was taken over by the European brewing giant Interbrew. More recently, Molson's announcement in June 2000 that the Canadiens were up for sale confirmed that the operating losses now associated with major league sports, said to be between $5–7 million per year in the case of the Canadiens, have risen to levels that even major brewing corporations cannot justify, in terms of the financial benefits that sports ownership brings to the company.

Over the 1990s, indeed, it became increasingly clear that only television or telecommunications companies can justify sports ownership, in the sense that it contributes to the corporate bottom line even when the team loses money on operations. Owning a team (or even better, several teams in a city) provides "content" in the form of popular sports programming for these types of companies. When this works, sports "rights," for example—to many more Blue Jays' baseball games or Canadiens' hockey games than will ever be available on the CBC, or to the Euro2000 soccer championships—help to sell cable or satellite subscriptions to people who need access to TSN or ExpressVu (or in Europe, SkyTV or Canal Plus) in order to watch the important competitions in their favourite sports. It may also help to sell Internet products in the future and assist in the development of online merchandising and advertising revenues. This model of integrating content ownership with distribution capacity was pioneered by the Turner cable network in Atlanta (which owned the Braves and a lot of movie rights), and by Viacom's ownership of Madison Square Gardens, the Rangers, and the Knicks. Now, however, ownership of sports teams by integrated communications giants is increasingly common in both the United States and Europe, and at the time of writing, this is the likely prospect for both the Canadiens and the Jays, with the dominant players in the Canadian communications industry in 2000—including Rogers, Canwest Global, and BCE (owners of CTV and TSN)—reportedly expressing interest.[7] The global giants of integrated entertainment and communications are, of course, Fox and Disney, and their models of integrating ownership of major entertainment "properties," including sports, with ownership of increasingly global distribution systems, are beginning to reshape the "playing field" on which others must compete.

The slogan "any sport, anywhere" expressed the strategic vision held in the early 1990s by ambitious marketers from Gary Bettman and David Stern to Rupert Murdoch (of Fox and SkyTV). At the turn of the century, it is possible to suggest that this vision remains unrealized, at least for now. Television audiences for hockey in the United States remain weak, while interest in the NBA (both abroad and at home) has declined since the retirement of Michael Jordan. The decision to hold the 1994 World Cup in America did not succeed in building audiences for professional soccer in the United States in any major way. Yet these efforts at expansion will clearly not be abandoned, and the point is that when sports are marketed in the ways the Raptors were in Toronto, or hockey is now in Atlanta or Nashville, sports "interests" are effectively repositioned as new and trendy consumer choices—as opposed to local (or national) traditions that, passed down through generations, help to sustain place identities. This celebration of globalism—the "excellence" of global products, and the excitement of global events—seeks precisely to undermine habits of loyalty to local institutions, and as Vancouver writer Brian Fawcett (1992) has observed, the entertainment industries, including professional sport, are among globalism's most effective ideological carriers. We are invited to think of ourselves as free-floating and discerning consumers, whose sophistication is demonstrated precisely in our taste for the "world-class" products that global promotion is making internationally known. When building global markets for products like hockey, moreover, national origins are likely to be played down, so that new audiences may more readily invest them with their own meanings.

In the new millennium, sport marketing will appeal to national identities when strategically useful. However, discourses that spoke to (and traded on) identities rooted in place are gradually being supplanted by marketing in which consumers around the affluent world are invited to identify with teams—and sports—on the basis of colours and logos, style and "attitude," and sheer ubiquitous presence in the media. What was also demonstrated in the selling of basketball in Canada in the late 1990s, as well as in the selling of hockey in southern California, is that these campaigns are pitched especially at the young, for whom their parents' sporting loves will have no privileged status (Chadwin, 1994). Sports that are not traditional local recreations are staged with all the techniques of show business, in turn forcing established games to adopt similar production values in order to compete. Team names and logos are chosen for their appeal to focus groups of pre-adolescent boys. The cumulative effect is a triumph of the values of marketing; and the progressive transformation of the sports fan, from member (i.e., of a face-to-face community, or a club) to loyal customer to global consumer.

CONCLUSION: "IT'S NOT OUR GAME ANY MORE": GLOBALIZATION AND NOSTALGIA

This emphasis on promotion and marketing, in which league officials and, increasingly, the rest of us, now talk of markets rather than cities, heralds a new stage in the economy of pro hockey, and one in which smaller Canadian cities may no longer matter. That cities like Winnipeg, Quebec, and perhaps Edmonton or even Montreal, may no longer be able to afford NHL hockey is difficult for many Canadians to accept. It is particularly unpalatable, not surprisingly, for fans in these cities that have loyally supported their teams and who, in Edmonton, have identified with the "City of Champions" version of civic pride. In these circumstances, it is not surprising that many Canadians resent that "our game" appears to be slipping away from us. There is nostalgia for the sense of national connection we used to experience around hockey, and for the pride we once took in our unchallenged prowess in the game. At the same time, though, the negative response of the Canadian public to the Manley proposals to assist Canada's NHL teams, cited at the outset of this paper, suggests that most Canadians have recognized that major league hockey is now a business rather than a national institution and are fed up with the claims on the public purse made by millionaire owners and players.

English sociologist Stuart Hall (1992, p. 293) has proposed that national identities are amalgams of ideas and images of "the nation" that ordinary people can identify with. These emerge out of communal historical experiences and practices, and out of stories of famous triumphs (and tragedies) that are retold in the media and in popular conversation till they become, literally, the stuff of legends. Together, they constitute a set of collective memories, as well as popular rituals that link the national present with the past, creating "imagined communities" in exactly the ways that Chaney (cited above) has suggested. In this spirit, sports can serve as anchors of meaning at a time when national cultures and identities are being affected by globalizing tendencies. The associations of sports with familiar places, with seasonal rhythms, even with particular weekends on the calendar, all contribute to a sense of the endurance of the imagined community of the nation (Maguire, 1993; Blake, 1996). Thus for many Canadians who grew up in the postwar decades, "our Canada" would surely include images and memories drawn from hockey: "*Hockey Night in Canada*" from Maple Leaf Gardens, Stanley Cup playoffs, and the 1972 victory over the Soviets. It might also include the memories of winter and childhood that anonymous municipal arenas can bring to mind for many Canadian men who grew up (or raised sons) in the postwar years (MacGregor, 1996).

Yet although revisiting such memories can help us to appreciate the powerful national significance that hockey continues to have for

Canadian men of these generations, it can also be suggested that nostalgia for the Canada of the 1950s or 1960s bucks the trend of new cultural realities that are emerging out of historically unprecedented patterns of global migration, global economic activity, and global communications.

All of these, as Hall and others have argued, are profoundly reshaping traditional national identities, and indeed the bases on which collective identities are formed (see, for example, Hannerz, 1996). In an earlier era, fan allegiances were expected to ritually reaffirm traditional, place-bound ways of defining "us" and "them," to register publicly the individual's membership in the local or national community. Now, fan affiliations are more likely to be "elective affinities" (see Hall, 1992; Blake, 1996). However, although the days are gone when most youths would automatically wear their local colours in preference to teal or black, it is also not unusual for young fans' identifications to reflect their own kinds of social choices: with the underdog, for example, or with an attitude or style of play. Thus, although it is tempting for older generations to treat as "natural" the identifying practices of our own youth, we need to recognize that "identity is no museum piece, sitting stock still in a display case" (Galeano, 1991). We need to acknowledge that in each generation, young people will construct both individual and collective identities out of the symbolic and narrative materials available to them, and that today, more of these materials will come from the marketplace.

We need, finally, as the 20th century passes, to acknowledge how much Canada, childhood, and hockey have all changed since the years when the baby-boom generation grew up. Certainly, Canada has undergone many changes that have made the equation between hockey and "Canadian-ness" increasingly problematic. Canada today is a much more heterogeneous and hybrid country than it was in the first two decades after the war, with the result that our culture is more diverse. We've always been a country peopled by immigrants; but in earlier times the popular culture of the anglophone and francophone majorities easily sustained pride of place. For many young immigrants between the 1930s and 1970s, learning to play hockey or even to watch the game knowledgeably was an actively pursued marker of becoming Canadian (Harney, 1985). Now hockey competes with many other activities for young Canadians' allegiances. Cable and network television now bring an unprecedented variety of sports into Canadian homes, while more Canadian boys and girls are playing basketball, soccer, and a wide variety of individual sports. Thus even though millions of children still play and watch hockey, they have choices, and hockey no longer constitutes the common experience of Canadian childhood that it did—for better or worse—among earlier generations (Gruneau and Whitson, 1993, pp. 268-269). Indeed hockey, and the associations of Canadiana that surround it, may have less appeal than other sports for those who have been marginal in the stories that an older, whiter, "two nations" Canada has told about itself (Abdel-Shehid, 1999).

It will be important, nonetheless, that Canadians continue to see through the idea promoted by the sports industries that cities without major league franchises are somehow dull and uninteresting places to live. Winnipeg and Quebec were culturally vibrant communities before the NHL arrived in 1979, and they continue to thrive, both economically and culturally, after the NHL's departure. Major league sports have promoted the self-interested notion that cities that will not meet their demands, in terms of tax breaks and subsidies, are thereby lesser places, and to the extent that this idea becomes "common sense," cities are judged even by their own people in terms of the access they offer to "world-class" entertainment and consumption. However, as Northrop Frye observed in one of his last published papers, "If Toronto is a world class city, it is not because it builds follies like the SkyDome or bids for the Olympics, but because of the tolerated variety of the people in its streets" (Frye, 1992, p. 16). Following Frye, then, our ideas of "civic culture" cannot be reduced to seeking the intermittent presence of famous entertainers, through whom boosters announce our status in the global village. We need to support the traditional cultural institutions that have made us distinct in the past, but we also need to nurture the cultural vitality and variety now present in our turn-of-the-century urban populations.

This leads us to a final comment on nostalgia, and on what rituals can and cannot do. Hockey has been a powerful and time-honoured Canadian ritual, connecting Canadians of different regions and ethnic origins and connecting our present with our past. Like other effective rituals it has worked, through most of the 20th century, because it has allowed us to suspend temporarily, in our common enjoyment of the game, differences that have divided us as Canadians for generations. Yet despite the emotional power of ritual, and despite the importance of rituals in allowing far-flung "imagined communities" to re-experience their sense of connection, we need to remember, following Chaney, that rituals and memories by themselves cannot hold together communities that are coming apart in other ways. As Rick Salutin (1977) suggested in an introduction to his play *Les Canadiens*, written in the aftermath of the election of the first Parti Quebecois government, the popular meanings of the Canadiens and of hockey in Quebec changed as Quebec society changed and started to assert its identity in more explicitly political ways. So, now, in Canada in 2000, hockey can remind Canadians of what we have shared in the past and can offer those who love the game a(nother) reason for searching for common ground. However, the tensions that divide our country and many of our cities today—tensions stemming from regional, ethnic, demographic, and economic differences—ultimately require political rather than symbolic solutions. To imagine that hockey, or any other ritual of identity, can defuse such tensions indefinitely is to make too much of what is, after all, a game.

NOTES

1. For further discussion of these events, see D. Whitson, J. Harvey, and M. Lavoie, "The Mills Report, the Manley Subsidy Proposals, and the Business of Major League Sport," *Canadian Public Administration*, 43 (2), 127–56.

2. See Shawna Richer and Allen Maki, "Molson No Longer Canadien," *The Globe and Mail*, 28 June 2000, pp. S1, S3.

3. See Marshall Berman, *All That Is Solid Melts into Air: The Experience of Modernity*, London: Verso, 1983, for one of the most influential discussions of the importance of urban public space. The references cited in the text explore the importance of leisure and sports, respectively, in this broader canvas.

4. The closest parallels in European sport are the ways that Rangers and Celtic Football Clubs have served as "representatives" for Scotland's Protestant and Catholic communities, and (perhaps even more) the way that FC Barcelona served as a representative of the Catalan minority in Spain. On the latter, see J. Burns, *Barca: A Peoples' Passion*, London: Bloomsbury, 1999.

5. In 1988–89, the average NHL salary was U.S.$180 000; by 1999–2000 this had risen to U.S.$1 350 000. For more details on these rises through the 1990s, see Marc Lavoie, *Avantage numerique, l'argent, et la Ligue Nationale de Hockey*, Hull: Vents d'Ouest, 1997.

6. See M. Ozanian, "Suite Deals: Why New Stadiums are Shaking Up the Pecking Order of Sports Franchises," *Financial World*, 9 May, 1995, pp.42–56.

7. As of July 2000, Bell Canada's purchase of CTV, itself a recent purchaser of TSN, required BCE to divest itself of CTV's all-sports channel, Sportsnet. Rogers' agreement to purchase the Blue Jays from Interbrew was reported to hinge on their offer to purchase Sportsnet being accepted by BCE and this realignment of the Canadian television industry being approved by the CRTC. See Wm. Houston, *The Globe & Mail*, 8 July 2000, p. S2. The sale of the Blue Jays to Rogers Telecommunications was finally completed in late 2000.

REFERENCES

Abdel-Shehid, G. (1999). Writing hockey through race: Rethinking black hockey in Canada. R. Walcott (ed.), *Rude*. Halifax: Fernwood, pp. 71–86.

Bellamy, R. and Walker, J. (1995). Foul tip or strike three? The evolving 'partnership' of major league baseball and television. *NINE*, 3(2), 47–56.

Betke, C. (1975). The social significance of sport in the city: Edmonton in the early 1920s. A. McCormick and L. McPherson (Eds.), *Cities in the west*. Ottawa: National Museum of Man.

Blake, A. (1996). *The body language: The meaning of modern sport*. London: Lawrence & Wishart.

Butsch, R. (ed.). (1990). *For fun and profit: The transformation of leisure into consumption.* Philadelphia: Temple University Press.

Chadwin, B. (1994). *Rocking the pond: The Mighty Ducks of Anaheim.* Vancouver: Polestar.

Chaney, D. (1985). A symbolic mirror of ourselves: Civic ritual in mass society. *Media, Culture and Society,* 5: 115–29.

————. (1993). *Fictions of collective life: Public drama in late modern culture.* London: Routledge.

Euchner, C. (1992). *Playing the field: Why sports teams move and cities fight to keep them.* Baltimore: Johns Hopkins University Press.

Fawcett, B. (1992). The trouble with globalism. In M. Wyman (ed.), *Vancouver Forum* (pp. 183–201). Vancouver: Douglas and McIntyre.

Frye, Northrop. (1992). The culutural development of Canada. *Australian/Canadian Studies,* 10, 9–16.

Galeano, E. (1991). *The book of embraces.* Trans. C. Belfrage. New York: W.W. Norton.

Gruneau, R. and Whitson, D. (1993). *Hockey Night in Canada: Sports, identities and cultural politics.* Toronto: Garamond.

Hall, Stuart. (1992). The question of cultural identity. In S. Hall, D. Held, and A. McGrew (Eds.). *Modernity and its Futures* (pp. 273–325). Cambridge: Polity Press/Open University.

Hannerz, U. (1996). *Transnational connections.* London: Routledge.

Harney, R. (1985). Homo ludens and ethnicity. *Polyphony,* 7(1), 1–12.

Hobsbawm, E. and Ranger, T. (1983). *The Invention of Tradition.* Cambridge: Cambridge University Press.

MacGregor, R. (1996). *The seven AM practice: Stories of family life.* Toronto: McClelland & Stewart

Maguire, J. (1993). Globalization, sport and national identities: The empire strikes back. *Loisir et société,* 16: 293–22.

Metcalfe, A. (1987). *Canada learns to play: The emergence of organized sport, 1807–1914.* Toronto: McClelland & Stewart.

Mills, D. (1995). The visible hand and the management of hockey. K.B. Wamsley (ed.), *Method and methodology in sport and cultural history.* Dubuque: Brown Benchmark, p. 244–80.

Mott, M. (1985). Flawed games, splendid ceremonies: The hockey matches of the Winnipeg Vics, 1890–1903. *Prairie Forum,* 10, 169–87.

Quirk, J. and Fort, R. (1992). *Pay dirt. The business of professional team sports.* Princeton, NJ: Princeton University Press.

Riess, S. (1989). *City games.* Champaign, IL: University of Illinois Press.

Rosentraub, M. (1998). *Major league losers: The real costs of sports and who's paying for it.* New York: Basic Books.

Rutherford, P. (1993). Made in America: The problem of mass culture in Canada. In D. Flaherty and F. Manning (Eds.). *The beaver bites back? American popular culture in Canada* (pp. 260–80). Montreal: McGill-Queen's University Press.

Salutin, R. (1977). *Les Canadiens.* Vancouver: Talonbooks.

Silver, J. (1996). *Thin ice: Money, politics, and the demise of an NHL franchise.* Halifax: Fernwood.

Wernick, A. (1991). *Promotional Culture.* London: Sage.

FURTHER READING

Andrew Blake. 1996. *The Body Language: The Meaning of Modern Sport.* London: Lawrence & Wishart.

Eduardo Galeano. 1998. *Soccer in the Sun and Shadow.* Trans. Mark Fried. London: Verso.

Richard Gruneau and David Whitson. 1993. *Hockey Night in Canada: Sport, Identities and Cultural Politics.* Toronto: Garamond

Roger Noll and Andrew Zimbalist (Eds.). 1997. *Sports, Jobs and Taxes: The Economic Impact of Sports Teams and Stadiums.* Washington: The Brookings Institution.

Larry Wenner (Ed.) 1998. *MediaSport.* New York: Routledge, 1998.

PART E

THE DYNAMICS OF CULTURE

Orchestra

Al Purdy

They do not know where their bodies are
their flesh has fled
inside the blonde cello
into warm red darkness
of the cherry-coloured violin
—and they are looking for their souls
bent over the crooked instruments
jagged shapes of sound
sheep-gut and horsehair
wire drawn thin as the tingle
of the seeking heart
that says "I want to know you"
See now
they are looking for their souls
and they are outside time
which is to say
their body-clocks have stopped
they have forgotten
wives husbands lovers
the cry of human gender
in one tumescent moment
solemn as eternity's
endless et cetera

None of all this do they know
not consciously
the space between thoughts
expanded to forever
where music is a continuous silence
except for the slight
"ping" sound of the absolute
—and when that other silence
applause begins
bodies are restored
souls unnecessary
doorknobs open doors
manhole covers murmur
buttons enter buttonholes
beasts die at the slaughterers
and the silver hiatus
ends

My Journey with Calixa: Reflections on Canadian Music

Allan Gordon Bell

Canada's national anthem was composed by a man who did not believe that the country had any future as a sovereign nation. When *O Canada* is performed during formal ceremonies or at the opening of cultural and athletic events (especially during the raising of the Canadian flag honouring gold medallists at the Olympic Games or international hockey tournaments), audiences may experience a tingling that is a physical manifestation of those sentiments that arise from the pride that they feel for their country. Or, as occurred recently in Montreal, audiences comprising a large number of *independists* may experience a revulsion for the song and choose to jeer because, for them, it is a symbol of a country to which they no longer wish to belong. Both of these reactions are a strange inversion for a piece of music that was originally composed as a patriotic song honouring the traditions and achievements of *les canadiens*, a 19th-century appellation for the national identity of the francophone population living in the provinces and territories of Canada. The anthem was composed by a man who believed that the best future for Canada would be annexation by the United States, a man who was the foremost Canadian composer of his generation, a man whom the majority of Canadians cannot identify by name.

When I completed my graduate studies in music, I too did not know who had composed the anthem. Nor did I have any idea that a vast body of Canadian repertoire existed. In my defence, I could state that during the 1970s, courses in Canadian music did not appear on the curriculum at any Canadian university. Although Radio Canada International and the Canadian Broadcasting Corporation had made recordings of some of the repertoire available to university libraries, the major sources that professors use in today's courses did not appear until the end of the decade and into the 1980s.[1] However, to be honest, I must confess that I did not become interested in the music of my own country until I had to face a personal crisis in my own creative work. After assimilating the compositional techniques passed down from the great masters as well as the new techniques invented by the major living European and American composers, I realized that I could not progress as an artist until I could learn how to create through my own voice. I began to try to capture the rhythms and the tonal colours of the land that had shaped me: the western part of a northern country.

My search for a creative direction ignited a passion for the music of other Canadian composers. In a single essay, I can only begin to convey the energy and the beauty of the music that I have encountered. Currently, the Canadian Music Centre has a collection of almost 20 000 scores created by close to 500 composers.[2] If I were a scholar, I would attempt to encapsulate this vast repertoire into intellectually manageable categories and to provide biographical sketches of selected composers and lists of works. However, as a composer, I would rather attempt to describe how the music sounds, how it is constructed, how it stimulates my own creative life. Therefore, for the purpose of this essay, I have created an alter ego with whom I can discuss the music, composer to composer. I have resurrected the ghost of the man who composed Canada's national anthem. His responses to and questions about the music that I have chosen serve to place a limit upon my passions.

Calixa Lavalée composed *O Canada* in 1880. Working from a French text by Adolphe-Basile Routhier, Lavalée created the work for a French-Canadian national convention that was held during the Saint Jean Baptiste festivities in Quebec City. At that time, Lavalée was a distinguished composer whose works were regularly performed in Canada and the United States. Born in Verchères, Lower Canada, in 1842, he began his musical studies in Montreal and then, in 1847, he went to the United States to perform and teach. In 1861, he became a musician in the Fourth Rhode Island Regiment. He fought in the Civil War and claimed that he had been wounded in the Battle of Antietam. After the war, he travelled back and forth between Quebec City, Montreal, and Boston, teaching music and giving recitals that also included many of his own compositions. His reputation in the United States was such that he was elected President of the Music Teachers' National Association in 1886. Despite the fact that he composed what was to become officially adopted as the national anthem of Canada in 1880, he publicly declared himself in favour of annexing Canada with the United States.[3]

I imagine a journey across North America with Calixa Lavalée. We travel by car from Quebec City, where he composed *O Canada*, to Calgary, where I live and work. We follow the route that would have been open to us in Lavalée's time: through Montreal and Toronto, crossing into the United States at Niagara, travelling south of Lake Superior, crossing back into Canada south of Winnipeg, heading west across the Prairies. Throughout the journey, we listen to the radio and to some compact discs that I have brought. After leaving Winnipeg, we stop listening and, after looking out of the windows at the passing fields of grain for perhaps an hour, we begin to discuss the music we have heard.

CL: *Alors, pour moi,* the experience of listening to so many radio broadcasts and to your compact discs has been as overwhelming as this prairie landscape through which we are now travelling. For long periods of time, everything seems the same—the endless fields of grain, the unchanging sky. But then the eye is drawn to a stand of trees, to a barn or a grain elevator, to a hawk circling above a field. Or the road drops down into a river valley or a coulee, and there is a rapid and magical transformation of the landscape. I am transfixed, and I feel that I see these events with an unimaginable clarity. *Pour moi, la musique, c'est comme ça.* When I reflect upon all of the music that you called popular, I regret to say that so much of it sounded the same to me, regardless of which side of the border we were on. *Vous savez,* long ago I came to the conclusion that it would be best for Canada if it were to be annexed by the United States. If what we have heard is any indication, a musical annexation has almost certainly occurred. *Aussi,* what truly surprised me was that so much of the music on the classical stations was exactly the same repertoire that I studied or heard during my lifetime. Then, just when I began to fear that the music, like this landscape, would overpower me with its sameness, I heard pieces that had such a distinctive voice that my ears were immediately stimulated, and I was drawn very deeply into their imagined sonic worlds.

AB: Did you hear them on the broadcasts or only on the compact discs that I selected for you?

CL: *Vraiment,* your question reveals a snobbishness that I am not certain you intend. Before we enter into a debate about the relative value of high and low art, which I found tiresome in my own time, let me state that I heard very intriguing as well as very boring pieces in both media.

AB: Tell me about the pieces that attracted your composerly mind.

CL: I found most of the popular music to be somewhat arid, drawing upon the same musical formulae, the same four-beat measures with that mind-numbing emphasis upon the second and fourth beats, the same four-measure phrases, the same instrumentation. However, when I heard the songs of Bruce Cockburn, Connie Kaldor, Jerry Alfred, and Stan Rogers and those groups with the strange names, Great Big Sea and Barenaked Ladies, I heard music by composers who have a very keen ear for the relationship between words and melodic line. They do not attempt to erase the regional accents from their singing voices. Instead, they splendidly capture the rhythm and tone of the language, arriving on just the right syllable at just the right time, with just the right inflection. I have been listening to the accents of the people we have met in restaurants on our journey. With these composers, I hear Ontario and Saskatchewan and somewhere in the Maritimes in their voices, unlike so many of the others who sound so anonymously North American. *Et plus intéressant,* they use local imagery in their lyrics in order to explore timeless themes.

AB: I admire these qualities as well. Can you give me an example of some musical selection that you found to be especially successful?

CL: I think that one line from the song about the Northwest Passage by Stan Rogers will haunt me for a long time: "Tracing one warm line through a land so wide and savage..."[4] *C'est magnifique, n'est ce pas?* The melody is so simple, beginning with descending steps and rising to the word "wide," dropping down slightly and then leaping back up from the first to the second syllable of "savage." Could there be anything more enchantingly Canadian than the way that he savours and lengthens the words with French roots ("tracing," "line," "savage") and he pushes the melody with the words with Anglo-Saxon roots ("one," "warm," "through," "land," "wide"). I also think that it is marvellous that he makes use of the alliteration that is generated by the way you English Canadians pronounce the initial phonemes of "one," "warm," and "wide." The effect would not be the same if it were said by the Americans that I lived among in Boston.

AB: Very few songwriters these days have such a sophisticated ear for the music that is inherent in a language.

CL: *C'est dommage.* Words reach more deeply into our souls when they carry their imagery in such a compact manner and when they resonate within an elegantly constructed melodic line.

AB: The rhythms and tonal colours of a spoken language become instruments in themselves. They carry a musical value even if you do not understand the meaning of the words.

CL: *Vraiment,* I thought about the same idea when I listened to the songs by Jerry Alfred, the Northern Tutchone singer from the Yukon. I could not understand the words, but I could hear the pain and the longing in the tonal quality of the vocatives and in the shapes of the melodic lines. I was also fascinated by the way in which he wove his music into the same harmonies and dance rhythms that I heard in so much popular music. *Mais,* his music has an admirable freshness.

AB: Perhaps that quality arises from his use of the techniques of native drumming to create a motoric energy similar to that formed in popular music but that does not rely on an emphasis on beats two and four.

CL: *Oui,* but I am also intrigued by the shape of his melodic lines. They begin very high in the head tones and then descend to the chest tones. The lines are very fluid in their phrasing and, when repeated, give the whole piece a cyclic form. *Pour moi,* this is very unusual and very attractive.

AB: Those melodic shapes are very common in traditional Aboriginal singing. As to the form, perhaps the cyclic phrasing is a musical way of incorporating the sacred Aboriginal symbol of the circle.

CL: *Mais, c'est très intéressant, ça.* I know nothing of this. In my time, we ignored the Native people. I never heard any of their music.

AB: Your time is not so very different from my time, I am ashamed to say.

CL: *Mais oui*, but this music is so compelling, so sophisticated. It suggests many possibilities for musical exploration.

AB: I share your enthusiasm, but I fear that this music will not have a widespread impact upon mainstream popular music because it is sung in a language that is understood by so few.

CL*: Mon ami, vous et moi*, as composers, let us celebrate the talent of Jerry Albert and not despair for the future of his music because we have no way of knowing what that future will be.

AB: Agreed.

CL: Besides, there is a great deal more music for us to discuss. I would very much like to respond to the music that you played for me on those compact discs. Clearly, what was called art music in my time has changed considerably in the past 100 years since I was composing.

AB: Since your time, there have been almost as many stylistic innovations as there have been decades. The vocabulary and instrumental resources available to a composer have increased geometrically.

CL: You have access to so much more music than I did because of your radios and your compact discs.

AB: Yes, but the challenge facing today's composer remains the same as always: how does one create an imagined world in sound that has a dramatic and musical unity and an individual voice?

CL*: D'accord.*

AB: I played you the music of four Canadian composers: Harry Somers, Hildegard Westerkamp, Alexina Louie, and Gilles Tremblay. I did so because I admire their work and because I believe that there are qualities in their music that could have been created only by composers who live in Canada. To badly paraphrase the great Canadian literary critic Northrop Frye, they all have come to know who they are as artists by first exploring where they are.

CL: *Mais, c'est curieux, cette idée.* To know the "who" by first knowing the "where"? For my colleagues Alexis Constant and Guillaume Couture, and me, such a question would never have been posed. We knew we were in a backward colony with only a nascent musical culture. We knew we had to go to Europe to study with the best teachers. And we knew that we lived and worked among philistines. Nonetheless, we composed, we performed. Of course we were "canadiens," and we were proud of our heritage. But we composed in the manner of all the best composers, and we felt very much a part of a great musical tradition.

AB: There are many composers working in Canada today who share your views. For me, it does not matter whether composers belong to an international community or whether their music attracts audiences in Paris, New York, or Tokyo. What matters is the quality of the music and the distinctive character of the composer's voice.

CL: *Je vous en pris,* I do not disagree with you as long as you are talking about songs. But if you are suggesting that some sort of regional dialect exists for pure instrumental music ... well that is absurd. That kind of music is abstract, its beauty lies in the fact that it has no reference to the rest of the world.

AB: What about your charming piano piece, *Papillons?* All those rapid passages, all of those light and delicate harmonies ...

CL: *Oui,* but I did not call it *The Monarch Butterfly near Moose Jaw.* I was referring only to the abstract quality of flight. The title is merely poetic.

AB: You remember the recording of *North Country* by Harry Somers?

CL: *Mais oui,* it began with those slow chords in the string orchestra and then moved to a second section where a very high and very slow violin melody was accompanied by some rapid and jagged lines in the lower strings.

AB: In northern Ontario, the landscape is filled with jagged granite and forests that, if you climb above them, are seemingly uninterrupted for kilometre after kilometre.

CL: *Mais non,* you are not suggesting a correlation between the land-scape and the music. *Pour moi,* the music is just a somewhat strange melody with a dissonant accompaniment.

AB: There are only a few places where these two elements co-exist. That someone should juxtapose them—is this merely an accident of his imagination, or does it arise from an aurage that he encountered that he then transformed into music.

CL: *Alors ...*

AB: Somers wrote that piece in 1948 when he was 23 years of age. The following year, he went to Paris to study with Darius Milhaud, supported by a scholarship from the Canadian Amateur Hockey Association.[5] But I hear nothing of Milhaud in Somers' music.

CL: Did his time in Paris not provide him with the opportunity to refine his raw talent, to hear the latest new music ...

AB: Perhaps. But remember the second piece that I played for you, *Evocations.* Somers composed it in 1966.

CL: *Oui,* I doubt that any European would have conceived of that kind of music. *Mon dieu,* what an opening passage: a quiet, delicate yet dissonant chord in the upper register of the piano followed by a long period of silence followed by a female voice imitating the cry of a northern loon.

AB: I can only speculate that the music arises from an aurage, in this case perhaps a sound memory of a time when Somers sat beside a northern lake, enchanted by the stillness and by the clarity of any small sound. As its title suggests, the piece evokes a sense of place, and it invites an emotional response. But, as the sounds are reiterated, developed, and folded into an overall rhythmic structure, the aurage becomes music, a wonderful abstract construction that still carries with it a connection to the original event. Convincing because of the integrity of its atmosphere, the piece also conveys a poignancy to any listener who remembers and yearns for a place of tranquility in the natural world.

CL: *Monsieur*, the relationship to the wilderness that you describe is far too romantic for my taste. *Alors*, what about all those mosquitoes and blackflies? In my time, we worked very hard to carve something civilized out of that forsaken landscape.

AB: In my time, we are struggling to understand our proper relationship to the natural world.

CL: Even if I did not find that to be such a strange concept, I would still find it hard to believe that music could have any role to play in that venture.

AB: R. Murray Schafer, one of Canada's most distinguished composers, wrote that "Northern geography is all form … The art of the North is the art of restraint … The art of the North is composed of tiny events magnified."[6] These kinds of distinctions are necessary if one is to be able to experience the beauty of all the Canadian land/sound-scape.

CL: *Vraiment*, the northern aesthetic proposed by Schafer seems too limited to encompass everything that is beautiful in a "land so wide and savage."

AB: It is a way of turning the ear toward what is actually present. But you are correct. The criteria cannot encompass some very compelling music composed by one of Schafer's protégés, Hildegard Westerkamp. She worked with him during the 1970s at Simon Fraser University on the World Soundscape Project dedicated to the study of humanity's relationship to the acoustic environment.[7] I played you her *Beneath the Forest Floor*.

CL: *Je me regrete*, but I cannot begin to understand her work as music. I cannot recognize any known musical instruments, I cannot hear any themes, there is no harmony, the rhythm has no pulse …

AB: This is a piece that is generated entirely by electronic means. She recorded the sounds of the British Columbia rainforest, and then she transferred those sounds into a digital sampler that stores the materials in the memory of a computer. She then manipulated the recorded sounds using specially developed music software. By digitally altering the time a sound lasts (stretching a sound that had an original duration of three seconds into a sound that has a new duration of thirty seconds, Westerkamp is able to take the listener inside a sound, making it possible to hear parts of a sound that go by too quickly when that same sound is heard in real time. She can also digitally filter out parts of a sound in order to radically change its colour. By combining many layers of these computer-altered sounds, she is able to create a musical texture that is composed of many transformations of a single sound.

CL: *Monsieur, je vous en pris, aidez-moi*. I did not understand any of what you just said. *Hiens*, I will trust that your marvellous technology can do what you say. But, my composerly mind is still baffled by these sounds.

Transformations occur so slowly that I can certainly follow them. I have time to contemplate each of the textures as it unfolds, and I must say that many of them are very pleasurable to my ear. But where is the musical structure …?

AB: I can think of few composers who explore a geographical place with as much depth and sensitivity as Westerkamp. Each piece is an exploration of a single idea that is dramatic without having to resort to excessive climaxes.

CL: What you are describing is akin to a Bach *Prelude.*

AB: Exactly. Except that the duration is expanded. And, she provides the listener with multiple layers of temporal events. One can listen with human ears, or one can listen with the imagined ears of a 200-year-old tree.

CL: *Pardonnez-moi*, but you have a rather *gauche* way of attempting to be poetic. I am still not convinced …

AB: As I listen to her skillfully constructed world derived from the sounds of that B.C. rainforest, I am drawn into a very intimate relationship with these sounds. Their strange beauty is seductive and ultimately subversive. I feel an artistic connection to the rainforest, and I would mourn the death of any part of it.

CL: I begin to understand your respect for this music, *mais, je regrete,* I cannot truly accept what I have heard as music. Perhaps if I listened to more of it, I would be able to abandon many of the principles of music that I worked so hard to learn and use in my own compositions.

AB: Preconceptions can radically affect our perceptions …

CL*: Monsieur,* before we stray into more philosophy, perhaps we can be composers again. You have been introducing me to music that celebrates the Canadian landscape, but a place is more than just geography. It also contains human society and all the traditions of a culture.

AB: Which is exactly why I played Alexina Louie's music for you.

CL: *Alors,* I found her symphonic piece, *Music for Heaven and Earth,* to be a very compelling work. It is exotic yet familiar, and it has a totally convincing architecture.

AB: She is a brilliant composer whose work embodies a common Canadian dilemma.

CL: You are no doubt referring to the fact that your Canadian society is an accommodation of many cultures.

AB: For Alexina Louie, the accommodation was more acute because her ancestors are Chinese. On numerous occasions she and I have discussed her music, and she has told me of her artistic journey. Her initial training was entirely devoted to the study of the Western masterpieces. She went to graduate school at the University California at San Diego where she wrote many pieces in the approved avant garde style of the 1970s.[8] But, she was unable to gain access to the full resources of her imagination until she undertook the study of the classical musics of Asia. The plural is important here because the principles of musical construction used in Chinese classical music and in the gamelan music of Java and Bali are radically different from those of the West.

CL: I do not know anything about these musics.

AB: Superficially, they make use of different scales and tuning systems than we have in the West. Neither tradition uses any harmony as you and I understand it. The gamelan tradition makes use of a battery of percussion instruments to create a flow of very complex rhythmic patterns. The Chinese tradition also uses percussion in addition to bowed and struck stringed instruments, flutes of many sizes, and reed instruments. Rhythm in Chinese music is very fluid, with long passages that have no perceivable pulse.

CL: So that would account for the very exciting percussion passages in Louie's music.

AB: Yes, but she is a much more subtle composer. She does not just transcribe the sounds of these other traditions and simply implant them into her pieces. Instead, she has fully incorporated both the Asian and Western aesthetics into her vocabulary. Using the harmonies and instrumental resources of the West and the melodic and rhythmic vocabularies of both traditions, her music is a compelling blend of many traditions.

CL: It is not a formless stew that might be one of the pitfalls of such an approach. Her musical architecture is very clear. It contains a very convincing balance of vigorous passages and slower, contemplative sections.

AB: In her more recent compositions, such as the prize-winning violin concerto entitled *Arc*, the blending of traditions is virtually seamless.

CL: *Sans doute*, I would very much like to hear more of her music. I am very attracted by her masterful use of instrumental colour.

AB: I think that she has found a very distinctive way of solving that very Canadian dilemma. Instead of merely participating in the mainstream of Canadian society and celebrating her Chinese heritage on occasion, she has found a way of creating a distinctive musical personality that revivifies both.

CL: *Je m'excuse*, but I must ask you about that other very Canadian dilemma. What has happened to "les canadiens"?

AB: Gilles Tremblay is a composer who has renounced Canada in favour of an independent Quebec. When we both served as adjudicators at a music festival in 1984, he told me that he had refused to accept the Order of Canada because it was a symbol of the country that had imprisoned many of his friends and colleagues during the October Crisis of 1970. But, like many Québécois, his political views are very complex. In fact, he has served on the board of the Canadian Music Council, which also named him Composer of the Year for 1977.[9]

CL: Perhaps it is best to leave political discussions to others and to just discuss his music.

AB: A very good idea.

CL: I am glad that you played his *Vers du soleil, Traçantes,* and *Jeux de solstices* for me. I was wondering whether composers today had entirely eschewed abstract music.

AB: No, in fact Gilles Tremblay is among the most intellectual composers in Canada. His music is above all concerned with sonority in all of its manifestations.

CL: *Sans doute,* but all composers must be concerned with how a piece sounds.

AB: Of course, but in Tremblay's case he is concerned with the elements that occur in a single sound. After exploring the physical properties of a sound, he isolates the more ephemeral elements of the sound and asks the performers to accentuate them. One example would be to ask the contrabass players to play the high harmonics of a structural pitch that is not sounded but rather implied by these harmonics.

CL: *Vraiment,* that is a very intellectual approach to music.

AB: For me, the analogy would be to imagine a lightning storm. The rapid flashes leave a momentary residue of light in the clouds. Now, imagine that you only saw the residue. The flashes would be implied by the residue. Of course, there is also the thunder, a sonic residue of the lightning but often delayed by time.

CL: That certainly accounts for the quality of that piano piece, *Traçantes,* where the punched chords are structurally less important than the ringing sounds that remain after the piano's pedal has been depressed. Mais, *Vers du soleil* and *Jeux de solstices* seem to be about a great deal more than just sonority.

AB: Both of these pieces seem to me to be the composer's way of reaching out, in a profoundly spiritual manner, to the powerful elements that make up this universe. Tremblay also told me about his studies with the French composer Olivier Messiaen who combines birdsong, avant garde textures, mathematics, and Indian classical rhythms in order to make personal statements of his own Catholic faith. *Vers du soleil,* with its joyous fanfare-like brass and percussion sections, its super-charged string and woodwind textures, and its reference to plainchant, seems to be a medium for the contemplation of transcendence.

CL: It is certainly a music that is filled with a joyous sonority, even if I think that its architecture is somewhat episodic. *Mais, disez-moi,* how is it that you think of this music as being distinctly Canadian, or in his case, Québécois?

AB: One of the themes that has run through many of the arts in Canada has been that of the wilderness and all of its elements being used as a place of spiritual purity.

CL: *Vous me moquez,* that was not a theme that was ever discussed in my time.

AB: But then you have not seen the paintings of the Group of Seven nor have you read the writings of Margaret Atwood.

CL: *Non, vraiment,* and I would rather have them explained to me by someone who is not a composer.

AB: Now, wait …

CL: *Monsieur, je voudrais vous remercier.* I see the lights of what must be Calgary in the distance. I have only one more thought that I would like to share with you.

AB: Go on …

CL: Had I not composed *O Canada,* and the government of Canada were to decide to commission an anthem today, who would compose it, and how would it sound?

AB: A very good question.

NOTES

1. Including *Anthology of Canadian Music* (begun 1978, completed 1989), *Canadian Music of the Twentieth Century* (1980), *Encyclopedia of Music in Canada* (1981), and *The Music of Canada* (1985).

2. See the CMC Web site <www.musiccentre.ca>.

3. *Encyclopedia of Music in Canada* (1981), pp. 527–28.

4. Stan Rogers, Northwest Passage. Halifax: Fogarty's Cove Music, 1981.

5. *Encyclopedia of Music in Canada* (1981), pp. 881–83.

6. R. Murray Schafer, "Music in the Cold," *On Canadian Music,* p. 65.

7. Composer Bio, "Hildegard Westerkamp," CMC Web site, <www.musiccentre.ca>.

8. Composer Bio, "Alexina Louie," CMC Web site.

9. *Encyclopedia of Music in Canada* (1981), pp. 932–33.

FURTHER READING

Cherney, Brian. *Harry Somers.* Toronto: University of Toronto Press, 1975.

Kallmann, Helmut et al., eds. *Encyclopedia of Music in Canada.* Toronto: University of Toronto Press, 1981.

———. *Encyclopedia of Music in Canada.* Toronto: University of Toronto Press, 1992.

McGee, Timothy. *The Music of Canada.* New York: W.W. Norton, 1985.

Proctor, George. *Canadian Music of the Twentieth Century.* Toronto: University of Toronto Press, 1980.

Schafer, R. Murray. *On Canadian Music.* Bancroft, ON: Arcana Editions, 1984.

ADDITIONAL INFORMATION ON CANADIAN COMPOSERS AND CANADIAN MUSIC

Canadian Music Centre Web site: <www.musiccentre.ca>.

COMPACT DISCS FOR LISTENING

Stan Rogers. *Northwest Passage.* Fogarty's Cove Music: Dundas, ON, 1981.

Jerry Alfred. *Jerry Alfred and the Medicine Beat: Nendaa (Go Back).* Caribou Records: CRCD002

Harry Somers. *The Spring of Somers.* CBC Records: SMCD 5162.

————. *Anthology of Canadian Music: Harry Somers.* RCI.

Hildegard Westerkamp. *Transformations.* empreintes DIGITALes: IMED 9631.

Alexina Louie. *Music for Heaven and Earth.* CBC Records: SMCD 5154.

————. *Shattered Night, Shivering Stars.* CBC Records: SMCD 5190.

Gilles Tremblay. *Tremblay / Mather.* SNE: 523-CD.

————. *Quebec-5 USA-3.* SNE: 553-CD.

FURTHER LISTENING

Introduction to Canadian Music/Florilège de la musique canadienne. NAXOS: 8.8.550171-2.

Contemporary Canadian Art: Locating Identity

Christine Sowiak

In her essay describing the arts in Canada during the 20th century, cultural historian Maria Tippett voiced her fear that Canadian culture and therefore Canadian identity are in a state of crisis. Due to factors ranging from ethnic diversity to globalization, "it [is] virtually impossible for writers, artists, musicians, and others to speak with one voice" (Tippett 2000, 18). Apparently, it is Tippett's view that if Canadian art does not speak with one voice then there can be no verifiable, definitive Canadian art. However, within a country such as Canada that takes pride in its diversity, such a vision of a unified, shared culture is as impossibly utopian as it is undesirable. There are many unique and disparate histories within Canadian art, ones that are distinct, individual, clashing, and fractious but also overlapping and related and even, at times, harmonious. These are the voices that add up to the sum of Canadian art. If a nation comes to be defined, at least in part, by its history, then the role of a nation's art history is not to provide a limited narrative common to all but rather to chronicle the courses and counter-courses of the nation's stories. The cultural history of any nation—its visual art, literature, drama, music, and media—is parallel to its social and political history, and Canada is certainly no exception to this truth.

The location of identity in Canadian art is not fixed. It can be found where the confluence of three key factors intersects with the individual. First, there is the participation and influence of the government on the arts in Canada—the marriage of art and the nation state—both by direct policy intervention and indirectly through agencies such as the Canada Council for the Arts and institutions such as the National Gallery of Canada. Patronage is always a determining factor in the growth and nature of an art, and the dominant role of government in the support of Canadian art has been influential. Secondly, there is the porous relationship between popular culture and the arts, that is, the effect engendered by dominant traits in public consciousness and current events on the visual arts. Third, and conversely, the work and production of artists can and have influenced public sentiment, motivated political opinion, and defined the nation's understanding of itself, so that the history of Canada's art might tell the story of a nation.

It is the purpose of this chapter to outline some salient moments in the visual arts in Canada, where art has been an active participant in shifting cultural views that, like all aspects of Canadian life, involve debates over nationalism, regionalism, politics, history, and daily life. It is important to acknowledge as well that the course of Canadian art did not proceed in isolation but has been in step with international developments and advancements, particularly in relation to Europe and the United States, although ultimately in ways that become specific to this country.

ESTABLISHING A TRADITION

The first Western art considered indigenous to Canada from the perspective of settler culture developed following the British conquest of New France in 1760. Most art of the French colonial period of Canada, while fascinating, was created all but anonymously in direct imitation of art from Europe or was directly imported to the colony and served chiefly ecclesiastic purposes. After British rule, Canadian art became more local in the form of topographical sketching and painting. This was landscape-based art created with the specific purpose of describing the geographic features of the New World.

The development of topographical art can be traced to the British officers stationed in Canada. At the time of colonization of Canada, it was still possible to buy commissions within the British army; as a result, most of the officers came from the wealthier upper classes and were accustomed to such "gentlemanly" pursuits as sketching and painting. In fact the education of these officers, most notably at England's Woolrich Academy, included training in topographical drawing and watercolour rendering. After 1763, when peacetime afforded more leisure time to the officers, landscape painting became one of the more popular diversions of the lively social life centred around the garrisons, and topographical art changed from a descriptive duty to a social pastime. Several commissioned officers produced a great number of highly accomplished topographical drawings.

Two aspects of European culture during the late 18th and early 19th centuries fostered an early concentration on landscape in Canadian art: the idea of the picturesque and the ideals of Romanticism. At the turn of the 19th century—the peak of Britain's colonial power—there was a growing fascination with travel books illustrated with engravings derived from sketches and watercolours. Professional artists began to tour North America, gathering sketches of the scenery for later publication. These illustrations of colonial Canada reflected the strong influence of Romanticism on painting from England and Northern Europe, in particular a fascination with nature—exotic, wild, and untamed—and within it, the presence of the Sublime. The paintings of J.W.M. Turner

(1775–1851), for example, capture a sense of raw emotion and depict the frailty and ruin of man confronted with greater powers amid atmospherically charged landscapes. Many of the topographical illustrations, through artistic devices such as contrived compositions and exaggerated scale, describe the almost overwhelming monumentality of the Canadian wilderness. As with Romantic painting, these illustrations were designed to stir the viewer's emotions, to create a sense of awe and wonder at the power of nature. This affinity between topographical work in Canada and the ideals of the Romantic landscapes of England and Northern Europe resulted in the portrayal of Canada's wilderness not for its own worth, but rather to serve as an exotic other for the amusement of distant Europeans.

By the mid-19th century, a more permanent art community took hold with the settlement in Canada of professionally trained European artists, primarily from England, rather than the itinerant artists who had previously travelled the colonies. The immigration of these artists was only one step in the development of a Canadian art, for although they took as their subject matter the Canadian landscape, they did so in a style heavily influenced by British academic training; "their work, like that of the vast majority of painters active in Canada at that time, was provincial; emulating conservative British art, they produced Canadian landscapes with a curiously English look to them" (*The Canada Company, 2000*). With more Canadian-born artists working alongside those who had immigrated, however, the profession developed at an increasingly rapid rate as artists' associations, societies, and annual exhibitions became established after 1860. Throughout this period, the wilderness landscape remained the primary subject matter for Canadian artists, and after confederation in 1867 and expansion to the Pacific Ocean in 1871, landscape painting became associated with the growing nationhood. A new spirit of national pride resonated in the representations of the beauty, grandeur, and unspoiled wilderness of the grand new country. The Royal Canadian Academy—"the culmination of the nationalist mood in Victorian Canada" (*The Canada Company*, 2000) established in 1880—was national in scope and intent and thus provided a centralized organization for artists otherwise separated by geography and, at times, language. That same year, the National Gallery of Canada was founded in Ottawa, and the basis of its national collection was established from the diploma pieces required for admittance into the Royal Canadian Academy.

The work of the early members of the Royal Canadian Academy was almost wholly influenced by the attitudes developed from the academies of English, German, and Dutch painting, with some influence from American painting. Canadian artists were producing landscapes generally referred to as academic, paintings realistic in style and imbued with a sober propriety and sentimentality that reflected tightly conservative ideals. With few exceptions, the influence of French work was slight until the mid-1870s. By this time, French painting had come to be regarded as the most advanced in Europe, and Paris was the centre of the art world. With the École des Beaux-Arts, numerous private academies, the annual Salon, and the many active French "masters," Paris was a city of great fascination to young Canadian artists, and several of them received up-to-date training in Paris. By 1907 two of these artists, Curtis Williamson and Edmund Morris, would become sufficiently disturbed by the tired and dull look of Canadian art following the English academic tradition that they would form the Canadian Art Club, the goal of which was to lure successful Canadian artists back home and infuse the national art scene with a current, modern sensibility.

While artists of the Royal Canadian Academy were critical of any developments considered "Frenchy" in Canadian art, the Canadian-born artists schooled in Impressionist then Post-Impressionist styles of painting began to peck away at the dominance of the academic style. The most notable and fascinating of these artists was James Wilson Morrice (1865–1924), who first arrived in Paris in 1890 after finishing his law degree at Osgoode Hall in Toronto. Morrice is positioned between two fashions of painting in Canada—the English academic and the Group of Seven—and fit in with neither group. Yet Morrice did share with the latter a contempt for the former, what Group member A.Y. Jackson referred to as the "stuffy stupid days when Dutch painting dominated Montréal" (Jackson, 1947, 93). Of the art scene in Montreal, Morrice himself found that "these English dealers with their ghostly Dutch monochromes have poisoned everything" (Buchanan, May 1946, 240).

With the Canadian Art Club, Williamson and Morris sought to break the cultural hegemony held by Paris at the turn of the century while establishing a distinctly Canadian art scene, and they formed a professional exhibition society supported by laypersons and composed only of invited, professional members. Only the most modern, up-to-date, and "subjective" work would be accepted for exhibition. When the Club formed in 1907, one of the first invited members was Morrice, and it was through these exhibitions that his work would influence the Group of Seven and, in particular, A.Y. Jackson.

The breach from academic, imported styles was achieved quite significantly in the first decade of the 20th century, "that bright, promising moment at the dawn of the century when the twentieth century was going to belong to Canada," (Moore, 2000, 83). This type of optimism is perhaps best typified by the type of social history popularized by George MacKinnon Wrong, the founding Head (1894–1927) of the first History Department in Canada at the University of Toronto. Wrong was confident that Canada was a success story of political reform and freedom. As Christopher Moore observes, "We mostly assume today that Canadian culture was born sometime about 1970. Yet in the early years of [the 20th] century, almost everyone in English Canada seems to have been writing, reading and publishing. Many writers, editors, and publishers shared George Wrong's sense that a heroic past could inspire the present and help prepare for the future" (Moore, 2000, 83).

TOWARD THE GROUP OF SEVEN

The nationalistic fervour of academic and literary circles at the turn of the 19th century was matched in artistic circles—an important recognition if one is to realize that the nationalism of the Group of Seven was not an anomaly but rather a natural counterpart to the popular concerns of the day. Several of the artists who would go on to form the Group of Seven, in particular Lawren Harris and J.E.H. MacDonald, were active at the beginning of the 20th century in Toronto associations such as the Toronto Art Students' League and the Arts and Letters Club. A reflection of the passionate optimism in Canada's future as a country, the sentiment among artists active in these organizations was that if nationalism were to be communicated through painting, it must be through painting that was distinctively and recognizably Canadian; "truly meaningful expression was accomplished only when the subjects dealt with were those the viewer shared with the artist. Canadian history, and even more assuredly the land itself, were the best vehicles for such communication" (Reid, 1987, 140). Following the European practice of *plein air* painting—painting nature directly in the outdoors—the Art Students' League had begun organizing sketching and painting trips as early as 1902. The opportunity for artists to travel and work directly from the landscape, combined with the strengthening association of the land with Canadian identity, bolstered the growing dominance of the landscape genre in Canadian painting.

In many respects, Canada emerged from World War I a grown-up country. For all of the stirrings of nationalism and celebratory history at play before the Great War, it was Canada's participation in and exposure to the horrors of war that gave life to a sense of nationhood within popular consciousness. Canada had paid its dues and was ready to be considered an equal of Britain and the United States. While it has "long been recognized that the Great War was a crucial factor in forging Canadian national identity in a political sense," claims Maria Tippett, "[t]his is no less true in a cultural sense. Thanks to the efforts of Lords Beaverbrook and Rothermere, who set up the Canadian War Memorials Fund in 1916, writers and artists were hired to record on canvas and in print Canada's participation on the home and war fronts. What was painted, written, composed and sung gave one sector of the country—the English-speaking community—a collective sense of identity for the first time" (2000, 19). That is to say, a *collective* national identity embraced and supported by the general public. There was a willingness and even on eagerness to celebrate pride of nation through the arts, and a corresponding surge of tangible support through public and private patronage for the arts. Everything seemed to indicate a growing belief that "culture had a role to play in the nation-building process" (Tippett, 2000, 19).

In all the discussions surrounding the Group of Seven, their ardent nationalism emerges as a central issue. It is valuable, however, to keep in mind that their beginnings took place in that sunny, celebratory climate before World War II. In the period following the war, when the public was prepared to accept a vision of their own nationalism reflected back to them in the arts, national pride and identity were already firmly entrenched in the artistic and moral visions of the Group of Seven, so much so that the catalogue to the first Group exhibition read:

> The seven artists whose pictures are here exhibited have for several years held a like vision concerning Art in Canada. They are all imbued with the idea that an Art must grow and flower in the land before the country will be a real home for its people. (Bice, 1989, 15)

Although the first official exhibition for the Group of Seven took place in 1920, it was not the first time they had shown or worked together. Rather, members of the Group began their social and professional relationships in that period before the war, amid growing calls for a distinctively Canadian art. When the call came again after the war, this time from the public, the Group was in place and prepared to answer it.

In the years just after the turn of the last century, the nucleus of artists that would form the Group gathered around two centres in Toronto: the Arts and Letters Club and the commercial art and design firm of Grip Ltd. When artist Lawren Harris saw J.E.H. MacDonald's 1911 exhibition at the Club, he initiated an acquaintance that would bring him into contact with the activities centred around the Grip firm. MacDonald (1873–1932) was senior artist at the firm, which also employed Tom Thomson (1877–1917), Frank Johnston (1888–1949), Franklin Carmichael (1890–1945), Arthur Lismer (1885–1969) and, for a brief time, F.H. Varley (1881–1969.)[1] Unofficially, the firm served as a focal point for the artists' discussions of painting and critical debates, for the encouragement and critique of each others' work, and for numerous weekend sketching and painting trips organized through the firm. Eventually these trips would focus on the raw, sparsely inhabited wilderness of northern Ontario, but they began in the areas immediately surrounding Toronto. To the artists, the north quickly became the true symbol of the Canadian spirit. Never before had landscapists painted the vast stretches of forests, lakes, and rock that make up the spectacular geography of the Canadian Shield. Of the Toronto painters, Tom Thomson in particular was an inspiration to the others.

> It was not the illustrated wonders of the tourist folders, the beauty spots portrayed on picture postcards which interested him; it was, rather, the authentic 'monotonous' North, the hillsides of ragged

timber, the rock-strewn slopes and the small lakes, repeating them-selves endlessly. These composed the landscape he [Thomson] loved, and these were the scenes he rendered with such passion and realism. (Buchanan, August 1946, 100)

Thomson was the first to venture beyond the immediate Toronto area, travelling to painting sites in ever-enlarging circles, and eventually to areas on Georgian Bay and then into Algonquin Park. His brightly coloured outdoor sketches, executed directly on canoe trips, became the basis for his large-scale, decorative studio canvases, the bold and stirring compositions of which were strongly influenced by the flat patterns of Art Nouveau graphic design (see illustration, Tom Thomson, *Autumn Foliage*). Many consider Thomson to have been the leader among those artists who would form the Group—if not organizationally, then through his passion and spirit—and only his untimely death in 1917 prevented him from becoming an official member.

By 1913, several factors had emerged to reaffirm for the artists their vision of a "living Canadian art." J.E.H. MacDonald and Lawren Harris trav-elled to the Albright Art Gallery in Buffalo, New York, to examine an exhi-bition of contemporary Scandinavian landscape painting. They discovered a kinship with those landscapes of a different North, and with it a confir-mation of their own ideals for Canadian art, "feelings of height and breadth and depth and colour and sunshine and solemnity and new wonder about our own country" (Bice, 1989, 14). That year, Harris and Dr. James MacCallum (a Toronto patron of the arts who would prove funda-mental to the development of the Group) founded and constructed the Studio Building, an affordable residence for artists that also provided studio spaces for them. At the prompting of Lawren Harris, Montreal artist A.Y. Jackson was persuaded to move to Toronto. During their time at the Studio Building, Jackson would be a most influential mentor to Thomson, whose talent and determination overcame his lack of formal training. November 1913 also saw the first exhibition of works by artists who would become the Group. Held at the Toronto Reference Library, the "First Exhibition of Little Pictures by Canadian Artists" was the beginning of the lively if polarized relationship between the painters and the press.

World War I, however, would interrupt the momentum forming behind the group.[2] Both A.Y. Jackson and F.H. Varley would go overseas as official artists of the Canadian War Memorials, Harris would be posted with the army within Canada, and Lismer would accept a teaching posi-tion in Halifax for the duration of the war. Thomson would take increas-ingly long canoe trips into the wilderness of Algonquin Park, also working as a guide, until his mysterious drowning death at Canoe Lake in 1917. Almost immediately after the war, the artists began regrouping. In late spring of 1918, Harris and Dr. MacCallum ventured into the Algoma region, a trip that would inspire the first of the Group's famous boxcar painting tours into the north country from 1918 through 1922.

In February 1920, the artists determined to form an exhibiting group, formalizing their kinship and realizing quite astutely that a combined presence would expand their opportunities and increase their impact. Their first official exhibition—of which there would be several until they disbanded in 1933—was at the Art Gallery of Toronto in May 1920 and included the work of Harris, MacDonald, Carmichael, Johnston, Lismer, Varley, and Jackson. The exhibition captured and conveyed to the willing public the rugged sweeping beauty of Ontario's near North, and by extension the mythic power of that landscape to represent the spirit of Canada. Theirs was an art that stated a firm nationalism by making full use of symbols of northern geography—towering pines, sun-bleached rocks, rugged hills, severe cloud formations—in a style fully informed by their knowledge of advanced contemporary painting, such as the almost scientific analysis of colour, light, and shadow learned from the Impressionists. Their patterned compositions simplified details, eliminating all but the most significant forms and shapes so that the viewer might concentrate on the whole; powerful landscapes that pulsate with pure colour and the dazzling play of full light and deep shadow (see illustration, Lawren Harris, *Above Lake Superior.*) The bold bravado of their style was deliberate and permeated their work and every discussion of it.

The Group would have seven more official exhibitions over the next 12 years, with a varying and growing configuration of artists. They were conscious too of their centralized Toronto location and attempted to expand their reach geographically, encouraging the work of British Columbia's Emily Carr and bringing Edwin Holgate of Montreal and L.L. Fitzgerald of Winnipeg into their membership. Eventually the Group of Seven dissolved and became, with their first exhibition in 1933, the Canadian Group of Painters. Within the space of a single generation, the Group of Seven rebelled against the dry conformity of the academic picturesque to such a point that their own rigorous and mythic paintings became the establishment of Canadian art, firmly embraced by the public.[3] They became in fact an almost unassailable icon of Canadian art and identity that, at least for a time, left room for no other painting.

LES AUTOMATISTES AND THE REFUS GLOBAL

If it can be said that English-speaking Canadians get a collective sense of identity by who they are not (not British, not American) it might be said that French-speaking Canadians have a somewhat stronger, more inherent collective sense of who they are as a culture. Distinct aspects of social and political history in Quebec have created unique circumstances from which artists have worked, and the premiere example would be *Les Automatistes,* the first group of French-Canadian artists to achieve recognition within the country and internationally. Centred around Paul-Émile Borduas, *Les Automatistes* produced the first truly abstract, non-representational painting in Canada. Influenced by European Surrealism, the work of *Les Automatistes* was nevertheless driven and determined by their very strong sense of individualism, what Maurice Gagnon (1987, p. 130) spoke of as the "moral suffering" experienced by the artists by striving to express complete personal honesty in their work. Theirs was bold and fiercely independent work, and they sought for it no labels of "Canadian" nor any further legitimization beyond its own aesthetic achievement. Where the Group of Seven developed a program to self-consciously create a distinctive Canadian art in both subject matter and a style suitable for that content, *Les Automatistes* were preoccupied with their exploration on aesthetic terms alone and produced work that is nevertheless wholly Canadian. Yet *Les Automatistes* had a political mandate as well, which was grounded in a bid for individual, personal, aesthetic, and cultural freedom from the restrictive parochial influence of the Catholic church in Quebec society and the oppressive government of Maurice Duplessis. *Refus Global* was a Surrealist-inspired manifesto, a passionate and poetic declaration of aesthetic ideals and cultural independence written by Borduas and signed by a cross-section of Quebec artists, writers, and dancers in 1948. It was a powerful aesthetic statement by the province's most forward-thinking artists, and, according to many the beginning of modern Quebec.

Paul-Émile Borduas (1905–1960) was a man of volcanic energy and fierce commitment to his work. He began his career as an ecclesiastic painter through the 1930s, a decorator of churches who studied and worked under Ozias Leduc. Later, he also studied at the École des Beaux-Arts in Montreal and, after 1928, at Atelier d'art Sacre in Paris. During the 1920s and 1930s, the nationalism and stylistic pursuits of the Group of Seven were of little interest to artists in Quebec, for whom the art and culture of France held a much stronger attraction. An early influence on Borduas was artist John Lyman, who had worked in Paris for 24 years before returning to Montreal in 1931 and who in 1939 founded the Contemporary Arts Society of Montreal. The group explored the most advanced painting of the time that considered the abstract interplay of formal elements—line, colour, shape, space, and volume—rather than the representation of nature to be the true essence of painting.

By the time Borduas joined the Contemporary Arts Society he had already turned increasingly away from any representational elements in his work toward pure abstraction. Through the writings of French Surrealist André Breton, Borduas became fascinated more with the ideas of Surrealism than with the actual artwork of European Surrealist artists. In particular, Borduas shared their fascination with the idea of "automatic writing," which is the free and spontaneous expression of the unconscious, the emotional, and the psychological. A series of gouache paintings from 1940 through 1942 were his first works that used abstraction as pure expression. He had his first solo exhibition in 1943, paintings of free-floating images made with a palette knife instead of a brush and achieving a sense of dynamic, enigmatic balance. A group of young artists—primarily students of his from the École du Meuble and from other schools in Montreal—began assembling around Borduas and his ideas, and had by the mid-1940s left the figurative emphasis of Lyman and the Contemporary Arts Society to pursue pure abstraction. After 1945 these artists—including Françosie Sullivan, Jean-Paul Rioppelle, Pierre Gauvreau, Fernand Leduc, Roger Fanteaux, Maurice Gagnon, and Marcel Barbeau—became recognized as a group fervently committed to art's potential for the expression of personal, spiritual, emotional, and psychological truths and freedoms, a commitment that was destined to clash with the grimly repressive control the Church and state held not only on Quebec society but also on individuals. Their first group exhibition in 1947, *Automatisme*, derived its title from a Borduas painting included in the show entitled *Automatisme 1.47* and in turn gave the group its name.

In 1948, those same artists would be among the 15 signatories of the *Refus Global*. The most notorious document in Canadian art history had a rather less than auspicious beginning. Of the 400 copies originally printed, only half sold at the modest price of one dollar each. *Refus Global* (Borduas, 1987b) was an aggressive and controversial cry for artistic, cultural, and by extension, social freedom that awakened the cultural community in Quebec, rankled officials of church and state, and forever changed the lives of Borduas and his co-signatures. For them and for officials opposed to them, the *Refus Global* was an explosion. Borduas was dismissed from his position at the École and soon after, finding that even the most advanced art scene in Montreal remained blocked by conservatism, chose self-imposed exile in New York and later, Paris.

Despite the sad removal of one of our finest creators from Canada, it is evident that Borduas did enjoy and protect the distinct character of Canadian *Automatisme*. Just as he would later stress in his writings, the divergent character of *Automatisme* from Surrealism, he had also in 1946 declined to participate in the *Exposition Internationale du Surrealism*, suspicious of the potential cultural hegemony of Parisian surrealists Breton and Marcel Duchamp. Nevertheless, Borduas placed his aesthetic ambitions ahead of any exhausted obligations to his native land and in 1953 moved to New York. There, he found interest and sympathy for his work amid artists engaged with Abstract Expressionism, such as Mark Rothko and Jackson Pollock. Here, he dropped his Surrealist tie with floating dream images in favour of canvasses that referred to nothing but their own making. Although sympathetic to Abstract Expressionism, Borduas as always followed his own distinct agenda, continuing to work on a smaller, more intimate scale than the monumental canvasses of the New York painters. He produced glowing and intense paintings in which the traditional relationship between figure and ground almost disappears into one taut dynamic surface. However, frustrated with the language barrier he faced in New York, Borduas moved to Paris in 1955 where he continued the work began in the States (see illustration, Paul-Émile Borduas, *Expansion rayonnante/Radiating Expansion*). He would live in Paris, exhibiting frequently and internationally until his death in 1960.

In 1958, Borduas wrote that "if the manifesto *Refus Global* has had an influence on Canadian thinking, this influence should be felt in the improvement of the critical sense in general and a new orientation for art in particular" (1987a, 126). At the time, the manifesto was undoubtedly a bomb in the lives of cultural Quebec, yet the aftershocks did not extend very far into mainstream society. Duplessis would be re-elected for two subsequent terms, and not until the present-day Quebec nationalist movement found its feet in the 1960s and claimed *Refus Global* as its own would the document be revived. When Liberals, under Jean Lesage, won the provincial election in 1960, the Quiet Revolution began and with it the quest for special status within confederation. Both *Les Automatistes* and the nationalists fought a common foe: the parochial Roman Catholic power that kept Maurice Duplessis in power and the Quebec people socially oppressed. *Refus Global* remains the most significant aesthetic document produced in Canadian history. That it would be claimed as the beginning of a political revolution is evidence enough of the influence of culture on all spheres of Canadian life.

THE GROWTH OF INSTITUTIONAL SUPPORT

The art of one generation is fated to be contested by the next. In Quebec, *Les Automatistes* were followed by *les Plasticiens*, a group of artists interested in a more controlled form of abstract painting that explored the dazzling relationships that occurred between stripes of pure colour, and then by the *Nouveaux plasticiens*. In English-speaking Canada, artists were still struggling against what had become the stranglehold of the Group of Seven "formula." Donald Buchanan, critic and later assistant to the Director of the National Gallery, saw regionalism as a way out from under the Seven. For Buchanan, however, regionalism was not the establishment of distinct styles or concerns but rather attention to the land known intimately by artists within the stylistic vocabulary of the Group. At the same time, the influence of the Group had been seen as a positive force for artists working in the regions:

> In the provinces, artists are more isolated and, literally, more lonely. In that situation, spiritual and literary art theories may help justify an activity which, in a hostile or apathetic community, might otherwise seem virtually pointless. (Fenton and Wilkin, 1978, 53)

By the early 1950s, the Group and its followers were the conservatives, and in Toronto younger artists chose to move away from them entirely by moving toward abstraction, to the incipient trajectory of increasingly non-representational painting now referred to as

Modernism. New York had replaced Paris as the centre of the art world following World War II, and it was to the New York artists and theorists, such as the preeminent Clement Greenberg, that Canadian abstract artists turned for leadership and standards. Greenberg established direct and substantial links with artists of central Canada and the Prairies that would, at least for a brief period, link Canadian art directly to all that was cutting-edge and modern in the New York art world. Greenberg's most direct routes of influence were through two groups of artists in particular. The Toronto-based Painters Eleven began showing their large scale, big attack abstract canvasses together as early as 1954. Like many groups, theirs was an alliance founded in order to exhibit their works in sympathetic contexts and create opportunities for those exhibitions. In 1957, amid internal dissent, the Painters Eleven invited Greenberg to discuss their works, and the critic took particular interest in championing the work of some of the artists, such as Jack Bush. The other group, based in Saskatchewan, fought their sense of regional isolation by inviting the New York art world to them, by bringing significant painters and critics to conduct the professional artists' summer workshops at Emma Lake. Through these, the Regina Five emerged with an exhibition at the National Gallery in 1961. Following Greenberg's residency at the workshops in 1962, he would catapult members of the Five to the international stage.

The American influence (some would say intrusion) on Canadian art and culture following World War II was only a small part of the changed world order that replaced Europe with the United States as the centre of world power. Canada enjoyed its own economic booms and surges through many levels of society, including the cultural realm. For example, Canadian historians had grown into a vastly different breed of scholar from the sunny optimistic Wrong and his fellow storytellers. They were "academics of formidable skill" with greater access to the resources of funding and archives and, thus, the production of new ideas. Of these, Donald Creighton rose to prominence. By the early 1950s, Creighton had dismissed Wrong's preoccupation with constitutional matters and the attendant problems of regionalism and equal representation as boring and irrelevant, and proposed instead a version of Canadian history driven by economics and geography—of a Canada built on geography, raw power, and visionary leadership—that became known as the Laurentian thesis. According to Christopher Moore (2000, 86), Creighton proposed that

> Canadian politics were all about power and leadership and authority. Creighton's heroes were the visionary elite who understood the Laurentian system and guarded it against dissidents, democrats, and small-thinking regionalists at every turn.

The swashbuckling nationalism of the Group provided, almost inadvertently and quite belatedly, the perfect images for the Laurentian thesis. The trends of culture, however, are often in advance of those of politics. If the Group produced images in the 1920s that foreshadowed Creighton's Laurentian thesis, artists in the 1950s were looking ahead to the next stylistic trend. At that time, that trend was Modernist painting, best exemplified by American abstraction:

> The mid-fifties was a period in which artists were repudiating local traditions and responding to the dynamism of American abstract painting. The trend made people nervous. It lacked grounding in transcendent values and national distinctiveness, and also in established standards of representation. (Ord, 1998, 68)

The early 1950s were also a period of rapid development in Canadian cultural affairs, under the federal Liberal government of Louis St. Laurent, a period in which the support structures still in existence today were created. In 1949, Vincent Massey was appointed head of the Royal Commission on National Development in the Arts, Letters, and Sciences and charged with seeking ways to encourage a distinctive Canadian culture. The Massey Commission Report was released in 1951 and recommended greater government intervention and support for the arts and social sciences through the creation of an arts funding agency. In 1957, this came to fruition when the Canada Council was created. The impact of the Canada Council on the arts cannot possibly be overstated. During the past four decades, the nature and role of the Council has grown and flexed yet has for the most part striven successfully to be an arm's-length organization that bolsters creation at both individual and institutional levels. It has improved conditions for cultural producers and caused such programs and institutions as the Art Bank, the National Library of Canada, and Telefilm Canada to come into being. The Council has also had its share of critics. There have been claims, at times well founded,[4] that accuse the Council of favouring Central Canada over the regions, English-speaking over French-speaking (or sometimes French- over English-), high culture over low, the professional over the amateur. At its inception, the tone of the Council was influenced by the Massey Commission, which sought to instill an institutionalized moral vision for Canadian art. Oddly, given this vision, neither the Commission nor the Council devised any formal means of repelling the infusion of American cultural goods into Canada.

Vincent Massey was also instrumental in bringing substantial changes to the National Gallery of Canada during the 1950s, including the hiring of Alan Jarvis as Director of the National Gallery. Enthusiastic, charming, and elitist, Jarvis was considered the person able to revive the Gallery and bring it in line with the progressive new relationship between art and state and the modernist surge in culture. The Gallery had become somewhat staid, and little abstract art had been purchased, a notable exception being the purchase of a Borduas. Jarvis, on the other hand, fell in well with artists who were turning against traditional

Canadian landscape in favour of American-style abstraction. He seemed, in fact, to mock the nationalist school, declaring "'that period is done with now' and as though to emphasize his point, Jarvis closed the Group of Seven room in the Gallery to allow for office space" (Ord, 1998, p. 8). His vision was to judge Canadian art against the standards of the world at large, yet he was thwarted in this somewhat by the National Gallery policy, bolstered in 1956, against the purchase of contemporary American art. The story of Jarvis' directorship is fascinating and controversial,[5] but he did achieve two major goals: first, the construction of a permanent pavilion for Canada at the site of the prestigious Venice Bienale of Contemporary Art and, second the acquisition of a new gallery. In many ways, Jarvis embodies the 1950s in Canadian art: a time of strengthening national institutions and their influence amid an art scene that was dismissing its nationalist past for an international present.

NEW VIEWS OF NATIONALISM

Generations of Canadian artists had traditionally combined in groups formed by like-minded individuals through a need to sustain one another's work and create exhibition and commercial opportunities. In the 1960s, this practice faded due to three factors: firstly, funding for the arts from the Canada Council lessened the stress on individual artists' needs to sell in order to survive; secondly, artists began responding to an increasingly unstable society where old rules no longer applied; and thirdly, the rules of art, its look, and its possibilities, were also undergoing the greatest changes of the century. If artists worked together, it was no longer in formal groups but in clusters of activists, as a collective that allowed for difference or in collaborations where individual identities were subsumed by the whole.

By the 1960s, the post–World War II optimism and boom were still hanging on, but in general North American culture had undergone such a revamping that cracks began to appear at first around the edges then at the centre of society. The first flight into space, the first man on the moon, the first birth control pill for women, and far too many assassinations of public figures all took place in the 1960s. It was the decade of civil rights, the building of the Berlin Wall, the peace movement and the onset of feminism, environmentalism, and activist groups such as Greenpeace. China exploded the hydrogen bomb, and the United States sent troops into Vietnam. And all of these events, accidents, and beginnings were linked by technology and communications in, according to Canadian communications theorist Marshal McLuhan, an increasingly global village.

The 1960s in Canada began with the start of Quebec's Quiet Revolution and ended with the Front de libération du Québec's October Crisis in 1970. The *Canadian Bill of Rights* was approved, and Aboriginal people won the right to vote in federal elections. Socialized medicine started in Saskatchewan, the Trans Canada highway opened, and Social Insurance Cards were issued. The CBC began broadcasting in colour, the new Canadian flag was inaugurated, and Canada celebrated its centennial anniversary by inviting the world to Expo '67 in Montreal. Amid the circus of Trudeaumania and its accompanying wave of nationalism, Pierre Trudeau was elected Prime Minister, a Royal Commission on the Status of Women was appointed, abortion laws were liberalized, and French and English were both recognized as official languages of Canada.

Amid such activities in the social and political arenas, it is inconceivable that the nature and content of art would not reflect similar changes. The very definition of what an art object could be underwent serious scrutiny in the 1960s. In an extensive essay on the Canadian art of the 1960s and 1970s, Catharine Mastin (1998) encapsulates some of the redefinition of the art object:

> While more established media, like painting, sculpture, and graphic arts, continued to absorb much attention in public art exhibitions and criticism, an alternative community of artists was simultaneously challenging the materials with which art objets were made, as well as what constituted art, and how the art object was to function beyond the confines of traditional media. New media and technology, such as the portapack video camera, film, and telex (an early version of today's fax machine) were being used for the first time for creative purposes. Among the many ephemeral forms of visual expression to grow from this era were 'happenings.' These publicly staged spontaneous and improvised performances focussed on the immediate experience. Usually no object was left behind except the promotional materials announcing them and, on occasion, some video-based documentation. (10–11)

Supporting changes to the approach of artists were institutional evolutions, many of which were facilitated by the Canada Council. When larger public galleries were somewhat slower to adapt to experimental media—grappling with issues such as how to collect and conserve ephemeral objects—a new system of artist-run galleries came into being. These were and are dedicated to exhibiting non-traditional work as well as art by emerging artists. Some centres, such as Vancouver's Western Front, are also dedicated to assisting artists in the production of their work.

After the massive diversification of artists, media, and ideas in the 1960s, singling out any group of artists to discuss is done so at the loss of countless other opportunities. Yet two artists are of particular relevance to this chapter not only for the significance of their work and their importance to successive generations of artists but also for the fundamental nationalism of their art. For Joyce Wieland, nationalism had a bearing on

the construction and exploration of personal identity. For Greg Curnoe—
"the most splendidly anti-American artist Canada has ever produced"
(Fetherling, 1993, 34)—nationalism mixed with healthy regionalism was
a central component of the belief system at the heart of his work.

For Greg Curnoe, a "sense of place was essential" (Fetherling, 1993,
34). Born in London, Ontario, Curnoe would study art there before
briefly attending Toronto's Ontario College of Art. There, he found the
hold of Modernist painting to be oppressive, particularly its elitism and
dictum that art should refer only to art at the expense of all other references, especially that unruly mix of popular culture that Curnoe
embraced. In the earliest stages of his career, Curnoe's work was identified with American Pop Art although it bore only a cursory, surface
resemblance to the Pop Art style. Perhaps this unfortunate categorization was in part what influenced his insistence that Canadian artists must
not be judged by critical standards imported from elsewhere.

Three considerations combine in any discussion of Greg Curnoe.
Foremost is his art—a body of work of diverse media and concerns that
can be examined through his early and sustained interest in combining
images with text or his sometime production of text-only pieces.
Secondly, his refusal to segregate his art from his life had profound
effects on both realities. Third, and underscoring all, Curnoe must be
known for his passionate belief in the importance of a person's local
reality, the regional, over any invented obligation to a distant art centre.
Throughout these considerations, Curnoe's nationalism is readily
apparent and informs all aspects of his life and work.

Curnoe's earliest works are notable for their lengthy text passages that
intertwine with images and his references to local specificities within that
text. By the end of the 1960s, his concentration on local and personal concerns was well developed. *View of Victoria Hospital, Second Series* (10 February
1969–10 March 1971) is a painting of the view from his studio window,
accompanied by eight pages of typewritten descriptions of 120 things that
happened to him during the two-year period of producing the painting.
Curnoe also produced pure text works, those paintings, drawings, and
books made painstakingly with rubber-stamp lettering that list Canadian
artists, musicians, and writers, provide text descriptions of the same landscape view of Victoria Hospital, or give an enumeration of all the things
that Curnoe was not. In the early 1970s, Curnoe—an avid cyclist and
founding member of the London Centennial Wheelers—also began an
extended series of images of his bicycle, a Mariposa 10-speed racer. The
reproduction in this chapter, *Mariposa 10 Speed* (25 March 1973–25 April
1973, see illustration), is a beautiful example of the artist's facility with
watercolour and his investigative representations of this personal icon. The
work also demonstrates the forthright connection of Curnoe's graphic
works to his life. One has to understand the significance of the text
appearing on the crossbar—Close the 49th Parallel!—to know the depth
of that connection.

In Curnoe's work, art unabashedly reflects popular culture, the mix of all things fascinating to his prodigious curiosity. From the focal point of the London community that was his studio, Curnoe and friends formed the Nihilist Party of Canada, a collective that apparently gave great picnics.[6] The Party also ran two politically charged campaigns, "Don't Vote," and "Close the 49th Parallel." Curnoe's nationalism involved a resolute anti-Americanism, a vigilance against the tidal wave of American culture that was rushing into Canada. For most of his career, Curnoe refused to let his work be exhibited south of the Canadian/American border, or reproduced in American publications, and his huge mural for Montreal's Dorval International Airport was removed from public display in 1968 for its overt anti-Americanism. Curnoe typified the increased social and political activities of artists in the 1960s and onward, by creating a seamless mix of his studio work and his community activities. He created the Nihilist Spasm Band, an ensemble of ebullient and rowdy would-be artist-musicians, and he took part in the first "Happening" in Canada at Canada's first artist-run centre, the Region Gallery, which he had helped found along with London's two subsequent artist-run galleries. Together with London artist Jack Chambers, Curnoe also created CARFAC in 1967, the important and influential artists' organization that was created to act as a professional standards union ensuring rights, adequate exhibition fees, and copyright protection strategies for Canadian artists.

London was Curnoe's home, and he turned it into a buzz of artistic energy that attracted national and international attention. Creating a culture around artist-run centres, Curnoe lent his support to other London artists such as Jack Chambers, David and Roydon Rabinowitch, Ron Martin, Murray Favro, Andy Patton, and Janice Gurney. Director of the National Gallery Pierre Théberge remembers Curnoe's London:

> When I think back on the London scene of the sixties, what strikes me most is how all the artists were proud of where they lived and of the institutions they had created and ran. Each had his own well-defined individuality and evinced a deep-rooted conviction that artistic creation was absolutely essential to his life. Yet, none of them tried to impose his stylistic preferences on the others. (Théberge, 1997, 165)

In the late 1960s Théberge curated an exhibition of 11 artists for the Gallery, significantly titled *The Heart of London*. Curnoe's achievements in carving out a niche in Canadian art for those in the regions was, according to Douglas Fetherling, at the very core of his way of being a Canadian artist:

> Musing on the meaning of being outside the mainstream is part of what it means to be a Canadian artist and thinker. London, Ontario, to him [Curnoe], was not simply the particular of

which Canada is the general. It was his own unique place away from the mainstream where one could lead a highly productive life: his London was to Toronto as Canada is to the rest of the world. (Fetherling, 1993, 39)

If Curnoe found his home and sense of place by burrowing deep into the local, Joyce Wieland found hers by a much different tack, that of the expatriate.

Joyce Wieland and her artist-husband Michael Snow had left Toronto in 1962 for what would be an eight-year stay in New York City. There, both their careers flourished, particularly Wieland's work with experimental film. She continued, however, to return to Canada for prolonged stays, visiting artist appointments and exhibition opportunities. It was during such a visit for a 1967 exhibition that she encountered and read *The Canadian Forum* magazine and the nationalist explorations of Melville Watkins, Walter Gordon, and George Grant—writings in which she found support for her own developing thoughts about nationalism, fostered by a New York–bred homesickness.

As her sense of nationalism grew, Wieland began to blend Canadian content into the mix of her art in such a way that both form and intent would be served. Wieland's work is an astonishing array of painting, drawing, printmaking, film, video, sculpture, assemblage, quilting, performance, and installation—all using innovative combinations of traditional and non-traditional forms and materials, and all imbued with Wieland's fearless and irreverent wit, joy, keen observation, feminism, sexuality, and humour.

Wieland began exhibiting her paintings in 1957, at the male-dominated Isaacs Gallery. Amid the glaring machismo of the "big-attack," male abstract painters, she produced paintings of dazzling colour and sensitivity to form and expression. At the same time, Wieland inserted her own wit and subversive, sexual femaleness into the paintings, creating phallic and vaginal forms with titles like *Balling, The Kiss, Heart On, Redgasm,* and *Laura Secord Saves Upper Canada.* In later years, Wieland would describe the thinly veiled content of these stained and sensual canvasses as "sex poems." When she and Snow moved to New York, Wieland concentrated on her film work. A 1968 film revealed Wieland as an innovator, able to create the appropriate form for an insightful commentary on politics, environmental issues, and of course, Canadian nationalism. *Rat Life and Diet in North America* is in part a commentary on the Vietnam war; a band of draft dodgers, played by Wieland's pet gerbils, bravely escape political oppression by fleeing to Canada. There they take up organic gardening and participate in flower festivals until the Americans eventually invade Canada. Like most of her work, *Rat Life* is equal parts politics and poetry, mixed with Wieland's humour.

Like Greg Curnoe, Joyce Wieland made no separation between her life and her art, and in fact used her work as an artist to pursue her never-ending quest to know and describe her own identity. For Wieland, this identity included being a woman and a feminist even before the feminist movement organized its own beginning. It meant being an alert and concerned citizen responding to the growing awareness of environmental issues. And it meant becoming an ardent nationalist in part because Trudeaumania was instilling a feverish pride across the country, as well as for deeply personal reasons. As Wieland expressed her thoughts, "I think of Canada as female.... All the art I've been doing or will be doing is about Canada. I may tend to overly identify with Canada" (Lippard, 2).

Indeed, Wieland blended the landscapes of Canada, the personal, and the feminine and by doing so found a success that, sadly, was uncharacteristic of women artists at that time. She was the first Canadian woman artist to be given a major retrospective exhibition at the National Gallery in 1971 and would subsequently receive the Order of Canada and have a retrospective of her work at the Art Gallery of Ontario.[7] The 1971 retrospective *True Patriot Love* perhaps best demonstrates the pointed diversity of this artist's work, a show not so much about creating a vision of Canada but rather reflecting on what things we might have in common in Canada:

> *True Patriot Love* took over the entire first floor of the gallery. Quilts, paintings, film and nationalistic paraphernalia were presented within an interior installation of pine trees, a pond with live ducks and the sounds of Canadian songbirds. At the opening, on Canada Day no less, a marching band crowded into the gallery, and to complete the festive occasion, Wieland had a huge, Arctic Passion Cake made for the guests and sold small bottles of a scent labeled *Sweet Beaver: the Perfume of Canadian Liberation.* (Contemporary Canadian Artists, 609–10)

While the artist's entire *ouevre* is too vast and complex to begin addressing in this chapter,[8] Wieland's quilts deserve special mention. Years before the *Dinner Party* by Judy Chicago, or the reinvestment in traditional women's work by the feminist movement, Joyce Wieland was making quilts that were to be seen as art, elevating craft to the status of high art and raising the value of women's work. At the same time, Wieland also used her quilts as a means of containing overtly Canadian content, such as her *Confedspread* of 1967, pictured on the cover of this text. It is a quilt that was created to celebrate Canada's centennial, in which the distinct and brightly coloured pieces of fabric are arranged and bound together into one stunning block, the whole of which is far more interesting than its separate parts. Her most well-known quilt, *Reason Over Passion,* takes Pierre Trudeau's comments on his own writing style and translates them into puffy, colourful balloon letters—somehow managing to invert his quote and to femininely assert the dominance of reason by passion. Another quilt of 1970, reproduced here, is *I Love Canada/J'Aime Canada* (see illustration), which combines in a pristine whiteness the political debates of official bilingualism and an expression of her passionate personal commitment to Canada. Wieland would return to Canada in 1971 and continue to have one of the most successful careers enjoyed by a female artist of her generation—one that would be an inspiration, a reference, and a call to action for countless women artists in Canada and abroad. Sadly, Joyce Wieland became afflicted with Alzheimer's disease and passed away in 1998.

LOCATING IDENTITY NOW

Clement Greenberg has been credited with saying that the history of Canadian art is written in landscape. Certainly, the landscape or at least the idea of landscape has appeared throughout the periods and artists examined in this chapter: the picturesque topographies of army officers and itinerant artists, the proud patriotic landscapes of the Group of Seven, the rejection of that landscape, and the witty, experimental landscapes of Greg Curnoe and Joyce Wieland. Maria Tippett would claim that this use of the Canadian landscape and all associated ideas are at the very core of the breakdown in our national art; "the symbols, on the other hand, which represent all Canadians—the country's vast geography, history, religious, ethnic, and linguistic diversity, the monarchy, and, in the last eighteen years, the Charter of Rights—have served to divide rather than unite its citizens" (Tippett, 2000, 18). Consider, however, the legacy of possibilities created for artists today:

> The almost unlimited possibilities of art now had begun to unfold in the 1960s and 1970s with the introduction of new media and new ideas about art's functions. During the past twenty years or so the spectrum of players in the art arena also has broadened dramatically. Art today includes those who had been excluded previously. The concerns and efforts of these new players have extended art's discursive terrain and introduced innovative artistic methodologies and forms. The playing field continues to expand: as new technologies (including, for example, digital and other electronic media) become more readily available, a new generation of players enters the game. (Hurtig, 1998, 9)

In so many words, artistic and cultural explosions have opened up art as a field of aesthetic and intellectual investigation that continues to expand. With the influx of Postmodern, Deconstructionist theory into the field, artists and cultural thinkers are also using art as a means of asking questions about Canadian identity and how that identity has come to be constructed. Without disparaging or dismissing the acknowledged mainstream history of art in Canada, contemporary artists and critics are also suggesting other, revisionist histories that include views of the mainstream by those who have until recently been excluded from it (women, First Nations, immigrants, gays, and lesbians).

Jin-me Yoon, an artist living and working in Vancouver, combines in her work an ongoing examination of her own Korean background with a questioning look at how Canada functions as a nation, both from the perspective of its official history and from the various histories of its less-than-mainstream citizens. For the 1996 exhibition *topographies: recent aspects of b.c. art*, Yoon worked with the Vancouver Art Gallery and in conjunction with the showing of *The Group of Seven: Art for a Nation* exhibition there, in order to produce her photographic installation, *A Group of Sixty Seven* (see illustration).

During the run of the Group of Seven exhibition, Yoon organized a series of dinners for a group of 67 Korean Canadians, each dinner being followed by a photographic session. With the photographer of the Vancouver Art Gallery, Yoon took portraits of the dinner guests with two paintings installed in the galleries; Emily Carr's *Old Time Coastal Village* from the Gallery's collection and Lawren Harris' *Maligne Lake, Jasper Park* (see illustration) from the *Art for a Nation* exhibition. In doing so, Yoon places newer histories together with old and the idyllic views of the Canadian landscape together with allusions to less than ideal aspects of Canadian history. If the number 67 refers obliquely to the Group of Seven, it also refers to the year of Canada's centennial celebrations—1967—which is also the year that the Canadian government lifted its immigration restrictions for certain East Asians. *A Group of Sixty Seven* is not, however, an easy dismissal of the Group of Seven as "agents of white imperialism," nor of Canada as a country with racist immigration policies. Rather, it points to truths both well and lesser known that are all part of the concept of national identity. Her guests, the 67 Korean-Canadian models, interact with the Canadian landscape, looking into the depths of Emily Carr's woods, peering out at us from Harris' majestic mountains, defining their place within the landscape. Yoon's models become part of our Canadian landscape and identity. *A Group of Sixty Seven* is in part an acknowledgment of Canada's past and the role of art within that past, and in larger part, it lets us know how our evolving history and identity will continue to be chronicled in the art of our nation.

NOTES

1. Varley would soon after move to the firm of Rous and Mann, following Thomson and Carmichael.

2. A.Y. Jackson would state that, had not World War I intervened, the Group would have formed several years earlier, and Thomson would have been a member (Bice, 1989,14).

3. A most thorough, researched, articulate, and balanced examination of the Group of Seven can be found in Charles C. Hill's catalogue to the 75th anniversary exhibition, *The Group of Seven: Art for a Nation.* Ottawa: National Gallery of Canada, 1995.

4. It must be noted that funds from the Canada Council are distributed by an arm's-length process that awards grants according to a juried selection process. As juries are composed of members from the arts communities, "the Council" should be used as a metonymic reflection of jury members and by extension, the larger arts community.

5. Please refer to Douglas Ord, "The Best Looking Man."

6. Other Canadian artists would enter the political sphere; in 1974 artist Victor Trasov ran for Mayor of Vancouver as his alter-ego, Mr. Peanut.

7. Wieland is most likely the only Canadian artist to show her work at the Cannes Film Festival *and* the Montreal Biennial of Tapestry.

8. Please refer to the catalogue of the Art Gallery of Ontario retrospective, Marie Fleming's *Joyce Wieland.*

REFERENCES

Bice, Megan. "Tom Thomson and the Group of Seven." *The McMichael Canadian Art Collection: Twenty-Fifth Anniversary Edition, 1965–1990.* Jean Blodgett, Megan Bice, David Wistow, and Lee-Ann Martin. Kleinburg: McMichael Canadian Art Collection and Toronto: McGraw-Hill Ryerson Ltd., 1989.

Borduas, Paul-Émile. "Global Refusal: Ten Years After." *Documents in Canadian Art.* Ed. Douglas Fetherling. Peterborough: Broadview Press, 1987a, pp. 126–27.

———. "Global Refusal." *Documents in Canadian Art.* Ed. Douglas Fetherling. Peterborough: Broadview Press, 1987b, pp. 113–25.

Buchanan, Donald W. "James Wilson Morrice—Pioneer of Modern Painting in Canada." *Canadian Geographical Journal* 32(5) (May 1946): 240–41.

———. "Tom Thomson—Painter of the True North." *Canadian Geographical Journal* 32(2) (August 1946): 98–100.

The Canada Company. <www.cyber-north.com/public/canart.htm>. Cited 2000, May 12.

Casson, A.J. "Group Portrait." *Documents in Canadian Art.* Ed. Douglas Fetherling. Peterborough: Broadview Press, 1987, pp. 56–65.

Charlesworth, Hector. "Canada and Her Paint Slingers." *Documents in Canadian Art.* Ed. Douglas Fetherling. Peterborough: Broadview Press, 1987, pp. 54–55.

Contemporary Canadian Artists. Toronto: Gale Canada, 1997.

Fenton, Terry, and Wilkin, Karen. *Modern Painting in Canada: Major Movements in Twentieth Century Canadian Art.* Edmonton: The Edmonton Art Gallery, 1978.

Fetherling, Douglas. "The Curnoe Story." *Canadian Art* 10(2) (Summer 1993): 28–39.

Fulford, Robert. "Regrouping the Group." *Canadian Art* 12(3) (Fall 1995): 68–77.

Gadsby, H.F. "The Hot Mush School, or Peter and I." *Documents in Canadian Art.* Ed. Douglas Fetherling. Peterborough: Broadview Press, 1987, pp. 43–48.

Gagnon, Maurice. "Automatism ... A New Canadian Painting." *Documents in Canadian Art.* Ed. Douglas Fetherling. Peterborough: Broadview Pess, 1987, pp. 128–32.

Hurtig, Annette. *Art Now: An Expansive Field of Play.* Kamloops: Annette Hurtig and Kamloops Art Gallery, 1998.

Jackson, A.Y. "James Wilson Morrice, by Donald W. Buchanan." *Canadian Art* 3(4) (Christmas 1947): 93.

Lippard, Lucy. *Watershed: Contradiction, Communication and Canada in Joyce Wieland's Work.* In Marie Fleming and Joyce Wieland (Eds.) Toronto: Art Gallery of Ontario, 1987.

Mastin, Catharine M. *Changing Spirits: Canadian Art of the 1960s and 1970s.* Kamloops: Kamloops Art Gallery, 1998.

Moore, Christopher. "Interpreting History." *The Beaver* 80(1) (February/March 2000): 82–88.

Ord, Douglas. "The Best Looking Man." *Canadian Art* 15(1) (Spring 1998): 64–70.

Reid, Dennis. *A Concise History of Canadian Art.* 2nd ed. Toronto: Oxford University Press Canada, 1987.

Théberge, Pierre. "London Recaptured." *Canadian Literature* 152/53 (Spring/Summer 1997): 160–66.

Tippett, Maria. "Expressing Identity." *The Beaver* 80(1) (February/March 2000): 18–27.

Yakabuski, Konrad. "Refus Global is Little Read, Highly Romanticized: A Documentary Explores the Contradictory Interpretations of a Document that Put Individual Freedom Above All." *The Globe and Mail,* 8 August 1998.

Wylie, Liz. "The True North?" *University of Toronto* XXVII(4) (Summer 2000): 35.

FURTHER READING

Fetherling, Douglas. ed. *Documents in Canadian Art.* Peterborough: Broadview Press, 1987.

Fleming, Marie. *Joyce Wieland*. Toronto: Art Gallery of Ontario, 1987.

Hill, Charles C. *The Group of Seven: Art for a Nation*. Ottawa: National Gallery of Canada and McClelland and Stewart, 1995.

Hurtig, Annette. *Art Now: An Expansive Field of Play*. Kamloops: Annette Hurtig and Kamloops Art Gallery, 1998.

Reid, Dennis. *A Concise History of Canadian Art*. 2nd ed. Toronto: Oxford University Press Canada, 1987.

From the Absent Audience to Expo-mentality: Popular Film in Canada

Charles R. Acland

At first blush, it may seem a bit ironic to address something that is absent. This is not, however, the case for Canadian cultural critics for whom absence is often a key term in debates and analyses. For instance, there is Margaret Atwood's (1972) resonant claim that the theme of "survival" in Canadian literature signals, in part, not its robust nature but the dismally low expectations about the culture's future. And Anthony Wilden (1980) suggests that Canadians live in "Notland," where we exist only in so much as we are not somewhere or someone else. Historically, the recipe for this "felt" national cultural absence has consisted of one part lost cultural potential, one part manifestos for corrective measures, and two parts self-loathing.

This tendency is amply evident in writing about Canadian cinema, whether it is Bruce Elder's (1988) modernist cries for "the cinema we need," Pierre Berton's (1975) observation that the images we and the world have of Canada are not our own but Hollywood's, or feminist film scholarship hoping to be "as Canadian as possible" given what are understood as dire circumstances (Berenstein, 1989). Interestingly, when Peter Harcourt (1978) wrote about "the invisible cinema" of Canada, he observed that the problem was not a lack of films but a lack of audiences for those films. In this chapter, I want to contextualize and challenge the notion of "absence" to show the way this assessment has restricted our ability to understand Canadian life. Doing so means understanding that a "national cinema" consists of much more than simply the films produced in a given country; a "national cinema" is also made up of the films people see, the people who work in the film industry, the places we go to see films, and the ideas about film that circulate. For the present argument, it is important to understand that cultural absence is one such idea that circulates. Far from being an empirical description of the state of things, cultural absence is an ideologically invested concept, one in which the politics of Canadian culture can be observed. To extend Harcourt's influential thesis, it is apparent that a blind spot in criticism has been popular film audiences and that the idea of absence has made it nearly impossible to recognize and appreciate the multitudes of Canadian cinemagoers.

TWO DIMENSIONS OF ABSENCE: ECONOMICS AND TASTE

Manjunath Pendakur (1990) characterizes the demise of the Allen Theatres circuit as a major part of the roots of Canada's dependent relationship to the United States in film (pp. 51–78). Starting in 1906, Allen Amusement Corporation exhibited and distributed film, capitalizing on a deal with Paramount Pictures in the United States, and became Canada's largest chain by 1920. That same year, however, Paramount Pictures created a rival in exhibition, Famous Players Canadian Corporation, run by Nathan Nathanson in an equal partnership. Through Famous Players, an American corporation involved in production, distribution, and exhibition had direct access to Canadian film audiences. And, without the arrangement with Paramount, the Allen chain collapsed by 1923. Famous Players embarked upon an aggressive strategy of building theatres, buying out those of competitors, and intimidation (Pendakur, 1990, p 61). So complete was their control of Canadian exhibition, even competing U.S. distributors had to deal with Famous Players (Pendakur, 1990, p. 72).

The historical control of theatres by U.S. distributors is perhaps the single most influential factor in the idea of cultural absence in Canadian film. Even today, Paramount owns Famous Players, whose parent corporation is the U.S. media giant Viacom. Similarly, the U.S.-based Universal has a stake in Cineplex Odeon, which merged with the Loews theatre chain in 1998 to create one of the largest exhibitors in the world, Loews Cineplex Entertainment. In 1998, Famous Players and Cineplex Odeon accounted for approximately 30 percent and 43 percent, respectively, of the total number of screens in Canada. This kind of concentration is unheard of in the United States, where no single chain reportedly had more than 10 percent before 1998 (Peers, 1998). The resulting industrial structure, and its close ties to U.S. corporations, make it such that domestic film is largely missing from traditional commercial exhibition channels; it occupies only 2 to 3 percent of the theatrical market (Report of the Feature Film Advisory Committee, 1999, p. 3). Even in Quebec, where the popular film culture is much stronger than in the rest of Canada, domestic film captures but 4 percent of the box office ("Report of the Feature Film Advisory Committee," 1999, p. 3).

A dominant paradigm for this subject is the dependency theory model, in which American economic might is singularly influential in structuring Canadian cultural life. The general story here is one of the failure of Canadian cultural enterprise to compete in an open market against the immense U.S. economies of scale. The U.S. control of

Canadian movie theatres is one consequence of U.S. economic influence on Canadian culture, and it is often indicated as a symptom of the "Americanization" of Canadian culture. Using traditional models of critical theory, cultural control is understood to be ideological control; this argument suggests that the economics of culture not only create barriers for Canadian artists and cultural entrepreneurs but also lead to the colonization of Canadian minds.[1]

Exhibitors are not blind to this argument, one that has a forceful presence in popular understanding as well as cultural policy. Industry participants, rather predictably, offer sympathetic responses, though the "realities" of the market tend to take precedence nonetheless. Canadian exhibitors will don the garments of nationalism, while finding rationales for the dismal invisibility of Canadian theatrical releases. Typical is Cineplex Odeon's Allen Karp, who maintained that exhibitors were doing their part to provide screen time for Canadian features but that "Canadian filmmakers must make more accessible films and distributors must make more efforts to market them..."(Harris, 1990).

Alternative strategies, ones that skirt the issue of the appearance of Canadian films on Canadian screens, are occasionally presented. Canada Film Year, with $2.5 million from Telefilm, was the Academy of Canadian Film and Television's attempt to expand non-commercial programs, especially away from urban centres (Harris, 1989). It was set to begin in late summer, 1990, with four main objectives: "to expand audiences of Canadian film by heightening public awareness; to create an appetite for more Canadian production by increasing the availability of Canadian film on both large and small screens; to develop greater awareness of Canadian film's past and present achievements, and future potential, and, finally to increase public consciousness of the cultural and economic importance of film production" (Harris, 1989, p. 5). By April, the project, however, was abandoned (Morgan, 1989).

Without necessarily having an impact upon the screen time of Canadian features, there has been a history of attempts to foster a national presence with other dimensions of cinemagoing. For instance, a 1994 deal between the Motion Picture Theatre Association of Canada and the Canadian Association of Film Distributors and Exporters created Canadian Project Pictures. In consultation with distributors, exhibitors select a film whose trailers and promotion will then appear regardless of what chain is actually playing the film (Armstrong, 1996). In another approach to the Canadianization of the film environment, but not of film, Famous Players offered a scheme that would match the advertising and promotional dollars for Canadian films screened at their cinemas.

In this way, attempts to "Canadianize" cinemagoing have often taken place around the central commodity of the feature. Unique in North America, Cineplex Odeon initiated a program to present specially commissioned works of Canadian art as permanent features in some of its lobbies. The first work, for the Beverly Center in Los Angeles, appeared in 1982; in 1989, 31 theatres in Canada and 21 in the United States had one of these art works (Adilman, 1989).

The advertisements and public service announcements, including Heritage Minutes, preceding the features are other points of visibility. A first reaction might be that this is an insignificant, and perhaps even demeaning, location to be promoting Canadian filmmaking. Even as advertisements were being introduced, an editorial in the Canadian industry publication *Playback* argued that "[a]dvertising has a place in movie theatre," but that with the saturation of our lives with commercials, Canadian audiences "want to preserve as many ad-free havens as they can" (Editorial, 1988, p. 4). Nonetheless, given their solid presence in other countries, advertisements in cinemas were not only inevitable but also may offer a space for Canadian filmmaking in Canadian theatres, even if it is commercial production rather than feature.

Of course, as solutions, these developments sidestep the questions of screen time and box office. Those who support sharing trailers consider "film absence" to be a problem of insufficient marketing; those supporting Canadian-made advertisements in cinemas believe this "minor" industry may spawn, eventually, feature work; and the recommendation of Heritage Minutes and Canadian lobby art sees national culture and history as an environment, a decor, that produces awareness, and hence affiliation, or so the argument goes. Stubbornly, it remains the case that the paltry number of Canadian films in the theatres cannot be addressed directly, because the economic incentives work against their attractiveness to exhibitors.

The political-economic analysis of cultural domination from without is hardly the exclusive domain of political economists. Instead, it is repeated and expanded by journalists, editorialists, policymakers, government representatives, and others. The pervasiveness of this argument leads me to suggest that it forms a part of our contemporary common sense. For example, one of the striking aspects of the state of Canadian film is the frequency with which popular periodicals report its absence, invariably citing the "colonization" of theatres as evidence. Film absence has an unusual presence in the popular imagination. An article on the Toronto Film Festival in the *Calgary Herald* ("Doubt clouds Canada's film future," 1997, p. C3) is a report on the uncertain future of Canadian film, especially when compared to the international success of Canadian television. *The Globe and Mail* reporter Robert Everett-Green (1997, p. C2) captured this thinking in the headline of an article on the topic, "Not coming soon to a theatre near you." Even industry sources habitually begin with this claim. For instance, an article in a trade publication on distribution opens with, "Theatrical distribution in Canada has long been plagued by problems of American domination" (Cuthbert, 1995, p. 6).

These examples are more than descriptions of the status of our film culture. They represent an agreement about its meagre existence; they are judgments and evaluations reflecting a particular history of film culture and criticism. In these judgments, there is no room to consider the experience and enjoyment of the Canadian audiences who frequent U.S. productions in our cinemas. So while the economic argument is indispensable, there has been an overinvestment in its explanatory powers, such that the multifarious pleasures, conditions, and operations of a travelling U.S. cinema are reduced to economic and ideological invasion only. Canadian distributors, producers, and filmmakers struggle for minor accomplishments in the context of the overwhelming presence of U.S. film. This, however, cannot substitute nor be taken as equivalent to the struggles and experiences of Canadian audiences who must live and negotiate the existing popular cultural scene. Put differently, our popular culture is not absent, it is made from an engagement with an internationally circulating popular culture. Further, it is also part of our popular culture that we talk about it as absent.

For this reason, a second, and traditionally underemphasized, notion of absence has to be elaborated upon. This dimension stems from the observation that Canadian film culture is not a part of the popular cinemagoing practices of Canadians. In this respect, the absence of Canadian audiences for Canadian film has to do, at least in part, with taste. While Seth Feldman wrote that Canadian film is located between centre stage and oblivion (1984, p. ix), in the popular imagination it is far closer to the latter. Harcourt has written that the first time he taught Canadian film, it was at York University in the mid-1970s, and that it was under the foreign cinema section of an introductory course (1994, p. 100). Take for example Bronwyn Drainie's (1996) commentary on Mort Ranson's 1996 film, *Margaret's Museum:* "It has been an extraordinary experience going to see *Margaret's Museum,* which I have done twice since it went into general Canadian release a couple of weeks ago. Extraordinary because for the first time I can ever recall in Toronto (outside the charged atmosphere of the annual film festival, that is), there was a lineup of people waiting in the February deep-freeze to buy tickets for an English Canadian movie." Part of the pleasure of the film, and part of its exceptionalism, was the anomalous presence of other people in the cinema. Statistics Canada (1999) reports that 1997–98 marked a nearly two-decade record of attendance at indoor theatres and drive-ins, just shy of 100 million. Considering only indoor theatre admissions, the 97.7 million attendance is a 36-year record. Obviously, Canadian audiences are not absent from theatres; however, audiences for Canadian film are typically sparse.

The experience of moviegoing in Canada can be a frustrating one. Though it offers a view to an exhilarating world movie culture, cinemagoing essentially takes you away from your national home. A seat in a Canadian movie theatre is essentially a seat on international territory; it offers the experience of being "anywhere" and of cosmopolitan connection to other world film audiences. Moviegoing, however, does not offer an experience of national spectatorship in the conventional sense; the idea of Canadians watching images of Canada at the movies is rarely realized. Canadians expect this, if only through a tacit agreement that U.S. culture is currently a brand of "degree zero" cultural specificity, finding itself at home in virtually any location.

Canadians live with a near total integration with U.S. cinema culture, involving not only the films and the industrial structures producing and distributing them, but also the movie magazines, the television shows about movies, the advertising, the Hollywood press junkets, the star interviews, the awards ceremonies, the popular criticism, the scholarly analyses, and so on. To round out our participation, we eagerly tap into the publicity machine of another country, from Barbara Walters to *Entertainment Tonight,* to help us assess our moviegoing choices, to see what interests other world movie audiences. Hence, it is important to recognize that the entwinement of the two cinema cultures includes a range of texts and practices beyond the films themselves.

The investment in a global cinema culture, and the experience of estrangement from our own domestically produced cinema, is familiar enough to popular film fans. It is not at all unusual to find a Canadian film in the "Foreign" section of the video rental store. While unfortunate part-time employees will try to explain that the section actually denotes "foreign language" videos, I wonder when French became such in Canada! And the excuse does not wash very well once one discovers, as I have at various times, the work of such English-language Canadian directors as Atom Egoyan, Guy Madden, William MacGillivary, Deepta Mehta, and Patricia Rozema, among the Kurosawas, the Truffaults, and the Arcands. Not bad company, but still, such cataloguing promotes our domestic cinema as a foreign cinema.[2]

Yet, this sense of estrangement from one's own culture is a banal fact of English-Canadian life; it makes sense to talk about how "at home" U.S. movies are here, and how "come-from-away" Canadian films are. While plenty of non-Hollywood texts, from James Bond to Mad Max, have made it into the mainstream of international popular culture, the expectation that Canadian films will do so is slim. In this respect, the "foreignness" of Canadian cinema concerns its affinity with an international art cinema. Here, "foreignness" does not designate a geographical distance from the national territory but a distance from popular taste.

To summarize, there is, on the one hand, the evidence of the inaccessibility (taken to mean its absence from cinemas and the tendency toward art cinema) of Canadian film to Canadian audiences, and, on the other, the critical paradigms available to explain this situation and recommend corrective measures. The continued focus on the economic explanation, as opposed to the second "taste" thesis, has led to a substantial misinterpretation of the "problem" of Canadian cinema culture. A fairly typical critical stance is to pronounce what a perfect film culture we would all enjoy if everyone went to see the latest Canadian film auteur instead of the latest Hollywood blockbuster in our cinemas. There are several problems with this assertion. First, to focus upon the space of the cinema ignores the fact that people see far more films in other locations. Second, even the film industry sees the box office as a receding measure of success of its movies, given the increasing importance of television, pay-per-view, and videotape as sources of revenue. Third, it suggests that popular taste is something to be combated for the way it suppresses an ideal Canadian popular culture. In the place of this argument, I suggest that we should be asking what is it about certain forms of cinema that confirm particular notions about what Canadian film is supposed to be? What gives some films and not others status as authentic, and appropriate, realizations of Canadian cinematic life? In order to respond to these questions, we must consider how Canadian audiences make sense of U.S. films.

INDUSTRIAL INTEGRATION AND CANADIAN READING STRATEGIES

Our film business is so integrated with the U.S. industry that it is said to be an industry of branch plants. Somewhat paradoxically, Canadian film largely acting in the service of U.S. productions has been responsible for the current unprecedented strength of the Canadian industry. This owes no small amount to the cheap Canadian dollar and tax breaks, making Canadian shoots and labour inexpensive to American investors. In 1994, $402 million was spent on film and television production in B.C. alone, generating an estimated $1 billion in other related spending. Approximately 75 percent of this came from Hollywood (Cernetig, 1995). By 1998, $1 billion was spent on film and television productions in that province (Saunders, 2000). Provinces compete with one another in their efforts to attract this influx of film activity, arguing that it keeps trained personnel working and at home.

Considering the economic and cultural impact of the U.S. productions shot in Canada using primarily Canadian crews, two issues are significant. First, what is the fallout of cultural policy that encourages U.S. shoots in Canada? Is it possible to argue that the bolstering of the résumés of Canadian film crews contributes to a vibrant indigenous film culture? Or are we in danger, as David Ellis has noted, of making Canadian talent into line producers, a position of little creative input or power (1992, p. 135)?[3] And second, should we consider that, in the context of such tightly entwined cinema industries, the Canadian branch plant film industry might offer unique forms of viewing, experiencing, and making sense of film?

A first step to moving beyond the economic model is to understand that there are ways of conceptualizing the pleasures of U.S. culture without celebrating their dominance in our lives. Many theorists, including Stuart Hall (1980), John Fiske (1987), and Janice Radway (1984), take the view that ideological effects are not written unambiguously into images, or into any sign, but instead are the product of the often unpredictable activities of "readers," interpreters, and media consumers. Replacing the certainty of finding dominant ideology in the messages of texts, contemporary theory suggests that the polysemic nature of signs, that is, their multiple meanings, open up a relative degree of freedom when it comes to the process of sense-making. This is influenced by context, social position, personal histories, and one's association with particular cultures and knowledge. Privileging the certitude of discovering ideological messages in culture has resulted in an historical misunderstanding of ritualized performance and popular pleasure; it has allowed for the simplistic view that U.S. images create an unproblematic "American" subject. This claim ignores the critical ability of people, the diverse and contradictory pleasures of culture, or even the possibility of saying "that movie was so terrible," or worse, that it was ideologically oppressive, yet "the company was good," or "the experience of watching was great."

Perhaps it would be advantageous to consider not so much an idea of a unified resistance to U.S. culture but to a structure of difference in Canadian life that facilitates a distinct reception of that culture. One thing that Canadians have in common with each other, and something that is not shared with U.S. audiences, is the recognition that U.S. popular culture is an imported culture. Further complicating this experience is the fact that some of this imported work might also be described as an export product of the Canadian industry. The unusualness of this import/export culture makes for some odd appeals to viewers. For instance, a U.S. network made-for-TV movie, called *How the West Was Fun* (Stuart Margolin, 1994) starring the Olsen twins, was shot in Alberta. When the television advertisements for the show ran, the local cable operator flashed a message across the bottom of the screen: "Shot in Calgary, shot in Calgary." This is hardly a form of subversion; but it is a recognition of the everyday appeal of reading the U.S. product through the eyes of the local viewer.

Further to this, the presence of Canadian talent in the United States, both in front of and behind the camera, provides another level of connection. The U.S. industry plays a role in the terms of success for Canadian talent; it also offers a way for Canadian audiences to view that success, to read a film as a mark of a Canadian achievement. There is a star-system-in-exile, as Canadian spectators watch local heroes in U.S. film and television, which both links and differentiates Canadian spectatorship to and from U.S. cinema. Some examples of southward-bound talent include Graham Yost, screenwriter for the movies *Speed* (Jan de Bont, 1994) and *Broken Arrow* (John Woo, 1996), John N. Smith, director of the Michelle Pfieffer vehicle *Dangerous Minds* (1995), *Screamers* (1995) director Christian Duguay, Matthew Perry of *Friends*, *VIP* star Pamela Anderson, actor Kate Nelligan, and the astronomically expensive Jim Carrey. This often-remarked-upon Canadian presence requires more than casual consideration. Is it possible to watch *Star Trek* (or *T.J. Hooker,*

Rescue 911, or *Tek Wars,* for that matter) and not be reminded of William Shatner's Canadianness, to see him as a local hero who has made good, or even as a CBC stock actor who graduated from the "protective wing" of public culture to the big-time down south? By contrast, it is entirely likely that *Top Cops,* which scores high on the Canadian-content point system, is seen as a U.S. import. These viewing practices are perfectly legitimate; there may be many opportunities to appreciate *Star Trek* from a "Canadian" angle, and there may be few such opportunities with the Canadian *Top Cops.*

John Caughie has noted that with the saturation of global media with U.S. products, viewing tactics develop to manage what I described as the experience of estrangement from one's national home. For instance, Caughie proposes that appreciation from an ironic angle is a tactic used by those who are suspicious of, yet still attracted to, the shiny surfaces of U.S. popular culture. Caughie writes that "television produces the conditions of an ironic knowingness, at least as a possibility, which may escape the obedience of interpellation or cultural colonialism and may offer a way of thinking subjectivity free of subjection. It gives a way of thinking identities as plays of cognition and miscognition, which can account for the pleasures of playing at being, for example, American, without the paternalistic disapproval that goes with the assumption that it is bad for the natives" (1992, p. 54). Not only have some, including Linda Hutcheon (1991) and Kieran Keohane (1997), pointed to irony as an especially Canadian literary tactic, but, arguably, English-Canadians are especially good at masquerading as Americans. The value of Caughie's approach is that this is seen as a coping mechanism, one that opens up the possibility of reading culture differently, rather than as a moment of psychic invasion.

POLICY AND ITS "CORRECTIVE" IMPULSE

The two aforementioned dimensions of absence—one economically determined and the other pertaining to popular taste—rest upon a concealment of actual cultural consumption (i.e., the habitual fashion in which Canadians make international culture their own). Due to the "absent-mindedness" of Canadian critical discourse, which sees Canadian culture for all it has never achieved, for its failures, programs have been initiated in the service of some imagined ideal national culture. A key goal of policy, for instance, has been to create new cultural relations as opposed to working with what is already present.

The relative misfires of policy, though, have been accompanied by serious misinformation about publicly funded culture. Part of a wider attack on publicly supported services, the argument that non-commercially viable culture is simply bad or elitist is utter nonsense. While there are struggles to assert popular sensibilities, our cultural policies are not conducive to ballet and opera only. Further, the claim that Canadian cinema is boring or amateurish does not hold water by any measure. This is driven home when we see the success of Canadian films in international festivals, indeed in international markets, yet not here. Something far more complex is afoot. There is often the obfuscation of the fact that government subsidy is not at all unusual in any number of industries, in particular those that require a boost to level the market playing field. Whatever the specifics of each instance of government support, the assumption is that there are other economic and social benefits to such subsidies and that these supports are not seen only in terms of an expenditure but also as an investment. Unfortunately, many have difficulty seeing the same claim in the cultural field.

National cultural policy refers to a structure of social power that has been involved historically in the making of the modern Canadian citizen through the making and appreciation of Canadian culture. It has attempted to incorporate a series of contradictory assumptions into a flexible, multidimensional idea of the national subject. For instance, national cultural policy corresponds to the federal governmental jurisdiction, but not, supposedly, in contradiction to the various provincial cultural policies. The centralizing pull of national policy has attempted to be balanced by a decentralizing agenda in the dissemination of funds. Policy has also projected an idea of unity comprising an image of multicultural diversity, always bumping up against competing discourses of Québécois nationalism. Canadian cultural policy articulates geographic, linguistic, ethnic, local, and provincial particularity back to a central location at which it is administered (that is, a specific level of government—the federal)—hence, to an imagined nation existing most vividly in the policy documents it produces.

To appreciate these tensions in the definition and administration of national cultural policy, one must turn to the 1920s and 1930s, the prehistory to our contemporary cultural policy framework. This period saw the emergence of attempts to define and respond to the threat of U.S. popular culture's omnipresence in Canada. A number of cultural critics and activists gained prominence, seeing a need to organize and develop Canadian culture in the service of democratic citizenship, often against the everyday cultural consumption of Canadians. These interwar cultural nationalists occupied the traditional ethical role of the State, meaning they took on the State's educational function in order to assure the stability of the social and political apparatus.[4] In so doing, they propagated their particular vision of culture and the country.

The many intellectuals and activists of this period, and the voluntary cultural organizations they founded, operated without official access to education or commercial culture; instead, they engaged alternate spaces of cultural activity, specifically leisure. Accordingly, the interwar period saw the cultivation of lecture circuits, travelling film projectionists, travelling art exhibits, radio forums, drama leagues, adult education, magazines, and conferences. In response to the seductions of U.S. culture, leisure was seen as a kind of work, and a work that built character and citizens, and was therefore in the service of the nation. After years of lobbying government for aid, this new cultural infrastructure of voluntary societies, along with its educative agenda, became embedded in Canadian film policy with the formation of the National Film Board of Canada (NFB) in 1939. With this institution, we see the linkage of (1) a particular idea about cinemagoing, associated with the lecture, the discussion, and the school and (2) the appreciation of certain film forms, in particular, experimental and documentary film, over the conventions of Hollywood narrative.

John Grierson (1988), the first film commissioner, departed in the mid-1940s, providing recommendations for the future of Canadian film policy; his argument essentially runs that Canada can't make Hollywood films as well as Hollywood, and why would you want to anyway? Peter Morris (1986) has effectively taken apart Grierson's au revoir recommendations, pointing out that they were rooted in an overinflated sense of the breadth of audience "captured" by NFB film.

By 1957, the NFB moved toward a reconceptualization of national film culture, favouring administrative decentralization. Symbolically, this was marked by the relocation of the NFB head office from Ottawa to Montreal; it was followed by the formation of the French-language film unit and the opening of regional offices in the mid-1960s. Also in the 1960s, the Challenge for Change/Société nouvelle film series provided incentives to those historically excluded from the filmmaking practice. From Challenge for Change/Société nouvelle, we see the emergence of the Mohawk Film Unit and a group of filmmakers who eventually go on to form Studio D, the famed and now-defunct women's filmmaking body. I would point out that in this re-formulation of what a national filmmaking institution is to engage—here involving a matrix of regional, ethnic, and gender identities—we still see the maintenance of a series of assumptions that can be condensed into a culture as education model. Even the NFB's earliest feature films represented a tendency toward the docudrama with Don Owen's *Nobody Waved Goodbye* (1964) and the experimental/personal film of Gilles Groulx's *Le Chat dans le Sac* (1964).

Feature film finally got the specific policy attention it deserved in 1967 with the formation of the Canadian Film Development Corporation (later renamed Telefilm). Here, in its mandate to spark production, the cultural model shifts drastically from the ethical ideal promoted by the voluntary societies of the 1920s and on. For the CFDC, the "feature" immediately signalled the commodity and the entrepreneur (Dorland, 1998). The definitions and criteria were almost exclusively economic; the problem of Canadian cinema, according to the CFDC, was the problem of investment. Many unabashedly popular films were produced, and the

CFDC was criticized for this. Marked with the taint of genre, they were seen as too American or too low-brow to be reasonable entrants to a national cinema. They included *Rabid* (David Cronenberg, 1977), *Meatballs* (Ivan Reitman, 1979), *Out of the Blue* (Dennis Hopper, 1980), and *Black Christmas* (Bob Clark, 1976). There were many other examples, and certainly, given the utter absence of virtually any feature filmmaking a few years earlier, the CFDC seemed a success. Nonetheless, the politics of government-supported *popular* culture led to a variety of attacks on the policies of the CFDC; one key example was the "scandal" of the CFDC's support of Denis Heroux's and Claude Fournier's sexploitation films, called "maple syrup pornography." Despite the burst of production activity, as well as the cultivation of audiences for these films, the question of national cinema has been ultimately one of aesthetics and taste. In other words, the process of evaluation involves both an ideal notion of what Canadian films should look like as well as a question of the "quality" of the audience they attract.

For all of its successes, the NFB, for years the centrepiece of film policy, sought a particular disposition in its film audiences, that of the student, and often acted as though the disposition of the student had become popular. Ultimately, it helped establish a radical disjuncture between an imagined ideal national (educated) subject and the actual cultural life of the nation. Canadian cinema has rarely been a popular cinemagoing practice, and when it has, the films have been treated disparagingly and rejected by critics. Instead, Canadian cinema culture has thrived in parallel locations—the school, the film festival or retrospective, the exposition, the community hall, the library, the museum—in this respect, building upon the structures established by the voluntary societies of the 1920s and 1930s. Importantly, all are locations with cultural dispositions, that is, ways of approaching and appreciating culture, distinct from those of popular cinemagoing or video-rental. For example, it is a common experience that a person's first encounter with Canadian cinema is in the classroom; here, the role of university-level Canadian film courses should not be underplayed.

THE EXPO-MENTALITY OF CANADIAN CINEMA

In light of the historical location of Canadian cinema culture in non-theatrical sites, in places parallel to commercial cinema, it can be said to demonstrate an "expo-mentality," an orientation to and for the special venue. The expo-mentality of Canadian cinema has led to the development of a lively and important circuit of film festivals. Much in the same way that many national cultures begin to cohere and appear whole at international festivals, Canadian film culture deploys the local festival to assert images of national participation. An incomplete list includes the Montreal World Film Festival, the Toronto International Film Festival (formerly the Festival of Festivals), the Canadian Screen Institute's Local Heroes International Screen Festival in Edmonton, the Canadian Independent Film Caucus's Hot Docs documentary film festival in Toronto, the Banff Television Festival, the Ottawa Animation Festival, Vancouver International Film Festival, Festival du cinema francophone international en Acadie, Saskatchewan's Yorkton Short Film and Video Festival (started in 1947, which makes it the oldest film festival in Canada), Rendez-vous de Cinema québécois, Dreamspeakers Film Forum, and Halifax's Atlantic Film Festival. Others include St. John's International Women's Film and Video Festival, Re-Visions Festival in Winnipeg, and Festival du Cinema International en Abitibi-Temiscamingue.

The economic significance of festivals is not lost on exhibitors. On the celebration of tastelessness at the Cult Film and Video Festival, Harvey Enchin (1992) noted, "as exhibitors continue to battle a decade-long slump in movie attendance, the popularity of film festivals seems to be growing. In fact, there is a proliferation of festivals catering to almost every taste or special interest, most of them more high brow than the cel-ebration of scuzz in Toronto" (p. 131). Another example is IMAX, a Canadian cinema practice, comprising its own technological system and chain of specially constructed theatres and production, that offers a film industry alternative to the conventions of Hollywood cinema. Initially associated with world fairs, science centres, and museums, IMAX is per-haps the quintessential example of Canadian film's "expo-mentality."[5] IMAX has now successfully begun to move into conventional multiplex cinemas.

Harcourt (1994) also notes the importance of the "Perspectives Canada" screening at the Festival of Festivals in Toronto. From its origins in 1984, it has become one of the main venues in which to see new Canadian film. While this festival and others like it serve as important markets for film, "Perspectives Canada" has a supplementary role as a "last chance" venue: see the film now because it will be nearly impossible to see it again. As Harcourt writes, the "yearly series of 'Perspectives Canada' screenings ... without exception, play to packed houses. The fact that when the films move from the festival to the commercial screens elsewhere in the city, they seldom last for more than a few weeks demon-strates that, in present-day consumer culture, people are more interested in events than in films" (1994, p. 116). While the latter comment is debat-able, the difficulty Canadian films have moving out of the festival circuit continues to be well documented. Robert Lepage's festival triumph, *Le Confessional* (1995), already a box-office hit in Quebec and promoted by excellent reviews, opened to dismal numbers in its theatrical run in Toronto (Kari, 1995).

As the above discussion should have made clear, this, then, is not the problem of absence; instead, it is a question of judgment that has pro-moted a particular cultural disposition—that is, certain kinds of cinemagoing practices—over others. In this vein, Pierre Bourdieu's (1984) notion of the *habitus* is illuminating, suggesting that there is a set of dispositions that structure the relations to culture. They include things like taste formation, like knowing how you are expected to act as part of a particular audience, and knowing whether you are invited to the show to begin with. As Bourdieu puts it, knowing the habitus is akin to having a "feel for the game" (1990, p. 9). One needs to ask what dispositions (involving both taste and criticism) are affirmed (not reflected) by the critically celebrated Canadian films, and why do so many Canadians not feel invited? This involves issues of exhibition, distribution, and marketing, that is, the economic explanation; but the response must also deal with a variety of other discursive and material conditions that act to position cultural products and our relations to them. The habitus of Canadian "expo-mentality" offers little to a popular disposition in which U.S. popular cinema is quite at home in Canada. One needs to take into account the fact that people don't go to the cinema only to see films; indeed people are increasingly becoming cinemagoers for special circumstances (weekends, movies "everyone" is seeing, to celebrate an event). One's pleasures may have to do with the cinematography, the kind of ending you are in the mood for, the quality of the company you share, and how close you are sitting to the bucket of popcorn. Further, as argued above, the claim that the space of film culture is the cinema is an increasingly arcane suggestion, one that itself bespeaks a particular cultural disposition. And, as Bourdieu (1984) reminds us, all dispositions, every habitus, are correlates of cultural capital and serve to establish social distinctions through cultural consumption. This is not to say that there is a national habitus but that there has been an attempt to situate a set of dispositions as central to a national character. In the end, an authorized language about Canadian culture has papered over its own investment in certain forms of social distinction and rendered the everyday pleasures of popular culture an absent location.

NOTES

1. For a complete rendering of the dependency theory history see Pendakur (1990), Smythe (1981), Crean (1976). For a critical re-examination of this history, see Magder (1993).

2. Blockbuster video argues that they receive the classification for their videos from the head office in the U.S., hence the penchant for the categorization of Canadian film as foreign.

3. For an extended analysis of the implications of location shooting in Canada, see Gasher (1995).

4. For more detailed treatment of this history, see Acland (1994), Litt (1992), and Vipond (1980).

5. Acland (1997) elaborates the argument of IMAX's "expo-mentality," placing it into the context of Canadian film history.

REFERENCES

Acland, Charles R. (1997). IMAX in Canadian cinema: Geographic transformation and discourses of nationhood. *Studies in Cultures, Organizations and Societies* (3), 289–305.

———. (1994). National dreams, international encounters: The formation of Canadian film culture in the 1930s. *Canadian Journal of Film Studies* 3(1), 3–26.

Adilman, Sid (1989, May 3–9).Thou 'art' the only cinema chain in U.S., Canada to seek original pieces. *Variety,* 463.

Armstrong, Mary Ellen. (1996, May 6). Are exhibitors doing their share? *Playback* 22.

Atwood, Margaret. (1972). *Survival.* Toronto: Anansi.

Ayscough, Susan. (1991, December 2). Stronghold for non-US fare weakens. *Variety,* 74.

Berenstein, Rhonda. (1989). As Canadian as possible: The female spectator and the Canadian context. *Camera Obscura* 20/21, 40–52.

Berton, Pierre. (1975). *Hollywood's Canada: The Americanization of our national image.* Toronto: McClelland and Stewart.

Bourdieu, Pierre. (1984). *Distinction: A social critique of the judgement of taste.* Trans. Richard Nice. Cambridge: Harvard University.

———. (1990). *In other words: Essays towards a reflexive sociology.* Trans. Matthew Adamson. Stanford: Stanford University.

Canadian movie attendance hit four-year high of 79 million in 1994. (1995, June 16). *Montreal Gazette,* D3.

Caughie, John. (1992). Playing at being American: Games and tactics. In Patricia Mellencamp (Ed.), *Logics of television: Essays in cultural criticism,* (pp. 44–58). Bloomington: University of Indiana Press.

Cernetig, Miro. (1995, May 13). Horray for Brollywood, *The Globe and Mail,* D1.

Crean, Susan. (1976). *Who's afraid of Canadian culture?* Toronto: General.

Cuthbert, Pamela. (1995, February 13). Distributors post record results. *Playback,* 6.

Dorland, Michael. (1998). *So close to the State/s: The emergence of Canadian feature film policy.* Toronto: University of Toronto Press.

Doubt clouds Canada's film future. (1997, September 9). *Calgary Herald,* C3.

Drainie, Bronwyn. (1996, February 22). Finally, a Canadian movie that ranks at the top. *The Globe and Mail,* A14.

[Editorial]. (1988, April 4). Advertising has a place in cinemas. *Playback,* 4.

Elder, Bruce. (1988). The cinema we need. In Douglas Fetherling (Ed.,) *Documents in Canadian Film.* Peterborough: Broadview Press, 260–71.

Enchin, Harvey. (1992, October 31). Ghoulish or grand, film fests pack'em in *The Globe and Mail*, B1.

Ellis, David. (1992). *Split screen: Home entertainment and new technologies.* Toronto: Friends of Canadian Broadcasting.

Everett-Green, Robert. (1997, January 18). Not coming soon to a theatre near you. *The Globe and Mail*, C2.

Feldman, Seth. (Ed.) (1984). *Take two: A tribute to film in Canada.* Toronto: Irwin.

Fiske, John. (1987). *Television culture.* New York: Methuen.

Gasher, Mike. (1995). The audiovisual locations industry in Canada: Considering British Columbia as Hollywood North. *Canadian Journal of Communication* 20, 231–54.

Grierson, John. (1988). A film policy for Canada. In Douglas Fetherling (Ed.), *Documents in Canadian film* (pp. 51–67). Peterborough: Broadview Press.

Hall, Stuart. (1980). Encoding/decoding. In Stuart Hall, Dorothy Hobson, Andrew Lowe, and Paul Willis (Eds.), *Culture, Media, Language,* (pp. 128–38). London: Hutchinson.

Harcourt, Peter. (1978, Spring/Summer). The invisible cinema. *Cine Tracts* 1(4), Spring-Summer, 48–49.

———. (1994). *A Canadian journey: Conversations with time.* Toronto: Oberon.

Harris, Christopher. (1989, January 23). Canada's year of film. *Playback*, 1.

———. (1990, May 14). Support our own, says Cineplex head. *Playback*, 3.

Hutcheon, Linda. (1991). *Splitting images: Contemporary Canadian ironies.* Toronto: Oxford University.

Kari, Shannon. (1995, December 8). From festival fanfare to box-office flop. *The Globe and Mail*, C2.

Keohane, Kieran. (1997). *Symptoms of Canada: An essay on Canadian identity.* Toronto: University of Toronto Press.

Litt, Paul. (1992). *The muses, the masses, and the Massey commission.* Toronto: University of Toronto Press.

Magder, Ted. (1993). *Canada's Hollywood: The Canadian state and feature films.* Toronto: University of Toronto.

Morgan, Joanne. (1989, August 7). Westerners upset by Festival of Festivals' rejection of nine films. *Playback*, 16.

Morris, Peter. (1986). Backwards to the future: John Grierson's film policy for Canada. In Gene Walz (Ed.), *Flashback: People and institutions in Canadian film history* (pp. 17–35). Montreal: Mediatexte.

Peers, Martin. (1998, January 26–February 1). Exhibs vexed by Wall St. hex on plex. *Variety*, 1.

Pendakur, Manjunath. (1990). *Canadian dreams and American control: The political economy of the Canadian film industry.* Toronto: Garamond.

Report of the Feature Film Advisory Committee. (1999). *The Road to success.* Ottawa: Canadian Heritage.

Radway, Janice. (1984). *Reading the romance: Women, patriarchy, and popular literature.* Chapel Hill: University of North Carolina.

Saunders, Doug. (2000, May 13). Trouble in Hollywood North: Controversy is rising over Canada's subsidies to U.S. movie moguls. *The Globe and Mail,* 1.

Smythe, Dallas. (1981). *Dependency road: Communications, capitalism, consciousness and Canada.* Norwood, N.J.: Ablex.

Statistics Canada. (1995). *Film and video 1992–1993.* Ottawa: Education, Culture and Tourism Division.

———. (1999). *Motion picture theatres survey,* 87F0009XPE, Ottawa.

Vipond, Mary. (1980, Spring). The nationalist network: English Canada's intellectuals and artists in the 1920s. *Canadian Review of Studies in Nationalism* V, 32–52.

Wilden, Anthony. (1980). *The imaginary Canadian.* Vancouver: Pulp.

FURTHER READING

Armatage, Kay, Kass Banning, Brenda Longfellow, and Janine Marchessault. (1999). *Gendering the nation: Canadian women's cinema.* Toronto: University of Toronto Press.

Canadian Journal of Film Studies.

Dorland, Michael. (1998). *So close to the state/s: The emergence of Canadian feature film policy.* Toronto: University of Toronto Press.

Magder, Ted. (1993). *Canada's Hollywood: The Canadian state and feature films.* Toronto: University of Toronto.

SECTION TWO

Regional Identities

Introduction

Beverly Rasporich

One way of considering the Canadian identity is to look at the country in its entirety and examine those issues that pertain to the national interest. Another is to narrow the focus to study the attitudes of Canadians closer to home—in the country's regions. In fact, regional self-determination has been centre stage in the country's development and has contributed to a contemporary postmodern reality where the parts of the nation may be greater than its whole. Certainly for the vast majority of the country's citizens, regional politics and local cultures play essential roles in determining their realities, their allegiances, and their senses of self. As William Wonders explains, "Geography and history have combined to endow Canada with strong regional identities. Whether such a variety makes for an interesting, rich and confident nation or for a diverse, inherently weak one may be debated" (Wonders, 1983, p. 345). Indeed, this tension between nation and regions has been a central issue in the Canadian political arena since confederation. In the 1990s it became a crucial and dangerous question as Quebeckers threatened to dissolve the country. Since that time, Western political disaffection has spawned the formation of a new political party, the Canadian Alliance, one that wants to reduce

293

the powers of central government. Yet since its inception, Canada has had faith that political federalism and regionalism were compatible. In his speech to the leaders of confederation from the Canadas in 1864, Joseph Howe made an early attempt to unify regions by proclaiming a dual identity: "I am not one of those who thank God I am a Nova Scotian merely, for I am a Canadian as well" (Hamilton, 1952, p. 29).

As students begin to examine regions and regionalism in Canada, they should first take note of the complexity of the term "region" and of the varieties of ways that the country can be divided into regions. Perhaps the most obvious regions are those of the provinces. Clearly political/provincial boundaries are important to regional identification, and Canadians are moved by provincial pride, particularly during elections and celebrations. Provincial economic interests are also very much bound to individual survival and, hence, to identity. Kathryn Welbourn in her personal essay "Outports and Outlaws" gives us a poignant picture of the loss of self-esteem and personal dislocation suffered by many Newfoundlanders on the death of the cod industry. Here, too, the federal government becomes the traditional villain as humanity is washed away by an out-of-touch and distant bureaucracy. In the urban context, city, too, can be a significant region. Harold Troper in "Immigrant City: The Making of Modern Toronto" gives us a full view of the new Toronto, a rich and vibrant multicultural city that can be seen to be a region unto itself.

Canadians are deeply affected, studied, and understood by a variety of regional identifications other than those determined by provincial, city, town, or hamlet boundaries. Geographers, for example, see connections between environment and culture, dividing the country into climactic regions, as climate affects behaviour; or studying population-dot and isopleth maps that divide Canada into distinctively different "settled" and "unsettled" regions; or making maps of language zones that link Canadians within, or across, the country according to linguistic criteria. As Emma LaRocque points out in "Native Identity and the Métis: *Otehpayimsuak* Peoples," the Métis in Canada had no landbase. Stripped of their land, they were often forced to live on road allowances, where they created small hamlets, or they had to wander like gypsies throughout the West. According to LaRocque, it was not so much geographic region as language that was key to the survival of Métis identity.

Region can also be as much a highly subjective, mythic place as an actual location or a region defined by rational criteria. Artists understand the imaginative foothold that place can provide both for their own identities and for those who wander into their artistic worlds. Eli Mandel, whose poem "the double world" introduces this book, is one of many literary geographers of the West. Eli's own sense of self was strongly rooted in the Jewish community of southern Saskatchewan. As much a region of memory and mind as a location, Eli's Estevan and Souris Valley become a mythic and legendary home that he memorializes in poetry for himself and his readers. This is also true of E.J. Pratt, whose classic poem

"Newfoundland," introduces Atlantic Canada in this volume as a powerful, sentient natural world—a mindscape of sea and wind, of storms and shipwrecks, of life and death. Similarly, Robert Kroetsch in "Stone Hammer Poem" reinvents the West in striking images of "ripening wheat" and "buffalo blood / hot in the dying sun." While Kroetsch magically traces Western Canadian narrative and lineage through a stone hammer, Morris Granatstein in "Kensington" brings to life a colourful Toronto multicultural landmark in the section on Ontario.

The concept of region then is a multiple abstraction—and a slippery idea for those geographers, historians, political scientists, and literary critics who use it as a conceptual tool. For the creative artist, region may even be an unconscious subject, or an imaginary construct, rooted in actual place but filtered through a personal vision. Yet artists are important contributors to regional identities. They are active creators of place, seducing us into seeing through their eyes and into claiming their experience and parts of Canada as our own.

As Eli Mandel pointed out in the first edition of this book, much of the character and quality of this country is not only an expression of diversity but also can be understood only in such terms. We have divided Canada into fairly large regional chunks—Atlantic Canada, Ontario, the West, and the North—understanding that there are provincial boundaries and factors of physical geography implicit in this division, and recognizing that regions overlap and that there are many regions within regions. Quebec has been omitted here, partly because of limitations of space, but largely because of its longstanding search for nationhood. Quebec is profiled in the first section of the book in this context. Atlantic Canada is really four provinces: New Brunswick, Nova Scotia, Newfoundland, and Prince Edward Island. Robert Finbow in his article "Atlantic Canada in a New Right Era: The Necessity of Unity?" addresses the potential for their amalgamation. Peter McCormick, looking at "Power and Politics in Western Canada" wisely suggests that the West is "less a coherent unit than four variations of a single theme." One of the most mysterious and value-laden areas of uncertain boundaries in the imagination of settler culture is "the North." Yet what is North? Karim-Aly Kassam in his article "North of 60°: Homeland or Frontier?" has provided some possible definitions of the North and considered the different perspectives of those who live in the North and of those "southerners" for whom it is a frontier. Graham White in "Government under the Northern Lights: Treaties, Land Claims, and Political Change in Nunavut and the Northwest Territories" focuses explicitly on two "regions," one that has been newly created.

There are many transformations occurring in all of our regions. Theresie Tungilik tells us in her own words the changes that the Inuit are experiencing. As well, globalization is as much a fact of life for regional cultures as it is for the national identity. Reg Whitaker makes the point in

"Revolutionaries out of Ontario: The Mike Harris Government and Canada" that it is quite possible that Ontario is assuming a North American regionalist role, that the Common Sense political revolution has been spawned from U.S. Republican sources, creating a north–south orientation for Ontario. He speculates that this may be difficult to reverse as we go into the 21st century and wonders if this orientation will spread to other provinces. Harold Troper's Toronto has also clearly gone global. There are now more Muslims in Toronto than Presbyterians—it is no longer the white, Christian culture that it once was. Miro Cernetig's British Columbia in "The Far Side of the Rockies: Politics and Identity in British Columbia" has also been dramatically altered by worldwide immigration, particularly from Asia. In the new Canada, multiculturalism is reshaping our communities.

Even if the world is shrinking, it is difficult to imagine a Canada without regional identities, however multifaceted and transformational. We know that in this section we can only begin to introduce students to the complexity of regions in this country and to a few of the issues that pertain to them. We are hopeful, though, that we can further our readers' understanding of Canadian places and of many regional points of view. In this last regard, the self-knowledge of the reader is most important. To have insight into one's own strongly felt regional identity enables one to understand others and ultimately be able to contribute to that which, in the fourth edition of this book, we still believe to be an ideal: a tolerant and an open Canadian society. In the words of prairie, western, northern, Albertan, Canadian—and perhaps even global— writer, Robert Kroetsch: "A local pride does not exclude the rest of the world, or other experience; rather, it makes them possible" (1983, p. 437).

REFERENCES

Hamilton, Robert. (1952). *Canadian quotations and phrases.* Toronto: McClelland and Stewart.

Kroetsch, Robert. (1983). On being an Alberta writer. In *A passion for identity,* 2nd edition. Scarborough, ON: Nelson Canada.

Wonders, William. (1983). Canadian regions and regionalisms: National enrichment or national disintegration? In *A passion for identity,* 2nd edition. Scarborough, ON: Nelson Canada.

ATLANTIC CANADA

Newfoundland

E.J. Pratt

Here the tides flow,
And here they ebb;
Not with that dull, unsinewed tread of waters
Held under bonds to move
Around unpeopled shores—
Moon-driven through a timeless circuit
Of invasion and retreat;
But with a lusty stroke of life
Pounding at stubborn gates,
That they might run
Within the sluices of men's hearts,
Leap under throb of pulse and nerve,
And teach the sea's strong voice
To learn the harmonies of new floods,
The peal of cataract,
And the soft wash of currents
Against resilient banks,
Or the broken rhythms from old chords
Along dark passages
That once were pathways of authentic fires.

Red is the sea-kelp on the beach,
Red as the heart's blood.
Nor is there power in tide or sun
To bleach its stain.
It lies there piled thick
Above the gulch-line.
It is rooted in the joints of rocks,
It is tangled around a spar,
It covers a broken rudder,
It is red as the heart's blood,
And salt as tears.

Here the winds blow,
And here they die,
Not with that wild, exotic rage
That vainly sweeps untrodden shores,
But with familiar breath
Holding a partnership with life,
Resonant with the hopes of spring,
Pungent with the airs of harvest.

They call with the silver fifes of the sea,
They breathe with the lungs of men,
They are one with the tides of the sea,
They are one with the tides of the heart,
They blow with the rising octaves of dawn,
They die with the largo of dusk,
Their hands are full to the overflow,
In their right is the bread of life,
In their left are the waters of death.

Scattered on boom
And rudder and weed
Are tangles of shells;
Some with backs of crusted bronze,
And faces of porcelain blue,
Some crushed by the beach stones
To chips of jade;
And some are spiral-cleft
Spreading their tracery on the sand
In the rich veining of an agate's heart;
And others remain unscarred,
To babble of the passing of the winds.

Here the crags
Meet with winds and tides—
Not with that blind interchange
Of blow for blow
That spills that thunder of insentient seas;
But with the mind that reads assault
In crouch and leap and the quick stealth,
Stiffening the muscles of the waves.
Here they flank the harbours,
Keeping watch
On thresholds, altars and the fires of home,
Or, like mastiffs,
Over-zealous,
Guard too well.

Tide and wind and crag,
Sea-weed and sea-shell
And broken rudder—
And the story is told
Of human veins and pulses,
Of eternal pathways of fire,
Of dreams that survive the night,
Of doors held ajar in storms.

Outports and Outlaws

Kathryn Welbourn

Jig a few cod or bag a moose for the winter larder? If you're a rural Newfoundlander, think again. Thanks to environmental crackdowns, your way of life is a crime.

Amid the black swells of a murderously cold October sea, Frank McCarthy leans straight into the North Atlantic wind, ball cap pointed toward the sky, hazel eyes searching for sunkers. Standing fast against the oncoming weather, he expertly guides the tiller of the small wooden boat he borrowed from a neighbour. She's cracked and chipped, stripped of both paint and, until Frank was in need of her, usefulness. She's just good enough to be out on the water, nothing more. Despite the forbidding weather we pass several other small boats—local fishermen jigging for cod. They pull their lines with ease, and given the customs of Newfoundland outport life, I assume we'll pull up alongside for a bit of gossip. When we wave a welcome, however, the men look up sharply and speed off in the opposite direction. With a resigned shrug, Frank explains that they don't know me; after all, I could be an undercover fisheries officer.

"No, they wouldn't stop for you now," he says of neighbours too fearful to pass a civil word. "They don't know who's in the boat with you. But you can't blame them."

We pull up smoothly by Dolly's Rock, a small knob of land on Newfoundland's northeast coast that's separated from the tiny village of Too Good Arm by this thin stretch of rock-spiked water. Settling in at his chosen spot, Frank, a lean slip of a man, begins flicking his jigger into the sea, testing the water for cod. It's hard to believe something so simple is such a serious crime. "Yeah, this is illegal, catching a few cod for your supper," he says. "Take it home and eat it and be called a criminal for that."

Frank McCarthy is in big trouble with the law. If the 49-year-old fisherman had slapped his wife or driven around town drunk, he would be in less trouble than he is in right now. Frank was convicted of doing what comes naturally—jigging a few codfish for his winter supply. He was fined $3500, which he can not afford to pay. Neither can he serve 90 days in jail, because he would lose the weekly payments of about $200 his family receives as compensation for the closure of the cod fishery. His wife, Ruby, and their two teenagers would have to go on welfare. The 17-foot fishing boat Frank's been working on all year will probably be repossessed. Frank could have escaped the fisheries officers when they came to arrest him here on the water. He saw them trying to sneak in around the cove in their fast boat. Frank laughs at the idea of the "fish police" going undercover in a community as small as Too Good Arm, population 162. As he pulls in a nice-sized cod for his dinner, he recalls that he made no effort to get away.

"I kept fishing while they were there reading me my rights. 'You have the right to remain silent,'" Frank laughs darkly, pulls out his knife, and bleeds his fish. "Well I'm not silent, I'm jigging." For the rest of Canada, the dominant story out of Newfoundland in the past few years has been the collapse of the Northern cod stocks and the subsequent closure of the food fishery in the summer of 1994. For the first time in nearly 400 years, Newfoundlanders no longer have the right to feed their families from the sea. And for the more than 250 000 rural Newfoundlanders who populate the hundreds of tiny outports snugged into coves straddling the rocky arms of the island's coasts, a more insidious trend is developing, one that cuts closer to their way of life. The locals have been read the environmental riot act, a sweeping assault on their traditional subsistence activities. Firewood and saw-log quotas have been cut. Controversial limits on the use of all-terrain vehicles keep outporters away from rabbit runs, berry patches, and moose trails.

Even the childhood pleasure of fishing conners and tom cods—small inshore fish—off the wharf is now against the law. In one of the most bizarre cases, a young man was fined more than $1000 for "molesting" a salmon. He was one of two boys throwing rocks at a large fish in a river.

From the outside, the zealous enforcement by federal and provincial governments of a battery of fisheries and wildlife regulations appears to be a legitimate conservation campaign, a sad but necessary evil. Rabbit populations are low, salmon stocks are slowly coming back, and the cod stocks remain depleted. "When you have a major problem with the conservation of resources, you just cannot carry on with traditions," says Ernie Collins, the recently retired chief of enforcement for the Department of Fisheries and Oceans (DFO) in Newfoundland. "Traditions will sometimes have to be curtailed or, indeed, ended."

But it is also true that corporate trawlers continue to drag up cod as a by-product of other activities, and which sells as a luxury item in the local supermarket. Pulp and paper companies clear-cut and spray huge tracts of Newfoundland forest, citing historic 90-year agreements. Outfitters and their wealthy, trophy-hunting clientele track their prey with the provincial government's active encouragement. For outporters being chased over the water and through the woods, the crackdown is traumatic. This is, after all, a population with the highest number of hunters per capita in Canada, a place where woodstoves heat homes, and winter larders are filled with bottled moose, salted fish, and wild-berry preserves. Norman Okihiro, a professor of sociology at Mount Saint Vincent University in Halifax, Nova Scotia, describes the government campaign as the criminalization of rural Newfoundland. "The way of life in outport Newfoundland depends, in large part, on people being able to sustain themselves from the land and from the sea," he says. "To have such severe penalties basically outlaws the way of life."

Jim Overton, a sociologist at Memorial University of Newfoundland in St. John's, sees the enforcement as part of a government effort to resettle the outports, shifting people out of the old economy and into supposedly more lucrative ventures such as tourism. "There's a very heavy hand, which is part of a war on people's traditional activities," he says. "The sentences are very harsh compared with the kinds of sentences that are handed out for, say, shoplifting or sexual abuse. The only way to interpret them is that the state has decided to teach people a lesson."

Resettlement is an old story in rural Newfoundland. The first time it came up was in the early 1600s, when English fish merchants persuaded the monarchy to enact laws to discourage and even stop outport settlements. Settlers from Britain, desperate to escape poverty and unemployment, had begun building permanent homes in small groups scattered thinly along the rocky coasts of the Southern shore and Conception Bay. Although there were fewer than 1000 permanent residents at the time, the fish merchants were annoyed by the settlers' presence. The merchants wanted a monopoly on the island's fabulous cod stocks, so the British government declared it illegal to bring new settlers over on fishing vessels, to allow fishermen to stay once the cod season was over, or to settle within 10 kilometres of the coast. The laws were repealed only in the late 1670s when Britain needed settlers to establish its sovereignty over the island.

In modern days, forcing people to move from the outports is a common trick of governments that want to reallocate the island's natural resources. In the 1950s through to the 1970s, Premier Joey Smallwood's resettlement program aimed to bring outporters into the mainstream by evacuating 440 small communities. Smallwood thought outporters' way of living was too backward for the 20th century. He wanted to modernize the small-boat fishing family and bring in high-tech, intensive fishing techniques such as draggers. He offered roads and services in larger centres and compensation for people who left their homes behind or who agreed to put them on floats and ferry them over to places like St. John's. More recently, the federal government offered relocation money as part of the federal fish aid package to entice at least half the coastal fishery workers to find employment elsewhere. The provincial government, meanwhile, is desperate for new economic development, such as big-game outfitting or foreign garbage disposal. Although nearly half the island's population lives in rural areas, the province is now cutting back essential services, such as snow clearing, in these regions—a subtle, yet effective, message that depopulating the outports is now under way.

Watson Lane knows all about resettlement. A retired school principal from Twillingate, just a few kilometres from Too Good Arm, Lane was raised in the traditional life of the outports on Bragg's Island in Bonavista Bay. Coming from a long line of fishermen, Lane gravitated to Memorial University in St. John's to pursue his interests in theology and the arts, but he chose to move back to work in rural schools. "The outport is the place where we play," he says. "It's our park, our back garden. Being part of all that gives you a big feeling. When I get to Bragg's Island, I'm lord and master, just like when I was a boy skipping 'round."

In the modest home he built for his retirement in nearby Glovertown, Lane seems the last person one would expect to thumb his nose at the authorities; but he sees no other option. "Our ingenuity, our self-respect, is being undermined. They have moved right into our living room," Lane says, his lilting voice tinged with contempt. "It puts me in mind of Victor Hugo's *Les Miserables* where the laws are such that you have to watch your back, be suspicious of the police. It puts shivers through you ... men out at night so they can jig a few cod."

The changes have been slow and steady but became strikingly apparent after the cod fishery was closed in 1992. A policy of zero tolerance for poaching of any kind was adopted, and governments began talking about new ways to use rural Newfoundland and its resources for tourism and industry. Most startling to outporters such as Lane was DFO's use of the term "recreational fishery" for what had always been known as the food fishery. In keeping with the new environmental attitude, regulations once ignored are now enforced. Lane recounts a litany of Orwellian regulations: he can cut a decreasing amount of firewood, but he can't give it to an aging neighbour; he can shoot a moose if he has a licence, but he can't sell the meat, even if he doesn't need it all; he can give the meat as a gift, but he must wrap it in a note to prove it came from legal hunting, like a report card pinned to the pocket of a wayward child.

To channel local frustrations, Lane started an outport lobby group. About 30 people attended the first meeting, and Lane says membership is growing. He is quick to emphasize that he and most other outporters are not against tourism or environmental protection. These days, for example, Lane is helping a friend build a wharf out on the ice for a new charter boat. As well, his lobby group is not protesting the closure of commercial industries such as the fishery. Inshore communities have been demanding and predicting the closure for years. The crackdown on rural life, however, has shifted the blame for the province's problems onto outport people, tagging them as abusive and destructive individuals. "It is not the Newfoundland man and woman and child going out in the boat on Sunday afternoon that did this," he says. "This is the price we're paying for the greedy money grubbers that swept the ocean floor clean."

Lane is not interested in going back to the days of kerosene lamps. Modern outport life is a clever combination of the old and the new; outboard motors in place of the old make-and-break engines, all-terrain vehicles instead of horses in the woods, wages for work rather than payment in supplies. "My way of life includes having a lobster on the beach and building my own home," says Lane. " A 55-year-old man sits on his wharf, and the ocean is just in front of him. What will he do? Don't ask me the question about whether I'll jig a fish or no."

Ernie Collins begs to differ. As the former chief of the DFO's enforcement in Newfoundland, Collins does not sympathize with poachers of any kind. "We're very proud of those fines," Collins says. "Traditions die hard, but we have no sympathy for these people. We've learned our lesson from the cod." Fisheries and wildlife officers have been told to be just as tough on those people out getting a bit of food as on those taking hundreds of pounds of fish for sale. The DFO has hooked up with provincial wildlife officers and the RCMP in an effort to crack down on local offenders. Enforcement officers now use DNA samples in courts and infrared glasses and cameras in the field. Wildlife officials admit it is difficult for officers to police their neighbours and sometimes their friends, but Collins says the laws must be enforced. "The message that's out there is, if you break these laws we're going to hit you where it hurts," he says.

But locals are hearing a different message. With the closure of the commercial fishery and commercial boats tied up, many believe that enforcement officers are at a loss for something to do. "So here you're having people watching the local villagers," says Norman Okihiro. "If somebody decides to go down the bay and just take a look around, you have a wildlife officer follow them. This is harassment." He illustrates his point with a true scenario: A family picnic on the beach, showing visiting relatives a good time. They lay out the food and settle in to eat, but the day is spoiled when they realize they are being watched by a fisheries officer. "Fisheries and wildlife officers have powers which most people would be surprised at," he says. "They can search your car, and they have powers of seizure. These authority figures are feared and may be given a bit too much respect. People have told me of searches of entire villages looking for poached meat—things that would not go on in the city, where you have lawyers and not as much fear."

In fact, some of the sentences being handed out seem to violate the *Charter of Rights and Freedoms*. A fisherman charged with lobster poaching was ordered by a judge not to buy, possess, or eat any lobster at all. Then there is the case of 24-year-old Troy Gilbert from St. Fintan's, on the island's west coast. The young man had been playing a large salmon with a single hook for three hours when he got fed up and put on a jigger (a kind of lure)—illegal now because its two hooks make it too efficient. Troy wanted the fish for his mother's table, and knew he couldn't miss with a double hook. When he pulled his catch out of the water, some fisheries officers who had been watching him for three hours came out of the woods and chased him through the bush. Troy takes a young man's pride in his escape that day, although one wonders what kind of shape the officers were in. Troy, after all, has a pronounced limp from a child-hood illness; but then, he knows the woods so well, fishing and hunting since he was 10 years old.

In the end, the officers had taken pictures, and Troy was convicted of jigging a salmon instead of catching it on a regular fly. He makes only about $150 per week at a local dairy farm, so he cannot pay the $4000 fine. Even worse is his probation order: for three years he is not allowed within 300 metres of an inland river. "I'd have to stay home and sit on my step all day just to keep the probation," he says in disgust. "I have to go to work—it's too close to the river. I have to cut wood for Mom—cross the river again. If I was to get sick tomorrow, I'd have to die on the doorstep or cross the river. So I have to watch out for the wildlife officers all the time."

It is a calm and warm evening in Sally's Cove, at the base of the Great Northern Peninsula. The water and sky form a seamless match, erasing the line of the horizon. Clarence Laing, a lobster and herring fisherman, heaves his boat down a roll of logs into the water, while his wife Margaret, and their youngest child, Jamie, 12, ready the herring nets. There is laughter and shouting as the boat hits the sea with a splash.

Clarence starts the motor, and the family moves out to their fishing berth. Tonight Jamie is getting a lesson in setting the net. He makes a few mistakes at the tiller, but his father rights the boat and Jamie tries again. His father, a 50-ish man with a bodybuilder's physique, smiles. Later, in the Laings' neat wooden home just steps from the sea, Margaret spreads out the family dinner of moose meat, homemade bread, fish, and veg-etables. Like all of their neighbours, the Laings built their home them-selves, harvesting the lumber from the woods. Most people in the area also build their own boats from raw logs, a skill passed down through generations. Hunting and trapping and berry picking are part of the cycle of work. Even the community store is heated with firewood to save on electric heat bills, which run up to $300 per winter month for the average saltbox house. Back in the early 1960s, the Laings started out with a tar-paper shack right on the beach and then built on as they could afford to. "I never borrowed anything in my life. I waited until I had a dollar," says Clarence, sitting back comfortably at the dinner table. "We went without many's the time. I kept my money and spent it on my (fishing) gear. I built up and built up until I got what I wanted. No dear, I don't owe no one. Not a cent."

Sally's Cove is one of the most beautiful places on the island. There are flat cleared fields leading to the beach, and the Long Range Mountains brood in the background. Parks Canada liked the area so much it offered in the 1970s to relocate the 54 families who lived there. When at least 12 families, including the Laings, refused to move, the gov-ernment set aside about 13 square kilometres of land as a community enclave and built Gros Morne National Park around Sally's Cove. Now, Margaret says, it is like living in a zoo. Residents are fenced in by the rules and regulations of the park, which ban all hunting and set out inadequate rabbit-snaring and woodcutting areas for local people. The Laings had to get rid of their sheep because the park did not want them grazing near the road or on the meadows. Two young men up the road have been banned from the park for refusing to give up their chain saw as evidence when they were investigated for allegedly cutting trees to build their new fishing boats. An 80-year-old trapper had his snowmobile confiscated for setting his trapline back in the hills on park land. For their part, Clarence and Margaret do not see anything wrong with such activities.

"No, I couldn't follow all the regulations," says Clarence. "I don't know if anybody knows what they all are, because they keep changing all the time. I say most people just goes on and does what they always do and hopes they don't get caught."

Wardens say they are just enforcing the rules set out by Parks Canada. You cannot advertise as a wilderness reserve and have tourists see moose entrails by the side of the road or locals cutting trees in the woods. The Laings, however, have different priorities. "A good citizen is a man who makes sure his family is warm and comfortable, a man who helps keep his neighbours and his community going," says Clarence. "Every law they're making now is making it harder to live."

A few kilometres up the road, the park has set up a fisherman's interpretive centre to show tourists how fishing families lived "30 years ago." The Laings only find it insulting, a parody of their daily work down on the beach.

The combination of the park and new provincial and federal crack-downs is almost enough to put the Laings out of business. Why don't they just pack up and leave or take wage jobs in the tourism industry in their area? Clarence answers the question with a sigh and a grin: "I don't think I'm made for going around trying to make someone else happy, make sure tourists, if they want their slice of bread, they got it, and their jam is on the right side of their plate, their bed is made up right. Fishing, that's what I'm made for. They'll be no punching a clock and begging a boss for me."

There has been a lot of charged writing about the death of the out-ports since the closure of the Northern cod fishery in 1992. National columnists, such as *The Globe and Mail*'s William Thorsell, have even gone so far as to claim it is immoral for people like the Laings to raise their children in rural Newfoundland. In subsequent media coverage, Newfoundlanders were called a burden on the rest of Canada. Michael Asch has heard this discourse before. The University of Alberta anthropology professor worked on the Mackenzie Valley Pipeline Inquiry in the 1970s, examining land use by native peoples in the Northwest Territories. The Canadian government, he says, is treating outport Newfoundland with the same disrespect that characterized its dealings with the Northern Dene.

"There was a presumed respect for a different way of life when we signed our treaties with native peoples, and the same for when

Newfoundland joined confederation. We're forgetting what our commitments were to these people and trying to force them into assimilation." The broken faith is based on ignorance about the lives of the people being regulated, he adds. "If people do not make a lot of money, then they're not considered to be up to some kind of modernizing concept of what a standard of living ought to be. It's part of an assumption about the outporters, that they're just savages who are plundering the resources."

Back in Too Good Arm, Frank McCarthy is trying to put together an appeal of his conviction. He cannot afford a lawyer nor can he get legal aid for a fisheries offence. "I'm going to tell the judge I was fishing out of necessity," he says. "Not just necessity, something I've always done. Something I wants to do. You can't call this justice." Taking a stand against DFO has exacted a big cost. Frank's marriage, already strained by unemployment, has disintegrated since his conviction. Ruby wanted Frank to stop jigging. "I'm not used to having the officers coming to the door," she said when Frank was first arrested. She wanted him to stay out of trouble. "I don't agree with what they done to Frank, but I want things to go back to the way they were."

But Frank just could not stop. In the room he has rented above an abandoned store in nearby Virgin Arm, he sounds tired—a man who has lost everything.

"I don't know why it hurts me so much," he says with resignation. "A whole way of life taken from you. I couldn't stand still for that."

✳✳✳

Since this award-winning article was first published in *Equinox Magazine* in October 1995, not much has changed in outport Newfoundland. A small cod fishery has been reopened. Inshore fishermen in some parts of the island asked DFO to allocate individual quotas so fishermen could take their time, fishing where and when it was best. Offshore boats voted for a competitive fishery—everybody fishes until the stock quota is taken—and that's what DFO agreed to. Far fewer than the half of the inshore fishermen the federal government hoped would leave the fishery have actually gone. Instead, inshore fishermen have diversified— fighting for crab and other permits. They have been refused the right to purchase bigger boats and so are forced to take their inshore boats offshore and pull crab pots under perilous conditions. As well, some fear the dragger shrimp fishery is destroying the crab fishery. Newfoundlanders are now allowed to fish cod for food one or two weekends a year. This has led to at least one drowning and fears of other tragedies as people go out in any weather during the "recreational fishery weekend." In Nova Scotia, New Brunswick, P.E.I., and Quebec, the food fishery is open year round. Since the cod stocks are the same, there has been no reasonable explanation given for this. Still, many Newfoundlanders eat fresh cod all summer. Some locals even take their cell phones out on the water, and when the fisheries officers leave the wharf, someone just gives them a ring.

FURTHER READING

Kurlansky, Mark. (1997). *Cod: A biography of the fish that changed the world*. Alfred A. Knopf Canada.

Morgan, Bernice. (1994). *Random passage*. St. John's: Breakwater.

———. (1994). *Waiting for time*. St. John's: Breakwater.

Atlantic Canada in a New Right Era: The Necessity of Unity?

Robert G. Finbow

INTRODUCTION

When many Canadians think of the Atlantic provinces, they envision a sleepy, picturesque region, bounded by the sea, beset by economic crises and the collapse of traditional resources. The physical beauty of its sea-coast, islands and peninsulas, lakes and rivers, hills and forests, and its well-preserved historical heritage make this region a favourite of travellers. The presence of a Diaspora of thousands who have "gone down the road" into all walks of life creates a residue of support nationwide. However, a more negative image is being propagated; that of client states, with dependent citizens, and a "parasitical" bureaucratic class. This view, expounded incessantly by our so-called "national" papers and think tanks, is taking on the quality of common sense. It is repeated with no critical scrutiny by those seeking to cut government, reduce taxes, and eliminate regulations at whatever costs to individuals and communities.

Like many stereotypes, this one contains a grain of truth. Many programs designed to foster development in the region have squandered public funds (albeit ones raised by national taxes paid by Atlantic Canadians, not plucked unilaterally from the wealthy provinces). Government's role in development must be reevaluated because of its inability to separate economic objectives from partisan, political ones. However, some critics present self-interested analyses for the politically and economically dominant regions and classes, rather than an even-handed evaluation of policy. When commentators refer to the entire region as a "gigantic make-work project," an "unnecessary ... parasite" that does "not deserve our respect or our tax dollars" (Francis, 2000, p. D02), it is hard to regard their advice as constructive.

This essay will outline the cultural and economic diversity of Atlantic Canada and question its depiction as an homogenous region. It will critically assess past development projects to search for better approaches in this era of technological change and global integration. But it will also attempt a rational response to the rabid ranting of the right-wing literati.

A critical assessment of Canadian federalism reveals that the Atlantic provinces are not the unilateral winners of confederation, sucking the life-blood from hard-working taxpayers in Ontario and the West. Instead, redistributive programs have provided inadequate compensation for centralist biases in the political and economic systems. National institutions, dominated by the two central provinces, prevent a fairer design of federal policies and expenditures. Withdrawal of redistribution will expose Atlantic Canada more nakedly to global pressures than the poorest U.S. state or European region. The essay will consider whether these four provinces will be forced to unite or cooperate to offset a decline in federal transfers and compensate for their marginal position in national affairs and global economics. The essay concludes by assessing alternative policies that are needed to provide the best opportunity for the region and its citizens in future.

THE ATLANTIC REGION AT THE TURN OF THE CENTURY

There are similarities among the four Atlantic provinces, notably proximity to the sea and the maritime orientation to economic life, resource dependence, high unemployment, and reliance on federal transfers for provincial and individual incomes. There are fewer recent immigrants, mostly old-stock British and Acadian, with Aboriginal and black minorities. But diversities are also evident, reinforced by the institutions of federalism. Newfoundland's historic dominion status, its late entry into confederation, and the isolation and distinct lifestyle of its dispersed outport communities separate it from the Maritimes. This province is overwhelmingly British and Irish in social origin and dependent on fishing, forestry, and mining. The collapse of cod, which was the mainstay for hundreds of isolated outports, was a profound economic and cultural blow. The people of Canada's poorest province were forced into even greater dependence on federal social assistance, as plans were devised to retire fishermen and retrain the young. Completion of the massive Hibernia offshore oil project, new hydro-electric developments, and the nickel find at Voisey's Bay in Labrador provide new potential. The government has tried to avoid disasters like the Churchill Falls hydro agreement (which drained revenues to Quebec) or futile subsidies to external investors. Though Newfoundland "neo-nationalism," based on oil has faded, cultural vibrancy remains evident in its Irish-based music, politicized theatre, and renowned satirical comedy.

The Maritimes are internally diverse, and citizens have generally frowned on unification. Nova Scotia's agrarian, fishing, mining, forestry, and urban communities are distinct worlds, making this province curiously difficult to govern. The economy has diversified beyond the primary sector, with the region's leading financial, educational, and medical services. Manufacturing includes aerospace, tires, food processing, and pulp and paper. Some primary sectors are in decline, with coal mines losing subsidies and affected by the Westray disaster. Fisheries are affected by groundfish bans, but shellfish flourishes. As the defence and civil service centre for the region, Nova Scotia has suffered greatly from cuts. Localism and patronage take their toll in waste and indecision, and the province remains among the worst in deficit reduction. Internal divisions are legion, and cooperation across diverse communities is difficult. Cape Breton is a distinct society with its economic hardships, scenic beauty, and distinct Gaelic culture. Halifax shares the cultural advantages of a metropolis (described by *Village Voice* as "Seattle East") but with violent crime, drug addiction, and some racial tension. Its leadership is generally resented by rural areas.

New Brunswick is the only officially bilingual province and was settled by both Acadians and Loyalists. Forestry is the largest primary industry, but potatoes spawned the multinational McCain's frozen-food empire. The Irvings built on cars and gas to become a provincial giant (including a near media monopoly). Mining is diverse led by zinc, lead, and silver. The province has innovated in municipal reform and has done more than other Atlantic provinces to adjust to fiscal constraint and the telecommunications revolution, especially under Liberal premier Frank McKenna. Despite occasional reactionaries, like the short-lived Confederation of Regions party, the province has bridged its ethnic and linguistic differences.

Prince Edward Island, the "garden in the gulf" is an insular community, where children's birthdays are noted on the provincial Web site. P.E.I. runs like a small city where local concerns dominate. The province relies on farming (especially potatoes), fisheries (notably shellfish), and tourism (around its remarkable beaches and gentle countryside). Often accused of traditionalism, it elected the first minority and female premiers (Joe Ghiz and Catherine Callbeck).

The enduring provincialism of those pre-confederation entities has recently been joined by a weaker regionalism based on grievance at marginalization and dependence on federal programs. "Atlantic Canadian regionalism in a very real sense can be considered a *creation* of the federal government or at the very least a socio-political phenomenon that exists, and has always existed, in symbiosis with the federal government" (Bickerton, 1990, p. 325). Atlantic Canada produced Ottawa's fiercest critics (including Nova Scotia separatists in the 1880s and the Maritimes rights agitation of the 1920s) seeking "better terms" as its influence in Ottawa waned. Later, the region supported federal cost-sharing in post-secondary education and health care, equalization grants to provinces facing fiscal shortfalls, and welfare and unemployment insurance for individuals. Ottawa poured millions into regional development agencies like the Department of Regional Economic Expansion (DREE), the Department of Regional Industrial Expansion (DRIE), and the Atlantic

Canada Opportunities Agency (ACOA), to reduce disparities in incomes and employment by attempting (largely unsuccessfully) to create regional industrial "growth poles."

Economic disparities have persisted, despite some industrialization. However, Ottawa's role has been challenged by Quebec nationalism and provincialist demands from the West and Ontario. While the threat of Quebec sovereignty (which would isolate the region geographically) has receded, decentralism in social policy is now preferred by some other provinces. To address political demands, development agencies cover the entire country, competing to attract investment even to areas with low unemployment; more is spent on Western diversification than on Atlantic development in some years (Savoie, 1997, p. 47). Fiscal constraints have eroded federal spending. Cuts to the federal Canada Health and Social Transfer have affected all provinces, but the Atlantic region has suffered disproportionately. An APEC study illustrates that over a 30-year period to 1995, transfers to Atlantic Canada for health, education, social assistance, and equalization declined by 3.8 percent a year compared with an average decline for all provinces of just over 2 percent. Ottawa's decreased contributions forced have-not provinces into debt to sustain services ("Social Security reform," 1995, p. 5). Equalization does not bring poorer provinces up to a national average since oil and gas royalties were excluded, and the standard was lowered to the average of five representative provinces.

Economic change is marked by the collapse of fisheries, which has forced thousands from their traditional livelihood. The number of fishermen decreased from 60 509 in 1986 to 49 957 in 1996 while the cod catch declined from 435 233 tonnes worth $224 million in 1989 to 15 480 tonnes worth $21 million in 1996 ("Cod chronicle," 1998, p. 29). Global commodity markets cuts prices for staples while consolidation into corporate forms in agriculture, fisheries, and forestry drives out small producers. Communities brace for the loss of traditional livelihoods while welcoming greater integration via new technologies.

There are promising developments, notably offshore energy in Newfoundland and Nova Scotia, which provides new revenue and new stimulus to industrial diversification. The completion of the fixed link to Prince Edward Island has created a tourism boom. Integration via trucking with regional markets heralds new efficiencies, but high energy costs hurt industrialization. Some cities have developed high-technology production capabilities with government help. Moncton, with its bilingual work force, has taken advantage of New Brunswick's efficient telecommunications infrastructure to become a telemarketing centre. Biotechnology, based on public research capacity and bioinformatics networks, has emerged in Metro Halifax, attracting capital and skilled labour from central Canada and overseas. Aquaculture has helped offset the decline in the fisheries in a few communities. The problem is whether there will be enough investment to sustain these developments.

Public spending has dropped significantly as a percentage of regional GDP. The Atlantic provinces cut bureaucracies significantly and, with the exception of Nova Scotia, have balanced budgets. Although there has been a decline in manufacturing, private enterprise helped build an urban, service economy led by managerial, sales, and professional occupations. Low labour costs, increased productivity, investments in machinery, as well as low energy, building, and land costs have aided job creation ("The changing face," 1997). Yet unemployment and dependence on federal expenditures remains high. The gulf in incomes and employment between rural areas and larger centres is wide. Cities are integrated with global economies, with suburbs complete with Walmart and warehouse outlets. Rural areas are stagnant, with older residents needing health and social services that are too expensive to supply. As well, globalization of economic activity reduces the capacity for governments to promote regional interests selectively. The mobility of capital makes these small units vulnerable to pressures to adjust wages and taxes downward while maintaining competitive services.

As their taxes increased and services decreased, some wealthier provinces grew more frustrated with interregional transfers. British Columbia has long been a critic of equalization payments. Ontario adopted a provincialist position after the Mulroney cutbacks, criticizing the equalization element in social assistance. Fiscal constraint has magnified the burden of interregional transfers, while globalization means that fewer transfers return to Ontario as purchases from local manufacturers and retailers (Haddow, 1994, pp. 484–5). A changing ethnic mix in other provinces results in declining psychological attachments to the policies of the past. This critique from other regions is founded on changing perceptions of their interests. Recent changes to the Canada Health and Social Transfer (CHST) reflect this pressure, as a per capita formula has been adopted. However, this trend has been fuelled by ideologues in the think tanks and the right-wing press that promote cuts, service depletion, and regional depopulation irrespective of the ultimate damage to the nation.

THE NEW RIGHT MANTRA

Atlantic Canada has long been derided for "transfer dependency," which made regional citizens and governments virtual "clients" of Ottawa. Citizens are said to be resistant to innovation, and lacking in political creativity, with values inherited from the 19th century. However, commentary has taken on a more fervent condemnatory tone in the past decade. With little historical perspective, conservative commentators allege that transfers (like unemployment insurance, equalization, development incentives, and health and education expenditures) are the *primary* cause of regional disparities. This approach was pioneered by Thomas

Courchene who suggested transfers deepened disparities by providing disincentives for Atlantic Canadians to adjust to change. He stated that transfers inhibit adjustment and lead to overpopulation, high unemployment, decreased incomes, and lower education (Courchene, 1981; Taylor, 1996–97).

This approach has been extended by think tanks in recent years. The C.D. Howe Institute targeted the UI "trap" as a source of stagnation (May and Hollett, 1995), and a Fraser Institute study by Filip Palda claimed that UI changes in the 1970s halted migration to other regions. Federal transfers to allow comparability of incomes and services (equalization, established program financing for health and education, social assistance, and tax transfers) harmed the economy by affecting individual choices respecting place of residence; "in the absence of such homogenizing action by Ottawa, some provinces would have offered more of those services to their residents, others less," promoting more effective adjustment (Palda, 1994, p. 1).

Analyses such as these contain important challenges to current development initiatives. ACOA's defenders cite its record in job creation, entrepreneurship, export development, business–state partnerships, and adjustment to the information economy (Mifflin, 1999, p. 7). But the Canadian Taxpayers Foundation's critique of ACOA notes the large percentage of funds channelled to large corporations despite evidence indicating that small and medium-sized enterprises generate most job growth. The high percentage of funds disbursed as non-repayable grants or vanishing as defaulted loans defies explanation as well, as funds disappear into a seemingly bottomless pit (Canadian Taxpayers Foundation, 2000, p. 6). Up to $70 million in defaulted loans was reported in 1998 alone (Beeby, 1999, p. C5).

Government has also supported inefficient sectors, notably the Sysco (Sydney Steel) and Devco (federally owned coal mines) regimes in Cape Breton, which have continued to soak up public funds rather than encourage adjustment to new opportunities. Many supporters of regional development initiatives accept that it is not possible to prop up some communities facing decline from collapse of resources like the fisheries. The region-specific elements of unemployment insurance were certainly a hindrance to adjustment. The system was too generous in the short time required to qualify and the lengthy benefits period. This caused seasonal workers to remain in jobs where they were not optimal, discouraging them from seeking off-season work. These policies contrast with European approaches, which phase out older industries and promote new opportunities.

But some critics espouse a "race to the bottom" in the North American context, with federal units competing to offer the low-tax, low-wage, weak regulatory environment that business in North America (as opposed to other trading blocs) now demands. In an era of open borders, this would force competition with sweatshop states in living standards and labour rights. The primary goal of these critics is to reduce the role of government in development. The Canadian Taxpayers Foundation is explicit:

> The function of the private capital market is to direct investment to projects, industries or firms that offer the best and most secure rate of return. To try and replace or mimic this judgment through government intervention is fundamentally flawed and unnecessary. (Canadian Taxpayers Foundation, 2000, p. 6)

New Right authors deny that equity in essential services is a national responsibility. Former Nova Scotia Premier John Savage argued that withdrawal of federal support for social programs would result in two classes of citizenship, with lower service levels in have-not provinces (Savage, 1996). Setting aside moral and constitutional issues of citizenship rights and government responsibility for community welfare, there are economic considerations. There would be increased pressure on education, training, health, and welfare programs in have regions from increased migration, and it is important to consider how this cost compares to the drain from current transfers. Higgins argues that one "should not recommend solving the problems of depressed areas by emptying them, as an alternative to regional development without knowing the costs; and *saving* the costs is one of the benefits of regional development" (Higgins, 1993, p. 115).

But most damaging to these perspectives is their weak argument that federal assistance plays a *causal* role in disparities. Despite some distorting effects, it is an exaggeration, without any historical context, to see transfers as the primary cause of underdevelopment. The investigations of the Duncan and White Commissions in the 1920s and the Rowell Sirois Commission in the 1930s did not reveal a region burgeoning under the laissez-faire system before equalization and unemployment insurance. These were impoverished provinces even then, suffering acute fiscal need as provincial responsibilities mounted but hampered by a federal system providing national policies for the benefit of the centre. Yet the New Right depiction of government aid as the main source of the problem has been taken as gospel by studies like the Macdonald commission in the 1980s without any consideration of "why such equilibrium theory had never worked to the Maritimes' advantage before the social programs were introduced." (Forbes, 1993, p. 27). Regional per capita incomes increased in the first years of equalization and regional development in the 1950s and 1960s before the oil shocks. Between 1920 and 2000, there is no clear negative correlation between federal spending and stagnant economies.

Whatever their merits, New Right critics have inspired a rethinking of commitments in the "have" provinces to redistribution unaccompanied by any revisiting of wasteful spending in other regions or the constitutional imbalances in the federation. For partisan purposes, politicians like Mike Harris and his "common sense revolution" and Stockwell Day of the Canadian Alliance Party advocate reduction of regional policies and social spending. Courchene's proposal for Ottawa to withdraw from transfers in social policy and turn over equalized tax points for provinces to run their own programs was recently supported by the "have" provinces plus Quebec. This approach would undermine quality programs in poorer provinces.

There is strong evidence of positive economic effects of some federal policies, such as equalization and support for education, training, health, and infrastructure on economic efficiency. In a decentralized federation, with inequitable patterns of taxation and services across the country, investors will be dissuaded from optimal investments in "have-not" regions, not based on economic factors of location, markets, or demand, but because of the higher fiscal burdens and lower service levels and workforce quality they face there. This will be an increasing problem in the information age, as skilled workers will not locate to areas bereft of strong public services. "Have-not" provinces would underinvest in education without a federal contribution, as mobility of the skilled would eliminate local benefits; this would impose greater costs on "have" provinces from net immigration of the unskilled. So a federal role in ensuring horizontal equity in taxes and services could have economically beneficial effects, if distorting subsidies and income security schemes are replaced by inducements to adjustment and entrepreneurship.

DISTORTIONS IN CANADIAN FEDERALISM

New Right authors single out this region, ignoring federal spending in the West, Ontario, or Quebec or commenting less virulently in those cases. They categorize "regional" policies selectively and do not examine the impact of so-called "national" policies, which may be regionally biased. And they overlook imbalances in Canadian federalism that transfers and development programs only partly address. Analysts need to consider the role of federal policies as compensation for constitutional and political distortions in the federation. These measures were instituted only after decades of Atlantic agitation against unfair national policies. They were adopted mainly to offset sovereigntist pressures from Quebec (as it is also a net recipient of equalization, UI, and development funds). Federal policies promoting distribution of economic activity or stimulative investments, as opposed to ameliorative redistribution, are biased toward the central region owing to deficiencies in regional representation in Ottawa. Centralization of Canada's economic and political systems means that Atlantic Canada is not supported by major economic policies, and is often overlooked by investors.

Analysts have criticized the adequacy of Canada's *Constitution* on two levels—intrastate (representation of regional interests at the centre) and interstate (intergovernmental sharing of powers and revenues between Ottawa and the provinces). Regional representation in Ottawa is weak because the Commons (based on representation by population) is dominant over the appointed Senate. Powerful regional ministers occasionally win concessions for peripheral regions, but their small weight in the government caucus limits the voice of Atlantic representatives (with less than one-third of Ontario's MPs). The Senate attempts regional representation inadequately as it is clearly subordinate, and its federal appointees owe allegiance to Ottawa not to the provinces. A parliamentary committee noted that the lack of influence of less populous provinces "could transform alienation into something much more destructive" (Canada, 1992, p. 17). The most frequent proposal for greater regional influence is a reformed Senate, with equitable numbers of representatives elected per province to counterbalance representation by population, but this proposal is now dormant.

Interstate problems can be traced to the imbalance between revenue sources and jurisdictional responsibilities under the *Constitution.* Ottawa has superior revenue-raising capacity, but its expenditure needs have declined in relative importance. As provincial responsibilities grew, Ottawa devised new means of support, through conditional and unconditional grants under the spending power. These include equalization, unemployment insurance, and health and education transfers used since the 1950s and 1960s to permit creation of programs of comparable quality across the country. This role was partially constitutionally entrenched in 1982 with the equalization clause, a vague commitment to comparable service levels across Canada. This intention has never been fully realized, and recent cutbacks have unravelled the redistributive element without increasing regional input on major national policies.

New Right economists support decentralization to address Quebec and Western grievances. They see this as inevitable because of both the fiscal crisis that weakened Ottawa's capacity to act and global forces favouring regionalization and north–south ties in the economy. The New Right believes that decentralization is needed to rationalize government, prepare for global competition, and reduce fiscal burdens (Reuber, 1991, p. 46; Courchene and MacDougall, 1991, pp. 33, 41). Atlantic Canada opposes decentralization, as it could entail the loss of beneficial national programs but has joined other provinces to demand consultation by Ottawa in the use of the spending power in the recent "social union" talks. Some cost-shared programs have a redistributive character that assisted service provision in the Atlantic provinces, so the spending power has been supported by those provinces. Critics view this as evidence of Atlantic dependence on Ottawa, not support for common citizenship rights.

While the Atlantic region is defined as supplicant, central Canada is seen as a self-generating economic dynamo that does not draw upon government subsidization. However, there is considerable evidence that the boom regions of the country have used their superior political power to secure most productive elements of federal spending, leaving mere redistributive sops to the peripheries. Larger provinces receive most stimulative spending on procurement, research and development, creation of state and quasi-state agencies, support for leading-edge industries (autos, aerospace, petrochemicals, etc.). For instance, it was recently reported that the federal government's Technology Partnerships Canada "has invested over $1 billion in Ontario and Quebec, creating 16 429 jobs. That program has provided only $15.3 million to the four Atlantic provinces, creating 290 jobs in this region" (Underhill, 2000, p. A1). Ottawa's recent emergence as a high-tech centre also has much to do with federal centralization of its research capacities in the region (especially in the National Research Council) (May, 2000, p. A1). Federal and provincial grants to industry are notably in regions of the country other than Atlantic provinces as governments engage in a destructive competition for investment via tax concessions, grants, and loans. Atlantic Canada's critics often comment uncritically on Montreal's role in aerospace or Sarnia's in petrochemicals despite federal government incentives. Many of Ottawa's incentives go to the country's largest companies, such as Bombardier. Payments from the Transitional Jobs Fund of Human Resources Development increased suspiciously in populous regions before the 1997 election. CIDA and Industry Canada spend disproportionately in the Central provinces, including many dollars squandered on failed ventures (Savoie, 1997, pp. 47, 51–53, 63). In the 1980s federal assistance to business increased to $252 per capita in other regions while falling to $133 per capita in Atlantic Canada (Savoie and Winter, 1993, p. 8).

Moreover, in assessing their inability to attract foreign investment, Atlantic business leaders argue that "federal officials working abroad not only prefer to promote other regions ... notably Ontario, Quebec and British Columbia, if only because most of them come from these provinces—but that they do not seem to possess the basic knowledge about Atlantic Canada's economic circumstances to promote the region to potential investors"(Savoie, 1997, p. 61). Centralization of capital markets and financial institutions created investment networks that marginalized the region, a problem exacerbated by the global scope of investment patterns in recent years. Skepticism about regional prospects makes it difficult for entrepreneurs with good ideas to secure financial support in Canada's centralized financial system One report indicated that only 1 percent, or $7 million, of the $669 million in venture capital invested in Canada went to the Atlantic region in 1995 (Campbell, 1997, p. 114). Major industrial potential in areas like shipbuilding has been neglected despite costly support for auto and aerospace industries in the central region; as former Premier McKenna of New Brunswick cynically observed, "if you could get ships in Oshawa, Ontario, or Ottawa, they would have a shipbuilding policy for this country"(McKenna, 1997, p. 1).

This does not mean that "have" provinces would be economically backward absent of federal largesse. But these contributions must be considered in assessing public policy. The New Right tendency is to arbitrarily label some programs "regional" and others as national. It is wrong to treat

> as regional subsidies programs that are, in the main, national programs. It is totally misleading to think of programs such as Unemployment Insurance (UI), family allowances, the Canada Pension Plan (CPP), Established Programs Financing (EPF), and the Canada Assistance Plan (CAP) as *regional*—these are clearly *national* programs. And ... it is important to consider the pattern of net federal spending (properly calculated) in all provinces, not just the Atlantic provinces. (Lynch, Locke, and Hobson, 1997, pp. 3–4)

Such programs are supported by national taxes (paid for by all Canadians). Other federal programs (not labelled "regional" by critics) draw on those same national taxes but are spent disproportionately in the centre or West. It could be quite appropriate, given imbalances in such spending, to describe federal research and development, procurement, and many other policies as "regional" programs for central Canada, as these often appear to lack any national vision or scope.

The right-wing press focuses heavily on relief for Atlantic fisheries workers while neglecting expensive examples of waste in other provinces. As one commentator noted:

> Where was the hue and cry when ... it was reported that the country's largest aerospace companies have paid back only fractions of the billions of dollars in repayable loans received under federal support programs between 1980 and 1996? (Dunn, 1998, p. 1)

Billions were also doled out for agricultural relief to grain farmers in the West and to poultry and dairy farms in central Canada (who also enjoy protections from marketing boards denied to the fisheries). Grants for culture are concentrated in the largest cities, and the national capital region is heavily subsidized. The St. Lawrence Seaway could be seen as regional development for the centre. Federal expenditures in wartime, even in shipbuilding, were concentrated in the centre. The *Bank Act*'s centralization of capital markets in the country (as contrasted with America's regionalized system) provided an unfair advantage to the central region in investment capital. Is it acceptable that the federal regime retains a percentage of revenues from offshore resources while turning over vast tracts of common territory in the North to the central and Western provinces? Ottawa refused to support Halifax's bid for the post-Panamax port development even though American competitors received significant local and federal support. The monetarism of recent policy has also been harmful; the Bank of Canada's use of interest rates to dampen inflationary growth at the centre worsened the performance of slow-growth regions when they could have used a stimulus from lower rates (or compensatory taxes as proposed by former Newfoundland Premier Clyde Wells). The list is potentially much longer, indicating the complexity of expenditures and taxes and the folly of the simplified balance sheets presented by the Right.

Dwelling on such slights is a favourite regional pastime that does not address the challenges of the present. Nonetheless, asymmetries in electoral strength and political power in Canada continue to cause biases in major policy decisions. These asymmetries are worse than in other federal systems, making the region vulnerable as the redistributive system is unravelled. For instance, the American Senate system, which guarantees equal representation for each state however populous and requires transregional coalitions for adoption of policy, encourages distribution of growth-inducing expenditures (in defence, aerospace, research and development, etc.) across the country. For Atlantic Canada to flourish, the federal system must change so that national policies reflect the interests of all regions. But such changes are unlikely, so Atlantic leaders must find alternatives to government support while coping with discriminatory effects of major national policies.

ATLANTIC CANADIAN COOPERATION AS A SOLUTION?

The fiscal and ideological climate in other regions points toward reduced support for transfers in the future, so the Atlantic provinces will have to find new ways to more effectively use limited resources. Many analysts have promoted a Maritime or Atlantic Union to help resolve chronic underdevelopment. But these provinces may need to go beyond creation of a single economic space to develop shared programs, if the citizens of this region are to retain services of national quality. Union into a single province has some potential advantages. It could consolidate resources and reduce expensive duplication, both legislative and bureaucratic. A single province could achieve greater economies of scale in key institutions (e.g., courts) or programs. It might allow more efficient provision of public services, especially in areas facing federal cuts (e.g., health and education). It could give the region a more coherent position in national forums, speaking with one voice. It would also produce the benefits of joint action in tourism promotion and resource management. It could promote a region-wide plan for industrial development and end the inefficiencies of interprovincial competition for limited investment dollars, via wasteful tax concessions, loans, or grants.

Some of these benefits have been attained through interprovincial cooperation. But while cooperation has advanced in some areas, important elements of industrial development have not been included. And these arrangements are transitory and subject to the electoral pressures in each province, which could inhibit new cooperation or unravel existing ventures. Essential cooperation can progress only so far without political integration. Governments change and may withdraw from agreements for their own electoral purposes. Maintaining separate provinces carries the risk of self-interested actions harmful to the region such as destructive competition for federal and private investment. Finally, a larger unit might be more credible as a voice for regional interests in the federation.

However, political union would be difficult if not impossible to implement. There is no means to force provinces together, given their constitutional vetoes over changes to their jurisdiction and borders. Also, the four provinces collectively hold a veto under the amendment formula calling for seven of ten provinces to agree to constitutional changes. As a single province, the region would lose this veto unless a unanimity rule was instated. (A similar argument applies to Maritime union; these three provinces would be reduced to one vote in intergovernmental and constitutional forums, while Newfoundland retained its own vote.) Union could end the "Senate floor" rule for smallest provinces (especially P.E.I., which could not keep four seats), prompting a decline in the relative number of MPs from the region.

There is also the argument that, for historical and cultural reasons, these provinces need status as separate units. They could lose distinctive identities that are important to residents. P.E.I. might reject submersion in a larger, impersonal unit. Acadians might resist becoming a smaller minority in a united province; "the distinct character of New Brunswick, Canada's only officially bilingual province, is without doubt the most precious gain of the Acadian people" (Société Nationale de L'Acadie, 1992, p. 5). It is unlikely that bilingualism would be extended throughout the Atlantic region. Newfoundland's cultural and historical distinctiveness make it resist union. Nova Scotia's unique diversity and parochialism would be hard to integrate, especially if the capital of the united province were located elsewhere.

There could be more tangible costs. There would be the inevitable (and fiscally desirable) loss of public employment, which would not be quickly replaced. Union would also end experimentation with better approaches by different regimes (e.g., the McKenna advances in New Brunswick). Efforts at union could be lengthy and may delay needed cooperation. Political opposition to union remained high in 1990s polls, which could indicate the need for a gradual integration to bring the population on-side by demonstrating the benefits of closer cooperation. This could perhaps take the form of constitutionalized agreements between provinces to enshrine cooperation and to prevent withdrawal by later governments. This could allow the merger of institutions and bureaucracies on a permanent (or semi-permanent) basis. A gradual integration could permit the creation of a single economic space that could not be reversed for electoral purposes. This could include coordination of taxation and social expenditures to prevent an American-style "race to the bottom." It could solidify current agreements on procurement for governments, municipalities, universities, and hospitals, and create durable arrangements to reduce interprovincial competition via costly investment incentives and tax breaks. And the provinces could create interprovincial agencies in areas such as transportation with their own sources of revenue independent of individual provincial regimes (e.g., by assigning fuel taxes directly to this agency). Eventually, the region might create joint bureaucracies in health and postsecondary education or create a common federal court. The Council of Atlantic Premiers could direct the process and assign major institutions to different provinces to share employment equitably. This cooperation could become an end in itself or a first step toward fuller political union later on, following the model of European Union integration.

Ottawa could contribute by ensuring certainty in cost-sharing arrangements and by tying its transfers to regional cooperation. It might make health and postsecondary education transfers to interprovincial agencies, not provincial governments. Ottawa may need to rethink its block grants scheme and provide funding clearly targeted to postsecondary education and advanced training to rectify underinvestment in education, which helps account for regional disparities. While many should probably be abandoned as inefficient patronage instruments, development and infrastructure agreements should be region-wide, not bilateral with individual provinces.

There would be challenges. Lack of complete political union means some benefits would be lost, especially the downsizing of legislatures (which have 200 members of the Legislative Assembly for 2.2 million people versus 130 for Ontario's 11 million plus). If there is no joint assembly, it might be difficult for citizens to keep these interprovincial institutions democratically accountable, to ensure that they are adequately scrutinized and sufficiently sensitive to public opinion. Careful steps are needed to ensure that these institutions do not become a supergovernment that fails to reduce costs. It is unclear whether economic union would be meaningful under this model or whether interprovincial competition would continue. It will be hard to promote cooperation in government services if separate bureaucracies persist, with their own interests at stake. But it is also uncertain whether job losses from bureaucratic coordination would be offset by savings from taxes, increased economic activity, and investment.

Some progress has been made toward joint action, with Maritime initiatives in higher education, municipal training, lotteries, and veterinary and police education. In the 1990s, Newfoundland joined in new Atlantic agreements on procurement and internal trade; integration of some regulations and insurance legislation has progressed more recently. A

Council of Atlantic Premiers was formalized in 1989. Despite this progress, the existence of four sovereign provinces has created continual problems of competition that the region can ill afford. Nova Scotia threatened to withdraw from the Atlantic Lottery Corporation and the police academy in P.E.I. to generate employment at home. P.E.I. and Newfoundland are at odds over shrimp quotas, while Nova Scotia and Newfoundland argue over the offshore boundary in the resource-rich Cabot strait. Intense economic need makes these provinces competitors, not cooperators. Substantial institutional integration is needed to end parochialism and electoral fetishism and encourage durable cooperation. But the harsh cutback of federal transfers has led to erosion of service quality. Regional leaders must realize that cooperation may be the only way to avoid closing hospitals and universities and downsizing or eliminating other services, which they would find electorally unpalatable.

THE WAY FORWARD

The New Right critique of Atlantic dependence indicates a need to end regionalized employment insurance (if alternative adjustment measures are adequate) and business subsidies (if similar measures are withdrawn for other provinces, where they are higher per capita). But proposed limits on federal transfers in health, education, welfare, and training, or decentralization with a transfer of tax points to provinces would be disastrous.

There must be a profound change in federal attitudes and priorities to distribute fundamental public investments equitably across the country. This may require reform of intrastate institutions to boost regional responsiveness. There is some evidence that the federal regime is getting the message on the need for pro-growth, spending on infrastructure, human development, and education. But the electoral predominance of the central provinces, and the economic vitality of the West, make the Atlantic region a forgotten periphery in most key policy decisions.

There is a need for reflection, rather than ideological fervour, in commentary and policy. There are complexities in the regional economy and society that, when coupled with politicization of development policies, created dysfunctions like regional unemployment benefits. Many industries are inherently seasonal, and it is not easy to simply abandon genuine markets for seafood, wood products, foodstuffs, and seasonal tourism. For instance, strawberry growers complain that changes to employment insurance have left them without seasonal workers to harvest their profitable crops. As APEC notes:

> Atlantic Canada faces income security reform with reservations. Most people in the region agree that change is necessary. In the same breath, most also realize that rapid wholesale change to programs could be devastating in the short-term, and quite

unpalatable despite the prospect of long-run benefits. So the pace of change is as important as reform itself. ("Social Security reform," 1995, p. 3)

Far from requiring an abdication of government responsibility, the situation requires more careful coordination of efforts across levels of government, and with private-sector actors, to plan for sustainability in seasonal sectors while seeking productive alternatives for employees.

Cooperation, including integration of policies and services, may be a necessary response to fiscal crisis and reduced transfers. The constitutional crises will not be resolved soon with PQ/BQ strength remaining high; while sovereignty has faded as an immediate threat, the region must prepare for decentralization and more provincial powers. Integration or cooperation must be implemented carefully to maximize savings and minimize costs. However, to expect this to occur voluntarily is an illusion.

Recent reports on Atlantic Canada's prospects indicate its strengths in environmental and social amenities and public services. But there are weaknesses in venture capital, export diversification, technological infrastructure, and human resources (Plumstead and McNiven, 1997, pp. 28–29). Atlantic leaders must find ways to keep more capital invested locally (e.g., through the use of public pension funds in investment pools as in the Quebec Société General de Financement for instance); or break down the centralization in the financial system through inducements to greater competition (not consolidation) among banks and investment houses. The smaller projects in the region have difficulties finding financial backing, a problem that the venture capital fund of the Business Development Bank and ACOA's ACF Equity Atlantic seek to address. Government must promote investment in internetworking, to encourage development of small enterprises linked to national and global centres but based in the attractive cities and rural areas of the region. These provinces must turn the offshore boom into permanent development by ensuring a regional role in managing these resources and limiting the drain of all profit to outside actors.

The goal must be to provide a skilled workforce and technological investments to encourage productivity improvements rather than relying on low-wage, low-skilled labour to bring investments (as some New Right thinkers suggest). As the North American Policy Group (NAPG) concludes, "Having a low-paid, un-skilled labour force in a developed country may not be competitive when compared with a lower-paid, un-skilled labour force in a developing nation" (McNiven, Plumstead, and Russell, 1997, p. 37). More importantly, since 20 to 33 percent of skilled workers migrate to opportunities elsewhere, retention of skilled persons becomes a priority; this requires higher, competitive wages and benefits, and better public amenities, not diminished ones as the New Right prescription would entail.

Despite the righteous predictions of the right-wing press, efforts to embarrass the region or to shock it into adjustment through rapid retrenchment will produce stronger resistance and make the task of improving policy more difficult. The strength of discontent can be seen in the violent responses to employment insurance cuts, privatization of DEVCO, fisheries quota limits and licence fee increases, and the end of The Atlantic Groundfish Strategy (TAGS). The region needs to overcome resistance to change by grassroots movements and foster an acceptance of adjustment to new economic realities. However, unilateral cuts without community planning spark aggressive responses. Surely European models of local consultation and planning of adjustment measures for both communities and individuals would be a better alternative

It will be difficult to break old patterns of patronage as the Liberals seek to recoup seats in the region to offset losses to the Canadian Alliance elsewhere. A Liberal initiative in June 2000 targeted communities, not individuals, for "new economy" spending (e.g., Moncton e-commerce, Sydney software, Halifax biotech, etc.) One could argue that such initiatives should focus on individual skills, entrepreneurship, and adjustment or mobility instead. There is considerable political appeal to the high-profile announcement of plans by regional ministers or MPs. As one national commentator notes, that "kind of old politics plays to the stereotype of Atlantic Canada as a region still in the grip of an entitlement culture, the old shibboleth that the number of votes a party can win is proportional to the amount of public money it doles out" (Wallace, 2000, p. 26). Perhaps this political style goes some way to explaining why analysts focus on regional policies in the East while overlooking region-specific benefits elsewhere. But political biases favouring the centre in government, media, and academe will keep the region marginalized. One would hope that analysts would produce more balanced, thoughtful policies and commentary in the future. But, more likely, this region will remain an easy target for intellectual bullies and their "ideological bull."

REFERENCES

Beeby, Deon. (1999, April 29). East Coast development loans overdue: $70 million in default. *Financial Post*, p. C5.

Bickerton, James. (1990). Creating Atlantic Canada: Culture, policy and regionalism. In James Bickerton and Alain-G. Gagnon (Eds.), *Canadian politics*. Peterborough: Broadview.

Campbell, Mark. (1997, April). Off the dole. *Canadian Business*.

Canada. (1992). Parliament, Special Joint Committee on a Renewed Canada: *A Renewed Canada*.

Canadian Taxpayers Federation. (2000). *ACOA: The lost decade: Overview*. Ottawa: Canadian Taxpayers Foundation, 6.

The changing face of Atlantic Canada: Factors behind private sector job growth. (1997). *APEC Bulletin* 4.

Cod chronicle. (1998, July–Aug). *Canadian Geographic* 118, 29.

Courchene, Thomas J. and MacDougall, John N. (1991). The context for future constitutional options. In Ronald L. Watts and Douglas M. Brown (Eds.), *Options for a new Canada*. Toronto: University of Toronto Press.

Courchene, Thomas J. (1981, Spring). Regions, transfers and growth. *Canadian Business Review*.

———. (1995). Glocalization: The regional/international interface. *Canadian Journal of Regional Science*, 18(1).

Dunn, Mark. (1998, June 23). All regions recipients of government largesse. *Canadian Press Newswire*.

Global challenges and opportunities: Atlantic export performance under free trade. (2000, Winter). *Atlantic Report* 34(4), 5.

Forbes, Ernest. (1993). Looking backward: Reflections on the Maritime experience in an evolving Canadian Constitution. In Donald J. Savoie and Ralph Winter (Eds.), *The Maritime provinces: Looking to the future*. Moncton: Canadian Institute for Research on Regional Development.

Francis, Diane. (2000, June 3). Time to cry out for the downsizing of the political class. *Financial Post*.

Haddow, Rodney. (1994). Ontario politics: 'Plus ca change...'? In James Bickerton and Alain-G. Gagnon (Eds.), *Canadian politics*. Peterborough: Broadview.

Higgins, Benjamin. (1990, Summer–Autumn). Subsidies, Regional Development and the Canada–U.S. Free Trade Agreement. *Canadian Journal of Regional Science* 13(2), 259–72.

———. (1993). Restructuring without tears in a free trade environment. In George J. De Benedetti, and Rodolphe H. Lamarche (Eds.), *Shock waves: The Maritime urban system in the new economy*. Moncton: Canadian Institute for Research on Regional Development.

Lamarche Rodolphe. (1993). The Maritime provinces in an information economy. In Donald J. Savoie and Ralph Winter (Eds.), *The Maritime provinces: Looking to the future*. Moncton, Canadian Institute for Research on Regional Development, 95.

Lynch, Scott, Locke, Wade, and Hobson, Paul. (1997). *Should our concern be the gift horse or the ideological bull? A critical economic assessment of "Looking the gift horse in the mouth: The impact of federal transfers on Atlantic Canada."* [Summary, pp. 3–4]. Moncton: Canadian Institute for Research on Regional Development, Maritime Series Monographs.

McKenna, Frank. (1997, October 9). Atlantic Canada: A vision for the future. An address to the Atlantic Vision Conference of Atlantic Canadian Premiers 9

October 1997, Moncton, N.B. [Online]. Available: <http://www.aims.ca/>. Cited 2000, July 13.

May, Doug and Hollett, Alton. (1995). *The rock in a hard place: Atlantic Canada and the UI trap.* Montreal: C.D.Howe Institute.

May, Kathryn. (2000, June 18). We made high-tech happen: PS chief; Government made Ottawa a dot-com boomtown, top bureaucrat insists. *Ottawa Citizen,* p. A1.

McNiven, J.D., Plumstead, J.E., and Russell, B.R. (1997). *Atlantic Canada and the future: Trends, challenges and opportunities.* Halifax: North American Policy Group.

Mifflin, Fred. (1999, July 12). Atlantic development agency is not just about roads any more: ACOA minister defends agency *Hill Times,* No. 497.

Palda, Filip. (1994). Provincial trade wars: Why the blockade must end. [On-line]. Available: <http://www.fraserinstitute.ca/publications/books/trade_wars/>.

Plumstead, Janice and McNiven, James. (1997, Summer). Benchmarking for the future of Atlantic Canada: A development comparison. *Economic Development Review.*

Reuber, Grant L. (1991) Federalism and negative-sum games. In Robert Young (Ed.), *Confederation in crisis.* Toronto: James Lorimer and Co.

Savage, John. (1996, November). Social service subsidies for have not provinces keep Canada together. *Canadian Speeches* 10(7), 38–42.

Savoie, Donald. (1997). *Rethinking Canada's regional development policy: An Atlantic perspective.* Moncton: Canadian Institute for Research on Regional Development.

Savoie, Donald J. and Winter, Ralph. (1993). Introduction. In Donald Savoie and Ralph Winters (Eds.), *The Maritime provinces: Looking towards the future.* Moncton: Canadian Institute for Research on Regional Development.

Social security reform (impact on Atlantic Canada). (1995, January). *Atlantic Report* 29(4), pp. 3, 5.

Société Nationale de L'Acadie. (1992, December 5). *Brief on the economic integration of the Atlantic provinces.* Submitted to the Council of Maritime Premiers.

Taylor, Peter S. (1996–97, Dec.–Jan.). Bye bye Bytown: Thomas Courchene is our most provocative, and best, policy thinker. And he thinks the provinces should run the country. *Saturday Night,* 111(10).

Tomblin, Stephen. (1995). *Ottawa and the outer provinces.* Toronto: James Lorimer.

Underhill, Bruce. (2000, June 28). High-tech handout for Atlantic Canada: PM, Boudreau to announce $700m fund. *Chronicle Herald,* p. A1.

Wallace, Bruce. (2000, May 22). New economy, old politics. *Maclean's,* 113(21), p. 26.

FURTHER READING

De Benedetti, George J. and Lamarche, Rodolphe H. (Eds.). (1993). *The Maritime Urban System in the New Economy.* Moncton: Canadian Institute for Research on Regional Development.

Mandale, Maurice and Milne, William J. (Eds.). 1996. *Has the Time Come? Perspectives on Cooperation.* Halifax: Atlantic Provinces Economic Council.

Savoie, Donald. 1997. *Rethinking Canada's Regional Development Policy: An Atlantic Perspective.* Moncton: Canadian Institute for Research on Regional Development.

Savoie, Donald J. and Winter, Ralph (Eds.). 1993. *The Maritime Provinces: Looking to the Future.* Moncton: Canadian Institute for Research on Regional Development.

Tomblin, Stephen. 1995. *Ottawa and the Outer Provinces.* Toronto: James Lorimer.

PART B

ONTARIO

Kensington

Morris Granatstein

Listen to the echoes
along the echo paths
in parchment
        ears
these streets
        the colours of
        this sky

the silver fishes in tanks
            in a Kensington
            fish store

footsteps in
sawdust
in the overrun
        lake smells
where we are
where
are
we

Listen to the echoes
on the echo paths
of these streets
these spotted surfaces

Crates with chickens
sidewalk strewn
with chicken feathers,

Look at the rooster crossing
recrossing the road
        from curb
        to curb

Men and women
in league
known as family
fathers and mothers
across at stands

selling fowl
fishes
yardgoods
footwear

And a cornerfront bakery
smells of dough,
of hot bread,
of kaiser rolls
coffee cakes
cookies in vast blue
arterioles
      monstrous loaves
      five feet high
      in yellow corner
      of window light

Listen to the echoes
along echo paths
in shadow of
      autumn blind
      heaven

The way the world ages
the way my parents age
solid black
solid grey
solid blue
under eyes
Between the seven heavens
and the seven earths
in vice
of a midnight
storyteller

Once upon a time
in mime
in pause,
in a story within a
story without a
story
in the gentle arms
of
a
story

Immigrant City: The Making of Modern Toronto

Harold Troper

Toronto is today a sprawling urban metropolis of almost 4 000 000 people. Toronto is also one of the most culturally and racially diverse cities in the world. The reason for both is immigration. Every year approximately one-third of all immigrants who enter Canada settle in the Greater Toronto Area. Statistics paint a remarkable picture. According to the 1996 Canadian census, while just over 17 percent of all Canadian citizens were born outside Canada, 42 percent of Toronto's population are foreign-born immigrants. Equally important, this influx of immigrants has arrived from every corner of the globe. There are in Toronto approximately 450 000 Chinese, 400 000 Italians, and 250 000 Afro-Canadians, the largest component of which are of Caribbean background, although there are separate and distinct groups of Somalis, Ethiopians, and other Africans. There are 200 000 Jews and large and growing populations from the Indian sub-continent, the Middle East, Greece, Portugal, Poland, Vietnam, Hispanic America, and various Slavic countries. There are more than 100 different languages spoken in the city. There are more Muslims than Presbyterians. And Toronto is now no longer the largely white city it once was. At some point during the next few years, the majority of those living in Toronto will be people of colour (Orenstein, 2000).

Nor is the impact of immigration likely to lessen in coming years. With the federal government promising to keep annual immigration numbers at or just under 1 percent of Canada's total population, there can be no doubt that immigration will continue to be a major shaping feature of Toronto's life and character.

IMMIGRATION BEFORE WORLD WAR II

Immigration is so important in Toronto today that it is impossible to understand the city without knowing the critical role the history of immigration has played and continues to plays in defining the city's course. Oddly, until after World War II, Toronto was not a major immigrant magnet. That is not to say that Toronto had no immigrants or foreigners, as immigrants were then commonly labelled. On the contrary. In the years before World War II, Toronto, like most Canadian cities, had its immigrant neighbourhoods. Best known is the Kensington Market area of Toronto. But, compared to today, Toronto's immigrant neighbourhoods were small and regarded by mainstream residents as neighborhoods apart, in the city but not really part of the city. And what of the immigrants? As far as most Canadians, Torontonians included, were concerned, immigrants were supposed to settle and work the land—not congregate in cities. The small number of immigrants who did settle in the city were expected to know their place, and their place was at the social and economic margins, corners of the larger urban landscape reserved for cheap labour, for people doing those jobs that "real" Canadians preferred not to do (Harney and Troper, 1975).

The policy connection between immigration and farming was so strong in the minds of most Canadians that they assumed that filling the land with farmers was what immigration was all about. This belief was prevalent from the earliest days of confederation. It became even more so after the completion of the first Canadian transcontinental railway in the mid-1880s and the opening of the vast Canadian prairie Northwest to intensive agricultural settlement. Importation of agricultural labour was then a national priority. And where would all the farmers come from? Toward the end of the 19th century, major population upheavals in central, southern, and particularly eastern Europe cut millions of people loose to seek new homes in the New World. The result was a huge wave of immigration out of Europe, some of which could be transplanted onto the vast agricultural expanse of Western Canada.

Of course, it should not be supposed that all immigrants were equally acceptable. Canada welcomed immigrants in a descending order of racial and ethnic preference. At the top were British and white American farmers followed closely by northern and western Europeans. Then came eastern Europeans—the fabled peasants in sheepskin coats. Closer to the bottom of the list came southern Europeans who, in both the public and government's mind, were regarded as less assimilable and less desirable. At the very bottom were Asians, Blacks, and Eastern European Jews, most of whom showed little inclination for farming. To guard against these less-desirable groups, government passed laws or instituted immigration regulations that stemmed the flow of Asian, Black, and Jewish immigration. When demand for agricultural or other labour exceeded the available pool of preferred immigrants, as it did at the turn of the last century, immigration authorities moved down their ladder of preference. This eventually allowed hundreds of thousands of eastern European settlers into Canada between the turn of the last century and the early 1920s (Troper, 1987).

These immigrants may have been critical to the economy, but they also caused anxieties. For many Canadians the influx of so many strange peoples speaking strange languages, people perhaps still loyal to foreign kings, people who prayed to alien gods and seemed so distant from mainstream Canadian ways raised fears about how or whether these foreigners could ever assimilate into Canadian society. But so long as Canadians were convinced immigration was good for the economy and these foreigners were content to remain on the land, fears were kept in check.

To the unease of many mainstream Canadians, however, not all foreigners were content with this arrangement. Some immigrants began moving into Canadian cities, including Toronto. The prosperity on Canada's Western agricultural, mining, and lumbering frontier that attracted so many immigrants to Canada in the first place also sparked economic growth and development in cities like Toronto. This meant jobs for unskilled immigrant workers. It was not long before immigrants were avoiding or abandoning the isolation of the bush or escaping the uncertainties and insecurities of life on the land in favour of wage labour in cities. Men ricocheted into Toronto where many found ready employment paving streets, laying trolley tracks, labouring in the expanding textile factories, and tunnelling the sewer systems. Women found work as household domestics, performed contract work at home, or took in boarders in order to make ends meet.

While immigrants laboured in Toronto, they also set down roots in the city. Many Torontonians looked on in shock. Immigrants were supposed to be on the land, not in their city. Reflecting the racism of their day, they regarded these foreigners as a threat. They believed immigrants were racially inferior and would bring an increase in crime, immorality, and political corruption. Immigrants also seemed so different, so determined to hold onto their old-world ways, many felt it would be impossible to turn them into Canadians. Their children offered little more hope. Some Canadian feared that, by the time they started school, these children would have absorbed their parents' "unCanadian" ways. And these children did not seem to know their place. It was one thing if these foreigners were content to spend their lives in sweat labour. It was another to find foreigners and their children competing successfully with skilled native-born craftsmen and small businessmen. The brightest among them were even starting to demand access to universities, professions, and the political arena. No, many mainstream Canadians urged, if foreigners in Toronto did not know their place they should be denied Canadian entry.

As hostility to immigrants in Toronto and other cities began to build, the federal government responded. In the mid-1920s Canadian immigration laws and regulations were modified so as to restrict Canadian entry to eastern and southern Europeans as well as continuing to bar Asians and Blacks (Kelley and Trebilcock, 1998). Following the economic collapse of 1929, with mass unemployment in urban Canada and a sharp decline in farm income, any remaining support for immigration evaporated. Canada's immigration door was sealed. Immigration officials who previously competed with other countries for immigrants now stood guard against any breach in the Canadian wall of restriction. So difficult was it to enter Canada during the 1930s and 1940s that Canada had arguably the worst record of all Western counties in the admission of refugees from Nazi Germany (Abella and Troper, 1982). Even those foreigners already in Canada were not safe from anti-immigration hostility. The pointed stick of racism seldom dug so deep as it did with the internment of Japanese-Canadians during the World War II (Sunahara, 1981).

THE POLITICS OF ETHNIC SELECTIVITY: TORONTO AND POSTWAR IMMIGRATION

But World War II and its aftermath also proved a critical watershed in the history of immigration into Canada and Toronto in particular. When the war ended in 1945, government policy planners at first feared Canada would backslide into the jobless depression of the 1930s. The exact opposite proved true. The postwar period proved an era of unprecedented prosperity and economic growth, especially for urban Canada. Toronto and the surrounding area led the way. Rather than a shortage of jobs, there was soon a massive shortage of labour. Industry that had grown up during the war, much of it in and around centres like Toronto, needed workers. Business leaders immediately began pressing government to throw open Canada's door to immigrant workers.

The government responded with caution. It approved a selective reopening of immigration that included holding the line against the immigration of non-British or non-western Europeans. In 1947 Prime Minister Mackenzie King was only reflecting the national mood when he declared that "the people of Canada do not wish to make a fundamental alteration in the character of their population through mass immigration." Discrimination and ethnic selectivity in immigration would remain. To quote King, "Canada is perfectly within her rights in selecting the persons whom we regard as desirable future citizens. It is not a 'fundamental human right' of any alien to enter Canada. It is a privilege" (*House of Commons Debates*, 1947, pp. 2544–47). So, as postwar Canada began admitting immigrants again, that privilege was denied those deemed ethnically or racially undesirable. Immigration preference was again given to northern Europeans. Southern and eastern Europeans were not favoured, and Asians and Blacks had very little chance of getting in.

The public seemed to support ethnic selectivity. Just over a year after the guns fell quiet in Europe, a public opinion poll on immigration found that Canadians would rather see recently defeated Germans allowed into Canada than eastern or southern Europeans. Jews fared better only than Japanese, a recently defeated enemy, in this ethnic public-opinion sweepstakes. Thus, public agreement with the government's reopening of immigration in late 1947 was very much predicated on holding fast to the ethnically and racially based immigration priorities of the 1920s.

Immigration might be tightly controlled by race and ethnic origin, but at least immigration was starting to move again. British, American, and northern Europeans, "the right types of immigrants," were actively courted. The government of Ontario was so concerned to get the "right type" of immigrant to come to Ontario that it inaugurated a highly publicized airlift of British families into the province. When British currency regulations threatened to choke off the flow of applicants, special transportation tariffs were negotiated to stimulate the inflow (Richmond, 1967, p. 9). When currency regulations similarly held up the immigration of other desirable western European groups, particularly the Dutch, the federal government intervened. In 1948 a three-year bilateral agreement was signed with the Netherlands to ensure the smooth removal of approximately 15 000 Dutch immigrants to Canada, many settling just north of Toronto (Paterson, 1955).

Employers were generally pleased by the government's growing commitment to immigration, but they were less pleased with continued restrictions against importing labour from outside the government's narrow circle of ethnic acceptability. Demanding that it must have access to an expanded pool of cheap imported labour to fill low-status jobs that native-born Canadians avoided, business warned that delay threatened the economic boom. Employers pressed Ottawa to open the door to immigration from southern and eastern Europe before other labour-short nations—including the United States and Australia—beat Canada to the punch. Responding to this pressure, the federal government slowly began enlarging the list of those immigrant groups approved for Canadian entry. Immigration was first approved for eastern Europeans, many of whom had been displaced by the war and then further expanded to include southern Europeans. Canada was finally and fully back in the immigration importation business, and Toronto was soon Canada's single most significant immigration destination.

In the postwar era Toronto's economy was especially strong and creating far more jobs than the existing labour pool could fill. Immigrants poured in to fill the demand for unskilled workers. Once established in the city, many wrote home encouraging family and friends to join them in Toronto. Immigrant communities grew quickly. Especially noteworthy was the arrival of a mass immigration from Italy, then still suffering the results of wartime devastation. Italy offered Canada a large pool of unemployed and unskilled labour that could easily be redirected to waiting employment in urban Canada.

When immigration from Italy opened up in the early 1950s, Ottawa, still thinking racially, may at first have hoped to attract the more "Germanic" northern Italians, but almost immediately southern Italians dominated the immigrant flow. By the mid-1960s Italian immigration into Canada climbed into the hundreds of thousands. In the industrial heartland of southern Ontario, and Toronto in particular, Italian labour soon became a mainstay of the booming construction industry. So extensive was the influx of Italians that within ten years Canada's Italian-origin population grew threefold from approximately 150 000 to 450 000. The inflow from Italy continued at a high rate, and Toronto absorbed the bulk of that immigration.

Mostly from rural areas, Italian immigrants to Toronto first located in residential working-class neighborhoods along major public transit routes and took up lower-status but often unionized manual labouring jobs, particularly in construction and related industrial sectors. As the city expanded in all directions, it was often Italian immigrant workers who laid the roads, built the homes and office towers, and installed the transportation network. And as Toronto prospered, so did the community. For many immigrants from Italy, residential property acquisition and bringing family from Italy were primary goals. Home ownership and a widening circle of kin also served to support the integrative process. Family often took in family, and together the extended family formed a strong social and economic unit, pooling money and resources, networking together for jobs, caring for one another's children, and sharing information.

Italian immigrants put their stamp on the areas of the city where they settled. Italian grocery stores, cafés, food wholesalers, newspaper publishers, parishes, and social clubs gave Italian neighbourhoods in Toronto a distinctive flavour and look. Other immigrant groups followed suit. Even as Italian immigration continued, large numbers of Greeks, Portuguese, and the peoples of the Balkan Peninsula began arriving in Toronto. Each group was unique in its cultural traditions, institutional organization, and economic priorities; each added its special character to the city; but each group also adopted many of the same family-based economic survival strategies so characteristic of postwar Italian immigrants (Iacovetta, 1992: Harney, 1998).

In 1951, for the first time since World War II, small numbers of non-Whites were also allowed into Canada. Many also settled in Toronto. Responding to a now multiracial British Commonwealth made up of independent former British colonial holdings, Canada set aside a small, but symbolically important, immigrant quota for non-White settlers from its new Commonwealth partners, India, Pakistan, and Ceylon. The numbers of non-Whites admitted to Canada was small, but the importance of this first postwar sanctioned admission of non-White immigrants to Canada should not be minimized.

The arrival of so many immigrants into Toronto from so many different countries and in so short a period had a dramatic impact on the city. Not only were immigrants an economic asset but they also slowly remade the Toronto urban landscape and urban life and attitudes. For example, immigrants gradually redressed the city's religious balance. Catholics have today replaced Protestants as Toronto's largest religious community. Immigrants also brought with them a diversity of cultural expressions and richness of traditions and languages greater than

Toronto had ever previously imagined, let alone known. Ready or not, Toronto was becoming a multicultural city.

At first, old-guard Toronto was unsure just how to respond to so many strangers in their midst. Of course, there were those Torontonians who recognized the benefits that came with immigration and responded with openness to the newcomers. These Torontonians welcomed the emerging cultural mosaic that was supplanting an image of Toronto as a staid backwater of British-style tradition.

Others Torontonians were less open and less welcoming. They felt ill at ease, uncomfortable with the changes that immigrants were bringing to the world around them. Some looked down their noses at immigrants, dismissing them as urban peasants. Some were even put off by things we now regard as part of our regular life style, like pizza. What kind of people, they asked, eat a pie made with melted cheese and tomato sauce? And would these immigrants ever change, ever become Canadian, they asked. Would these foreigners ever learn to be like us? Can we force them to be like us? In the late 1950s Toronto police, enforcing restrictive liqueur legislation, descended on picnicking Italians immigrants for daring to drink a glass of wine in a public park let alone for allowing their children take a sip. Municipal health authorities tried to close down new European-style cafes that violated city ordinances by serving food outside at sidewalk tables.

Immigrants felt the cold wind of rejection and discrimination. Many immigrants speaking their mother tongue in the street or on public transit can remember being told to "Speak white!" School teachers and administrators in Toronto schools, thinking they were doing immigrant children a favour, helping them become a little more Canadian, robbed many an immigrant child of his or her most personal possession—a name. At the hands of teachers, Gabriella became Gail, Luigi became Louis, Olga became Alice, and Hershel became Harold. And as immigrants struggled to build new lives in a new land, they heard local politicians and editorialists railing against the evils of immigrant overcrowding, ghettoization, and crime.

EMBRACING MULTICULTURALISM: THE MAKING OF THE NEW TORONTO

But this too passed. Slowly at first, Torontonians became more comfortable with the new foods, the polyphony of languages, and distinctive ethnic neighbourhoods that immigration brought in its wake. And for some, comfort gradually turned to pride in Toronto's newfound cosmopolitan feel. A new Toronto was taking shape. But what of that deep stain of anti-immigrant racism that was so much a part of Toronto's past? How was it that in less than one generation Toronto's self-image shifted so dramatically from an Anglo-Saxon town to a culturally pluralist city? Put simply, by the late 1960s a new postwar generation of Torontonians was coming of age, a generation that grew up with immigrants from Europe as a fact of city life. What's more, the hundreds of thousands of European immigrants who had come to Toronto, and their children, were becoming a major social and political force in the city. If it would take time for this new reality to soak in, the election of Nathan Phillips, a Jew and a child of immigrants, as Toronto's first mayor of the 1960s, something that nobody would have believed possible only a few years earlier, was a clear sign of the enormous changes immigration was bringing to the city.

Nor was it just attitudes that changed in Toronto during the decades following the war. Laws had to change as well. As immigrants in Toronto came to regard themselves and be regarded by others as equal partners in the community—deserving all the rights, privileges, and responsibilities of native-born Canadians—law had to reflect this new reality. This change began with Canadian citizenship itself. Little remembered today is the fact that until 1947 there was legally no such thing as Canadian citizenship. Instead, those living in Canada were designated as British subjects resident of Canada, not Canadian citizens.

Pressure for a distinct Canadian citizenship began in the postwar period. The politician most associated with that change was Paul Martin. In his autobiography Martin described how his conversion to the idea of a separate and distinct Canadian citizenship came during an official visit he made to recently liberated Europe in 1945. While in France he was taken to visit the Canadian military cemetery at Dieppe. Walking amid the rows of Canadian graves, some still fresh with wooden markers, he reported being deeply moved by the incredible diversity of names found among the Canadian fallen—names that spoke to the pluralism of origins even then making up Canadian society. As Martin later wrote, "Of whatever origin, these men were Canadians" (Martin, 1983). They had fought and died for Canada. They deserved to be remembered as Canadians. In their memory he championed the creation of a Canadian citizenship.

It took time, but Canadian citizenship became law on January 1, 1947. And the adoption of Canadian citizenship turned out to be far more than simple postwar flag-waving sentimentalism. It proved a far-reaching act. Henceforth, individual Canadian citizens were promised that everyone would be treated equally irrespective of whether they were Canadian or foreign born, and irrespective of any claim that any group might make to being more Canadian than any other.

The inauguration of a distinct and separate Canadian citizenship paved the way for subsequent human rights initiatives so important to immigrants in urban Canada. Immigrants in cities like Toronto demanded laws guaranteeing equal access to public institutions, and they wanted the laws to have teeth. These immigrants were supported by a coalition of organized labour, liberal-minded politicians and churches, and older Canadian ethnic communities who had embraced the Canadian war effort, who had sent their children off to fight for Canada and who, in the aftermath of war, refused to ever again accept second-class status for themselves or their children. Their human-rights agenda was simple; clear away any and all roadblocks that prevented immigrants or ethnic community members from enjoying full and equal social, economic, and political rights in society.

Nowhere was the push for legal protections against racial, religious, or ethnic discrimination more important than in Toronto where people from all over the world now lived and worked together. And the human-rights crusade made gains. In the first decade after the war, province after province enacted fair employment and accommodation legislation barring discrimination on account of race, religion, or country of origin. In the international arena, Canada signed the Universal Declaration of Human Rights, which added urgency to the new Canadian human-rights agenda. Canadian courts were soon responding to the more progressive spirit of the day by using their powers to expand society's human-rights agenda.

The new spirit of human rights and equality began to have an impact. Immigrants were no longer commonly referred to as foreigners; they were New Canadians. And, for that matter, they were no longer spoken of as unwelcome intruders. They were in cities like Toronto by right, and now by right of law. It was only a matter of time before the domestic human-rights upheaval impacted on Canadian immigration legislation and administration.

In Toronto, where immigrants were growing rapidly in number, they were also now a significant political force. It was not long before urban politicians, once hostile to foreigners, began appealing to "New Canadian" voters. Issues important to immigrant communities were now important at city hall. Schools, previously dedicated to assimilation, to turning "them" into "us," were forced to reinvent themselves to be open to and inclusive of different cultures. And in the streets of Toronto, the public expression of racism, once so common, not only became socially unacceptable but also a legally punishable violation of community standards.

Meanwhile the number and diversity of immigrants in Toronto continued to grow at a pace that few would previously have imagined possible. In 1956 a failed revolt against Soviet control in Hungary sent thousands of refugees into flight. This first refugee crisis of the Cold War eventually brought 37 000 Hungarian refugees to Canada. These Hungarian arrivals also foreshadowed two trends that would reshape the immigration flow heading for Toronto in the decades that followed. First, unlike much of the previous postwar immigration, this wave of Hungarian refugees included many skilled workers or educated professionals. With time and English-language training, many found employment in high-paying professions or entered the growing white-collar workforce. As the Canadian economy changed, immigration policy shifted from encouraging the immigration of unskilled labour toward encouraging the immigration of highly skilled and educated immigrants to meet a growing need for a better-educated workforce.

Also, while the government of the day thought the Hungarian refugee movement would prove a one-time Cold War event, it was wrong. During the next few decades Canada would again and again find itself called upon to offer new homes to group after group of refugees, all of whom feared persecution in their homeland. For the majority of these refugees, their new home would be Toronto. This proved the case with the next big refugee influx in 1968. Reminiscent of Hungary, a movement for democratization in Soviet-controlled Czechoslovakia collapsed under the heel of invading Soviet troops. Refugees again fled westward. Approximately 12 000 Czech refugees soon resettled Canada, the majority again coming to Toronto (Dirks, 1977). They were followed in 1972 by about 5600 Ugandan Asian refugees expelled from Uganda by Idi Amin and, starting the next year, by about 2000 refugees from a brutal 1973 right-wing coup d'état against Salvador Allende's democratically elected government in Chile.

The Ugandan Asian refugee movement represented another shift in Canadian immigration that would have far-reaching impact on the face of Toronto—the Ugandan Asians were not white. Their arrival in 1972 would have been unthinkable a decade earlier when immigration policy still blocked entry to most non-Europeans. But, in part to bring immigration legislation in line with major human-rights initiatives at the provincial and federal levels and in part to remove irritants between Canada and the newly independent nations in the developing world, in 1962 the federal government lifted most racial and ethnic restrictions on the processing of immigration applicants. The government stopped just short, however, of removing all racial barriers. To prevent a feared anti-Asian backlash in British Columbia, racial restrictions remained in place, preventing Asians in Canada from sponsoring their families. This last immigration barrier was finally removed in 1967, Canada's Centennial year. Canadian immigration officials soon began processing applications from Asia, Africa, and the Caribbean.

The government also overhauled procedures by which immigration applicants were assessed, ensuring that immigration better met urban Canada's constantly changing needs. A point system, as it come to be known, was instituted. Simply stated, points were granted to each applicant for specific skills, background, or Canadian links. In addition to education and employment experience, points were assigned for character, Canadian demand for the applicant's skills, English and French language proficiency, age, and proposed Canadian destination. If an applicant amassed the requisite number of points, he or she was granted Canadian admission. When Canadian economic conditions or skill demands changed, the point system could be quickly adjusted to give an applicant greater or fewer points according to these new priorities.

All these changes had a dramatic impact on Toronto. Following the removal of racial selection criteria and the opening of immigration offices in previously unserved areas, the admission of persons of colour, most from the developing world, increased. In 1967, shortly after Canadian immigration operations were upgraded in Asia and the Caribbean, less than 15 percent of immigrants into Canada were of African or Asian descent. In the early 1970s economic pressures in both the Caribbean and South Asia caused many to consider relocating abroad. As a result, in 1971, for the first time, members of visible minorities constituted the majority of immigrants entering Canada. This trend has continued each year since and has so altered Toronto's racial composition that soon visible minorities will be in the majority.

This has not occurred without some heightened racial anxiety and tensions. But if the potential for racial tension cannot be denied, what is remarkable is the degree to which Toronto has also made an effort to accommodate to the racial pluralism that now makes Toronto one of the most racially and ethnically diverse cities in the world.

But what does it mean for a city like Toronto to be diverse or multicultural? With immigration expanding the mosaic of peoples who call Toronto home, in 1971 the federal government announced its support for a policy of multiculturalism. The policy symbolically recognized the positive and enduring impact of past immigration on Canadian society and set forward a pluralist model for nation-building. While observers at the time and since have debated the complex political pressures that prodded the government of Pierre Elliott Trudeau to adopt its multiculturalism policy, there is no doubt the policy posed a radical reconstruction of Canadian cultural definitions. It rejected the notion of a single overriding national cultural tradition. In so doing, the federal multicultural policy statement affirmed English and French as the two official national languages but rejected biculturalism—an image of Canada as a product of the nation-building efforts of two charter groups, the English (British) and French, in which their two cultures hold a privileged position in determining the boundaries of Canadian identity. Instead, multiculturalism affirmed respect for cultural diversity and acceptance of pluralism as the best base on which to build an inclusive Canadian identity. As the policy statement asserted, "there is no official culture, nor does any ethnic group take precedence over any other. No citizen or group of citizens is other than Canadian, and all should be treated fairly." Instead, the government declared that the binding force in the Canadian social compact would henceforth be based on mutual respect rooted in acceptance of cultural diversity, the same cultural diversity that was now the reality of the urban Canadian street. What is more, the government pledged that, no matter what a person's cultural heritage, all had equal rights in the eyes of the law.

In recent years multiculturalism has been attacked as a barrier to the development of a singular and bonding Canadian identity, but at the time Torontonians were generally supportive of the policy (Bissoondath, 1994). It spoke positively to Torontonians about the diversity that was now their urban reality. Multiculturalism, they were told, was a logical next step in ensuring the rights of all citizens—a right to cultural respect. More than that, the policy asserted than an individual's or group's desire to maintain and develop a cultural heritage, if exercised in accord with Canadian law, was natural; it enhanced the common good and was in harmony with citizen participation in the civic society. Put simply, in the Toronto of the early 1970s, the multiculturalism simply translated as "live and let live" (Burnet, 1976, 1979).

Toronto's embrace of multiculturalism and seemingly growing comfort level with the pluralism in its streets, classrooms, and workplaces made easier the federal government's implementation of a new *Immigration Act* in 1978. Under the new legislation immigration authorities for the first time began working under a form of quota system. In consultation with the provinces, Ottawa established a yearly target for the total number of immigrants, and for the various categories of immigrant, it hoped to admit the following year. The Canadian immigration target, more a goal than a commitment, served as a guide allowing provinces and municipalities to prepare in advance for immigrant arrivals. That goal could be adjusted up or down depending on existing conditions at home and abroad. But, it was hoped that by agreeing on a target figure, the resources necessary for the smooth integration of immigrants would be in place as immigrants arrived. As a rule of thumb, in recent years the immigration target has remained at about 1 percent of the total Canadian population each year or, by the late 1990s, about 250 000 immigrants per year (Orenstein, 2000).

That number was for all of Canada. The Greater Toronto area receives one-third of all these immigrants, yet it is not officially party to federal–provincial discussions. No city is officially part of these consultations. Toronto's interests are represented by the government of Ontario. No doubt federal and provincial officials are well briefed on the special needs of the Toronto immigration catchment area. However, being briefed and making Toronto's needs a priority are not one and the same. As a result, Toronto politicians, public servants, social agency officials, and ethnic leaders remain concerned that the city be adequately funded to meet the needs of new arrivals. And it is the municipality that is largely responsible for much of the hands-on delivering of services to immigrants such as health, education, social services, and policing. Sometimes stretched to the financial limit, Toronto service providers can only hope for the generosity of federal or provincial governments. This is not assured. Too often, when the cheque comes, it is not enough.

The 1978 *Immigration Act* also impacted Toronto in another important way. In addition to setting a goal for the number of immigrants who would enter Canada, the act also opened the door to easier entry of two specific classes of immigrant: business-class immigrants and refugees. Business-class immigrants are divided into several categories, including entrepreneur and investor classes. As part of their admissions process, possible entrepreneur-class immigrants were required to submit a business plan to Canadian authorities that offered promise of employing Canadians. Investor-class immigrants were required to show a net worth of $500 000 and be ready to invest half of that amount in a job-creating project. Some critics attacked the business immigrant scheme as little more than "Canadian citizenship for sale." Critics, however, ignore the fact that immigration has always been a vehicle for national economic development. From this perspective, adjusting the immigration system to favour those who will best serve Canadian business is not different in any meaningful way from the immigration system previously favouring immigrants who promised to prime the national economic pump with their professional training or unskilled labour.

In the years after the business category was initiated, entrepreneurial immigration jumped by 600 percent, and Toronto became a favoured destination for those seeking to tie immigration with financial investment. Among those business-class immigrants who came to Canada before 1997 were many from Hong Kong. With the then-impending Chinese takeover of the British colony, many Hong Kong business-people, looking for a safe haven for family and money, welcomed opportunities for capital investment in Toronto. Chinese immigration from mainland China, Taiwan, and the Chinese Diaspora so increased the previously small Toronto Chinese population that the Chinese now constitute the largest ethnic community in the Greater Toronto area, more than 500 000 strong.

THE REFUGEE ISSUE

The new 1978 *Immigration Act* also solidified Canada's international humanitarian commitment to refugee resettlement. Of course, Canada had previously accepted large numbers of refugees—displaced persons, Hungarians, Czechoslovakians, Ugandan Asians, Chileans—but each of these refugee movements was treated as a special case requiring special permission to enter Canada. Under the new immigration legislation this changed. Henceforth those who were "displaced or persecuted," those defined by the 1951 United Nations Convention on Refugees as having "a well-founded fear of persecution," would now be included as a class of immigrant eligible for admission to Canada, even though as individuals or as a group they might not meet Canada's strict selection standards.

The 1978 *Immigration Act*'s refugee provisions were quickly put to the test during the Vietnamese "boat people" crisis. Stirred by press and television reports of desperate refugees fleeing Vietnam by sea in tiny boats, sometimes hardly more than a crowded raft, pro-refugee sympathy in Canada took Ottawa by surprise. While some in government and among the larger civic society may have harboured private doubts about the wisdom of Canada accepting any large body of "boat people," influential public and media spokespersons demanded action. And, moved by compassion, all across Canada friend joined with friend, neighbour with neighbour, and church group with church group in applying to sponsor Vietnamese refugees.

Ottawa responded to these sponsorship requests with both humanity and dispatch. The government promised that it would work in concert with private sponsorship groups and match private sponsorships refugee for refugee. By the end of 1980 the government agreed to the admission of more than 60 000 Vietnamese, Cambodian, Laotians, and ethnic Chinese from Southeast Asia in a blend of government and private sponsorship programs unique in Canadian history. By the time this refugee crisis subsided, Canada could boast that it had the highest per capita "boat people" resettlement of any country. Toronto soon became home to the majority of these Southeast Asian refugees, adding yet another layer to the city's remarkable ethnic and racial mix.

Since the "boat people" episode, refugee admissions have continued to centre on Toronto, and refugees have emerged as a controversial part of Canada's immigration program. In 1980, at the height of the "boat people" crisis, slightly more than 28 percent of all immigrants admitted to Canada were refugees. During the subsequent ten years, the percentage hovered between 14 and 20 percent (Statistics Canada, 1990, p. 28). But the core of the controversy regarding refugees had little to do with the number of refugees admitted to Canada. That number moves up or down on a year-by-year basis depending on federal quota negotiations with the provinces and the state of international refugee problems. The big issue for government and the source of much heated public and media debate is inland applicants. Instead of being selected and processed abroad by Canadian authorities—as were the Vietnamese refugees—inland applicants are those who somehow arrive in Canada and claimed refugee status once they arrive. Canada does not select these refugees. They pick Canada, and Canada has to determine on a case-by-case basis whether or not an individual claimant is a legitimate refugee entitled to remain in Canada. From the beginning, these claimants arrived in Canada in unexpected numbers. Numbers soon overwhelmed the refugee determination process. It often took months or even a year or more before a claim was heard and a decision rendered. And until each claimant was individually assessed and either granted refugee status or not, the legal status of these people remained in limbo.

If the refugee backlog was a national problem, it was most problematic in Toronto. In Toronto, where so many refugee claimants waited for their refugee hearing, questions about the municipality's responsibilities to the refugees remained to be answered. Were they entitled to social assistance or municipal housing? If not, who would pay their living expenses until their status was decided? What about educating refugee children? Were children of refugee claimants entitled to be in public school before refugee status was decided? Again, who would pay the costs

—the federal government, the province, the municipal taxpayer, individual refugee claimants? Would claimants be allowed to work? And what would become of those eventually judged not to be legitimate refugees? Would they be sent home? Easier said than done. By making a refugee claim in Canada, a claimant was asserting that he or she had been persecuted at home. True or not, after making such a claim, how would claimants denied refugee status in Canada be received if deported back to their home country?

Even as the government was considering ways of tightening Canadian inland refugee procedures, the issue heated up still more. Two ships illegally stranded their respective refugee cargoes on Canadian shores in the dead of night—155 Tamils in Newfoundland in 1986 and 174 Sikhs in Nova Scotia in 1987. Refugee claims were not unknown in Newfoundland. Gander Airport, a regular refuelling stop for flights to and from eastern Europe to Cuba, was often the jump point for passengers requesting asylum in Canada. Nevertheless, the arrival of the Tamils was a surprise, and the Canadian public and media responded as much with curiosity as with concern. The landing of the Sikhs a year later raised the issue once again. Across Canada attention became riveted on the refugee issue as the media warned that boatloads of additional refugees might be on their way to Canada. Over the protest of those who warned against overreacting, Parliament was recalled and passed legislation that it hoped would slow the flow, including denying refugee status to individuals who had passed though another country, such as the United States, where a refugee claim might have been made. This move alone would sharply curtail the number of Latin American claimants who might be eligible for refugee status. However, this was not the end of Canada's effort to control the flow of inland refugee claimants. In 1992, in the midst of the sharpest economic slump since the 1930s, the government introduced yet another package of major revisions to the *Immigration Act*, making it still more difficult for inland refugee claimants to reach Canada or make refugee claims.

In spite of legislative and regulatory changes, refugees continued to arrive, many ending up in Toronto, and Canadian immigration and refugee policy continued to be a political hot potato. In the federal election of 1993, the Reform Party, parent of the current Alliance Party, fanned the flames of anti-immigrant and anti-refugee sentiment. While it is hard to know how much playing on concerns over immigration helped the Reform Party, Reform came out of the election only one seat shy of forming the official opposition. A measure of how immigration and refugee issues registered in Toronto where pluralism and refugee arrivals are a fact of life, was that the Reform Party came out of the 1993 election carrying zero ridings in the city and its suburbs. But if the Reform Party was frozen out of Toronto, its willingness to play on public anxiety over immigration and the party's suddenly powerful voice in Ottawa has given pause to those in Toronto who look to Ottawa for leadership and financial assistance in addressing municipal immigration and intergroup issues (Soberman, 1999).

In 1999, with Canada's refugee policy still a flashpoint of controversy, yet another refugee crisis exploded. Late in the summer of 1999 almost 400 illegal Chinese migrants, including women and children, were apprehended while smuggling themselves into British Columbia aboard three small and dangerously overcrowded vessels. The vessels' crews were arrested and charged with various violations of the Canadian *Criminal Code*. The migrants faced a different and uncertain future. Once in Canadian custody, most of the migrants claimed to be refugees fleeing persecution in China. In accord with established Canadian immigration procedures, a review process was set in motion to determine the legitimacy of each individual's claim. While the refugee determination process was fast tracked for these migrants, the process has been difficult and lengthy. It has also been controversial. The vast majority of those who have gone through the assessment process have been judged not to be legitimate refugees and, at this writing, are awaiting removal back to China.

Through the initial stages of this crisis, the media proved generally unsympathetic to the migrants but no more so than many Canadians. If radio talk shows and letters to the editor were in any way reflective of the public mind, the Chinese migrants sparked widespread Canadian anger not only at the migrants for attempting to smuggle themselves into Canada but also against the government for its seeming laxity in dealing with those who enter Canada illegally. Many feared that Canadian immigration and refugee regulations were little more than a sieve permitting almost everyone and anyone to slip into Canada. No other country, some charged, would stand for this kind of wholesale violation of its borders. If these illegal Chinese migrants were allowed to remain, they warned, Canada would become an international laughingstock. And to make matters worse, weren't Canadian tax dollars paying the bills to feed, house. and clothe these migrants, let alone pay for all the legal and administrative overhead involved in processing their refugee claims? Some charged that needy Canadians were being denied assistance while undeserving foreigners, illegal immigrants, were quick to get government handouts. While public and media attention gradually refocused elsewhere, the potential that immigration and refugee issues will again explode in the public eye always remains. The impact on Toronto will be direct.

THE GREAT PLURALIST EXPERIMENT: TORONTO IN THE 21ST CENTURY

The issue of refugee determination continues to smoulder, and large numbers of refugee and immigration arrivals create other issues that need to be addressed. In spite of thorny problems as the millennium dawned, the Canadian and local Toronto economy is very strong, and the flow of immigration into Canada and into the Greater Toronto area shows no signs of slowing. The extent of that immigration is not only measured in its numbers but also in its diversity and impact—an impact that not even the most far-seeing policy planner of an earlier era could have predicted. As both the hub of Canadian economic development and the gateway to Canada for most immigrants, Toronto is projected to remain a magnet for immigrants.

What has been the result? As noted, immigration has transformed and is transforming the city. Since World War II, the Toronto that was has given way to a city composed of numerous ethnic villages, an urban complex where ethnic and racial neighbourhoods nuzzle against one another in an overlapping pattern stretching from the inner city to the outer suburban ring. Some of these villages are characterized by single family homes while others are vertical villages, high-rise apartment complexes dominated by one or another ethnic or racial community. These villages are commonly served by ethnic shopping, business, and cultural areas where any one of many home languages or dialects coexist alongside English. Here one can find immigrants and their children negotiating a middle way between mainstream Canadian culture and a familiar culture of the homeland. It is immigrant children who often face the difficult task of walking these two roads at one time—one dominated by a richness of family and ethnic heritage and tradition and the other a road dominated by the signposts of school, popular culture, the marketplace, and the larger society.

With so great a pluralism of racial and ethnic communities in Toronto the potential for tension is also present. Nevertheless, the level of civic harmony in Toronto remains remarkably high. This is partly due to the hard work and sensitivity of city officials supported by the community at large. Municipal officials in Toronto, recognizing the potential for ethnic and racial misunderstanding, continue to seek ways of better adapting municipal services to the city's changing racial and ethnic reality. Important public notices are now being printed in a number of the more common languages spoken. In some parts of the city where immigrants who are not familiar with the Latin script have settled, public street signs are written in both English and the other language. And civic institutions are being forced to readjust as well. In order to stay on top of Toronto's ever-changing population mix, the police are redefining their role and image. Among other things, this has meant vigorous race sensitivity training for police officers and a determined program of minority hiring. The police are not alone. Other public institutions—the courts, social welfare agencies like children's aid societies, hospitals, libraries, and schools—are also determined to reflect the new reality of Toronto.

What is true of the public sector in Toronto is also increasingly true of the private sector. And it is proving good business. Banks, once thought of as a white, male Anglo-Saxon club, are determined to break that image both in their hiring policies and by delivering services in a culturally caring fashion. Many businesses make sure that they have translation services available as needed for those who are not yet comfortable in English. Even supermarket chains are responding. Stores are no longer carbon copies of one another. Instead, many are adapting to the ethnic character of their neighbourhoods by stocking food and consumer items that reflect the taste of the surrounding community.

For all this there remain areas of difficulty and even conflict. While Toronto can be described as a city of many ethnic villages, the boundaries between those villages are not fixed. As a new immigrant community begins to move into a more established neighbourhood, changing the existing racial or ethnic population balance, turf wars sometimes result. This phenomenon is as much a feature of the suburban ring around Toronto as it is of the inner city. For example, in Toronto's upmarket suburban northeast corridor, an infusion of often well-heeled Hong Kong immigrants in the early 1990s caused alarm among some in the previously dominant community. Disagreements erupted over how far high-profile community institutions should bend to reflect the incoming Chinese. When several large neighbourhood shopping centres adopted a Chinese-language sign policy, the reaction from some non-Chinese speakers was anger. Controversy also dogged new arrivals who purchased "tear down" homes on large lots and built what came to be called "monster homes" which, some charged, destroyed the character of the neighbourhood.

Closer to the city core, there have been confrontations and even shooting incidents involving police and youth, particularly black youth and so-called "Asian youth gangs." Problems can erupt even over small things. Recently, two Toronto neighbours settled a much-publicized dispute over the smell of ethnic cooking. One neighbour sued the other over what were claimed to be disagreeable cooking odours vented out of the kitchen of the other. While the problem was eventually resolved by an agreement to extend and redirect the kitchen vent, the whole affair was played out on a canvas of misunderstanding.

What of the future? What, for example will be the long-term impact of moves by the Harris government to downsize the public sector? Will it scuttle efforts, initiatives that cost money, to accommodate and integrate immigrants within the larger society? In the case of Toronto, the provincial government is downloading the cost of many services onto the municipality while siphoning educational dollars out of the city's schools to support schools in the rural ring around the city. Toronto, relying on its property tax base, is finding it increasingly difficult to sustain adequate level of services without driving up taxes to impossible levels. With less money come fewer services, and services essential to immigrant integration are not likely to escape the chopping block. Toronto schools, for example, have already cut back on programs of English as a second language for immigrant children, and language programs for adult learners have been eliminated almost completely. Low-end property rentals are disappearing just as financial support for refugee claimants is also being slashed, making affordable housing difficult to find. All the while, immigrant and refugee arrivals continue.

For all its problems and with all the potential for tension, Canada's largest city remains Canada's largest immigrant city. Indeed, nothing so defines Toronto as the breadth of its cultural and racial pluralism. And with immigration from around the world likely to continue as a feature shaping Toronto life for years to come, there is little doubt that this cultural and racial pluralism will be even more pronounced in the future.

REFERENCES

Abella, Irving, and Troper, Harold. (1982). *None is too many: Canada and the Jews of Europe, 1933–1948.* Toronto: Lester, Orpen and Dennys.

Bissoondath, Neil. (1994). *Selling illusions: The cult of multiculturalism in Canada.* Toronto: Penguin.

Burnet, Jean. (1976). Ethnicity: Canadian experience and policy. *Sociological Focus* 9, 199–207.

———. (1979). Myths and multiculturalism. *Canadian Journal of Education* 4, 43–98.

Dirks, Gerald. (1977). *Canada's refugee policy.* Montreal: McGill-Queens University Press.

Harney, Robert F., and Troper, Harold. (1975). *Immigrants: A portrait of the urban experience, 1890–1930.* Toronto: Van Nostrand Reinhold.

Harney, Nicholas DeMaria. (1998). *Eh, paesan! Being Italian in Toronto.* Toronto: University of Toronto Press.

House of Commons Debate. (1947, May 1). 2644–47.

Iacovetta, Franca. (1992). *Such hardworking people: Italians in postwar Toronto.* Montreal and Kingston: McGill-Queen's University Press.

Kelley, Ninette, and Trebilcock, Michael. (1998). *The making of the mosaic: A history of Canadian immigration policy.* Toronto: University of Toronto Press.

Martin, Paul. (1983). *A very public life: Far from home.* Ottawa: Deneau.

Orenstein, Micheal. (2000). *Ethno-racial inequality in the City of Toronto: An analysis of the 1996 census.* Toronto: Access and Equality Centre.

Paterson, William. (1955). *Planned migration: The social determinants of the Dutch-Canadian movement.* Berkeley: University of California Press.

Richmond, Anthony H. (1967). *Post-war immigrants in Canada.* Toronto: University of Toronto Press.

Statistics Canada. (1990). *Immigrants in Canada: Selected highlights.* Ottawa: Statistics Canada.

Soberman, Liane. (1999). Immigration and the Canadian federal election of 1993: The press as a political educator. In Harold Troper and Morton Weinfeld (Eds.), *Ethnicity, politics and public policy: Case studies in Canadian diversity* (252–81). Toronto: University of Toronto Press.

Sunahara, Ann. (1981). T*he politics of racism: The uprooting of Japanese Canadians during the Second World War.* Toronto: Lorimer.

Troper, Harold. (1987). Jews and Canadian immigration policy: 1900-1950. In Moses Ruskin (Ed.), *The Jews of North America* (44–61). Detroit: Wayne State Press.

FURTHER READING

Breton, Raymond, Isajiw, Wsevolod, Kalbach, Warren, and Reitz, Jeffrey. (1990). *Ethnic identity and equality: Varieties of experience in a Canadian city.* Toronto: University of Toronto Press.

Burnet, Jean, and Howard Palmer. (1988). *Coming Canadians: An introduction to a history of Canada's peoples.* Toronto: McClelland and Stewart.

Henry, Francis, Tator, Carol, Mattis, Winston, and Rees, Tim. (1995). *The colour of democracy: Racism in Canadian society.* Toronto: Harcourt Brace.

Troper, Harold, and Weinfeld, Morton (Eds.). (1999). *Ethnicity, politics and public policy.* Toronto: University of Toronto Press.

Whitaker, Reg. (1987). *Double standard: The secret history of Canadian immigration.* Toronto: Lester & Orpen Dennys.

Revolutionaries out of Ontario: The Mike Harris Government and Canada

Reg Whitaker

In 1995 the Conservative party under Mike Harris won a majority government in Ontario. There seemed nothing remarkable about this. After all, the Conservatives had governed Ontario from 1943 until 1985, an extraordinary unbroken run of 42 years. After brief turns of the Liberals (1985–90) and the New Democratic party (1990–95) in provincial office, the Tories were back in their accustomed place of power at Queen's Park.

Any idea that this was just a return to business as usual was quickly shattered. The Tories of the past were cautious, pragmatic moderates who governed firmly from the centre. The 1990s-version Tories came armed with an ideological text called "The Common Sense Revolution" (CSR), and they were determined to impose their blueprint on the province. Tories of the past were accommodative, given to compromise, and fond of forging a broad consensus around their policies. The new Tories were confrontational, uncompromising, and disdainful of opposition, indifferent to the bitter divisions they were opening up in Ontario society. The old Tories had built modern Ontario, including the basis of the welfare state, and were protective of the fabric of the society they had helped fashion. The Harris Tories were convinced that the system was broken and needed revolutionary restructuring.

Within the first few years of their mandate, the Harris Conservatives had bulldozed over opposition to bring in a sweeping series of reforms the speed and scope of which few provinces have ever seen. Ontario was transformed in the eyes of the rest of Canada from the placid, complacent industrial heartland to a site of violent protests, general strikes, and a level of political vituperation that seemed almost "un-Canadian." Ontario had spawned a (counter)revolution, and the rest of the country was watching closely.

Re-elected to a second consecutive majority in 1999, the Harris government began its next mandate with somewhat diminished revolutionary fervour and perhaps more concern to consolidate and digest the reforms and restructuring of its first four years. We can now pause, along with the government and take measure of the changes wrought in the name of the CSR, and their implications and ramifications for the rest of the country.

I would like to pose two questions: first, what is new in the Ontario Tory experiment. Second, what is likely to be lasting about the CSR reforms? The answer to the first question can be divided into a number of areas: first, innovative uses of the party as a vehicle; second, innovation in political marketing; third, the shift to programmatic as opposed to pragmatic, brokerage politics; fourth, a new style and method of governing; fifth, the reorientation of Ontario from a historic east–west Canadian federal alignment to a north–south North American regional alignment; and sixth, the degree to which the changes in Ontario may be reflected in new political directions at the national level.

FROM PARTY TO "VIRTUAL" PARTY

In recent years, political parties in Canada have been "shape-shifting." Once organizations with structure, hierarchy, sharply defined organizational boundaries, and continuity over time, they have been transforming into "virtual" parties. Like "virtual" corporations in the networked information economy, virtual parties form and reform for specific purposes. With more tasks "outsourced" and fewer done in-house, the virtual party networks across traditional organizational boundaries, drawing in specialists who perform specific functions to meet specific, market-driven needs. Virtual parties form around politicians seeking the leadership of parties as relatively small entourages or coteries of political strategists, marketing and communications experts, "spin doctors," PR flacks, policy "wonks." If successful, the same coterie then colonizes the party and runs the subsequent election campaign. The party, as such, serves as little more than a convenient franchise with brand recognition, marketing "location," and ready source of campaign funding. Sometimes it is more convenient to "re-brand" the old party for better location. The real campaign dynamic derives from the virtual party within the shell of the traditional party. If the electoral campaign is successful, the virtual party then colonizes the strategic heights of government itself, around the office of the prime minister or premier, setting policy priorities, interfacing with the permanent bureaucracy and managing the government's image and media presentation. All this is dependent upon the leader, who is the product being marketed (Noel, 1996).

Nowhere has the "virtual" party been better illustrated than by the small group of young activists who formed to back the leadership candidacy of Mike Harris, the Tory MPP from North Bay, in 1990. In the years following its traumatic defeat in 1985, the party was "hollowed out, broke, leaderless" (Ibbitson, 1997, p. 39). This represented an opportunity for ideologically committed young right wingers to seize the party franchise. The Ontario Tories had been known and feared for the "Big Blue Machine," the Conservative party organization that raised lavish funds from Bay Street, ran one successful electoral campaign after another, and then discreetly and efficiently managed the patronage that came with seemingly perpetual political power. The Big Blue Machine was now defunct, the party a shell that could be taken over. Moreover, the moderate "Red Tory" policy orientation of the past could be discarded and replaced with a hard right neoconservatism. Mike Harris, an affable yet ambitious MPP with few ties to the crumbling party establishment, was the young Turks' chosen instrument (Woolstencroft, 1997).

The first run was unpromising. Liberal premier David Peterson called what many Ontarians considered an unnecessarily early election just two months after Harris took over his party's leadership. Neither Harris nor his handlers were prepared, and they were woefully short of cash to run the kind of media campaign that would make Harris known to the voters. Nor did they have a platform, apart from a promise to cut taxes. The PCs finished last, with less than a quarter of the popular votes. The surprise winner was Bob Rae's New Democrats.

If the young neoconservatives who had taken over the Tory franchise seemed to have lost the first round to left-wing opponents, in reality the stage was being set for eventual triumph. An untried and inexperienced social democratic party was coming to office just as Ontario slipped into a very serious recession. Handcuffed by ballooning deficits and shaken by the implacable hostility of business, the NDP were unable to deliver on their promises of better social programs. By the end of their mandate, the NDP had become locked in a bitter conflict with the public sector unions—normally NDP supporters—over the "Social Contract," which imposed restraint on public employees. Many union supporters of the NDP simply sat out the subsequent election; at the same time, the NDP's move to the right won it no new friends in business. The Harris Conservatives not only profited from the debacle of Ontario "socialism" but also took due note of the disastrous effects on a party of alienating its own core supporters. This was a mistake they would never make.

FROM MASS TO NICHE MARKETING

New media and new information technologies have been shifting consumer marketing strategies from the mass marketing of mass production products to niche or "micro" marketing of products and services more closely tailored to the consumption profiles of identifiable groups. While this trend has been proceeding in the private sector for some time, it was the Harris Tories who, more than any other political party in Canada, appropriated these techniques for political campaigning. The Harrisites set out in the early 1990s to identify their core potential political markets throughout the province. Partly the choice was negative: which groups were most distressed and outraged by the NDP and by the relatively free-spending Liberals who had preceded the NDP? But the marketing genius of the Harrisites was to fashion a positive program to speak specifically to the needs of their potential voters. Thus the CSR was crafted to offer potential buyers precisely what they wanted from Queen's Park: less government, lower taxes, fiscal responsibility, an Ontario that was once again open for business, and a sharp back of the hand to all those groups perceived as having their fingers in the taxpayers' pockets. These groups included labour unions, welfare recipients, Aboriginal, ethnic, feminist, and other minority groups, unruly youth, and overprivileged elites on the public payroll and insulated from the free market, like bureaucrats, teachers, and professors. Upper-middle income earners in the private sector, especially in the smaller urban centres and the large "905" suburban belt around Toronto (Dale, 1999), skilled workers, and older and more rural Ontarians, were all prime targets as potential voters. The typical Tory voter was more likely male than female, more likely white than a visible minority, and generally better off than the average—although suffering considerable anxiety about his family's economic security, and very worried about crime, disorder, and the declining moral fibre of society. All these are familiar ingredients of conservative populism. What distinguished the Harrisites was not only their effective identification of their potential markets but also the sophistication with which they devised policies targeted specifically at the buyers.

Having put together a sufficient number of these market niches to assemble a winning coalition in 1995, the PCs were very careful in office to deliver the policies and programs they had promised their voters, thus retaining their fidelity in their re-election campaign in 1999. Unlike the NDP, which had alienated its core supporters, the Harris Tories have been assiduous in constantly steering government actions in the direction of pleasing their core constituents. Although presented as in the "public interest," Tory policies have always had very specific political markets as their targets. All parties of course try to do this, but few have been as single-minded or as efficient as the Harris Tories. The secret of their success has been that in practice they recognize that the "public" is divided, that the "public interest," as such, is a chimera, and that their political success comes from identifying, targeting, and delivering to *their* Ontario.

In the 1980s, the Reagan Republicans fashioned a political model in which they energized their own upper-income constituents with designer public policies, while enervating and disorganizing their Democratic opponents' potential supporters. The result was an overall low voter turnout but a relatively high voting rate by Republicans. Precisely the same scenario has characterized Ontario in the 1995 and 1999 elections: overall participation rates have fallen to their lowest levels ever, but core Harris constituents turned out in larger numbers than their Liberal and NDP counterparts, who divided the anti-Harris vote. This is symptomatic of a successful niche marketing strategy, albeit dubious from the point of view of healthy democracy, as just 26 percent of eligible voters produced a majority government.[1] When over two out of five citizens do not vote, and the opposition is divided between two relatively large parties, one quarter of the citizenry can produce an effective mandate for government. So long as they can retain their core constituencies, the Tories can afford to ignore or at least downplay the interests of the other three-quarters of Ontarians.

FROM PRAGMATIC TO PROGRAMMATIC POLITICS

The Harris marketing strategy was so successful because his handlers realized that selling a personality was not enough. The personality was just the recognizable face that was placed on a programmatic approach to politics. To a degree this shift from pragmatic to programmatic politics simply mirrors changes that were going on at the federal level in the 1990s with the decline of the brokerage-style Progressive Conservatives and the rise of the relatively programmatic Bloc Québécois and Reform parties (Whitaker, 1997). The Reform party and its successor, the Canadian Alliance, have stressed the importance of a clearly articulated program, which has been spelled out in detail and widely circulated prior to elections. Even the very pragmatic Liberal party released its *Red Book* of policy promises prior to the 1993 and 1997 elections. The Tory policy document, the *Common Sense Revolution*, that preceded Harris's first election victory is distinguished by its powerful and consistent ideological tone and by the strong commitment of the Harris government to actually implement its promises as fully as possible. The CSR is no pluralist grab bag of promises to all but a decisively conservative ideological construction, a blueprint for change (in fact the 1999 follow-up document was called exactly that, *Blueprint*). The Liberal record of implementation of its *Red Book* promises is spotty at best, and the document proved no guide at all to the main agenda of the first Chrétien government, Finance Minister Paul Martin's deficit elimination priority. The CSR on the other hand spelled out a Tory program that the Tories proved very energetic and attentive in implementing.

The salient features of the CSR can be broken down into six broad categories:

1. 30 percent provincial income tax cut
2. 20 percent cut in "non-priority" government spending
3. Reduce barriers to job creation, investment, growth
4. Spend "smarter"
5. Balance the budget
6. Create jobs (750 000 in first mandate)

Category 2 on spending cuts can be further subdivided into subcategories:

2a. Fewer and cheaper politicians

2b. 15 percent cut in number of bureaucrats

2c. Cut welfare and introduce "workfare"

2d. Reduce spending on and restructure education

2e. Eliminate or reform wasteful government programs

2f. Protect priority areas: health, law enforcement

There were numerous detailed specifications within these categories, including some that were to prove major undertakings, such as a promise under (4) to "de-layer" government, leading to municipal amalgamation plans, or the restructuring of school boards under (2d). Some of the promises were purely negative, such as the repeal of the NDP government's labour and employment equity laws, which was quickly accomplished. Many of the others would require a sharp change in direction in Ontario traditions and practices (most of them rooted in former Conservative governments), some major restructuring of the institutional framework of the province, and the inevitable reaction and resistance of major entrenched interest groups, especially the trade unions representing public sector workers and teachers.

The CSR generally resembles the so-called "neo-liberal" agendas associated with the Reagan and Gingrich Republicans in the U.S., or the Thatcher Tories in Britain (Ralph et al,. 1997). It appears that the architects of the CSR were especially drawn to Republican administrations in certain eastern U.S. industrial states such as New Jersey and Michigan in looking for immediate models. However, there are some distinctive features as well. Notably absent from the CSR was any mention of the kind of "moral" or Christian Right issues associated with the social conservatism that coexist beside neoliberal economics among U.S. Republicans, or among some Canadian Alliance members and supporters. The Harris governments have in fact steered well clear of such hot-button moral issues as abortion or homosexuality, thus distinguishing themselves sharply from their U.S. counterparts. Also distinctive was the top priority accorded tax cuts, which were seen as the centrepiece of the CSR. It might also be noted that the leader of the British Tories, knocked out of office by "New Labour" in 1997 and casting about for an ideological *raison d'être*, actually came on a pilgrimage to Ontario and took back parts of the CSR to incorporate into British Tory policy. Thus, even if inspired by foreign models in the first instance, the CSR has itself become a sort of model to be emulated elsewhere.

Another distinctive feature of the CSR was its clarity and its wide dissemination as an explicit guide to what could be expected from a Harris government. Neither Reagan nor Thatcher presented voters with such a categorical and detailed set of promises. The Gingrich Republicans who took control of the U.S. Congress in the mid-1990s did promote a detailed "Contract with America," but they were simply dominant in the legislative branch, not in control of the executive. Not only did the Harrisites present the public with their program in advance, but they were relatively tenacious in putting their promises into action, and provided a report card to voters on their record when they sought re-election in 1999. Given their track record, voters were inclined to believe that their re-election promises could be taken seriously. Thus when the Liberals and NDP dismissed the Tory 1999 promise to spend more on health care as deceitful, voters were more inclined to take the Tories at their word. This kind of programmatic politics pays a particular dividend in a climate in which voters have become increasingly distrustful and cynical about politicians and their promises. Whether one agreed with them or not, the Harris Tories were widely seen as trustworthy, no small matter in an age of political cynicism.

During the first Harris mandate, polls showed that the public reacted in variable ways to the changes that were being imposed so forcefully. Not surprisingly, some groups reacted sharply, especially those who felt themselves to be the targets of the CSR. However, there was apparent consistency on one point: when asked if the government was "on the right track," a majority of respondents always answered in the affirmative.[2] In other words, even when people felt threatened by particular policies in the CSR, they were still inclined to grant that the CSR was generally on the right track, despite the deep divisions the Tory program was opening up in Ontario society. To understand how the CSR has struck such remarkable resonance in Ontario, we might look to the specific context of the Harris victory in 1995.

After 42 years of uninterrupted Tory rule, Ontario went through a decade from 1985 to 1995 in which both opposition parties had a turn at government. The Liberals initiated what Courchene has called Ontario's "Quiet Revolution" (Courchene, 1998, pp. 70–121). The social agenda was significantly expanded. Unfortunately for the Liberals, this coincided with a sharp downturn in federal transfer payments, especially the "cap" imposed by Ottawa on CAP (the Canada Assistance Program), which had the effect of treating Ontario inequitably in relation to other provinces. Inevitably, taxes rose in Ontario, and by the end of Liberal rule in 1990 a substantial deficit awaited the NDP. The latter came to office with a social democratic agenda at precisely the moment when the Ontario economy was entering its most serious postwar recession. While unable to implement many of their promises to their supporters, they found themselves sucked into a "fiscalamity" (Courchene, 1998, pp. 122–68). The first NDP budget registered a record high deficit of close to $10 billion. By the end of the NDP mandate, the cumulative provincial debt was over $100 billion, with more than $8 billion per year allocated to debt servicing alone. This coincided with a broad shift in Canadian public opinion to identify deficits and public debt as a major, if not the major, public policy problem facing both federal and provincial governments. The NDP could be portrayed as profligate and fiscally irresponsible, and the loss of jobs and drying up of investment that accompanied the recession (which, in fact may have had little directly to do with the NDP, as such) was widely attributed, especially by a hostile Bay Street, to the NDP's "socialist" policies. Ironically, NDP supporters were angered by the government's failure to implement even the mild social democratic promises of their campaign.

The NDP responded to this crisis in part by challenging Ottawa to rewrite the rules of fiscal federalism to remove Ontario's penalization ("Fair Shares Federalism"), a campaign that failed. The other response was to restrict the earnings of public sector workers, which alienated supporters at the same time as it failed to attract non-supporters to the government. The NDP did attempt to implement parts of its agenda that did not carry a high price tag. Two pieces of legislation in particular, a revised and liberalized labour law and an *Employment Equity Act,* did bear a distinctive NDP stamp. But these fit into a right-wing stereotype of special legislation targeted to "special interests," trade unions in the one case and women, ethnic minorities, Aboriginals, and people with disabilities in the other. Repeal of these laws was an explicit promise of the CSR. Rightly or wrongly, this image of left-wing bureaucrats favouring special interests over the taxpaying majority did seem to strike a chord with many voters—certainly among those targeted by the Tories.

In other words, there was never a better time and place for constructing a right-wing populist constituency for a radical conservative program to roll back a decade of Liberal and NDP policies. Economic recession and decline were identified with both the other parties. But the CSR message was that to get back to the old Tory days of postwar prosperity and sound economic management it would first be necessary to destroy the entire edifice of "leftist" mismanagement of the past ten years. "The system," the Tories said in 1995, "is broken." The restoration of conservatism required revolutionary reconstruction. And the economic and political circumstances of the mid-1990s commended this radical course to a large number of Ontarians.

If the circumstances conspired to advance a programmatic politics in 1995, economic developments during the first Harris government seemed to confirm that the new directions of the CSR were indeed on the right track. The Ontario economy turned around dramatically. Unemployment fell, plant shutdowns slowed while new investment poured in, and Ontario once again assumed its normal role as the leading engine of growth in Canada. Premier Harris was quick to argue in 1999 that "Ontario's turnaround in the past four years didn't happen by accident. Thanks to some key decisions we were able to get rid of the roadblocks that held us back" (Harris, 1999). Chief among these roadblocks was seen to be high provincial income tax rates, which the Tories slashed by 30 percent. As the centrepiece of the CSR, tax cuts were accorded major credit by the Tories for the economic recovery. Economists questioned the causality of this link and noted that the Ontario recovery was mainly being driven by the boom in the U.S. economy to the south. No matter, the simple equation of "tax cuts = prosperity" was a powerful message to the public. Moreover, it strongly reinforced the basic ideological thrust of the CSR: what was good for the individual pocketbooks of taxpayers (especially the upper-middle and upper income earners who reaped the main benefit of percentage cuts on higher incomes, and who disproportionately voted Conservative) was good for the health of the Ontario economy in general. Left-wing critics argued that the cost of the tax cuts was being borne by the poorest and most vulnerable members of society through the slashing of welfare costs and social programs that was the other side of the CSR. The Tory response was to reiterate the traditional argument that a rising tide lifts all boats, at least after short-term adjustments.

The emphasis on tax cuts tended to undermine somewhat the fiscal conservatism of the CSR. The promise of deficit reduction was placed in effect on the backburner. The federal Liberal government, which inherited from its Conservative predecessor an even more alarming fiscal position, was able to move into a surplus position at the outset of its second term. Even some poor provinces, like Newfoundland and Saskatchewan (under Liberal and NDP governments), were able to rid themselves of deficits. Only in their second term have the Harris Tories been able to put the provincial finances in balance. This tardiness is of course attributable to the fall in revenues generated by tax cuts. In effect, the CSR paid for tax cuts through borrowing. Although this might seem suspicious to hard-line fiscal conservatives, it has elicited remarkably little critical comment from the business community.

The persistence of a deficit permitted a tough position on spending cuts. The Harrisites will now fall victim to their own success and lose the protection offered by deficits. With the province moving into a surplus position, they will have to revert to being brokers of demands from various sectors for new programs and improved funding of existing programs. Moreover, a province with a surplus finds itself more handicapped in making demands of Ottawa for increased transfers. Indeed, as if in anticipation, the 1999 successor to the CSR, *Blueprint*, specifies a "guaranteed 20% increase in health care funding," "guaranteed funding" in education, and a $20 billion "SuperBuild" growth fund to renew infrastructure networks for hospitals, schools and universities, and highways (Harris, 1999).

Although *Blueprint* speaks about "an end to red ink and waste" in government and promises to further reform the welfare system by refocusing on workfare and retraining, most of its bows in the direction of neoconservative thinking tend to the symbolic, with low price tags, such as promises to institute school uniforms and strict conduct codes for students, and the highly publicized aim of driving so-called "squeegee kids" off the streets of Toronto. In short, moving into Harris's second term and into a new era of relative prosperity and fuller government coffers, the CSR has begun to lose the sharp ideological edge it possessed when the Tories were outsiders storming Queen's Park. Running against government is a program best suited to right-wing radicals unencumbered by a record in office. The longer they remain in office, the less credible an antigovernment agenda appears. In this sense the CSR was perhaps a self-limiting revolution. Nevertheless, it remains a remarkable example of relatively uncompromising programmatic politics.

CONFRONTATION OVER CONSENSUS

From the moment they assumed the reins of government in 1995, there was no mistaking the revolutionary intent of the Harris Tories. The Harris style was uncompromising and confrontational and even seemed to actively avoid consensus building.

Steamrolling the opposition was made easier by a smooth and efficient transition from the NDP to the PCs (White, 1997). The Harrisites hit the ground running. Less than a month after assuming office, and well before the first meeting of the legislature, the Tories lopped a whopping $1.9 billion off provincial spending. A thorough fiscal review laid the necessary groundwork and caught the major interest groups unprepared. The promised tax cuts followed, staged over the life of the government. As well as the 30 percent personal income tax cut, the new government also moved to slash payroll taxes on employers, seen as a barrier to investment and growth.

Those on social welfare felt the immediate impact: welfare benefits were slashed by 21.6 percent. Controversy erupted over the effects on the poor. Opponents tied this to the tax cuts, arguing that the CSR was being financed on the backs of the poor. To show how serious they were about restructuring, the government in the fall of 1995 rammed the so-called "Omnibus Bill" through the legislature, which gave the cabinet powers to impose restructuring on municipalities and school boards and abolish various provincial agencies and authorities without recourse to the legislature. Courchene finds it "passing strange" that an anti–big government party should "enact legislation that put their own decisions beyond the reach of traditional democratic processes" (Courchene, 1998, p. 203). Administratively, Harris centralized political control of the bureaucracy. The cabinet secretary, Rita Burak, was designated by the premier as the sole channel through which the deputy ministers could communicate to the cabinet. This centralization facilitated the policy influence of the premier's office, staffed by the CSR backroom boys and girls. Sometimes the pace of the CSR meant that the government was running ahead of the capacity of the bureaucrats to lay the administrative groundwork for the avalanche of changes. The Tories generally pressed on regardless.

Early in January 1997, the government launched the second wave of the CSR, an extraordinary series of initiatives dubbed "Megaweek." This involved the following elements (Courchene, 1998, pp. 198–209):

1. Structural reorganization of education, removing education costs from the property tax base, and slashing the number of school boards by more than half and the number of school trustees by almost two-thirds.

2. Reorganization of welfare responsibility toward 50/50 cost-sharing between provinces and municipalities; responsibility for child care, social housing, many public health programs, and ambulance services transferred to municipalities, while Children's Aid societies and women's shelters would be funded by the province.

3. Massive shifts in responsibility from the province to municipalities in a series of areas, including policing, public transit, water, and sewage.

4. Property taxes to be reassessed on market value; municipalities to have more freedom to set commercial rates to attract business, while province eliminates $1.6 billion Business Occupancy Tax.

In the end, the government compromised with the municipalities on revenue restructuring, which was no doubt wise given the inevitable unanticipated consequences of such massive change. Despite this uncharacteristic indication of willingness to negotiate change, the Tories did achieve much of the CSR's projected "rationalization" of government. Some of the unanticipated effects of these rapid changes, taken as they were with much administrative improvisation, may come back to haunt the Conservatives. In the spring of 2000, e-coli bacteria contaminated the municipal water supply of the town of Walkerton, resulting in a number of deaths. Many blamed privatization of water testing and the shunting of responsibility from the ministry of the environment onto a municipality that was unprepared for the task of safeguarding the water supply. An official inquiry was established to assess responsibility for the tragedy. But Walkerton is just one of a number of time bombs that may go off in the future before the administrative infrastructure is properly in place for the new divisions of responsibility.

Compromise and caution were certainly not on the Harris agenda for the biggest change of all its municipal restructuring projects: the amalgamation of the city of Toronto with a number of suburban municipalities to form a "megacity" of some 3 000 000 people. Bitterly opposed by all the municipal governments involved, and apparently deeply unpopular with local voters, amalgamation was pursued with fierce and uncompromising determination by Queen's Park. Local referenda were called by municipal councils in which voters registered opposition by large margins: the Tories merely shrugged and went on with it. A local paper depicted the minister of municipal affairs as a "Borg" from *StarTrek* intoning: "Resistance is futile, you will be amalgamated." And so they were.

While the administrative rationale for amalgamation comes right out of the CSR, the long-term consequences of this transformation may not necessarily be to the liking of the Tories. A "megacity" now elects a "megamayor" with a direct mandate from 3 000 000 citizens—considerably more than the direct electoral mandate of the premier of the province, whose own votes come from a single constituency. The new Toronto may well in future begin to wield its considerable weight (political, but also economic as an emerging "world-class" metropolis), to the acute discomfort of provincial governments.

If the Tories hit the ground running in 1995, their opponents were also quickly off the mark, as soon as the seriousness of the CSR program became apparent. However, protest against the government slipped out of the hands of the parliamentary opposition parties, both of which sought new leaders following poor electoral performances. The Liberals had no alternative program to the CSR, while the NDP, still disoriented from their humiliating rejection by the voters, had themselves while in office alienated many of the groups, especially the unions, which now were feeling the brunt of the Tory program. The result was a relative vacuum in the parliamentary opposition and its displacement outside parliament.

One of the first tests Harris faced was a strike in early 1996 by OPSEU, the provincial government employees' union. For five weeks, striking public servants tried to shut down the provincial government sometimes clashing violently with provincial police. The strike was mainly about job security, which was a forlorn hope in the era of the CSR: within a year of the strike's end, 11 500 jobs had been eliminated (Ibbitson, 1997, p. 177). Later, teachers' strikes were launched against government plans to restructure the schools. Even though angry teachers successfully targeted the minister for personal defeat in 1999, they won few of their points. Labour protests were organized under a coordinated series of "days of action" held in different urban centres across Ontario, culminating in a massive two-day protest in Toronto, the first given to one-day strikes and the second to a huge parade of protestors through the downtown, culminating in a mass rally. These protests attempted, with some success, to mobilize not only public and private sector unionized workers but also a panoply of other groups, from various social movements, churches, welfare and poor peoples groups, feminists, environmentalists, gays and lesbians, etc. Yet for all the feelings of solidarity and common cause that may have been forged, after the Toronto culmination the protests lost all direction and momentum and petered out. Even the hope of a parliamentary riposte to the CSR came to an abrupt halt with the Harris government's relatively easy re-election victory in 1999 (the Tories actually increased their share of the popular vote over 1995).

Looking back over the rise and fall of protests in the streets against the CSR, it is hard to escape the sense that the main beneficiaries of extra-parliamentary protest were the Tories themselves. The Tories were ready and able to outlast and exhaust their opponents. They were able to do this because they knew that the public broadly supported the main objectives of the CSR and wanted the government to continue on the "right track." Opponents were "special interests," the enemies of the public interest, an equation made manifest by the group-based nature of the extra-parliamentary protest movements. Even more pointedly, the Tories understood that their opponents were never going to vote for them anyway. Their constituents, whom they had very carefully identified and targeted and for whom they had tailored their policies, were grateful to the government and deeply resentful of the "special interests" as having hijacked the taxpayers' money during the NDP and Liberal era. The more the protestors demonstrated, the more the core Harris constituencies were confirmed in their resolve to enable the government to see the CSR through. To Harris supporters in the suburbs and smaller towns and rural areas, it was a case of "know (and love) them for their enemies." In any event, none of the protest momentum was transferred to one of the opposition parties in the legislature, where division continued. With the Harris constituencies united, and the opposition divided, government by confrontation proved politically effective for the Tories.

In the 1999 election, the labour movement tried to encourage "strategic voting," whereby anti-Tory votes in local contests would be directed to whichever opposition candidate was better positioned to win. There is little evidence that this strategy actually paid off. Worse, given the policy differences between the Liberals and the NDP, the anti-Tory front was purely negative, an ideological vacuum set against a government with a clear program.

It is important to recognize the innovative nature of the Harris Tory party. Long-time observers of Ontario party politics were puzzled by the Tory enthusiasm for restructuring the very institutions that had been the basis for Conservative organization in the past. For example, the sharp reduction in the number of school boards and elected school trustees seemed to undermine one of the traditional career paths for Tory politicians, who often began as local trustees, graduating to council office and finally to MPP nominations. But the "virtual" Tory party has no need of this antiquated patronage structure. Now it is all media image management, effective niche marketing, spin doctoring, and shaping policies to market demands. Programmatic politics and confrontational government sold.

Given the popularity of the CSR program with business, the Tory party in office became a mighty engine for corporate fund-raising (MacDermid, 1999a). Between and during election campaigns, the Tories raised many times more dollars than their opponents, both of whom ended their 1999 campaign millions in debt (MacDermid, 1999b).

Even more interesting was what the Tories concentrated their money on: television advertising and polling. In fact, the Harris party has pioneered a new kind of perpetual media campaign. Even between elections a constant barrage of TV and radio ads communicate the Tory message. Moreover, borrowing from their American cousins, the Tories also tend to target attack ads against their opponents. For instance, even before the opening of the 1999 campaign, a series of TV ads attacked Liberal leader Dalton McGuinty. McGuinty suffered from low name recognition among voters; the Tories seized the opportunity to define him negatively in voters' minds before the Liberals could even get their own campaign in gear. It worked.

FROM EAST—WEST TO NORTH—SOUTH?

Traditionally, Ontario has been the industrial heartland of Canada and the key link in the east–west alignment of the economy since the National Policy of the late 19th century. This has not always pleased other regions, which have often felt that Ontario smugly expresses its own interest in self-serving "national" terms. A few years ago, an Ontario cabinet minister incautiously blurted out that "what's good for Ontario is good for Canada."

Ontario premiers have sought to play the role of the "statesmen of confederation," especially with regard to the tensions between Quebec and the rest of Canada since the 1960s. Former Tory Premier Bill Davis was one of only two premiers who supported Pierre Trudeau in the patriation of the *Constitution* in the early 1980s. Liberal Premier David Peterson strongly supported the Meech Lake accord, and NDP Premier Bob Rae was a leading actor in the Charlottetown process. Mike Harris has shown little inclination to play a leading or even active role in relation to the constitutional issues that followed the Quebec referendum on sovereignty in 1995. On the other hand, unlike his Liberal and NDP predecessors, Harris unreservedly welcomes free trade with the United States, the NAFTA treaty, and more generally the forces of economic globalization. This suggests a reorientation away from the old east–west alignment of confederation toward a new north–south continental focus.

In 1998 Thomas Courchene authored the provocative thesis that Ontario was moving away from its position as the Canadian heartland and becoming a North American "region-state" (Courchene, 1998). By 1994, 90 percent of Ontario's exports were to the United States, and Ontario ranked as the United States' second-largest trading partner. Ontario is strategically located at the heart of North American consumer and industrial markets, as well as the transportation and communication networks. Courchene argues that the CSR could be interpreted as a more or less systematic strategy for building this region-state and for penetrating the North American market. He further argues that the Harris government's actual role in Canadian federalism—focusing on maximizing fiscal autonomy and seeking transfer of economic powers to the provinces—could best be understood as disentangling itself from many of its traditional federal obligations in order to maximize Ontario's leverage on the continental stage.

The Courchene thesis has generated much comment and debate (IRPP, 2000). While it is unclear to what degree the CSR was actually driven by the kind of strategy Courchene describes, and to what extent it was driven by narrower ideological concerns, there is some considerable "fit" between its policy prescriptions and a North American regionalist role for Ontario. The pollination of policy ideas and political strategies from U.S. Republican sources, especially those states regionally linked to Ontario like Michigan and New Jersey, also speaks to this north–south alignment. To the extent that this shift is correctly described, the very thoroughness of the CSR suggests that any future attempt by other parties to change this north–south orientation will be difficult. That may be one of the lasting legacies of the CSR.

EXPORTING THE REVOLUTION?

The final question about the CSR is whether, or to what degree, this revolution is exportable to the rest of Canada. If Ontario is really becoming a powerful new North American region-state, perhaps the CSR is an ideology that will not be exportable to other, less economically favoured, regions.

Yet Ontarians have not in fact demonstrated a notable sense of estrangement from the national political culture nor shown much willingness to pursue any go-it-alone strategy (Wiseman, 2000). While Ontario voters have bestowed two successive provincial mandates on the right-wing Tories, they have also given two overwhelming mandates in federal elections to the centrist Liberals (who have held almost every seat in Ontario since 1993). The Liberals have often been criticized for allegedly failing to attend closely to the specific needs of what is now their national electoral stronghold. Yet Ontario voters appear indifferent to such criticism, continuing to lavish high levels of approval on a Chrétien government that addresses national, and Quebec, issues with more attention than regional Ontario concerns. Indeed, the federal Liberals have consistently fared better with Ontario voters than have the provincial Tories. Ontarians, it would appear, are content to act in provincial politics from a provincial perspective but in national politics from a national perspective. If the CSR represents an emergent Ontario region-state, that regionalism has not yet translated onto the national stage, as indeed the regional concerns of the West have translated into support for the Reform/Canadian Alliance party, and Quebec nationalism has translated into francophone support for the Bloc Québécois.

Premier Mike Harris has tended to avoid any partisan commitments in national politics; "not my problem," he once tersely rebuffed media questions on the subject. During Harris's first term, he was reluctant to engage in "Ottawa-bashing," even though his NDP predecessor had freely criticized Ottawa for unfair treatment of the province. Prime Minister Chrétien and Premier Harris have shown that they can work with one another when it is mutually beneficial. Initially reluctant, the premier signed on to the Social Union framework agreement. On the eve of the 1999 provincial election, Ottawa promised to transfer billions of dollars for health care back to the provinces. Since concern over health care cutbacks was the weakest point in the Tories' public image, this had the effect of allowing them to promise to spend more on health without affecting the provincial budgetary situation. There is a tradition in Ontario politics whereby Liberal governments in Ottawa and Tory governments at Queen's Park usually enjoyed *modus vivendi* that sacrifice partisanship for effective intergovernmental relations. Harris and Chrétien have sometimes followed that tradition.

Since their re-election, however, the Tories have gone on the offensive against Ottawa, producing ads that not only attack the Liberals for not providing sufficient health transfers but also, more controversially, demand bigger federal tax cuts—an area outside of provincial jurisdiction, suggesting an effort to impose CSR principles on the federal government. The provincial treasurer has announced plans to disconnect the Ontario tax collection system from the federal system with which it is harmonized, as are all other provinces save Quebec. This move would have serious consequences for federal–provincial fiscal relations.

At the same time, key elements of the "virtual" Tory party that constructed the CSR have shown strong inclinations to intervene in national politics, to export the revolution, in effect, to Ottawa. The challenge to the federal Conservatives posed by the new Canadian Alliance has centred on the old Reform party's efforts to enlist the Harris Tories on their side and against Joe Clark's party. It is clear that Ontario is the major battleground between the two federal parties of the right, which split the conservative vote 50/50 in the last two federal elections, leaving Ontario to the Liberals. The campaign for the leadership of the fledgling Alliance by Tom Long, considered one of the architects of the CSR, was organized by virtually the same team that made Harris PC leader and premier and lavishly financed by the same Bay Street sources that funded the provincial Tories. Despite these advantages, Long finished a distant third behind two Alberta candidates. It remains to be seen whether the new party under the leadership of the former Alberta treasurer Stockwell Day can consolidate the right-of-centre vote in Ontario, thus threatening to realign national politics and challenge the national Liberal hegemony. If so, it will not be a simple export of the CSR to Canada, but rather an alliance of Ontario with conservative forces in the West.

In shifting from the federal Conservative party, the CSR people disdain tradition. Alister Campbell, one of the leading architects of the CSR, and a former federal PC official, wrote an open letter to PC supporters urging them to abandon their party for the Alliance (Campbell, 2000). His language is purely instrumental as he complains about his "wasted investment" in this "brand"; "it was time to invest elsewhere." He went on: "If the federal PC party in which you have invested so much was a mutual fund, you would have dumped it years ago." His words capture precisely the logic of the new "virtual" party, now shifted from the provincial to the federal level.

The CSR is likely not exportable in its full Ontario manifestation. It arose out of a very specific political and economic conjuncture unlikely to be replicated at the national level. National politics has moved decisively into the post-deficit era, not the most favourable ground for radical fiscal conservatism. Ontario is more homogenous than the national political culture—Quebec, for instance, remains barren ground for the Alliance and for the ideas of the CSR, as such. The kind of compromises and accommodations required in federal politics seem alien to the spirit of the CSR. And to the extent that the CSR actually is specifically designed as an expression of Ontario's emergent region-state status, its transposition onto the national stage might well be viewed as a device to free Ontario from its federalist constraints and would consequently be distrusted by other regions.

Given the enthusiasm and commitment of financial and human resources that the core CSR "virtual" Tory party is investing in the Canadian Alliance, it is likely that the CSR activists recognize the continuing relevance of the Canadian federation and of national issues to the future of their brand of conservatism. While they may well make a mark on Canadian politics, it will not be in the old form of "what's good for Ontario is good for Canada." Rather, in the transposition to the national stage, the CSR will have to accommodate itself to the complex and variegated realities of a diverse and regional country.

Meanwhile, in the birthplace of the CSR, the consolidation of the changes brought down so quickly and relentlessly will no doubt progressively moderate the Harris government. All revolutions, even common sense revolutions, run their course and become institutionalized, finally becoming part of the establishment they once attacked from the other side of the ramparts.

I would like to offer special thanks to Steve Patten for his detailed and very useful comments on the first draft of this essay.

NOTES

1. Turnout, which registered over 90 percent at the beginning of the 20th century and over 70 percent in the 1930s, declined to 63 percent in 1995 and then to a low of 58 percent in 1999: Statistics from Elections Ontario Web site at <http://www.electionsontario.on.ca/>. The turnout may actually be lower yet, as inadequately updated voters lists left some potential voters ineligible.

2. According to Angus Reid, in January of 1997, when conflict over the introduction of the CSR program was at its height, 52 percent of Ontarians agreed that the Tories were on the "right track." Six months later this had risen to 61 percent, a figure that still held firm by January 2000, into the government's second term (Angus Reid Web site: <http://www.angusreid.com/>.

REFERENCES

Campbell, Alister. (2000, March 9). A "Dear Tories" letter. *National Post.*

Courchene, Thomas J. with Colin R. Telmar. (1998). *From heartland to North American regional state: The social, fiscal and federal evolution of Ontario.* Toronto: University of Toronto Press.

Dale, Stephen. (1999). *Lost in the suburbs: A political travelogue.* Toronto: Stoddart.

Harris, Mike. (1995). *The common sense revolution.*

Harris, Mike. (1999). *Blueprint: Mike Harris' plan to keep Ontario on the right track.*

Ibbitson, John. (1997). *Promised land: Inside the Mike Harris revolution.* Scarborough: Prentice-Hall.

Institute for Research on Public Policy (IRPP). (2000, January–February). Is Ontario a region-state? *Policy Options/Options Politiques,* 21(1), pp. 83–105.

MacDermid, Robert. (1999a). Funding the common sense revolutionaries: Contributions to the Progressive Conservative Party of Ontario, 1995–97. [Online]. Available: <http://www.socialjustice.org/PCPAPER.html>.

MacDermid, Robert. (1999b, December). Money and the 1999 Ontario election. *Canada Watch,* 7(6).

Noel, Sid. (1996). Patronage and entourages, action-sets, networks. In Brian Tanguay and Alain-G. Gagnon (Eds.), *Canadian parties in transition,* 2nd ed. (pp. 238–51). Scarborough: Nelson.

———. (1997). *Revolution at Queen's Park: Essays on governing Ontario.* Toronto: James Lorimer.

Progressive Conservative Party of Ontario Web site: <http://www.OntarioPC.on.ca/>.

Ralph, Diana, André Régimbald, and Nérée St-Amand (Eds.) (1997). *Open for business, closed to people: Mike Harris's Ontario.* Halifax: Fernwood Books.

Whitaker, Reg. (1997). Canadian politics at the end of the millennium: Old dreams, new nightmares. In David Taras and Beverly Rasporich (Eds.), *A passion for identity: An introduction to Canadian studies*. Toronto: ITP Nelson.

White, Graham. (1997). Transition: The Tories take power. In Sid Noel, *Revolution at Queen's Park: Essays on Governing Ontario*. Toronto: James Lorimer (pp. 139–50).

Wiseman, Nelson. (2000). Ontarians still identify with their nation-state, not their region-state. Institute for Research on Public Policy, *Policy Options/Options Politiques*, 21(1), pp. 83–84.

Woolstencroft, Peter. (1997). Reclaiming the "Pink Palace": The Progressive Conservative party comes in from the cold. In Graham White (Ed.), *The government and politics of Ontario*, 5th ed. (pp. 365–401). Toronto: University of Toronto Press.

FURTHER READING

Courchene, Thomas J. with Colin R. Telmar. 1998. *From Heartland to North American Regional State: The Social, Fiscal and Federal Evolution of Ontario*. Toronto: University of Toronto Press.

Dale, Stephen. 1999. *Lost in the Suburbs: a Political Travelogue*. Toronto: Stoddart.

Harris, Mike. 1995. *The Common Sense Revolution*.

Harris, Mike. 1999. *Blueprint: Mike Harris's Plan to Keep Ontario on the Right Track*.

Ibbitson, John. 1997. *Promised Land: Inside the Mike Harris Revolution*. Scarborough: Prentice-Hall.

Institute for Research on Public Policy. 2000. "Is Ontario a region-state?," *Policy Options/Options Politiques*, 21:1, January–February, pp. 83–105.

Noel, Sid. 1997. *Revolution at Queen's Park: Essays on Governing Ontario*. Toronto: James Lorimer.

White, Graham, ed., 1997. *The Government and Politics of Ontario*, 5th ed. Toronto: University of Toronto Press.

PART C

THE NEW WEST

Stone Hammer Poem

Robert Kroetsch

1.

This stone
become a hammer
of stone, this maul

is the colour
of bone (no,
bone is the colour
of this stone maul).

The rawhide loops
are gone, the
hand is gone, the
buffalo's skull
is gone;

the stone is
shaped like the skull
of a child.

2.

This paperweight on my desk

where I begin
this poem   was

found in a wheatfield
lost (this hammer,
this poem).

Cut to a function,
this stone was
(the hand is   gone–

3.

Grey, two-headed,
the pemmican maul
fell from the travois or

a boy playing lost it in
the prairie wool or
a squaw   left it in
the brain of a buffalo or

it is a million
years older than
the hand that
chipped stone or
raised slough
water (or blood) or

4.

This stone maul
was found.

In the field
my grandfather
thought
was his

my father
thought was his

5.

It is a stone
old as the last
Ice Age, the
retreating/the
recreating ice,
the retreating
buffalo, the
retreating Indians

(the saskatoons bloom
white (infrequently
the chokecherries the
highbush cranberries the
pinchberries bloom
white along the barbed
wire fence (the
pemmican winter

6.

This stone maul
stopped a plough
long enough for one
Gott im Himmel.

The Blackfoot (the
Cree?) not

finding the maul
cursed.

?did he curse
?did he try to
go back
?what happened
I have to/I want
to know (not know)
?WHAT HAPPENED

7.

The poem
is the stone
chipped and hammered
until it is shaped
like the stone
hammer, the maul.

8.

Now the field is
mine because
I gave it
(for a price)

to a young man
(with a growing son)
who did not

notice that the land
did not belong

to the Indian who
gave it to the Queen

(for a price) who
gave it to the CPR
(for a price) which
gave it to my grandfather
(for a price) who
gave it to my father
(50 bucks an acre
Gott im Himmel I cut
down all the trees I
picked up all the stones) who

gave it to his son
(who sold it)

9.

This won't
surprise you.

My grandfather
lost the stone maul.

10.

My father (retired)
grew raspberries.
He dug in his potato patch.
He drank one glass of wine
each morning.
He was lonesome
for death.

He was lonesome for the
hot wind on his face, the smell
of horses, the distant
hum of a threshing machine,
the oilcan he carried, the weight
of a crescent wrench in his hind pocket.

He was lonesome for his absent
son and his daughters,
for his wife, for his own
brothers and sisters and
his own mother and father.

He found the stone maul

on a rockpile in the
north-west corner of what
he thought of
as his wheatfield.

He kept it (the
stone maul) on the railing
of the back porch in
a raspberry basket.

11.

I keep it
on my desk
(the stone).

Sometimes I use it
in the (hot) wind
(to hold down paper)

smelling a little of cut
grass or maybe even of
ripening wheat or of
buffalo blood hot
in the dying sun.

Sometimes I write
my poems for that

stone hammer.

Native Identity and the Metis: Otehpayimsuak Peoples

Emma LaRocque

INTRODUCTION: HALFBREED AND METIS PEOPLES

There have been a number of odd definitions of "Metis." Several years ago I read in a college report that the Metis are neither Indian nor Inuit. There was no further explanation. Even the Royal Commission on Aboriginal Peoples (RCAP) begins its chapter on the Metis by defining them more in terms of who they are not, instead of who they are: "Metis are distinct Aboriginal peoples, neither First Nations or Inuit" (1996, p. 199). They have also been defined as "half white, half Indian" persons, or "halfbreeds." More often, people who have some combination of both White and Indian ancestry are lumped together into the category "metis." Others make a distinction between those Metis whose origin can be traced back to the Red River and those "metis" who are of mixed Indian and non-Indian ancestry with no direct links to the Red River Metis. Metis have also been described as people "between two worlds" (Harrison, 1985)[1] who lack a core culture with distinct cultural markers (Sawchuk, 1978).[2] But all these descriptions are either misleading or inadequate as Metis and Halfbreed histories and identities cannot be so easily generalized or fused together. It is only recently that scholars and perhaps politicians have begun to recognize that Metis peoples are an Aboriginally based ethnic group who are more than the sum of white and Indian mix.

There is much misunderstanding and misperception about Aboriginal peoples generally, but there is even greater and more widespread confusion about Metis people. Stereotypes, politics, and government policies have contributed much to the confusion. Misrepresentation in colonialist narratives and subsequent cultural popular productions have almost totally negated Metis' presence in North America, both in terms of Metis ethnicity and of Metis significance in historical and cultural roles. Although various archival sources throughout the 1700s and 1800s commented on the growing numbers of Metis communities scattered along trade routes in the Old Northwest (Peterson and Brown, 1985), as a rule, Metis peoples were treated not as ethnic collectivities but as unpredictable "halfbreed" individuals without a community who could either be romanticized or demonized, depending on the needs of fictionalists and historians (LaRocque, 1983). And even though the Red River Metis were acknowledged as a "population," they and their leader Riel were dismissed as confused, volatile half-savages who embodied presumed conflicting forces of "civilization" and "savagery" (Stanley, 1960; Morton, 1950).[3]

Such Eurocentric interpretations of history were popular until about the 1970s when some scholars began to review Native–white relations in Canada. Since about the 1980s and in response to the commemoration of Riel's political death in 1885, there has been a growing recognition that the Western Metis, particularly those of Red River ancestry, are a culturally distinct ethnic group. Today, this group refers to themselves as Metis Nation peoples. However, there are many different Metis communities across Canada, and not all of them originate in Red River. The Royal Commission on Aboriginal Peoples (RCAP) makes a distinction between the "Metis Nation" (of Red River origins) and the "other Metis" such as Eastern and Labradorian Metis. It is not clear whether RCAP recognizes that in the Prairie provinces and the Northern territories there were also "other Metis" ethnic groups who developed independently of Red River. It is not surprising that, given the differences among Metis peoples, some Metis groups object to the universal application of the term "metis." In 1984 the Metis National Council proposed using uppercase M to refer to those Metis "originally of mixed ancestry who evolved into a distinct indigenous people," specifically those in Western Canada who were dispossessed by Canadian governments in the late 1870s on, and lowercase m "metis" for all the other persons of mixed ancestry (Peterson and Brown, 1985, p. 6). Peoples of Metis Nation origins argue that the term "Metis" belongs to them, and its generalized application serves to obscure their distinct identity.

There has especially been much confusion in the lumping together of any persons or peoples with any "Indian" in them as "Metis," no matter their generational, historical, or cultural differences. Perhaps the term "halfbreed" has added to the confusion. It was often used as a self-designation by most Metis groups throughout the 1800s, whether they were of Anglo-Saxon/Indian or of French/Cree ancestry, or whether they were from James Bay, Red River, Batoche, or Lac La Biche areas. Some Metis still prefer to identify themselves as "halfbreed." Prior to the *Canadian Constitution* of 1982, the federal government used the hyphenated "half-breed" especially in the context of the scrip and land grant programs in Western Canada.[4] There are of course, first-generation peoples who are "half white and half Indian" or are "part Indian" in their family history, but it is not the case that all such peoples are necessarily or automatically Metis, ethnically speaking. The fact is, there may be no historical or cultural connection between those persons who have a "mixed" ancestry consisting of Indian and non-Indian, and those peoples of a distinctly Metis ethnicity whose roots go back to the fur trade alliances between European and Indian traders, but over time married within their own group from which grew a distinctly Metis peoplehood or ethnicity. Such peoples and communities developed throughout North America and Canada. They are not "half white, half Indian" or people in-between cultures; they are a distinct ethnic group with undisputed Aboriginal connections and identity (RCAP, 1996).

The Royal Commission on Aboriginal Peoples (1996) attempts to clarify the situation by focusing on culture as an objective criteria by which the Metis can be identified:

> It is primarily culture that sets the Metis apart from other Aboriginal peoples. Many Canadians have mixed Aboriginal/non-Aboriginal ancestry, but that does not make them Metis or even Aboriginal. Some of them identify themselves as First Nations persons or Inuit, some as Metis and some as non-Aboriginal. What distinguishes Metis people from everyone else is that they associate themselves with a culture that is distinctly Metis. (p. 202)

While this may be helpful in considerable ways, for example, in the recognition that Metis have a distinct culture, it certainly does not answer everything. The phrase "associate themselves" can be problematic as anyone can "associate themselves with a culture" that is Metis. Further, ethnic identity is more than about "association," especially when such an association is purely self-declared rather than historically and culturally rooted. Anthropologists and sociologists generally make distinctions between peoples based on objective cultural markers. In addition to political consciousness, which is an important aspect of contemporary identity, Metis Nation peoples do have such cultural markers, which form a foundation to their identity.

METIS ETHNICITY

In an attempt to clarify the matter of the Metis as a distinct Aboriginal culture in Canada, I will here briefly trace the development of Metis ethnicity and will refer to my family and community history. The emergence of Halfbreed and later Metis peoples is directly related to the commercial partnerships between European men and the Original societies. Relationships between European men and Indian women facilitated trade through kinship between the two worlds. In areas of languages, geography, foods, clothing, medicines, transportation, and other technologies, not to mention cross-cultural diplomacy, the significance of Indian women in these circumstances and relationships cannot be overemphasized as they provided companionship, knowledge, and skills to the European men (Van Kirk, 1983). They also inculcated their Halfbreed children with Aboriginal values and life skills.

From these early relationships grew families who in time became Halfbreed peoples, some segments of which eventually became Red River Metis peoples and whose descendants in Western Canada now identify themselves as The Metis Nation. In order to best understand this development, it may be useful to look at the various components of identity such as biology, culture, and endogamy (marriage within one's own group), the combination of which can create a new ethnic group. Naturally, all human beings begin by biological processes: Halfbreed peoples are the result of two different "racial" groups. Generally speaking, by the 1600s, there were Halfbreed individuals everywhere there was significant contact between Indians and Europeans. All humans, no matter their racial ancestry, are born into human cultural groups. Initially, Halfbreed children were usually raised by their mother's cultural group, that is, by Aboriginal cultures. Over time, as the population of Halfbreed persons grew, Halfbreed individuals began to marry other Halfbreed persons. The practice of endogamy is a very common tendency among humans. As more and more Halfbreed peoples practised endogamy, it became possible to develop communities of people who really were no longer "half white, half Indian" but an entirely new ethnic group. Such peoples were/are of Metis–Metis ancestry.[5] As this new unified population grew, they began to develop a culture that we may call Metis. Such a culture was at once unique and yet one that naturally blended both Indian and European cultures.

By the mid-1700s, a number of white travellers began to notice and comment on this group of Metis populations and communities, which were quite distinct from both Indians and Europeans. Such metis communities were acknowledged throughout the Great Lakes and the Ohio Valley. These peoples were identifiable in terms of family connections, occupational identification, dress, speech (usually trilingual, and eventually Michif),[6] recreation, and geographic location (Peterson and Brown, 1985). Many towns and cities throughout North America got their beginnings as early Metis settlements or trading towns.

Some scholars (Peterson and Brown, 1985) theorize that social and economic networks linked the Old Northwest (Great Lakes/Ohio Valley) with the Far Northwest (Red River/Rupertsland). They believe that the cultural and national development of the Red River Metis was related to the early sense of cultural distinctiveness of the Old Northwest Metis.

"Metis" is a French word that simply means "a person of mixed ancestry." It is not clear when Halfbreed peoples were first called "Metis," and, more important, when they first called themselves "Metis." We do know that French/Indian Halfbreeds in Red River called themselves "Metis" in the early 1800s, but it is not a term that was widely used by anyone until about the 1970s when contemporary Metis organizations were established. We also know that other Halfbreed peoples preferred to call themselves "Halfbreed," especially in James Bay and in areas now known as Saskatchewan, Alberta, and the Northwest Territories. We also know that Anglo-Saxon/Indian Halfbreed peoples referred to themselves as Halfbreed in Red River.

The complexity of Metis origins and history has been obscured because much of the focus has gone to the Red River Metis. The French-connected Metis of Southern Manitoba gained attention partly because of the fact that the Red River community, unlike many other Halfbreed-concentrated communities in North America, developed not only cultural distinctiveness but also a strong sense of nationalism. The Red River Metis were culturally distinct, geographically concentrated, and politically and militarily organized. Throughout the 1800s the Metis did not hesitate to protect their interests by a show of force, whether against the Sioux or against the Hudson's Bay Company. In 1869, in the face of imposing confederation, they were prepared to defend their culture and their homelands, a fact that caught John A. Macdonald with his eastern prejudices against "half castes" off-guard. Unfortunately for the Metis people, and in no small measure due to the prejudices of the times, their Provisional Government, under the leadership of Riel, fell.

I read these events in Red River as a people's resistance to colonial incursion and prefer to call it the First Metis Resistance, but of course it was Riel who caught the imagination of scholars and artists. So much so that it was long assumed by historians that when Riel died, the people died with him. But in fact, the Metis as a cultural group never died, and they have certainly refused to disappear. They did, however, suffer great losses and dispersal. About 83 percent of the Red River Metis lost their lands due to various administrative and legal manoeuvres of both the federal and Manitoba governments throughout the 1870s. Dispirited and systematically dispossessed, a great many of these Metis moved out of their homelands, a movement that has been characterized as an "involuntary exodus" (Sprague, 1980). The majority moved west and northwest, creating new communities all along the way or joining other existing Halfbreed communities of the Northwest. The Second Metis Resistance, better known by non-Native Canadians as the 1885 Northwest Rebellion, produced much the same results for the Metis as the Red River Resistance: marginalization and landlessness. The Metis had neither treaty rights nor private property. And after 1885 the Metis became, and perhaps continue to be, Canada's "forgotten people" (Sealey and Lussier, 1975). Their expertise, skills, and ways of life (largely land-based: hunting, trading, fishing, some farming), which had sustained the commercial flow between East and West, North and South, Indian and White, became irrelevant in a new Canada bent on white settlement, agriculture, and urban and industrial "development."

LEGISLATIVE DISCRIMINATION AND METIS' IDENTITY

The Canadian government has not been kind to the Metis. Its history of dismissing and dispossessing Metis peoples has greatly contributed to the confusion about the Metis. Not only has the Canadian government consistently refused to recognize the Metis as a distinct ethnic group, it has consistently divorced the Metis from their Indian or Aboriginal roots. Generally, Aboriginal peoples refers to those peoples whose ancestors and whose cultural, social, and racial attributes can be identified as Aboriginal. Until recently, most Aboriginal peoples of Canada have been known as "Indians," a term inherited from Columbus and later defined by colonial legislation. In Canada, the first statutory definition of who was an Indian was enacted in 1850, and with the establishment of the *Indian Act* (1876), the term "Indian" became a legal definition. The problem with the *Indian Act* is that it is not all inclusive. The *Indian Act* has created Aboriginal sub-groups and identities with unequal rights. Not only did it exclude the Inuit[7] and the Metis from being considered "Indian," it created a legal loophole known as enfranchisement by which status Indians would lose their status. Enfranchisement created a new group: the non-status Indians.

Enfranchisement was a legal process by which status Indians lost or gave up both the "benefits and burdens" of the *Indian Act.* "Benefits," or "rights" as is interpreted by Indians, include such things as reserved lands, health care, and schooling within specified terms. "Burdens" means that the *Indian Act* has had total control of Indian peoples in areas of identity, religious practices, education, fiscal development, and expropriation of lands. It is only since the 1970s that status and treaty Indians have begun to pry apart this control. Many Indian people gave up their status as a way of getting away from this totalitarianism as well as accessing what mainstream Canadians assumed to be basic rights such as the federal vote, public schools, joining the army, or simply being able to go into Liquor Commission premises. In the 1900–50s era, many Indian agents coaxed Indians to give up their status; often, the Indian people did not understand the full implications of doing so, for example, enfranchised Indians had to leave their reserves as well as lose other interests in reserve communities. There was also involuntary enfranchisement. For example, under Section 12(1)(b) of the *Indian Act* Indian women (and their children) lost their status if they married any man who was not legally a status Indian. Indian women also automatically lost their status if their status husbands enfranchised voluntarily or not. Between 1876 and 1985 approximately 25 000 Indians directly lost their status, not counting the descendants who also automatically became non-status (Frideres, 1998). Enfranchised Indians became classified as non-status Indians.

Non-status is not to be confused with either non-treaty status Indians or the Metis. Non-status is a legal not a racial designation; however, there is now a complex connection between non-status and various

Metis/metis communities. When Indians lost their status, most of them had to move out of their reserves and, since they were not welcomed by Canadian society, many moved into Metis communities, especially to those Metis communities located close to reserves. Because many Indians and Metis were related to each other, it was not surprising that many non-status Indians joined the Metis. Over time, in some communities it has become virtually impossible to make a distinction between non-status Indians and Metis as some Metis may also be legally non-status, and some non-status Indians may be racially and culturally Metis.

Nor has Bili C-31 clarified the identity situation. Bill C-31 amended the *Indian Act* with respect to Indian status and band membership and became effective April 17, 1985. Although Bill C-31 ended sexual discrimination and provided a mechanism for non-status Indians to re-apply for status, it clouded the issue of membership with complex and confusing eligibility rules. Many say Bill C-31 has become as contentious, unfair, and divisive as the old 12(1)(b) of the *Indian Act.* In any event, Bill C-31 has had quite an impact on both Indian and Metis populations. By 1996, 99 710 non-status peoples, many of whom had considered themselves Metis, had been reinstated as status (Frideres, 1998). This of course means that the Metis population has been substantially reduced.

METIS AS DISTINCT ABORIGINAL CULTURES

The Canadian government has also failed to protect or advance the Metis as a distinct Aboriginal culture with legitimate land rights. Section 12 of the *Indian Act* excluded any person who "has received or has been allotted Half-breed lands or money scrip," which generally referred to those Metis in the Prairie provinces who "chose" scrip under the Halfbreed Scrip Commission terms as an alternative to treaties. "Scrip" was a voucher that could have either money or land value and was given to "eligible" Metis individuals on a raffle-like basis. As noted above, the Metis suffered massive land loss from the Red River area in the 1870s and again in the Northwest areas in the 1880s largely through legalese and the unsubtle maladministration of the scrip system (Sawchuk et al., 1981; Sprague, 1988; Chartrand, 1991; RCAP, 1996).

Some continue to believe that the Canadian government acted properly and that whatever losses the Metis suffered were due to their primitive passions, poor leadership, and fear of "progress." Frankly, I find such accusations incredulous in the face of overwhelming documentation that the Canadian governments aggressively facilitated white settlement of Western Canada.[8] The vast majority of the Red River and Northwest Metis who lost their homelands (or lots as in Red River) were land-based Cree-(and/or Michif) speaking hunters and traders who found John A. Macdonald's schemes, bureaucracy, and legalese as culturally foreign as Plains Cree leader Big Bear found treaties and reserves to be. It is important not to confuse these Cree-Metis with the French-speaking, Eastern-educated, urbanized Riel. In an effort to secure homelands for the Metis, Riel did lose his life, but he was in many respects an anomaly both in cultural orientation and education.

But despite the losses, the dispersals, and the prejudices experienced by the Metis, they were and remain survivors. They continued to live off the land by hunting, trapping, fishing, gardening, or picking berries and roots wherever possible. They supplemented their land-based resource-fulness with wage labour wherever they could: working the sugar beet fields, cutting and selling wood, picking rocks, stooking hay, picking and selling blueberries and seneca roots, sewing, and so forth. Many Metis, especially during the Depression, became gypsy-like labourers, moving from place to place on horse-drawn wagons, looking for work. The women and children would frequently stay in one place, usually small Metis hamlets, while the men mobilized in search of work. Throughout Canada's history, Metis have been the labouring backbone of this country, serving first as portaging and fur-packing *coureur de bois*, defining the buffalo industry with their organization and technologies, then building railroad lines and roads, clearing fields for farmers, or fighting fire for the forestry. Today countless Metis continue to form part of the modern labouring class that sustains this country.

After the dispersals, most Metis were forced to become "Road Allowance people" (Campbell, 1973, p. 8). Through assorted federal and provincial legislation that facilitated immigration, agriculture, and indus-trialization with its Westernized concepts of land improvements, Metis were legally rendered "squatters" on the very homesteads and home-lands they had possessed (both in the sense of Aboriginal use and occu-pancy or through *scrip*). As "squatters" such Metis were forced onto unsurveyed Crown lands or "road allowance" strips of land. In these places scattered throughout north-central and northern areas of the Prairie provinces, they developed all-Metis hamlets and retained much of their culture. Left largely to themselves, they were able to retain their Cree and/or Michif language, their freedom, and their love of land, as well as their worldviews. They were, however, extremely poor and often confronted with deadly epidemics such as tuberculosis or influenza. They were also extremely vulnerable to repeated neocolonial incursions. From the late 1880s to about the 1970s, such Metis remained marginalized from Canadian cultural and economic life. For example, in Alberta, formal education was generally inaccessible for the Northern Metis until the mid-1950s when they began to trickle into public schools. Because Metis were/are not "Indian" under the terms of the *Indian Act*, most Metis could not attend residential schools. But even if they could, it is doubtful that Metis parents would have allowed their children to go to these schools for many Metis of my parents' generation viewed schools, residential or public, as a threat to their cultural integrity.

Most Metis in the Western provinces represent the blending of the Red River and locally developed Northwest Metis, and yet our great grandfathers and mothers ended up on road allowance strips of lands. For generations now, very little has changed for such Metis in regards to land ownership. Many Metis do not own the lands they live on and use for traditional pursuits. Alberta is the only province in Canada that did set aside lands for 12 Metis settlements (only 8 are in existence; 4 were rescinded at various times) in 1938 through the *Metis Betterment Act.* Pressured by Metis leaders, the Alberta government established the Ewing Commission in 1934 to study social conditions facing the Metis. Although the Metis settlements began essentially as patronizing welfare schemes to assist the destitute Metis, they did at the time provide a land-base for several thousand Metis, and since the late 1980s the people have gained some control in terms of governance, lands, and resources. Today there are about 5500 Metis (Dickason, 1992, p. 364) in the settlements or "colonies" as they were called.

The Royal Commission on Aboriginal Peoples takes these settlements as possible models for Metis self-government. But the majority of Metis did not get into these settlements because either they did not know about them or they were afraid. My father, who was born before the province of Alberta, explained to me that many Northern Metis were afraid that these settlements were reserves and that the people would become politically and geographically confined like their status Indian friends and kin. Metis such as my parents and grandparents, whose ancestors were free traders, were proud and protective of their freedom and independence. In fact, in Cree they were known as *Otehpayimsuak,* the independent and self-reliant ones. Geographical and agricultural restrictions conflicted with their hunting, trapping, or fishing. Reserves and residential schools were anathema[9] to *Sagaweenuak,* or bush people, as we also called ourselves. Not surprisingly, we were among the numerous Metis communities throughout central and northern Alberta who did not get into these settlements. My community of people owned no land, and to this day, we own no land. We were able only to rent acreages or traplines.

My father used to say that we are nothing without land. He represented a generation of people who associated their identities inextricably with the land. Our linguistic, epistemological, and economic way of life was nurtured by the ecology, seasons, and spirit of the land. To use more familiar phraseology, I come from a Metis peoples whose primary culture throughout much of the 1900s was traditionally land-based, that is, Cree-speaking (with some forms of Michif) hunters, trappers, fishermen and women, berry and root pickers, as well as gardeners. In summers, men turned to wage labour for railroads, forestry, and farmers. Because we did not have geographically contained or legally protected land bases, my parents' generation had to practise their hunting and trapping in creative ways. In practical terms this meant, for example, that my parents leased and lived on an acre of land where they built a cabin. This cabin was situated so that we could be bussed to school. Our everyday family life took place in this cabin. For hunting and trapping, Metis men (families could not go during school seasons) had to travel considerable distances to satellite campsites inside their traplines, which were leased from provincial Natural Resources departments. But long before the province of Alberta was born, long before confederation was born, my paternal and maternal Plains and Woodlands Cree/Metis ancestors filled these lands, if not by population, by indigenous use and love of the land. Like other Metis, my parents knew every nook and cranny of those lands ranging several hundred miles.

Such Metis communities existed throughout Northern Alberta, and in fact, throughout the northern parts of most provinces. But little has been known about such communities because much of the research or interest about the Metis has been about Riel and Red River. And in Alberta the Metis settlements have overshadowed the unpropertied Northern Metis. Yet it is these unpropertied but traditionally land-based peoples whose lives have changed most dramatically due to waves of urban and industrial encroachments that really began to overrun the Metis in the postwar years. In an era when the Metis were most defenceless in terms of representation, literacy, or familiarity with mainstream bureaucracy and legislation, provinces and industries went about assuming ownership of lands and traplines upon which the people depended. There was no protection for these Metis' way of life. For example, in the early 1950s people in my hamlet lost their traplines when the province simply declared their trapping area a bombing range. Within a decade many families were forced to accept social welfare to feed their children. Some people even lost their own backyards as various urban aggressions impinged on our communities. Needless to say, all this, among other socioeconomic injuries, had a very demoralizing effect on the people.

Many Metis, including my father, refused to take any social assistance. My parents had to make difficult decisions in order to be able to keep practising their independent way of life. They moved (or commuted by train to accommodate the school schedule) 100 miles further north where my father found stable seasonal (summer) work for the Northern Alberta Railways (NAR) and trapped with my uncle in the winters. There were self-sufficient Cree-Metis communities strung all along the NAR line, which stretched from Lac La Biche to Fort McMurray. But by the 1960s, oil and gas companies were everywhere, bulldozing over campsites and traplines with their huge machines. They may as well have been army tanks for they destroyed hunting areas and dispossessed the Metis as effectively as any army. There I watched my uncle's backyard turned into a man-made lake (the reasons for which remain unknown to us). By the 1980s, neither traplines nor trapping were available or feasible for most Metis in these areas. The Metis youth faced an untenable situation: they could no longer make a viable living based on an indigenous relationship with the land, yet were ill equipped to enter mainstream culture on any equal footing. Public schools we attended hammered us with assimilation policies just as effectively as residential schools battered status Indian children. The accumulative effect of all these pressures turned our worlds into sociocultural war zones.

To put it mildly, the results have been heartbreaking. Forced to make a new world for ourselves, many of us had to leave families and homes we loved, especially if we wanted to pursue education beyond grade school. Those who stayed faced their own difficulties. But whether we moved or stayed, few survived unscathed, and many became lost or actually died in the chaos of urban and industrial invasion that has come with neocolonialism. Such industrial aggressions have been rationalized as progress by so-called developed nations. In this country, particularly since the World Wars, both the governments and society have been aggressively whipping Native peoples into "modernization." There is powerful evidence that forced modernization batters and disorients Indigenous peoples even as it is dispossessing them.[10] Whatever awareness there is about this process in Canada has been largely focused on status Indians who have experienced forced relocation.[11] There has hardly been any notice taken about all the cultural stress and dispossession the unpropertied Metis have endured. Nor is there any notice that federal and provincial governments continue to allow industries to overtake lands that properly belong to *Sagaweenoo-Apeetowgoosanak,* or Metis bush peoples.

What has happened in the area I come from is not an atypical example of what happens to contemporary Metis generations when the unprotected lands upon which their parents depended are no longer meaningfully accessible to them. Given the array of assaults the Indigenous-based Metis have sustained, it should come as no surprise that many Metis communities throughout Western and Eastern Canada are disappearing or fragmenting, and this does have implications for Metis identity. There is a direct connection between cultural erosion and lack of legal protection for lands upon which these Metis cultures and communities were built.

However, cultural erosion does not mean cultural amnesia. The relationship between dispossession and cultural survival is of course a complex discussion, a discussion that demands much greater attention than I can give it here. Dispossessed peoples do not necessarily forget or abandon their languages, beliefs, traditions, values, arts, skills, or human connections, all of which weave into a people's culture. This fact is now better appreciated by modern anthropology, but the old stereotypes that "natives" are Stone Age primitives unable to cope with "civilization" or "progress" have long served colonial interests. There is nothing inherently moribund about Aboriginal cultures. And certainly Metis peoples, to the extent we have had choices, have always integrated various components of Indigenous and Canadian cultures. What needs to be understood is the interplay between forced change and change that can be seen as "normal" in any given culture. There is no question that Metis peoples have undergone various phases of forced change throughout the past century, yet they have also engaged in cultural exchange as a vibrant people who were often at the forefront of innovation prior to confederation's takeover of Western Aboriginal lands. It is true of course that colonization continues to impact negatively on Aboriginal cultures and persons, particularly in the area of lands and resources, but it is just as true that Aboriginal peoples are not cardboard caricatures without cultural elasticity or political agency.

What is remarkable is that, despite the relentless pressures the Metis have suffered, many of us managed to build some sense of cultural continuity meaningful to us, whether in places of origin or in the cities. We still know ourselves in Cree as *Apeetowgoosanak* or "Half-sons." Our traditions and cultural expressions remain uniquely Metis. Our legends and ghost stories, our Cree chants or Red River jigs, our humour and temperament, the embroidery on our moccasins or pillowcases, as well as our protocols for familial and social behaviour, remain distinctly Metis. We do have our own beliefs and practices that reflect our syncretistic religion (Cree/Roman Catholic) and language (forms of Michif), as well as our integrated approach to lands and technology. And both individuality and social responsibility are still highly valued.

I found it surprising that RCAP restricted its assessment of "cultural loss" of the Metis to "traditional Aboriginal activities" that are "cultural, spiritual, ceremonial or recreational in nature" (1996, 214–15). By "Aboriginal" RCAP here really means "Indian," and reflects the common tendency to evaluate the Metis in terms of Indian traditions (often associated with and confined to elders and powwows). Elders and powwows were not familiar to many Metis until about the 1970s. What is not well understood is that there were and are cultural differences between Indian and Metis peoples, a point Maria Campbell made in her book *Halfbreed*. Some of these differences may be more subtle than others, but were the Metis properly assessed in terms of Metis traditions, the profile on cultural loss or retention would come out quite differently.

Nonetheless, while it is true that the Metis are a remarkably resilient people and will continue to forge and re-forge the identities meaningful to them, they have sustained heavy cultural damage with respect to land-based traditions. Not only is a certain way of life ultimately lost but so are the resources upon which a new life could be developed. And unpropertied people become marginalized and dispirited, often falling into a cycle of poverty. As people whose core culture has been the blending of two distinct societies, it is not "progress" nor change nor any technological developments per se that the Metis have feared, it is the choicelessness that has always come with colonization. Even though we may optimistically believe that culture is what people do together and as such is dynamic and portable, dispossessed peoples do become landless and can respond only within certain parameters. With respect to being able to carry on in our places of origin, my brother is an example of how many Metis struggle heroically to maintain their *sagaweenuak* independence by combining land-based resources with wage labour. But my brother's remaining tiny land base is diminishing before his eyes as provincial and global corporations, not to mention animal-rights politics, continue to encroach upon these lands and his way of life.

Metis must take active steps to prevent the cultural erosion that comes from lack of legal protection for their lands and cultures. RCAP takes the position that the federal government has a legal and moral mandate to assist the Metis in the rebuilding and retaining of their identity. RCAP recommends that the federal government must end legal discrimination against the Metis with respect to Aboriginal rights and homelands and take remedial action in areas of cultural redevelopment.

While the *Canadian Constitution* (1982) included the Metis as one of the Aboriginal peoples, many issues on Metis land rights and identity remain unresolved. In Manitoba, legal and historical debate continues concerning Metis lands arising from the *Manitoba Act* (1870), Sections 31 and 32. In Alberta, some 50 000 to 70 000 Metis do not live in the settlements, and many remain as landless and marginalized as the vast majority of Metis across Canada.[12] The federal government has persisted in its refusal to recognize the Metis as "Indian" under the terms of section 91(24) of the *Constitution Act, 1867,* a refusal that is tantamount to withholding Aboriginal rights from the Metis. But Metis peoples have held to the view that they are Aboriginal, ancestrally, culturally, and now constitutionally, and should qualify for land claims on the basis of Aboriginal rights. RCAP concurs:

> The refusal by the Government of Canada to treat Metis as full-fledged Aboriginal people covered by section 91(24) of the constitution is the most basic form of government discrimination. Until that discriminatory practice has been changed, no other remedial measures can be as effective as they should be. (1996, pp. 219–20)

In this context the status Indian adoption of the term "First Nations" (which excludes the Metis) is unfortunate because it has resulted in disconnecting the Metis from their Aboriginality as the media and the public increasingly make a terminological distinction between "Aboriginal" or "Native" and "Metis." It would appear that this is convenient for the provincial and federal governments; the further removed the Metis are from their Aboriginality, the less pressure for governments to address Metis land and resource claims.

But Metis are Aboriginal and in fact it is this that contributes to the complexity of Metis' identities. While scholars generally restrict and divide differences among the Metis to their Anglo-Saxon or francophone origins, Metis' cultural differences are more than equally determined by connections to different Aboriginal cultures. For example, that the Metis of Labrador are different from the Metis of Red River or the Metis from British Columbia speaks to the many cultural differences among Indigenous peoples, whose cultural stamp on various Metis ethnicities is considerable. At the point of European arrival, there were perhaps several hundred different Original cultures consisting of about 11 linguistic families representing about 50 different languages (Dickason, 1992). There were great diversities among the Original cultures ranging from the fishing coastal peoples along the Atlantic and Pacific, the great hunters of the Boreal Forest and of the Plains, the Iroquian farmers of the Woodlands, to the tundra peoples of the Arctic. It is estimated that there were about 500 000 to a possible 2 000 000 Original peoples when Europeans arrived (Dickason, 1992). Not only was there intermarriage between various Original peoples, undoubtedly, giving rise to many Aboriginal peoples of "mixed ancestry," but each locality where there was significant contact between European and Indian peoples generated its own Halfbreed peoples who then developed their own distinct Metis identities. Of course, not all such communities survived, but as we do more research we will uncover more such histories.

There are of course, historical and cultural differences among the Metis. As the Royal Commission on Aboriginal Peoples discovered, there are many such communities throughout Canada outside the Prairie provinces, for example, in British Columbia, Ontario, Labrador, or Nunavut. There are also regional differences among the Metis Nation peoples. That we are able to trace our roots to Red River does not mean that we are necessarily the same. There are, for example, some fundamental differences between French-connected Metis of southern Manitoba and Cree-oriented Metis of northern Alberta, or even of northern Manitoba. Some of the differences include linguistics, lifestyles, and worldviews as well as experience and education. A Metis who grew up speaking French Michif with a Roman Catholic religion in an urban area is different from a Metis who grew up speaking Cree Michif with an Aboriginal epistemology in a bush or rural setting. There are also persons who can clearly trace their family histories to the Red River Fur Trading systems but who were not raised in a Metis culture. Then there are those who have only one Metis parent. The other parent may be Salish, Stoney, Micmac, Irish, Ukrainian, black, Asian, and so forth. There are still those who are "half white, half Indian" and do adopt Metis values and communities and remain strong supporters of the Metis. To what extent these peoples of various origins have a rightful claim to Metis identity with Aboriginal rights remains to be determined. In the words of historian Olive Dickason: "... the many backgrounds of individuals of mixed ancestry has complicated the matter of identity for the Metis" (Dickason, 1992, pp. 365).

That there are cultural differences, some even substantial, among the Metis does not mean that the Metis lack distinct cultural markers. It means only that they reflect their many origins and levels of political awareness. Scholars have been slow to sort out these differences. The public has been singularly unable to fathom the fact of these differences among the Metis. In their minds, the word "metis" represents a hodge-podge in which is thrown any person who claims some Indianness, no matter how remote or questionable. It appears this has been inversely convenient for various parties. On one hand, employers such as the civil service, universities, or even Metis organizations can fulfill human rights mandates to hire "minority" or "Aboriginal" staff by hiring anyone who claims metisness but can confirm little, if any, such background or identity. On the other hand, provincial and federal governments continue to deny or contest Metis claims to Aboriginal rights based on the confusion surrounding Metis' identity! Both the public and politicians have failed to respect the Metis Nation peoples as a distinct Aboriginal group. For these reasons the Metis Nation peoples have emphasized their distinctive and Aboriginally based ethnicity among a people with such a complex history.

CONCLUSION

How to maintain an ethnic identity in the face of imposed change and/or legislation is a challenge for any group. For the Metis, it has been particularly taxing. Peoples usually maintain their identity through "enclavic factors" such as (a) geographical concentration or isolation; (b) language retention; (c) shared lifestyles, and so on. Different histories and ethnicities, government policies, industrial encroachment, urbanization, and lack of legally protected Metis' homelands continue to threaten Metis identity (or identities). Still, despite all odds, the Metis continue to survive as a distinct ethnic group with strong Aboriginal ties in terms of kinship, language, land use, and spirituality. The racial and cultural connection is indisputable. Depending on terms of reference, estimates on Metis/metis populations range from about 500 000 to over 1 000 000 (Frideres, 1998).

The Metis Nation community is often put in an awkward position of having to make a distinction between itself and non-Metis persons (presumably of mixed ancestry) who pass themselves as Metis. There are those who appropriate Metis identity in an attempt to secure employment or services and rights that should properly go to Metis peoples. In an attempt to address these concerns, Metis organizations have established criteria for membership that usually requires community confirmation or documented evidence of one's Metis ancestry. This is particularly important for purposes of identifying the Metis population entitled to Metis-specific land grants or Aboriginal rights. Within the context of self-government negotiations, a Metis Nation–controlled national registry was proposed by the Metis National Council (MNC) during the Charlottetown deliberations. MNC defined "Metis" as "(a) an Aboriginal person who self-identifies as Metis, who is distinct from Indian and Inuit and is a descendant of those Metis who received or were entitled to receive land grants and/or scrip under the provisions of the *Manitoba Act, 1870*, or the *Dominion Lands Act*" and "Metis Nation" as the "community of persons in subsection (a) and persons of Aboriginal descent who are accepted by that community" (RCAP, 1996, p. 377).

For those who insist that anyone should have the right to become "metis" merely by self-declaration is engaging in colonial imposition. If Aboriginal self-government or the actualization of land grants and Aboriginal rights is to mean anything for the Metis, they must have the right to define and determine their constituencies. Such rights are not disregarded for status Indians or for many other Canadian groups. This is not an issue of discrimination on the part of the Metis, it is simply an attempt to ensure that Aboriginal and other rights flow properly to them. They also wish to clarify anthropological and historical factual differences about their ethnicity. Naturally, the Metis are interested in maintaining their identity in much the same way that any other ethnic or cultural group, such as the Blackfoot, the Mohawks, the Ukrainians, the English, or the French, is working to maintain its identity. The Metis Nation peoples make no claim to racial or ethnic purity or cultural superiority; if anything, they have been open and generous to numerous individuals of many backgrounds who have come to their doors claiming kinship. But poor history and generalized terminology has long resulted in the obscuration of Metis identity as well as legislative and sociological discrimination with respect to their Aboriginality, land, and resource rights. Although some scholars have rightly pointed out there are "many roads to Red River" (Peterson and Brown, 1985), that is, the Metis/metis have many origins, clearly there are substantial cultural and historical differences among peoples and persons who claim "some Indian" in them. The generalized notion and usage of the term "metis" remains a question of some contention within Metis communities. Perhaps the Metis Nation peoples should adopt a different name, say, *Otempayimsuak*, for their identity in order to foreground the point: that they are an Indigenous-based distinctive ethnic group who have constitutional, historical, cultural, and moral claims to Aboriginal rights. To be unique among many remains an important emotional, psychological, and spiritual fact among human groups. *Otempayimsuak* Metis are no different. They simply want recognition that they are indeed an ethnic group with a distinct culture whose rights and roots go back to the very bones of this land.

NOTES

1. In part reflecting her sources, many of whom seem equally confused, Julia D. Harrison in *Metis: People between Two Worlds*, seems unable to make sense of those Metis who "have a clear sense of their own identity as they individually define it," yet "see themselves as a distinctive people" (p. 15). Metis identity is based on much more than individual definitions, or individuals caught between two worlds. It is true that the Metis have suffered marginality, but as repeatedly established, the marginality is in large part due to the persistent refusal by society and governments to accept the Metis as a cohesive Indigenous-based distinctive ethnic group.

2. Sawchuk argued that the Manitoba Metis were less a "culture bearing" unit with distinct cultural markers than a reformulated politically determined group (1978, p. 10). In response to this limited vision of Metis ethnicity I wrote a playful review "Conversations on Metis Identity" (*Prairie Fire* 7.1 [Spring 1986]: pp. 19–24). Certainly, political consciousness has played an important role in strengthening contemporary Metis identity, and the ebb and flow of cultural expression does change from generation to generation, but just as certainly, Metis peoples have always had strong cultural identities. Sawchuk was confused between people of Metis Nation backgrounds and those who appropriated Metis identity. Sawchuk has since broadened his understanding of the Metis in subsequent works.

3. Echoing G.F. Stanley's thesis (1936), W.L. Morton declared: "This admixture of civilized life and barbaric ... indeed occurred in the very persons of the half-breed population of Red River and the West" (1950, p. 2).

4. For example, in the aftermath of the Metis Resistance movements, the federal government set up *scrip* for Half-Breed Heads of Families, and after 1885, the Half-Breed Land Grants Commission. In 1935 Alberta set up the Half-Breed Commission, later known as the Ewing Commission. For a good overview of official attitudes reflected in these various programs, see Sawchuk et al., *Metis Land Rights in Alberta: A Political History.*

5. For example, both of my parents were Metis, all four of my grandparents were Metis, and three of my great grandparents were Metis. My family is not at all atypical in Western Canada. It would be ludicrous to describe such a family or community of people as "half white, half Indian."

6. RCAP describes Michif as a "unique language that blends components of French and Aboriginal language." For an overview of issues surrounding the development of Michif see "What is Michif? Language in the metis tradition" by John C. Crawford in Peterson and Brown, 1985. The use and extent of Michif varies among Metis of Red River origins. In my family we put French prefixes and suffixes to many of our Cree words, but I did not learn of "Michif" until I came to Winnipeg, where some Metis have a conversational knowledge of Michif. I have noted differences in Michif depending whether the speaker is French or Cree in linguistic orientation.

7. In *re Eskimo 1939*, the Supreme Court of Canada held that the Inuit were "Indian" within the meaning of section 91(24) of the *BNA Act*. The Metis have not been so considered, an issue taken up by RCAP.

8. Earlier scholars and, more recently, Flanagan (1983) have blamed the Metis for losing their lands and have justified government actions with the Eurocentric myth that the Indian-related Metis feared and resisted "progress" by "rebelling" and then retreating to "the chase." White expansionism is here associated with Manifest Destiny, that is, that as a "civilization" Euro-Canadians had some inherent moral and racial right to dispossess Aboriginal peoples whom they predetermined as "primitive" or "savage."

9. In this respect, I am frankly puzzled to read in Dickason, in the context of counting federal land "allotments" to Aboriginal peoples, that "Alberta, with only ninety-six reserves (eight of which are Metis settlements) has by far the highest allotment" (Dickason, 1992, p. 325). This is incorrect on two counts: the Metis settlements are provincial, not federal, arrangements, and they are not reserves. Elsewhere in the textbook, Dickason provides a fine summary of the settlements.

10. Most Aboriginal communities have been battered and/or dispossessed by urban and industrial aggressions. For an excellent overview (though there are only oblique references on the Metis) see Geoffrey York, *The Dispossessed: Life and Death in Native Canada.* See also Boyce Richardson, ed. *Drumbeat.* For more personal observations on "modernization" see my autobiographical essay "Tides, Towns and Trains."

11. Shkilnyk in *A Poison Stronger Than Love* locates forced relocation in 1963 (ostensibly to accommodate the Native people's access to the modern amenities of a nearby town) as the source for the social disintegration of an Ojibiwe community in Northern Ontario. Shkilnyk provides a disturbing but intelligent and compassionate portrait of a traditional people who suffered "collective trauma" (p. xvi) as a consequence of forced modernization (capped with industrial poisoning in 1970).

12. It is impossible to get precise figures for Metis populations. In 1981 the Metis Association of Alberta provided an estimate of 75 000 Metis in Alberta, with 3400 in the Metis settlements. RCAP uses the 1991 Aboriginal Peoples Survey figure of 56 310 who identified as Metis in Alberta. Dickason (1992) provides an estimate of 55 000 who live off the settlements. Taking into account these discrepancies, I have used a range of 50 000 to 70 000 Metis who live outside Metis settlements.

REFERENCES

Adams, Howard. (1995). *A tortured people: The politics of colonization.* Penticton: Theytus Books.

Campbell, Maria. (1973). *Halfbreed.* Toronto: McClelland & Stewart.

———. (1995). *Stories of the road allowance people.* Penticton: Theytus Books.

Chartrand, Paul L.A.H. (Fall 1991). Aboriginal rights: The dispossession of the Metis. *Osgoode Hall Law Journal* 29.3: 457–82.

Dickason, Olive P. (1992). *Canada's First Nations: A history of founding peoples from earliest times.* Toronto: McClelland & Stewart.

Flanagan, Thomas. (1983). *Riel and the rebellion of 1885 reconsidered.* Saskatoon: Western Producer Prairie Books.

Frideres, James. (1998). *Aboriginal peoples in Canada: Contemporary conflicts.* Scarborough: Prentice Hall Allyn and Bacon Canada (1st edition, 1974).

Harrison, Julia D. (1985). *Metis: People between two worlds.* Vancouver: Douglas & McIntyre.

LaRocque, Emma. (1983). The Metis in English Canadian literature. *The Canadian Journal of Native Studies,* 3.1: 85–94.

———. (1986). Conversations on Metis identity. *Prairie Fire,* 7.1: 19–24.

———. (1990). Tides, towns and trains. Joan Turner, ed. *Living the changes.* Winnipeg: University of Manitoba Press.

Morton, W.L. (September 1950). The Canadian Metis. *Beaver:* 3–7.

Peterson, Jacqueline and Jennifer S.H. Brown, Eds. (1985). *The new peoples: Being and becoming Metis in North America.* Winnipeg: University of Manitoba Press.

Richardson, Boyce, ed. (1989). *Drumbeat: Anger and renewal in Indian country.* Toronto: Summerhill Press, Assembly of First Nations.

Royal Commission on Aboriginal Peoples. (1996). Volume 4, Chapter 5. Metis perspectives: 198–386.

Sawchuk, Joe. (1978). *The Metis of Manitoba: Reformulation of an ethnic identity.* Toronto: Peter Martin Associates Limited.

Sawchuk, Joe, Patricia Sawchuk, Terry Ferguson, and Metis Association of Alberta. (1981). *Metis land rights in Alberta: A political history.* Edmonton: Metis Association of Alberta.

Sealey, D. Bruce and Antoine S. Lussier. (1975). *The Metis: Canada's forgotten people.* Winnipeg: Manitoba Metis Federation.

Shkilnyk, Anastasia M. (1985). *A poison stronger than love: The destruction of an Ojibwe community.* New Haven: Yale University Press.

Sprague, Doug N. (1988). *Canada and the Metis, 1869–1885.* Waterloo: Wilfrid Laurier University Press.

———. (1980). Government lawlessness in the administration of Manitoba land claims, 1876–1887. *Manitoba Law Journal* 10: 415–41.

Stanley, George F. (1960). *The birth of Western Canada: A history of the Riel rebellion.* Toronto: University of Toronto Press.

Van Kirk, Sylvia. (1983). *'Many tender Ties': Women in fur trade society 1670–1870.* Norman: University of Oklahoma Press.

York, Geoffrey. (1990). *The dispossessed: Life and death in native Canada.* London: Vintage U.K.

Power and Politics in Western Canada

Peter McCormick

Twenty years ago, the notion of "Western alienation" was a staple of journalistic comment about contemporary Canadian politics. The provinces of Western Canada repeatedly articulated a distinct set of political and economic grievances with deep historical roots, a dissatisfaction that was reinforced by the perceived biases of contemporary federal policies, and federal priorities that worked consistently to disadvantage the West. The showcase complaint (particularly for Alberta) was Pierre Trudeau's National Energy Program, which capped provincial revenues from booming energy prices. Brian Mulroney's subsequent decision on the CF-18 (awarding an aircraft maintenance contract to a Montreal consortium despite a superior bid from a Winnipeg consortium) suggested that the problems ran too deep to be resolved by simply putting a new prime minister or even a different political party in office. The immediate response to the CF-18 decision included the formation of the Reform Party, with its slogan "The West Wants In!"

After Quebec made constitutional demands to remedy its isolation from the 1981/82 patriation process, the West likewise sought remedies for its grievances through the aggressive pursuit of constitutional change; if Quebec had opened the constitutional door, then the West could walk through it as well. The "Triple-E" Senate, first brought into the debate by Alberta Premier Don Getty, was the centrepiece of Western demands, although British Columbia's preferred Senate vision always owed more to the German model than to the American and Australian. To put the matter a little too simply (because changes to the federal–provincial division of powers were also routinely advanced), if "distinct society" became the core of Quebec's concerns in the constitutional debates of the 1980s, Senate reform emerged as the West's vehement *quid pro quo*. One reason for the tragedy of end-of-the-century constitutional change was the fact that each lump was too large for the other side to swallow.

Today, at the turn of the new century, the mood is distinctly different. Demands for formal constitutional change are clearly off the agenda—they survive only in such forms as Alberta Premier Ralph Klein's farcical Senate nominee elections, an increasingly irrelevant sideshow even in the province that once made "Triple E" the Western battle cry. The Western premiers still grumble about Ottawa, but they no longer do so in ways that make them distinctly different from other premiers. Issues like demanding the restoration of funding for health care and social services are serious concerns and sources of genuine complaint, but they make up a chorus that any provincial premier can sing. Today, sweeping proposals for radical change are more likely to come from Mike Harris's Ontario than from any of the Western provinces. The memory of past grievances, economic and political, has not completely faded, but the temperature level has gone down; Jean Chrétien may not be loved in the West, but he cannot realistically be described (as Trudeau and Mulroney in turn clearly could have been) as the most hated man west of the Lakehead.

It is probably less true than it was 20 years ago (and it was not particularly true then) that "the West" could usefully be treated as a coherent unit for purposes of political interaction. Today, there is no support anywhere even for the concept of "one Prairie province" (a theme explored at a 1971 conference, of which the Canada West Foundation is the lasting product), and even the conventional "three Prairie provinces" label may have outlived its usefulness. The notion of a "four-province" Western bloc is even less credible; British Columbia has always been one of a kind, more prone to think of itself as comprising (with the Yukon) a "fifth Canadian region" than part of any larger Western entity. Economically, the West is less a coherent unit than four variations of a single theme, four resource-based export economies with limited interprovincial trade as either a current reality or a serious future prospect. Although the discussion that follows will try to identify some general themes, each one is more true of some of the Western provinces than others, and all such generalizations must be qualified.

POLITICAL CULTURE AND IDEOLOGY

At first glance, ideology would seem to be the most promising approach to an understanding of Western Canada at the turn of this century. In the 1997 federal general election, the Reform Party (subsequently transmogrified into the Canadian Alliance) captured a solid majority of the seats in the four Western provinces but not a single seat east of the Manitoba/Ontario border. Since all commentators agree that Reform/Alliance is a "right-wing" party (and some, including the current national government, would characterize it as being on the "extreme" right), this would seem to identify a clear ideological divide with the right-wing West on one side and the rest of the country on the other.

But simply shifting the focus from federal to provincial politics tells quite a different story. At the turn of this century, three of the four Western provinces had the only New Democratic Party governments in the country. Indeed, this understates the matter, because nowhere east of the Manitoba border is the NDP strong enough even to form the official opposition. But all commentators would agree that the NDP is the most "left-wing" of Canada's major parties, a valid generalization even if the balance between purity and pragmatism varies from one provincial NDP party to another. A survey of provincial politics, then, would seem to identify an ideological divide with the left-wing West on one side and the rest of the country on the other. But the West cannot be simultaneously the most right-wing region of Canada (in federal politics) and the most left-wing region of Canada (in provincial politics), so the simple ideological explanation falls of its own weight.

This is not to deny some limited utility to the ideological argument. If there is a "right wing" in Canada, it is almost certainly found in the West, in a mixture of social conservatism, nostalgia for an economy and society organized around such institutions as the "family farm," traditional "family" values, and a greater salience for religious convictions that carry over into public action. But the "Bible belt" includes at most the British Columbia interior and the rural areas of central and southern Alberta. Any attempt to broaden the generalization to include Calgary (let alone Vancouver) must fail. Alberta's Video Lottery Terminal debate in 1998 demonstrates the strength of the churches, as they provided the major organizational muscle for an unprecedented massive petition drive that forced a province-wide referendum on a reluctant provincial government. But it also shows their limitations, as the referendum vote went against them in almost every part of the province.

On the other hand, the Western outcry against gun control is best thought of in terms other than ideology. This is not some reflex northern version of America's NRA, replete with patriotic slogans and images of a vigilant citizen militia but rather a reflection of the simple fact that there are still some parts of the country where the word "gun" conjures up visions, not of armed robbery, but rather of the .22 calibre rifle kept on the porch in case the coyotes show up near the chicken run. The demographics of the new century, in the West as elsewhere, are still dominated by urban growth and rural decline, but in Western Canada rural votes and rural interests are still strong enough to make a difference.

THE ECONOMY

The Free Trade deal delivered the goods for Western Canada. Not only is the overall volume of trade with the United States up, but the content of that trade has shifted from unprocessed raw materials to semi-processed and manufactured goods. Alberta, for example, no longer counts energy and grain as the two most valuable elements of provincial exports; grain has been pushed into third place by telephone and switching equipment. On a lesser scale, the same story can be told of other sectors of the economy and other provinces.

This observation seems somewhat out of place in light of the economic crisis that has recently hit Western agriculture. In 1999, the premiers of Saskatchewan and Manitoba were obliged to press the federal government for urgent funding for disaster relief for their grain farmers, who were hard hit by rising costs, low prices, the trade war between the United States and the European Community, and extreme weather conditions; the problems have persisted into the new century, with serious flooding in parts of both provinces after record-breaking thunderstorms. The plight of the farmers, and the limited capacity (or willingness) of governments to assist them, is one of the reasons why the Filmon government was defeated in Manitoba and the Romanow government in Saskatchewan reduced to the minority status that necessitated coalition with the small Liberal caucus. The broader social problem underlying this particular emergency is the demise of the family farm on the Prairies and the frustration of the generation of farmers who are seeing the end of a way of life.

But the general observation remains valid: agriculture is a smaller element of the Western economy than it has been in the past. The only province that still fits the "Prairie province" stereotype of reliance on the long trains of grain cars is Saskatchewan; Manitoba's major export is airplane and helicopter parts. The diversification that was (unsuccessfully) pursued in the 1980s through government-sponsored mega-projects has emerged in the era of NAFTA and globalization. There is also a message in the fact that it was two premiers, not three, who were importuning Ottawa for assistance for the farm sector. In Alberta, not only has the economy swung away from agriculture to processing but also within the agricultural sector there has been a swing away from grain mono-culture to a wider and more flexible diversity of crops. This hardly suggests immunity from the broader problems affecting the family farm and export crops, but in that province those problems have been of more modest proportions.

All of the Western provinces are heavily dependent on export trade, and most of that trade is with the United States. British Columbia, however, is a special case—more so than any other Western province—it has a "Pacific Rim" presence with strong exports to southeast Asia. In the early 1990s, this meant that B.C. was still booming while the rest of the country was in recession; in the late 1990s, it meant that B.C. was in a slump (due to the sharp contraction of the Asian economies) while the rest of Canada was in a strong recovery. The general lesson is that the B.C. economy may often be out of step with the rest of the country. What B.C. shares with most of the Western provinces is a heavy reliance on a single economic sector. In B.C., it is the forest industries, the largest single employer and the largest single exporter in the province. In Alberta, it is the energy sector, which accounts for fully half of Alberta exports. In Saskatchewan, as noted above, it is agriculture. The above comments about recent diversification are true only in a comparative context—more diverse than five or fifteen years ago—and do not defeat the generalization that these provinces are heavily dependent on exports of raw materials into international markets subject to strongly cyclical prices.

It is one of the enduring problems of the Canadian union that, for all provinces and for the Western provinces in particular, interprovincial trade counts for such a small proportion of the total economic activity, much less than that consumed within the province as well as that shipped to the United States. This is aggravated by the fact that the various provinces have been so creative in devising a bewildering diversity of barriers to interprovincial trade, from preferential procurement policies to labelling and licensing requirements to tax breaks, but the basic problem would not be fully resolved even by a genuine Canada-wide free trade zone.

EVOLVING FEDERAL PARTY SYSTEMS

In any single election, we tend to take the parties—the governing party, its major challenger or challengers, and the "splinter" movements that threaten to split the government or the antigovernment vote—very much for granted. They are simply there, natural forces around which opinion organizes and through which issues are identified and debated. And under normal circumstances, the party system tends to endure for considerable periods of time, subject to some adaptation of the major parties, some oscillation back and forth in terms of their major class and regional support, some successes (sometimes short-lived "raids" and sometimes persistent additions to the debate) on the part of "third parties."

But we are wrong to take the party system for granted as an enduring feature of our politics. Sometimes new political forces emerge, and their impact can displace one or more of the long-standing parties with newcomers, the process being less a simple substitution than a reconfiguration of the major cleavages and the major issues that divide the significant contenders for political power. Canada is going through such a period now, and like several of the previous major challenges to the national party system (by the Progressives after World War I and by the CCF and Social Credit during the Great Depression), the West is the major source of the challenge. And—again like the previous major challenges—the transformation will be contained or turned back, an episodic raid rather than a transformation, if it cannot transcend its Western regional roots.

The displacement of the ruling Progressive Conservatives by Reform in the West and by the Bloc Québécois in Quebec, accomplished in 1993 and confirmed in 1997, is an episode without precedent in Canadian politics. It was as true in 1988 as it had been a century earlier that only two parties—the Liberals and the Conservatives—had any reasonable chance of forming a national government, and although other "third parties" had existed for decades, the only practical impact of their "high-water" marks was a greater likelihood of Liberal or Conservative minority governments and some concomitant shadings to policy. Suddenly in the 1990s, this was no longer the case: one of the two historic national parties became the smallest of the five parties represented in the House of Commons, and the official opposition oscillated between two parties that had not even existed a decade earlier.

There are, of course, parallels in the experiences of other democratic countries. In the United States, the national party system was initially disrupted, and ultimately transformed, by the emergence of the Republican Party in the 1850s. In Great Britain, there was a period of political uncertainty and a string of minority governments as the Liberal Party that had created the welfare state was displaced by the Labour Party in the 1920s. Both episodes signalled major changes in the configuration of political forces and issues at the core of national politics, and the same is true of the events in Canadian politics in the 1990s.

There are several elements that are represented by the new political party that is trying to replace the Conservatives and redefine the issues. A very important one, frequently misinterpreted as hostility toward francophone Quebec, is a repudiation of French/English duality as the central axis, often expressed as the feeling that the "real" issues are being neglected while Ottawa worries about bilingualism or the latest separatist threat. (To this extent, the two successor movements to the Mulroney Conservatives—Reform/Alliance and Bloc—play off each other, each finding its fears confirmed by the very existence of the other.) This is reinforced by the long-standing heartland/hinterland confrontation that is inevitable in any geographically extensive polity and that represents the current face of what used to be called Western alienation.

Another important element is a repudiation of the post–World War II Canadian national consensus, which supported a strongly interventionist role for government involving a significant degree of the redistribution of wealth. This has been a consistent focus of national governments, Liberal and Conservative alike, for several decades; the disagreement between the two is often presented as stark ideological confrontations when they really constitute disagreements about the pace but not the direction of government policy—Tweedle-Grit and Tweedle-Tory, in Reformist rhetoric. For the new Reform party, the debt-and-deficit crisis of the early 1990s carried a double message—not just the need for a balanced budget ("you get only the government you can pay for"), but also the need for a smaller government, with fewer employees, smaller budgets, and a less aggressive interventionist and redistributionist role. The first message may have become the new common sense, directly challenged by very few, but the second message certainly has not.

It is a hallmark of eras of consensus that changes of government are often accompanied by continuity in major policies. This means that the sound and fury of election campaigns is often followed by the anti-climax of minor adjustments—election promises notwithstanding, the Chrétien Liberals did not tear up the free trade agreement or scrap the GST. But the Reform/Alliance challenge contests a long-standing consensus, and this means that much more will hang in the balance of the next few federal election campaigns.

Reform was, and the Alliance presumably will be, strongest in British Columbia (especially the interior) and Alberta (especially outside of Edmonton). It is weaker in Saskatchewan and in Manitoba, the latter being the only province to elect MPs from four different parties in 1997. The challenge, which defeated Manning and may doom Day, is to win seats in Ontario (and possibly the Atlantic) without compromising the regional protest from which the movement was born—failing that, Joe Clark's dreams of a Tory comeback may not be as fanciful as they now appear.

PROVINCIAL PARTY SYSTEMS

British Columbia is also undergoing a modest realignment in the provincial party system—one major political party (Social Credit) has vanished, and a new party (the provincial Reform party) is trying to become a significant force. But the realignment is only a modest one because it does not effect the basic logic of B.C. politics for most of the century, with a strong left-wing party facing one or more "free-enterprise" parties, and usually forming the government only when two free-enterprise parties split the vote. For almost 40 years, the free-enterprise vote was generally concentrated behind the Social Credit party; today, much of it has gone to the B.C. Liberal party with a challenge (particularly in the interior) from the B.C. Reform party. This challenge split the vote just enough to keep the NDP in office into the new century, but recent by-elections suggest that it may be fading. The most likely (but by no means inevitable) prospect is that the NDP will go back into opposition for a decade, waiting for the next strong third-party challenge to give it another "turn" in office. Geographically, the major political split is between the lower mainland (i.e., greater Vancouver) and the interior; socially, it is more strictly class-based than in any province in Canada, with an aggressive and unusually radical union movement and a bitter partisan cast to political commentary.

In Alberta, the province that defeats provincial governments only once in a generation, the Conservatives have won eight elections in a row and are entering their fourth decade in office. The elections of the 1990s saw the Liberals displace the New Democrats as the alternative "government in waiting," the final element being the departure from politics of the NDP's colourful Pam Barrett after a religious experience in a dentist's chair. The problem is that under both the NDP and the Liberals, the opposition is able to do well only in Edmonton, and it is also worth noting that on those rare occasions when Alberta governments fall, they are not usually replaced by the official opposition. The popularity of the Klein government having survived (albeit in a somewhat bruised condition) the imposition of controversial changes to the Alberta health system, the opposition's next opportunity will probably come when the Tories have to pick a new leader, something that is always difficult (especially in this age of personalized politics) but now has become even more problematic with Stockwell Day's departure for federal politics removing the prime contender. There is a double axis to the political cleavages of Alberta: the first is a surprisingly persistent partisan differentiation between Edmonton and Calgary, the two major urban centres that now share more than two-thirds of the provincial population. The second is the rural/urban split, its importance gradually shrinking as urbanization shrinks the rural voting base, although persisting malapportionment continues to delay its political demise. The political dominance of Calgary reflects the fact that it has been on the winning side of both cleavages; free-enterprise Calgary better reflects the style and spirit of the province than the "government town" of Edmonton.

In Saskatchewan, the return of the New Democrats to office in the 1990s was followed by an apparently never-ending string of scandals that saw many members of the earlier Conservative caucus (including some members of the government itself) charged, tried, and convicted; yet the third-party Liberals were unable to capitalize because of leadership problems. The outcome was the formation of the Saskatchewan party, which pulled together dissatisfied fragments of both the Liberals and the Conservatives under the leadership of a one-time federal Reform member of Parliament. Despite early doubts as to whether the loose alliance could even hold together, it took more votes (but not more seats) than the NDP in the 1999 election. This forced the NDP into a lopsided coalition with the surviving handful of Liberal members, the ultimate effect of which may well be to solidify both the bipolarization of Saskatchewan politics and the Saskatchewan party itself. The major axis of political cleavage in the province has long been urban versus rural areas, never more starkly so than in 1999.

In Manitoba, the replacement of the Conservatives by the NDP in the 1999 election is the latest chapter in a 40-year struggle between the Conservatives and the NDP, the two parties that have shared the government of the province to the exclusion of anyone else. (The ebb and flow of Liberal fortunes in that province usually just means the possibility of minority—but, since 1958, not coalition—government; now that the Liberals have shrunk to a single seat in the legislature, they do not even have this limited impact.) The "sharing" of office has been less than even, less than a perfectly regular alternation—the Conservatives have tended to win more elections and serve for longer stretches—but there is still no need to talk of partisan realignment as opposed to a simple turning of the wheel of political fortune. The major axis of political cleavage in the province, again surprisingly persistent, is a straight line from the southeast corner of the province running north and west through Winnipeg; the Conservatives tend to do well south of this line, the NDP does well north of it, and the ridings along the line decide the outcome.

POLITICAL ISSUES OF THE NEW CENTURY

As in the rest of the country, the major debate of the next few years will be about the appropriate role and scope of government. The paradox pointed out in the first section—of a region that is the most right wing in the country in federal politics but the most left wing in the country in provincial politics—strongly suggests that there is no consensus on this matter. Even at the provincial level, the experiences have been rather different. Alberta and Manitoba led the way for the whole country in identifying the debt-and-deficit issue, in passing balanced budget legislation and moving toward a balanced or surplus budget, and in doing so by containing the scope of government spending. In Saskatchewan, by contrast, the move toward balancing the budget was accomplished more by higher taxes than by lower spending, and British Columbia alone among the provinces has continued to carry deficit budgets into new century.

To be sure, this does not in any way distinguish the West from the rest of the country, and that is the reason why it should be emphasized. Western Canadians, like other Canadians, worry about the future of their health care programs and their public pension plan. These are "hot button" issues that can provoke demonstrations and swamp the talk shows. But at the same time Western Canadians are aware that they pay higher taxes than most of the rest of the world, and particularly more than the economic superpower that is our southern neighbour, with which we conduct most of our trade and whose high salaries attract some of our best and brightest. Arguing over the appropriate balance between these two considerations will dominate politics for years.

There will also be ongoing friction with the national government over the federal–provincial division of powers—more in the sense of disagreement over what the *Constitution* really says right now than in the sense of seeking formal constitutional change. In part, this will grow out of the federal role in the social programs that are delivered by the provinces; since Ottawa seeks to maintain a strong role even while its funding share falls, this creates a fiscal box within which the provinces constantly struggle, whether it is Alberta exploring the idea of private hospitals or British Columbia trying to establish a residency period for social assistance. Whether it is a question of rethinking the social programs themselves, or simply exploring alternative mechanisms for their delivery, the political realities of the postwar "social safety net" guarantee friction.

Friction is also generated by the fact that the Supreme Court has recently given the federal government a significant (but not exclusive) role in environmental decision making. The problem is that all of the Western provinces are heavily—perhaps excessively—reliant on the export of natural resources (lumber, coal, oil, natural gas, grain, copper, electrical power), and that any resource extraction, transportation, or processing must necessarily have a significant environmental impact. You cannot cut down trees, or drill for oil, or bury a natural gas pipeline without having an impact on watercourses and animal habitat; and there is no reason to expect that the federal and provincial governments will want to strike the same balance between today's economy and tomorrow's environment.

A special case in point is the Kyoto Accord, an international agreement through which Ottawa has committed the country to a significant reduction in the generation of greenhouse gases. But the Western provinces—particularly, but by no means only, Alberta—are massively reliant on the extraction and export of the energy resources that contribute to the production of these gases. The extent of the impact will depend on how quickly, and through what means, the Kyoto Accord is implemented, but no provincial premier (above all the premier of oil-rich Alberta) has trouble generating nightmare scenarios that devastate the provincial economy. To date, there has been more noise than action, but delay just means that even more forceful action will be necessary if Canada is even to approach the deadlines for its commitments. For many Canadians, the term "carbon tax" carries no immediate meaning, but it generates apoplexy among Western politicians, and every federal budget cycle is coloured by Western accusations (and Ottawa denials) that such a tax is being considered on energy sources such as oil, natural gas, and coal. If any single issue threatens to re-ignite the vehement Western alienation of the 1970s, this is the one.

Aboriginal issues will be a major issue for the country but more so for the Western provinces. This is partly because 60 percent of Canada's Aboriginal peoples live west of the Ontario–Manitoba border and constitute a larger share of the population of the four Western provinces than of any other part of Canada. For the 1996 census 2.8 percent of Canadians met the Statistics Canada definition, but the corresponding figure was 3.8 percent for British Columbia, 4.8 percent for Alberta, and almost 12 percent for Saskatchewan and Manitoba. These numbers are trending upward because the rate of natural increase is much higher among the Aboriginal peoples than among the rest of the population. Most Aboriginal peoples do not live on reserves but among the general population, generally in the larger cities, and many have not fared well at the margins of Canadian society. They generally constitute a much larger proportion of the prison population than their numbers would normally lead one to expect, a fact that has generated major reviews of the justice system in several of the Western provinces and a number of experiments with models of Aboriginal courts and sentencing procedures. As well, there are major reserves very close to a number of Western cities (most notably Calgary), and this also gives the issue greater prominence. The Aboriginal issue is a major challenge for Western provinces.

It is even more so for British Columbia, given the fact that Canada's treaty system with the First Nations was never completed. The 11 "numbered Treaties" signed between 1871 and 1921 included First Nations people in an enormous area that included the three Prairie provinces, much of the territories, and most of Ontario (that part that drains into Hudson Bay)—but included only the northeast corner of British Columbia. To be sure, even in those territories the treaty system was never complete—the Lubicon Band in northern Alberta is still trying to negotiate its own reserve—and controversies remain about the application of their terms, but they do constitute a relatively unambiguous foundation from which to work on relations between Aboriginal people and the federal and provincial governments. But in British Columbia, that process was barely begun, and the regime has been much more fragmented and ad hoc. The negotiations resulting in the treaty with the Nisga'a people of northwestern British Columbia show how protracted, and how politically divisive and controversial, the process is going to be—and that treaty dealt (as many of the future ones will not) with a relatively isolated region of the province and a modestly sized community.

A final major challenge (although for British Columbia and Alberta more than the other two) is what we might think of as cultural integration and accommodation. The West, particularly the major urban areas, continues to be transformed by waves of immigration. To consider only the two most dramatic examples: the "Hong Kong" Diaspora (in more prosaic terms, the relocation of many Hong Kong entrepreneurs when that territory was returned to Chinese control) has transformed the appearance and the economy of British Columbia; and the Sikh community has become a significant political presence in both Alberta and British Columbia, reflected in the fact that B.C. now has Canada's first Indo-Canadian premier. English is the first language for only a minority of the students attending primary school in Vancouver; and there are communities within Vancouver (most strikingly Strathcona) where more people report Chinese as a first language.

The positive side of this development, in the West as in the rest of Canada, is the emergence of a new multiethnic society that is less visibly dominated by the European groups whose immigration largely predated World War II. Sino-Canadian and Indo-Canadian professionals and business people are playing an increasingly important role. Just as the earlier European immigrants continued to maintain some contact and identification with their "mother countries," so the newer elements of society are contributing to a greater understanding and closer contact with larger parts of the planet, particularly along the Pacific Rim.

But at the same time, there are negative aspects that cannot be overlooked. The most serious is the most obvious—an element of racism that seeks to exclude the new elements, or to limit their growth by controlling immigration, and that objects to their full participation in (for example) the processing of nominating political candidates or selecting party leaders. Societies with visible minorities do not need to be racist, but they unquestionably provide the context within which racism can operate if it is not controlled.

The second problem is that for many Western Canadians, the francophone group becomes just another ethnic community and not even one of the larger ones. In Vancouver, French is the first language of fewer people than is German or Italian—let alone Punjabi or Chinese. If we had a second language, Western Canadians often say, it would be Chinese (in Vancouver) or Ukrainian (in Edmonton, although in fact there are more people in the city who speak Chinese and German), or German (in Regina). The logical solution to a multiethnic situation is either a single shared *lingua franca* or (less practicably) a multiplicity of official languages. Neither of these observations is particularly helpful in the context of Quebec's concern with its place in Canada; my point is not to endorse them, but simply to report their experiential basis in the lives of Western Canadians and the reason Western public opinion is so often unhelpful in terms of dealing with Canada's most longstanding political and cultural cleavage.

FURTHER READING

Barman, Jean. (1996). *The west beyond the west: A history of British Columbia.* Toronto: University of Toronto Press.

Cairns, Alan C. (2000). *Citizens plus: Aboriginal peoples and the Canadian state.* UBC Press.

Conway, John C. (2000). *The west* (revised edition). James Lorimer.

Flanagan, Tom. (1996). *Waiting for the wave: The Reform party and Preston Manning.* Don Mills, ON: Stoddart Publishing.

The Far Side of the Rockies: Politics and Identity in British Columbia

Miro Cernetig

In 1942, when *The Unknown Country* hit bookstores, it was immediately heralded as a unique insight into the collective psyche of a young nation called Canada. Yet when its author found himself west of the Rocky Mountains, he admitted to being baffled by the odd sensation that came over him. "Being in British Columbia," wrote Bruce Hutchison, was unlike the life of the Prairies or the East,

> so unlike it that, crossing the Rockies, you are in a new country, as if you had crossed a national frontier. Everyone feels it, even the stranger, feels the change of outlook, tempo, and attitude. What makes it so, I do not know. The size of everything, I suspect, the bulk of mountains, the space of valleys, the far glimpses of land and sea, the lakes and rivers, all cast in gigantic mold. They make a man feel bigger, more free, as if he had come out of a crowded room ...[1]

Those words now have the ring of prophecy as British Columbia marches into the 21st century. Long stereotyped as carefree lotus land by the rest of Canada, which justifiably envies countrymen counting daffodils in February, Canada's third-largest province remains an enigma to those who cross the continental divide. Yet the province's sense of being a nation within a nation, a sentiment manifested by decades of stubbornly claiming it must be regarded as its own Canadian region, is beginning to be recognized. In 1996, Prime Minister Jean Chrétien finally bowed to the obvious and designated B.C. Canada's "fifth region," giving it the power to veto constitutional change.[2] What is more fundamental, though, is the tacit acknowledgment of what West Coasters have always felt in their rain-soaked bones: from the beaches of Tofino to the gas fields of the Peace River Country, British Columbia is and always has been its own distinct society.

What makes this so is the subject of perpetual debate. Is it the province's trademark hedonism and insouciance, fostered by a temperate coastal climate and sense of frontier, that makes outsiders think

B.C. is so strangely un-Canadian? After all, where else in Canada is there a nude beach in the city centre and an annual race in which people pile into bathtubs juiced up with outboard motors and surf the waves on the Strait of Georgia, the blue expanse of Pacific that separates Vancouver from Vancouver Island? And what of the names of Spanish explorers affixed to landmarks along the coast, just another sign of a markedly different early history from the rest of Canada? What other Canadian city can claim one in four residents are of Asian descent, the legacy of an immigration wave that has given the city the highest real estate prices in the country but lifted the economy in many important ways? "Touch down on the far side of the Rockies and you've entered not just a different province but a different country," author Richard Gwyn observed in 1996, echoing the same sense that Mr. Hutchison had a half-century earlier. "The climate—the psychological climate—changes totally. The prevailing mood is laid back, open-air, hedonistic. Little if any of the Calvinistic ethic of reserve and of public duty, and of guilt, that so defines the East penetrated here."[3]

Practically everyone who makes it to the West Coast for the first time seems to experience this sense of apartness from the rhythms of the East. When I landed in Vancouver in 1986, a forced transplantation from Toronto because the *Vancouver Sun* was the only newspaper generous enough to give a job to a 22-year-old who aspired to write, I too was struck by the distinctiveness. Boarding the DC-10 in Toronto, I had been in the middle of cold Canadian winter. Four hours later, on the other side of the Rockies, I walked out of Vancouver International Airport, a suitcase in each hand, and entered a city that seemed like a dream.

Warm rain drizzled down from a pewter sky, flowers were blooming in February, wild ducks waddled in the gardens near seaside apartments, and relaxed-looking people sat outside drinking *cafe latte* at dusk, breathing in air sweetened with the Pacific and waterlogged cedar. My first impulse was to find a pay telephone near the beach, drop in all the change I could find in my pocket, and dial back three time zones to pass on this exotic and exhilarating discovery. I had discovered what longtime Premier W.A.C. Bennett liked to trumpet as "The Good Life."[4]

Lotus land's sensuousness has always cast this powerful and beguiling spell. Yet it's also a distraction to the newcomers, who miss British Columbians' deep desire to be viewed as not only another province but also a society as distinct in Canada as Quebec. At first glance, through the Eastern eye, all that really seems different in B.C. is its famous good life, which has consequently led to the rest of Canada stereotyping the province as little more than a laid-back homeland for a breed of Canadians who aspire to beaches, sailboats, and other pursuits that make them the nation's version of Californians. "Top-flight people can't stand slowness like this," Judy LaMarsh declared in 1976, a tongue-in-cheek remark, but one that hit on the common perception in the rest of

Canada and always leaves British Columbians fuming and feeling profoundly misunderstood.[5]

As an Easterner, I've always been more forgiving of such slights than the people who are born here. It takes time to decompress and absorb the cultural shock of B.C. life. When you first get to the West Coast, you are ebullient that the B.C. lifestyle is now yours. But that intoxication wears off after a while. Soon, if you stay, which most Eastern writers don't, you begin to be overwhelmed by a sense of alienation from the Golden Triangle of Toronto, Ottawa, and Montreal, where the bulk of Canadians live, and all the major decisions seem to be made. Eventually, you begin to nod your head at the famous adage of former Premier Edward G. Prior, who in 1903 coined the now oft-repeated West Coast lament: "Victoria is 3000 miles from Ottawa whereas Ottawa is 30 000 miles from Victoria."[6] You know you're becoming a British Columbian in mind and spirit, though, when you begin to understand that the old Premier's observation isn't so much a complaint as a considerable blessing.

THE BRITISH COLUMBIA DIFFERENCE

It was Lord Durham, in his report back to Britain on the affairs of British North America, who gave Canadians what has become the enduring definition of Canada's peculiar contradiction as a nation. "I expected to find a contest between a government and a people; I found two nations warring in the bosom of a single state; I found a struggle, not of principles, but of races."[7] From that, Canada's Founding Fathers, and the statesmen who have followed them since confederation in 1867, embraced the bicultural concept of Canada as a touchy meeting of English and French. But on this mist-shrouded coast, where more people speak Cantonese than French, one has to wonder whether Lord Durham would have drawn the same conclusion if he had come to the top half of North America after 1871, when British Columbia had joined Canada. For from that day forward, an even deeper existential crisis took root, one that might be best called three nations warring in the bosom of the state.

Like Quebeckers, British Columbians were reluctant Canadians, a people more used to basking in their own political and cultural isolation on the Pacific Coast. Even today, with their economy in the doldrums and a resulting drop in the heady optimism of the 1980s that their "Pacific Perspective" would give them more independence from Toronto's Bay Street, British Columbians prefer to look westward to Asia, not eastward to Ottawa. They want to be masters on their far side of the Rockies. And while most of them are now staunch Canadians, few forget that the seeds of their own nationhood were planted long before they joined Canada. Those roots of a unique B.C. identity are still deep.

Nationhood is a slippery concept, particularly in the context of the British Empire colonies, settlements most often dominated by men who had first come to plant the Union Jack on foreign shores and then, often unintentionally, grew their own unique brands of nationalism, some that took root and some that did not. As good a working definition as any of what makes a nation, though, is straight from the *Oxford English Dictionary*. There, we are told a nation is "a distinct race or people, characterized by common descent, language, or history, usually organized as a separate political state and occupying a definite territory." By that measure, it is difficult to dismiss the argument that at the time it entered confederation, B.C. was already well on its way to being a nation on the Pacific coast. True, by the act of joining the union, British Columbia's leaders had made a decision that truncated any dream of nationhood, opting to become a part of a larger whole. Yet it is still British Columbia's distinct political, cultural, and economic history from before that period that defines its attitude to this day.

The land west of the Rockies has always been a particularly strong magnet for wacky visionaries who fitted in nowhere else, from the entrepreneur who brought in camels as pack animals during the gold rush to a Founding Father and premier who, as an adult, one day renamed himself Amor de Cosmos (lover of the universe) and encouraged what Easterners call the "spoiled child" syndrome of the province. "I would not object to a little revolution now and again in British Columbia, after Confederation, if we were treated unfairly; for I am one of those who believe that political hatreds attest the vitality of the state."[8] Despite being an unapologetic eccentric, Amor de Cosmos still managed to get elected, an early sign that marching to a different drummer would be indulged in B.C. A lot of longtime British Columbians bristle when Easterners call their politics wacky, but where else would a premier buy a castle from Expo '86 and then move it through the streets of Vancouver during the night to put it in his Fantasy Garden World theme park, as Bill Vander Zalm did? "Part of it is that crazy Jack Kerouac thing," says B.C. writer Brian Fawcett. "It's the end of the world. You know, I didn't really know what Canada was, really, until I got to the other side of the mountains."[9]

To understand the B.C. mindset toward the rest of Canada, it must be understood that from the start, its residents expressed a pronounced ambivalence toward the prospect of becoming Canadians and were enticed more by the economic arguments of belonging to the new country than by the poetry of being the Pacific bookend for a new nation that sprawled from sea to sea, the lofty goal that had so many hearts fluttering to the east. Historian George Woodcock masterfully summed up the zeitgeist of the day in his sweeping history, *British Columbia*:

> British Columbians entered the confederation of Canada with
> an eye to the main chance. They were members of a community
> in crisis; the prosperity flowing from the gold rush had dwin-

dled, and a diminishing white population hung on in the surviving but shrinking communities. The undulating pattern of mining, rush followed by recession, had led to chronic business instability. And nothing by 1871 had yet replaced gold as an effective stimulus to the nascent economy or as a lasting means of attracting population ...

What British Columbia needed, to solve both the fiscal problems of the government and the economic difficulties of the colony in general, was the means of emerging from an isolation in which its principal trading partners were California, the Oregon Territory, and the Sandwich Islands. Such emergence required the development of better means of transportation than the sea routes around Cape Horn and the primitive land routes that then existed into Washington Territory. And it was for the possibility of linking up with a larger economy that would activate their own that the British Columbians grasped at the straw of a union with Canada, which would offer them merely a wagon road on which traffic might move slowly to Lake Superior.[10]

Eventually, the promise of a winding wagon trail was converted by the government of Canada into a transcontinental railway to be completed within 10 years of B.C. joining Canada. Tied around a pro-confederation package that also promised to settle the colony's debts, that "ribbon of steel" was enough to entice British Columbians into Canada in 1871. There was euphoria to the east, where the presumption was, and still tends to be, that Canada's westernmost province joined because without unification it was destined to remain a far-flung and hard-up cousin of the empire that would otherwise be swallowed up by the Americans. Closer to the truth, though, were the words spoken a year before, by Dr. John Sebastian Helmcken in the Pacific colony's debate on the wisdom of confederation: "No union between this colony and Canada can permanently exist, unless it be to the material and pecuniary advantage of this colony to remain in the Union."[11]

While British Columbians indeed felt a pressing economic need to join Canada, they also understood that they brought with them a natural bounty second to none. At the time of union, there were 40 000 inhabitants of the colony, with 30 000 of those being Aboriginal, and the population was shrinking thanks to the slump that followed the earlier gold rush boom. And as a whole, the populace was undoubtedly depressed, as Woodcock notes, "by a sense of their lack of resources in manpower and money."[12] Still, their land base was almost as large as the original Dominion of Canada and larger than any European country after Russia. So while the province was under duress, it was obvious a formidable economic engine was, as Woodcock notes, beginning to hum: timber mills were emerging on an unlogged coast, canneries were beginning to profit from the extraordinary runs of salmon, collieries were harbingers of a future mining industry, cattle ranches in the Cariboo were thriving, as were the dairy farms sprawling through the Fraser Valley. And the sheltered waters of Burrard Inlet had emerged as a great natural harbour, which a century later would make Vancouver one of the world's foremost Pacific ports. B.C. was never destined to be a pauper.

Thus, from the start, Helmcken's *quid pro quo* was the underpinning of the B.C. logic to attaching itself to Canada. It was the new nation's duty to aid the young province in developing its natural bounty or risk losing its loyalty. Proof that this was no bluff bubbled to the surface remarkably quickly when it became obvious in 1873 that Ottawa had reneged on its promise of beginning the railway within two years of B.C.'s joining confederation. Victorians stomped into the legislature, with some reports of pistols being drawn. By 1878, there was enough disgruntlement for the legislature to pass a resolution 14 to 9 that "British Columbia should hereafter have the right to exclusively control her Customs and Excise and to withdraw from the union ..."[13] Whether or not British Columbians would have acted on this impulse is a moot point, because by October 1878 the national government vowed to make good on its promise.

Antics like these, repeated in various forms since, have earned B.C. the title "the spoiled child of confederation." But there is an often overlooked reason behind the obstreperousness. Unlike the other Western provinces, B.C. entered confederation as an equal partner, not a vassal of the state carved out of federal lands. The first non-Aboriginal inhabitants of British Columbia governed their own Crown colony, making them self-reliant and largely unconnected to the affairs in Ottawa. From the beginning, B.C. felt it was a master of its own fate, a free spirit unyoked to a central government in Ottawa. "From the beginning, when they debated the advisability of joining the United States, British Columbians have been part of Canada in the Constitution, in law, in the written word, but not much in the spirit," Hutchison wrote in *The Unknown Country*. "From the beginning it was the land of men who wanted to get away from everything, to start afresh, to be on their own."[14]

IT'S THE MOUNTAINS

In 1965, Quebec chansonnier Gilles Vigneault hit the charts with *Mon Pays*, whose first line was *"Mon pays ce n'est pas un pays, c'est l'hiver."*[15] And though it was Québécois, the lyric to this day still seems to catch something fundamental about one of the natural bonds defining the spirit of 30 million Canadians. Except, however, the country's 3.7 million British Columbians, the majority of whom live on the coast. In their province, the country is defined by the sea and salmon, the claustrophobic coastal fogs, and the bald eagles that hover above them and occasionally fly through downtown Vancouver. And, of course, the balmy weather. But above all, British Columbians are shaped by the craggy peaks that have historically separated them from the rest of Canada. "It's the mountains," said Terry Glavin, a B.C. writer who lives on Mayne Island, making him one of the many British Columbians who use boats more than cars to get into the city. "Yes, they have been a barrier. But they have also protected us from the outside, allowing peculiar things to develop and take root."[16]

One of those peculiarities is B.C.'s nearly forgotten language. More than 20 years ago, when Vancouverites saw a fast car, they sometimes called it *skookum*. Thirty years before that, a newscaster began nightly radio shows with the words *"Klahowyah, tillicums."* Today, British Columbians still call the Pacific the *salt chuck*. Those words are echoes from the past, when the West Coast had its own exotic tongue known as Chinook. Today, most people don't know that *skookum* means powerful or fast, that *Klahowya, tillicums* is "Hello, friends," and that *chuck* is Chinook for water. But that language is now often pointed to as proof of B.C.'s unique cultural antecedents, and it still explains the geography surrounding the place, as the town named Skookumchuck attests.[17]

Indeed, the development of Chinook, a fusion of English, French, and Indian languages, was a rare happening in post-contact North America. The other occurrence of such a sophisticated trade language blossoming in the New World was in the U.S. gulf states more than a century ago, based on English, French, and Choctaw. It is tempting to write Chinook off as a sort of pidgin tongue of passing significance, but it resonated on the Coast, so much so that from 1862 to 1899, one Victoria publishing company produced "no less than seven editions of its Chinook dictionary." Almost a century later, a Vancouver publisher is planning a new edition. Nobody expects Chinook to flourish as an official language. But Glavin is one of many in the intelligentsia who believe its re-emergence is a symbol that the province is on the verge of a cultural rediscovery, perhaps even the sort of renaissance that a generation earlier revived Quebec nationalism.[18]

There can be no mistake that the West Coast political scene is original in Canada, if not North America. While most Canadians enter the political fray every four years or so, when the government's mandate comes up, British Columbians seem to relish being in a state of perpetual political debate. Just tune in to the West Coast's hot-line radio shows, a genre that was actually pioneered in B.C. by Pat Burns, the talk show radio host who was a North American sensation in the 1960s when he began calling up politicians unannounced to grill them on the air. The genre has since proliferated on the Coast like mushrooms in the rain forest. Day in, day out, the airwaves bristle with talk radio, where British Columbians call up to grouse about their politicians (or roast them live if they happen to be in the studio). Part of the reason hot-line radio is so popular in B.C. is that few other Canadians seem as eager as British Columbians to pick a side in politics and then defend it to the death, or at least until their larynx wears out. Indeed, no other province can lay claim to the degree of polarization that defines the B.C. political psyche, which is defined by a deep cleavage between rich and poor, left and right. In B.C., it is a requisite of residency to know which side you are on.

Since World War II, the province has been predominantly governed by the Social Credit Party, a coalition of right-of-centre interests that coalesced under the Socred umbrella to keep the New Democratic Party from power. Until 1991, that strategy worked magically, keeping the "socialist hordes," as the Socreds liked to demonize the New Democrats, out of office for all but one term since the end of the war. This lock on power helped to make politics in B.C. the most strife ridden and bitter in perhaps all of English Canada. Only Quebeckers, where separatists fight federalists, seem to have the same emotional tie to political life.

In the 1990s, however, the B.C. political scene was undergoing an unexpected transformation. The Social Credit Party imploded after a series of political scandals, dissolving the right-of-centre coalition. That enabled the NDP to win power in 1991 and then, for the first time in the province's history, win a second majority government in 1996. By re-electing the NDP, who campaigned on the theme that going into debt isn't necessarily bad for a fast-growing province such as B.C., British Columbians also turned their back on the neoconservative wave that gripped Canada in the 1990s.

That may be about to change. The NDP is now in disarray following the resignation of Premier Glen Clark, who ran one of the most turbulent and unfocused governments in B.C. history. British Columbians are on the verge of electing a Liberal government, one that will bring in spending cuts and shift the province back to the right of the spectrum. But there has been one telling development after Clark's departure: he was replaced by Ujjal Dosanjh, a Sikh who will now go down in Canadian history books as the first premier in Canada of Indian heritage. Dosnajh is evidence of another distinction that sets the province apart: the political influence of the Asian community. Asian immigration has long played a role on the West Coast, most notably with Chinese labour being brought in to build the transcontinental railway that cemented B.C.'s place in confederation. But the history is not a proud one for Canadians. From the start, racism has been rampant on the Coast, with support of head taxes on the Chinese at the turn of the century and the forced internment of Japanese-Canadians during World War II. But a new relationship was forged in the 1990s.

A profound transformation began a decade ago, when a new wave of Asian immigration began to arrive on the West Coast. The catalyst was the decision of the British government to return the Crown colony of Hong Kong to the Chinese government in 1997. Canada, and in particular the West Coast, quickly emerged as a popular destination for those seeking to flee the return of the communists. Of late, Hong Kong immigration has slowed. But it has been replaced by immigrants from mainland China itself. Tens of thousands of Chinese now arrive each year, and they are not the impoverished immigrants of the past. Most of the new

Hong Kong arrivals were—and continue to be—wealthier than average British Columbians. They enter at the top of the economic food chain, and their spending power transformed the once-sleepy real estate market, driving housing prices in the province to the highest in Canada. An average bungalow on Vancouver's west side now costs over $500 000, about three times what it was a decade ago. Early on in this unprecedented immigration boom, there was resentment, with Vancouverites complaining their city was becoming Hongcouver. The new arrivals altered neighbourhoods by building sprawling homes that came to be called, much to the new arrivals' chagrin, "monster homes." Chinese quickly became the second language in many Vancouver schools, where administrators were poorly prepared for the influx.

In the past few years, however, British Columbians have come to embrace—or at least adjust to—these profound changes in their society, through which one in four Vancouverites are now of Asian descent. In fact, 1996 can fairly be characterized as the beginning of a new era in political life. In that year's provincial election, the politicians aggressively courted the new Asian voters. Campaign literature was frequently written in Chinese; one party took to driving a van full of Chinese campaign literature around the Asian malls. When Premier Glen Clark then was appointed to his job in early 1996, his first words were in Cantonese, when he offered voters the traditional Chinese greeting of good luck for the Chinese New Year.

B.C. AND THE REST OF CANADA

Newfoundlanders, of course, might say they are different too. They also came into confederation as a self-governing colony, and as anyone who has had to kiss a cod knows, they have their own proud history and cultural idiosyncrasies. But their province has been a "have-not" in confederation almost from the start. British Columbia, endowed with rain forests of 90-metre-high cedars, bays full of salmon, and mountain ranges full of minerals, had one big advantage. It was—and is—rich. Moreover, B.C. did not come into confederation with the bitter aftertaste of a conquest by the English, as did Quebec. Joining Canada was a choice, albeit one preceded by an acrimonious political dispute in the colony pitting pro-Canada forces against B.C. sovereignists who preferred independence or annexation by the United States to joining Canada, sentiments that linger on with a small fraction of the population today. "British Columbia was a separate colony when it joined the country," notes Gordon Campbell, leader of the provincial Liberal Party, and a staunch federalist who nevertheless believes his province needs greater power in the running of the federal state. "It was equivalent to Quebec and Ontario when we decided to come together as Canada. We were on the same level."[19] And that, as any British Columbian will tell you, is what makes the provincial psyche so different from that of the Prairies, which has a long history of being subjugated by politicians to the east.

When Canada expanded after 1867, the three Prairie provinces were later carved out of the federal territory, getting self-government only after they had sufficient population and political clout. For most of their early history, they were necessarily beholden to Ottawa, which even controlled the natural resources of the new Western provinces. It was not until 1930 that Alberta was given control of the vast pools of oil that lay beneath its wheat fields, the "black gold" that enabled it to move beyond the agrarian-based economy that still defines Saskatchewan and Manitoba. And it was control of its petroleum wealth that allowed Alberta to join B.C. in its demand for a greater voice in confederation.

Most Canadians remain blissfully unaware of these distinctions, preferring instead to take the egregious view that the four Western provinces are a homogeneous unit. Just how cemented this view has become was crystal clear in the constitutional conference of 1969, when B.C. Premier W.A.C. (Wacky) Bennett unveiled his own innovative map of Canada, which boldly suggested five regions instead of ten provinces. The Premier's idea was to recognize the *de facto* economic boundaries of the country through regions. These he called the Atlantic (the four Eastern provinces), Quebec, Ontario, the Prairies and, finally, shaded in a glowing green, British Columbia. Reaction, as the Premier noted, was a mixture of derision and shock. "The prime minister nearly had a fit when he saw this map."

True, the map was a bit of the showmanship that made Wacky famous, but it was also the beginning of a contemporary fight for B.C. to carve out its own distinct national niche. "You must plant seeds," Bennett said. "All my political life I've been a planter of seeds, of ideas. The only trouble with the five regions idea is that it's too logical."[20] Twenty-seven years later, the "seed" sprouted when the federal government, seeking to make constitutional peace with Quebec and the West, finally agreed that British Columbia is a different region from the Prairies.

This recognition wasn't munificence on the part of Ottawa. It was an admission that B.C., with just under 4 000 000 people, and expected to pass Quebec's population in a generation, is an emerging political and economic force in Canada that simply can't be ignored. In a very real sense, British Columbia is now undergoing its own version of the Quiet Revolution, the rise of an intelligentsia, an ambitious, educated middle class that transformed Quebec and Canada. During that period in the 1960s, the seeds were also planted for the Quebec separatist movement, run by francophones who believed only secession would allow them political freedoms and a sense of identity. In B.C., only one in ten British Columbians now say they wish to leave Canada, about the same level of support that Quebec separatists had in the 1960s. However, with the Quebec question on the backburner at the start of the 21st century, most British Columbians are hopeful that the West Coast's Quiet Revolution can take place without seeding a future secessionist movement, a view espoused by historian David Mitchell:

> First of all, Quebec's Quiet Revolution of the early 1960s was not about separatism; it was a defining period of intense and dramatic change, allowing that province to assert itself in new, creative ways within Confederation. The move toward political independence was by no means inevitable; it was inspired by forceful political demagogues such as [Premier] Rene Lévesque, and unwittingly fostered by feeble responses from Ottawa to Quebeckers' ambition to become "maitres chez nous." To some extent, British Columbians also want to become "masters in our own house," but fortunately no West Coast Rene Lévesque has yet emerged.[21]

What definitely has emerged, though, is a new attitude, part pique and part nationalism, that's upsetting the status quo of federal politics. It's been a long time in the making, but it emerged forcefully in the 1990s and has began to reshape the country. In 1990, it was British Columbians who were most rabidly opposed to the Meech Lake Accord, a constitutional change that would have given Quebec status as a distinct society. In 1992, when the federal government held a national referendum on another package that would reform the *Constitution* and recognize only Quebec as a distinct society, British Columbians again led the charge, with more than two out of three of them voting down the changes.

Helping bring this fierce independence to a boil was the hot-line radio culture, a cauldron for B.C.'s volatile populism. The loudest voices in B.C. aren't the status quo federalists, but rather hot-line radio hosts and the faceless people who call them, expressing disdain for the two-founding-nations paradigm of the country. The hot-line powerbrokers can—and do—rally their considerable audience behind what often seems a jingoistic and isolationist call to arms. It can often sound suspiciously like a call to secede. "The trouble is it is going to happen," wrote radio hot-line host Rafe Mair. "... We should have a plan if the wheels fall off. And I think, given our natural blessings and the already deep feeling British Columbians have for their province, that B.C. could go it alone—and very nicely too."[22]

That's not the view of the majority. But what British Columbians are demanding in the new century is the sort of devolution of federal powers that has been a hobbyhorse from the start. After a long history of pretty much calling the shots for the West, the federal government is facing demands from B.C. and Alberta to devolve powers to the provinces, demands that will have to be addressed if the confederation is to survive into the next century. "But now things are changing," B.C. author, pundit, and one-time politician Gordon Gibson has noted. "The centre is weakening. Ottawa is out of money and the foundations of the country are under attack by Quebec sovereignists. To save itself, this country will have to change in rather dramatic ways. This will involve a rebalancing of federalism: some stronger powers (such as internal trade) to the central government to be sure, but mostly decentralization to the provinces, cities or private sector."[23]

There will be some powerful people from B.C. pushing ahead such sentiments on the national stage. Stockwell Day, the born-again Christian who has taken the helm of the Canadian Alliance, the country's right-wing opposition Party, has chosen to run for the House of Commons in British Columbia instead of his native Alberta. More interesting is that he chose to move further west, rather than move east to Ontario, where his party needs to build support. But in a way it is an instinctive thing for him to do. Day will be pushing through a realignment of the federal structure and political culture—and in B.C. he will find himself in the movement's heartland.

Canada is not facing another secession crisis on the West Coast. Going it alone is by no means the preferred alternative of lotus-landers. A Decima Research poll in 1993 found that 76 percent of British Columbians viewed themselves as Canadians first, and British Columbians second. Only 17 percent identified themselves as British Columbians first. That bespeaks deep loyalty to the maple leaf.[24] But it shouldn't be construed as contentment with status quo federalism. There is a ravenous appetite for the enshrinement of equality of provinces. The call to empower the Senate by making it elected, with an equal number of senators from each province, is a demand for a fundamental shift of power to the West. British Columbians no longer see Ottawa's focus on Quebec as either wise or defensible. The once sacrosanct policy of official bilingualism, meant to be a shining symbol of the two-nations model of Canada, makes less and less sense in B.C. and the rest of the West, for that matter. Eighty percent of Westerners speak English today and only 2 percent French, a language that under the *Official Languages Act* must be inscribed on the cereal boxes British Columbians see each morning. In Vancouver, people like to point out that it would make far more sense to write the ingredients in Chinese, now the second-most-spoken language after English. Boast about taking French classes, and you are likely to draw a quizzical look. "French?" a B.C. teenager asked me when I told her I was taking lessons in the country's other official language. "Why would you bother with that anymore?"

As they enter what they like to call the Pacific Century, when the rising economic forces are on the Western curve of their ocean's horizon, British Columbians aren't asking their fellow citizens to rewrite history or ignore the French Fact in Canada. They just want to move beyond what always has seemed—and always will seem—a simplistic myth from the East: that Canada is the product of two founding cultures. West Coasters have always known it's much more than that. If you don't believe it, just turn on the radio and listen. They'll be happy to explain at length.

NOTES

1. Bruce Hutchison, *The Unknown Country* (Toronto: Longman, Green & Company, 1942), p. 315.

2. Susan Delacourt and Miro Cernetig, "B.C. wins constitutional veto," *The Globe and Mail* (Dec. 8, 1995).

3. Richard Gwyn, *Toronto Star.*

4. David J. Mitchell, *W.A.C. Bennett and the Rise of British Columbia* (Vancouver: Douglas & McIntyre, 1995), pp. 376–416.

5. John Robert Colombo, *New Canadian Quotations* (Edmonton: Hurtig Publishers, 1987), p. 402.

6. Ibid., p. 40.

7. Ibid., p. 141.

8. George Woodcock, *British Columbia* (Vancouver, Douglas & McIntyre, 1990), p. 143.

9. Miro Cernetig, "B.C. reveals its own unique culture," *The Globe and Mail,* (Dec. 5, 1995).

10. Woodcock, *British Columbia,* p. 142.

11. Ibid.

12. Ibid., p. 122.

13. Ibid., p. 149.

14. Hutchison, p. 315.

15. Colombo, p. 348.

16. Cernetig, "B.C. reveals its own unique culture."

17. Miro Cernetig, "Ancient language offers doorway to past," *The Globe and Mail* (March 8, 1996).

18. Robie L. Reid, *The Chinook Jargon. Vol. VI* (Victoria: Archives of British Columbia, 1942), pp. 1–11.

19. Cernetig, "B.C. reveals its own unique culture."

20. Mitchell, p. 395.

21. David Mitchell, "What B.C.'s quiet revolution is really about," *The Globe and Mail* (Jan. 30, 1996).

22. Miro Cernetig, "Canadians feel strain from sea to sea," *The Globe and Mail* (July 1, 1994).

23. Gordon Gibson, "The new west will define the new Canada," *The Globe and Mail* (Jan. 9, 1996).

24. Roger Gibbins and Sonia Arrison, *Western Visions: Perspectives on the West in Canada* (Peterborough: Broadview Press, 1995), p. 65.

FURTHER READING

Gibbins, Roger and Arrison, Sonia. 1995. *Western Visions: Perspectives on the West in Canada.* Peterborough: Broadview Press.

Hutchison, Bruce. 1942. *The Unknown Country.* Toronto: Longman, Green & Co.

Mitchell, David. 1995. *W.A.C. Bennett and the Rise of British Columbia.* Vancouver: Douglas & McIntyre.

Woodcock, George. 1990. *British Columbia.* Vancouver: Douglas & McIntyre.

PART D

THE NORTH

The Inuit

Theresie Tungilik

I would like to take this opportunity to open eyes on who we are, where we come from, what we are like, and where we are heading.

In my parents' and grandparents' generations, their main goal was to survive. They could only survive by constant communication and cooperation. These skills were taught to us at an early age, so it too ensured that we would survive in our harsh and merciless environment.

As Inuit were nomadic people, different responsibilities fell among family members. The man of the igloo was expected to come home with the food to feed the whole family as well as to maintain his dog team, and to make household and hunting tools. He was also responsible for teaching his skills to his sons.

The woman of the igloo was responsible for making the clothing for all family members and for the social well-being of the whole household. She was also in charge of teaching her daughters the same duties she had.

The animals within our environment provided us with food, clothing, and shelter. Even the snow played an important role in our lives.

All parents' roles of teaching were by doing and through oral tradition, the teaching of good behaviour and basically being a good person. It was believed that in order to be treated with respect, you too had to treat everyone with respect.

You were taught to respect your elders and your parents the most. Their survival against our different and difficult climate proved that they had conquered many hardships in order for us to be alive today. It was they who taught us the survival skills.

The Inuit had gone without any professional medical assistance, but that did not mean people were not cured of their illnesses. Among a chosen few, we had shamans. Shamans did not only perform evil deeds, as suspected by the arrivals of the missionaries.

Shamans in our ancestors' days were at that time very powerful and feared. Their shamanistic power depended on the individual. They were a chosen few for a purpose. Not just anyone could become a shaman. If one were to become a shaman, their preparation began at a very early age. The Inuk whom the Inuit would depend on to cure the sick, find the migrating animals that did not migrate in their expected path, or communicate with the sea mammals to find food for his or her people, fight off evil doers, and who would be your judge and jury, if you committed any crime, had to certainly be the right ones.

Shamans were our source of living when mother nature did not offer. Shamans were our powerful prophets, the guardians to survival of the Inuit life, but all ordinary people were taught orally of all survival skills, before other forms of surviving techniques were introduced to us. Teaching of the survival skills really saves lives in the North. You had to hear and remember and know all that we taught to you. Then when you became a parent, it was your responsibility to carry out the tradition.

These are just a few of the things that make us distinct from other societies.

Time changes people, and we were no different from anyone. We were continuously changing toward improving our tools, our clothing, and our skills, but the fact remained that all parents wanted their children to be good people, people who would be responsible, practical, accountable, and most of all kind, considerate, and good to others.

In the 50s we experienced one of the fastest changes in Inuit culture, it was destructive but progressive later on.

It was destructive when Inuit families were ordered not to live a nomadic way of life. They were colonized and expected to live a completely different life style. For a high percentage of them, it was not their choice, though they were not given any choice. Those who opposed were given a hard time by the authorities and other non-Inuit community members.

This practice took away not just the freedom of living wherever you wanted to, but it became difficult for them to provide and sustain themselves. There were no job opportunities, nor did they know English as a second language. This made it difficult for them to communicate what they needed or wanted in their communities to the government authorities. For the women it became very difficult to maintain the care of fur and skin clothing. With this handicap, traditional clothing was slipping away fast. The hunters no longer took care of the animal skins as much as they used to. A lot of our traditional values were no longer being practiced. Christianity played an important role in the Inuit life, but how much of it was meaningful? Was everyone just following a trend? Where had our dignity, joy of freedom gone?

It was progressive because once we became educated, we were more determined to be tax payers instead of tax users. With the knowledge and skills we acquired, we determined the fact that we wanted our own identity. We wanted our own territory, so we negotiated, and now we are in the process of implementing Nunavut.

Today when I look at Nunavut, I can feel the pride of the Inuit people.

Yes, we are on our way to recovery. We are going to be in charge. If we make mistakes, it won't take long to correct them. We can be in partnership with the world. Only we can limit ourselves. But all this will come with a big price tag if we are not careful on how we do things, in timing of events, and watching our budget very closely.

The Inuit of Nunavut need not feel an intruder in the house, demanding changes without the consent of the host. There will not be such strangers.

We have to be like blind people to see the true picture. We shall not see race, nor any other form of discrimination when we become decision makers. We will need to judge "whose cry is real." We must capture the young from falling through the cracks. It is they who will look after our grandchildren's affairs. Prevention of disaster will be the best key for looking after healthier people.

We do not have a whole lot of time, but the excitement is already in the air. There are different plans already underway for April 1, 1999. Think of us and remember us as the same as you, and we shall rejoice together, though distant from one another, we shall be one on that day.

© Theresie Tungilik, Rankin Inlet, Nunavut, Canada. Speech given at Canadian Centre for Management Development, Ottawa, Ontario, August 1997.

North of 60°: Homeland or Frontier?[1]

Karim-Aly S. Kassam

INTRODUCTION

What is North? The Canadian North tends to be classified politically as Yukon, the Northwest Territories, and Nunavut,[2] but fundamentally, the North is a combination of a geographic and a mental orientation. Canada as a nation is itself Northern. Geographically, the North is a cardinal point marking the direction toward that part of the earth most remote from the midday sun in this hemisphere. As a mental abstraction, it is consciousness of location based on the interplay of geography and culture. In essence, it is a vision of one's place, a source of identity.

The aim of this chapter is to contrast two competing visions of the North as homeland or frontier (see Table 1). The vision of the North as homeland originates from those who live, work, and play there, whereas its conception as a frontier has Southern roots. The latter is solely motivated by a desire to exploit natural resources, whilst the former is informed by thousands of years of indigenous use of the land and sea. The notion of the North as frontier is myopic and simplistic. In contrast, the reality of the North as homeland is characterized by diversity and complexity in the population demographic, culture, and economy. The North as homeland has withstood the test of time, showing resilience and sustainability of indigenous life style. Development in the North inspired by the frontier mindset is invasive and dogged by boom and bust cycles. The North as homeland is conducive to circumpolar linkages to communities across national borders in meeting the challenges of globalization. As frontier, the North is constrained to supplying natural resources to southern markets. In essence, one point of view is indigenous and shaped by a relationship with the natural ecology, whilst the other is informed by industrial capitalism and is exogenous.

Staples development is a policy of dependence on natural resource exploitations for the purposes of economic and social development. Frontier is a perception of the North as a harsh environment that contains enormous wealth. The idea of frontier has its roots in the stories of

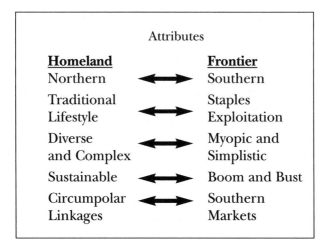

the early explorers and the fur trade. The search for the Northwest Passage as a means to the riches in the East was accompanied by a desire to discover great wealth in the North (Kassam and Maher, 2000). Northern homeland is a regional consciousness linking local geography to culture and economic life (Bone, 1992). To call the North a homeland is to recognize its autochthonous political and social reality (West, 1995).

In this chapter, varying conceptions of "Northernness" will be explored; the image of the three Canadian territories as frontier will be examined critically; and an explanation for the persistence of this image will be given based upon the staples development of northern economies. The North as homeland will also be considered on the basis of the human ecology of the region and the traditional economy. This vision of the North has withstood the test of time and sustained life for thousands of years. The economic and demographic diversity of three Northern territories will be explored. Finally, the prospect of Canada as a member of the circumpolar community will be presented as a challenge for an integrated Canadian economic and cultural consciousness in the forthcoming decades.

DEFINING NORTHERNNESS

One method of delineating Northerliness is by the Arctic Circle (66.67° latitude). In this area, inhabitants experience some of the winter months in total absence of direct sunlight and summer months in continuous sunshine. All three of the territories have regions above and below the Arctic Circle.

A second approach to demarcating the North is by the area of permafrost. Permafrost is perennially frozen ground. This climatic measure of the North is useful when undertaking geological work, archaeological excavation, or simply constructing buildings. All three of Canada's

Northern territories are largely within the continuous permafrost region with Southern parts in discontinuous permafrost. As we move south, the line of discontinuous permafrost extends to large areas of the provincial North across Canada, depending upon annual climatic variations.

A third way of defining the North is the separation into Arctic and sub-Arctic regions. Figure 1 illustrates these two regions of Canada.[3] The Arctic is within the continuous permafrost region of Canada. It supports quick-maturing and shallow vegetation; it is tundra. The sub-Arctic is characterized by deciduous and coniferous trees of the boreal forest and wetlands; it is taiga. The Arctic encompasses 3 000 000 square kilometres of Canadian territory. The sub-Arctic comprises 4 500 000 square kilometres of the region of Canada (Bone, 1992, p. 4). Yukon, Northwest Territories, and Nunavut contain both Arctic and sub-Arctic regions.

A fourth and more sophisticated attempt to define the North is Louis-Edmond Hamelin's concept of "nordicity" (1979). The degree of northerliness of a region goes beyond measurement of latitude to include factors such as climate, geography, and psychology. Hamelin's measure of nordicity is Polar Value (*valeurs polaires* or VAPO). He developed four regional categories: extreme North, far North, middle North, and near North. Figure 2 illustrates these four regions of Canada.[4] Hamelin's aims were to illustrate and thereby encourage Southerners to

Figure 1

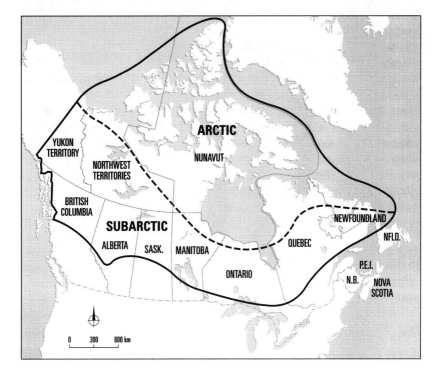

Figure 2

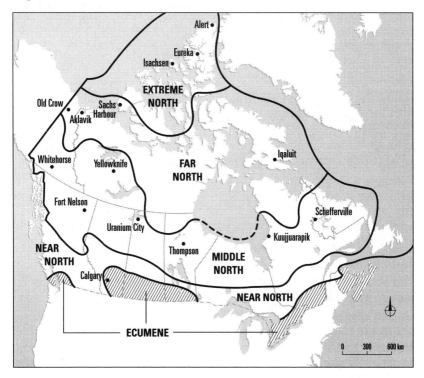

recognize their country's northerliness and to appreciate the cultural pluralism that is prevalent in the Canadian North.

For example the North Pole (90° latitude) in the extreme North has a VAPO of 1000. Iqaluit, the capital of Nunavut (63.75° latitude), in the far North has a VAPO of 584. Yellowknife, capital of the Northwest Territories (62.45° latitude), in the middle North has a VAPO of 390. Whitehorse, capital of Yukon (60.71° latitude) in the middle North has a VAPO of 283. Calgary, Alberta (51.05° latitude), has a VAPO of 94 (Hamelin, 1979, pp. 71–74). Using Hamelin's criteria Yukon, the Northwest Territories, and Nunavut occupy the extreme, far, and middle Norths.

Despite their arrangement of increased sophistication, the four approaches to defining northerliness outlined above emerge essentially from a Southern Canadian perspective in an effort to study the North. The urge to define the North according to scientific disciplines is comforting and useful in specific studies but does not necessarily relate to the reality of the perceptions of the people living in the three territories or the rest of Canada.

For most Canadians, the North is approached through films, television and radio programs, and literature rather than personal experience or travel. The nature of this engagement tends to emphasize discovery, vast riches, and the exotic. At best these characterizations are romantic and at worst they are tantamount to intellectual colonialism (Coates and Morrison, 1996). The following quote from Robert Service's famous poem *The Cremation of Sam McGee*, one that has been taught to generations of Canadian school children, illustrates this perception of a mysterious gold-laden North:

> There are strange things done in the midnight sun
> By the men who moil for gold;
> The Arctic trails have their secret tales
> That would make your blood run cold;
> The Northern Lights have seen queer sights,
> But the queerest they ever did see
> Was the night on the marge of Lake Lebarge
> I cremated Sam McGee.
>
> *Robert Service, 1890, p. 159*

These Southern constructions suggest an indifference to the reality of the North as a homeland.

This attitude is also found in other circumpolar countries, such as the United States. A particularly brazen example of Southerners regarding Northern lands as an "empty frontier," despite their being populated continuously for almost 10 000 years, was the U.S. Atomic Energy Commission's plan in the 1950s to detonate nuclear devices on the coast of Northwestern Alaska. Point Hope, Alaska, the site for the detonation, has one of the longest histories in North America of being continuously inhabited by indigenous people. Because of intense efforts by community members and a small group of scholars, the Atomic Energy Commission's plan was finally derailed (O'Neill, 1994).

Differing visions of the North exist between those who live or are committed to the North and those who view it from solely a Southern lens. Conflicting views of the North as homeland or frontier will be considered below. A rich history and diversity of culture inform the conception of the North as homeland. The perception of the North as a frontier is relatively more recent and homogenous.

FRONTIER: STAPLES EXPLOITATION AND GOVERNMENT INTERVENTION

The vision of the territorial North as a hinterland for natural resource development is firmly embedded in Canadian public policy. This is readily illustrated by the names of federal government departments responsible for the territorial North: Department of Resources and Development (1950–53); Department of Northern Affairs and National Resources (1953–66); and Department of Indian Affairs and Northern Development (1966–present). The Department of Indian Affairs and Northern Development (DIAND) is accountable for all Aboriginal communities across Canada and Northern affairs including economic development (Dickerson, 1992, pp. 61–63).

This notion is wedded to a staples view of the economy, a thesis that was advanced by Harold Adams Innis after undertaking a critical analysis of Canada's economic development and an examination of the formation of Canada's political institutions. A staple is the basic or most important good that is produced in a particular region. It refers to renewable or non-renewable natural resource exploitation for economic gain. Innis maintained that Canada, as a nation, has emerged from staple exploitation of renewable and non-renewable resources such as fur, fisheries, timber, wheat, and minerals. More recently, staples development has included oil and gas, hydroelectricity, and strategic minerals such as gold and diamonds. Innis was a political economist who clearly understood the relationship between geography and economic development. To personally experience the diverse economic geography of the Canadian North, Innis, in 1924, undertook an exciting journey up the Mackenzie River to see the rich diversity of peoples supported by this natural transportation network. He understood the significance of a country separated by wide distances and the implications of vast geography on the development of political and economic institutions (Innis, 1995).

Innis observed that in the 19th century staples exports united the nation on an east–west trade axis connecting Canada, as hinterland, to its metropolitan centre in Britain. In the 20th century, staples exports reoriented and fragmented the national economy by creating a north-south trade axis connecting the provinces to metropolitan centres mainly in the United States and other parts of the globe (Wright, 1993).

The hinterland–metropolis relationship that Canada maintains under international trade mirrors Canadian policy toward its own territories. In other words, as Canada is a hinterland to other more industrialized nations, the territorial North is a hinterland to the more developed regions of Southern Canada (Lipscomb, 1999).

Figure 3 illustrates staples dependence on the basis of the percentage of gross domestic product by industry for Canada and the three Northern territories in 1996. Government services (Yukon, 18.7 percent and Northwest Territories/Nunavut, 17 percent) support staples extraction in terms of mining, quarrying, and oil industries (Yukon, 17.1 percent and Northwest Territories/Nunavut, 17.2 percent).

Mining activities span Canada, reiterating Canada's role as a supplier of raw materials to the world. As the possibilities for mining in Southern Canada are exhausted, the North is increasingly regarded as a supplier of raw materials. Figure 4[5] illustrates productive mines across Canada. Gold and silver mines are operative in the Yukon (1, 2); gold and diamond mines are active in the Northwest Territories (3, 4); and lead, silver, and zinc mines are present in Nunavut (5, 6). The majority of staples-extraction activities are foreign owned (Lipscomb, 1999, p. 87; Yukon, 2000). In a staple-dependent economy, the federal government supports natural

Figure 3

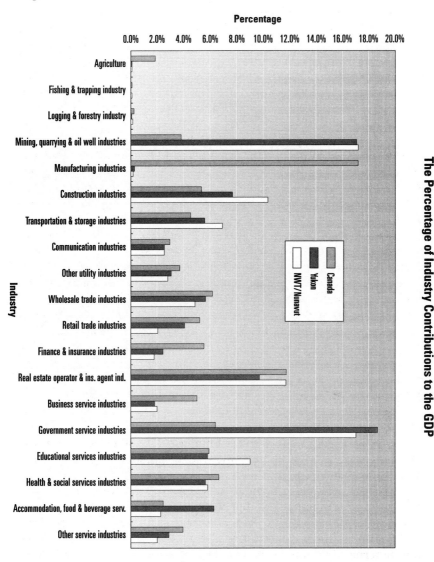

Source: Statistics Canada, Provincial Gross Domestic Product by Industry (in 1992 prices), Catalogue No. 15-203, based on 1996 Census data.

resource extraction by corporations whilst seeking to maintain a comfortable level of welfare for its citizens. Government services for staples exploitation range from underwriting loans for private corporations to develop resource-extraction activities to building infrastructure transportation networks such as roads and social infrastructure. The role of

Figure 4

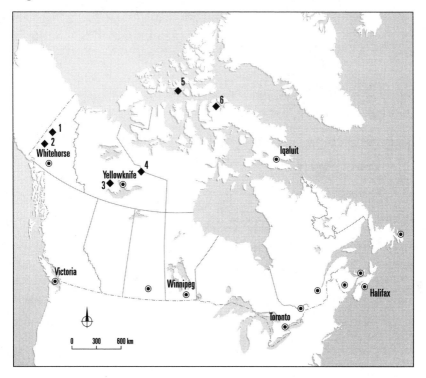

government in supporting the unstable market variations of staples exports is articulated in the *Yukon Economic Review 1998, 1999*, p. 1:

> The closure of the Faro mine and falling mineral prices were the main factors causing the further contraction in mining and related industries and contributed to an out-migration of more than 1,400 people from the territory. The slump in the mining industry was alleviated by continued strong growth in tourism, government and related service sector industries.

In 2000–01, total federal government transfers will be $1.5 billion to the three territories (Northwest Territories, $578 million; Nunavut, $588 million; and Yukon, $342 million), which is small in comparison to the total of $39 billion for remaining provinces. However, when federal transfers are represented on a per capita basis for the three territories in proportion to the Canadian average (Figure 5),[6] it is clear that government transfers pay for territorial welfare whilst staples extraction takes place by large foreign corporations.

The staples thesis is particularly relevant in understanding the persistence of the view of the three territories as a frontier.

First, staple exports are financed primarily by foreign capital to serve foreign markets. The need to develop these staple exports requires the

Figure 5

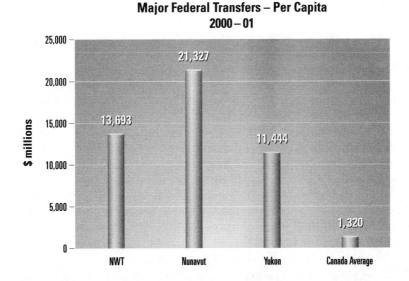

Major Federal Transfers – Per Capita
2000 – 01

Source: Reproduced with permission of the Minister of Public Works and Government Services Canada, 2000.

building of physical infrastructure such as roads or railway to gain access and support resource extraction. The federal government borrows from foreign lenders to build such infrastructure. The cost of building the physical infrastructure is ultimately paid for by the Canadian taxpayer. For example, the saying "all roads lead to Rome" is particularly germane to understanding the significance of staples development in linking the hinterland with the centre. This sentiment was reflected in Prime Minister Diefenbaker's policy of the Roads to Resources program in the late 1950s. The federal government undertook to finance the building of a road system linking Alberta to Fort Smith, Fort Simpson, Hay River, and Yellowknife in the Northwest Territories. The aim of the road network was to enable Cominco to export lead and zinc from its Pine Point Mine to Southern markets (Dickerson, 1992, p. 66).

Second, as staples development requires a large initial input of capital investment followed by a long period of extraction, the foreign investor is able to exercise considerable leverage over the policies of the government. The government itself is guided by its own objectives such as job creation and re-election.

Third, due to the high capital requirements for staples extraction, larger foreign companies have greater advantage over smaller domestic firms. Smaller Canadian firms are unable to compete with large foreign companies in raising the funds necessary to undertake massive capital investments.

Fourth, as distribution of resources in Canada is uneven, there is regional concentration of staples industries. In other words, there are regions that have resources for exploitation and regions that do not. Staples development, therefore, is dependent primarily on the timing of discovery and foreign demand. The rise and fall of the fur industry based on the transitory demand of the European fashion industry is a compelling and sadly tragic example of the staples thesis. The livelihoods of communities were dramatically altered by the collapse of the fur industry (Porter, 1990; Kakfwi, 1985).

Fifth, as the staples export is intended for foreign markets, it reflects instabilities due to variations in international market prices and variability in supplies. Northern communities are therefore, subject to the boom and bust cycles associated with export of commodities.

Sixth, due to their large scale, staples industries tend to dwarf local economies, dominate local communities, and dictate their political, economic, and physical infrastructure (Lipscomb, 1999; Innis, 1995; Wright, 1993).

The result is a political structure that favours economic dependence on staples production. For example, the Klondike gold rush led to the signing of Treaty 8 in 1899, and Imperial Oil's discovery of oil led to the signing of Treaty 11 in 1921 (Usher, 1981). Government policy is geared to meet the needs of staples production. Similarly, the moratorium on oil and gas development activities resulting from the Mackenzie Valley Pipeline inquiry in 1977 enabled the process of land claims to be settled first so that natural resource extraction could proceed once again. Arguably, in each of these instances, recognition of Aboriginal rights and settlement of their claims was not primarily motivated by a sense of justice but by systemic dependence upon exploitation of non-renewable resources for sale to foreign markets.

The implications of staples development is that political and economic structures are oriented to further reinforce staples dependence. Domestic capital is drawn into the staples sector at the expense of building a locally sustainable economy because valuable human and capital resources are directed to staples development. Staples development leads to a trap in which the potential for economic diversification is severely limited. Staples dependence leads to underdevelopment in the long run because socioeconomic policies are not geared to sustainable development based on local needs. Ultimately, staples development removes cultural and economic leverage from the people who live within the region and places it firmly on foreign markets (Pretes, 1988).

Sarah Jerome, a Gwich'in leader from Fort McPherson, Northwest Territories, comments on the vagaries of the staples-oriented resource development and its implications for men in her community. Jerome's description of the collapse of the fur industry and the short-lived impact of exploration activities in the Mackenzie Delta are typical of staples dependence. In each instance, the promise of staples development is replaced by the reality of the impacts on families and individuals. Communities are left with very few resources and many broken individuals in the wake of unstable staples development. Demand for staples production is controlled from outside the region where most of the benefits accrue. Whether it's the fur industry, oil and gas development, or mining, the result is much the same. The common thread is that the impact of development is short-lived with considerable social costs. Communities are left weakened by the boom and bust cycles of staples exploitation.

> We went through a transitional period during the 1970s when the whole subsistence economy of the community went to a wage economy. The trapping lifestyle of the trappers was sort of being phased out and the wage economy was coming in and this is where a lot of women in the community who had the education and who had the time to get the jobs, who were willing to be trained, got into the wage economy, and they gradually became the breadwinners of the community. Which left our men sort of in limbo, there was no more trapping to be done, they didn't have the skills or the education to get into these job situations, so they were sort of just stuck.
>
> I know that a lot of the men were not comfortable with that [changing gender roles], but they had no choice, so they automatically turned to the next thing they could think of, which was drinking, which created a lot of social problems within the community. But it wasn't their fault, because they didn't have the education, they didn't have the skills to go out there and get jobs. A lot of them had skills to go out [on the land] and work with the oil companies with the boom that they had in the Beaufort Delta region of exploration, gas exploration ... they were making a lot of money in a very short time frame. I remember being so afraid thinking, what are we going to do with these people when the oil boom is over and they're back, what are we going to do with them? (Kassam and Wuttunee, 1997, p. 58)

HOMELAND: APPREHENDING ANOTHER VISION

The reality of the three Canadian territories is beyond superficial characterizations seen through Southern eyes. Most important, there is a significant tension between the Southern approach to economic exploitation and the traditional indigenous economy. Below we will examine three aspects of life north of 60°: population, cultural pluralism, and the indigenous traditional economy. A key feature of the North is that diversity exists in the population structure, in the economic realm, and in the peoples that live there.

A. Population

Compared to the total population in Canada, Aboriginal peoples are a minority. In Canada's Northern territories, however, they range from a significant portion (Yukon, Northwest Territories) to a relative majority (Nunavut) of the population.

In Canada, as a proportion of the total population, the Aboriginal population is 2.8 percent. In Yukon, Aboriginal peoples comprise 20.1 percent of the total population; in the Northwest Territories, 48.2 percent; and in Nunavut, 83.7 percent. Aboriginal peoples in the territories have been calling this region of the Canadian North home for many thousands of years.

In addition to a strong presence in the territories, the population of Aboriginal peoples is growing. In the 1996 Census, Aboriginal youngsters represented 75 percent of all the children under the age of 15 in the Northwest and Nunavut Territories (Statistics Canada, 1998, p. 12). The proportion of Aboriginal population will grow in the next decades as these young people become adults, have their own families, and play a significant role in the life of Northern communities. In fact, the total population (Aboriginal and non-Aboriginal) tends to be young in all three territories compared to the Canadian average.

A youthful population carries with it a promise for the future as well as a legitimate demand for those education, social, and health services available to all Canadians and an expectation of employment opportunities. How these needs will be met is being currently debated amongst policymakers and communities in the North. For instance, the possibility of the construction of a gas pipeline in the Mackenzie Valley is currently being discussed by affected communities along the Mackenzie River. Discussion of impact on future generations, Aboriginal cultures, and the environment is very much at the forefront of the discussions. What distinguishes this debate from the one in the 1970s is that Aboriginal communities are now suggesting that they retain control of the pipeline such that its ownership not be entirely in the hands of distant or foreign companies (Chief Pierrot, 2000). Equity ownership of resource development initiatives by Northerners is a direct means of enabling environmental and economic sustainability in the territories. The youth in the territories are looked upon by Aboriginal elders to provide the leadership that will achieve development consistent with indigenous culture.

B. Cultural Pluralism

A strong Aboriginal demographic and a mainly youthful population is combined with a rich cultural diversity in the Northern territories of Canada. This diversity is manifested in the assertion of Aboriginal identity, through language and other means. For instance in 1996, almost three-quarters of those who identified themselves as Inuit reported that they could conduct a conversation in Inuktitut (Statistics Canada, 1998, p.11). Inuktitut is itself marked by a significant diversity of dialects and is representative of a language group. Some of the other language groups in the territories include Chipewyan, Cree, Dogrib, South Slave, Kutchin-Gwich'in, and Tlingit. Cultural pluralism is an attribute of the Canadian North.

There is an increasing self-confidence exercised by Aboriginal communities about their own culture and traditions, particularly as a result of assertion of Aboriginal rights and the settlement of comprehensive land-claim agreements in all three territories. The poem by René Fumoleau (below) about building bridges across cultures is particularly relevant to the diversity of the Canadian and circumpolar North. In a context where many Aboriginal and non-Aboriginal communities live united by a common geography, pluralism is achieved through recognizing and respecting cultural diversity. Distinctiveness is a form of legitimacy. By recognition of the specificity of a people, community, or individual, a genuine bridge or relationship will be built for mutual benefit and support. Only after we accept diversity can we talk about what unites this diversity (Carrithers, 1992). In the Canadian Territories, cultural diversity is very much a part of Northern consciousness.

Bridge

A meeting in Yellowknife gathered Dene and whites
coming from a variety of races,
religions, political and economic systems.

Members of the dominant society
were preaching accommodation
to those who have already been
so accommodating for two hundred years:

"We can all meet halfway ..."
"We can find a middle ground ..."
"We must all compromise at the centre ..."
"It's easy to start from a midway location ..."
Not new ideas for Benitra, a Dene elder:
"We've walked halfway long time ago,
and halfway again,
and halfway many more times.

Now I have a question for you:
Have you ever heard
of anybody building a bridge
by starting at the centre?"

René Fumoleau, 1997
Reprinted with permission.

Cultural diversity is not only present among the Aboriginal communities but also manifest amongst the non-Aboriginal Northerners. According to 1996 census data some of the other languages spoken in the Territories range from Italian to Tagalog. In addition to Aboriginal peoples and northern Europeans, people originating from eastern Europe, southern Asia, the Far East, and the Mediterranean also call the North their home.

C. Indigenous Ecology and Economy

The Mackenzie Valley Pipeline Inquiry under the leadership of Justice Thomas Berger in the latter half of the 1970s was a turning point in heightening Southern Canadians' awareness of Northern Aboriginal and environmental issues. The title of his report, *Northern Frontier, Northern Homeland: The Report of the Mackenzie Valley Pipeline Inquiry* (1977), illustrates the two competing visions of the Canadian territorial North. The result of the inquiry was a wider consciousness among all Canadians of Aboriginal concerns and a realization of the delicate ecological balance in this region.

The differences between conceptions of the North as frontier and as homeland are easily illustrated by the use of maps. Maps are a way of visualizing the land—at once representing a geographical area and the perspective or worldview of the map's creator. Figure 6 is a representation of the Mackenzie Valley in the Northwest Territories where the pipeline was proposed. In Figure 6, the Mackenzie Valley is empty space, barren, ready for exploration and resource extraction. Figure 7 is a hypothetical

Figure 6

Figure 7

map depicting the human ecology of the region. The symbols represent the diversity of life and cultures of people who live within the region. Human ecology describes the relationships between people and their habitat. It includes the relations among humans, other animals and plants, and their habitats. The figure portrays how indigenous people within a specific geographic region rely on the land and sea. The map contains ethnographic, historical, and current information on land- and marine-use patterns. A map may contain specific ecological knowledge as well as information on hunting, fishing, herding, plant species, trapping, forestry practices, migration patterns of wildlife, and location of sites that are sacred to indigenous communities. Traditional land- and marine-use mapping is not restricted solely to any one or all of these details (Kassam and Graham, 1999, p. 206). The struggle to define the Canadian North of the 1970s as either a resource frontier or an indigenous homeland was decided in part based on the ability of the peoples of the Mackenzie Valley to definitively map out their activities on the land. Based on the maps and testimonies produced during the inquiry, a 10-year moratorium was placed on staples exploitation of oil and gas through the Valley (Kassam and Maher, 2000).

In contrast to the Southern Canadian experience of regularly going shopping at a grocery store to purchase food that is cleaned, portioned, and wrapped, where the customer has no knowledge of, or connection to, the meat, fruits, or vegetables being purchased, in Northern communities people continue to retain a direct relationship with the web of life that sustains them. The surrounding wildlife is a key part of the life of Northern communities. People hunt, fish, and gather living resources from the land and sea. Notwithstanding the intrusive and disruptive political, social, and economic changes caused by colonization, forced settlement, and industrial development, the indigenous economy has proven a resilient way of life. It continues to be a viable source of living. In fact, the indigenous economy makes an essential contribution to the welfare of Northern peoples (Usher, 1981; Cox, 1985; Kakfwi, 1985; Porter, 1990).

Considerable evidence from all three of the territories indicates that the fruits of the land and sea contribute not only to the physical welfare of Northerners but also to their psychological well-being and sense of community spirit (Condon et al., 1995; Wein and Freeman, 1995; Wein et al., 1996; Collings et al., 1998). The psychological effects of indigenous hunting activities indicate a continuum of community tradition that spans thousands of years. It heals the rupture caused by drastic social change, making the past relevant to the present. Traditional harvesting of marine mammals, terrestrial mammals, fish, and plants are at once a manifestation and the defining means for retaining a connection to the land and indigenous history. Likewise, the subsequent sharing of country foods is both a formal and informal mechanism of maintaining the integrity of the community and its identity. For example Photo 1[7] illustrates seal flensing in the Inuit community of Holman, Victoria Island, Northwest Territories. In June the community celebrates its traditions by displaying skills associated with traditional harvesting activities. Other communities from the surrounding area also participate.

Similarly, other indigenous communities across the circumpolar North celebrate their traditions through sharing of foods harvested from the land and sea. For example, the Inupiat community of Wainwright, Alaska, celebrates a successful whale harvest and the cooperative effort required to hunt a large marine mammal such as a bowhead whale through a community feast, *nalukataq*. Community members gather to share food, dance, and celebrate.

Various estimates have been made of the economic value as food of the many animals and plant species harvested. For instance, in 1990, the food value of Barren Ground caribou was estimated at $27.6 million for the Northwest Territories (Ashley, 1998). In 1999, it was estimated that

the replacement food value for caribou, seal, and three species of fish (Arctic char, lake trout, and whitefish) for Nunavut was over $25.6 million (Nunavut Wildlife Harvest Survey, 1999). The various techniques for measurement of food values are open to debate, but the point is clear—wildlife is fundamental to the physical health and the economic welfare of Northern Aboriginal peoples. Furthermore, the harvesting of the fruits the land and sea are intimately linked to the spiritual and cultural well-being of Northern communities.

Indigenous use of the fruits of the land and sea has withstood the test of time, revealing sustainable use of renewable resources. Even today in a wage economy supported by staples exploitation, indigenous utilization of renewable resources results from a time-tested relationship with the natural environment. For example, the seasonal profile of the community of Holman, Northwest Territories, expresses this relationship. The seasonal round shows the activities of the community in a calendar year based on the rhythms of nature and the resources found in the region (Kassam, 2000, p. 28). It is a conception of time that is cyclical rather than linear. Figure 8 illustrates the human ecology of Holman in terms of sustainable harvest of marine and terrestrial mammals, fish, birds, and plants. The shaded areas indicate the length of the yearly harvest season and its intensity (Kassam, 2000).

Seasonal representation of sustainable harvesting of diverse food resources in Holman is an example of similar harvesting cycles found in other Arctic and sub-Arctic communities across the circumpolar North.

A Circumpolar Perspective

Canada shares its geography—the Arctic (tundra) and sub-Arctic (taiga)—with other circumpolar nations. The boreal forest encircles the North as a protective skin. This unity of geography is matched by the diversity of indigenous people, who have been living on these lands for thousands of years.

At the dawn of the 21st century, key events force a re-examination of Canada's role in a circumpolar context. The collapse of the Soviet Empire has had significant global implications. Whilst Russia remakes itself, important energies have been released on both sides of the great divide known as the "iron curtain." Mutual belligerence is no longer the primary objective. Valuable national resources may be utilized in other ways.

The collapse of the Soviet Empire has been accompanied by rhetoric of increasing globalization. The decline of communism is self-validating and has been touted as a victory for the market system (Goldsmith, 1996; Korten, 1996). However, staples development in the Canadian North warns of an unstable future based on international markets for finite raw materials and foreign ownership of the means of production. Globalization is not a new concept. Its roots in the Canadian North go at least as far back as first contact and the search for the Northwest Passage.

Figure 8

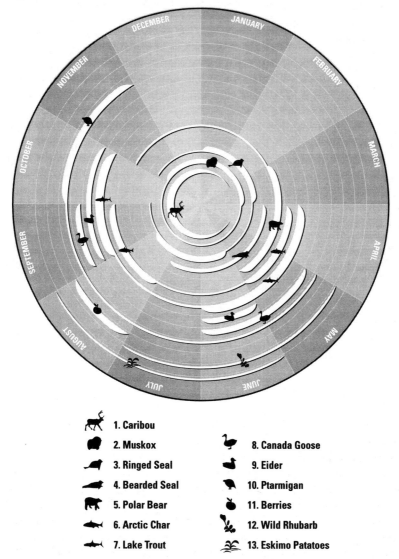

1. Caribou
2. Muskox
3. Ringed Seal
4. Bearded Seal
5. Polar Bear
6. Arctic Char
7. Lake Trout
8. Canada Goose
9. Eider
10. Ptarmigan
11. Berries
12. Wild Rhubarb
13. Eskimo Patatoes

In its early manifestations, globalization is synonymous with colonization. These first attempts at globalization brought about critical changes with tragic consequences for the lives of indigenous peoples. In a similar manner, the nation as it has developed in the 19th and 20th centuries is undergoing dramatic changes. Economic liberalism, international trade agreements, and the emergence of economic unions are significantly limiting the socioeconomic independence of the individual nation-state. In many respects, the powers of the nation are withering in comparison to supranational economic structures (Kassam, 1997). In the Canadian North, the persistence of the indigenous economy based on sustainable harvesting of fruits of the land and sea has moderated the vagaries of staples development. In Russia de-industrialization is taking place, and Northern indigenous communities of that country are relying primarily on hunting and fishing for their survival (Robinson and Kassam, 1998; Kassam and Avdeeva, 1997). After several decades of industrial development, it is hunting and fishing activities that literally put food on the tables of Northern families. Government services and industrial development provide little if any hope for survival. In such a context, communities have a significant role to play not only in terms of basic survival but also cultural survival. Communities maintain the fabric of society. A circumpolar perspective enables interaction with similar communities across the circumpolar north. If globalization is indeed inevitable, as its proponents claim, then it must carry with it the seed of pluralism, which still characterizes the Canadian and circumpolar North.

The Canadian federal government recognizes the opportunities afforded by pluralism. At a Canada–EU (European Union) seminar on Circumpolar Co-operation and the Northern Dimension, Lloyd Axworthy, Canadian Minister for Foreign Affairs, describes the government's objectives for circumpolar collaboration: "There are also exciting new possibilities for partnership with other countries of the North, particularly Russia and the Baltic States; as well as with the various communities within the North, especially Indigenous peoples" (Axworthy, 1999, p. 62).

DISCUSSION

The tension between frontier and homeland will continue to manifest itself in the Canadian context. In Canada the notion of the North as both homeland and frontier co-exist. The North as homeland has withstood the test of time and contains the seed of cultural pluralism. The North as frontier is motivated by the promise of wealth and is short sighted. Other circumpolar regions such as Russia and Alaska also display a similar dual conception of their Northern territories. During recent efforts to build a pipeline along the Mackenzie Valley, some leaders in the oil and gas industry referred to the proposed initiative as the "frontier" pipeline. The discussions on development in the territorial North will be framed by a delicate balance between staples development of non-renewable resources and sustainability of indigenous livelihoods. Northern Aboriginal people will deservedly play a significant and decisive role in this debate.

The historic significance of an indigenous economy accompanied by the presence of cultural diversity in Northern peoples is and will continue to be a key feature of Northern Canadian identity. Moreover, the increasing role of Canada as a member of a community of circumpolar nations is a challenge that can be creatively turned into an opportunity for collaboration and a meaningful articulation of Canadian identity. Circumpolar trade can also take the form of ideas and mutually agreed-upon approaches to solving common problems rather than simply the exchange of raw materials. It is likely through linkages with communities across the circumpolar world that the tension between homeland and frontier will be resolved, and Canadians will recognize the reality of the North as a homeland.

NOTES

1. I acknowledge the support of my student research assistants Jennifer Cardiff, Sean Maher, Ciara McNiff, and Kenneth Robertson in preparing the graphs and tables used in this chapter and Mr. Hassan Lalji for drawing the seasonal profile. I note Dr. Mark O. Dickerson's and Dr. David W. Norton's contributions in reviewing this article.

2. Arguably the North also includes Northern portions of provinces. Much of what is discussed regarding the three Canadian territories in this paper may also be applied to the provincial North.

3. Adapted from Robert M. Bone, *The Geography of the Canadian North: Issues and Challenges* (Toronto: Oxford University Press, 1992), p. 5; Energy, Mines and Resources Canada, "Canada Indian and Inuit Communities and Languages," *The National Atlas of Canada,* 5th edition (Ottawa, ON: Surveys and Mapping Branch, Department of Energy, Mines and Resources, 1980).

4. Adapted from Robert M. Bone, *The Geography of the Canadian North: Issues and Challenges* (Toronto: Oxford University Press, 1992), p. 10.

5. Adapted from Natural Resources Canada, <http://mmsd1.mms.nrcan.gc.ca/maps>, May 23, 2000.

6. Adapted from Finance Canada, <http://www.fin.gc.ca/FEDPROVE/ftpe.html>, May 1, 2000.

7. Photograph by Karim-Aly Kassam.

REFERENCES

Ashley, Bruce. (1998). *The economic value of country food: The case of barren ground caribou in the NWT.* Yellowknife: Resources, Wildlife and Economic Development.

Atwood, Margaret. (1995). *Strange things: The malevolent north in Canadian literature.* Oxford: Clarendon Press.

Axworthy, Lloyd. (1999). Circumpolar co-operation key to Canada's new northern vision. *Canadian Speeches,* 13(5), 62–67.

Berger, Thomas R. (1977). Northern frontier, northern homeland. *The report of the Mackenzie Valley pipeline inquiry: Volume one.* Ottawa: Department of Indian and Northern Affairs Canada.

Bone, Robert M. (1992). *The geography of the Canadian north.* Toronto: Oxford University Press.

Carrithers, Michael. (1992). *Why humans have cultures: Explaining anthropology and social diversity.* Oxford: Oxford University Press.

Chief Pierrot, Delphine. (2000, May 10). Personal Communication.

Coates, K. S. and W. R. Morrison. (1996, Fall). Writing the north: A survey of contemporary Canadian writing on northern regions. *Essays on Canadian Writing,* 59, 5–25.

Collings, Peter, George Wenzel, and Richard Condon. (1998). Modern food sharing networks and community integration in the central Canadian Arctic. *Arctic,* 51(4), 301–14.

Condon, Richard, Peter Collings, and George Wenzel. (1995). The best part of life: subsistence hunting, ethnicity, and economic adaptation among young adult Inuit males. *Arctic,* 48(1), 31–46.

Cox, Bruce A. (1985). Prospects for the northern Canadian native economy. *Polar Record,* 22(139), 393–400.

Dickerson, Mark. (1992). *Whose north.* Vancouver: UBC Press.

Fumoleau, René. (1997). *The Secret.* Ottawa: Novalis.

Goldsmith, Edward. (1996). Development as colonialism. In Jerry Mander and Edward Goldsmith (Eds.), *The case against the global economy.* San Francisco: Sierra Club Books.

Hamelin, Louis-Edmond. (1979). *Canadian nordicity: It's your north too.* Translated by William Barr. Montreal: Harvest House Ltd.

Innis, Harold A. (1995). *Staples, markets and cultural change.* Montreal and Kingston: McGill-Queen's University Press.

Kakfwi, Stephen. (1985, Winter). Our land, our life: The role of the subsistence economy in native culture. *Information North.*

Kassam, Karim-Aly S. (1997). Review of northern peoples, southern states. *Arctic,* 50(1), 77–78.

Kassam, Karim-Aly S. (2000). *Human ecology research, Holman, Northwest Territories.* Calgary: Arctic Institute of North America. (In Press).

Kassam, Karim-Aly S. and Sean K. Maher. (2000, May 26). Indigenous, Cartesian, and cartographic: Visual metaphors of knowledge in Arctic (tundra) and Sub-Arctic (taiga) communities. Presentation to the Association for the Integration and Unity of Knowledge, 2000 Congress of the Social Science and Humanities. (In Press).

Kassam, Karim-Aly S. and John Graham. (1999). Indigenous knowledge, community participation and traditional land-use mapping." In Delaney, R., Brownlee, K., and Sellick, M. (Eds.), *Social work with rural and northern com-*

munities (pp. 195–219). Thunder Bay: Centre for Northern Studies, Lakehead University.

Kassam, Karim-Aly S. and Larissa Avdeeva. (1997, Winter). The life of a sami dom cultura (cultural centre) in the Russian Arctic. *Museums Review,* 23(4).

Kassam, Karim-Aly S. and Wanda Wuttunee. (1997). Development and the changing gender roles of Gwich'in women. In Debrah Poff and Toni Fletcher (Eds.), *Northern visions: Northern futures.* Prince George: UNBC Press.

Korten, David C. (1996). Mythic victory of market capitalism. In Jerry Mander and Edward Goldsmith (Eds.), *The case against the global economy.* San Francisco: Sierra Club Books.

Lipscomb, David Robert. (1999). International trade and northern Canada. In Lise Lyck (Ed.), *Arctic international trade.* Copenhagen: New Social Science Monographs.

Nunavut Wildlife Harvest Study data. (1999). Unpublished

O'Neil, Dan. (1994). *The firecracker boys.* New York: St. Martin's Griffin.

Porter, David P. (1990). Conservation strategies and the sustainable development of northern sources. In Elaine Smith (Ed.), *Sustainable development through northern conservation strategies.* Calgary: University of Calgary Press.

Pretes, Michael. (1988). Underdevelopment in two norths: The Brazilian Amazon and the Canadian Arctic. *Arctic,* 41(2), 109–16.

Robinson, Michael P. and Karim-Aly Kassam. (1998). *Sami potatoes: Living with reindeer and perestroika.* Calgary: Bayeux Arts.

Service, Robert. (1990). *The best of Robert Service.* Philadelphia: Running Press Book Publishers.

Statistics Canada. (1998). *1996 census: Aboriginal data.*

Usher, Peter. (1981). *Staple production and ideology in northern Canada in culture, communication and dependency.* New Jersey: Ablex Publishing.

Wein, Eleanor E. and Milton M.R. Freeman. (1995). Frequency of traditional food use by three Yukon First Nations living in four communities. *Arctic,* 48(2), 161–71.

Wein, Eleanor E., Milton M.R. Freeman, and Jeanette C. Makus. (1996). "Use of and preference for traditional foods among the Belcher Island Inuit. *Arctic,* 49(3), 256–64.

West, Douglas A. (1995, Summer). Limits of northern identity: an assessment of W. L. Morton's northern vision. *Northern Review,* 14, 92–115.

Wright, Robert W. (1993). *Economics, enlightenment and Canadian nationalism.* Montreal & Kingston: McGill-Queen's University Press.

Yukon. (1999). *Yukon Economic Review 1998.* Whitehorse: Department of Economic Development.

Yukon. (2000). *Yukon Economic Outlook 2000.* Whitehorse: Department of Economic Development.

FURTHER READING

Bone, Robert M. 1992. *The Geography of the Canadian North.* Toronto: Oxford University Press.

Dickerson, Mark. 1992. *Whose North.* Vancouver: UBC Press.

Fumoleau, René. 1997. *The Secret.* Ottawa: Novalis.

Government under the Northern Lights: Treaties, Land Claims, and Political Change in Nunavut and the Northwest Territories

Graham White

Canadian identity is intimately linked to the country's northern character. Yet for many Canadians the reality of being "northern" goes little beyond vague ideas about pristine wilderness expanses, a fondness for Group of Seven paintings or Inuit art, and unfulfilled aspirations to someday "go North." The little southern Canadians do know of the far North rarely extends to even the basics of its government and politics. This is unfortunate since some of the most interesting—and difficult—political questions in Canada are to be found in the territorial North and since the responses to the political and social problems there have often been distinctive and original. Many of the distinctive features of northern politics reflect the involvement of Aboriginal people in governance.

As well, northern politics are noteworthy for the extent of change they have exhibited over the past two or three decades. Politics in southern Canada has certainly undergone substantial change in this period: new issues and new priorities have emerged, once-powerful political parties have declined or disappeared altogether, and remarkable ebbs and flows have marked the politics of national unity and constitutional change. Yet political change in the North has been far more sweeping.

The pace of change has been extraordinary (though many in the North continue to be frustrated by what they see as lack of progress). Barely three decades ago, the North was governed by Ottawa bureaucrats with negligible local participation or influence. Today the northern territories are entirely self-governing and enjoy nearly all the powers of provinces. As well, many of the changes—both actually achieved and under serious discussion—go far beyond simply replacing one party with another at an election. They entail changes to the basic political regime: the fundamental organizing principles and structures of governance. Far-reaching as it may be, for example, the creation of Nunavut in April 1999 was only one of these changes.

This chapter examines some of the basic political questions facing Nunavut and the Northwest Territories as well as some emerging and proposed responses to them. Many of the social and economic problems facing the North[1]—and by extension the politics around them—would be familiar to all Canadians: growing disparity between rich and poor, the implications of global economic forces on the local economy, cynicism about government and the public sector's capacity to respond to society's key priorities, concerns about essential public services such as health and education. Yet the Aboriginal presence in the North raises fundamental issues of governance that, though by no means unknown "south of 60," are central to political life in ways scarcely imaginable in most of Canada.

This is not simply a question of numbers, though it is crucially important that the proportions of Aboriginal people are much higher in Nunavut (85 percent) and the NWT (50 percent) than elsewhere in Canada.[2] While substantial variations are evident among Aboriginal peoples along many dimensions, including the political—indeed, this is an important subtheme of the chapter—in overall terms, Aboriginal culture (and political culture) differs in fundamental ways from those of mainstream Euro-Canadian society. Simply put, Aboriginal and non-Aboriginal Canadians conceive of politics and governance very differently. Aboriginal people have a holistic understanding of nature, human society, and politics; they prefer inclusive, consensus decision making respectful of all views, and leaders whose power is diffuse and sharply limited by community direction; they give primacy to local community interests and respect to the wisdom and experience of elders. By contrast, the governance system standard throughout Canada (and to a substantial degree imposed on Aboriginal peoples) emphasizes extensive concentration of power, rigidly hierarchical and compartmentalized governmental structures, formalized bureaucratic processes, and indirect democracy realized though divisive elections and confrontational political processes. Thus it is not merely that the interests of Aboriginal people in the North differ from those of non-Aboriginal people; their most basic understandings and ideas about the nature of politics and governance are incongruent.

Moreover, Aboriginal people have a unique relationship to the Canadian state, by virtue of the treaties they and their ancestors signed with British and Canadian authorities. As discussed below, this includes the modern-day treaties known as land-claim settlements.

Although fundamental political distinctions between Aboriginal and non-Aboriginal people are found throughout Canada, it is in the territorial North that they come particularly to the fore and that the scope exists for truly significant and innovative political accommodation of Aboriginal peoples. The people of the North have opportunities to determine how they govern themselves that southern Canadians have never enjoyed. Basic questions of governance remain open in the North to an extent unknown elsewhere in Canada.

NUNAVUT AND THE NWT: AN OVERVIEW

For many Canadians, "the North" is a huge, undifferentiated land mass, cold and barren, though rich in natural resources. Not surprisingly, given that Nunavut and the NWT make up some 40 percent of Canada's territory (as trivia buffs know, the country's geographical centre lies just outside Baker Lake, Nunavut), their physical features exhibit tremendous variation, from the forests and mountains of the western NWT, through the flat "barrenlands" between Great Slave Lake and Hudson Bay, to the breathtaking fiords and glaciers of Baffin and Ellesmere islands. So too do the people.

If the precise boundary between Nunavut and the NWT is artificial and arbitrary, it nonetheless does reflect very real differences between the territories, for it roughly follows the tree line (which is not a line as such, but a zone, beyond which the climate is too harsh for trees). In turn, the tree line marks the primary division between Inuit and Dene, who are, ethnographically, culturally, and linguistically, quite separate peoples. The Inuit live north and east of the tree line; their traditional culture and economy centred on the sea and sea mammals, while the traditional lands of the Dene were the boreal forests of the Mackenzie Valley, which shaped their economy and culture in quite different ways.[3] Although the Inuit and the Dene, along with the Métis (who have Dene and European ancestry), co-existed in reasonably amicable fashion in the pre-division NWT, their interests, situations, and political approaches diverged substantially. After all, the pre-1999 NWT had no organic unity; it was simply the territory left over after the provinces and Yukon Territory were carved out of the lands Canada acquired from Britain in the 19th century.

The Canadian Arctic is among the most sparsely populated regions on earth. In the NWT some 41 000 people inhabit roughly 1 200 000 square kilometres, while Nunavut is even more thinly settled: 27 000 residents spread across 2 100 000 square kilometres. Together their area is larger than India and nearly twice the size of Western Europe.

Nunavut is overwhelmingly Inuit (approximately 85 percent of its population, according to the 1996 census); virtually everyone else is non-Aboriginal. By contrast, the social composition of the NWT is far more complex. About 50 percent of the population is non-Aboriginal, with the balance divided between Dene (28 percent), Métis (10 percent), and Inuvialuit (Inuit of the Mackenzie Delta and the Western Arctic islands; 10 percent). Not only is Nunavut's Aboriginal population much larger, proportionately, than is the case in the NWT, but also is more homogeneous. Regional tensions certainly exist in Nunavut, and Inuktitut (the Inuit language) has distinct regional dialects, but the overall sense of Inuit unity is strong. In the NWT, the Inuvialuit differ markedly from the Dene, and important regional and tribal divisions are evident among the

Dene, symbolized by the five Dene languages. And if the Métis share much in common with the Dene, they also have a well-developed sense of themselves as a distinct people, in some measure derived from legal distinctions between Métis and "status Indians" under the federal *Indian Act*.[4] Inuit are not subject to the *Indian Act*, and no equivalent to Métis exists in Inuit society; one is either an Inuk or not (in legal terms, a "beneficiary" of the land claim).

Other important distinctions between the NWT and Nunavut can be noted only briefly here. Transportation, which can be crucial for natural resource development, is far better in the NWT; indeed, Nunavut has virtually no roads. The private sector is more extensive and diversified in the NWT; among other things, this means the Nunavut government has less capacity to generate tax revenue. Close to half the NWT population lives in Yellowknife, which is a predominantly non-Aboriginal community, whereas Iqaluit, in which Inuit are in the majority, represents only about 18 percent of Nunavut's population. Inuktitut, spoken by virtually all Nunavut Inuit, is relatively healthy in comparison to the Aboriginal languages of the NWT, some of which are spoken by only a few hundred, mainly older, people and are in serious danger of dying out.

A final key difference between Nunavut and the NWT relates to historical treaties. Whereas most of the NWT was covered by Treaty 8 (1899) and Treaty 11 (1921), none of Nunavut was ever subject to a treaty or any formal agreement between the Inuit and the British or Canadian authorities.

To be sure, the two territories share many important similarities. Distance from southern markets, high living costs, low levels of education, small, dispersed populations, and of course a brutal climate pose tremendous challenges for economic development. By every indicator of economic well-being—unemployment rates, welfare dependency, income, job status—Aboriginal people rank substantially below non-Aboriginal people. Although Aboriginal development corporations, built on land-claims money, are becoming increasingly important players, control of the private sector is largely in the hands of non-Aboriginals. The large oil, gas, and mining operations are owned entirely by southern Canadian or foreign interests.

In turn, economic problems are linked to pervasive social pathologies in Aboriginal communities. The roots of these social dislocations are not, of course, limited to economics. The colonization of northern Aboriginal peoples by powerful southern, Euro-Canadian forces—the churches, the Hudson's Bay Company, the government—led to endemic loss of control by Aboriginal peoples over their own lives, loss of culture, and social marginalization. Until well into the 20th century, most northern Aboriginal people were nomadic, but with virtually all now living in permanent settlements, central, defining elements of traditional culture, lifestyle, and economy have been lost or transformed.

The social consequences of economic disadvantage and cultural dislocation are numerous and severe: high rates of criminal offences and violence, particularly family violence; widespread drug and alcohol abuse; high youth suicide rates; extensive welfare dependency; substandard and overcrowded housing. In Nunavut, these problems are compounded by high birth rates, which are placing tremendous demands on social services and on the economy's job-creation capacity.

TREATIES AND GOVERNMENT

"Government" in any formal sense is relatively new to the Canadian North. Explorers and fur traders had reached the Mackenzie Valley by the late 18th century, though Euro-Canadian presence was minimal until the latter part of the 19th century. By the turn of the 20th century, the Canadian state had begun to expand its institutions into the western Arctic and to negotiate treaties with the Dene, though government activity remained limited. In the eastern and central Arctic, isolated contact between Inuit and Europeans occurred from the time of the Frobisher expeditions of the 1570s, but extended contact with Euro-Canadian society came later than in the west (some central Arctic Inuit were said not to have encountered white men until the 20th century). Emanations of the Canadian government were correspondingly slower to reach Nunavut.

Experience in the North conforms to the pattern typical of Canada's treaties with its indigenous peoples, whereby fundamental disagreement marks the government's and the Aboriginal peoples' understanding of the treaties' nature and meaning. For the government, these were land deals, through which the Dene agreed to, in the words of the treaties, "cede, release, surrender and yield up ... all their rights titles and privileges whatsoever"[5] to their lands and accept the sovereignty of the Canadian state and its authority to direct their affairs. In return Canada would look after their health, education, and other needs. The Dene, however, regarded the treaties as solemn commitments to peace and friendship between independent nations, under which Canadians would be allowed to live on and use Dene lands, and the government agreed to provide benefits and assistance to the Dene. The notion that the treaties in any way entailed "selling" their land was literally inconceivable to the Dene, who had neither a concept of privately held (and thus alienable) property nor leaders or organizations with the authority to agree to such an arrangement. Similarly, Dene leaders reject the notion that their forefathers gave up the right to govern themselves.[6]

For many years, however, Dene interpretations of the treaties carried no political weight. The Canadian government acted on the assumption that it owned the land, and it proceeded to establish authoritative institutions of government (as it did, somewhat later, in the eastern Arctic). The limited and extremely localized nature of resource extraction and the lack of arable land meant that the NWT never experienced the pressures to clear Aboriginal people off the land for white settlers and farmers that characterized southern Canada. In turn, reserves based on the southern model were largely unnecessary. Accordingly, the NWT contains only two small reserves.

With the treaties effectively ignored as a basis of governance, for most of the 20th century, the NWT was governed—or more accurately, administered—as a colony of the federal government, with little or no involvement of the Aboriginal people. The "government" of the NWT consisted of a committee of federal bureaucrats under the direction of an all-powerful figure, the Commissioner. Ottawa, thousands of kilometres distant from the NWT, served as the territorial capital until 1967. Only in the 1950s did the federal government permit election of a few members to serve with the appointed officials on the territorial Legislative Council. At first only the more populous centres of the western Arctic, which were dominated by non-Aboriginal people, were permitted to elect representatives to Council. Even when elected representation was extended to all parts of the NWT, few Aboriginals held office. Virtually no Aboriginal persons held positions of authority in the bureaucracy.

From the late 1960s to the mid 1980s, pressure from Northerners and accommodation on the part of Ottawa and its representatives made for a dramatic shift of power and authority to territorial institutions and people. By 1985, the government of the Northwest Territories (GNWT) was no longer in the hands of federal officials but consisted of a cabinet responsible to a democratically elected legislature. Major devolutions of government programs gave the territorial government effective control over most of the powers exercised by provinces, including health, welfare, transportation, education, economic development, and local government. The major exception was (and remains) jurisdiction over lands and non-renewable natural resources, which—as in the Prairie provinces prior to 1930—Ottawa retained.

If the outline of territorial governance—premier, cabinet, legislature, British-style "responsible government"—seemed to replicate southern models, important northern variations characterized both the structure and the operating principles of the central institutions of the GNWT. Disagreement exists as to whether these unique modifications of the "Westminster model" arise from northern Aboriginal political culture or are simply consistent with it (Dacks, 1986; White, 1991). What is not in dispute is the distinctiveness of the so-called "consensus government" system.

The most unusual feature of "consensus government" is that it functions without political parties. Candidates for the legislature run as independents, and while groupings based on region, culture, or other factors are certainly evident in the legislature, nothing like political parties exists there.[7] This may not seem remarkable—almost all Canadian municipal governments lack organized political parties—until it is recalled how central parties are to most Canadians' understanding of parliamentary government. Many people, academics and practising politicians among them, cannot conceive of Westminster-style responsible government without parties. Yet it is alive and well in the NWT and in Nunavut, which effectively inherited the consensus system.

In the absence of parties, the premier and the cabinet ministers are chosen by secret ballot of all members of the Legislative Assembly (MLAs); by the same token they may be, and some have been, removed from office by majority vote of the legislature. This makes for cabinet–legislature dynamics quite unknown in Ottawa and the provinces. Since ministers owe their elevation into cabinet to the MLAs rather than to the premier, the premier has far less power over them than do first ministers in Ottawa and the provinces. Similarly, the private members, who are in a position to out-vote cabinet at any time, wield far more influence than their counterparts in the south. Conflict, power politics, and backroom dealing are unquestionably part of Northern legislative life, but overall the atmosphere is far less adversarial and confrontational than in other Canadian legislatures. The more cooperative style is in part realized through a uniquely Northern parliamentary institution: caucus. In other Canadian parliaments, caucuses exist, but in a very different form: they are the regular meetings each party holds of its elected members to determine strategy and (to a limited extent) policy. In Nunavut and NWT, caucus consists of all MLAs meeting in private to discuss major issues and determine policy. Though less powerful than cabinet, it plays an important role in guiding cabinet and in developing consensus around difficult issues.

Like any political system, "consensus government" has its strengths and weaknesses. Whether Northerners would be better served by a party system is hotly debated (Widdowson and Howard, 1999a, 1999b; White 1999, 2000); for present purposes, the key point is the preference of many Northerners for the existing system over a party system.

Those pressing most vigorously for an end to "consensus government" and the introduction of political parties are mainly non-Aboriginal. Since 1975 Aboriginal MLAs have outnumbered non-Aboriginal members in the NWT (both pre- and post-division), and most ministers and premiers have been Aboriginal. Yet, paradoxically, important elements in NWT Aboriginal organizations are not at all satisfied with the NWT political system. They argue that the NWT legislature is at best a pale imitation of true consensus decision making found in their communities, and that the GNWT is far more Euro-Canadian than Aboriginal in its structure and orientation. This is particularly so, they point out, in the composition and culture of the bureaucratic apparatus of the territorial state, which for most people is the everyday face of government. Relatively few senior bureaucratic positions are held by Aboriginal people, Aboriginal languages are rarely heard in GNWT offices, and the routines and processes of the modern bureaucracy run directly counter to traditional Aboriginal values and approaches.

Most significantly, however, many Aboriginal people simply do not consider the GNWT legitimate. Legitimacy refers to people's fundamental acceptance of the state's existence; while they may disagree with specific government policies and oppose particular people who hold office, they do not dispute the state's authority over them. Simply put, many Dene and Métis believe that their treaties affirmed their status as self-governing peoples and established nation-to-nation relations between themselves and the government of Canada. They thus regard the GNWT as a foreign, colonially imposed, and illegitimate government, created without consultation with Aboriginal people, let alone their agreement. Inuit, who had if anything even stronger grounds for denying the legitimacy of the GNWT and indeed the Canadian state—they were never conquered militarily, they signed no treaties, but one day found strangers in their lands who claimed to represent a distant entity called "government," which would henceforth control their lives—were less inclined to the rhetoric of anticolonialism of the Dene-Métis. They spoke of the GNWT as a "temporary" or "interim" government.

ABORIGINAL POLITICAL ASPIRATIONS

By the 1960s and 1970s, a new generation of Aboriginal leaders, educated in the white man's schools, fluent in his language, and knowledgeable in his ways, had emerged in both the eastern and western NWT. Encouraged by the retreat of colonialism in Africa and Asia and linked into the growing activism and militancy of Aboriginal peoples throughout North America, these leaders mobilized for political action. The organizations they created directly challenged the legitimacy of the existing political order and propounded far-reaching schemes for fundamental change.

From the outset it was clear that save for a largely abstract sense of mutual support, the Aboriginal organizations of the east and the west would not make common cause in practical political matters. (Indeed, in the critical question of the boundary between their homelands, they found themselves in direct conflict.) Division of the NWT may not have been inevitable, but at a minimum, very different political solutions were sure to develop in the two regions.

The Inuit and the Dene adopted quite different strategies and objectives rooted in their different circumstances and outlooks. Dene lands contained far more of the natural resources, such as fur, minerals, and oil, that drew Canadians north than did Inuit lands; as well, travel was comparatively easier in the west. Accordingly, Dene contact with Southerners and their governments had historically been more extensive, more exploitative, and more harmful to their culture than in the east. These experiences inclined them toward vehement rejection of the existing political regime and to greater militancy in pursuing political solutions that would enable them to regain control over their own affairs.

Moreover, whereas Inuit remained an overwhelming majority in their territory, non-Aboriginal residents had already reached numerical equality with the Dene and Métis, who faced the prospect of becoming an increasingly small minority of the population. Finally, the distinct political approaches of the Dene and the Inuit may in part reflect their different characteristics as a people. Whereas the Inuit, though unwavering in their objectives, are pragmatic about methods and patient in working toward them, the Dene seem to place greater store in political symbolism and are less willing to compromise on means of attaining their goals. (Whether such differences are inherent to the character of the Inuit and the Dene or reflect their different experiences with Euro-Canadian society and governments is a matter of debate.)

Accordingly, whereas Inuit were content with a "public government" model, many Dene and Métis leaders pushed for some form of Aboriginal self-government. Public government is the standard in southern Canada, to the point where the very term would appear redundant to most people. The authority and jurisdiction of public government applies to all residents, who are in turn eligible to hold political office and to participate (usually through voting) in the selection of office-holders. By contrast, only Aboriginal people hold office or select office-holders in Aboriginal self-government regimes, whose services and programs generally extend only to Aboriginal people. Many different models for Aboriginal self-government, and for their links to public government, have been proposed for the North and in other parts of Canada.[8] Preference for Aboriginal self-government among Dene and Métis is to an important extent rooted in their rejection of the territorial government as illegitimate.

The goal for the Inuit was clear and essential: protection and promotion of Inuit culture through creation of a separate political jurisdiction, which would effectively become an Inuit homeland—Nunavut ("our land" in Inuktitut). Avoiding the roadblocks that Ottawa was sure to place in the way of an "ethnic government," the Inuit opted for a public government model, secure in the knowledge that their numerical advantage would ensure its Inuit character. In the Mackenzie Valley no such unity of vision was evident, and divisions within Aboriginal ranks continue to this day. Some Aboriginal leaders, though interested in self-government possibilities, looked to extend Aboriginal influence through involvement in public government structures and were prepared to reach what they saw as realistic compromises on matters of treaty, land, ownership, and Aboriginal rights to expedite essential action on economic and social problems. Others held out for nothing less than creation of a Denendeh Territory in which government of Dene for Dene would replace the public government of the GNWT. Métis, who were found in both camps, found their perspectives and strategies coloured by their vulnerability stemming from their lack of a land base and their exclusion from treaty provisions.

Throughout the North, however, much of the Aboriginal groups' strategy hinged on the pursuit of what are termed "comprehensive land claims."

LAND CLAIMS

In essence, land claims are demands by Aboriginal people that their interests, especially in terms of territory, be formally integrated into the Canadian system of governance. Land claims are based on Aboriginal peoples' assertion that in the many parts of Canada where treaties were never signed (or were flawed in important ways), Aboriginal title was never "extinguished"— in other words, Aboriginal people still owned the land and resources and could thus exercise legal control over them. In the early 1970s, landmark court decisions forced the federal government to entertain Aboriginal land claims seriously and to begin negotiations on them. Both Dene and Métis organizations and the Inuit Tapirisat of Canada (ITC) launched massive land claims in the 1970s.

To describe the progress and politics of the northern claims as tortuous scarcely begins to tell the tale. Only the outcome of the lengthy and complex negotiations can be sketched here. The Inuvialuit, who had initially been part of the ITC claim, opted for a separate claim in order to deal with intense oil and gas development pressures on their lands and waters. The Inuvialuit Final Agreement, settled in 1984, was the first claim to be resolved in the territories.[9] The Dene and Métis signed an agreement-in-principle with Ottawa in 1988 on a massive claim covering the entire Mackenzie Valley, but it fell apart due to dissension among Aboriginal peoples on the question of extinguishing Aboriginal land rights. Subsequent regional claims were settled with some of the groups that had initially signed on to the failed Dene-Métis claim: the Gwich'in of the Mackenzie Delta in 1992 and the Sahtu Dene and Métis (in the area around Great Bear Lake) in 1993. The Dogrib, whose lands lie between Great Slave and Great Bear lakes, reached an agreement-in-principle in 1999 and were moving toward ratification at the time of writing. Arguing that if government honoured the spirit and intent of the existing treaties their land and governance issues would be resolved to their satisfaction, the Deh Cho First Nations in the Southwest NWT and the Akaitcho Dene First Nations (primarily south of Great Slave Lake) have refused to enter into land-claims negotiations and are dealing with Ottawa through other mechanisms. The federal government has begun what amounts to land-claims negotiations with the South Slave Métis Tribal Council (the only Métis organization in Canada to have such a claim accepted by Ottawa).

Once ratified by vote of the affected Aboriginal people and authorized by act of Parliament, these land-claims settlements gain constitutional status under section 35 of the *Constitution Act, 1982*. Accordingly, they are nothing less than modern-day treaties. Although each comprehensive claim settlement is unique, all share important common features. These include

- extinguishment of Aboriginal title; that is, legal acknowledgment by the Aboriginal people that they are giving up their rights over the land except as specified in the agreement (Aboriginal rights not pertaining to land are unaffected).

- cash compensation, over a period of years, for the land (the payments are collective and are made to the organizations representing the Aboriginal people rather than to individuals); this can amount to substantial amounts of money—$1.14 billion over 14 years in the case of the Inuit claim.

- formal Aboriginal ownership ("fee simple" title) of specified tracts of land (again, collectively rather than individually held). Under the four settled claims in the NWT/Nunavut, the Aboriginal groups gained title to between 18 to 35 percent of the total land in the claim area; subsurface (oil, gas, and mineral) rights were included for a ninth to a quarter of this land.

- recognition of Aboriginal rights to hunt, trap, and fish throughout the claim area.

- creation of co-management boards with regulatory and decision-making authority over such issues as wildlife management and environmental protection.

- establishment of frameworks or processes for working toward new governance regimes. The Nunavut claim is unique in its commitment to create a new territory, with a public government system; the Inuvialuit, Gwich'in, and Sahtu claims contain provisions relating to self-government, but these amount only to commitments to negotiate, lists of possible jurisdictions of self-government institutions, and vague prescriptions that self-government is to be realized "within the framework of public government." The Dogrib claim entails an extensive self-government regime.

As this summary suggests, land-claims settlements have many far-reaching effects on the Northern political landscape. Among the most important but least known is the network of co-management boards. Composed of members nominated (but not controlled) by the federal and territorial governments and by the Aboriginal organization responsible for the claim, they are part of neither the federal nor the territorial governments and hence effectively operate as a distinct level of governance. Though many of their decisions about land use, environmental protection, and wildlife management are subject to federal veto, this has not occurred to any significant degree so that these boards possess substantial influence over critical decisions affecting resource development. It would be, for example, very difficult—legally and politically— for a major project such as a mine or road to go ahead without approval from the various boards involved. The co-management boards are institutions of public government but clearly bring a strong Aboriginal involvement in decisions relating to land and wildlife issues, which are fundamental—culturally, spiritually, and economically—to Aboriginal people of the North.

NUNAVUT: PROSPECTS AND PROBLEMS

The celebrations marking Nunavut's official creation on April 1, 1999, attracted international attention. Journalists, camera crews, and the merely curious came from across North America, Europe, and Asia to Iqaluit for the event. Following a midnight fireworks show, a formal ceremony featured political speeches, traditional rituals presided over by Inuit elders, Inuit dances, and rock music from Susan Aglukark and other Inuit performers. The Governor General, the Prime Minister, and other dignitaries rubbed shoulders with Inuit hunters, mothers carrying toddlers in their amoutit (women's parkas with special pouches for children), and all manner of ordinary Nunavummiut (residents of Nunavut). It was quite a party.

The pragmatism of Inuit leaders may have inclined them to accept a public government for Nunavut, following the essentials of the GNWT model, but it also meant that they expected to adapt the new government to make it conducive to their needs and values. The success of these adaptations will be key to the success of the entire Nunavut enterprise.

At root, Nunavut is about Inuit cultural survival. Thus, although non-Inuit will be included and accommodated, Nunavut is primarily to be a government of, by, and for Inuit. The population and the politicians they elect are overwhelmingly Inuit, but this is only part of what an "Inuit government" entails. Also critical are use of Inuktitut as a working language within government and high proportions of Inuit in bureaucratic and staff posts. As well, on a more intangible level, congruence with Inuit cultural values and approaches to governance must inform the practice of governing.

Fostering use of Inuktitut is central to the health of Inuit culture. And of course the government of Nunavut (GN) must be able to communicate with its citizens, many of whom have limited facility in English. Accordingly, extensive use of Inuktitut as a—perhaps the—language of work in the GN is a key goal with symbolic as well as practical overtones. Significant as it may be in its own right, though, Inuktitut capacity in the GN will very much be a function of an even more critical issue: Inuit representation within the territorial bureaucracy.

Quite simply, if over the long term the GN requires substantial numbers of southern and/or non-Inuit staff (few of whom would have any Inuktitut capacity) in order to operate effectively, a key purpose of creating Nunavut will have been defeated. The Inuit land-claim negotiators understood this and included a provision committing all parties "to increase Inuit participation in government employment in the Nunavut Settlement Area to a representative level." The practical difficulties in reaching this lofty goal, however, are daunting. The GN is much less transfixed than other governments by the need for staff to possess formal credentials; nonetheless, Inuit with the requisite skills and experience to fill all the government jobs are simply not available in anything like the numbers needed. At start-up in April 1999, the interim target of 50 percent Inuit representation among GN was met, but moving beyond that proportion, especially in the higher reaches of bureaucracy and in professional categories (such as lawyers and accountants), is proving difficult.

The level of Inuit staffing in the GN touches on more than questions of language and bureaucratic character; it is also an economic, and by extension, a social issue. The jobs—generally well-paid, secure jobs—available in the GN represent an important source of employment and economic mobility for the Inuit of Nunavut. By no stretch of the imagination will these jobs solve the territory's severe unemployment problems, or the social pathologies so often rooted in them, yet they are the best hope for many Inuit.

Training and education were top priorities for those who designed the GN and remain at the top of the political agenda. As well, attempts are being made to create a governmental structure and atmosphere compatible with Inuit lifestyles and values and thus conducive to Inuit involvement in the Nunavut bureaucracy. The government will be physically decentralized to a remarkable degree. In addition to a network of field offices, which provide government presence in all communities, many departmental headquarters and operational divisions, which in other governments are almost invariably located in the capital city, are being located in small communities throughout Nunavut. This will not only distribute the economic benefits of government employment throughout the regions but also create career opportunities for Inuit unwilling or unable to leave their home communities. As well, non-traditional work arrangements, such as job sharing, flexible work schedules, and telework (working from home via computer) are being developed in order to facilitate integration into the bureaucratic milieu of those wishing to retain elements of traditional Inuit lifestyle.

The Nunavut government has also committed itself to principles of Inuit Qaujimajatuqangit (IQ—roughly, "Inuit knowledge" or "the Inuit way"). The essential idea is to ensure that government operates and makes decisions on the basis of traditional Inuit values and approaches. Though the general objective is clear, precise specification of how IQ is to inform government operations and the day-to-day work of the GN is only slowly emerging.

If the extent to which the GN will be distinctive in terms of its Inuit character is as yet uncertain, in another respect the Nunavut political system is unquestionably unique in Canada, and quite possibly in the world. Nunavut has a public government, but Nunavut Tunngavik Incorporated (NTI), the Inuit land-claim organization, plays a fundamentally important role in territorial governance. Aside from its legal status as the body responsible for administering key elements of the land claim (for example, in nominating members of the co-management boards), it is a major political power in its own right. NTI is no simple "interest group": it can legitimately claim to speak for 85 percent of Nunavut residents; since the NTI president is elected on a territory-wide basis, and the Nunavut Premier represents a single constituency, the leader of NTI holds office by virtue of many more personal votes than the head of the GN.[10] NTI has neither the resources nor the inclination to act as some sort of alternate government, and the early relationship between NTI and the GN has been amicable and generally cooperative. Still, nothing like the GN–NTI relationship exists anywhere else in Canada.

NWT: THE SEARCH FOR A NEW CONSTITUTIONAL ORDER

When division occurred in 1999, the NWT essentially inherited a scaled-down version of pre-1999 political institutions. The post-division GNWT thus faces none of the major capacity-building issues of the GN. However, the political challenges facing the leaders and people of the NWT are in some ways far more difficult and potentially conflict-ridden than those in Nunavut. A small illustration of these issues was the nasty political fight over the distribution of seats in the new NWT Assembly. The successful political and legal campaign to boost the number of Yellowknife seats waged by a non-Aboriginal interest group, the "Friends of Democracy," involved far more than the usual political manoeuvring that accompanies legislative redistribution of seats. In directly pitting Aboriginal against non-Aboriginal people's visions for the new territory, it portended serious future conflict.

Establishing a widely acceptable political order will be much more problematic in the NWT than it was in Nunavut. The large non-Aboriginal population, the diversity of Aboriginal peoples (and their manifest political divisions), and greater Aboriginal hostility to Euro-Canadian political institutions (both their forms and the power configuration they represent) all add complexity to the situation. With several separate sets of negotiations under way on the realization of Aboriginal self-government, and no agreement in sight on the form or powers of the central territorial government, the basic nature of the governmental system remains in some doubt.

It is a measure of the distance to be travelled that some involved in attempting to craft the new political order take comfort in the implicit agreement that there will indeed be a central territorial government. (Leadership of the Deh Cho First Nations continues to pursue the goal of a separate Deh Cho territory, but this is not an option with much prospect of success.) Regional, tribal, and community loyalties are very strong in the NWT, and Aboriginal conceptions of power emphasize community over distant, central institutions. Thus strong sentiment exists for locating as many real powers as possible at the regional or community level, which would leave the central territorial government with only a vaguely defined capacity to set standards and to coordinate public policy. At the same time, neither the federal government nor large segments of the non-Aboriginal population would likely countenance reducing the central government to little more than a hollow shell.

Another source of conflict is the basic design of the central territorial government. Many Aboriginal people wish to see the end of the current British cabinet–parliamentary system. Their distaste for it reflects both its symbolic status as a residue of the colonial system of government and the incompatibility between its formality, adversarial nature, and concentration of power and key tenets of their political culture. A related concern—evidenced in the Friends of Democracy battle—is the composition of the legislative and executive bodies of the central territorial government and the weighting of Aboriginal and non-Aboriginal interests in important decisions. The essential issues are these: Should various Aboriginal and non-Aboriginal groups be guaranteed representation in the legislature and in the cabinet? If so, what proportions of legislative seats and cabinet posts should be reserved for various groups? Should certain types of issues be subject to group veto or require majority support among both Aboriginal and non-Aboriginal legislators?

The profound disagreements on these matters reflect both divergent understandings of society and politics and practical political calculation. Northern Aboriginal peoples conceive society in group terms and thus accept the legitimacy of formal political involvement of tribal and national groupings to a far greater extent than most non-Aboriginals. Non-Aboriginals' Euro-Canadian orientation to society and politics accords pride of place to individualism and to egalitarian principles. Granting what seems "special status" to some on the basis of culture or ethnicity is an anathema to this way of thinking.

Aboriginal leaders also look to the immediate and distant future. Though the Aboriginal and non-Aboriginal populations are effectively equal in size today, Aboriginal leaders worry that, in decades to come, extensive migration of non-Aboriginals to the NWT could turn the Aboriginal population into a small minority, as has happened everywhere else in Canada save Nunavut. The Métis feel especially vulnerable since they do not constitute a majority in any part of the territory and thus, unlike the other Aboriginal groups, cannot count on local concentration of numbers to ensure the election of MLAs.

Yet another set of troublesome issues involves the melding or coordination of public and Aboriginal self-governments. Self-government regimes may be slow in emerging, but they will be a reality in the NWT: the federal government recognizes the inherent right of Aboriginal people to self-government; land-claims settlements include commitments by federal and territorial governments to negotiate self-government; and the treaties carry important self-government implications. Yet public and self-governments cannot exist in watertight compartments; they must be reconciled on two dimensions. At the level of principle, the jurisdiction and authority that each has over residents as well as procedures for joint policymaking must be established. At the level of on-the-ground government activity, practical mechanisms are needed to ensure efficient administration of programs and effective delivery of services. While the principles have to be addressed, and indeed have been considered in myriad discussion papers and endlessly debated in settings formal and informal, the practicalities of providing services lie at the heart of the matter. This is particularly so in view of the small scale of many Aboriginal communities and the limited financial resources available to them.

Enormous time and energy have been devoted over the past two decades to establishing a political framework that could successfully accommodate both the self-government aspirations of Aboriginal people and the liberal, public government preferences of most non-Aboriginal residents. Any number of conferences, working groups, discussion papers, and the like have failed to find a satisfactory basis for a new governmental regime in the NWT.[11] Though we usually do not speak of provincial, let alone territorial, "constitutions," truly what is under way in the NWT is a dauntingly difficult exercise in constitution making.

Not the least of the difficulties lies in the importance of wide public involvement in developing and approving any new constitutional order, which is essential to ensuring legitimacy for the new system. A particularly serious impediment may lie in the repeated commitments by political leaders to put any proposed constitutional settlement to a public vote. Michael Lusztig has argued that in systems characterized by deep ethnic or cultural divisions, any constitutional package requiring approval in a plebiscite is doomed to failure because the necessary elite level compromises will be unacceptable to the general public (Lusztig, 1994) His thesis has obvious applicability in the NWT. Another sticking point is the form a plebiscite might take: non-Aboriginals insist on a one-person, one-vote formula, but some Aboriginal leaders prefer an approach based on local community approval (which would dilute the power of non-Aboriginal voters), and still other Aboriginal leaders altogether reject the notion that their political future should in any way be determined by a vote of non-Aboriginals.

Yet for all the complex, daunting constitutional issues and the potential for deep-seated conflict, significant goodwill and optimism remain. Aboriginal and non-Aboriginal residents of the NWT alike know that both are there to stay and that only in partnership can a viable political system be devised and maintained. For most people in the NWT, of course, politics is far from their main preoccupation; they are more concerned with the realities of day-to-day living. At the same time, they realize that however they define a good life—a vibrant economy, strong Aboriginal cultures, good social services in healthy communities—effective political institutions are essential. And to be effective, those institutions must enjoy legitimacy among all NWT residents.

CONCLUSION

Much of this chapter will seem foreign to southern Canadians whose notions of politics largely encompass images of MPs engaged in mindless partisan wrangles in the House of Commons, party leaders competing for the best "photo ops" and "sound bites," and federal and provincial politicians endlessly pointing fingers at one another for all manner of alleged evils. So too, southern Canadians, whose political culture is so strongly liberal (that is, individualistic and egalitarian) are inclined to assume that ideological disputes occur mainly over the nature and extent of state intrusiveness in the economy and in people's personal lives, may have difficulty coming to grips with a politics so based in unfamiliar conceptions of society and authority. It is precisely these variations from the standard Canadian model of government and politics that render northern governance so challenging.

In Nunavut the broad outline of government is clear and well accepted, but the difficulties in realizing the objective of a government run along Inuit principles are formidable. In the NWT, the basic principles of governance remain at issue; fundamental disagreement exists as to how political life ought to be organized.

This chapter has surveyed some of the unconventional structures and processes of governance in the NWT and Nunavut that have emerged in response to the unique political situations there. In turn, the politics of the North very much reflects the aspirations of its Aboriginal peoples. The North differs from the rest of Canada not only in its geography and climate but also in its society and politics, which stand in sharp contrast to those south of 60°.

NOTES

1. Obviously, "the North" includes Yukon and the northern reaches of most provinces, but for purposes of this discussion "northern" and "the North" will be taken to mean only Nunavut and the NWT.

2. The Aboriginal population of Yukon is approximately 20 percent; according to the 1996 census, roughly 11 percent of both Manitoba's and Saskatchewan's population is Aboriginal; no other province has nearly as high a proportion of Aboriginal residents. Other statistical data reported in this paper have been taken from the Government of the Northwest Territories and the Government of Nunavut Bureaus of Statistics, <www.stats.gov.nt.ca; www.stats.gov.nu.ca>.

3. Both Dene and Inuit historically hunted in the barrenlands. Attachment to these traditional hunting territories gave rise to significant conflict over the location of the boundary between the territories (not, as might be surmised, the diamonds that were found in abundance near the border after the boundary had been settled).

4. The distinction between Dene and Métis is often less a case of blood relations than of legal definitions and of historical anomalies. Some status Dene are in fact of mixed Dene-European descent, while a substantial number of the members of certain NWT Métis organizations are status Indians.

5. This wording is found in several of the post-confederation "numbered treaties," including Treaty 8, signed June 21, 1899. For full text of this and other treaties, see the Department of Indian Affairs and Northern Development Web site, <www.inac.gc.ca/pr/trts/index_e.html>.

6. If the language of the treaties ("cede, release ...") is so clear, how can Aboriginal people interpret them as they do? Because extensive evidence exists that the written documents do not accurately represent the oral agreements that the Dene reached with the representatives of the Canadian government. The signatories to the treaties spoke little English, and many were illiterate. As one current Dene leader put it, "In my language, there is no word for 'surrender'. I cannot describe surrender to you in my language. So how do you expect my people to put their X on surrender?" (Quoted in RCAP, II 44). The strong oral tradition of the Dene—their equivalent to the paper version of the treaties—provides powerful support for their interpretation. See Fumoleau, 1967.

7. Federal politics in the territories are premised on parties, and many territorial politicians belong to federal parties. The NDP ran seven candidates in the 1999 NWT election, but none were successful.

8. Non-public governments are unusual but not unknown in Canada. For example, Ontario's separate school system, in which only Roman Catholics vote for and serve as trustees, and that only admits Catholic students, could be thought of as a limited form of Catholic self-government. For an insightful, plain-language discussion of Aboriginal self-government in the

northern context, see the series of booklets "Aboriginal Self-Government in the Northwest Territories," published by the GNWT, available at <www.gov.nt.ca/Publications/ASG/unde.pdf>.

9.   The Inuvialuit Final Agreement was not the first comprehensive claim settled in Canada's North; the James Bay and Northern Quebec Agreement was finalized in 1975, but the circumstances of its development and its provisions differ in important respects from the claims north of 60°.

10.   Paul Quassa was elected president of NTI in late 1999 with 2093 votes; in the 1999 Nunavut election Paul Okalik, who went on to become Premier, won the riding of Iqaluit West with 334 votes.

11.   See for example, in the 1990s, Commission for Constitutional Development 1992 and Constitutional Working Group 1996 and 1998.

REFERENCES

Commission for Constitutional Development. (1992). *Working toward a common future.* Yellowknife, NWT.

Constitutional Working Group. (1996). *Partners in a new beginning.* Yellowknife, NWT.

———. (1998). *Common ground.* Yellowknife, NWT.

Dacks, Gurston. (1986). Politics on the last frontier: Consociationalism in the Northwest Territories. *Canadian Journal of Political Science,* 19(2), 345–61.

Fumoleau, René. (1967). *As long as this land shall last.* Toronto: McClelland and Stewart.

Lusztig, Michael. (1994). Constitutional paralysis: Why Canadian constitutional initiatives are bound to fail. *Canadian Journal of Political Science,* 27(4), 747–71.

Royal Commission on Aboriginal Peoples. (1996). [Final] *Report.* Ottawa: Supply and Services Canada.

White, Graham. (1991). Westminster in the Arctic: The adaptation of British Parliamentarism in the Northwest Territories. *Canadian Journal of Political Science,* 24(3), 499–523.

———. (1993). Structure and culture in a non-partisan Westminster Parliament. *Australian Journal of Political Science,* 28(2), 322–39.

———. (1999). The tundra's always greener: A response to Widdowson and Howard. *Policy Options,* 20(4), 59–63.

———. (2000). Letter. *Policy Options,* 20(2), 59.

Widdowson, Frances and Albert Howard. (1999a). Corruption north of 60. *Policy Options,* 20(1), 37–40.

———. (1999b). Duplicity in the north: A reply to Graham White. *Policy Options,* 20(7), 66–68.

FURTHER READING

Cameron, Kirk and Graham White. (1995). *Northern governments in transition: Political and constitutional development in the Yukon, Nunavut and the western Northwest Territories.* Montreal: Institute for Research on Public Policy.

Clancy, Peter. (2000). The Northwest Territories, old and new: Class politics on the northern frontier. In *The provincial state*, second edition, eds. Keith Brownsey and Michael Howlett. Peterborough: Broadview Press.

Gombay, Nicole. (2000). The politics of culture: Gender parity in the Legislative Assembly of Nunavut. *Inuit Studies* 24, 125–48.

Hicks, Jack and Graham White. (2000). Nunavut: Inuit self-determination through a land claim and public government? In *The provincial state*, second edition, eds. Keith Brownsey and Michael Howlett. Peterborough: Broadview Press.

McCormick, Floyd. (2000). Still frontier, always homeland: Yukon politics in the year 2000. In *The provincial state*, second edition, eds. Keith Brownsey and Michael Howlett. Peterborough: Broadview Press.

Contributors

Charles R. Acland teaches media and cultural studies in Communication Studies, Concordia University, Montreal. His books include *Youth, Murder, Spectacle: The Cultural Politics of 'Youth in Crisis'* (Westview Press, 1995) and *Harold Innis in the New Century: Reflections and Refractions* (McGill-Queen's University Press, 1999), co-edited with William Buxton of Concordia University. His research on Canadian film history, popular culture, and IMAX has appeared in *Cultural Studies, Canadian Journal of Film Studies, Communication,* and *Wide Angle,* among other scholarly and popular venues. His current work involves cinemagoing, globalization, and the rise of the megaplex cinema.

Allan Gordon Bell is a composer and Professor of Music at the University of Calgary. He has created works for solo instruments, chamber ensembles, orchestra, and electroacoustic media. His music has been performed and broadcast throughout Canada, the United States, Europe, and Japan. In 1999, CBC Records released *Spirit Trail: The Music of Allan Gordon Bell,* a CD containing five orchestral works. From 1984–88, Bell served as President of the national board of the Canadian Music Centre

J.M. Bumsted is a Fellow of St. John's College and a Professor of History at the University of Manitoba. Among his recent publications are *Fur Trade Wars: The Origins of Western Canada* (1999) and *The Dictionary of Manitoba Biography* (1999).

Miro Cernetig is the Beijing Bureau Chief for *The Globe and Mail.* Before that he was the paper's Vancouver Bureau Chief.

Janice Dickin is Director of the Law and Society Program at the University of Calgary. Her work on legal topics includes articles on pornography, prostitution, crime comics, and legal education. She is general editor of the *Legacies Shared* series for the University of Calgary Press.

Robert G. Finbow is Associate Professor of Political Science and Canadian Studies at Dalhousie University. He holds degrees from Dalhousie, York University, and the London School of Economics. He has published articles on Atlantic Canada and the Constitution, comparative public policy and political culture, and labour adjustment in free trade areas.

Anne Hébert was born at Sainte Catherine de Fossambault, Quebec. A poet, novelist, short-story writer, and dramatist, she is perhaps best known for her novel, *Kamouraska,* which was turned into an award-winning movie by Claude Jutra. Her latest novel, *L'Enfant chargé de songes* (1992), is a celebration of the country of her childhood. Her writing is as well known in French-speaking Europe as it is in Quebec. Hébert's essay is abridged from *Century 1867–1967* (published by Southam Press, 1967).

Rob Huebert is an Assistant Professor in the Department of Political Science at the University of Calgary. He is also the Associate Director of the Centre for Military and Strategic Studies and the editor of the Centre's e-journal *Journal of Military and Strategic Studies.* His areas of research include strategic studies, Canadian defence policy, the law of the sea, and circumpolar relations.

Matt James will be a graduate of the Ph.D. program in Political Science at the University of British Columbia by the time of this book's publication. His academic work, which focuses on questions of prestige, social movements, and citizenship, is in the areas of Canadian political science and social and political theory. He is a native of Kingston, Ontario.

Karim-Aly S. Kassam is the first Murray Fraser Professor of Community Economic Development at the University of Calgary. He developed and established the Theme School in Northern Planning and Development Studies and is currently its Director. Professor Kassam's circumpolar research projects range from human ecology and the impact of chemical pollutants, sea ice, and climate change, to empowerment of indigenous women. He has undertaken research work in the Canadian, Alaskan, and Russian Arctic and sub-Arctic. You can comment on, and discuss, this chapter with Professor Kassam by e-mail at <kakassam@ucalgary.ca>.

Emma LaRocque teaches in the Native Studies Department at the University of Manitoba (since 1977). Author, educator, historian, social and literary critic, and poet, LaRocque has lectured and published extensively on colonization, historiography, and Native literature and identity. She served as consultant on Métis identity in Christine Welsh's film *Women in the Shadows* (1993). She is Plains Cree-Métis, originally from Northern Alberta, and author of *Defeathering the Indian.*

Peter McCormick is a Professor and Chair of the Department of Political Science at the University of Lethbridge. He is the author of *Supreme at Last: The Evolution of the Supreme Court of Canada* (2000) among other works. Professor McCormick serves as an advisor to Alberta Premier Ralph Klein on national unity and the *Constitution.*

Anne McGrath is a doctoral candidate in Education at the University of Calgary. She has worked for Oxfam Canada and as a commentator for the CBC. She lives in Ottawa.

J.R. Miller teaches Canadian history at the University of Saskatchewan. His research and teaching focus on the history of relations between Aboriginal peoples and newcomers in Canada from contact to the present. Among his publications are *Skyscrapers Hide the Heavens: A History of Indian–White Relations in Canada, Sweet Promises: A Reader on Indian–White Relations in Canada, Shingwauk's Vision: A History of Native Residential Schools, Big Bear (Mistahimusqua)*, and (with Arthur J. Ray and Frank Tough) *Bounty and Benevolence: A History of Saskatchewan Treaties.* His scholarship has been recognized by election as President of the Canadian Historical Association (1996–97) and installation as a Fellow of the Royal Society of Canada (1998).

Réjean Pelletier is a Professor in the Department of Political Science at Laval University. A specialist in Canadian and Quebec politics, he has published more than 70 articles on party politics, federalism, women and politics, new nationalism, parliamentarism, and the State. His publications include: *Partis politiques et société québécoise* (1989), *Que font-elles en politique?* (with M. Tremblay, 1995); he has co-edited *Le parlementarisme canadien* (with M. Tremblay and M. Pelletier, 2000), *L'engagement intellectuel, Mélanges en l'honneur de Léon Dion* (with R. Hudon, 1991), *Minorités et État* (with J. Zylberberg, P. Guillaume and J.M. Lacroix, 1986), *L'État du Québec en devenir* (with G. Bergeron, 1980), *Partis politiques au Québec* (1976).

Beverly Rasporich is a Professor in the Faculty of Communication and Culture at the University of Calgary. She is the author of *Dance of the Sexes: Art and Gender in the Fiction of Alice Munro* and numerous interdisciplinary articles, and has edited books on Canadian culture. Her latest project is a compact disc entitled *Western Place/Women's Space.*

Christine Sowiak is the Curator of Art at The Nickle Arts Museum at the University of Calgary and is an Adjunct Professor (Painting) to the Department of Art. She holds a Master of Fine Arts degree in Painting, as well as undergraduate degrees in both Art History and Painting. Recent exhibitions curated by Sowiak, with accompanying catalogues, include *M. N. Hutchinson: vistarama 7, Sandra Vida: Kitchen Freedom, Blue,* and *John Will... ain't paralyzed yet* (forthcoming February 2001.)

David Taras is a Professor in the Faculty of Communication and Culture at the University of Calgary. He is the author of *The Newsmakers: The Media's Influence on Canadian Politics* and *Power and Betrayal in the Canadian Media.* He is a frequent media commentator on Alberta and Canadian politics.

Wisdom J. Tettey is an Assistant Professor in the Faculty of Communication and Culture, University of Calgary. He teaches in the areas of Development Studies, African Studies, and International and Intercultural Communications. His research interests include intercultural communications and the representation of Africans in the mass media.

Harold Troper is a Professor in the Department of Theory and Policy Studies at the Ontario Institute for Studies in Education, University of Toronto. He is the co-author of *None Is Too Many: Canada and the Jews of Europe, 1933–1948* (with Irving Abella) and *Old Wounds: Jews, Ukrainians and the Hunt for Nazi War Criminals in Canada* (with Morton Weinfeld) among many other works.

Theresie Tungilik was born on the sea ice in an igloo between Harbour Islands and Repulse Bay and spent most of her childhood in Repulse Bay, Wager Bay, and their surrounding areas. Theresie went to residential school in Chesterfield Inlet, Nunavut, and high school in Churchill, Manitoba. She has lived in Rankin Inlet since the fall of 1979. Theresie is now employed by the government of Nunavut as the Senior Advisor, Arts Economy, in the Department of Sustainable Development.

Cora Voyageur teaches in the Department of Sociology at the University of Calgary. She has written extensively on First Nations' history and society.

Kathryn Welbourn is an award-winning radio documentary maker and publisher of the *Portugal Coast St. Phillips Times*.

Reg Whitaker is Professor of Political Science at York University in Toronto. He has published *The End of Privacy* (New York, 1999); *Cold War Canada* (Toronto, 1994); *A Sovereign Idea* (Montreal, 1992); *Double Standard* (Toronto, 1987); and *The Government Party* (Toronto, 1977).

Graham White is Professor in the Department of Political Science, University of Toronto. He has written widely on Canadian political institutions, especially at the provincial and territorial level. He is a frequent and enthusiastic visitor to the North.

David Whitson is a Professor of Canadian Studies at the University of Alberta. He is the co-author of *Hockey Night in Canada: Sport, Identities and Cultural Politics* (with Richard Gruneau) and *The Game Planners: Transforming Canada's Sport System* (with David Macintosh). He has also published numerous articles on sports, leisure, and popular culture, including "The Mills Report, the Manley Subsidy Proposals, and the Business of Major League Sport," which appeared in *Canadian Public Administration* in the Summer 2000 issue. Despite all of this, he remains a sports fan.

INDEX OF NAMES

INDEX OF SUBJECTS

PERMISSIONS